# Basic Marketing Research
## Using Microsoft® Excel Data Analysis

### Second Edition

**ALVIN C. BURNS**

Louisiana State University

**RONALD F. BUSH**

University of West Florida

PEARSON
Prentice
Hall

Upper Saddle River, New Jersey 07458

Library of Congress Cataloging-in-Publication Data
Burns, Alvin C.
  Basic marketing research: using Microsoft Excel data analysis/Alvin C. Burns,
    Ronald F. Bush—2nd ed.
      p. cm.
  Includes bibliographical references and index.
  ISBN 0-13-205958-4
  1. Marketing research. 2. Microsoft Excel (Computer file) I. Bush, Ronald F. II. Title.
  HF5415.2.B7787 2008
  658.8'30285554—dc22

                                                          2007039014

Acquisitions Editor: Melissa Sabella
AVP/Editor in Chief: David Parker
Manager, Product Development: Ashley Santora
Editorial Project Manager: Melissa Pellerano
Editorial Assistant: Christine Ietto
Permissions Project Manager: Charles Morris
Marketing Manager: Anne Howard
Marketing Assistant: Susan Osterlitz
Senior Managing Editor: Judy Leale
Production Project Manager: Debbie Ryan
Senior Operations Supervisor: Arnold Vila
Operations Specialist: Michelle Klein
Senior Art Director: Janet Slowik
Cover Designer: Karen Quigley
Cover Photo: John Foxx/Stockbyte/Getty Images, Inc.
Interior Designer: Karen Quigley
Director, Image Resource Center: Melinda Patelli
Manager, Rights and Permissions: Zina Arabia
Manager: Visual Research: Beth Brenzel
Manager, Cover Visual Research & Permissions: Karen Sanatar
Senior Image Permission Coordinator: Cynthia Vincenti
Composition: GGS Book Services
Full-Service Project Management: Ann Courtney
Printer/Binder: Phoenix Color/Hagerstown
Typeface: Berkeley, 10.5 pt

Credits and acknowledgments borrowed from other sources and reproduced, with permission, in this textbook appear on appropriate page within text.

Pearson Education LTD.
Pearson Education Singapore, Pte. Ltd
Pearson Education, Canada, Ltd
Pearson Education–Japan

Pearson Education Australia PTY, Limited
Pearson Education North Asia Ltd
Pearson Educación de Mexico, S.A. de C.V.
Pearson Education Malaysia, Pte. Ltd.

10 9 8 7 6 5 4 3 2
ISBN-13: 978-0-13-205958-9
ISBN-10: 0-13-205958-4

# BRIEF CONTENTS

# CONTENTS

## CHAPTER 3:  STEPS IN THE MARKETING RESEARCH PROCESS INCLUDING DEFINING THE PROBLEM AND RESEARCH OBJECTIVES  60

## CHAPTER 8:  USING MEASUREMENT SCALES IN YOUR SURVEY  230

## CHAPTER 15:  PREPARING AND PRESENTING THE RESEARCH RESULTS  466

## WHAT MAKES BASIC MARKETING RESEARCH: USING MICROSOFT® EXCEL DATA ANALYSIS, 2ND EDITION, UNIQUE?

This book provides:
- a concise presentation of the fundamentals of marketing research
- an improved software package, XL Data Analyst™, which runs using Microsoft® Excel 2003 or later versions
- input from many professionals in the marketing research industry
- an integrated case complete with a data set that gives students an experiential learning exercise throughout the course

## WHY EXCEL FOR DATA ANALYSIS?

Most students will not become marketing researchers and only a small percentage of them, in their future careers, will have access to powerful software programs designed specifically for data analysis. By having this book, they will continually have access to our Excel add-in program, XL Data Analyst™. In this course students will learn how to use this powerful software program, which they can access as long as they can access Excel. Instructors told us they want to teach students a software program they will have and use in the future. Once students learn to use XL Data Analyst™ they can use it with their Excel programs for years to come.

A powerful computing tool, Excel is widely used and understood by students. To increase the usage of Excel, add-ins are commonly developed to address many applications far beyond the intentions of the original Excel spreadsheet. Our add-in, XL Data Analyst™, opens up Excel's computing capabilities for marketing research applications in an easy-to-use format. Many features of XL Data Analyst™ make it more desirable than some of the most widely used dedicated stat packages.

# OUR INTENDED AUDIENCE

This book is written for the introductory marketing research course at the undergraduate level. We assume students have not had a prior course in marketing research, and that they have had at least one elementary statistics course. We focus on teaching the process of marketing research so that students will be better users of marketing research. They should be able to evaluate the need for marketing research and also determine the adequacy of research proposals. At the same time, we give the students of this book the tools to conduct basic analysis techniques on their own.

## A Concise Presentation

We wanted to provide a book with the basics of marketing research. Adopters have told us they want to teach the basics of marketing research in depth as opposed to covering a large amount of material superficially. Many professors desire to teach a course with less text material, allowing them to supplement the course with projects or to spend more time on the basics. *Basic Marketing Research: Using Microsoft® Excel Data Analysis* is shorter in length but covers the essential, basic components of marketing research. We made every effort to write a shorter book without sacrificing knowledge on what we consider the "basics."

## New Features for XL Data Analyst™

XL Data Analyst™ is unique in that it only requires Excel, to which many students have access, and it is written expressly for the purpose of conducting marketing research data analysis. When we wrote the first edition of this book we knew we didn't want to just write a shorter version of a marketing research book. We wanted a new approach to data analysis. Specifically, we wanted a program that would operate without statistical terms that are difficult for students to navigate. We wanted the program to operate in a user-friendly format that was intuitive. Secondly, with many years of teaching marketing research experience, we wanted our program to offer output in a way that allowed students to interpret the output correctly and more easily. Those who have studied statistics realize that many of the

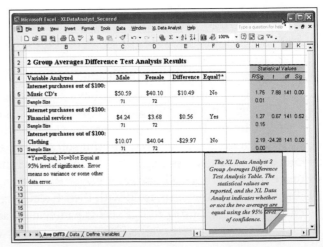

**Download XL Data Analyst at www.prenhall.com/burnsbush**

presentations of statistical output are based upon tradition. We offer users an alternative. The XL Data Analyst™ has both traditional and classical statistical format as well as output in our new easy-to-interpret format. However, the essence of our new software is output that students can immediately interpret without a need to consult the statistical values: our program generates polished tables with "plain English" presentations of the various findings. This allows students to have greater focus on using marketing research to make decisions; the purpose of marketing research.

We have made several new changes in XL Data Analyst™ based upon our experience with the first edition of this book. The new utilities menu item allows for: (1) importing a csv data file and setting up the worksheets, (2) Clean-up checks for errors in the Define Variables value codes and value labels, (3) Filter allows users to select subsets of data for analysis, and (4) Unfilter returns the full data set.

The new version has been tested and is fully compatible with Excel 2007. Students may download XL Data Analyst™ at **www.prenhall.com/burnsbush**.

## ABOUT THE TEXT: KEY STRENGTHS

Aside from being the first marketing research text to fully integrate Excel for data analysis, this book offers several key strengths.

### Time-Tested, 11-Step Approach

The framework of our best-selling SPSS® text is the same framework for our Excel version. Our logical 11-step process is a time-tested process used throughout this book.

### New Examples

In every chapter we searched for new examples for opening vignettes that would wake the students' interest and understanding of marketing research. Several of these vignettes were supplied from our professional contacts in the marketing research industry. Several of them reflect current marketing research practice. In addition to these all-new chapter-opening vignettes, new examples, many from marketing research industry sources, are integrated throughout the text.

### Integrated Case with Data Set

In the first edition we wanted an integrated case which related to students' interests. Our experience has shown that the "College Life E-Zine," a case about four college graduates who want to start an e-zine targeting the college population, was a good choice. The case is discussed throughout the course. The case resonates with students' interests and, at the same time, is an excellent example of teaching the marketing research process. The cases and topics covered are:

- **Chapter 1, Case 1.2:** "The Need to Conduct Marketing Research"
- **Chapter 2, Case 2.2:** "Searching for a Marketing Research Firm"
- **Chapter 3, see within the text of the chapter:** "Putting It All Together Using the Integrated Case for This Textbook: Defining Problems and Research Objectives"
- **Chapter 4, Case 4.2:** "Appropriate Use of a Focus Group"
- **Chapter 7, Case 7.2:** "Determining the Data Collection Method"

*Where We Are*
1. Establish the need for marketing research
2. Define the problem
3. Establish research objectives
4. Determine research design
5. Identify information types and sources
6. Determine methods of accessing data
7. Design data collection forms
8. Determine sample plan and size
9. Collect data
10. Analyze data
11. Prepare and present the final research report

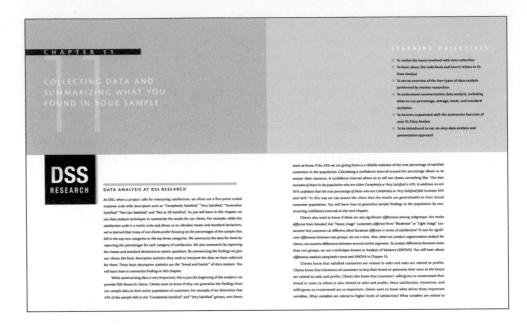

- **Chapter 9, see within the text of the chapter:** "Marketing Research Application 9.1: The College Life E-Zine Survey Questionnaire"
- **Chapter 9, Case 9.2:** "Questionnaire Design"
- **Chapter 10, Case 10.2:** "Sampling Decisions"
- **Chapter 11, Case 11.2:** "Summarizing Findings"
- **Chapter 12, Case 12.2:** "Generalizing Findings"
- **Chapter 13, Case 13.2:** "Market Segments Analysis (Differences Analysis)"
- **Chapter 14, Case 14.2:** "Relationships Analysis"
- **Chapter 15, Case 15.1:** "Organizing the Written Report"
- **Chapter 15, Case 15.2:** "Appropriate Visuals"
- **Chapter 15, Case 15.3:** "PowerPoint Presentations"

---

### CASE 11.2 — Your Integrated Case

#### The College Life E-Zine Survey Summarization Analysis

Bob Watts was happy to inform Sarah, Anna, Wesley, and Don that the College Life E-Zine survey data were collected and ready for analysis. Bob had other marketing research projects and meetings scheduled with present and prospective clients, so he called in his marketing intern, Lori Baker. Lori was a senior marketing major at State U., and she had taken marketing research in the previous semester. Lori had "aced" this class, which she enjoyed a great deal. Her professor had invited Bob Watts to give a talk on "a typical day in the life of a market researcher," and Lori had approached Bob the very next day about a marketing research internship. Like every dedicated marketing major, Lori had kept her Burns and Bush marketing research basics textbook and her XL Data Analyst software for future reference. Bob called Lori into his office and said, "Lori,

it is time to do some analysis on the survey we did for the College Life E-Zine project. For now, let's just get a feel for what the data look like. I'll leave it up to your judgment as to what basic analysis to run. Let's meet tomorrow at 2:30 P.M. and see what you have found."

Your task in Case 11.2 is to take the role of Lori Baker, marketing intern. As we indicated in this chapter, the College Life E-Zine data set is included with your XL Data Analyst software that accompanies this textbook. We have used this data set in some of the examples of various types of descriptive analysis in this chapter. Now, it is time for you to use the XL Data Analyst on these and other variables in the College Life E-Zine survey data set.

1. Determine what variables are categorical, perform the appropriate descriptive analysis, and interpret it.
2. Determine what variables are metric scales, perform the appropriate descriptive analysis, and interpret it.

Also, we use the College Life E-Zine case data set to illustrate all of our data analyses procedures discussed in our four data analyses chapters.

## Our New Approach to Teaching Data Analysis

When we introduced the first edition of this book we said "Finally there is an alternative!" After many years of teaching marketing research and talking with dozens of colleagues who do the same, the authors decided it was time to do some things a different way. Weary of students struggling with levels of measurement, we present measurement in terms of categorical or metric variables. Instead of having students baffled by data analysis, we present data analysis in an easy-to-learn six-step process. Data analysis keystrokes are illustrated through colorful, annotated screen captures. Experience has shown us that the students, using XL Data Analyst™, quickly learn the tools of data analysis and complete their projects much faster than with traditional software programs. They focus more on getting the answers and writing their reports instead of staring at hard-to-interpret output.

## Ethics, Globalization, and Online Research

As we did in the first edition, when we touch on ethical issues or give examples of the global use of research, we use icons to alert readers to these special topics. We also highlight references to the use of online research, now dominant in the industry, through the use of the online icon. Finally, when we use a practical application we denote this with an icon.

## Marginal Notes, Key Terms, and Learning Outcomes

These proven pedagogical aids are included in *Basic Marketing Research: Using Microsoft® Excel Data Analysis*, 2nd Edition.

# TEACHING AIDS

## Instructor's Manual

(0-13-205959-2) A complete instructor's manual, prepared by the authors, can be used to prepare lecture or class presentations, find answers to end-of-chapter questions and case studies, and even to design the course syllabus.

## Test Item File

(0-13-205995-9) The test bank for the 2nd Edition contains over 50 questions for each chapter. Questions are provided in both multiple-choice and true/false format. Page numbers corresponding to answers to the questions are provided for each question.

This Test Item File supports Association to Advance Collegiate Schools of Business (AACSB) International Accreditation.

Each chapter of the Test Item File was prepared with the AACSB learning standards in mind. Where appropriate, the answer line of each question indicates a category within which the question falls*. This AACSB reference helps instructors identify those test questions that support that organization's learning goals.

## What is the AACSB?

AACSB is a not-for-profit corporation of educational institutions, corporations and other organizations devoted to the promotion and improvement of higher education in business administration and accounting. A collegiate institution offering degrees in business administration or accounting may volunteer for AACSB accreditation review. The AACSB makes initial accreditation decisions and conducts periodic reviews to promote continuous quality improvement in management education. Pearson Education is a proud member of the AACSB and is pleased to provide advice to help you apply AACSB Learning Standards.

## What are AACSB Learning Standards?

One of the criteria for AACSB accreditation is the quality of the curricula. Although no specific courses are required, the AACSB expects a curriculum to include learning experiences in such areas as:

- Communication
- Ethical reasoning
- Analytical skills
- Use of information technology
- Multiculturalism and diversity
- Reflective thinking

These six categories are AACSB Learning Standards. Questions that test skills relevant to these standards are tagged with the appropriate standard. For example, a question testing the moral questions associated with externalities would receive the Ethical Reasoning tag.

## How can I use these tags?

Tagged questions help you measure whether students are grasping the course content that aligns with AACSB guidelines noted above. In addition, the tagged questions may help to identify potential applications of these skills. This, in turn, may suggest enrichment activities or other educational experiences to help students achieve these goals.

## Instructor's Resource Center

All your teaching resources in one place. Electronic versions of the instructor's manual, test item file, TestGen test generating software, plus PowerPoints are available online at **www.prenhall.com/burnsbush** (Select Instructor Resource Center). All of these resources (with the exception of TestGen) are also available on CD-Rom (0-13-205997-5) for your convenience.

## Companion Website

At **www.prenhall.com/burnsbush**, students will be able to take self-study quizzes on each chapter in the 2nd Edition and have them automatically graded. Students should study the chapter first, then take the sample test to assess how well they have learned chapter material.

*Please note that not all test questions will indicate an AACSB category.

# ACKNOWLEDGMENTS

We could not write books about the marketing research industry without our extensive, expert assistance from many people. We wish to acknowledge the help of many people in writing this book. First, we thank our Editor-in-Chief, David Parker. Melissa Pellerano served as Project Manager, Editorial. Melissa could not have been more helpful. Even though we have been through this process several times, we constantly fired questions to Melissa. Each time she responded quickly and professionally. Thank you, Melissa! Judy Leale is Senior Managing Editor, Production. She is very knowledgeable of many technical production issues and we owe her a special "thanks" for her very capable production assistance. Debbie Ryan served as our Project Manager, Production. Thank you Debbie for your able assistance. We have been with Prentice Hall now for well over a decade and we are forever grateful we found such a great partnership. The entire Prentice Hall staff is courteous and professional. Thank you all for being so good at what you do!

In the 2nd Edition we again benefited from the capable experience of Heather Donofrio, Ph.D. Heather has been involved in different aspects of helping with our textbook for several years. Her highly qualified editorial assistance is reflected throughout this book. Having editorial assistance from someone who has actually taught the course is a bonus. We also wish to thank Ashley Roberts who cheerfully and professionally helped us with many tasks during the preparation of this book.

We both enjoy keeping up with industry trends and practice through our extensive contacts in the marketing research industry. For this edition we want to particularly thank Dan Quirk of *Quirk's Marketing Research Review*. When we began working on this 2nd Edition we asked Dan if he would introduce us to some practitioners who wanted to share some of their insights with us for this edition. The following professionals made contributions to the 2nd Edition:

Baltimore Research – Ted Donnelly
Common Knowledge Research Services – Shawna Fisher
Decision Analyst – Cristi Allen
e-Rewards Market Research – Sheri Hayes
EyeTracking, Inc. – Sylvia Knust
Fieldwork – Molly Lammers
I.think_inc. – Beth Mack
Irwin – Kathryn Blackburn
Knowledge Networks – Erica Demme
Maritz Research – Tom Evans
TAi Companies – Hal Meier
Western Wats – Jeff Welch

Over the years we have made many friends in the industry and we rely on them to provide us with current information about the industry. We want to thank the following individuals for contributing to the 2nd Edition. (A few of these are internal suppliers of marketing research, but most represent external supplier firms.)

Arbitron – Jessica Benbow
American Marksman – Mark Eberhard
Bluetooth SIG – Kari Hernandez
Burke, Inc. – Andrea Fisher
Claritas, Inc.– Stephen F. Moore
CMOR – Patrick Glaser
DSS Research – Kevin Weseman
ESRI – Brent Roderick
Experian Simmons & Experian Vente – Dave Aneckstein
Harris Interactive – Tracey McNerney
Inside Research – Jack Honomichl & Laurence Gold
Insight Express – Jenny R. Donohue
Market Research Insight – Verne Kennedy
Momentum Market Intelligence – Doss Struse
MRA – Linda Schoenborn
MRSI – Holly Ford
ProQuest – Alexandra Barcelona
*Quirk's Marketing Research Review* – Dan Quirk and Joseph Rydholm
Survey Sampling International – Joan Nadel
VISIT FLORIDA – Marsha Medders

We'd like to thank the professors who took part in our focus groups and shared their ideas for this text and XL Data Analyst:

## Reviewers

| | |
|---|---|
| Greg Broekemier | University of Nebraska-Kearney |
| Jim Cox | Illinois State University |
| Alan Dick | State University of New York at Buffalo |
| Michael T. Greenwood | Suffolk University |
| Douglas R. Hausknecht | The University of Akron |
| Craig Kelley | California State University, Sacramento |
| Aron Levin | Northern Kentucky University |
| Susan Logan | Nelson University of North Dakota |
| Raymond Liu | University of Massachusetts, Boston |
| Frank Philpot | George Mason University |
| Raj Sethuraman | Southern Methodist University |
| Minakshi Trivedi | State University of New York at Buffalo |

As always, we wish to thank our life partners who put up with our book writing exploits and, no matter what, always smile. Thank you, Jeanne and Libbo, for your steadfast support of our professional endeavors.

**Al Burns**
*Louisiana State University*
*alburns@lsu.edu*

**Ron Bush**
*University of West Florida*
*rbush@uwf.edu*

# CHAPTER 1

## INTRODUCING MARKETING RESEARCH

## WHY DO WE LOVE THE MOVIES?

There are many factors that go into making a great movie; good scripts, directors, producers, actors, and all the support staff are fundamental. But movies have been improved by using marketing research to gather consumer reactions for many years. Two of the earliest users of marketing research, though primitive, were Carl Laemmie and Adolph Zukor. In the early 1900s small, neighborhood theaters called Nickelodeons showed films of the day; admission was a nickel. Laemmie observed audience and sales data for

Welcome to the exciting world of marketing research! As you can see by our opening vignette on the motion picture industry, marketing research can help provide information to aid in making decisions. In this chapter, we will introduce you to marketing research by: (a) examining how marketing research is a part of marketing, (b) exploring definitions and purposes and uses of marketing research, (c) learning how to classify marketing research studies, (d) providing you with an understanding of how marketing research fits into a firm's marketing information system, and (e) introducing you to some "hot topics" in marketing research.

This is an exciting time to learn about marketing research, because there are many innovations going on in the field. One change that is impacting marketing research is the development of new software technology. In light of that fact, we are pleased to introduce you to the second edition of the first comprehensive marketing research textbook ever written that uses Microsoft Excel as the sole, primary, integrated analysis program throughout the book. Not only is Excel a powerful analysis tool, it is widely available and is used by many marketing research firms. We have developed *XL Data Analyst*™ to allow you to easily tap the power of Excel for purposes of marketing research analysis. Now, we will show you *why* you conduct marketing research analyses by introducing you to the field of marketing research.

> This is the second edition of the first comprehensive marketing research textbook ever written that uses Microsoft Excel as the sole, primary, integrated analysis program throughout the book. With your new book, you also can download a copy of *XL Data Analyst*™, which will allow you to easily tap the power of Excel for marketing research analysis.

## WHAT IS MARKETING?

If this is a book about marketing research, why do we need to first discuss marketing? The answer is that because marketing research is part of marketing, and you cannot fully appreciate marketing research and the role it plays in the marketing process unless you know how it fits into the marketing process. What is **marketing**?

> Because marketing research is a *part* of marketing, we must first understand marketing in order to understand marketing research.

*The American Marketing Association has defined marketing as an organizational function and a set of processes for creating, communicating and delivering value to customers and for managing customer relationships in ways that benefit the organization and its stakeholders.*[2]

> What is **marketing**? "The American Marketing Association has defined marketing as an organizational function and a set of processes for creating, communicating and delivering value to customers, and for managing customer relationships in ways that benefit the organization and its stakeholders."

The way we view marketing is shifting away from thinking that we create a physical product and then optimize profits by making efficient promotion, distribution, and pricing decisions. For many years marketing focused on providing the customer with value through a physical product that emerged at the end of the distribution channel. Current thinking, proposed primarily by Vargo and Lusch (2004)[3], calls for a framework that goes beyond a "manufacturing-tangible product" view of marketing (i.e., GM creates value by building cars). Rather, Vargo and Lusch argue that we should adopt a service-centered view of marketing which (a) identifies core comepetencies, the fundamental knowledge and skills that may represent a potential competitive advantage; (b) identifies potential customers that can benefit from these core competencies; (c) cultivates relationships with these customers that allow customers to help create values that meet their specific needs;

> By listening to the consumer, companies know what it takes to *satisfy* consumer wants and needs.

Hale's Tours in Chicago. He made notes on what types of people saw the films and determined the most popular hours of the day. Zukor, a Nickelodeon operator in New York, watched audience faces to see their reactions to different parts of the films and claimed he learned "feel" reactions of laughter, pleasure, and boredom. Both Laemmie and Zukor must have learned something. They created the two companies Universal and Zukor Paramount—both large motion picture giants even today.

Over the years marketing research has increasingly played a role in movie making. When marketing research, conducted by the Gallup Poll, predicted a huge market success for the movie *Gone With the Wind*, MGM decided to price the movie between $.75 and $2.20 when the average movie ticket of the day was about $.25! The result was huge profits, as the Gallup predictions turned out to be correct. Marketing research has continued to be used to determine if scripts are profitable, rate the market attractiveness of the actors and actresses, profile the movie-going market segments, determine the effectiveness of advertising, and determine which type of movie ending the audience most prefers. Today, marketing research is heavily used by Hollywood to help make movies you love to see![1]

and (d) gauge feedback from the market, learn from the feedback, and improve the values offered to the public. One implication of this new framework is that firms must be *more* than customer oriented (making and selling what firms think customers want and need). Rather, firms must *collaborate with* and *learn from* customers, adapting to their changing needs. A second implication is that products are not viewed as separate from services. Isn't Toyota really marketing a service, a service that happens to include a by-product called a car?[4] This new framework is referred to as the "Service-Dominant Logic for Marketing."

Our point here is not to provide a discourse on how marketing thought is evolving. After all, we are still trying to answer the question: Why do we need to know about marketing in order to better understand marketing research? The answer is, in order to practice marketing, marketing decision makers need information in order to make better decisions. And, in our opinion, current definitions and frameworks of marketing mean that information is *more* important, not less important, in today's world. For example, the "Service-Dominant Logic for Marketing," implies that decision makers need information to know what their real core competencies are; how to create meaningful relationships with customers; how to create, communicate, and deliver value to customers; how to gather feedback to gauge customer acceptance; and how to determine the appropriate responses to the feedback. Keeping these information needs in mind, think about the information needed by these successful firms: Toyota, whose hybrid, the Prius, far exceeds all other hybrid cars in market share; Louis Vuitton, who creates and delivers such value in their handbags that customers pay as much as $1,200 for them; ABC, whose TV production of *Grey's Anatomy* enjoys very high viewer ratings; The Red Cross, which earns donations and support by creating value in the sense that it provides donors with "peace of mind for helping others"; or Apple, which has been so successful in noncomputer areas such as its iPod and iTunes that it has dropped the word *computer* from its corporate name. In order to make the decisions necessary for the success of these

> ■ Marketing decision makers need information in order to make better decisions and current definitions and frameworks of marketing mean that information is *more* important, not less important, in today's world.

The Toyota Prius hybrid car outsells all other hybrids because Toyota executives used their core competencies to create a competitive advantage in the marketplace.

■ NewProductWorks, a division of the Arbor Strategy Group, is a new-product-development consulting organization. Explore what they offer their clients at www.newproductworks.com. Also see how the experts rate the success of new products by going to Interactive Learning at the end of this chapter.

organizations, decision makers needed information. As you will learn, marketing research provides information to decision makers.

Of course, not all firms enjoy marketing success. Products and services fail. General Motors' all electric vehicle, the *EV1*, was a failure. McDonald's veggie-burger, the MacLean, was taken off the market. There are thousands of examples of product failures including the examples below of *IncrEdibles* "push-up," eat-on-the-go scrambled eggs, and *Hey! There's A Monster In My Room* spray.

**IncrEdibles Breakaway Foods, L.L.P,** launched IncrEdibles in late 1999, touting its "Push n' Eat" self-serving unit as fast, easy, and convenient. The breakfast fast-food alternative was available in three scrambled egg flavors—cheese, cheese and sausage, and cheese and bacon. However, because of some operational problems, the product was pulled with the hope that it would be retooled and relaunched, but to no avail. It was an interesting concept, but the execution was riddled with problems. The product was frozen, and according to reports, when you started eating it on the run, it fell over onto your lap.

**Hey! There's A Monster In My Room spray:** In 1993, OUT! International, Inc., introduced this monster-buster spray to rid children's rooms of scary creatures. The spray came in a bubble gum fragrance. The idea was cute, but the name was not, and it set up a fright for the kids.

■ There are thousands of product failures every year, and one way managers avoid failure is by having the right information so they can make the best decisions.

■ In addition to having the right information, managers should have the right philosophy to guide their daily decisions; they should adopt the marketing concept.

Peter Drucker wrote how firms can avoid failure. He said that successful companies know and understand the customer so well that the product conceived, priced, promoted, and distributed by the company is ready to be bought as soon as it's available.[5] (Notice how this is consistent with Vargo and Lusch's view of collaborating and learning from the consumer.) Drucker, as usual, is right on target, but how can a marketer know and understand how to deliver value to the customer? By having the right information. So, to practice marketing correctly, managers must have information. This is the purpose of marketing research, and it's why we say that marketing research is a part of marketing; it provides the necessary information to enable managers to *properly* market ideas, goods, and services. But how do you *properly* market ideas, goods, and services? You've probably learned already in your studies that you must begin by having the right philosophy, followed by proper marketing strategy. We call that philosophy the "marketing concept."

## The "Right Philosophy": The Marketing Concept

A philosophy may be thought of as a system of values, or principles, by which you live. Your philosophy is important because it dictates the decisions you make and what you do each and every day. To illustrate this point, you likely have a philosophy similar to this: "I believe that higher education is important because it will provide the knowledge and understanding I will need in the world to enable me to enjoy the standard of living I desire." Are we right? Probably. So, does this philosophy affect your daily life and the decisions you make every day? We think so. Think about what you are doing right now. You are reading this book, aren't you? Enough said. Well, the same is true for business managers. A manager's philosophy will affect how he or she makes day-to-day decisions in running a firm. There are many different philosophies that managers may use to guide them in their decision making. "We are in the locomotive business; we make and run trains." Or "To be successful, we must sell, sell, sell!" The managers who guided their companies by these philosophies guided those companies right out of business. A much better philosophy is called the marketing concept. One of the most prominent marketing professors, Philip Kotler, has defined the marketing concept as follows:

> The **marketing concept** is a business philosophy that holds that the key to achieving organizational goals consists of the company's being more effective than competitors in creating, delivering, and communicating customer value to its chosen target markets.[6]

■ The philosophy called the marketing concept emphasizes that "the key to achieving goals consists of the company's being more effective than competitors in creating, delivering, and communicating customer value to its chosen target markets."

For many years, business leaders have recognized that this is the "right philosophy." And although the *marketing concept* is often used interchangeably with other terms such as *customer oriented* or *market driven*, the key point is that this philosophy puts the customer first. Time has proven that such a philosophy is superior to one in which company management focuses on production, the product itself, or some promotional or sales gimmick. If you satisfy consumers, they will seek to do business with your company. Thus, we've learned that having the right philosophy is an important first step in being successful. Still, just appreciating the importance of satisfying consumer wants and needs isn't enough. Firms must put together the "right strategy."

## The "Right Marketing Strategy"

A strategy is nothing more than a plan. The term *strategy* was borrowed from military jargon that stressed developing plans of attack that would minimize the enemy's ability to respond. Firms may also have strategies in many different areas, such as financial strategy, production strategy, technology strategy, and so on. So, what exactly is marketing strategy?

> A **marketing strategy** consists of selecting a segment of the market as the company's target market and designing the proper "mix" of product/service, price, promotion, and distribution system to meet the wants and needs of the consumers within the target market.

■ Marketing strategy consists of selecting a target market and designing the "mix" (product/service, price, promotion, and distribution) necessary to satisfy the wants and needs of that target market.

Note how this definition *assumes* that we have already adopted the marketing concept. A manager not having the marketing concept, for example, wouldn't be concerned that his or her plan addressed any particular market segment and certainly wouldn't be concerned with consumers' wants and needs. So, to continue, we are thinking like *enlightened* managers; we have adopted the marketing concept. Now, as we shall see, because we have adopted the marketing concept, we can't come up with just any strategy. We have to develop the "right" strategy—the strategy that allows our firm to truly meet the wants and needs of the consumers within the market segment we have chosen. Think of the many questions we now must answer: What is the market? How do we segment the market? What are the wants and needs of each segment? How do we measure the size of each market segment? Who are our competitors, and how are they meeting the wants and needs of each segment? Which segment(s) should we target? Which model of a proposed product will best suit the target market? What is the best price? Which promotional method will be the most efficient? How should we distribute the product/service?

Now we see that many decisions must be made in order to develop the right strategy in order to succeed in business. In order to make the right decisions, managers must have objective, accurate, and timely information. Not only do managers need information to implement the right strategy now, but because environments are forever changing, this means marketers constantly need updated information about those environments. A strategy that is successful today may need to be changed as the competitive, economic, social, political, legal, global, and technological environments change. Managers must have the right information to understand when and how to modify their company's strategies. The bottom line of this entire discussion: To make the right decisions, managers continuously need information. As we shall learn next, marketing research supplies much of this information.

■ In order to make the right decisions, managers must have objective, accurate, and timely information.

■ Since environments are forever changing, this means marketers constantly need updated information about those environments.

## WHAT IS MARKETING RESEARCH?

■ Marketing research is the process of designing, gathering, analyzing, and reporting information that may be used to solve a specific marketing problem.

We've established that managers need information in order to carry out the marketing process. Now you are ready to learn exactly what marketing research is.

> **Marketing research** is the process of designing, gathering, analyzing, and reporting information that may be used to solve a specific marketing problem.

■ The AMA has defined marketing research as "the function that links the consumer, customer, and public to the marketer through information—information used to identify and define marketing opportunities and problems; generate, refine, and evaluate marketing performance; and improve the understanding of marketing as a process."

This definition tells us that marketing research is a *process* that results in reporting information and that information can be used to solve a marketing problem such as determining price, how to advertise, and so on. The focus, then, is on a *process* that results in information that will be used to make decisions. (We introduce you to this 11-step process in Chapter 3.) Notice also that our definition refers to information that may be used to solve a *specific* marketing problem. We are going to explain the importance of this later on in this chapter. Ours is not the only definition of marketing research. The American Marketing Association formed a committee several years ago to establish a definition of marketing research. The AMA definition is:

> **Marketing research** is the function that links the consumer, customer, and public to the marketer through information—information used to identify and define marketing opportunities and problems; generate, refine, and evaluate marketing actions; monitor marketing performance; and improve the understanding of marketing as a process.[7]

■ Sometimes managers say, "market research" when they mean "marketing research." Market research is appropriate when marketing research is being conducted on a specific customer group in a specific geographic area.

Which one of these definitions is correct? They are both right. Our definition is shorter and illustrates the process of marketing research. The AMA's definition is longer because it elaborates on the function (we call it the *purpose*) as well as the *uses* of marketing research. Note that **market research** refers to applying marketing research to a specific market area. One definition of market research is "the systematic gathering, recording, and analyzing of data with respect to a *particular market, where 'market' refers to a specific customer group in a specific geographic area.*"[8] In the next two sections, we will talk more about the purpose and uses of marketing research.

*Market* research, as opposed to market*ing* research, is the systematic gathering, recording, and analyzing of data with respect to a *particular market, where "market" refers to a specific customer group in a specific geographic area.*

## WHAT IS THE PURPOSE OF MARKETING RESEARCH?

By now you've probably guessed that the purpose of marketing research has to do with providing information to make decisions. That is essentially correct, but the AMA definition includes a reference to the consumer: The **purpose of marketing research** is to link the *consumer* to the marketer by providing information that can be used in making marketing decisions.

The AMA definition expands on our definition by telling us that the information provided by marketing research for decision making *should represent the consumer.*

Marketing research is not always right. Seinfeld was predicted to be a failure by marketing researchers.

In fact, by mentioning the consumer, this implies that marketing research is consistent with the marketing concept because it "links the consumer … to the marketer." The AMA definition is normative. That is, it tells us how marketing research *should be* used to ensure the firm is consumer oriented. We certainly agree with this, but what *should be* done isn't always followed. Kevin Clancy and Peter C. Krieg, in their book *Counterintuitive Marketing: Achieve Great Results Using Uncommon Sense,* argue that many failures can be attributed to managers just making "intuitive" decisions.[9] These well-known authors implore managers to use marketing research in order to make better decisions. While the AMA definition makes the point that marketing research links the firm to the consumer, we want to point out that marketing research information is also collected on entities other than the consumer. Information is routinely gathered on members of distribution channels, employees, and competitors as well as the economic, social, technological, and other environments.[10] Of course, one could argue that the point of all this research is to do a better job of satisfying consumers.

*Sometimes marketing research studies lead to the wrong decisions.* We should point out here that just because a manager uses marketing research doesn't mean that the decisions based on the research are infallible. In fact, marketing research studies are not always accurate. There are plenty of examples in which marketing research said a product would fail, yet it turned out to be a resounding success.

Jerry Seinfeld's popular TV program, *Seinfeld,* is a good example. The marketing research conducted on the pilot for *Seinfeld* stated the show was so bad that executives gave up on the idea. It was six months before another manager questioned the accuracy of the research and resurrected the show, which became one of the most successful shows in television history.[11] Likewise, marketing research studies also predicted that hair-styling mousse and answering machines would fail if brought to market.[12] Also, there are plenty of failures where marketing research predicted success. Most of these failures are removed from the shelves with as little fanfare as possible. A classic example of this was Beecham's cold-water wash product, Delicare. The new product failed even though marketing research predicted it would unseat the category leader, Woolite. When this happened, there was a great deal of publicity because Beecham sued the research company that had predicted success.[13] As we noted earlier in this chapter, there are many examples in which products or services have failed; for many of those, marketing research studies were conducted that supported them. But this doesn't mean marketing research is not useful. Remember, most marketing research studies are trying to understand and predict consumer behavior, and that is a difficult task. The fact that the marketing research industry has been around for many years and is growing means that it has passed the toughest of all tests to prove its worth—the test of the marketplace. If the industry did not provide value, it would cease to exist.

## WHAT ARE THE USES OF MARKETING RESEARCH?

### Identifying Market Opportunities and Problems

Now that you understand the purpose of marketing research, let's take a closer look at the *uses* of marketing research. In our short definition, we simply refer to the use of marketing research as providing information to solve a specific marketing problem, and the AMA definition spells out what some of these problems may be.

---

■ The purpose of marketing research is to link the consumer to the marketer by providing information that can be used in making marketing decisions.

■ Marketing research *should* be used to ensure the firm is consumer oriented, but some firms do not use marketing research.

■ Sometimes marketing research predicts failure, yet the product or service is a success.

■ Sometimes marketing research predicts success yet the product or service is a dismal failure.

■ The fact that the marketing research industry has been around for many years and is growing means that it has passed the toughest of all tests to prove its worth—the test of the marketplace.

For example, the *identification of market opportunities and problems* is certainly a use of marketing research. Mintel, a British consumer market research firm, looks for opportunities for new products. Some of its interests include baby milk sold in disposable bottles, tea and coffee that heat themselves, and a spray that temporarily whitens teeth.[14] Many research studies are being conducted today to determine the health effects of ingredients such as omega-3s, lecithin, and soy and how best to offer these ingredients in new foods.[15]

■ The identification of market opportunities and problems is a use of marketing research.

## Generate, Refine, and Evaluate Potential Marketing Actions

Marketing research can also be used to generate, refine, and evaluate a potential marketing action. For example, as AT&T grew from being "the long-distance telephone company" to participating in all forms of the fast-paced telecommunications industry, it wanted a brand image that would connote being a dynamic, unique, creative, and fast-moving company with advanced products and services in many areas. It conducted research that generated the "Boundless" brand advertising campaign. Then it conducted research to evaluate the effectiveness of the campaign.[16] Thus, AT&T is a good example of a firm using marketing research to generate, refine, and evaluate a marketing action. In this case, the "action" was developing a brand that conveyed the image AT&T wanted in the marketplace.

■ Another use of marketing research is to generate, refine, and evaluate a potential marketing action.

## Monitor Marketing Performance

The AMA definition also states that marketing research may be used to *monitor marketing performance*. Everyone talks about the Super Bowl commercials in which companies spend millions of dollars for a 30-second spot during the most-watched TV event of the year. Bruzzone Research Company monitors the effectiveness of these high-priced ads in order to provide information to companies that want to monitor the impact of their investment.[17] Another example of monitoring research is called tracking research. Tracking research is used to monitor how well products of companies such as Hershey's, Campbell's, Kellogg's, and Heinz are performing in the supermarkets. These "consumer packaged-goods" firms want to monitor the sales of their brands and sales of their competitors' brands as well. Research firms such as ACNielsen and Information Resources, Inc., are two of several firms monitoring the performance of products in supermarkets and other retail outlets. They monitor how many units of these products are being sold, through which chains, at what retail price, and so on. You will learn more about tracking studies later on in this book.

■ Another use of marketing research is to monitor marketing performance.

MRSI is a marketing research firm that specializes in helping firms find opportunities in the marketplace.

■ Visit MRSI at www.mrsi.com.

## Improve Marketing as a Process

■ Finally, a use of marketing research is to improve marketing as a process by expanding our basic knowledge of marketing.

Finally, our AMA definition says that a use of marketing research is to *improve marketing as a process*. This means that some marketing research is conducted to expand our basic knowledge of marketing. Typical of such research would be attempts to define and classify marketing phenomena and to develop theories that describe, explain, and predict marketing phenomena. Such knowledge is often published in journals such as the *Journal of Marketing Research* or *Marketing*

---

# MARKETING RESEARCH APPLICATION 1.1

PRACTICAL

APPLICATIONS

## Successful New Products Don't Just Happen

**Sherwin Williams uses marketing research to produce products customers want.**

Adam J. Chafe, Vice President of Marketing for Sherwin Williams, oversaw the research used to develop the company's successful Dutch Boy brand "Twist and Pour" paints container. Research had shown that the percentage of women buying paints had increased from 35% in 1993 to 52% in 2001. Women particularly disliked the old standard steel paint cans. The wire steel pail handles hurt the hand, the can did not pour easily or neatly, and it was difficult to seal the can to store leftover paint. Sherwin Williams used the following marketing research to develop the "Twist and Pour" packaging program platform.

**Focus Groups I** Investigated new concepts for paint cans.

**Focus Groups II** Refined design alternatives for test-market prototype tooling.

**Test Market** Produced 10,000 units to test price-point sensitivity, consumer acceptance, and operational impact with regional Home Center postpurchase interviews. Interviewed purchasers and nonpurchasers at the store and postuse to understand why they bought the product, what influenced them in the in-store marketing and media mix, and their experience after product trial—e.g., did it make the process neater and easier?

**In-Home Video** Taped consumers using the product to understand the subtleties of actual product use as it related to design.

**Web/Phone-In** Merchandised an opinion line (stickered on the package) to capture consumer thoughts pre- and postuse.

**Axiom Concept Testing** Used theater-style (200 people in 3 cities) concept testing against 11 other concepts to validate the concept in a quantitative execution (it tested at the highest levels) for uniqueness, believability, need, and purchase intent.

**McCollumn Speilman Testing** Online quantitative testing of media ads (TV) for breakthrough, persuasiveness, and recall.

As you can see, Sherwin Williams went to considerable effort, using marketing research to make better decisions regarding new product design, pricing, distribution, and media decisions.

*Source:* Courtesy of Sherwin Williams.

*Research.* Much of this research is conducted by marketing professors at colleges and universities and by other organizations, such as the Marketing Science Institute. The latter use could be described as the only part of marketing research that is basic research. **Basic research** is conducted to expand our knowledge rather than to solve a specific problem. Research conducted to solve specific problems is called **applied research**, and this represents the vast majority of marketing research studies. We will revisit the idea that marketing research provides information to solve *specific problems* later in this chapter. Marketing Research Application 1.1 illustrates how Sherwin Williams used applied marketing research to design a better paint can.

> ■ Basic research is conducted to expand our knowledge rather than to solve a specific problem. Research conducted to solve specific problems is called applied research, and this represents the vast majority of marketing research studies.

## CLASSIFYING MARKETING RESEARCH STUDIES

Another way to introduce you to marketing research is to look at a classification of the different types of marketing research studies being conducted in the industry. In Table 1.1 we organize the major types of studies under the usage categories from the AMA definition. Under each of these four categories we provide examples of studies.

## THE MARKETING INFORMATION SYSTEM

So far we have presented marketing research as if it were the only source of information. This is not the case, as you will understand by reading this section on marketing information systems.

> ■ Marketing research is not the *only* source of information.

Marketing decision makers have a number of sources of information available to them. We can understand these different information sources by examining the

**Table 1.1**
A Classification of Marketing Research Studies

### A. Identifying Market Opportunities and Problems

As the title implies, the goal of these studies is to find opportunities or problems with an existing strategy. Examples of such studies include the following:

  Market-demand determination
  Market segments identification
  Marketing audits SWOT analysis
  Product/service-use studies
  Environmental analysis studies
  Competitive analysis

*(Continued)*

**Table 1.1**   *cont.*

### B. Generating, Refining, and Evaluating Potential Marketing Actions

Marketing research studies may be used to generate, refine, and then evaluate potential marketing actions. Marketing actions could be as broad as a proposed marketing strategy or as narrow as a tactic (a specific action taken to carry out a strategy). Typically these studies deal with one or more of the marketing-mix variables (product, price, distribution, and promotion). Examples include the following:

- Proposed marketing-mix evaluation testing
- Concept tests of proposed new products or services
- New-product prototype testing
- Reformulating existing product testing
- Pricing tests
- Advertising pretesting
- In-store promotion effectiveness studies
- Distribution effectiveness studies

### C. Monitoring Marketing Performance

These studies are control studies. They allow a firm that already has a marketing mix placed in the market to evaluate how well that mix is performing. Examples include the following:

- Image analysis
- Tracking studies
- Customer satisfaction studies
- Employee satisfaction studies
- Distributor satisfaction studies
- Web site evaluations

### D. Improving Marketing as a Process[a]

A small portion of marketing research is conducted to expand our knowledge of marketing as a process rather than to solve a specific problem facing a company. By having the knowledge generated from these studies, managers may be in a much better position to solve a specific problem within their firms. This type of research is often conducted by institutes, such as the Marketing Science Institute, or universities. Examples include the following:

- How managers learn about the market
- Consumer behavior differences in e-business transactions
- Determining the optimum amount that should be spent on e-business and measuring success in e-business
- Predictors of new-product success
- The impact of long-term advertising on consumer choice
- Measuring the advantage to being the first product in the market
- Marketing-mix variable differences over the Internet

[a] These study topics were taken from the Marketing Science Institute's research priorities list and former award-winning research papers. See **www.MSI.org** for additional studies designed to improve marketing as a process.

components of the **marketing information system (MIS)**. An MIS is a structure consisting of people, equipment, and procedures to gather, sort, analyze, evaluate, and distribute needed, timely, and accurate information to marketing decision makers.[18] The role of the MIS is to determine decision makers' information needs, acquire the needed information, and distribute that information to the decision makers in a form and at a time when they can use it for decision making. However, this sounds very much like marketing research—providing information to aid in decision making. We can understand the distinction by understanding the components of an MIS.

> ◼ An MIS is a structure consisting of people, equipment, and procedures to gather, sort, analyze, evaluate, and distribute needed, timely, and accurate information to marketing decision makers.

## Components of an MIS

As noted previously, the MIS is designed to assess managers' information needs, to gather this information, and to distribute the information to the marketing managers who need to make decisions. Information is gathered and analyzed by the four subsystems of the MIS: internal reports, marketing intelligence, marketing decision support system (DSS), and marketing research. We discuss each of these subsystems next.

> ◼ The four subsystems of an MIS are the internal reports system, marketing intelligence system, marketing decision support system (DSS), and marketing research system.

### Internal Reports System

The **internal reports system** gathers information generated by internal reports, which includes orders, billing, receivables, inventory levels, stockouts, sales-call records, and so on. In many cases, the internal reports system is called the accounting information system. Although this system produces financial statements (balance sheets and income statements, etc.) that generally contain insufficient detail for many marketing decisions, the internal reports system also contains extreme detail on both revenues and costs, which can be invaluable in making decisions. A good internal reports system can tell a manager a great deal of information about what has happened within the firm in the past. When information is needed from sources *outside* the firm, other MIS components must be called upon.

> ◼ The internal reports system gathers information generated by internal reports, which includes orders, billing, receivables, inventory levels, stockouts, sales-call records, and so on.

### Marketing Intelligence System

A second component of an MIS is the **marketing intelligence system**. The marketing intelligence system is defined as a set of procedures and sources used by managers to obtain everyday information about pertinent developments in the environment. Such systems include both informal and formal information-gathering procedures. Informal information-gathering procedures involve such activities as scanning newspapers, magazines, and trade publications. Formal information-gathering activities may be conducted by staff members who are assigned the specific task of looking for anything that seems pertinent to the company or industry. They then edit and disseminate this information to the appropriate members or company departments. Formerly known as "clipping bureaus" (because they clipped relevant newspaper articles for clients), several online information service companies, such as LEXIS-NEXIS, provide marketing intelligence. To use its service, a firm would enter key terms into search forms provided online by LEXIS-NEXIS. Information containing the search terms appears on the subscriber's computer screen as often as several times a day. By clicking on an article title, subscribers can view a full-text version of the article. In this way, marketing intelligence goes on continuously and

> ◼ The marketing intelligence system is defined as a set of procedures and sources used by managers to obtain everyday information about pertinent developments in the environment.

searches a broad range of information sources in order to bring pertinent information to decision makers.

### Marketing Decision Support System (DSS)

■ A marketing decision support system (DSS) is defined as collected data that may be accessed and analyzed using tools and techniques that assist managers in decision making.

The third component of an MIS is the decision support system. A **marketing decision support system (DSS)** is defined as collected data that may be accessed and analyzed using tools and techniques that assist managers in decision making. Once companies collect large amounts of information, they store this information in huge databases that, when accessed with decision-making tools and techniques (such as break-even analysis, regression models, and linear programming), allow companies to ask "what-if" questions. Answers to these questions are then immediately available for decision making.

### Marketing Research System

Marketing research, which we have already discussed and defined, is the fourth component of an MIS. Now that you understand the three other components of an MIS, we are ready to discuss the question we raised at the beginning of this section. That is, if marketing research and an MIS are both designed to provide information for decision makers, how are the two different? In answering this question, we will see how marketing research differs from the other three MIS components.

■ Marketing research provides information not available from other components of the MIS. Marketing research studies provide information to solve specific problems and are sometimes referred to as "ad hoc studies." They also have a beginning and an end. Hence, they are also referred to as marketing research "projects."

First, the **marketing research system** gathers information not gathered by the other MIS component subsystems: Marketing research studies are conducted for a *specific* situation facing the company. It is unlikely that other components of an MIS have generated the particular information needed for the specific situation. When *People* magazine wants to know which of three cover stories it should use, can its managers obtain that information from internal reports? No. From the intelligence system or the DSS? No. This, then, is how marketing research plays a unique role in the total information system of the firm. By furnishing information for a *specific problem at hand,* it provides information not available from other components of the MIS. This is why people in the industry sometimes refer to marketing research studies as "ad hoc studies." *Ad hoc* is Latin, meaning "with respect to a specific purpose." (Recall that earlier in the chapter when we defined marketing research, we told you we would revisit the word *specific.* Now you see why we used that word in our definition.)

There is another characteristic of marketing research that differentiates it from the other MIS components. Marketing research projects, unlike the previous components, are not continuous—they have a beginning and an end. This is why marketing research studies are sometimes referred to as "projects." The other components are available for use on an ongoing basis. However, marketing research projects are launched only when there is a justifiable need for information that is not available from internal reports, intelligence, or the DSS.

## HOT TOPICS IN MARKETING RESEARCH

At this point, you should understand how marketing research is used by marketing managers to help them develop the "right" strategies using the marketing concept. You also know how to define marketing research, and you know the purpose and uses of marketing research as well as some of the different types of studies conducted. We conclude this introductory chapter by telling you about some "hot topics" in marketing research.

## Online Marketing Research

There is little doubt that the hottest topic in the marketing research industry for the last several years has been online marketing research.[19] We define **online research** as:

> *The use of computer networks, including the Internet, to assist in any phase of the marketing research process, including development of the problem, research design, data gathering, analysis, and report writing and distribution.*

Computer networks, particularly the Internet, have brought about many changes not only in terms of how people shop, learn, and communicate but also in how businesses operate. Computer networks have impacted how businesses market to one another (B2B) and how businesses market to consumers (B2C). They have affected virtually every type of business worldwide. Marketing research is no exception. The authors of *Online Marketing Research* state: "The advent of the Web has led to a revolution in the research community. Web technology has astronomically reduced the cost of conducting numerous types of research and simultaneously enabled the execution of more complicated and rigorous study designs."[20] The industry has developed many applications of online research. Today RFPs (*requests for proposals* to do research), sample design and ordering, data collection (online survey research), data analysis, and report writing and distribution are carried out through online tools and services. You will learn more about these throughout this book, and we will note them using our online research icon that you see at the beginning of this section. Before we move to the next "hot topic," you should know that some other terms are often confused with online research. First, by **Web-based research**, we mean research that is conducted *on* Web applications. This type of research, sometimes confused with online research, may use traditional methods as well as online research methods in conducting research on Web-based applications. Some Web-based applications include research on the popularity of the Web pages themselves, such as "site hit counts," effectiveness studies of pop-up ads on Web sites, and research measuring consumers' reactions to various components of Web sites. Any of these Web-based projects could be researched using either online research or traditional research. Because online research refers to using computer networks in conducting the research process, it may be used regardless of the application.

Second, another type of research, online *survey* research, is confused with online research. Online survey research has experienced rapid growth in the last several years, and many erroneously think this is the same as online research. **Online survey research** refers to the *collection of data* using computer networks. Collecting employee satisfaction data using a company's intranet would constitute online survey research. Many research firms, such as Greenfield Online and Insight Express, were created for the purpose of using the Internet to gather survey data. Because online survey research uses computer networks to collect

■ Online research is the use of computer networks, including the Internet, to assist in any phase of the marketing research process, including development of the problem, research design, data gathering, analysis, and report writing and distribution.

■ Web-based research is research conducted *on* Web applications. This type of research, sometimes confused with online research, may use traditional research methods as well as online research methods.

■ Online survey research refers to the collection of data using computer networks. It is a subset of online research.

data (part of the research process), we would consider it to be a subset of online research.

Worldwide Internet research revenues have been growing at double-digit rates for the last few years. The top 50 U.S. marketing research firms generated 56% of their revenues outside the United States.[21] Eastern Europe, Southeast Asia, and Central America are "hot" markets for marketing research.[22]

■ For excellent information on Internet and e-business research, see www.eMarketer.com.

■ Weary of abuse from telemarketers and other direct marketers, consumers resent invasions of privacy more and more, including requests for information from legitimate marketing researchers.

## Growing Consumer/Respondent Resentment

Another hot topic in marketing research is that of growing consumer resentment toward invasions of privacy. Marketing research, because it often seeks information from consumers, is "invasive." Weary of abuse from telemarketers and other direct marketers, potential respondents have grown resentful of any attempt by others to gather information from them. Finally, consumer rights groups have grown so powerful that the government, acting through the Federal Trade Commission (FTC), introduced a national "**Do Not Call**" list in the summer of 2003, to curb calls made by telemarketers to anyone requesting that the calls be stopped (**www.donotcall.gov**). So far, thanks to intense lobbying efforts by industry professional associations, the marketing research industry is excluded from the ban placed upon telemarketers in the Do Not Call regulations. However, the industry is very concerned about this trend. The Council of Survey Research Organizations (CASRO) reported research that showed 97% of consumers felt that telemarketers should be excluded through Do Not Call legislation but, alarmingly, CASRO found that 64% of consumers felt the legislation should also apply to marketing researchers.[23] The marketing research industry payed close attention to a bill that is similar to the Do Not Call legislation but directed at Internet spam. Called the "**Can Spam**" bill, it would have authorized the FTC to create a Do Not Spam list.[24] Depending on the wording of that legislation, this may have greatly impacted online survey research. However, Congress dropped the Can Spam bill due to inability to enforce it. Now, more legislation that can affect marketing researchers is being considered in several state legislatures. The **Do-Not-Mail** movement, as of summer 2007, is being considered by more than a dozen states. The intention is to allow consumers to sign up and be free of junk mail.[25] Will this legislation include legitimate surveys sent out via the mail by marketing research firms? The research industry realizes that gaining consumer willingness to participate in research is an important issue facing the research industry. Some firms are battling the rising nonresponse rates by investing in panels of consumers who are recruited to be available for several research requests. Still, the cost of recruiting such panel members is increasing yearly. The industry must devote considerable time and effort to maintaining trusted relationships with consumer respondents, who are the lifeblood of the marketing research industry. Presently the industry has considered developing a signature logo or seal that would identify firms as legitimate research firms that can guarantee anonymity and confidentiality and reassure potential respondents that these firms are not attempting to sell them anything. Ethical treatment of respondents is necessary if marketing research firms are to stop the growing consumer resentment. We will discuss this topic throughout the text, in those sections identified with the ethical icon you see at the beginning of this section.

■ A hot topic in marketing research is determining how to combat growing consumer resentment and falling response rates to marketing research requests. Ethical treatment of respondents is necessary.

## Globalization

As marketing firms spread globally during the 1990s, marketing research firms followed them to their distant markets. In the 2006 Honomichl Global Top 25 annual report, Jack Honomichl reported that about 70% of the revenues of the worlds top marketing research firms were generated from outside the United States.[26] Also, firms from other countries have been purchasing U.S.-based firms. The largest of these firms is VNU, a Dutch-based publisher that owns ACNielsen. To illustrate the influence of global marketing research, a research firm, Opinion Access Corporation, advertised that they do business in 10 languages![27] You will see many global applications as you learn about marketing research in this book. We will highlight them for you by using the global icon you see at the beginning of this section.

Marketing research firms followed their globe-trotting clients by locating and operating in markets around the world. Likewise, marketing research companies located in other countries have moved into the United States.

# SUMMARY

Many firms use Excel to conduct marketing research. Add-ins are written to make Excel more suitable for a particular application. *XL Data Analyst*, provided with this book, is Excel add-in software that will allow you to easily analyze data for marketing research projects. Marketing research is part of marketing. The American Marketing Association has defined marketing as an organizational function and a set of processes for creating, communicating, and delivering value to customers and for managing customer relationships in ways that benefit the organization and its stakeholders. The new "Service-Dominant Logic for Marketing" means that marketers need *more* information. In order to practice the marketing concept and to develop sound marketing strategy, managers must make many decisions. The marketing concept is a philosophy that states that the key to business success lies in determining and fulfilling consumers' wants and needs. Marketers attempting to practice the marketing concept need information in order to determine wants and needs and to design marketing strategies that will satisfy customers in selected target markets. Environmental changes mean that marketers must constantly collect information to monitor customers, markets, and competition.

We defined marketing research as the process of designing, gathering, analyzing, and reporting of information that may be used to solve a specific problem. The purpose of marketing research is to link the consumer to the marketer by providing information that can be used in making marketing decisions. Not all firms use marketing research and sometimes marketing research leads to the wrong decisions. But marketing research has been around for many years and is growing—it has passed the "test of the marketplace."

The uses of marketing research are to: (1) identify and define marketing opportunities and problems; (2) generate, refine, and evaluate marketing actions; (3) monitor marketing performance; and (4) improve our understanding of marketing. We classified marketing research studies using the above four types of studies, and we identified specific types of marketing research studies that would be found within each type of use of marketing research. Marketing research is one of four subsystems making up a marketing information system (MIS). Other subsystems include internal reports, marketing intelligence, and decision support systems. Marketing research gathers information not available through the other subsystems. Marketing research provides information for the specific problem at hand. Marketing research is conducted on a project basis as opposed to an ongoing basis. Hot topics in marketing research are online marketing research, growing consumer/respondent resentment toward invasions of privacy, and the continued globalization of marketing research.

## KEY TERMS

Marketing (p. 4)
Marketing concept (p. 7)
Marketing strategy (p. 7)
Marketing research (p. 8)
Market research (p. 9)
Purpose of marketing research (p. 9)
Basic research (p. 13)
Applied research (p. 13)
Marketing information system (MIS) (p. 15)
Internal reports system (p. 15)

Marketing intelligence system (p. 15)
Marketing decision support system (DSS) (p. 16)
Marketing research system (p. 16)
Online research (p. 17)
Web-based research (p. 17)
Online survey research (p. 17)
Do Not Call (p. 18)
Can Spam (p. 18)
Do Not Mail (p. 18)

## REVIEW QUESTIONS

1   Explain how marketing research can be used in the movie industry.
2   What is marketing? Explain the role of marketing research in the process of marketing management.
3   Give some examples of products that have failed.
4   Why are philosophies important to decision makers? What is the marketing concept?
5   What is strategy, and why is marketing research important to strategy makers?
6   Define marketing research. Define market research.
7   What is the purpose of marketing research?
8   Name the uses of marketing research.
9   Which use of marketing research is considered basic research?
10  Give two examples of the types of studies in each of the four classes of marketing research studies provided in this chapter.
11  Distinguish among MIS (marketing information system), marketing research, and DSS (decision support system).
12  Name three "hot topics" facing the research industry.
13  What is the difference between online research, Web-based research, and online survey research?
14  Why does the Do-Not-Mail legislation threaten marketing research?

## APPLICATION QUESTIONS

15  Go to your library, either in person or online, and look through several business periodicals such as *Advertising Age*, *Business Week*, *Fortune*, and *Forbes*. Find three examples of companies using marketing research.

16 Select a company in a field in which you have a career interest and look up information on this firm in your library or on the Internet. After gaining some knowledge of this company, its products and services, customers, and competitors, list five different types of decisions that you believe this company's management may have made within the last two years. For each decision, list the information the company's executives would have needed to make these decisions.

17 What are the differences among online research, Web-based research, and online survey research? Give some examples as to how a manager in a firm may use each of these three types of research.

18 Think of the following situations. What component of the marketing information system would a manager use to find the necessary information?

    a A manager of an electric utilities firm hears a friend at lunch talk about a new breakthrough in solar panel technology she read about in a science publication.

    b A manager wants to know how many units of each of three of the company's products were sold during each month for the past three years.

    c A manager wants to estimate the contribution to company ROI (return on investment) earned by 10 different products in the company product line.

    d A manager is considering producing a totally new type of health food. But first, he would like to know if consumers are likely to purchase the new food, at which meal they would most likely eat the food, and how they would prefer the food to be packaged.

19 Assume you are the manager of a successful marketing research firm located in Southern California. Discuss how the "hot topics" in marketing research presented in this chapter may affect your firm.

## INTERACTIVE LEARNING

 Want to know how good you are at "hearing the voice of the consumer" by evaluating new products for success or failure? Go to **www.newproductworks.com**. This is an organization devoted to helping companies avoid product failure by studying why products fail. Go to "NewProductWorks" and then to "HITS or MISSES." Also visit the Burns and Bush Web site at **www.prenhall.com/burnsbush**. For this chapter, work through the Self-Study Quizzes, and get instant feedback on whether you need additional studying.

| CASE 1.1 | Starlight Films |
| --- | --- |

Daniel Lee Yarbrough is a director and producer with *Starlight Films* in San Francisco, California. As part of his normal duties as a director and producer, Daniel constantly seeks scripts that he can turn into successful movies. The movie business is strongly driven by profits. While a few firms exist to make films purely for their artistic value, the cost of movie making is so huge today that few firms can afford to make movies that do not earn a respectable ROI for their investors. Daniel knows he must make "good" decisions; those that will result in a film that will attract sufficient audience numbers to earn a good return.

Daniel has recently received a manuscript by a successful author, Warren St. John. St. John wrote the highly successful book "Rammer Jammer Yellow Hammer" (a book about football fans following their team in RVs). Recently St. John turned out another manuscript about a boy's soccer team that has Yarbrough's interest. As he reads through the manuscript, Yarbrough begins thinking about decisions he will need to make if he wants to turn the manuscript into a movie.

How much should he offer St. John for the manuscript rights? Daniel knows the manuscript is very good and he assumes other film companies are going to make offers. While Daniel has paid for manuscripts in the past, it has been about three years since he was actively involved in bidding for an author's script.

Though the amount paid the author will be a small part of the total cost of the movie, it could still be a significant amount of money.

Casting decisions must be made early because they could greatly influence costs. Who should play the lead roles? Supporting roles? As always, there is a plentiful stock of talented, yet unknown actors available. On the other hand, there are "hot" actors who are very popular and draw audiences just due to name recognition.

Daniel's filmmaking experience allows him to adequately predict many of his costs. He knows, for example, what it takes to film on location versus in a studio. He also knows the costs of equipment and costs of various personnel such as cameramen, grips, and copyeditors. However, of all the issues facing Daniel Yarbrough, the most important issue will be: How many people will buy a ticket to see this movie? Emmy Awards are great but to make the needed ROI, Daniel knows he needs people to walk into movie theaters to see his movies. Of course, while some can estimate this number, no one can assure Daniel of the exact number. But, he can get some good estimates as to whether samples of an audience like the script.

1  Do you think Daniel Yarbrough needs to conduct some research? Why? Why not?

2  Just based on the case material alone, list decisions that Daniel needs to make.

3  For each decision you list in number 2 above, provide a description of the information that you think Daniel needs in order to make the decision.

## CASE 1.2   |||  Your Integrated Case

### College Life E-Zine

### Friends

Sarah Stripling, Anna Fulkerson, Wesley Addington, and Don Cooper were good friends who had met while students at State University. All four graduated with B.S. degrees in marketing five years ago and found careers in the same city in which State University was located. Sarah worked for a large firm that published books and periodicals, including magazines targeted to special market segments ranging from seniors seeking vacation resorts to avid teenage tennis players. Wesley

and Anna had both taken elective courses in computer technology and Internet marketing, and both worked for a local consulting firm that specialized in creating e-commerce systems for small and medium-sized firms. Don had started his career with the local newspaper in sales. He had a talent for writing and wrote short articles for the newspaper about new business openings. The editor of the paper recognized Don's talent and moved him into a writing position. Don had just been promoted to editor of the Entertainment section of the newspaper. The four were still good friends and often socialized together.

## Future Entrepreneuers?

One thing the four friends had in common was a desire to go into their own business. Each had dabbled with a few business ideas and shared them among the other three friends but, thus far, no one had had an idea that succeeded in generating significant interest. Still, the four constantly talked about potential ways to serve the market's wants and needs. Two more years passed. Each person was successful in their line of business, and had seven years of good experience in their chosen field.

## A Business Idea

As the four gathered for a Saturday afternoon of watching State U football and grilling burgers, Sarah suggested a new business idea. "Hey, guys. I've been thinking about a business idea for us. I've been watching the sales of our magazines that are targeted at special markets. Their growth rates surpass all our other publications. Also, our online subscriptions, our 'e-zines,' have been growing each year, especially in publications targeted at younger audiences."

"Yeah," Anna said, "I subscribe to three e-zines myself. I like them because I can read them wherever I have access to a computer, and if I want the actual hard copy, I can always print out an article. But what's your point, Sarah?"

Now, with everyone's attention on her, Sarah replied, "I think there is a huge market that has been missed by all the publishers . . . the college student market."

Don argued, "College students have their own student newspapers, and when they want more, they can read our newspaper."

Not deterred, Sarah said, "Of course they have their own student newspapers, but those newspapers offer stories and information mostly about what's happening at the college or university. I think college students want more than just knowing the dates for early withdrawal from classes or which sorority won first place for the homecoming float. They want the news and entertainment stories targeted for college students. And Don, no disrespect for the newspaper—you guys do a great job—but how many of us read the local newspaper when we were in college?"

"I guess you're right, we sure didn't read the newspaper!" Don replied. As Don recalled his college days his creative juices were beginning to flow. He asked, "What would college students today want to know about? More than just sports. They'd want to know the inside story about teams, players, coaches . . . . The major media cover the major sports events. They don't cover State U's championship softball games, and lots of students would like to watch the basketball games but don't go to the game . . . . Also, they want more than what the mass media provides in terms of politics and foreign policy. Political stories are intriguing, but they aren't written for college students in the major media. I didn't get interested in politics until I was older and read the paper daily, which allowed me to keep up with the intricacies of the political arena. You could write the stories of politics with a different slant for college students. I would think college students want to know the basics of the political stories and they want visuals. They want to know more about the people themselves. A *People* magazine approach may appeal to them. They don't want the standard line they read in all the other publications." As Don talked aloud, his rising voice level clearly indicated that his excitement about the idea was growing.

Wesley, sensing everyone's attention turning to the new business idea, mentioned that he and Anna could easily put the concept online in the form of an e-zine targeted to college students. Sarah, now taking the burgers off the grill, set the plate down and said in a serious tone, "Listen up! We may have something here that uses all of our talents. I know the publishing business, and Don has a flair for writing and creating features, and Anna and Wesley can handle the technical aspects needed to make an e-zine a reality. What should we do to follow up on this idea?"

1 Do you think the four friends should now conduct marketing research? Why or why not?
2 If you feel they should conduct marketing research, what questions should they seek to answer?

2

# UNDERSTANDING THE MARKETING RESEARCH INDUSTRY

## Which Research Company Would A Client Choose?

Build a Foundation to Build your Business.
*For information on Professional Researcher Certification, visit www.mra-net.org/prc.*

By permission, MRA

Clients seeking the services of marketing researchers now have a choice; certified or noncertified marketing researchers. One of the most significant events to happen in the marketing research industry occurred in 2005, when a certification program was introduced for the industry. The Marketing Research Association, working with several other industry associations, created the process leading to Professional Researcher Certification, PRC. The goal of PRC is to encourage high standards within the opinion and marketing research profession in order to raise competency, establish an objective measure of an individual's knowledge and proficiency, and to encourage continued professional development. Certification requires passing rigorous tests, and maintaining one's PRC requires keeping current on new knowledge, techniques, and technologies in the marketing research industry.

- To understand how the marketing research industry evolved
- To learn about the marketing research industry today, including the major firms and professional organizations
- To learn how to classify firms in the marketing research industry
- To know examples of the different types of external suppliers
- To appreciate some of the challenges to the industry and consider some proposed suggestions for improvement
- To understand how a researcher's philosophy might dictate behavior
- To appreciate the ethical issues involved in marketing research
- To learn the ethical standards for conducting online survey research

## About MRA

The Marketing Research Association is the leading and largest association of the opinion and market research profession, a multibillion-dollar-a-year industry dedicated to providing valuable information to guide the decisions of companies that provide products and services to consumers and businesses. Established in 1957, MRA's international membership encompasses companies and professionals engaged in all segments of marketing and opinion research including end users, full service researchers, data collectors, and support service providers. MRA publishes the annual Blue Book Research Services Directory which is widely known throughout the opinion and marketing research profession. Their Web site is **www.mra-net.org.**

The MRA is one of several professional organizations that support the marketing research industry. In this chapter, you will learn about these organizations and about the marketing research industry. We will begin with a short discussion about how the industry came into being, followed by a look at the industry today. Next, we will learn how to classify different members of the industry, and we will take a look at some examples of each of the different types. We will also examine some of the criticisms of the industry and consider some proposed resolutions. The second part of this chapter is devoted to ethical issues facing the research industry and what the industry is doing to deal with these issues. When you finish this chapter, you will have finished our two-chapter introduction to marketing research. We include two appendixes at the end of this chapter: Appendix A gives you more detailed information on how to conduct an online survey without spamming, and Appendix B provides information on careers in marketing research.

# THE MARKETING RESEARCH INDUSTRY

## Evolution of the Industry

### The Beginnings

Robert Bartels, a marketing historian, wrote that the earliest questionnaire surveys began as early as 1824, and that in 1879 a study was conducted by N. W. Ayers and Company to examine grain production by states for a client. However, Bartels believes the first continuous and organized research was started in 1911 by **Charles Coolidge Parlin**, a schoolmaster from a small city in Wisconsin. Parlin was hired by the Curtis Publishing Company to gather information about customers and markets to help Curtis sell advertising space. Parlin was successful and the information he gathered led to increased advertising in Curtis's *Saturday Evening Post* magazine.[1] Parlin is recognized today as the "Father of Marketing Research," and the AMA provides an award in his name each year at their annual marketing research conference.

### Growth of the Need

While there are a few reported instances of the use of marketing research in the early days of the history of the United States, it wasn't until the 1930s that marketing research efforts became widespread. Prior to the Industrial Revolution, businesses were located close to the consumers. In an economy based upon artisans and craftsmen involved in barter exchange with their customers, there was not much need to "study" consumers because business owners saw their customers daily. They knew their needs and wants, and their likes and dislikes. However, when the Industrial Revolution led to manufacturers producing goods for distant markets, the need for marketing research emerged. Manufacturers in Boston needed to know more about the consumers and their needs in "faraway" places like Denver and Atlanta. Marketing research firms began to appear to meet this need. A. C. Nielsen started his firm in 1922. In the 1930s, colleges began to teach courses in marketing research, and during the 1940s, Alfred Politz introduced statistical theory for sampling in marketing research.[2] Also during the forties, Robert Merton introduced focus groups, which today represent a large part of what is known as qualitative marketing research. Computers revolutionized the industry in the 1950s.[3] By the 1960s, marketing research had not only gained acceptance in the business world but also was recognized as being a key to understanding distant and fast-changing markets. It was needed for survival.

Since the 1960s the marketing research industry has seen technological advances, in the form of many new products and services, which have increased productivity in the industry. As you learned in the previous chapter, the research industry is truly a global industry. As firms spread their business throughout the markets of the world, the marketing research industry followed those firms to their distant markets.

---

■ Go to Interactive Learning at the end of this chapter to learn how to find out more about the AMA's Charles Coolidge Parlin Award.

Read more about Charles Coolidge Parlin by going to www.advertisinghallof fame.org, go to Members, and search under "P."

■ While there are a few reported instances of the use of marketing research in the early days of the history of the United States, it wasn't until the 1930s that marketing research efforts became widespread.

■ When the Industrial Revolution led to manufacturers producing goods for distant markets, the need for marketing research emerged.

■ By the 1960s, marketing research had not only gained acceptance in the business world but also was recognized as being a key to understanding distant and fast-changing markets. It was needed for survival.

# The Marketing Research Industry Today

## World Revenues

The marketing research industry accounts for over $15 billion spent annually to better understand customers, markets, and competitors. In 2005 the world's top 25 marketing/advertising/public opinion firms accounted for over $14 billion of total revenues, which represents a 5.4% growth rate from 2004 to 2005. So, the top 25 global firms account for a major share of total revenues, due to the increase of acquisitions made by these top 25 companies. The top 25 global research organizations list is compiled by Jack Honomichl and reported as the **Honomichl Global Top 25** annually in *Marketing News*.[4] Take a look at the latest report by visiting **www.marketingpower.com/honomichl**.

The top 25 firms are from all over the world. Home countries include the Netherlands, Japan, Germany, Italy, France, the United Kingdom, and the United States. Reflecting the true global nature of marketing research, 67% of the total revenues generated by the top global 25 firms come from operations or subsidiaries outside the home country (see Figure 2.1). The largest research firm in the world is The Nielsen Company, which is based in Haarlem, the Netherlands. This firm, which owns ACNielsen, has revenues of over $3.5 billion, of which only a small share comes from the Netherlands.[5]

▪ Mr. Honomichl's report is highly regarded as the best measure of revenue and change in the marketing research industry. You can view "The Honomichl Top 50" table with hyperlinks to the companies at **www.marketingpower.com** (do a search for "Honomichl").

Visit ACNielsen at **www.acnielsen.com**.

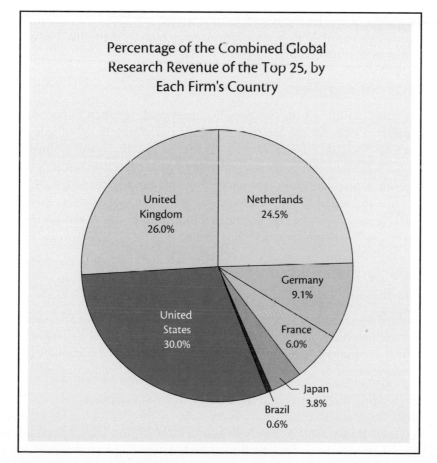

**Figure 2.1**

Source: Honomichl, Jack (2006). No great growth. Compared to prior years, revenue gains small. *Marketing News*, August 15, H3.

## The Honomichl Top 50

### Revenues of the U.S. Firms

The top 50 U.S.-based firms, based upon revenues, are reported each year in the **Honomichl Top 50** in *Marketing News*. Honomichl reported the top 50 earned total revenues in the United States of $6.7 billion in 2005, and this was an increase of 5.3% over 2004. CASRO, the council of American Survey Research organizations, has many member firms not large enough to make the top 50, and when CASRO firms are added, the total number of U.S.-based research firms climbs to 193. When U.S. revenues for these additional firms are added to the top 50 firms' revenue, the total climbs to $7.5 billion, an increase of 5.5% from 2004.[6] Figure 2.2 depicts U.S. revenue growth, actual and adjusted for inflation, from 1995 through 2006.

### Competition in the Industry Is Very Keen

Inefficient or ineffective firms are quickly removed by market forces. There has been a growth in strategic alliances among competitor firms in recent years. **Strategic alliances** allow firms with strong expertise in one area (data collection) to form partnerships with firms offering expertise in another area (data analysis). This increases competition within the industry. ACNielsen acquired 61% of Net Ratings which now gives ACNielsen a leadership role in Internet audience measurement.[7]

■ Strategic alliances allow firms with strong expertise in one area to form partnerships with firms offering expertise in another area.

## Classifying Firms in the Marketing Research Industry

Providers of marketing research information are known as **research suppliers**. In Figure 2.3, modified from a classification by Naresh Malhotra,[8] suppliers are classified as either internal or external.

## Internal Suppliers

An entity within a firm that supplies marketing research is known as an **internal supplier**. Firms having internal suppliers spend about 1% of sales on marketing research.[9] Kodak, General Mills, General Motors, Ford, and DaimlerChrysler have research departments of their own. AT&T has an in-house research department that constantly monitors consumer satisfaction and environmental trends. It also provides research support to AT&T's advertising agencies. Internal suppliers exist not only in for-profit firms but also in not-for-profits. For example, The American Heart Association has its own marketing research department.

## How Do Internal Suppliers Organize the Research Function?

Internal suppliers of marketing research can elect several organizing methods to provide the research function. They may: (1) have their own formal departments, (2) have no formal department but place at least a single individual or a committee in charge of marketing research, or (3) assign no one responsibility for conducting marketing research.

■ Internal suppliers may: (1) have their own formal departments, (2) have no formal department but at least a single individual responsible for marketing research, or (3) assign no one responsibility for conducting marketing research.

### Organizing the Formal Department of Internal Suppliers

Most large organizations have the resources to staff their own formal marketing research departments. Firms with higher sales volumes (over $500 million) tend to have their own formal marketing research departments, and many large advertising

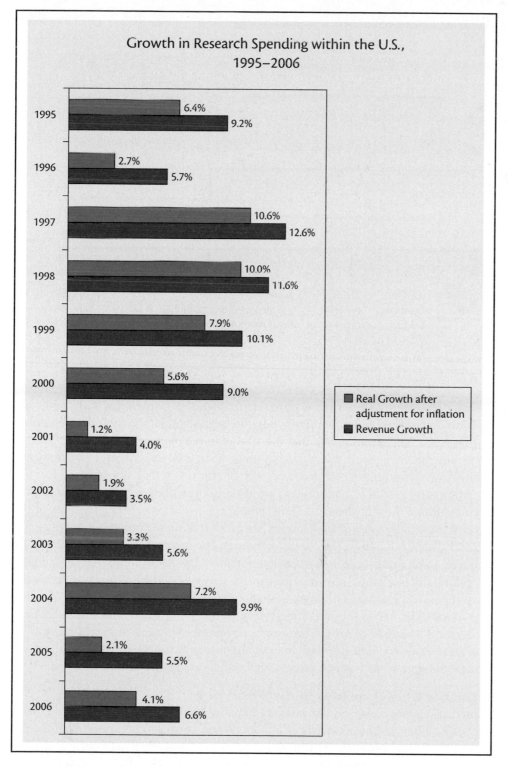

Growth in Research Spending within the U.S.,
1995–2006

1995: 6.4% | 9.2%
1996: 2.7% | 5.7%
1997: 10.6% | 12.6%
1998: 10.0% | 11.6%
1999: 7.9% | 10.1%
2000: 5.6% | 9.0%
2001: 1.2% | 4.0%
2002: 1.9% | 3.5%
2003: 3.3% | 5.6%
2004: 7.2% | 9.9%
2005: 2.1% | 5.5%
2006: 4.1% | 6.6%

■ Real Growth after adjustment for inflation
■ Revenue Growth

**Figure 2.2**

Source: Honomichl, Jack (2006). Honomichl Top 50. *Marketing News*, June 15, H3; and information provided to the authors by Jack Honomichl.

**Figure 2.3** A Classification of Marketing Research Suppliers

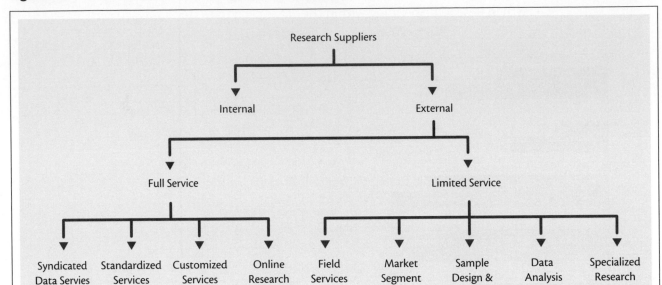

agencies have their own formal research departments.[10] Companies with their own research department must justify the large fixed costs of supporting the personnel and facilities. The advantage is that the staff is fully cognizant of the firm's operations and the changes in the industry, which may give them better insights into identifying opportunities and problems suitable for marketing research action.

■ Marketing research departments are usually organized according to one or a combination of the following functions: area of application, marketing function, or the steps of the research process.

Marketing research departments are usually organized according to one or a combination of the following functions: *area of application, marketing function,* or *the research process.* By "area of application," we mean that these companies organize the research function around the "areas" to which the research is being applied. For example, some firms serve both ultimate consumers as well as industrial consumers. Therefore, the marketing research department may be organized into two divisions: consumer and industrial. Other areas of application may be brands or lines of products or services. Secondly, marketing research may be organized around *functional areas* (the 4 P's) such as product research, ad research, pricing research, channel of distribution research, and so on. Finally, the research function may be organized around the *steps of the research process* such as data analysis or data collection.

### Organizing When There Is No Formal Department

If internal supplier firms elect not to have a formal marketing research department, there are many other organizational possibilities. When there is no formal department, *responsibility for research may be assigned to existing organizational units* such as departments or divisions. A problem with this method is that research activities are not coordinated; a division conducts its own research, and other units of the firm may be unaware of useful information. One way to remedy this is to organize by having a *committee or an individual assigned marketing research* to ensure that all units of the firm have input into and benefit from any research activity undertaken. In some cases, committees or individuals assigned to marketing research may actually conduct some limited research, but typically their primary role is that of helping other managers recognize the need for research and coordinating the purchase of research from external research suppliers. Obviously, the advantage here is limiting fixed costs incurred by maintaining the full-time staff required for an ongoing department. *No one may be assigned* to marketing research in some organizations. This is rare in large companies but not unusual at all in smaller firms. In very small firms, the owner/manager plays many roles, ranging from strategic planner to salesperson to security staff. He or she must also be responsible for marketing research, making certain to have the right information before making decisions.

> ■ It is rare to find no one responsible for marketing research in large organizations; small-business owners who see their customers daily conduct their own "informal" research constantly.

## External Suppliers

**External suppliers** are outside firms hired to fulfill a firm's marketing research needs. In most cases, internal suppliers of marketing research also purchase research from external suppliers. Both large and small firms, for-profit and not-for-profits, and government and educational institutions purchase research information from external suppliers.

> ■ External suppliers are outside firms hired to fulfill a firm's marketing research needs.

Of course, there are many other research firms in the marketing research industry. These research firms range in size from one-person proprietorships to the large, international corporations you will find in the Honomichl Global 25. You can get an idea of the type, number, and specialities of these firms by looking at some online directories of marketing research firms. For example, take a look at the New York chapter of the American Marketing Association's Web site, and look through the *Greenbook*, a directory of marketing research firms. Go to **www.greenbook.org**. Explore this Web site and you will get a better understanding of how to classify external supplier firms. Also visit the different "directory" listings at **www.quirks.com**. The MRA publishes the bluebook which can be viewed at **www.bluebook.org**.

> ■ Go to www.greenbook.org. Explore this Web site and you will get a better understanding of how to classify external supplier firms. Also visit the different "directory" listings at www.quirks.com and the MRA Bluebook directory at www.bluebook.org/.

## How Do External Suppliers Organize?

Like internal supplier firms, external supplier firms organize themselves in different ways. These firms may organize by function (data analysis, data collection, etc.), by type of research application (customer satisfaction, advertising effectiveness, new-product development, etc.), by geography (domestic versus international), by type of customer (health care, government, telecommunications, etc.), or some combination. We also see research companies changing their organizational structure to accommodate changes in the environment. For example, as online research grew in the last several years, Burke, Inc., added a division to Burke Marketing Research called Burke Interactive. Finally, many companies use multiple bases for organizing. Opinion Research Corporation (ORC) is organized by geography, type of research application, and function. ORC's three divisions are ORC International, which conducts global marketing research; ORC Macro, which specializes in global social research such as health issues; and ORC ProTel, which is a provider of teleservices.[11]

> ■ Many external supplier firms use multiple bases for organizing the research function.

> ■ Take a look at some of the company Web sites listed in the Honomichl Global 25 or Honomichl Top 50. You can see how these external supplier firms organize themselves by looking at their divisions and departments.

## Classifying External Supplier Firms

As you may recall from Figure 2.3, we can classify all external supplier firms into two categories: full-service or limited-service firms. In the following paragraphs, we will define these two types of firms and give you some examples of each.

> ■ External suppliers can be classified as either full-service or limited-service supplier firms.

### Full-Service Supplier Firms

**Full-service supplier firms** have the ability to conduct the entire marketing research project for the buyer firms. Full-service firms will often define the problem, specify the research design, collect and analyze the data, and prepare the final written

■ Full-service supplier firms have the ability to conduct the entire marketing research project for the buyer firms. Full-service firms can be further broken down into syndicated data service firms, standardized service firms, customized service firms, and online research services firms.

report. Typically, these are larger firms that have the expertise as well as the necessary facilities to conduct research studies in their entirety. For example, The Nielsen Company offers services in more than 100 countries and has 41,000 employees. The company can provide marketing research services in any area and has divisions for tracking retail sales, consumer panels, modeling and analytical services, and customized research that can be tailored to the individual needs of the client. The Kantar Group (TKG) operates around the world with several research businesses, including Millward Brown Group, Research International, the Ziment Group, Mattison Jack Group, and Lightspeed Research.[12] These divisions give TKG the ability to conduct many different forms of research. Most of the research firms found in the Honomichl Global 25 and Honomichl Top 50 would qualify as full-service firms.

### Syndicated Data Service Firms

■ Syndicated data service firms collect information that is made available to multiple subscribers.

**Syndicated data service firms** collect information that is made available to multiple subscribers. The information, or data, is provided in standardized form (the information may not be tailored to meet the needs of any one company) to a large number of companies, known as a syndicate. Therefore, these companies offer syndicated data to all subscribing members of the syndicate. Information Resources, Inc., and ACNielsen are two large syndicated data service firms. We will discuss syndicated data service firms in greater detail in Chapter 6.

### Standardized Service Firms

■ Standardized service firms provide syndicated *services*, as opposed to syndicated data. Each client gets different data, but the *process* used to collect the data is standardized so that it may be offered to many clients at a cost less than that of a custom-designed project.

**Standardized service firms** provide syndicated marketing research services, as opposed to syndicated data, to clients. Each client gets different data, but the *process* used to collect the data is standardized so that it may be offered to many clients at a cost less than that of a custom-designed project. Burke's Customer Satisfaction Associates provides the service of measuring customer satisfaction. RoperAWS offers several segmentation services. ACNielsen and several other companies offer the service of test marketing.

### Customized Service Firms

■ Customized service firms offer a variety of research services that are tailored to meet the client's specific needs.

**Customized service firms** offer a variety of research services that are tailored to meet the client's specific needs. Each client's problem is treated as a unique research project. Customized service firms spend considerable time with a client firm to determine the problem and then design a research project specifically to address the particular client's problem.

### Online Research Services Firms

■ Online services firms specialize in providing marketing research services online, such as surveys, concept testing of new products, and focus groups.

**Online research services firms** specialize in providing services online. Recall in Chapter 1 that we defined online research as the use of computer networks, including the Internet, to assist in any phase of the marketing research process, including development of the problem, research design, data gathering, analysis, and report distribution. Virtually all research firms today use online research in the sense that they make use of online technology in at least one or more phases of the research process. Most of these firms would be better categorized in one of the other types of firms shown in Figure 2.3. However, there are many firms that *specialize* in online services. Their "reason for being" is based on the provision of services online. Affinnova, for example, exists because it has proprietary software that allows consumers to design preferred product attributes into new products online. Knowledge Networks came into being because its founders wanted to provide clients with access to probability samples online. Insight Express was formed by NFO, Inc., to allow clients to easily develop questionnaires and quickly conduct surveys online. Active Group was formed to conduct focus groups online. Certainly, there are overlapping categories in Figure 2.3. We do not claim that the categories are mutually exclusive. In fact, we could argue that some of these, because they specialize in one step of the research process, could be placed in one of the limited-service supplier categories that follow.

### Limited-Service Supplier Firms

**Limited-service supplier firms** specialize in one or, at most, a few marketing research activities. Firms can specialize in types of marketing research techniques such as eye-testing (tracking eye movements in response to different promotional stimuli) or mystery shopping (using researchers to pose as shoppers to evaluate customer service), or specific market segments such as senior citizens, or certain sports segments such as golf or tennis. The limited-service suppliers can be further classified on the basis of their specialization. These include field services, market segment specialists, sample design and distribution services, data analysis, and specialized research technique service suppliers. Many of these limited-service firms specialize in some form of online research.

**Field service firms** specialize in collecting data. These firms typically operate in a particular territory conducting telephone surveys, focus-group interviews, mall-intercept surveys, or door-to-door surveys. Because it is expensive and difficult to maintain interviewers all over the country, firms will use the services of field service firms in order to quickly and efficiently gather data. There is specialization even within firms that specialize in field services. Some firms, for example, conduct only in-depth personal interviews; others conduct only mall-intercept surveys. Some firms, such as Irwin and Mktg., Inc., are known as **phone banks** because they specialize in telephone surveying. Irwin collects data using door-to-door, executive interviewing, and mystery shoppers, among others.

Other limited-service firms, called **market segment specialists**, specialize in collecting data for special market segments such as African Americans, Hispanics, children, seniors, gays, industrial customers, or a specific geographic area within the United States or internationally. Strategy Research Corporation specializes in Latin American markets. JRH Marketing Services, Inc., specializes in marketing to ethnic markets, especially to black markets. Other firms specialize in children, mature citizens, pet owners, airlines, beverages, celebrities, college students, religious groups, and many other market segments. C&R Research has a division called Latino Eyes that specializes in U.S. Hispanic and Latin American markets. They have another division specializing in kids, tweens, and teens, called KidzEyes and another division specializing in the 50-year-and-over market called Sage Advice.[10] By specializing, these limited-service suppliers capitalize on their in-depth knowledge of the client's industry.

Survey Sampling, Inc., and Scientific Telephone Samples (STS) are examples of limited-service firms that specialize in **sample design and distribution**. It is not uncommon, for example, for a company with an internal marketing research department to buy its sample from a firm specializing in sampling and then send the samples and a survey questionnaire to a phone bank for completion of the

Irwin is an example of a Field Services Firm.

■ **Survey Sampling, Inc. (SSI), is one of the oldest and best-known firms specializing in providing samples to marketing research firms. SSI is also an example of a company using online research. Users can design their sample plan online (see SSI SNAP on the company's Web site) and receive their samples online. Go to www.surveysampling.com.**

■ **Specialized research technique firms address very specific needs such as eye-tracking, package design, or brand name testing. Visit Eye Tracking, Inc., at www.eyetracking.com.**

survey. This way, a firm may quickly and efficiently conduct telephone surveys using a probability sample plan in markets all over the country. Survey Sampling, Inc., provides Internet samples, B2B samples, global samples, and samples of persons with characteristics that are hard to find (low-incidence samples).

There are limited-service marketing research firms that offer **data analysis services**. Their contribution to the research process is to provide the technical assistance necessary to analyze and interpret data using the more sophisticated data analysis techniques such as conjoint analysis. SDR Consulting, SPSS MR, and Applied Decision Analysis LLC are examples of such firms.

**Specialized research technique firms** provide a service to their clients by expertly administering a special technique. Examples of such firms include Eye Tracking, Inc., which specializes in eye movement research. Eye movements are used to determine effectiveness of ads, direct-mail pieces, and other forms of visual promotion. Other firms specialize in mystery shopping, taste tests, fragrance tests, creation of brand names, generating new ideas for products and services, and so on.

We should not leave this section without saying that our categorization of research suppliers does not fit every situation. Many full-service firms fit neatly into one of our categories. However some do not: Taylor Nelson Sofres, for example, is a large, full-service firm, but it also offers very specialized data analysis services.

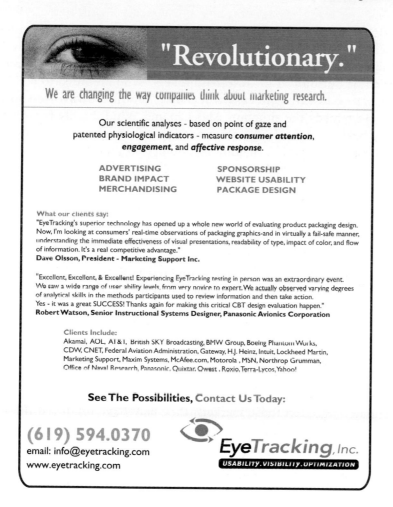

Eye Tracking, Inc. is an example of a Specialized Research Technique firm.

In addition, there are other entities supplying research information that do not fit neatly into one of our categories. For example, universities and institutes supply research information. Universities sponsor a great deal of research that could be classified as marketing research.

## CHALLENGES TO THE MARKETING RESEARCH INDUSTRY

Studies evaluating entire industries are conducted from time to time. Such is the case in the marketing research industry. These reviews indicate that, although the marketing research industry is doing a reasonably good job, there is room for improvement.[11] Here are some striking examples indicating marketing research needs improving: Sony, Chrysler, and Compaq did not use marketing research when they introduced the Walkman, minivan, and PC network servers—all very successful products. Coca-Cola's first attempt at New Coke and McDonald's McLean Burgers both failed but, in each case, were supported by extensive marketing research.[12] Critics Vijay Mahajan and Yoram Wind suggest, however, that

There are examples of successful products produced without any marketing research as well as product failures that received extensive marketing research.

■ Some industry critics believe marketing research can add more value if marketing researchers are more involved in upper-level strategic decisions rather than as providers of research services viewed as commodities.

marketing research is not fundamentally flawed but that many executives misapply research by not having research professionals involved in high-level, strategic decision making. Instead, too many executives view marketing research as a commodity to be outsourced to "research brokers" who are hired to conduct a component of the research process when they should be involved in the entire process. To remedy the situation, Mahajan and Wind, highly regarded in academics and business consulting, recommend that researchers: (1) focus on diagnosing problems, (2) use information technology to increase speed and efficiency, (3) take an integrative approach, and (4) expand the strategic impact of marketing research.

## Marketing Researchers Should Focus on Diagnosing Problems

Mahajan and Wind suggest that marketing researchers should stop using marketing research only to test solutions, such as testing a specific product or service. Instead, researchers should diagnose the market. As an example, consider that customers didn't "ask" for a Sony Walkman or a minivan. Marketing researchers would not have known about these products by asking customers what they wanted. Without having ever seen these products, it is unlikely that customers would have been able to articulate the product characteristics. But had marketing researchers focused on diagnosing the market in terms of unserved markets and unarticulated needs in those markets, they may have produced these products. The Walkman was successful because it met an unserved market's need for portable entertainment. The minivan was successful because it met an unserved market's need for additional space in family vehicles. Marketing research can improve by properly diagnosing the market first, then testing alternative solutions to meet the needs discovered in the market.

■ Marketing researchers need to diagnose market needs first and then test proposed alternative solutions to market needs.

## Marketing Researchers Should Speed Up Marketing Research by Using IT

It has long been recognized that there is a trade-off between quickly producing marketing research information and doing research in a thorough manner. Marketing researchers want time to conduct projects properly. However, Mahajan and Wind point out that researchers must remember that time is money. Companies face real dollar losses when they are late in introducing products and services to the marketplace. So much so, in fact, that many of them cut corners in the research they conduct or don't do any marketing research at all. This, of course, often leads to disaster and has been labeled "death-wish" marketing.[16] The suggested prescription is for marketing researchers to make use of information technology (IT) for speed and economic efficiency. This is exactly why online research has become such a significant part of the research industry. Decision Analysts, Inc., allows companies to test product concepts quickly using online respondents. Affinnova is a new company that allows a company to actually design new products online. Harris Interactive, Knowledge Networks, Greenfield Online, and many others allow surveys to be conducted online. All of these firms use IT to speed up and reduce the cost of research.

■ Online research has grown significantly because it can speed up the research process.

## Marketing Researchers Should Take an Integrative Approach

Marketing researchers have created "silos," or individual compartments, which separate and isolate different types of information. For example, by separating research into qualitative and quantitative research, researchers tend to use one or the other when, in fact, more insights may be gained by integrating the two approaches. Other silos are created when decision support systems are not linked with marketing research. Firms should integrate experiments they conduct instead of conducting one-shot projects that investigate a single issue. Mahajan and Wind also suggest greater integration of marketing research with existing databases and other information sources such as customer complaints, other studies of product/service quality, and external databases. In other words, marketing researchers would improve their results by taking a close look at all existing information instead of embarking on isolated research projects to solve a problem.

■ Marketing researchers would improve their results by taking a close look at all existing information instead of embarking on isolated research projects to solve a problem.

## Marketing Researchers Should Expand Their Strategic Impact

Marketing research has become too comfortable providing standard reports using simple measures. This information, although useful, does not allow marketing research to contribute to the important central issues of determining overall strategy. Research becomes relegated to a lower-level function providing information for lower-level decisions. As an example, Mahajan and Wind refer to marketing research periodically providing a report on market shares. Although this information is useful for making tactical decisions for each brand, marketing research should be providing information such as defining the market. Should the company look at a broader market than the one defined? Should global market share be considered? How can the company get more from total spending in the market? These are broader, more strategic issues that, if addressed properly by marketing research, would add value to the function of marketing research.

■ Marketing researchers can add greater value if, instead of providing tactical reports, they provide information useful for determining and guiding the overall strategy of the firm.

## Other Criticisms

There have been several other investigations of the research industry over the years. Some of these reviews have been made by knowledgeable persons' critiques, and others have asked buyers of marketing research studies whether the value of the research performed by the suppliers in the industry is worthwhile. Criticism has focused on the following areas of concern: There is a lack of creativity, the industry is too survey oriented, the industry does not understand the real problems that need studying, market researchers show a lack of concern for respondents, the industry has a cavalier attitude regarding nonresponse error, the price of the research is high relative to its value, and academic marketing research should be more closely related to actual marketing management decisions.[17]

Critical reviews are good for the industry. John Stuart Mill once said that "custom is the enemy of progress."[18] One entire issue of *Marketing Research*, edited by

■ Other criticisms of the industry include not being creative, focusing too much on survey research, not knowing the real problem of the client, not caring about respondents, not addressing the problem of nonresponse error, and price being high relative to the value of the research provided.

■ Critical reviews have stirred debate in the marketing research industry.

Chuck Chakrapani, was devoted to a number of articles questioning customary practices in marketing research.[19] The debate these articles stirred is good for the industry. In summary, the basic conclusion of these evaluations is that the industry has performed well, but there is room for improvement. We discuss some of the suggestions for improvement in the following paragraphs.

## Improvements: Certification, Auditing, and Education

Even though there have been criticisms of the marketing research industry, the industry has performed well by the toughest of all standards, the test of the marketplace. As we noted earlier in this chapter, revenues in the research industry now total nearly $16 billion, and these revenues have been increasing each year. Clients obviously see value in the marketing research that is being generated. However, the industry is not complacent. Many suggest that the problems are created by a very small minority of firms, most of which simply are not qualified to deliver quality marketing research services. There is obviously a concern among buyers and suppliers with the lack of uniformity in the industry as well. In a study of buyers' and suppliers' perceptions of the research industry, Dawson, Bush, and Stern found that the key issue in the industry is a lack of uniform quality; there are good suppliers and there are poor suppliers.[20]

> ■ Many of the problems in the research industry are created by a very small minority of firms, most of which simply are not qualified to deliver quality marketing research services.

### Certification

**Certification** is a designation that indicates the achievement of some minimal standard of performance. As we noted at the beginning of this chapter, marketing researchers can now be certified. Over the years many have argued that marketing research attracts practitioners who are not fully qualified to provide adequate service to buyer firms. There were no formal requirements, no education level, no degrees, no certificates, no licenses, and no tests of any kind required to open up a marketing research business. Certainly, the vast majority of research firms have staffs thoroughly trained in research methods and have years of excellent performance. However, some say it is those few firms with unqualified personnel and management that tarnish the industry's image.

As other professions such as accounting, real estate, and financial analysis have learned, certification programs can raise the overall level of competence within an industry.[21] Alvin Achenbaum[22] as well as Patrick Murphy and Gene Laczniak[23] have proposed a professional designation of certified public researchers (CPRs), analogous to CPAs or CFAs. Those who argued against certification pointed out that it would be difficult, if not impossible, to agree on defining certification standards, particularly for the creative aspect of the research process.[24] The MRA worked very hard to bring about the **Professional Researcher Certification**. This is a program explained more fully in Marketing Research Application 2.1.

> ■ The marketing research industry is discussing certification and auditing programs. It has also recently implemented new professional development programs for members of the industry.

### Auditing

**Auditing** has also been suggested as a means of improving the industry. The concept is to have marketing research firms' work be subject to an outside, independent review for the sake of determining the quality of their work. An audit would

## MARKETING RESEARCH APPLICATION 2.1

PRACTICAL

APPLICATIONS

### Professional Researcher Certification

*By Jessica Wilson*

February 28, 2005, was a significant day for the marketing research profession. On this day, the Marketing Research Association (MRA) announced its new certification program, the Professional Researcher Certification. The paragraphs below contain the essentials of the program. Interested parties should consult the MRA Web site, which is also shown below.

### Certification Overview

#### WHO DESIGNED THE CERTIFICATION PROGRAM?
The MRA assumed the leadership role in developing the Certification program. However, to ensure widespread industry input and participation, the Certification Task Force included both MRA and non-MRA members. Members included representatives from MRII, IMRO Division of MRA, CMOR, and AMA. Also, Task Force members represented all segments of the marketing research industry from Data Collectors to End Users.

#### WHAT IS THE CERTIFICATION DESIGNED TO DO?
The Certification program is designed to accomplish the following three objectives:

- reflect all segments of the marketing research profession
- be recognized by industry-related associations and experts
- meet all requirements of NOCA (certification authorization entity) and IACET (CEU [continuing education unit] authorization entity)

### WHO BENEFITS FROM CERTIFICATION?
The MRA Certification program is beneficial for both the individual and the industry. For the individual, it will be a means of differentiating oneself from others. A "badge" of competence in the given areas gives assurance to others that the certified individual meets some minimal level of knowledge and experience. The Certification program benefits the industry in that it aids in the development of a pool of well-trained, competent marketing researchers, thereby improving standards in the industry.

### Certification Recognizes the Diversity within the Profession
In order to address the diversification of the work collectively known as "marketing research," job descriptions throughout the industry were analyzed and sorted into categories consisting of levels of responsibility, levels of specialized knowledge, and levels of required knowledge. The three major segments are: Data Collection, Research Suppliers/Providers, and End Users. And there are subgroups within each industry segment such as the subgroups of Mall, Telephone, Online, and Ethnographic Research within the Data Collection segment. Then, within each subgroup there are job titles. For example, for the Data Collection segment subgroup of Mall the job titles include: Facility Owner, Facility Manager, Supervisor, and so on. The skills required for a title within a subgroup of a particular segment determined the criteria for certification as well as the requirements for maintaining certification.

### Criteria for Levels of Certification
Certifications are awarded at three levels of experience and knowledge. Each level and their respective criteria are:

#### EXPERT
Candidates are expected to have a thorough and detailed knowledge and comprehension of topics classified for this level. Applicants must have no known ethics complaints in the past three years, and must currently be a member of at least one marketing research professional organization that adheres to a code of ethics *or* sign MRA's code. Applicants must also have five or more year's experience in a senior-level or equivalent position and have attended at least one industry conference in the past three years.

## PRACTITIONER

Candidates are expected to have a working knowledge and comprehension of the topics classified for this level. Applicants must have no known ethics complaints in the past three years. Topics at the expert level are central or mainstream and arise frequently in day-to-day professional practice. Applicants must also provide documentation of each skill area on the application, document hours for each skill area on application, list courses/conferences related to skill area on application and be a member of at least one marketing research professional organization that adheres to a code of ethics *or* sign MRA's code.

## ASSOCIATE

Candidates are expected to have a basic understanding of the topics classified at this level. These topics may arise less frequently in day-to-day practice or are emerging, specialty, or peripheral topics. Candidates are expected to have a general familiarity with those topics and understand their broad implications. Applicants must also have at least one year in current or similar position, one letter of recommendation, and no known ethics complaints in the past three years and must document hours for each skill area upon application.

## EXAMINATION

An exam developed by the Certification Development Committee is required for all applicants, excluding grandfathering applicants. Exams have been developed using resources within the profession and based on topic areas directly related to the skills and knowledge required for a specific position. A list of study guides will be provided for approved applicants. All exams will be reviewed and critiqued by the Committee, some of whom have taken the exams. This is to ensure the accuracy and appropriateness of the questions that comprise the exams. These exams will test the comprehension of topics central or mainstream to the candidate's daily professional practice.

## MAINTAINING CERTIFICATION

Knowledge and skills acquired through contact hours and/or CEUs will be the primary method for maintaining certification; CEUs (Continuing Education Units) are required for advancing to a different level of Certification. In order to maintain Certification, individuals must accrue a specified number of contact hours in the field in which they are certified. Contact hours can be earned by attending an approved educational program, such as an MRA national or chapter educational event or activity that offers programming in research skills, management, or support skills. With such education, individuals can develop skills in order to keep up with industry trends and techniques.

## GRANDFATHERING

Current marketing researchers may be eligible for Certification without taking an exam as long as they satisfy all criteria. The ability to grandfather is allowed only during a two-year period after the certification process began.

## CERTIFICATION VERSUS ACCREDITATION?

Certification applies to individuals. Accreditation applies to an organization. A company may become accredited if it can show evidence of and maintain standards set by the accreditation agency. The MRA program addresses certification of individuals. However, the MRA also intends to sponsor an accreditation program.

## WANT TO LEARN MORE ABOUT PROFESSIONAL RESEARCHER CERTIFICATION?

Go to the MRA's Web site at **www.mra-net.org**. See the menu item "PRC website."

Source: This paper was adopted from information provided by the MRA, particularly from materials posted on its Web site at **www.mra-net.org**. Also, much of the material was adapted from the writings of John Burns of Teradyne, Inc., who was the Chair of the Certification Workgroup. See, for example: Burns, J. (2005). Certification: The five key questions. Retrieved April 19, 2005, from the Marketing Research Association Web site at **www.mra-net.org**.

MRA Exesecutive Director Larry Brownell has spearheaded and supervised the development of the new Professional Researcher Certification. MRA Staff Members Linda Schoenborn and Elyse Gammer have shared major responsibility as well.

involve procedures such as retabulation from raw data of a random sample of descriptive surveys, validation of a sample of questionnaires, and even checking questionnaires for evidence of selling under the guise of marketing research.[25] (We discuss the latter in the following section on ethics.)

Though proposed several years ago for the marketing research industry, the audit concept has lain dormant and, now, with a certification program in place, auditing is not likely to gain industry acceptance. However, auditing is increasing in other areas and this may create renewed interest in the concept for marketing research. The Audit Bureau of Circulations (ABC), the auditor of magazine and other periodical circulation for many years, formed ABCi (ABC Interactive) in 2001 for the purpose of auditing traffic on Web sites.[26] Survey Sampling, Inc., a marketing research firm specializing in the provision of samples, has asked ABC to audit its samples. Thus, the use of auditing *may* still be an alternative for the industry.

## Education

Although debate continues over the issue of certification, and auditing may make a comeback bid, the key issue is that the industry recognizes it has certain problems, and efforts are being made to remedy them. The industry has been involved in very good continuing education programs. The AMA sponsors programs designed to increase skills in the industry. One program, the AMA School of Marketing Research, is conducted at Notre Dame University and is designed to benefit the analyst, project supervisor, or manager of marketing research. The AMA also holds an annual conference on advanced analytical techniques. The Marketing Research Association (MRA) offers an introductory program on marketing research. Coordinated at the University of Georgia, this program is designed to develop the research skills of those being transferred into marketing research or those who want to enter the profession. The MRA, CASRO, and the Advertising Research Foundation (ARF) have many excellent training classes and programs frequently scheduled to meet industry needs. Several universities now offer master's-level training in marketing research. (See Appendix B at the end of this chapter.) Certain firms also provide excellent training for the industry. The Burke Institute, a division of Burke, Inc., has provided training programs for many years that are highly regarded in the industry. The institute teaches classes throughout the year on a

■ Visit the Marketing Research Association's Web site at **www.mra-net.org.**

Tony Zahorik of The Burke Institute teaches a class on online research to marketing research practitioners in San Francisco.

number of topics, including online research, multivariate techniques, questionnaire design, focus-group moderating, basic marketing research, and many others. Any review of the industry would agree that it is healthy and is being responsive to its many challenges.

# ETHICS AND MARKETING RESEARCH

ETHICS

■ We think these ethical issues are so important that we call your attention to them throughout this book, using the ethical issue icon that you see here.

■ The marketing research industry is not immune to ethical issues.

As in most areas of business activity, there exist many opportunities for unethical (and ethical) behavior in the marketing research industry.[27] A study by the Ethics Resource Center of Washington, DC, states that the most common ethical problem in the total workplace is "lying to employees, customers, vendors or the public" (26%), followed by "withholding needed information" from those parties (25%). Only 5% of those in the study reported having seen people giving or taking "bribes, kickbacks, or inappropriate gifts." Ninety percent of American workers "expect their organizations to do what is right, not just what is profitable." But one in eight of those polled said they "feel pressure to compromise their organization's ethical standards." And among these respondents, nearly two-thirds said pressure "comes from top management, their supervisors and/or coworkers."[28] Unfortunately, the marketing research industry is not immune to ethical problems.[29] Our purpose here is to introduce you to the areas in which unethical behavior has existed in the past and hopefully to give you some framework for thinking about how you will conduct yourself in the future when confronted with these situations. We think these ethical issues are so important that we call your attention to them throughout this book using the "Ethics" icon that you see at the beginning of this section.

■ Ethics may be defined as a field of inquiry into determining what behaviors are deemed appropriate.

**Ethics** may be defined as a field of inquiry into determining what behaviors are deemed appropriate under certain circumstances as prescribed by codes of behavior that are set by society. Society determines what is ethical and what is not ethical. In some cases, this is formalized by our institutions. Some behavior, for example, is so wrongful that it is deemed illegal by statute. Behavior that is illegal is unethical, by definition. However, there are many other behaviors that are considered by some to be unethical but are not illegal. When these types of behaviors are not spelled out by some societal institution (such as the justice system, legislature, Congress, regulatory agencies such as the FTC, etc.), then the determination of whether the behaviors are ethical or unethical is open to debate.

## Your Ethical Views Are Shaped by Your Philosophy: Deontology or Teleology

There are many philosophies that may be applied to explain one's determination of appropriate behavior given certain circumstances. In the following discussion, we use the two philosophies of deontology and teleology to explain this behavior.[30] **Deontology** is concerned with the rights of the individual. Is the behavior fair and just for each individual? If an individual's rights are violated, then the behavior is not ethical.[31] For example, consider the marketing research firm that has been hired to study how consumers are attracted to and react to a new form of in-store

■ One's philosophy usually determines appropriate, ethical behavior.

display. Researchers, hidden from view, record the behavior of unsuspecting shoppers as they walk through the supermarket. A deontologist considers this form of research activity unethical because it violates the individual shopper's right to privacy. The deontologist would likely agree to the research provided the shoppers were informed beforehand that their behaviors would be recorded, giving them the option to participate or not to participate.[32]

On the other hand, **teleology** analyzes a given behavior in terms of its benefits and costs to society. If there are individual costs but group benefits, then there are net gains and the behavior is judged to be ethical.[33] In our example of the shopper being observed in the supermarket, the teleologist might conclude that, although there is a violation of the right to privacy among those shoppers observed (the cost), there is a benefit if the company learns how to market goods more efficiently, thus reducing long-term marketing costs. Because this benefit ultimately is shared by many more individuals than those whose privacy was invaded during the original study, the teleologist would likely declare this research practice to be ethical.

Thus, how you view a behavior as being ethical or unethical depends on your philosophy. Are you a deontologist or a teleologist? It's difficult to answer that question until you are placed in an ethically sensitive situation. One thing that is for certain is that you will come across ethically sensitive situations during your career. Will you know it's an ethically sensitive situation? How will you respond? We hope you will at least know when you are in an ethically sensitive situation in marketing research. The rest of this section is devoted to teaching you this sensitivity.[34]

## Ethical Behavior in Marketing Research

As noted previously, there are many ways a society may prescribe wanted and unwanted behaviors. In business, if there are practices that are not illegal but are nevertheless thought to be wrong, trade associations or professional organizations will often prescribe a **code of ethical behavior**. This has been the case in marketing and, more specifically, in marketing research. The American Marketing Association has a statement of ethical norms and values for all marketers (**www.marketingpower .com**). The AMA exhorts their members to be honest, responsible, fair, respectful, open, and to demonstrate good citizenship.[35] The AMA directs its members to refer to subdisciplines (i.e., marketing research, for codes specific to the subdiscipline). Some of the larger organizations serving the marketing research industry and who have codes of ethics are: The Council of American Survey Research Organizations (**www.casro.org**), the Qualitative Research Consultants Association (**www.qrca.org**), the Marketing Research Association (**www.mra-net.org**), and the Canadian-based Professional Market Research Society (**www.pmrs-aprm.com**) all have a code of ethics. The European-based ESOMAR, the European Society for Marketing Research (**www.esomar.org**), has a code of ethics that is adopted by many marketing research organizations around the world, such as the Market Research Society of Australia, Ltd.

All over the world, marketing research organizations are striving to achieve ethical behavior among practitioners of marketing research. Marketing Research Application 2.2 illustrates how one firm follows the MRA's code of ethics.

■ One philosophy is called deontology, which focuses on the rights of the individual. If an individual's rights are violated, then the behavior is not ethical.

■ Teleology is a philosophy that focuses on the trade-off between individual costs and group benefits. If benefits outweigh costs, the behavior is judged to be ethical.

■ In the beginning of this chapter we introduced you to the MRA. Check out their Web site at www.mra-net.org.

■ The British-based MRS has a code of ethics. Visit its Web site at www.mrs.org.uk. Also, the Market Research Society of New Zealand has a code of ethics. Visit its Web site at www.mrsnz.org.nz.

## MARKETING RESEARCH APPLICATION 2.2

PRACTICAL

APPLICATIONS

### Baltimore Research Follows MRA's Code of Ethics

Baltimore Research is a full-service marketing research firm. One of the many services we offer our clients is focus group research. There are ethical concerns with focus group facilities that "cut corners" in recruiting respondents. A given focus group will have strict specifications for the profile of qualified candidates, which can include household composition, demographics, brand and category usage, as well as a number of lifestyle and personality variables. Ideally, the focus group should be comprised of a cross section of consumers that meet the exact criteria needed by the client. For example, Frito-Lay may have a new, nutritious snack that they want to test with mothers of young children who purchase similar foods. While it takes time and effort to find the right individuals, we will only recruit the types of consumers our client expects to have in our focus groups. Baltimore Research utilizes a number of creative methodologies to target the harder-to-find segments. You will read more about this concept in this book when your authors discuss "incidence rates."

Clients expect us to recruit "typical" consumers into our focus groups. There are individuals who try to get into as many focus groups as possible to make a living from participation. This presents a number of concerns to researchers. For example, they may lie in the screening process and not really be the type of consumer sought. Consequently, their experiences may not be truly relevant. For a number of other reasons, these "professional respondents" may not be representative of the average consumer. We have implemented many procedures to safeguard against professional respondents, including software to track respondent participation by a number of variables, such as frequency and research topic. At Baltimore Research, we know that our enduring profitability and existence depends on providing quality information that will help our client solve their research problems. If we give them the information that leads them to be more profitable, they will return to us when they have a future need for marketing research.

At Baltimore Research we "take the pledge" to avoid unethical shortcuts to ensure the long-term health of our industry. Many of our employees hold PRCs (Professional Researcher Certifications) from the MRA (Marketing Research Association). We are committed to continuing education for our employees and are proud custodians of the MRA's Code of Ethics.

Ted Donnelly, Ph.D., PRC

Vice President

Baltimore Research

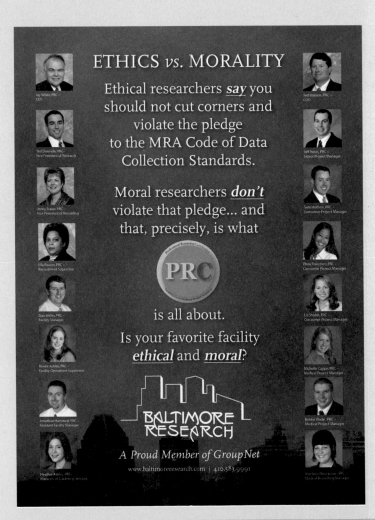

## Codes of Ethics

As noted previously, the Marketing Research Association has a code of ethics. You can read the code in entirety at its Web site (**www.mra-net.org**). However, some of the issues covered are:

- prohibiting selling ("sugging") or fund-raising ("frugging") under the guise of conducting research;
- maintaining research integrity by avoiding misrepresentation and omission of pertinent research data;
- treating outside clients and suppliers fairly.

## Sugging and Frugging

Market Researchers are prohibited from selling or fund-raising under the guise of conducting research. **Sugging** refers to "selling under the guise of a survey." Typically, sugging occurs when a "researcher" gains a respondent's cooperation to participate in a research study and then uses the opportunity to attempt to sell the respondent a good or service. Most consumers are quite willing to provide their attitudes and opinions of products and services in response to a legitimate request for this information. Suggers (and fruggers), however, take advantage of that goodwill by deceiving unsuspecting consumers. Consumers soon learn that their cooperation in answering a few questions has led to their being subjected to a sales presentation. In sugging and frugging, there is no good-faith effort to conduct a survey for the purpose of collecting and analyzing data for specific purposes. Rather, the intent of the "fake" survey is to sell or raise money. Of course, these practices have led to the demise of the pool of cooperative respondents. The Telemarketing and Consumer Fraud and Abuse Prevention Act of 1994 made sugging illegal. Under this act, telemarketers are not allowed to call someone, say they are conducting a survey, and then try to sell a product or service. Although telemarketers are not able to legally practice sugging, the act does not prohibit sugging via the mails.[36] **Frugging** is closely related to sugging and stands for "fund-raising under the guise of a survey." Because frugging does not involve the sale of a product or service, it is not covered in the Telemarketing and Consumer Fraud and Abuse Prevention Act of 1994, but it is widely considered to be unethical. Actually, sugging and frugging are carried out by telemarketers or other direct marketers. Researchers do not practice sugging and frugging. However, we cover this topic because both sugging and frugging are unethical treatments of potential respondents in marketing research.

> Sugging refers to "selling under the guise of a survey." It is now illegal for telemarketers to engage in sugging. Frugging refers to "fund-raising under the guise of a survey." Frugging is unethical.

> Sugging is illegal.

> Frugging is unethical.

## Research Integrity

Sometimes research is not totally objective. Information is withheld, falsified, or altered to protect vested interests.

Marketing research information is often used in making significant decisions. The outcome of the decision may impact future company strategy, budgets, jobs, organization, and so forth. With so much at stake, the opportunity exists for a lack of total objectivity in the research process. The loss of **research integrity** may take the form of withholding information, falsifying data, altering research results, or misinterpreting the research findings in a way that makes them more consistent with predetermined points of view. As one researcher stated, "I refused to alter research results and as a result I was fired for failure to think strategically."[37] We now know

ETHICS

that this was all too common in the field of auditing. The Enron fiasco of 2002 taught the world that even the once highly esteemed field of auditing is subject to a failure of research integrity. A breakdown occurred when Anderson was the auditing firm and also the managerial consulting firm.[38] The impetus for a breach in research integrity may come from either the supplier or the buyer. If a research supplier knows that a buyer will want marketing research services in the future, the supplier may alter a study's results or withhold information, so that the study will support the buyer's wishes. Breaches of research integrity need not be isolated to those managing the research project. Interviewers have been known to make up interviews and to take shortcuts in completing surveys. In fact, there is some evidence that this is more of a problem than was once thought.[39] Maintaining research integrity is regarded as one of the most significant ethical issues in the research industry. In a study of 460 marketing researchers, Hunt, Chonko, and Wilcox found that maintenance of research integrity posed the most significant problem for one-third of those sampled.[40]

### Treating Others Fairly

Several ethical issues that center around how others are treated may arise in the practice of marketing research. Suppliers, buyers, and the public may be treated unethically.

**Buyers.** In the Hunt, Chonko, and Wilcox study cited previously, the second most frequently stated ethical problem facing marketing researchers was fair treatment of buyer firms. *Passing hidden charges* to buyers, *overlooking study requirements* when subcontracting work out to other supplier firms, and *selling unnecessary research* are examples of unfair treatment of buyer firms. By overlooking study requirements, such as qualifying respondents on specified characteristics or verifying that respondents were interviewed, the supplier firm may lower its cost of using the services of a subcontracting field service firm. A supplier firm may oversell research services to naive buyers by convincing them to use a more expensive research design.

■ Sharing of "background knowledge" among firms raises ethical questions.

■ Marketing researchers try to avoid conflicts of interest by not working for two competitors.

*Sharing confidential and proprietary information* raises ethical questions. Virtually all work conducted by marketing research firms is confidential and proprietary. Researchers build up a storehouse of this information as they conduct research studies. Most ethical issues involving confidentiality revolve around how this storehouse of information, or "background knowledge," is treated. One researcher stated, "Where does 'background knowledge' stop and conflict exist (as a result of work with a previous client)?"[41] It is common practice among research supplier firms to check their existing list of buyer-clients to ensure there is no conflict of interest before accepting work from a new buyer.

**Suppliers.** *Phony RFPs.* Buyers also abuse suppliers of marketing research. A major problem exists, for example, when a firm having internal research capabilities issues a **request for proposals (RFPs)** from external supplier firms. External firms then spend time and money developing research designs to solve the stated problem, estimating costs of the project, and so on. Now, having collected several detailed proposals outlining research designs and costs, the abusing firm decides to do the job internally. Issuing a call for proposals from external firms with no intention of doing the job outside is unethical behavior.

*Failure to honor time and money agreements.* Often buyer firms have obligations such as agreeing to meetings or the provision of materials needed for the research project. Supplier firms must have these commitments from buyers in a timely fashion in order to keep to their time schedules. Buyer firms sometimes abuse their agreements to deliver personnel or these other resources in the time to which they have agreed. Also, buyers sometimes do not honor commitments to pay for services. Although this happens in many industries, research suppliers do not have the luxury of repossession; they do, however, have legal recourses.

**The Public.** Sometimes researchers are asked to do research on products thought to be dangerous to society. Ethical issues arise as researchers balance marketing requirements with social issues. This is particularly true in the areas of product development and advertising. For example, marketing researchers have expressed concern over conducting research on advertising to children. Some advertising has had the objective of increasing the total consumption of refined sugar among children via advertising scheduled during Saturday morning TV programs. Other ethical concerns arise when conducting research on products researchers felt were dangerous to the public, such as certain chemicals, and cigarettes.

> Ethical concerns arise when marketing researchers are asked to conduct research on advertising to children or on products they feel are dangerous to the public, such as certain chemicals, cigarettes, alcohol, or sugar.

### Respondents

Respondents are the lifeblood of the marketing research industry. Respondent cooperation rates have been going down and the industry is concerned with the ethical treatment of the existing respondent pool.[42] In 1982, CMOR (Council for Marketing and Opinion Research) began monitoring survey response cooperation. CMOR surveys a large number of consumers from time to time to determine the percentage of the population that has refused to take part in a survey in the past year. The percentages have risen sharply: from 15% in 1982, to 31% in 1992, 40% in 1999, and 45% in 2002.[43] More recent data are proprietary but it is known that refusal rates have continued to climb.[44]

Marketing researchers must honor promises made to respondents that the respondent's identity will remain confidential or anonymous if they expect respondents to cooperate in requests for information in the future.

### Respondent Fairness

In the following paragraphs, we consider some of the issues marketing researchers must face in order to treat respondents fairly.

**Deception of Respondents.** Respondents may be deceived during the research process. Kimmel and Smith point out that **deception** may occur during subject recruitment (respondents are not told the true identity of the sponsor of the research, etc.), during the research procedure itself (they are viewed without their knowledge, etc.), and during postresearch situations (there is a violation of the promise of anonymity).[45]

**Confidentiality and Anonymity.** One way of gaining a potential respondent's trust is by promising confidentiality or anonymity. **Confidentiality** means that the researcher knows who the respondent is but does not identify the respondent with any information gathered from that respondent and provided to a client. So the respondent's identity is confidential information known only by the researcher. A stronger appeal may be made under conditions of **anonymity**. The respondent is, and remains, anonymous or unknown. The researcher is interested only in gathering information from the respondent and does not know who the respondent is. Ethical issues arise when the respondents are promised confidentiality or anonymity and the researcher fails to honor this promise.

**Invasions of Privacy.** Marketing research, by its nature, is invasive. Any information acquired from a respondent has some degree of invasiveness. Ethical issues, some of them legal, abound in the area of invading others' privacy. The two areas that are most responsible for consumer concern are unsolicited telephone calls and spam. Since marketing researchers rely heavily on telephone surveys and, more recently, online survey research, both these areas are very significant to the marketing research industry.

**Unsolicited Telephone Calls.** Telemarketers' abuse of consumer privacy by flooding consumers with unsolicited telephone calls has resulted in consumers' putting pressure on Congress for relief. In the summer of 2003, the FTC introduced a national "Do Not Call" registry (**www.donotcall.gov**). So far, marketing research firms, calling for consumers' opinions only, have been excluded from the Do Not Call legislation.[46] But recall what we told you in Chapter 1: CASRO reported research that showed 97% of consumers felt that telemarketers should be regulated through Do Not Call legislation but, alarmingly, CASRO found that 64% of consumers felt the legislation should also apply to marketing researchers.[47] Marketing researchers must work especially hard to encourage consumer goodwill and ensure that they are viewed separately from telemarketers.

**Spam.** When online survey research was made possible by the growing use of the Internet, some organizations viewed this as an easy, fast way to gather survey information. They gave little concern to ethical issues when they obtained e-mail lists to use to target survey recipients. They began sending out thousands of surveys to unwary persons. The practice of sending unwanted e-mail is called spamming. An electronic message has been defined as **spam** if: (1) the recipient's personal identity and context are irrelevant because the message is equally applicable to many other potential recipients; (2) the recipient has not verifiably granted deliberate, explicit, and still-revocable permission for it to be sent; and (3) the transmission and reception of the message appear to the recipient to give a disproportionate benefit to the sender.[48] The name *spam* comes from a Monty Python skit in which a restaurant customer is deluged with repeated requests to order canned Spam. Finally, the customer yells, "I don't want any Spam!"[49]

The practice of sending spam continues today and there are consumer organizations to fight it such as CAUCE, Coalition Against Unsolicited Commercial Email (**www.cauce.org**), and MAPS, Mail Abuse Prevention System (**www.mail-abuse.org**). Since improper online surveying could be considered spam, the marketing research industry has worked hard to establish codes of ethics dealing with proper online surveying. We present this information to you in Appendix A: Marketing Research and Spam Surveys.

◼ The name *spam* comes from a Monty Python skit in which a restaurant customer is deluged with repeated requests to order canned Spam. Finally, the customer yells, "I don't want any Spam!"

◼ It is important to know how to properly conduct online surveys to make certain you are not spamming.

In conclusion, marketing research firms are working hard to protect the privacy of their respondents. The firms in the industry realize that they must rely on consumer cooperation for information requests. In order to achieve a cooperative pool of potential respondents, marketing researchers must attempt to separate themselves from unscrupulous direct marketers. The industry has been considering developing and using an "industry identifier" such as a "Your Opinion Counts" to help consumers more easily identify legitimate marketing research firms. While this idea has been around for several years,[50] it is being discussed again among industry leaders. However, in the meantime, the future is cloudy in terms of how legal actions will affect research. Already, research firms, realizing that respondents are their lifeblood, are moving in the direction of recruiting their own panels of willing respondents. Recruiting and maintaining a panel requires a considerable investment. **Panel equity**, the value of readily available access to willing respondents, may become more and more important in the future. Marketing research firms, recognizing the value they have in panels, will make even greater effort to ensure fair and ethical treatment of their panel respondents.

▨ In an attempt to help consumers distinguish marketing research firms from unscrupulous direct marketers such as telemarketers and spammers, the industry is considering an "industry identifier" similar to the "Good Housekeeping" seal of approval.

▨ Realizing that respondents are their lifeblood, many research firms are recruiting their own panels of willing respondents, which requires a considerable investment. The value of panels, known as panel equity, may become very important in the future.

## SUMMARY

This chapter covered four introductory topics. First, it reviewed how the marketing research industry evolved. Although surveys were conducted for business purposes in the early 1800s, Charles Coolidge Parlin is given credit for conducting the first continuous and organized marketing research, for the Curtis Publishing Company beginning in 1911. Parlin is recognized as the "Father of Marketing Research." Prior to the Industrial Revolution, there was little need for formal marketing research. Business proprietors—artisans who bartered with their customers—knew their customers' needs and preferences. However, once mass production led to producing goods for distant markets, managers needed information about these distant markets. By the 1930s the marketing research industry was becoming widespread, and by the 1960s the practice of marketing research gained wide approval as a method for keeping abreast of fast-changing, distant markets.

The marketing research industry today is a $15+ billion industry with firms operating all over the globe. The Honomichl Global 25 is a listing of the top 25 firms, in terms of revenue, operating around the world. The Honomichl Top 50 is a list of U.S.-based firms ranked by revenues generated in the United States. These 50 firms generate almost $7 billion in revenue. Strategic alliances in the industry make it very competitive.

The marketing research industry is composed of research suppliers. Suppliers may be broadly classified as internal (research is provided by an entity within the firm) or external. Internal suppliers may be found in for-profit as well as not-for-profit firms and in service firms as well as product firms. Internal suppliers organize by having their own formal departments, having a committee or individual responsible for research, or by not having anyone responsible. Formal departments use a variety of ways of organizing themselves. External suppliers organize by function, research application, geography, type of customer, or some combination. External supplier firms may be classified as full-service or limited-service firms. Each of these types may be further classified.

The marketing research industry's performance is evaluated from time to time. In general, these reviews show that the industry is doing a reasonably good job but there is room for improvement. Suggestions are made for some of these improvements. There is now a certification program in place, the PRC. Some industry leaders have called for an auditing system to ensure consistency of performance across the industry. The marketing research industry has started several professional development programs for its members in recent years. These educational programs come from industry professional organizations such as CASRO, MRA, ARF, and the AMA. Also, there are private educational programs of excellent quality, such as the Burke Institute.

Ethical issues in marketing research are more important today than ever. Ethics is defined as a field of inquiry into determining what behaviors are deemed appropriate under certain circumstances as prescribed by codes of behavior that are set by society. How you respond to ethically sensitive situations depends on your philosophy: deontology or teleology. Several organizations in the research industry have codes of ethical behavior for both buyers and suppliers of research. Sugging is illegal. Frugging is very unethical. Ethical issues include research integrity, and treating others (buyers, suppliers, the public, and respondents) fairly. Respondent fairness issues include deception, confidentiality, and invasions of privacy. Unsolicited telephone calls and e-mail spam are an invasion of privacy. Special standards, reported in Appendix A, are provided to online marketing researchers to protect the privacy of online respondents. In the future, we can probably expect more legislation affecting access to respondents. Research companies, faced with a declining pool of willing respondents in the general public, will rely more heavily on recruiting their own panel members. We believe that by recruiting and maintaining their own panels of respondents, research companies will come to value their "panel equity" and we will see even fairer treatment of respondents in the future. Appendix A is provided to examine how the research industry is conducting online surveying without spamming. Appendix B is provided for readers who are interested in a career in marketing research.

## KEY TERMS

Charles Coolidge Parlin (p. 26)
Honomichl Global 25 (p. 27)
Honomichl Top 50 (p. 29)
Strategic alliances (p. 29)
Research suppliers (p. 29)
Internal suppliers (p. 29)
External suppliers (p. 31)
Full-service supplier firms (p. 31)
Syndicated data service firms (p. 32)
Standardized service firms (p. 32)
Customized service firms (p. 32)
Online research services firms (p. 32)

Limited-service supplier firms (p. 33)
Field service firms (p. 33)
Phone banks (p. 33)
Market segment specialists (p. 33)
Sample design and distribution (p. 33)
Data analysis services (p. 34)
Specialized research technique firms (p. 34)
Certification (p. 38)
Professional Researcher Certification (p. 38)
Auditing (p. 38)

Ethics (p. 42)
Deontology (p. 42)
Teleology (p. 43)
Code of ethical behavior (p. 43)
Sugging (p. 45)
Frugging (p. 45)
Research integrity (p. 45)
RFPs (p. 46)

Deception (p. 47)
Confidentiality (p. 47)
Anonymity (p. 48)
Spam (p. 48)
Panel equity (p. 49)
Can Spam Act (p. Appendix A-55)
"Opt-out" standard (p. Appendix A-56)
"Opt-in" standard (p. Appendix A-56)

## REVIEW QUESTIONS

1  Name three professional organizations serving the marketing research industry.
2  Who is given credit for conducting the first continuous and organized marketing research? (He is also known as the "Father of Marketing Research.")
3  Explain why marketing research was not widespread prior to the Industrial Revolution.
4  The marketing research industry, worldwide, is about a $__ billion industry. Marketing research, in the United States, is about a $__ billion industry.
5  We categorized firms as internal or external suppliers of marketing research information. Explain what is meant by each and give an example of each type of firm.
6  Distinguish among full-service, limited-service, syndicated data service firms, standardized service firms, customized service firms, and online research services firms.
7  How would you categorize the following firms?
   a  a firm specializing in marketing to kids (ages 6–12)
   b  a firm that specializes in a computerized scent generator for testing reactions to smells
   c  a firm that offers a package for running test markets
   d  a firm that offers clients samples drawn according to the client's sample plan
   e  a firm that collects data over the Internet
8  Explain why certification is beneficial to the marketing research industry.
9  What is the advantage in a firm having its own formal marketing research department? Explain different ways such a department may be internally organized.
10  On evaluating the marketing research industry, what was suggested in the text as indicating there is room for improvement?
11  What were the recommendations for improving marketing research given by Professors Mahajan and Wind?
12  What have been some suggested remedies for improving the marketing research industry?
13  Do you agree or disagree with the question "Should marketing researchers be certified?" Why or why not?
14  What are the two fundamental philosophies that can be used as a basis for making ethical decisions?
15  Name four ethical issues facing the marketing research industry.

# APPLICATION QUESTIONS

**16** Go to the Web site for any three companies listed in the Honomichl 50. Study the Web site and compare and contrast the services the three firms offer.

**17** Look up "marketing research" in your yellow pages directory. Given the information provided in the Yellow Pages, can you classify the research firms in your area according to the classification system we used in this chapter?

**18** Comment on each practice in the following list. Is it ethical? Indicate your reasoning in each case.

**a** A research company conducts a telephone survey and gathers information that it uses later to send a salesperson to the home of potential buyers for the purpose of selling a product. It makes no attempt to sell the product over the telephone.

**b** Would your response to the preceding case change if you found out that the information gathered during the telephone survey was used as part of a "legitimate" marketing research report?

**c** A door-to-door salesperson finds that, by telling people that he is conducting a survey, they are more likely to listen to his sales pitch.

**d** Greenpeace sends out a direct-mail piece described as a survey and asks for donations as the last question.

**e** In the appendix of the final report, the researcher lists the names of all respondents who took part in the survey and places an asterisk beside the names of those who indicated a willingness to be contacted by the client's sales personnel.

**f** A list of randomly generated telephone numbers is drawn up in order to conduct a telephone survey.

**g** A list of randomly generated e-mail addresses is created using a "Spambot" (an electronic "robot" that searches the Internet looking for and retaining e-mail addresses) in order to conduct a random online research project.

**h** Students conducting a marketing research project randomly select e-mail addresses of other students from the student directory in order to conduct their term project.

# INTERACTIVE LEARNING

 To learn more about the Charles Coolidge Parlin Award, go to the American Marketing Association's Web site at **www.marketingpower .com**. In the "search" box, type in *Parlin*. Click on "Parlin Award." Be sure you take a look at the former awardees and, while you are there, explore the AMA's Web site. You will likely find some very useful information for this course and other courses you are taking. Also, don't forget you can go to this book's Web site at **www.prenhall.com/burnsbush**. For this chapter, work through the Self-Study Quizzes, and get instant feedback on whether you need additional studying.

*The authors wish to thank Jeff W. Totten, D.B.A., PCM, McNeese State University, for preparing this case.*

*We strongly suggest you read Appendix A before attempting to answer the questions for this case.*

Dr. Chris Andrews leaned back in his office chair, contemplating how best to collect data for a project he wanted to do. Andrews, a marketing professor at Northern Minnesota State University, taught the marketing research course, among others. He was interested in learning more about two new data collection methods: e-mail surveys and Internet surveys. He had done some reading on the methods, and wondered how marketing research companies were using the new methods, if at all.

Andrews looked through the two main directories of marketing research companies, the American Marketing Association March 2007 membership directory and the Researcher SourceBook from *Quirk's Marketing Research Review* (September 2007 issue). The latter directory was more up to date, so he decided to use it for his sampling frame. He randomly selected approximately 450 firms out of those that had e-mail addresses. He developed a survey that consisted of general questions about the two new methods. The major problem he faced was the lack of funding support from his school, which quickly ruled out a mail survey, since he didn't have the personal resources to pay for printing and postage. He also didn't have the time to call 450 research companies, given his teaching load. Then he noticed that many of the firms in the sampling frame had e-mail addresses, and the proverbial lightbulb went on. *I'll send my survey out as an e-mail survey!* he thought.

Andrews went back to his stack of articles on the new methods and read about the strengths and weaknesses of e-mail surveys. The research industry and member associations like The Council for Marketing and Opinion Research (CMOR), CASRO, and American Association for Public Opinion Research (AAPOR) were just starting to address the issues of privacy and ethical use of these methods. Andrews leaned back and thought about the best approach to take to get his questionnaire out to his targeted population. Several options came to mind:

1 "The quickest way to get this survey out would be to load all the 450 or so e-mail addresses into one address book 'nickname.' Then I prepare one basic message, put the 'nickname' in the To: slot, and attach the survey. Then I press the Send button. My message would read: 'Dear marketing research firm, You have been randomly selected to participate in a survey about the use of e-mail and Internet surveys. Please complete the attached survey and return it as an attachment to me at **candrews@nmnsu.edu**. Thanks for your help. Sincerely, Chris Andrews, D.B.A.'"

2 "Let's see. Another way I can do this is to first e-mail the research companies, requesting permission to send them a survey. The easiest way would be to do one mass e-mail, as mentioned in my first option above. I will then send each firm that responds an individual e-mail, with the same message above, and the survey as an attachment."

3 "Hmm. Oh, yeah. The Human Subjects guidelines. Better check that out. Okay—maybe I should say this in my message: 'Dear Ms. Betty Jones, Your firm was randomly selected from the 2007 Researcher SourceBook, published by *Quirk's Marketing Research Review*. The questionnaire will be sent to you as an attachment to an e-mail message, in the form of a Microsoft Word 97 document. All information that you provide will remain confidential. There will be no company identification information included in the survey data that will be analyzed. Only some basic classification information will be gathered and used in the analysis. You are free to participate or decline to participate in this study. If you would like to receive a copy of the findings, please e-mail me at **candrews@nmnsu.edu**.' Then I do the mass e-mailing as a prenotification, followed up by individual messages with the survey."

4 "Perhaps I should first have my student worker make phone calls to the 450 or so companies, asking permission to send them the survey via e-mail. Or I should develop a basic message and get it printed on postcards. I could probably afford to pay for the postcards, and perhaps there's a way to mass-print postcards using a laser printer. The

student worker could hand-address each postcard, or create mailing labels for me. That would delay my data collection process by a week or so, but maybe that's best. Let's see, the postcard prenotification message should say this: 'Dear Ms. Betty Jones, I am conducting a survey of marketing research firms regarding their use of e-mail surveys and Internet surveys. Your firm was randomly selected from the 2007 Researcher SourceBook, published by *Quirk's Marketing Research Review*. Please notify me by e-mail (**candrews@nmnsu.edu**) if you are willing to participate in this study. The questionnaire would then be sent to you as an attachment to an e-mail message, in the form of a Microsoft Word 97 document. Let me know if some other method of delivering the survey electronically is better for you. The questionnaire should take approximately 10 to 15 minutes to complete. All information that you provide will remain confidential. There will be no company identification information included in the survey data that will be analyzed. Only some basic classification information will be gathered and used in the analysis. You are free to participate or decline to participate in this study. If you would like to receive a copy of the findings, please e-mail me at **candrews@nmnsu.edu**. Sincerely, Chris Andrews, D.B.A., Northern Minnesota State University.' Similar wording would be used in the e-mail 'cover letter' message that would carry the attached survey."

5  "You know, I should be able to get permission by e-mail. I will create the message mentioned in option 4 above and copy it into 450 individual e-mail messages and send them out. That should work. Then I'll use similar language in the messages I send out that carry the attached survey. That just might work."

1  Evaluate each of the five options that Dr. Andrews has developed, using the CASRO guidelines and research principles.

2  Are any of the options illegal? Unethical? Why?

3  Which option would you recommend that Andrews use?

---

## CASE 2.2 ||| Your Integrated Case

### College Life E-Zine

*This is the second case in our integrated case series. If you have not already done so, you will need to read Case 1.2 before reading this case.*

The four friends have decided they may need the services of a research firm to help them with their business idea. Wesley and Anna are both concerned about exposing their business idea. They worry about telling a marketing research firm about their idea and the firm "selling" their idea to another party.

Don is much less concerned about this. He says, "Those firms are in the marketing research business. They're not magazine publishers and they don't want to be. At the newspaper, our local advertisers confide in us frequently about new business ventures they are considering. They know we're in the newspaper business and we aren't going to steal their business idea."

"That's not what I'm concerned about," says Anna. "What worries me is the research firm we confide in may already have a big magazine publisher as a client. What's to keep them from sharing our idea with their longtime, big-money customer?"

Don agrees but suggests they ask the research firm what their policy is on this. "Let's confront them with it right up front and see what they say. If we're still concerned, we'll talk to other research firms until we find one we can trust."

Now the friends have to select the "right" research firm. Wesley says, "Let's call our old marketing research professor at State U, Dr. Smith. He can tell us where to start."

The next day, they call Dr. Smith. He tells them, "Well, you can take a look in the Yellow Pages for starters, but you may want to also go to some Internet sites to learn more about the companies. I would recommend you take a look at **www.greenbook.org**. This is the Web site of the New York chapter of the American Marketing Association. They have maintained a directory of research firms for years. Take a look at their search screens and the types of research firms. You should be able to make some decisions about the type of firm you want depending on the nature of your project."

They also asked Dr. Smith about the issue of the confidentiality of their business plans. Dr. Smith told them, "There is always a chance you will deal with someone who is unethical. This is just one of several reasons you should take some care in selecting the research firm. I recommend you take a look at some of the codes of ethics to which these firms should adhere. Go to **www.casro.org**. 'CASRO' stands for Council of American Survey Research Organizations, and their code of ethics is posted on the Web site. All of their members will be familiar with that code. Check it to see if it deals with confidentiality of client business plans. Good luck and let me know if I can help you in any other way."

1  Go to the CASRO Web site. Can you find anything in their code of ethics that addresses the four friends' concern about the confidentiality of their business plans?
2  Go to the Greenbook Web site. Take a look at the different types of marketing research firms and services offered by firms in the research industry. Develop some criteria the four friends should use in selecting a research firm.

## APPENDIX A

# MARKETING RESEARCH AND SPAM SURVEYS

As we have noted previously, the Internet provides researchers with the ability to access millions of potential respondents. However, *how* they access these potential respondents is critical in determining whether unethical practices are being used. In this appendix, we present information that clarifies whether an e-mailed survey is or is not ethical.

ETHICS

## The Can Spam Act

In 2003, Congress heard complaints that one-half of all e-mail traffic is spam, that spam is increasing, that U.S. firms alone lose $10 billion annually in lost productivity and cost for spam-filtering software, and that 70% of e-mail users report that spam e-mails make the online experience annoying.[51] The new legislation will not make all spam illegal. Rather, it will require spam to be truthful and will give government agencies the authority to fine and, in some cases, imprison offenders. It will require spammers to use real e-mail addresses (many presently disguise their true identity) and to provide proper subject lines indicating the true nature of the e-mail message. The law also forbids "harvesting"—the gathering of e-mail addresses without owners' awareness. And, as of this writing, there *may* be a "Do Not Spam" registry similar to the "Do Not Call" registry.[52] However, some legal experts believe the **Can Spam Act** will be ineffective because most spammers operate in foreign countries and will not be subject to U.S. law. Some even believe the act will harm efforts to curb spam because it supersedes states' laws, some of which (such as California's) are more strict. At least one legal expert believes that the remedy to spam will have to come from technology instead of the legal system.[53]

■ The "Can Spam Act" is not likely to "can" spam.

Unfortunately, spam will continue and this will further alienate potential respondents to online research requests from legitimate online marketing research firms.

## Opt-Out Versus Opt-In Standards

There is an ongoing debate regarding what practices actually constitute invasions of privacy. Slowly, legislation is being adopted around the world that helps to define this issue. One common theme in the legislation has been the individual's right of consent. One consent standard is the **"opt-out" standard**. Under this standard, individuals are given the opportunity to not be contacted again and/or to limit the manner in which the information they provide may be used. On the other hand, the alternative standard, the **"opt-in" standard**, provides that individuals must specifically and affirmatively consent to a specified activity, such as being given an online survey via their e-mail. Opt-in is referred to as "active consent" and has been preferred by many privacy advocates for the reason that it allows the individual full control. That is, respondents never receive the survey unless they have opted to take it. Others argue that the ability to opt out, also known as "passive consent," provides ample control to individuals.

Legislative bodies will likely continue the debate as to which standard, opt-in versus opt-out, should be used in privacy laws. The marketing research industry has been regulating itself through codes of ethics that specify the opt-in standard. CASRO has been an industry leader not only in helping to shape ethical standards for the industry but also in trying to ensure that legislation passed to deal with telemarketers does not include legitimate marketing researchers.[54]

■ Marketing researchers cannot send unsolicited e-mails. Consumers sent e-mails should have a "reasonable expectation" of receiving the e-mail.

## What Does the CASRO Code of Ethics Say About Online Survey Research and Spamming?

### Who May Be Surveyed?

We summarize procedures that marketing research firms should follow in order to conduct online survey research without spamming. As a general rule, marketing research organizations believe that survey research organizations should not use unsolicited e-mails (spam) to recruit respondents for surveys. And, in order to send e-mail surveys, research organizations are required to verify that individuals contacted for research by e-mail have a reasonable expectation that they will receive e-mail contact for research. CASRO states that such a reasonable expectation can be assumed when *all* of the following conditions exist.[55]

1 A substantive preexisting relationship exists between the individuals contacted and the research organization, the client, or the list owners contracting the research (the latter being so identified). Examples would include when there has been a business transaction or correspondence with the e-mailed person and that person has voluntarily supplied his or her e-mail address for future research, marketing, or correspondence contact. The relationship must be evident to the person being e-mailed and the client firm or the research firm must be identified.

2 Individuals have a reasonable expectation, based on the preexisting relationship, that they may be contacted for research. This means that there must be a sufficient belief, based upon the preexisting relationship, that an individual may be contacted via e-mail for purposes of research.

3 Individuals are offered the choice to be removed from *all* future e-mail contact in each invitation (the opt-out standard).

4 The invitation list excludes all individuals who have previously taken the appropriate and timely steps to request the list owner to remove them. In other words, researchers or clients must maintain a "Do Not E-Mail" registry.

■ CASRO's code of ethics identifies conditions under which consumers may be sent e-mails from marketing research firms.

### Gathering E-Mail Addresses

Codes of ethics followed by the research industry prohibit research organizations from using subterfuge in obtaining e-mail addresses of potential respondents, such as using technologies or techniques to collect e-mail addresses without individuals' awareness. Research organizations are prohibited from using false or misleading return e-mail addresses when recruiting respondents over the Internet. CASRO's code further states: When receiving e-mail lists from clients or list owners, research organizations are required to have the client or list provider verify that individuals listed have a reasonable expectation that they will receive e-mail contact, as defined previously.

## APPENDIX B

# CAREERS IN MARKETING RESEARCH

Marsha Medders received her B.S.B.A. in marketing with a concentration in marketing research at the University of West Florida in 2003. She developed an interest in marketing research during her coursework and elected to take additional courses that helped her learn more about the field. She developed expertise in SPSS. She accepted her first position upon graduation as a Market Research Analyst with the Florida Agency for Health Care Administration. She planned and implemented research studies there before accepting another position as Research Associate in the Florida Department of Education. At the Department of Education, she continued to develop her analytical skills using Excel and SAS. Presently, Ms. Medders is Market Research Analyst with VISITFLORIDA, where she is responsible for conducting

studies to measure and evaluate tourism in the state of Florida. She is a member of the Marketing Research Association and has the PRC certification.

Maybe you have been thinking about marketing research as a career choice. There are many career opportunities in the industry, and we have prepared this appendix to give you some information about those career choices. More importantly, we give you some sources from which to pursue additional information about a career in the marketing research industry.

## What Is the Outlook for the Industry?

Before you seek employment in any industry, you should ask about the total outlook for the industry. Buggy whip manufacturing is not exactly a growth industry! What are the growth rates in the industry? What do the experts have to say about the future of the industry?

A good place to find information about the outlook of an industry is the *Occupational Outlook Handbook*. You can access it online at **www.bls.gov/oco/home.htm**. Enter "marketing research" in the search box, then click on "Market and Survey Researchers."

The *Occupational Outlook Handbook* forecasts that jobs in economics and marketing research will grow "faster than average" through 2014. Demand for qualified market research analysts should be healthy because of an increasingly competitive economy. Marketing research provides organizations valuable feedback from purchasers, allowing companies to evaluate consumer satisfaction and more effectively plan for the future. As companies seek to expand their market and consumers become better informed, the need for marketing professionals will increase.

Opportunities for market research analysts with graduate degrees should be good in a wide range of employment settings, particularly in marketing research firms, as companies find it more profitable to contract out for marketing research services rather than support their own marketing department. Other organizations, including financial services organizations, health care institutions, advertising firms, manufacturing firms producing consumer goods, and insurance companies may offer job opportunities for market research analysts.

Opportunities for survey researchers should be strong as the demand for market and opinion research increases. Employment opportunities will be especially favorable in commercial market and opinion research as an increasingly competitive economy requires businesses to more effectively and efficiently allocate advertising funds.[56]

Also, recall that we showed you in this chapter that the research industry has been growing. One of the largest concerns expressed by members in the industry in a 1999 survey conducted by the Advertising Research Foundation was a concern that too few qualified researchers would be available to handle industry needs. The report suggested increasing college graduate recruiting and working with universities to offer meaningful internships and enrichment of existing marketing research courses.[57]

## What Are the Salaries?

Another question you should ask is how much the people in this profession earn. As in many professional services, salaries vary widely in the marketing research industry. Nevertheless, we can give you some general guidelines. The *Occupational Outlook Handbook* separates marketing research analysts from survey researchers. The primary difference is that analysts are involved with the total research process, whereas their definition of survey researchers closely matches what we categorized in this chapter as field data collection firms (limited-service firms). Median annual earnings of market research analysts in 2004 were $56,140. The middle 50% earned between $40,510 and $79,990. The lowest 10% earned less than $30,890, and the highest 10% earned more than $105,870. Median annual earnings in the industries employing the largest numbers of market research analysts in 2004 were as follows:

| | |
|---|---|
| Management of companies and enterprises | $58,440 |
| Computer systems design and related services | $58,100 |
| Insurance Carriers | $51,030 |

Median annual earnings of survey researchers in 2004 were $26,490. The middle 50% earned between $17,920 and $41,390. The lowest 10% earned less than $15,330, and the highest 10% earned more than $56,740.[58]

## What Kind of Jobs Are There?

Okay, so you are still interested! What types of jobs are there in the marketing research industry? We suggest you go to the MRA Web site at **www.mra-net.org** and click on "Education" and then on "Career Guide I" and "Career Guide II." Once you are familiar with these guides, go to the Honomichl 50 table cited in this chapter and go to the Web sites of the companies listed. Most of them will have a "Careers with Us" or similar link. Check out the types of jobs they are describing. You should, of course, go to your career center and find out what resources your college or university has to help you find the job you want.

## What Are the Requirements?

Do you have what it takes? The traits associated with the most successful and effective marketing researchers include the following: curiosity, high intelligence, creativity, self-discipline, good interpersonal and communication skills, the ability to work under strict time constraints, and proficiency in working with numbers. The field is becoming gender neutral. About half of all new researchers are women.[59] Information Resources, Inc. (IRI), states it prefers a degree in marketing or a related area. Although an undergraduate degree is required, there has been a trend toward requiring postgraduate degrees in some firms. Most universities do not offer a degree in marketing research. There are some, reported later, that are quite good. Thus, an M.B.A. with a marketing major is one of the more common combinations for people employed in marketing research. Other possibilities are degrees in quantitative methods, sociology, or economics. Undergraduate training in mathematics or the physical sciences is a very suitable (and employable) background for anyone considering a career in marketing research.

## Are You Interested in a Master's Degree in Marketing Research?

Graduate degrees are highly recommended in the marketing research industry. Go to the CASRO Web site at **www.casro.org** and click on "The World of Research" and then "Colleges and Universities." Also, go to the MRA Web site at **www.mra-net.org** and click on "Education & Events" then "Education" and you will see a listing of schools offering specializations and degrees in marketing research. You will find graduate programs in marketing research and in related areas at these sites.

# 3

# STEPS IN THE MARKETING RESEARCH PROCESS INCLUDING DEFINING THE PROBLEM AND RESEARCH OBJECTIVES

## BLUETOOTH SIG USES MARKETING RESEARCH TO ASSESS BRAND NAME AWARENESS

Though many of you are familiar with the *Bluetooth* brand you probably did not know that Bluetooth SIG doesn't make wireless headsets in sunglasses or wireless printers. Rather, the Bluetooth SIG coordinates the design of wireless technology among manufacturers of wireless-capable products, so wireless products from different manufacturers can "talk to each other." The Bluetooth Special Interest Group (SIG) is a privately held, not-for-profit trade association. The SIG is composed of over 8,000 member companies that are leaders in the telecommunications, computing, automotive, music, apparel, industrial automation, and network product industries. The Bluetooth SIG has a small group of dedicated staff in Hong Kong, Sweden, and the USA. The Bluetooth SIG global headquarters are in Bellevue, Washington, USA, with local offices in Hong Kong, and Malmo, Sweden.

## LEARNING OBJECTIVES

- To learn the 11 steps of the marketing research process
- To understand the importance of properly defining the problem
- To understand the sources of problems
- To know the difference between problems and symptoms
- To understand the researcher's role in problem definition
- To see how research objectives are constructed and to understand their relationship with the problem
- To learn what is contained in the marketing research proposal
- To allow students to experience defining the problem and research objectives through an in-depth case situation

The Bluetooth SIG staff is comprised of a small team of marketing, engineering, and operations professionals. While they are of course responsible for coordinating the development of future versions of *Bluetooth* technology, they also are responsible for creating a high level of public awareness of the *Bluetooth* brand and maintaining a positive image toward the brand.

### Why is *Bluetooth* Brand Name Awareness and Image Important?

The *Bluetooth* brand is the primary asset of the Bluetooth SIG. Strong customer demand for licensed and qualified *Bluetooth* products allows the Bluetooth SIG to hold manufacturers to a high standard in qualifying their products, ensuring that licensed products work properly together.

While the SIG's member companies contribute to brand awareness by actively marketing their own products, the Bluetooth SIG's marketing team works to ensure that consumers are aware of the fact that *Bluetooth* products from different manufacturers work together. SIG marketing efforts highlight all of the possible uses for *Bluetooth* technology, from hands-free calling to wireless printing, and work to ensure that the *Bluetooth* brand continues to stand for reliability, interoperability, and ease of use.

*Bluetooth* **Monitors its Brand Awareness and Image by Using Marketing Research**

As with any new technology, *Bluetooth* wireless technology experienced growing pains, and some early *Bluetooth* products worked together less reliably than manufacturers and users hoped. Marketing research studies which measured brand awareness and image, along with diligent monitoring of print and online media, gave the SIG early warning of potential problem areas and allowed the marketing staff to adjust its communications strategy while the SIG's technical staff worked to address these initial shortcomings. These early efforts paid off, and today *Bluetooth* name recognition stands at well over 80 percent in many countries, while more than one billion *Bluetooth*-enabled products were sold by the end of 2006.

With the image of the *Bluetooth* headset now firmly ingrained in the popular culture, current SIG marketing initiatives focus on building awareness that *Bluetooth* technology means more than just talking hands-free. Other scenarios include printing photos wirelessly from a camera phone to a printer, streaming stereo music to wireless headphones, sharing files between a laptop and PDA, or connecting a laptop PC to the Internet wirelessly using a mobile phone's data service.

T he *Bluetooth* vignette you just read illustrates how a company used marketing research to help them recognize they had a problem and to ensure that they had corrected their problem in the eyes of consumers. The Bluetooth SIG hired Millward Brown, a global research company with communications and branding expertise to help them design and implement marketing research that helped Bluetooth SIG monitor brand awareness and image. In conducting the research for Bluetooth SIG, Millward Brown went through steps involved in the marketing research process. Marketing researchers are familiar with these steps, and their knowledge of them helps make better decisions regarding how to conduct the marketing research. In this chapter, we will introduce you to these important steps, and these steps will serve as a framework for the rest of this book. Also in this chapter, we begin the steps of the marketing research process by "determining the need for marketing research" and "defining the problem and research objectives."

■ Visit Millward Brown at www.millwardbrown.com.

## THE MARKETING RESEARCH PROCESS

### An 11-Step Process

Thus far you've learned what marketing research is and how it is used to facilitate decision making. You've also learned about the marketing research industry and some of the issues facing the industry. You are now ready to learn the steps in the marketing research process. By introducing you to these steps, we are also giving you a preview of what's in store for you as you read this book. We identify the 11 **steps in the marketing research process** in Figure 3.1.[1] The steps are: (1) establishing the need for marketing research, (2) defining the problem, (3) establishing research objectives, (4) determining research design, (5) identifying information types and sources, (6) determining

■ It is very important for you to learn the 11 steps in the marketing research process.

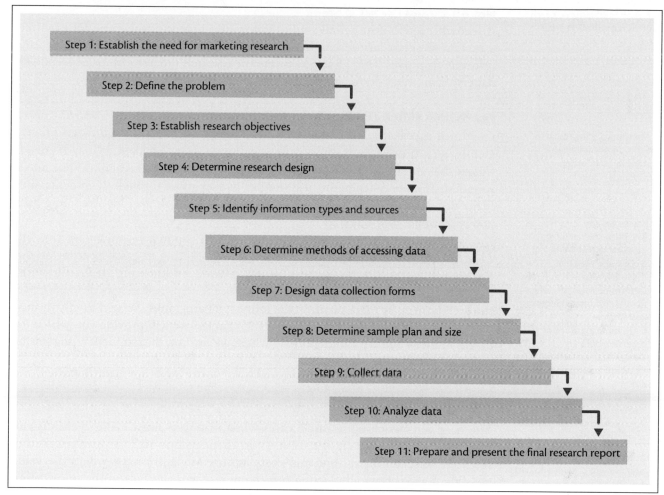

**Figure 3.1** Eleven Steps in the Marketing Research Process

methods of accessing data, (7) designing data collection forms, (8) determining the sample plan and size, (9) collecting data, (10) analyzing data, and (11) preparing and presenting the final research report. We will discuss each of these steps in the following paragraphs, but first, you need to understand there are some caveats associated with using a step-by-step approach to understanding the process of marketing research.

## Caveats to a Step-by-Step Process

### Why 11 Steps?

You should know that there are caveats to presenting all research projects in an 11-step process. First, while we conceptualize the research process as 11 steps, others may present the process in fewer steps or even more steps. There is nothing sacred about 11 steps. We could present research as three steps: defining the problem, collecting and analyzing data, and presenting the results; but we think this oversimplifies the research process. Or we could present you with 20-plus steps, but in our opinion, this would provide more detail than is needed. We feel that 11 steps is explicit enough without being overly detailed. But you should know that everyone doesn't present the research process in the same way we have presented it here.

■ While we think 11 steps is a good number of steps to adequately explain the marketing research process, others may use fewer, or more, steps.

■ Not all marketing research projects require all 11 steps.

### Not All Studies Use All 11 Steps

A second caveat is that not all studies follow *all 11* steps. Sometimes, for example, a review of secondary research alone may allow the researcher to achieve the research objectives. Our 11 steps assume the research process examines secondary data and continues on to collect primary data.

■ Many marketing research projects do not follow the 11 steps in exact order.

### Few Studies Follow the Steps in Order

Our third caveat for you is that most research projects do not follow an orderly, step-by-step process. Sometimes, after beginning to gather data, it may be determined that the research objectives should be changed. Researchers do not move, robotlike, from one step to the next. Rather, as they move through the process, they make decisions as to how to proceed in the future, which may involve going back and revisiting a previous step.

While you are forewarned about using a "list" approach, remember that our 11 steps are very useful in understanding the marketing research process. In our opening vignette, the researchers benefit greatly by knowing the steps of the research process. Knowing the steps in the process helps researchers design a better research project for their client. In the following paragraphs, we will briefly discuss the 11 steps. Also, at the beginning of each chapter, we will provide you with a list of the 11 steps and we will highlight "where we are" on the list, depending on the topics covered in the chapter. See "Where We Are" in the margin.

■ *Where We Are*

1  Establish the need for marketing research
2  Define the problem
3  Establish research objectives
4  Determine research design
5  Identify information types and sources
6  Determine methods of accessing data
7  Design data collection forms
8  Determine sample plan and size
9  Collect data
10  Analyze data
11  Prepare and present the final research report

■ At the beginning of each chapter, we will provide you with a list of the 11 steps and we will highlight "where we are" on the list, depending on the topics covered in the chapter.

## Step 1: Establish the Need for Marketing Research

The need for marketing research arises when managers must make decisions and they have inadequate information. Not all decisions will require marketing research. Research takes time and costs money. Managers must weigh the value possibly derived from conducting marketing research and having the information at hand against the cost of obtaining that information. Fortunately, most situations do not require research, for if they did, managers would be mired down in research instead of making timely decisions. We will discuss situations that dictate the use or nonuse of marketing research later in this chapter.

■ Defining the problem is the most important step, because if the problem is incorrectly defined, all else is wasted effort.

## Step 2: Define the Problem

If it is decided to conduct marketing research, the second step is to define the problem. This is the most important step, because if the problem is incorrectly defined, all else is wasted effort. As examples, consider the following problems: "Which of three proposed TV advertising commercials will generate the highest level of sales of our line of baked cookies?" "Which media, or combination of media, should we use to promote our line of baked cookies?" "What message should we use in our promotions to gain sales for our line of baked cookies?" "What should be our overall marketing strategy for our line of baked cookies?" "Should we be in the baked cookie business?" As you can see, problems may vary considerably from being specific and narrowly focused (i.e., which of three TV ads should we use?) to being very general and not narrowly focused (i.e., should we even be in the baked cookie business?). Problems stem from two primary sources: gaps between what is *supposed* to happen and what *did* happen and gaps between what did happen and what *could* be happening. We will devote a latter section of this chapter to issues that should be considered to properly define the problem.

## Step 3: Establish Research Objectives

Research objectives, step 3, when achieved, provide the information necessary to solve the problem identified in step 2. Research objectives state what the *researchers* must do. For example, if the problem is to determine the level of customer satisfaction with product X, a research objective could be to survey 400 users of product X and measure their level of satisfaction on six different attributes as well as the likelihood of their purchasing the product again. We will explore research objectives in more depth later in this chapter.

■ Research objectives state what the *researchers* must do in order to carry out the research.

## Step 4: Determine Research Design

By *research design* we are referring to the research approach undertaken to meet the research objectives. There are three widely recognized research designs: exploratory, descriptive, and causal designs. Exploratory research, as the name implies, is a form of casual, informal research that is undertaken to learn more about the research problem, learn terms and definitions, or identify research priorities. Going to the library and looking for background information on a topic is an example of exploratory research. Descriptive research refers to research that describes the phenomena of interest. A marketing executive who wants to know what type of people buy the company's brand wants a study *describing* the demographic profile of heavy users of the company brand. Many surveys are undertaken to describe things: level of awareness of advertising, intentions to buy a new product, satisfaction level with service, and so on. The last type of research approach is causal research design. Causal studies attempt to uncover what factor or factors *cause* some event. Will a change in the package size of our detergent cause a change in sales? Causal studies are achieved from a class of studies we call experiments. You will learn about these three research designs and when it is appropriate to use each in Chapter 4.

■ There are three widely recognized research designs: exploratory, descriptive, and causal designs.

## Step 5: Identify Information Types and Sources

Since research provides information to help solve problems, researchers must identify the type and sources of information they will use in step 5. There are two types of information: primary (information collected specifically for the problem at hand) and secondary (information already collected).

Secondary information should always be sought first, since it is much cheaper and faster to collect than primary information. A company franchising car washes, for example, may use secondary data to make decisions as to where to locate new car washes based on the number of vehicles per square mile and the number of existing car washes in different market areas. This is information that has been collected and is available in published sources for a small fee. Sometimes research companies collect information and make it available to all those wishing to pay a subscription to get the information. This type of information is referred to as syndicated data; Neilsen Media Research's TV ratings, which report the numbers of persons who watch different TV programs, is an example of syndicated data. Secondary information is discussed further in Chapters 5 and 6.

However, sometimes secondary data are inadequate. What if our car-wash franchiser wanted to know how car owners in Austin, Texas, would respond to a one-price ticket good for as many car washes as needed in a year? This information is not available. Primary data must be collected specifically for this problem. Beginning with Chapter 7, the rest of this book teaches you how to gather, analyze, and report primary data.

## Step 6: Determine Methods of Accessing Data

Data may be accessed through a variety of methods. While secondary data are relatively easy to access, accessing primary data is much more complex. When the researcher must communicate with respondents, there are four main choices of accessing data: (a) have a person ask questions (i.e., conduct an in-home survey or a telephone survey), (b) use computer-assisted or direct questioning (i.e., CATI or computer-assisted telephone interview or online survey delivered to an e-mail address), or (c) allow respondents to answer questions themselves without computer assistance (i.e., mail survey), or (d) use some combination of two more of the above three modes. There are several methods of accessing data within the three broad choices, and each of these, along with its pros and cons, is discussed in Chapter 7.

## Step 7: Design Data Collection Forms

■ Care must be taken to ask the questions that will generate information needed to solve the research objectives and to ask them clearly and without bias.

Step 7 is designing the form upon which we gather the data. If we communicate with respondents (ask them questions), the form is called a questionnaire. If we observe respondents, the form is called an observation form. In either case, great care must be given to designing the form properly. Care must be taken to ensure that the questions asked will generate answers that satisfy the research objectives and that can therefore be used to solve the problem. The questions must be worded properly so that they are clear and unbiased. Care must also be taken to design the questionnaire so as to reduce refusals to answer questions and to get as much information as desired from respondents. You will learn how to design questionnaires and observation forms in Chapters 8 and 9.

## Step 8: Determine Sample Plan and Size

■ Sample plans describe how each sample element, or unit, is to be drawn from the total population. The sample plan determines whether the sample is representative of the population.

Typically, marketing research studies are undertaken to learn about populations by taking a sample of that population. A population consists of the entire group that the researcher wishes to make inferences about based upon information provided by the sample data. A population could be "all department stores within the greater Portland, Oregon, area" or it could be "college students enrolled in the College of Business at XYZ College." Populations should be defined by the research objectives. One firm, for example, defines their survey population as between 17 and 70 years old and who make buying decisions for the household regarding technology products. A sample is a subset of the population. Sample plans describe how each sample element, or unit, is to be drawn from the total population. The objectives of the research as well as the nature of the sample frame (list of the population elements or units) determine which sample plan is to be used. The type of sample plan used determines whether or not the sample is representative of the population. Secondly, there is the issue of sample size. How many elements of the population should be used to make up the sample? The

## MARKETING RESEARCH APPLICATION 3.1

PRACTICAL

APPLICATIONS

### Sampling Around the World

Survey Sampling International (SSI) began operations in 1977 and is a major player in the marketing research industry. The company provides services that allow clients, both companies conducting their own research as well as other marketing research firms to solve complex sampling problems. Using the firm's SSISNAP® program, clients may design their own sample plans online and receive samples electronically in a matter of minutes. The company has access to huge databases and can provide client firms with RDD (random-digit-dialed) samples for households or business firms. They offer samples that have been screened for disconnected numbers and they also provide a service, LITe® samples, which targets selected populations such as pet owners or frequent travelers.

Responding to globalization, SSI now offers sampling services in over 20 countries around the world. This is a significant undertaking, as the various differences in infrastructure makes sampling much more complex. Just think of the differences between countries in address format, telephone numbering systems, and information sources containing databases of mailing addresses, telephone numbers, and Internet addresses.

Visit the SSI website at **www.surveysampling.com** Go to "Sampling Solutions by Country" and see to which countries SSI offers sampling services.

Canada is the second-largest country in the world. It is in northern North America, bordering the North Atlantic Ocean and North Pacific Ocean, north of the United States. Canada is a self-governing dominion with ties to the British crown. The capital city is Ottawa.

The population is approximately 31,592,805. The bulk of the population (68%) is between the ages of 15 and 64 years; nearly 19% is 14 years and younger; and nearly 13% is 65 years and older. The languages spoken are English 59.3% (official), French 23.2% (official), and other 17.5%. The country has 16,840,000 Internet users.

*Source: The World Factbook 2002 and Wikipedia: The Free Encyclopedia*

---

size of the sample determines how accurately your sample results reflect values in the population. In Chapter 10 you will learn about step 8, which deals with how you draw elements, or units, from the population to form a sample. You will also learn sample size theory, which will teach you how *many* elements to draw for your sample. Read marketing Research Application 3.1 for a discussion of Survey Sampling International. This firm specializes in sampling.

## Step 9: Collect Data

In Chapter 11 you will learn what issues to consider in collecting data. Errors in collecting data may be attributed to fieldworkers or to respondents, and they may be either intentional or unintentional. What is important is that the researcher knows the sources of these errors and implements controls to minimize them. For example, fieldworkers, those collecting the data, may cheat and make up data they report as having come from a respondent. Researchers minimize this from happening by undertaking a control referred to as "validation." Validation means that 10% (the industry standard) of all respondents in a marketing research study are randomly selected, recontacted, and asked if they indeed took part in a research study. You will learn the sources of the data collection errors and how researchers control for them in Chapter 11.

■ How many elements of the population should be used to make up the sample? The size of the sample determines how accurately your sample results reflect values in the population.

■ Mktg. Inc., is a marketing research firm that specializes in data collection. Visit the company Web site at www.mktginc.com.

■ It is important that researchers know the sources of data collection errors and how to implement controls to minimize these errors.

## Step 10: Analyze Data

Marketing researchers transfer data from the data collection forms and enter the data into software packages that aid them in analyzing the data. In this book you will learn how to enter data into Excel and how to conduct data analysis using the XL Data Analyst™, a new data analysis software program that comes with this book. You will learn basic descriptive analysis in Chapter 11. In Chapter 12 you will learn how to estimate values in the population based upon your data, and you will also learn how to test hypotheses. In Chapter 13 you will learn how to test for differences between groups. For example, are there differences in intention to buy a new brand between different demographic groups? Determining relationships among variables and using regression to predict are the topics covered in Chapter 14. The objective of data analysis is to use the statistical tools that come with XL Data Analyst™ to present data in a form that satisfies the research objectives. If the research objective was to determine if there are differences in intention to purchase a new product between four levels of income groups, data analysis should be used to determine if there are any differences in intention to purchase between the income groups and to determine if these differences (based upon sample data) actually exist in the population.

## Step 11: Prepare and Present the Final Research Report

The last step in the research process is preparing and presenting the marketing research report. The report is very important because it is often the client's only record of the research project. In most cases, marketing research firms prepare a

Sean Meckley, a Bluetooth SIG Market Research Analyst, makes a presentation of the results of the Millward Brown study at a meeting in Seattle, WA.

By permission, Bluetooth SIG.

written research report and also make an oral presentation to the client and staff. Marketing researchers follow a fairly standard report-writing format, which is illustrated for you in Chapter 15. Care must be taken to write clearly and to present data accurately using the most appropriate figures and tables. The most important criterion for the report is that it clearly communicate the research findings to the client.

We've just outlined and briefly discussed the steps in the marketing research process. If care is exercised by the researcher and the client, the research process will produce information that can be used to resolve the problem. Pay attention to "Where We Are" in these steps at the beginning of each chapter. This will help you appreciate the research process more as you learn more about the details of each of the steps in the marketing research process. Now, in the following sections of this chapter, we begin the steps in earnest by examining the first three steps in depth.

■ In most cases, marketing research firms prepare a written research report and also make an oral presentation to the client and staff.

■ We have now finished our overview of the 11-step marketing research process.

■ Begin step 1! This section begins our journey through the 11 steps.

## ESTABLISHING THE NEED FOR MARKETING RESEARCH

### When Is Marketing Research Not Needed?

#### The Information Is Already Available

Managers make many decisions. Many of these decisions are routine and the manager has the experience to make the decision without any additional information. When decisions do require additional information, remember that there are other components of the marketing information system (MIS) that the manager may use. Can the needed information be obtained from the internal reports system? Marketing intelligence system? The decision support system? All of these information systems are ongoing sources of information. Marketing managers can quickly and inexpensively access this information. Consider the following examples: A manager at Kodak wants to make a decision regarding the need to spend more dollars on R&D technology. She consults the marketing intelligence system to see what new technology breakthroughs have been brought to market by Kodak's competitors. A manager at Roche Pharmaceuticals needs to make a decision regarding adding to the sales force. He consults the company's decision support system to do an analysis on which colleges and universities produced the salespeople who most consistently meet or exceed their sales quota. But when information is *not* available, the researcher should consider conducting marketing research.

#### The Timing Is Wrong to Conduct Marketing Research

Time often plays a critical role in decision making, and that is true with marketing research as well. It may be that there isn't enough time to conduct marketing research. Consider this situation: The candy bar business is highly competitive. Mars introduces a new flavor and sales skyrocket. Market share is gained at the expense of competitors such as Hershey. Should managers at Hershey launch marketing research to determine if the new flavor is acceptable to the market? No. There isn't time. Mars' new product's success is all the evidence that should be needed to demonstrate that the new flavor has market acceptance. Instead of conducting research, Hershey needs to launch a competitive product, with the same flavor as the new successful Mars brand, to take back some of the losses they've already experienced.

■ Sometimes the need to respond quickly to competition means there isn't time to conduct marketing research.

Time may also be a factor for products that are nearing the end of their life cycle. When products have been around for many years and are reaching the decline stage of their life cycle, it may be too late for research to produce valuable results.

### Funds Are Not Available for Marketing Research

Small firms or firms that are having cash flow problems may not conduct marketing research simply because they cannot afford it. Research, if conducted properly, can be expensive. A study gathering primary data for a representative sample can cost hundreds of thousands of dollars. Also, in many cases the total cost of the research project is not calculated. Conducting the research is one cost, but firms must also consider what it may cost to *implement* the research recommendations. The owner of a pizza restaurant saved money for a research project but was then unable to fund the resulting recommendations (that the restaurant offer drive-through and delivery service). In this case, the research money was wasted.

### Costs Outweigh the Value of Marketing Research

Managers should always consider the cost of research and the value they expect to receive from conducting the research. While costs are readily estimated, it is much more difficult to estimate the value research is likely to add. As an example, consider a decision as to how best to package a new brand of toothpaste. The packaging required to send a few sample boxes to a new-products trade show would certainly not warrant research. The packaging only needs to assure safe transit. If the packaging fails, little is lost and recovery is simple. However, what about the packaging of the toothpaste itself? The toothpaste must sit on a shelf among many other brands, many of which have packaging that is easily recognized by brand-loyal customers. Chances are a consumer quickly scanning the toothpaste section will see his or her favorite brand and make the purchase without even being aware of the existence of the new brand. If research can identify a package design that will cause greater attention and awareness of the brand on the shelf, sales will go up. This gives the research value. How much value? Managers must try to estimate what impact will there be on sales if 2 out of 10 shoppers are aware of the brand instead of 1 out of 20. Though placing a dollar figure on value is difficult, value *can* be estimated and a more informed decision may be made as to whether or not marketing research is justified. Some managers fail to compare research cost with its value, which is a mistake.[2]

**When Will Research More Likely Have Greater Value?** Some guidelines for answering this question are: Will the research help clarify problems or opportunities? Will research identify changes that are occurring in the marketplace among consumers or competitors? Will research clearly identify the best alternative to pursue among a set of proposed alternatives? Will the research help your brand establish a competitive advantage?[3] Once a decision is made that research is needed, managers (and researchers) must properly define the problem and the research objectives.

## The Impact of Online Research and Determining the Need to Conduct Marketing Research

ONLINE

A primary advantage of online research is speed. Managers today may use an online research company to obtain information in a matter of days, whereas traditional research would require weeks or even months to gather the information. What this means is that online research will lead to more decisions to use research in situations where timing ruled out research in the past. Hershey managers, for example, by using online research, would be able, during the short time it would take to develop the proper recipe and tool up for production, to quickly test several marketing-mix decisions related to the new bar before introducing it to the market. They could test brand names, package designs, effectiveness of new promotional materials, and the like.

Another favorable point to be made about online research is that, in many circumstances, it is less costly than traditional research. Savings in time and money means managers may look to conduct online marketing research projects when, in the past, they may have felt traditional research took too much time or did not offer enough value for the cost.

## DEFINE THE PROBLEM

### The Importance of Properly Defining the Problem

Sometimes problems are easy to define: "What are the media habits of the heavy users of our brand?" Sometimes problems are very difficult to define: "Our sales are increasing but our market share is going down. Is there a problem and, if so, what is it?" But regardless of how difficult or easy it is to define the problem, we can state that properly defining the problem is *the* most important step in the marketing research process. While this may sound like a dramatic statement, it is indeed true. Why? You've just learned that there are 11 steps in the marketing research process. You also learned that, after determining whether or not research is needed, defining the problem is the next step in the research process. If the wrong problem is defined, what impact does this have on the rest of the research process? *Everything* else is wrong! It doesn't matter if you collect data properly, analyze it properly, and report it in a meaningful fashion if it addresses the *wrong* problem. Great care must be exercised in properly defining the problem. Let's look at a couple of examples to illustrate improper problem definition.

■ Begin step 2!

■ Properly defining the marketing management problem is *the* most important step in the marketing research process.

#### How Can We Beat Burger King?

McDonald's conducted marketing research for a new burger, the McDonald's Arch DeLuxe. The burger, targeted for adults, received a less-than-hoped-for result even though McDonald's spent large sums of money on marketing research. What happened? The analysis points to "improper problem definition." McDonald's management was eager to match the Burger King Deluxe burger. All research was focused on measuring consumer preferences for different sizes and tastes of hamburgers. McDonald's researchers would likely have been better off by not defining the problem as "How can we beat Burger King" but, instead, focusing on *adult* fast-food customers' preferences, including nutritional content. They may have produced a product that was better tasting than the Burger King product but they didn't come up with a product that appealed to adults. Improperly defining the problem leads to lost time and money.[4]

#### How Can We Win a Taste Test?

The following example, well known among researchers, also illustrates the costs and wastes associated with improper problem definition. Coke was continually losing in taste tests against Pepsi, a cola with a sweeter taste than Coke. Though Coke had significant market share and an established brand name, its executives defined their problem as not having a product as tasty as that of their major competitor. This led to over four years of research in which they developed a sweet-tasting cola. The new flavored beverage beat the competitor's cola in taste test after taste test. Thinking they had solved the "taste test problem," Coke management dropped its old product and introduced the new, sweeter-tasting cola. To their surprise, sales plummeted and consumers, missing their old drink, protested by the thousands. What happened? Many believe Coke did not define the problem correctly. They defined the problem as "How can we beat the competitor in taste tests?" instead of "How can we gain market share against our competitors?" They already had a sizeable share of the market with their non-sweet-flavored cola. When they stopped producing the old drink, their customers only had the sweet-flavored beverage to buy, which they didn't want; they had already shunned sweeter-tasting Pepsi in favor of Coke. Losing the taste tests led Coke to improperly define the problem; they wanted to beat their competitors. They did, but by dropping their existing product in favor of the new "better-tasting" cola, they lost their own customers. With 20/20 hindsight, they should have kept their existing Coke product and introduced a new brand to compete for the market preferring a sweeter cola. Eventually they did reintroduce the old cola as Coke Classic and they kept the new, sweeter version. By not focusing research on the right problem, management learned a hard lesson and wasted much time and millions of dollars.[5]

These examples illustrate the importance of properly defining the problem. Not only does improper problem definition waste valuable resources such as time and money, but it also prevents proper marketing research information that may set management on the right track sooner, and, as we saw in the case of Coke, another problem is lost goodwill from brand-loyal customers.

> ■ "A problem well defined is a problem half solved." It is an old but still valid adage. A bad problem definition dooms the entire project from the start.

Lawrence D. Gibson, an independent consultant and Senior Associate at Eric says, "A problem well defined is a problem half solved." It is an old but still valid adage. How a problem is defined sets the direction for the entire project. A good definition is necessary if marketing research is to contribute to the solution of the problem. A bad definition dooms the entire project from the start and guarantees that subsequent marketing and marketing research efforts will prove useless. Nothing we researchers can do has so much leverage on profit as helping marketing define the right problem."[6]

## Two Sources of Problems

> ■ Managers recognize problems when gaps exist between what was *supposed* to happen and what *did* happen or when there is a gap between what *did* happen and what *could have* happened.

First, we must understand that problems may come from two different sources. A **problem** exists when there is a gap between what was *supposed* to happen and what *did* happen.[7] Failure to meet an objective, for example, creates a gap between what was *supposed* to happen and what actually *did* happen. This situation is what we normally think of when we use the term *problem*. The manager must now determine what course of action to take in order to close the gap between the objective and actual performance. The second type of problem, however, is not often immediately recognized as a "problem". This second type of problem, called an **opportunity,** occurs when there is a gap between what *did* happen and what *could have* happened.

> ■ An opportunity is a form of a problem in that managers must determine whether and how to take advantage of it.

This is an opportunity because the situation represents a favorable circumstance or chance for progress or advancement.[8] Put another way, a **marketing opportunity** has been defined as an area of buyer need or potential interest in which a company can perform profitably.[9] For example, our sales were $X but *could have been* $Y had we introduced a new, more competitive product. Even though we refer to this as an opportunity, managers still have a problem in that they must determine whether and how to take advantage of an opportunity.

## Recognizing the Problem

Good managers will be aware of problems or they will soon cease to hold management positions. For managers to recognize a problem, they must be knowledgeable of objectives and actual performance. They should be setting objectives and have a control system in place to monitor performance. This is just sound management practice. Many experienced managers would agree that what is worse than discovering you have a problem is to continue to operate in ignorance of the problem. Unless managers have a control system, they will not likely identify problems arising from failure to meet objectives. Managers must also be aware of opportunities, and unless they have a system for monitoring opportunities, sometimes referred to as a process of **opportunity identification,** they will not likely identify these problems.[10] Table 3.1 shows the sources of problems and the systems needed to recognize them, along with examples.

■ Unless managers have a control system, they will not likely identify problems arising from failure to meet objectives. Managers must also be aware of opportunities, and unless they have a system for monitoring opportunities, they will not likely identify these problems.

## The Role of Symptoms in Problem Recognition

The classic statement "We have a problem . . . we are losing money" illustrates why researchers and managers, in properly defining problems, must be careful to avoid confusing symptoms with problems. The problem is not that "we are losing

| Sources of Problems | Examples | System Required in Order to Recognize Gap |
|---|---|---|
| Gap between what is *supposed* to happen and what *did* happen (Failure to meet objectives) | Sales calls below target number | Control system based upon setting objectives and evaluating them against actual performance |
| | Sales volume below quota | |
| | ROI below goal | |
| Gap between what *did* happen and what *could* happen (Should we and how do we take advantage of opportunities?) | Increase in sales if we change product features | System for identification of opportunities |
| | Increase in profits if we expand into new territory | |
| | Increase in ROI if we diversify into growing new field | |

**Table 3.1**
**Problem Recognition**

Some marketing management problems come from a failure to meet objectives, and other problems stem from determining if and how to take advantage of opportunities. In either case, managers must select the proper course of action from several alternative choices.

■ Managers and researchers must be careful to avoid confusing symptoms with problems.

money." Rather, the problem may be found among all those factors that cause us to make (or lose) money, and the manager, with help from the researcher, must identify all those possible causes in order to find the right problem or problems.

**Symptoms** are changes in the level of some key monitor that measures the achievement of an objective; for example, our measure of customer satisfaction has fallen 10% in each of the last two months. In this case, the role of the symptom is to alert management to a problem; there is a gap between what *should* be happening and what *is* happening. A symptom may also be a perceived change in the behavior of some market factor that implies an emerging opportunity. A pharmaceutical company executive sees a demographic forecast that the number of teenagers will increase dramatically over the next 10 years. This may be symptomatic of an opportunity to create new drugs designed for teen problems such as acne or teenage weight problems. Note that symptoms may be *negative* but still bring about opportunities; for example, say that the forecast for teens is that their numbers will *shrink* in the next 10 years. Should the company shift R&D from developing new drugs for teens to the growing aging–Baby Boomer market? Both types of symptoms should be identified by either the control system (objectives/monitoring) or by the system in place for opportunity identification. The key lesson, however, is that symptoms are not problems; they should be used to alert managers to recognize problems.

■ The key lesson is that symptoms are not problems. Rather, symptoms should be used to alert managers to recognize problems.

## Types of Problems

Not all problems are the same. We have already established that the sources of problems may differ: Some arise through recognition of a failure to meet an objective, and others from a recognition of an opportunity. We can also characterize problems in terms of their being specific versus general. Some problems are very specific: The Director of Marketing Research at Kraft Foods may want to know "What is the best package design to create awareness and interest in our Maxwell House coffee brand?" or "Which of three new cookie recipes is the most preferred?" Sometimes the problem can be very general: "Should we change our entire marketing plan?" "Should we even be in the coffee business?" Clearly, these two extremes illustrate there are wide differences in the types of problems confronting managers. Generally, the more specific the problem, the easier the marketing researcher's task. When a problem is defined very narrowly and in specific terms by management, it is much easier for the researcher to transform this type of problem into well-defined and specific research objectives. Alternatively, the researcher has a much more challenging task when presented by management with a vague, general problem.

## The Role of the Researcher in Problem Definition

Regardless of the type of problem, the researcher has an obligation to help managers ensure they are defining the problem correctly. This is particularly true when the researcher is called in by the manager who already has the problem defined in very specific terms. The manager who thinks that the problem is coming up with a better cookie recipe may be startled to learn that total cookie sales have been falling for the last five years. Perhaps the researcher should ask the manager the question "Are you sure you should be in the baked cookie business?" Problem definition expert Lawrence Gibson wrote, "Researchers must resist the temptation to 'go along' with the first definition suggested. They should take the time to conduct their own investigation and to develop and consider alternative definitions." [11] This additional investigation may take the form of a situation analysis. A **situation analysis** is a form of preliminary research undertaken to gather background information and gather data pertinent to the problem area. (We will discuss several methods of conducting exploratory research, used in a situation analysis, when we introduce you to this type of research design in Chapter 4.)

The researcher should be interested in the long-term welfare of the client. Because researchers are accustomed to dealing with problem definition, they should help managers define the problem accurately. By doing so, the research they provide will add real value to the client's bottom line, helping to ensure the long-term relationship.

> Researchers must resist the temptation to accept the first problem defined. They should conduct their own research to determine if there are alternative problems.

## Impediments to Problem Definition

You've read some examples illustrating how companies have not defined the problem correctly. Properly defining the problem may be hampered due to two factors: (a) managers may fail to recognize the importance of changing their behavior in order to communicate and interact closely with researchers, and (b) the differences between researchers and managers may hamper communications.

### Failure to Change Behavior for Problem Definition Situations

Managers sometimes do not recognize that they need to change their normal behavior in order to properly define the problem. Managers are accustomed to dealing with outside suppliers efficiently. Suppliers are asked to present their products or services, they are evaluated against established purchasing criteria, and a decision is made. A minimum of interaction and involvement is required to make most purchasing decisions, and this is viewed as desirable; it leads to accomplishing business activities efficiently. Unfortunately, this behavior does not necessarily change when dealing with an external supplier of marketing research. To a lesser extent, you could say this is also true of managers dealing with other divisions within the same firm, as would be the case when an internal marketing research department is supplying the marketing research. However, to find possible causes for changing symptoms or to identify and determine the likelihood of success of pursuing opportunities requires in-depth communications over an extended period of time. Often, to be effective, this process is slow and tedious. Managers often are unaware of the required change in their behavior and this causes problems in identifying the real problem. Veteran researchers are well aware of this situation, and it is up to them to properly inform management of their expected role and the importance of this initial step in the research process.

> Managers are accustomed to dealing with suppliers in an efficient manner. They must change this behavior when working with marketing research suppliers in order to properly identify the problem.

### Differences Between Managers and Researchers

Marketing managers and marketing researchers see the world differently because they have different jobs to perform and their backgrounds differ markedly. For example, managers possess line positions; researchers are in staff positions. Managers are responsible for generating profits; researchers are responsible for generating information. Managers are trained in general decision making, and researchers are trained in research techniques. All of these differences hinder communications between the two parties at a time when in-depth, continuous

> Managers historically have been generalists and researchers have been technical specialists.

communications and trust are required. However, these differences have improved over the years and are growing smaller. The reason is that college students today, tomorrow's managers, are in a better position to learn and have greater appreciation for the technical side of marketing research. Many of the analyses you will learn using XL Data Analyst™, for example, were once only available to computer specialists who could write the code required to run these analyses on mainframe computers. You will be far better equipped to communicate with marketing researchers than your predecessors.

## The Role of ITBs and RFPs

ITBs are "invitations to bid" and RFPs are "requests for proposals." Companies use these documents to alert research firms that they would like to receive bids or proposals to conduct research to solve a particular problem.

**ITBs** are "invitations to bid." Alternatively, some firms use **RFPs**, which stands for "requests for proposals." Companies use these documents to alert research firms that they would like to receive bids or proposals to conduct research. In either case, the roles of the researcher and manager have changed in the problem definition process. When a company uses an ITB or RFB, they have already defined the problem and, in some cases, the research objectives. At the very least, management has thought through many of the issues revolving around defining the problem. This means much of the dialogue normally necessary between researchers and managers may be avoided. For example, managers in a firm decide they need to assess customer satisfaction in a way that will allow them to prescribe remedial actions. The problem has been defined. They submit an ITB or RFP to several research firms, who now bid on doing the necessary research.

Although RFPs and ITBs are all different, they contain some common elements. Commonly found sections are:

- **Introduction.** Identification of the company or organization that originates the RFP, with background information about the company.
- **Scope of Proposal.** Description of the basic problem at hand.
- **Deliverables.** Specification of the tasks to be undertaken and products to be produced and delivered to the company soliciting the proposal or bid. For example, the deliverable may be "a survey of 1,000 representative recent users of the company's services, described in a report with text, tabulations, figures, and relevant statistical analyses."
- **Evaluation Criteria.** The criteria or standards that will be used to judge the proposals, often set up as a point system in which the proposal is awarded a number of points for each area based on the quality of the work that is proposed.
- **Deadline.** The date by which the deliverables must be delivered.
- **Bidding Specifics.** Necessary items such as the due date for the proposal or bid, specific information required about the bidding company, proposal length and necessary elements (such as sample questions that may appear on the questionnaire), intended subcontract work, payment schedule, contact individual within the origination company, and so on.

As you may remember from our discussion of ethics in Chapter 2, ITBs and RFPs are sensitive issues in terms of appropriate ethical behavior. A firm that sends out phony ITBs (or RFPs) simply to get ideas for research is practicing highly unethical behavior.

We have discussed the importance of properly defining the problem, and we have learned several things about the nature of problems—how to recognize a problem, different sources of problems, different types of problems, and impediments to properly defining the problem—and the role of ITBs and RFPs. Next, we look at a process a researcher may use in defining the marketing manager's problem.

Want to take a look at some ITBs or RFPs? See Interactive Learning at the end of the chapter.

## A PROCESS FOR DEFINING THE PROBLEM AND ESTABLISHING THE RESEARCH OBJECTIVES

There is no universally accepted, step-by-step approach used by marketing researchers to define the problem and establish research objectives. In fact, Lawrence D. Gibson, a recognized authority on defining the problem, wrote that "defining problems accurately is more an art than science."[12] Although there are a number of problem-solving techniques that individual managers can use,[13] we will describe a process that works for the manager–researcher situation. We outline this process for you in Table 3.2. But, before you examine Table 3.2, recall that there are *two* sources of problems: one when there is a failure to meet an objective and the other when there is an opportunity. The process for defining these two problems is different, though they both end up determining research objectives. The major difference is that, for opportunities, the firm must do research to determine the attractiveness and probability of success of any opportunity. This process Kotler refers to is **Market Opportunity Analysis (MOA)**.[14] We are not going to discuss MOA here but we want to point out that after a company conducts an MOA they now have a problem choosing from among several alternative opportunities or evaluating different alternative means to take advantage of the opportunity selected. It is at this point that the two types of problems are similar, and therefore, we are going to discuss only the process involved when there is a failure to meet an objective. As you will see, the problem and research objectives are intertwined. The problem definition process results in definitions of the research objectives.

- Assess the background and the manager's situation
- Clarify the symptoms of the problem
- Pinpoint suspected causes of the symptom
- Specify solutions that may alleviate the symptom
- Speculate on anticipated consequences of the solutions
- Identify the manager's assumptions about the consequences of the solutions
- Assess the adequacy of information on hand to specify research objectives

**Table 3.2**

A Process for Determining the Problem and Establishing Research Objectives *When the Source of the Problem Is a Failure to Meet an Objective*

## Assess the Background and the Manager's Situation

The process may begin with the researcher learning about the industry, the competitors, key products or services, markets, market segments, and so on. The researcher should start with the industry in order to determine whether any symptoms, to be identified later, are associated with the entire industry or only with the manager's firm. The researcher should then move to the company itself: the history of the company, its performance, products or services, unique competencies, marketing plans, customers, major competitors, and so on.

Also, the researcher should try to find out about the manager's unique situation. What constraints is this manager operating under? Why does this manager believe research is needed? Do other managers agree? Does this manager have a particular objective he or she is trying to achieve? At this stage, the researcher is gathering information and will have considerable homework to do after the first meeting with the manager. The researcher must conduct some exploratory research to learn more about the industry, the company, and its competition and markets. Will this information conflict with the information the manager is providing? Recall Larry Gibson's admonition that researchers should not accept the problem without question. Researchers understand the importance of properly defining the problem, and managers, if inexperienced with research, may not be aware of this issue. Researchers add value by ensuring the proper problem is being addressed.

> ■ The researcher is gathering information and will have considerable homework to do after the first meeting with the manager. The researcher must conduct some exploratory research to learn more about the industry, the company, and its competition and markets.

## Clarify the Symptoms of the Problem

You have already learned that symptoms are important in helping to identify the problem. Without symptoms, problem definition is virtually impossible. The researcher needs to understand what control system is in place. Companies vary greatly in terms of defining their objectives, monitoring their results, and taking corrective action. Does the company have an adequate control system? Is the manager alert to symptoms? What are they? Are they accurate measures of performance? Are they reported in a timely fashion? You are beginning to see, no doubt, that the researcher acts much like a detective. It is the researcher's role to explore and to question, in order for the problem to be defined properly. (You may now better understand why we told you earlier that this process requires managers to change their normal behavior. They must enter into an open and trusting relationship with the researcher, and they are not accustomed to doing this with an outside supplier.)

> ■ Without symptoms, problem definition is virtually impossible.

## Pinpoint Suspected Causes of the Symptom

At this point the manager and the researcher should be in agreement on which symptom or symptoms are in need of attention. Symptoms do not just happen. There is always some **cause** or causes for the change. Profits do not go down by themselves. Sales do not drop without customers doing something differently than they have done in the past. Satisfaction scores do not drop without some underlying cause. It is important to determine *all* **possible causes**. If only some of the possible causes are listed, it is possible that the real cause will be overlooked. In this case the problem will not be defined properly, and all research efforts will be wasted. We will next look at the example of University Estates apartments to help illustrate the problem definition process.

> ■ It is important to determine *all* possible causes.

### University Estates: An Example of the Problem Definition Process

University Estates is an apartment complex that targets students attending a nearby college. Last year, University Estates experienced a decline in its occupancy rate from 100% to 80%. The researcher and the manager of University Estates met and began discussing this symptom, asking themselves why the occupancy rate declined. Over the course of their discussion, they identified four general areas of possible causes: (1) competitors' actions, which had drawn prospective student residents away; (2) changes in the consumers (the student target population); (3) something about the apartment complex itself; and (4) general environmental factors. The results of their brainstorming session are presented in Table 3.3. Given this long list, it was necessary to narrow down the possible causes to a small set of **probable causes**, defined as the most likely factors giving rise to the symptom.

> Probable causes are those possible causes that are highly likely to be culprits.

The researcher and the University Estates manager systematically examined every possible cause listed in Table 3.3 and came to the realization that only a few could be probable causes of the decline in the occupancy rate. For example, the manager was vigilant in monitoring what rents were being charged, and he knew that no competitor had lowered its rents in the past year. Similarly, no new apartment complexes had been built or opened up in the past year. Through this dialogue, the researcher and the University Estates manager narrowed the list down to two probable causes: (1) competing apartment complexes had added digital cable television in every apartment, and (2) some apartment complexes had added

**Table 3.3**

Possible Causes for University Estates Occupancy Rate Decline

**1. Competitors' Actions**

| | |
|---|---|
| a. Reduced rents | d. New facilities |
| b. New or additional competitors | e. Better advertising |
| c. New services | f. Financial deals such as no deposit |

**2. Consumers (Current and Prospective Student Renters)**

| | |
|---|---|
| a. Loss of base numbers of students | e. Gravitating to condominiums |
| b. Change in financial circumstances | f. Want more value for the money |
| c. Better living opportunities elsewhere | g. Negative word-of-mouth publicity |
| d. Concern for personal safety | |

**3. University Estates Itself**

| | |
|---|---|
| a. Traffic congestion | d. Aging facilities and equipment |
| b. Noisy neighbors | e. Image as "old" apartments |
| c. Advertising cutback, change | f. Upkeep issues |

**4. The Environment**

| | |
|---|---|
| a. Less student financial aid | d. Change in students' preferences |
| b. Increased crime rate | e. Cost of commuting increase |
| c. Housing market oversupply | f. Other living alternatives |

on-site workout facilities. With a little more background investigation, it was found that only one competing apartment complex had added a workout facility, and most of the complexes, including University Estates, did not have any workout facility. Thus, the cable television deficiency of University Estates was narrowed down as the most probable cause for its occupancy decline.

## Specify Possible Solutions That May Alleviate the Symptom

Managers have at their disposal certain resources, and these resources may provide the solutions they need to address the probable cause of the symptom. Essentially, possible **solutions** include any marketing action that the marketing manager thinks may resolve the problem, such as price changes, product modification or improvement, promotion of any kind, or even adjustments in channels of distribution. It is during this phase that the researcher's marketing education and knowledge fully come into play; often both the manager and the researcher brainstorm possible solutions.

Once again, it is for the manager to specify *all* of the solutions needed to address the probable cause of the symptom. In fact, one marketing research consultant has gone on record with this bold statement, "Unless the entire range of potential solutions is considered, chances of correctly defining the research problem are poor."[15]

### Back to University Estates

Returning to our University Estates example, the manager realized that he needed to look into *all* types of television-delivery systems. After a thorough review of the alternatives, the manager was not content to just match the competition, so he began considering a satellite television system such as DishTV's Multiple Dwelling Unit Program with its 150 channels; four premium channels of HBO, Starz, Showtime, and Cinemax; plus pay-per-view, as one of his likely plans of action. In fact, the manager was quite pleased with his discovery that he could offer satellite television connections in every apartment, because the satellite programming seemed far superior to basic cable television.

## Speculate on Anticipated Consequences of the Solutions

Research on anticipated **consequences**, or most likely outcomes, of each action under consideration will help determine whether the solution is correct or not. For example, a solution might resolve the problem; on the other hand, it might intensify the problem if the solution is not the correct action. To avoid resolving the problem incorrectly, the manager asks "what if" questions regarding possible consequences of each marketing action being considered. These questions include:

- What will be the impact not only on the problem at hand but also throughout the marketing program if a specific marketing action is implemented?
- What additional problems will be created if a proposed solution is implemented?

■ To help resolve problems, managers ask "what if" questions.

Typically, the range of consequences of possible marketing actions is readily apparent. For example, if your advertising medium is changed from *People* magazine to *USA Today*, customers will either see less, see more, or see the same amount of advertising. If a nonsudsing chemical is added to your swimming pool treatment, customers will either like it more, less, or have no change in their opinions about it. Most marketing research investigates consumer consequences of marketing solutions, but it is also possible to research dealers' reactions or even suppliers' reactions, depending on the nature of the problem.

### Back to University Estates

It seemed reasonable to the University Estates manager to speculate that if University Estates added a satellite television system connection in each apartment, University Estates would be seen as more attractive than the other apartment complexes that had surged ahead in occupancy.

## Identify the Manager's Assumptions About the Consequences of the Solutions

As they attempt to define the problem, the manager and the researcher make certain **assumptions**, which are assertions that certain conditions exist or that certain reactions will take place if the considered solutions are implemented. For example, the manager may say, "I am positive that our lost customers will come back if we drop the price to $500," or "Our sales should go up if we gain more awareness by using advertising inserts in the Sunday paper." However, if a researcher questions a manager about his or her beliefs regarding the consequences of certain proposed actions, it may turn out that the manager is not really as certain as he or she sounds. Conversely, the manager may be quite certain and cite several reasons why his or her assumption is valid. It is imperative, therefore, that the manager's assumptions be analyzed for accuracy.

> ■ The manager's assumptions deserve researcher attention because they may be incorrect or uncertain.

Assumptions deserve researcher attention because they are the glue that holds the decision process together. Given a symptom, the manager *assumes* that certain causes are at fault. She or he further *assumes* that by taking corrective actions (solutions) the problem will be resolved and that the symptoms will disappear. If the manager is completely certain of all these assumptions, there is no need for research. But typically, uncertainty prevails, and critical assumptions about which the manager is uncertain will ultimately factor in heavily when the researcher addresses the problem. Research will help eliminate this uncertainty.

> ■ Research will help to eliminate a manager's uncertainty and therefore aid in decision making.

### The Role of Hypotheses in Defining the Problem

**Hypotheses** are statements that are taken for true for the purposes of argument or investigation. In making assumptions about the consequences of solutions, managers are making hypotheses. For example, a successful restaurant owner uses a hypothesis that he must serve X amount of food in an entrée portion in order to please his customers. This restaurant owner bases his decisions on the validity of this hypothesis; he makes sure that a certain quantity of food is served on every plate regardless of the menu choice. Businesspeople make decisions every day based upon statements they believe to be true. Sometimes those decisions are very important and the businessperson may not be confident that he or she is

> ■ Hypotheses are statements that are taken for true for the purposes of argument or investigation.

entirely correct in making the hypothesis. This is very similar to what we have been discussing in the paragraphs previously about assumptions, isn't it? Sometimes the manager makes a specific statement (an assumption) and wants to know if there is evidence to support the statement. In the instances where a statement is made, we may use the term *hypothesis* to describe this "statement thought to be true for purposes of a marketing research investigation." Note that not all research is conducted through hypotheses. A research question is often used to guide research. In this case, the question, not being a statement, is not considered a hypothesis. You will learn how to test hypotheses using your XL Data Analyst™ later on in this book. However, for now, you should understand that when a manager makes a statement he or she believes to be true and wants the researcher to determine if there is support for the statement, we call these types of statements hypotheses.

■ A research project may or may not use hypotheses. When a manager makes a statement he or she believes to be true and wants the researcher to determine if there is support for the statement, we call these types of statements hypotheses.

### Back to University Estates

The key assumptions underlying the University Estates manager's proposed solution are that students (1) know about and understand the advantages of satellite television over basic cable TV and (2) they want satellite television more than they want cable television in their apartments. And, most importantly, the manager was also assuming that (3) adding a satellite television connection in each apartment would render University Estates more desirable than the other apartment complexes targeting university students.

## Assess the Adequacy of Information On Hand to Specify Research Objectives

As the manager and researcher go through this process, available information varies in both quantity and quality. As just noted, the manager may have information that greatly reinforces his or her beliefs, or he or she may not have anything more than an intuitive feeling. You should recall that it is the researcher's responsibility to provide information to the manager that will help resolve the manager's problem. Obviously, if the manager knows something with a high degree of certainty, it is of little value for the researcher to conduct research to reiterate that knowledge. It is vital, therefore, that the researcher assess the existing **information state**, which is the quantity and quality of evidence a manager possesses for each of his or her assumptions. During this assessment, the researcher should ask questions about the current information state and determine the desired information state. Conceptually, the researcher seeks to identify **information gaps**, which are discrepancies between the current information level and the desired level of information at which the manager feels comfortable resolving the problem at hand. Ultimately, information gaps are the basis for establishing research objectives.

■ Information gaps are discrepancies between the current information level and the desired information level. Information gaps are the basis for setting research objectives.

### Back to University Estates

With the University Estates situation, the manager felt quite confident about the accuracy of his information that cable television was offered by his competitors, because they had advertised this new feature as well as announced this new service with signs outside the apartment complexes. He was also confident that students were into cable television; however, he was not sure about how much they desired the additional programming available on satellite television. Thus, the manager had an information gap because he was unsure of what the reactions of prospective University Estates residents would be if the satellite program package was included in the apartment package. Would they see it as competitive to the other apartment complexes that had cable television? Would they want to live at University Estates more than at an apartment complex that had only basic cable?

As you may have noticed in the University Estates example, whenever an information gap that is relevant to the problem at hand is apparent to the manager, the manager and researcher come to agree that it is a research objective. That is, **research objectives** are set to gather the specific bits of knowledge that need to be gathered in order to close the information gaps. Research objectives become the basis for the marketing researcher's work. In order to formulate the research objectives, the marketing researcher considers all the current information surrounding the marketing management problem. We have created Table 3.4 to identify the information gaps and appropriate research objectives in the case of University Estates.

> ■ The manager and researcher come to agree on research objectives that are based on the information gaps.

Now we must relate to you the most important difference between the marketing manager and the market researcher. The entire time that the dialogue is going on between the manager and the researcher, the manager is fixed on one goal: "How can I solve this problem?" However, the researcher is fixed on a different but highly related goal, "How can I gather information relevant to the problem that will help the manager solve his or her problem?" The researcher knows that if the right information is provided to the manager, the problem will be solved. This is why we said the problem and the research objectives are "intertwined" at the beginning of this section. Next, the researcher must focus on the action standard and the research proposal, which we take up next.

### The Role of the Action Standard

We've seen how the problem definition and research objectives development process works with our University Estates case. However, there is another important element that we have not yet covered: we must specify the Action Standards. An **Action Standard** is the predesignation of some quantity of a measured attribute or characteristic that must be achieved for a research objective in order for a predetermined action to take place. The purpose of the action standard is to define what action will be taken given the results of the research findings. For example, in our University Estates case, we have determined that one research objective should be to collect

> ■ An Action Standard is the predesignation of some quantity of a measured attribute or characteristic that must be achieved for a research objective in order for a predetermined action to take place.

**Table 3.4**
Information Gaps and Research Objectives for University Estates

| Information Gap | Research Objective(s) |
|---|---|
| How will prospective residents react to the inclusion of the satellite television programming package with the base price of the apartment? | *To what extent do prospective student residents want satellite television?* |
| Will University Estates be more competitive if it adds a satellite television package? | *Will University Estates be more attractive than competing apartment complexes if it has the satellite television progamming package?* |

information which measures *the extent to which prospective students want satellite television* (see Table 3.4). Let's assume that we measure this using a 5-point scale measuring the preference for satellite TV ranging from 5 "Very Strongly Prefer" to 1 "Very Strongly Do Not Prefer" satellite TV (see operational definitions in the following section). When we get our research results, how do we know whether or not students prefer satellite TV? What if our results show that 50% of the students "very strongly prefer" satellite TV? Some could argue that 50% is not enough preference stating "Half the students do not want it!" Others may argue that this is a large amount: "Half the students want it!"

Action Standards require you to make important decisions before you collect your information and serve as clear guidelines for action once the research is over. Ron Tatham, former CEO of Burke, Inc., and a veteran of the problem definition process with many clients, told the authors, "The action standard is an important component of the problem definition and research objective formulation process because it requires the client to focus on predetermining what information he or she will need in order to take action. Using action standards helps the researcher determine the appropriate research objective because the specification of the

By permission, Decision Analyst.

Decision Analyst helps their clients interpret and act on advertising research results by establishing meaningful Action Standards.

action standards tells the researcher what information and in what format they must provide the client. Secondly, action standards allow clients to take action on research results. Without action standards, managers will often say 'The results of the research are interesting. I learned a lot about the market but I am not sure what to do next.'"[16] Decision Analyst has a database that helps them determine appropriate action standards. The following quote, in italics, supplied to us by Decision Analyst, explains the role Action Standards play when they conduct research on the effectiveness of a given advertisement for their clients. By using an "Action Standard" Decision Analyst's clients know, after an advertising test, whether to run a proposed ad or kill it.

*"Advertising testing systems have long relied on normative data to help determine if a given advertisement is likely to be successful. 'Normative data' simply means historical averages of how other advertisements in the same or similar product category have scored. If a company's new ad scores above the 'norm,' or average, then the advertising agency is happy and the client's marketing director is happy. However, it is Decision Analyst's position that normative data are insufficient as benchmarks. A simple average of historical test scores sets too low a standard, because the normative data includes many failed advertisements (i.e., low-scoring commercials), which pull down the historical averages. Normative data sets the bar too low.*

*That is why Decision Analyst focuses on 'normative action standards' as the appropriate benchmarks. One might think of an 'action standard' as normative data with the low-scoring advertisements removed (at a minimum). The search for a meaningful action standard is the goal of an advertising testing program. As advertisements for a brand are tested and then run or put 'on air,' actual sales responses are monitored to see if the ads appear to be working. Over time through trial and error, a company will begin to develop an understanding of the testing scores that correlate with positive sales response. This point at which the testing scores begin to signal an effective advertisement is where the action standard should be set. Advertisements that score near or above the action standard go forward, while ads that score below the action standard are killed."* (By permission, Decision Analyst).

## FORMULATE THE MARKETING RESEARCH PROPOSAL

As you have learned, the research objectives are the all-important results of the dialogue between the manager and researcher in their quest to specify the problem. That is, the marketing researcher's first task is to talk to the marketing manager and to develop as complete a picture of the problem as possible. With the problem statement agreed to, the marketing researcher develops the research objectives and quickly moves to the formulation of a marketing research proposal. A **marketing research proposal** is a formal document prepared by the researcher, and it serves three important functions: (1) it states the problem, (2) it specifies the research objectives, and (3) it details the research method proposed by the researcher to accomplish the research objectives. Proposals also contain a timetable and a budget.

## Problem Statement

The first step in a research proposal is to describe the problem. This is normally accomplished with a single statement, rarely more than a few sentences long, called the problem statement. The problem statement typically identifies four factors: (1) the company, division, or principals involved; (2) the symptoms; (3) the probable causes of these symptoms; and (4) the anticipated uses of the research information to be provided. The problem statement section of the formal marketing research proposal is necessary to confirm that the researcher and the manager fully agree on these important issues.

## Research Objectives

After describing the problem in the marketing research proposal, the marketing researcher must reiterate the specific research objectives. As we just described, the research objectives specify what information will be collected in order to address information gaps that must be closed in order for the manager to go about resolving the problem. The proposal provides a mechanism to ensure that the manager and researcher agree as to exactly what information will be gathered by the proposed research.

■ **Research objectives must be precise, detailed, clear, and operational.**

In creating research objectives, researchers must keep in mind four important qualities. Each research objective must be *precise*, *detailed*, *clear*, and *operational*. To be precise means that the terminology is understandable to the marketing manager and that it accurately captures the essence of each item to be researched. Detail is provided by elaborating each item perhaps with examples. The objective is clear if there is no doubt as to what will be researched and how the information will be presented to the manager. Finally, the research objective must be **operational**. By this we mean that the research objective should define how the construct being evaluated is actually measured. These definitions are referred to as operational definitions. An **operational definition** is a definition of a construct, such as intention to buy, or satisfaction (see next section), that describes the operations to be carried out in order for the construct to be measured empirically.[17] For example, if we want to measure students' preference for apartment complex characteristics, we can do this with a 7-point rating scale for each characteristic, which ranges from 1 = Strongly Not Preferred to 7 = Strongly Preferred.

By Permission, Bluetooth SIG.

■ **As we discussed at the beginning of this chapter, the Bluetooth SIG measures the following two constructs: awareness of their brand and their brand image.**

■ **The researcher uses marketing constructs and envisions operational definitions of these constructs.**

### The Role of Constructs

A construct is an abstract idea inferred from specific instances that are thought to be related.[18] For example, marketers refer to the specific instances of someone buying the same brand 9 out of 10 times as a construct entitled "brand loyalty." A construct provides us with a mental concept that represents real-world phenomena. When a consumer sees an ad for a product and states "I am going to buy that new product X," marketers would label this phenomenon with the construct called "intention to buy." Marketers use a number of constructs to refer to phenomena that occur in the marketplace. Preference, awareness, recall, satisfaction, and so on are but a few. Marketing researchers find constructs very helpful because, once it is determined that a specific construct is applicable to the problem, there are customary ways of operationalizing, or measuring, these constructs.

**Table 3.5** How the "Hierarchy of Effects" Model Can Frame Research for University Estates' Satellite Television Decision

| Hierarchy Stage | Description | Research Question |
|---|---|---|
| **Unawareness** | Not aware of your brand | What percentage of prospective student residents are unaware of satellite television? |
| **Awareness** | Aware of your brand | What percentage of prospective student residents are aware of satellite television? |
| **Knowledge** | Know something about your brand | What percentage of prospective student residents who are aware of it know that satellite television (1) has 150 channels, (2) premium channels, and (3) pay-per-view? |
| **Liking** | Have a positive feeling about your brand | What percentage of prospective student residents who know something about satellite television feel negatively, positively, or neutral about having it in their apartment? |
| **Intention** | Intend to buy your brand next | What percentage of prospective student residents who are positive about having satellite television in their apartment intend to rent an apartment with it? |
| **Purchase*** | Have purchased your brand in the past | What percentage of the market purchased (tried) your brand in the past? |
| **Repurchase/Loyalty*** | Purchase your brand regularly | What percentage of the market has purchased your brand more than other brands in the last five purchases? |

*Not applicable to University Estates as the satellite television feature is not currently available.

This knowledge becomes very useful in developing the research objectives. Additionally, many constructs have relationships that are explained by models, and these relationships can be useful in solving problems. For example, Table 3.5 illustrates how certain constructs are related using a model referred to as the "hierarchy of effects." Note how useful this would be to you if you were the researcher in our University Estates example.

## Detail the Proposed Research Method

Finally, the research proposal[19] will detail the proposed **research method**. That is, it will describe the data collection method, questionnaire design, sampling plan, and all other aspects of the proposed marketing research in as much detail as the researcher thinks is necessary for the manager to grasp the plan. It will also include a tentative timetable and specify the cost of the research undertaking. Proposals vary greatly in format and detail, but most share the basic components we have described: problem statement; research objectives; and proposed research method, including timetable and cost. You will study in detail all of these topics in chapters that follow, so we will not delve into them now.

What does a marketing research proposal look like? We have prepared Marketing Research Application 3.2, which is the proposal written for University Estates based on the way it has been described in this chapter.

## MARKETING RESEARCH APPLICATION 3.2

**PRACTICAL**

**APPLICATIONS**

**Marketing Research Proposal for University Estates: Proposal to Determine the Attractiveness of Satellite Television to Prospective Student Residents of University Estates**

### INTRODUCTION

This proposal responds to a request on the part of the principals of University Estates, 2525 Bright Drive, New Haven, Connecticut, to provide assistance in its deliberations of adding satellite television to attract prospective university student residents.

### BACKGROUND

University Estates is experiencing an occupancy drop from 100% to 80%. This decline coincides with the addition of cable television now available in all University Estates competitiors but not at University Estates. University Estates principals are contemplating the addition of a satellite television system that will include 150 channels, four premium channels, and pay-per-view. Information is needed to assess prospective student residents' reactions to this possible additional service.

### RESEARCH OBJECTIVES

Discussion with University Estates managers suggests that answers are desired to the following questions:

- To what extent do prospective student residents want satellite television?
- Will University Estates be more attractive than competing apartment complexes if it has the satellite television programming package?

### RESEARCH FRAMEWORK

Based on Research Associates' understanding of the decision facing University Estates principals, and further using the Company's experience in these types of questions, the Company proposes to use the "hierarchy of effects" model as a framework in which to cast the research questions to be used in the proposed survey.

This framework addresses the decision by breaking it into constructs or factors that delineate a complete picture of the factors that may facilitate or hamper the attractiveness of the satellite progamming package.

Using this model, the research questions are:

- What percentage of prospective student residents are aware of satellite television?
- What percentage of prospective student residents who are aware of it know that satellite television (1) has 150 channels, (2) four premium channels, and (3) pay-per-view?
- What percentage of prospective student residents who know something about satellite television have a positive feeling (as opposed to negative or neutral feelings) about having it in their apartment?
- What percentage of prospective student residents who are positive about having satellite television in their apartments intend to rent an apartment with it?
- Is University Estates with satellite television more attractive than competing apartment complexes with cable television?

Action Standards are to be determined for each question above.

### RESEARCH METHOD

Research Associates proposes to undertake a telephone survey of 500 full-time university students who live off-campus. Research Associates will prepare and pretest the survey questionnaire, subcontract the telephone survey work, analyze the data, and present the findings to University Estates principals within six weeks of the execution of a contract. The cost of the proposed survey work is $10,000.

## PUTTING IT ALL TOGETHER USING THE INTEGRATED CASE FOR THIS TEXTBOOK

In this section, we are going to continue with our integrated case study, "College Life E-Zine." You were introduced to this case in Chapter 1, Case 1.2, and also in Chapter 2, Case 2.2. Please go back and read these two cases, as the information in these two cases sets the scene for the description we are about to provide for you in this chapter. Again, this integrated case appears in the case section of several chapters and is the basis for most of the examples we will use in teaching you data analysis in the latter chapters of this book. Your instructor may assign these to you either as written assignments or as class discussion items throughout your course. Here is the continuation of our integrated case.

| | |
|---|---|
| **INTEGRATED CASE** | **College Life E-Zine** |

*This is the third case in our integrated case series. If you have not already done so, you will need to read Case 1.2 before reading this case. You may find it helpful to also read Case 2.2.*

## ORS Marketing Research

Sarah, Anna, Wesley, and Don were now firmly committed to their business idea of providing an e-zine targeted to college students. They had scheduled their second appointment with Bob Watts of ORS Marketing Research. ORS stood for Online Research Solutions, and the firm was committed to providing high-quality online research. It had the capability of conducting online survey research as well as conducting research using traditional data collection methods such as conducting focus groups, person-to-person, and telephone surveys.

## The Need for Primary Data

Bob described some of the secondary data collected by ORS. It was clear that e-zines were growing, especially among younger and more educated segments of the market. All of this was very favorable for the new business venture. "However," Bob stated, "we have no secondary data to tell us if an e-zine targeted specifically to college students will be feasible." Bob went on to explain the need to collect primary data. "We'll need to get some feedback from the students at State U to tell us whether or not to proceed with this business idea and, if we do proceed, how to design the e-zine so that we maximize its appeal. We're going to need to construct the research project so that we can project the findings to the entire student population at State U with an accurate level of precision."

"You're talking about using those sample size formulas we learned in college to give us the margin of error we want, aren't you?" asked Wesley.

"Exactly. I think that it'll be important to have a representative sample and the right sample size if we're going to try to make some accurate estimates of the entire campus population," Bob replied.

## Determining Feasibility

Anna asked how ORS could determine "feasibility." Bob explained that the word had many different meanings and that they themselves would have to determine what was feasible and what was not feasible. "The four of you will have to make the 'go/no-go' decision. Obviously you want to earn a reasonable return on the savings you're going to invest, so one definition of 'feasible' would be for the business to project an ROE at the level you desire. But, before we get too far, maybe we should do some work to determine how many subscriptions you will need to break even. We often recommend this to clients so they can make an early decision as to whether to continue or drop the project idea."

"That makes a lot of sense," said Don. "We were always working on break-even analysis in college. If we project that we will need more students to subscribe than there are students at State U, we're in trouble."

Laughing, Bob agreed, "Yes, you remember your college work well. Break-even analysis is a tool for helping us to determine if the demand required to break even is a reasonable demand level for us to achieve. It doesn't tell us how many people will actually buy the e-zine."

They all agreed break-even analysis would be a great tool to help them begin determining feasibility.

"You all have degrees in marketing," said Bob. "Why don't the four of you work the break-even analysis and call me when you're ready to go over it."

"That'll be no problem," said Sarah. "We can get together tonight at my house and start trying to determine our expenses."

All agreed that that would be a great start.

### Estimating Expenses, Determining a Price, and Calculating the Break-Even Point

That evening, the group met at Sarah's to begin working on the break-even analysis. Fortunately, given their work experience, they had little difficulty in estimating most of the expenses. Determining the price they would charge was more difficult. Since the e-zine would be updated often and because it contained "interactive" components, it wasn't comparable to a regular monthly magazine. Also, they knew from their work experiences that many advertisers would offer the students many specials to get their business and, at least for the students who used the specials and coupons, this would represent a significant value. After much discussion, the group decided on a price of $15 per month that could be billed automatically to a credit card. They would offer six-month subscriptions. Wesley was concerned that this was too expensive.

"That's why we're conducting marketing research," said Anna. "We can do some focus groups first to determine students' reactions to this price once they fully understand the concept. If those focus groups tell us we're way out of line, we can revisit the price."

Wesley felt relieved they were doing the research to help them make this important decision.

At a price of $15 per month for a subscription, the break-even analysis indicated they needed 6,000 subscriptions. Now the four friends weren't sure what this meant to them in terms of a "go/no-go" decision. They agreed that at least it wasn't a number like 30,000, which they knew they could never achieve. On the other hand, it wasn't a small number, like 2,000, which they felt they could more easily achieve. After some discussion they agreed that they needed to ask Bob at ORS if they could obtain research information that would help them make the decision to "go or not go" with the e-zine business. The next day, they called and set up another meeting with Bob Watts to discuss their break-even point of 6,000 subscriptions.

## Information Needed to Confirm Meeting the Break-Even Point

At the meeting, Bob asked to see their analysis. The group discussed the assumptions they had made, and Bob approved of the decisions they used in the break-even analysis. He then asked the group, "Okay, so now what do you think?"

Sarah spoke up and said, "Well, since State U has 35,000 students, the four of us felt that 6,000 subscriptions could be achieved, but we are very uncertain about that assumption. We need some kind of information that will help us confirm our decision that we can reach at least 6,000 subscriptions."

Bob replied, "Yes, I agree that you need that information. Once you get it you'll really see the value of doing marketing research."

"You bet we will," Wesley said, "but what information can ORS gather that will help us with this uncertainty?"

Bob said, "We can conduct research that tells us what percent of the campus population is intending to purchase a subscription." He went on to discuss how they could measure the construct of "intention to subscribe" with a scale ranging from "very likely" to "very unlikely." "Of course," Bob continued, "people don't always do what they say they intend on doing, but if we use only the respondents who say they are 'very likely' to subscribe, this may give us a pretty good estimate of the percentage of students who actually will subscribe." Bob then explained that they would not count on the "somewhat likely" or "undecided" respondents even though they knew some of them would subscribe.

Wesley said, "I see. We need to know what percentage of 35,000 students equals 6,000 students?" As they all nodded in agreement, Wesley was already entering the figures in his calculator. "If we divide 6,000 by 35,000, we get 17.14%. So, we should be pretty confident in our decision to continue on as long the percentage of those saying they are 'very likely' to subscribe is better than, say, 18%."

"Yes," says Bob. "If the number turns out to be 3%, we know the e-zine is probably ahead of its time. On the other hand, if it exceeds 18%, you should be in good shape, at least from a break-even standpoint."

The friends agreed that this would give them a good criterion upon which they could make a decision to move forward or not. Once they knew exactly what percent was willing to subscribe, they would be able to get a better estimate of total sales revenue, expenses, profits, and, eventually, ROE.

## Accuracy of the Estimate of the Percent Very Likely to Subscribe

Sarah, after quietly listening, said, "Okay, I understand trying to determine the percent of the students in the sample you're going to study who want to subscribe, but I'm having trouble understanding how we're going to apply that percentage to the entire campus population. How do we know that the percentage you calculate from your one sample study is *the* correct percentage of students who are 'very likely' to subscribe? Would that percentage change if you did the study again the next day?"

Bob replied, "You are exactly right, Sarah. The percentage we get from the sample data will be our best estimate of the percent of the campus that we expect to subscribe. But it's only an estimate. There is a statistical tool that we can use that will help us identify a range within which the real population value is likely to fall. And we'll be able to say we're 95% confident that the true population percentage falls within that range. I'll go over that tool with you later, but you have an excellent point.

For now, please understand that ORS will be able to provide you with that information, which really gives you greater confidence in using the estimate we get from the sample."

## Other Revenue Sources: Advertising, Affiliated Marketing, and Pay-Per-View

After the group finished discussing the break-even analysis, Bob reminded them that they had intentionally prepared a conservative break-even analysis in that they had assumed revenues flowing only from subcriptions. Now it was time to discuss the other potential revenue sources: (a) advertising, (b) affiliated marketing programs with online vendors, and (c) "pay-per-view" revenues for special events provided over the e-zine. The group had intentionally omitted these revenues from their break-even analysis because they all agreed that it would take time to generate ad revenue, since advertisers would not want to place money in the e-zine until they were confident that it was an established product. Also, they weren't sure if the student subscribers to the e-zine were purchasing over the Internet, so they didn't want to base any revenue on affiliated marketing. (Affiliated marketing is an e-commerce arrangement whereby a Web page owner, A, establishes a link for Web page owner B's Web page. If a Web page visitor clicks through A's Web page to B's Web page and buys something, B provides A with a fee. Sometimes this fee can be 15% of the sale, and it can result in substantial revenues.) Finally, they didn't want to use pay-per-view revenues without having any idea as to whether students would be willing to pay extra for these events.

All five members of the group felt that if subscription fees could carry the costs of the e-zine, the other sources of revenue would just add icing on the cake. "I agree with your thinking wholeheartedly," said Bob. "In fact, most of the time, we have to discourage would-be entrepreneurs at this stage. Usually, they want to count every conceivable revenue source and we try to bring them back to reality. I think your conservative estimate, based solely on subscription revenue, is a good idea. But in planning the research we're going to conduct, we need to think about what information you're going to need in order to help you make the decisions you'll need to make concerning these other revenue sources. When we conduct our research, we want to be sure we gather that information for you."

### Information Needed for Potential Advertisers

"Let's focus first on what information we need for potential advertisers in the e-zine," said Bob.

Don, being very familiar with ad revenue for publications, noted that the group should consider local advertisers such as the movie theaters, restaurants, pizza parlors, and entertainment spots that surrounded State U. He also reminded the group that State U was only the first of what they hoped would be a national market of colleges and universities and that national advertisers seeking to target the college student market would likely be very interested in advertising in the e-zine.

Bob then made the statement "Okay, Don and Sarah both work for publishers that earn their living by selling advertising space. What information do we need to collect in order to appeal to potential advertisers in our e-zine?"

Both Sarah and Don agreed that their advertisers first want to know if their customers, the people who buy their goods and services, read their publications. Don said, "I would have to say that is the foremost criterion our advertisers use. They want to make certain that the types of people who are their potential customers are actually reading the newspaper."

Sarah agreed and pointed out that the reason many of their specially targeted magazines had been so successful was that they allowed advertisers to target the most likely buyers of their goods and services.

Bob said, "Great, this gives us direction. Now, let's determine what kinds of advertisers we want to gather this information for."

The five brainstormed and came up with the following: soft drinks, non-fast-food restaurants, fast-food restaurants, pizza delivery chains, automobile dealers, real estate (for local student apartments), clothing stores, and local night entertainment spots.

## Information Needed for Potential Affiliated Marketing Programs

"Okay, team," Bob said, "we can generate the information you're going to need to help you attract advertisers. Now, let's talk about what information we can provide that will help you establish good affiliated marketing contracts."

Again, everyone launched into a discussion of what potential affiliated partners would want them to demonstrate. First, they agreed that affiliated partners would want to know if subscribers to e-zines are e-commerce users. In other words, do they make purchases over the Internet? Secondly, for those e-zine subscribers that do make purchases, on which types of products and services do they spend their money? Looking ahead to the research, Bob said it would be beneficial if they could come up with categories, as they had with advertising, of products or services bought over the Internet. The five-member team did some exploratory research by searching the Internet and came up with the following: books, gifts for weddings and other special occasions, music CDs, financial services such as insurance and loans, clothing, and general merchandise for home and car. Bob assured the group that he could design the research project so that they would have that information.

## Information Needed for Potential Pay-Per-View Programs

Bob also told them they needed to decide if they wanted a flat fee for everything or if there was a market that would pay extra for pay-per-view events.

Don immediately threw in, "Yes, like streaming video of the school's sporting events."

The group talked about costs, and they were a little uncertain as to what the cost would be to get into pay-per-view offerings. Nevertheless, they all felt strongly that there was great potential in pay-per-view and it could be a way of differentiating their offering from competitors. Don said, "If we are the first in the market and we get the contracts with the universities to video their sports events, we'll have a definite strategic advantage over competitors, who are bound to arise if we are successful."

Bob advised, "Okay, I'm hearing a lot of enthusiasm about the potential of pay-per-view in the future. For now, let's see what kind of response we get if we ask potential subscribers their preference for a type of pay-per-view event. How they answer that question will tell you how much you should pursue this idea after you get the basic e-zine up and running."

Sarah, speaking softly to Anna, said, "Am I glad we hired ORS. I'm feeling much better about these tough decisions we are going to have to make."

Anna nodded her agreement.

## Related Advertising/Affiliated/Pay-Per-View Decisions

Anna said, "Back to measuring this construct you called intentions. Aren't we going to have to adequately describe the concept to them first? I can't tell you if I'm going to buy something until I know what the 'something' is."

Bob agreed and stated that he realized the four had not decided on what the features and articles would actually be, but told them, "We can describe the general idea to them and get their likelihood to subscribe. This is pretty standard in marketing research. Once we determine who intends to subscribe and who doesn't, we can examine some relationships to get a better understanding of profiling our subscriber target market."

Sarah said, "We'll want to have a good profile of our subscribers. Not only will this help us make better marketing decisions, but it will be necessary when we try to sell other companies on advertising in our e-zine or establishing affiliated marketing partners." Bob agreed.

## What Features Should Be Included in the E-Zine?

Bob stated that ORS could also provide information that would help determine potential subscribers' preferences for various types of features in the e-zine.

Don said, "Some hard data would be very helpful to us in making those decisions. We have to remember not to put ourselves in the place of our customers. We haven't been college students for several years now! I've been thinking about the different types of features we can offer, and I'll bring the list of ideas to our work session tonight."

Bob said, "That sounds great. We may also want to consider doing some focus groups right away with college students. They're likely to have some great ideas about exactly what they would like to see in the e-zine. Focus groups may give you some good ideas on what to name your e-zine as well, and they'll give us some idea about students' willingness to accept the $15-per-month subscription fee."

## Are All College Students the Same?

Anna spoke up: "All this sounds great, but I keep thinking we shouldn't treat all college students alike. I lived at home my first two years of college, and I doubt I would have been interested in an e-zine about college. I was too busy watching my parents' big-screen TV and going to the movies with my old high school buddies. But when I moved to campus, my life changed. I think I would have loved an e-zine."

"Good point!" Bob said. "We'll want to know if there is a difference in preferences for the e-zine between on-campus versus off-campus students, and we may find some differences between part-time and full-time students."

Wesley added, "I'll bet we find that freshmen will have different preferences for reading material and topics covered than juniors and seniors. As a freshman, my world revolved around the latest Britney Spears CD. By the time I was a junior, I was hooked on world affairs!"

Bob assured the group that the marketing research project could be constructed so as to help them make the proper decisions regarding differences between these groups.

### Expanding Beyond State U

Everyone agreed that the real potential in the e-zine was in expanding the concept to other universities. Since many of the features in the e-zine would remain the same, this would lower the incremental costs of adding other colleges and universities. Targeting the right colleges and universities would be very important to the success of the e-zine. Bob said ORS could design the research so that they could use the information gathered to determine other colleges or universities with the best potential. He explained, "For example, if we find that a large proportion of, say, engineering students subscribe, we'll target universities with large engineering colleges. Or, if we find that most subscribers live on campus, we can target universities with large on-campus enrollments. Colleges and universities publish this type of information, so we'll be able to select those colleges and universities that have the greatest potential."

Later that evening, the four friends met at Wesley's home. Everyone was pleased with the meeting at ORS, and Don said, "I'm very pleased with Bob Watts. I feel like hiring ORS to help us has been a smart decision."

Anna agreed, "Yes, it was a good idea, and when we get the results of the research, we'll have the information that we need to make several decisions."

The group spent a couple of more hours discussing the various features and their contents. They knew that, as entrepreneurs, their work had only just begun.

### QUESTIONS

1 Define the problem or problems.
2 What are the research objectives?

## SUMMARY

This chapter begins with a description of an 11-step marketing research process. It is important for students to know these 11 steps, though there are caveats to such a step-by-step approach—not everyone agrees that there are 11 steps, not all studies use all 11 steps, and few studies follow the steps in the exact order. Students should use the "Where We Are" list of steps at the beginning of each chapter, which highlights the step or steps the chapter is presenting. Each of the 11 steps is briefly discussed, and the steps are: (1) establishing the need for marketing research, (2) defining the problem, (3) establishing research objectives, (4) determining research design, (5) identifying information types and sources, (6) determining methods of accessing data, (7) designing data collection forms, (8) determining the sample plan and size, (9) collecting data, (10) analyzing data, and (11) preparing and presenting the final research report.

The rest of the chapter is devoted to discussing the first three steps in the research process. Establishing the need for marketing research involves knowing when and when not to conduct marketing research. Marketing research is not needed when information to make a decision is already available, the timing is wrong, there are insufficient funds, or when costs outweigh the value of doing research. Several reasons are provided to illustrate when you should conduct marketing research, when the research is likely to have great value. These situations include when research will help clarify problems or opportunities, identify changes in the marketplace, identify the best alternative to action, and help establish a competitive advantage. Defining the problem, step 2, is the most important of all the steps. A problem well defined is a problem half solved, and a bad problem definition will doom the entire project. There are two sources of problems. One arises when there is a gap between what was supposed to happen and what did happen. This type of problem is attributed to failure to meet an objective. The second type of problem arises when there is a gap between what did happen and what could have happened. We refer to this type of problem as an opportunity. Managers recognize problems through either monitoring of control systems or systems to recognize opportunities. Symptoms are not problems. Rather, symptoms are changes in the level of some key monitor that measures the achievement of an objective. Symptoms alert managers to problems. Problems may be general or specific, and the researcher is responsible for ensuring that management has properly defined the problem. In some cases, a situation analysis is required to help define the problem. Problem definition is sometimes impeded because (a) managers fail to change their normal behavior in order to interact closely with researchers, and (b) managers are usually generalists and researchers tend to be technical. ITBs are "invitations to bid." Alternatively, some firms use RFPs, which stands for "requests for proposals." Companies use these documents to alert research firms that they would like to receive bids or proposals to conduct research.

The process for defining the problem when the source of the problem is a failure to meet objectives is: (1) assess the background and the manager's situation, (2) clarify the symptoms of the problem, (3) pinpoint suspected causes of the symptom, (4) specify solutions that may alleviate the symptom, (5) speculate on anticipated consequences of the solutions, (6) identify the manager's assumptions about the consequences of the solutions, and (7) assess the adequacy of information on hand to specify research objectives. When faced with an opportunity, management should conduct a Market Opportunity Analysis to determine which opportunities to further pursue with additional marketing research. A case example of University Estates apartments was discussed in the chapter to illustrate the process of defining the problem when there has been a failure to reach an objective. Both problem definition processes lead to generating research objectives. Research objectives gather the specific bits of knowledge needed to close information gaps. Action Standards help researchers determine the appropriate research objectives and their format. Action Standards also determine client actions.

Marketing research proposals are formal documents prepared by the researcher and serve the functions of stating the problem, specifying research objectives, detailing the research method, and specifying a timetable and budget. Research proposals typically identify marketing constructs and the operational definitions specifying how the constructs will be measured. The chapter ends with the integrated case, College Life E-Zine.

## KEY TERMS

Steps in the marketing research
    process (p. 62)
Problem (p. 72)
Opportunity (p. 72)
Marketing opportunity (p. 73)
Opportunity identification (p. 73)
Symptoms (p. 74)
Situation analysis (p. 75)
ITBs (p. 76)
RFPs (p. 76)
Market Opportunity Analysis (MOA)
    (p. 77)
Cause (p. 78)
Possible causes (p. 78)

Probable causes (p. 79)
Solutions (p. 80)
Consequences (p. 80)
Assumptions (p. 81)
Hypotheses (p. 81)
Information state (p. 82)
Information gaps (p. 82)
Research objectives (p. 83)
Action standard (p. 83)
Marketing research proposal
    (p. 85)
Operational (p. 86)
Operational definition (p. 86)
Research method (p. 87)

## REVIEW QUESTIONS

1 What are the steps in the marketing research process?
2 What are the caveats to studying marketing research in terms of a "step-by-step" process such as the 11 steps given to you in this chapter?
3 Which step in the 11-step process we present in this chapter is the most important step? Why?
4 Explain what research objectives are.
5 Name the three types of research design.
6 What are the different types of information?
7 What is the difference between the sample plan and sample size?
8 What is the name of the software you will use in this course to help you analyze data?
9 What makes the final research report important?
10 Name the situations when marketing research is not needed.
11 Name the situations when marketing research is needed.
12 What is the impact of online research in terms of determining the need for marketing research?
13 Give an example of a research project that was conducted with the wrong problem definition.
14 What are the two sources of marketing problems?
15 Explain how managers should recognize they have a problem.
16 What is the role of symptoms in problem recognition?
17 Explain how problems may vary, and give some examples.
18 What is the role of the researcher in problem definition, and what are the impediments to problem definition?
19 What is the process for determining the problem and establishing research objectives?

20   Explain how the process for determining the problem and establishing research objectives differs when a manager is faced with an opportunity instead of a failure to reach an objective.

21   Explain the role of an Action Standard and give an example.

22   What are the components of the marketing research proposal?

## APPLICATION QUESTIONS

23   Sony is contemplating expanding its line of three-inch and six-inch portable televisions. It thinks there are three situations in which this line would be purchased: (1) as a gift, (2) as a set to be used by children in their own rooms, and (3) for use at sporting events. How might the research objective be stated if Sony wished to know what consumers' preferences are with respect to these three possible uses?

24   Take the construct of channel (that is, "brand") loyalty in the case of teenagers viewing MTV. Write at least three different definitions that indicate how a researcher might form a question in a survey to assess the degree of MTV loyalty. One example is, "Channel loyalty is determined by a stated preference to view a given channel for a certain type of entertainment."

25   You just started a new firm, manufacturing and marketing MP3 players. Since your design offers more storage and several other features at two-thirds the cost of the lowest-priced competitor, your sales have been very good and it has been difficult to keep up with production. Describe the systems you need to put into place in order to detect problems your firm may have now or in the future.

26   The local Lexus dealer thinks that the four-door sedan with a list price in excess of $50,000 should appeal to Cadillac Seville owners who are thinking about buying a new automobile. He is considering a direct-mail campaign with personalized packages to be sent to owners whose Cadillac Sevilles are over two years old. Each package would contain a professional video of all the Lexus sedan's features and end with an invitation to visit the Lexus dealership. This tactic has never been tried in this market. State the marketing problem and indicate what research objectives would help the Lexus dealer understand the possible reactions of Cadillac Seville owners to this campaign.

## INTERACTIVE LEARNING

In this chapter you learned about ITBs and RFPs. Take a look at some real *"Invitations to Bid"* or *"Requests for Proposals"* by going to a search engine (**google .com, yahoo.com**) and entering either of these terms with quotes as shown. Take a look at some of the documents posted on the Web. Can you identify any of the components of an ITB or RFP we discussed in the chapter? Visit the Web site at **www.prenhall.com/burnsbush**. For this chapter, work through the Self-Study Quizzes, and get instant feedback on whether you need additional studying. On the Web site, you can review the chapter outline and case information for Chapter 3.

## CASE 3.1 ||| Washington Suites

Bob Smith is in the corporate marketing office of Washington Suites, a national motel chain. Occupancy levels have been good but Bob is interested in increasing the occupancy rates. He is convinced that Washington Suites needs to put in place more 1-800-reservation operators. The last three times he's called for a reservation himself, he has been put on hold. Even with 10 years of experience in the lodging industry, Bob decides to call in a marketing researcher. He has never used anyone from a research company, and he's interested in getting some fresh ideas from someone with experience from working with a variety of industries. Bob is put in contact with Doss Struse of Momentum Marketing Research. They schedule their first meeting for next Monday morning.

1 Outline the questions Struse should ask Smith in the first meeting.
2 What role should Struse play in the problem definition process?
3 What pitfalls will Struse need to warn Smith of as they embark on the research process?

## CASE 3.2 ||| AJResearch

Five years ago, when Allison James started her marketing research firm, she had no idea she would be working with so many clients at one time. You are her new research assistant. She asks you to review her five new clients to determine the research objectives to each of their problems. The five new clients and their marketing research problems are as follows:

1 Wired, Inc., an electronics firm, has developed a new flat-screen television that will sell for one-third of the price of those currently on the market. Problem: Will there be enough demand to offset the large fixed costs of retooling to make the new television sets?

2 Wacky Znacks, a large snack foods firm, has made a name for itself with wild flavored snacks like licorice cookies and jalapeño sunflower seeds. Problem: They feel that customers expect even wilder flavors. Wacky Znacks wants to know what consumer reactions would be to even more unusual flavored snacks (e.g., watermelon-flavored corn chips and barbeque-flavored chewing gum).

3 Wild About Toys is a large toy firm that enjoys surprising consumers with innovative new toys. They have developed an edible clay for children. Problem: Will parents want to purchase a toy that their children can also eat?

4 Jimmy Roberts wants to start a small catalog business that caters to new parents. He wants to offer a variety of high-quality, higher-priced items. Problem: So many different baby products exist. Roberts needs to start with a limited product line. Which products should he start his business with?

5 The Better Butter company has spent many years researching and developing a butter product that the company believes is truly superior to other butters on the market. Problem: There are a plethora of butter products. How can Better Butter package its product to call attention to it while portraying the idea of a superior product?

Using the information above, determine the research objectives for each client.

# CHAPTER 4

# RESEARCH DESIGN

# *Momentum*
## *Market Intelligence*
### *Predictive Insight*

You can visit MMI at **www.miontel.com.**
By permission, Momentum Market Intelligence.

## RESEARCH DESIGN AT MOMENTUM MARKET INTELLIGENCE

Momentum Market Intelligence (MMI) is located in Portland, Oregon.[1] The firm supplies strategic research to customers in the Information Technology, Financial Services, Health Care/Life Sciences, Public Utilities, and Consumer Packaged Goods (CPG) industry sectors. Doss Struse is Senior Partner and CEO. Doss has several years of high-level marketing research experience with firms such as Oscar Mayer, Carnation/Nestle, and General Mills. He also has served as an executive with ACNielsen, Research International and Knowledge Networks. In the following paragraphs, Doss describes some different client problems and how knowledge of research design would enable him to make advance decisions regarding methods and procedures needed to solve the client's problem.

- To understand what research design is and why it is significant
- To learn how exploratory research design helps the researcher gain a feel for the problem by providing background information, suggesting hypotheses, and prioritizing research objectives
- To know the fundamental questions addressed by descriptive research and the different types of descriptive research
- To explain what is meant by causal research and to describe types of experimental research designs
- To know the different types of test marketing and how to select test-market cities

*Research design refers to a set of advance decisions that make up the master plan specifying the methods and procedures for collecting and analyzing the information needed to solve a problem. The benefit of knowledge of research design is that, by knowing which research design is needed to solve a client's problem, a good researcher can predetermine certain procedures that will likely be needed. This not only leads to a more efficient research planning process but it enables a good researcher to advise the client early on as to the advantages and disadvantages that will be experienced with the chosen design. Let me give you some examples to illustrate my point.*

Doss Struse, Senior Partner and CEO Momentum Market Intelligence

*Let us assume we have a client that is a consumer packaged goods manufacturer with a well-established brand name. The client has focused on manufacturing and distribution for years while the marketing program has been set on "auto pilot." All had worked fine though there was a hint of emerging problems when, in the preceding year, market share had fallen slightly. Now, let us assume our client is reviewing the current market share report and notices that over the previous 12 months their share has gradually eroded 15%. When market share falls clients are eager to learn why and to take corrective action. In these situations we know immediately the problem is that we don't know what the problem is: there are many possible causes for this slippage. In this situation we would follow a research design known as exploratory research which means exactly what the name implies. We would begin to explore by examining secondary data about the industry, the market, submarket's served, and competitors. We would likely conduct some focus groups, often used in exploratory research, of both consumers and distributors. In quick order the client's problem (or problems) would begin to emerge and, once identified, we could begin solving the problem. By knowing we needed to know more about the problem itself we would know we would be using an exploratory research design. By knowing we needed this research design, the researcher would be in a position to select from a variety of procedures used with this design, such as secondary information search or focus groups and make advanced decisions early in the life of the project. The client could also be apprised of the advantages and disadvantages of the procedures early on in the project.*

*As another example, let us assume we have a manufacturer of several baked goods products sold in grocery stores throughout the country. Marketing is divided up into five regional divisions in the United States. The five divisions have had total autonomy over their advertising though all of them have used TV advertising almost exclusively. Each division has tried several different TV ad campaign; some were thought to be successful and others not as successful, but no one had ever formally evaluated the ad expenditures. A new Marketing VP now wants to evaluate the advertising. She's interested in knowing not only the sales of the client's products during the different campaigns, she also wants to know what happened to sales of competitors' brands. In this case, the client needs us to* describe *sales by SKU in the client's product category for each TV market and for each time period associated with each ad campaign. When we need to describe something, such as consumers' level of satisfaction with brand X or the percentage of the target population that intends to buy a new product, we turn to* descriptive research *design. Again, by knowing we are going to be doing descriptive research, we are in a better position to determine, in advance, what methods and procedures we will be using to solve the client's problem.*

*To complete our discussion, let's look at one more situation. Imagine a client that is in a very competitive category with equal market share of the top three brands. Assume the client is convinced that they have changed every marketing mix variable possible except for package design. Since the three competitive brands are typically displayed side-by-side, they want us to determine what factors of package design (i.e., size, shape, color, texture, and so on, cause an increase in awareness, preference for, and intention to buy the brand). When clients want to know if they change x what happens to y, we know the appropriate research design is* causal research*. By knowing this we know we will be using* experimental design *research and, once again, this helps us plan many decisions in advance. You will learn more about research design by reading this chapter. After you've read the chapter, come back to this page and reread the examples I've given you. You will have a better appreciation of how important research design is to those of us in the marketing research profession.*

**Doss Struse, Momentum Market Intelligence**

**Where We Are:**
1 Establish the need for marketing research
2 Define the problem
3 Establish research objectives
4 Determine research design
5 Identify information types and sources
6 Determine methods of accessing data

Doss Struse's discussion of research design at MMI provides you with an excellent introduction to the concept of research design. You will notice that while they do many types of studies, these studies fall into one of three categories: exploratory, descriptive, or causal (experiments). Thus, they use all three types of research design that you will learn about in this chapter. In the following pages, we will introduce you to the concept of research design. An overview is provided of the various types of research design: exploratory, descriptive, and causal. The chapter concludes with a discussion of test marketing. When you finish this chapter, you should be able to determine what type of research design is appropriate for a given problem and research objective.

7 Design data collection forms
8 Determine sample plan and size
9 Collect data
10 Analyze data
11 Prepare and present the final research report

## RESEARCH DESIGN

Marketing research methods vary widely. Some projects are experiments of food tasting held in kitchenlike labs; others are focus groups, simulated test markets, or large, nationally representative sample surveys, among many others. Some research objectives require only library research, whereas others may require thousands of personal interviews; other studies require observation of consumers in supermarkets, while another may involve two-hour-long, in-depth, personal interviews in respondents' homes.

Each type of study has certain advantages and disadvantages, and one method may be more appropriate for a given research problem than another. How do marketing researchers decide which method is the most appropriate? After thoroughly considering the problem and research objectives, researchers select a **research design**, which is a set of advance decisions that makes up the master plan specifying the methods and procedures for collecting and analyzing the needed information.

■ There are some basic marketing research designs that can be successfully matched to given problems and research objectives. In this way, they serve the researcher much like the blueprint serves the builder.

■ A research design is a set of advance decisions that makes up the master plan specifying the methods and procedures for collecting and analyzing the needed information.

### The Significance of Research Design

Marketing researcher David Singleton of Zyman Marketing Group, Inc., believes that good research design is the first rule of good research.[2] Every research problem is unique. In fact, one could argue that, given each problem's unique customer set, area of geographical application, and other situational variables, there are so few similarities among research projects that each study should be completely designed as a new and independent project. In a sense this is true; almost every research problem is unique in some way or another, and care must be taken to select the most appropriate set of approaches for the unique problem and research objectives at hand. However, there are reasons to justify the significance placed on research design.

First, although every problem and research objective may seem totally unique, there are usually enough similarities among problems and objectives to allow us to make some decisions in advance about the best plan to use to resolve the problem. Second, there are some basic marketing research designs that can be successfully matched to given problems and research objectives. In this way, they serve the researcher much like the blueprint serves the builder.

Once the problem and the research objectives are known, the researcher selects a research design. The proper research design is necessary for the researcher to achieve the research objectives. However, sometimes the wrong research design is formulated and this leads to disaster.

■ Although every problem and research objective may seem totally unique, there are usually enough similarities among problems and objectives to allow us to make some decisions in advance about the best plan to use to resolve the problem.

## THREE TYPES OF RESEARCH DESIGNS

Research designs are classified into three traditional categories: exploratory, descriptive, and causal. The choice of the most appropriate design depends largely on the objectives of the research. It has been said that research has three objectives: to gain

■ The choice of the most appropriate design depends largely on the objectives of the research.

background information and to develop hypotheses, to measure the state of a variable of interest (for example, level of brand loyalty), or to test hypotheses that specify the relationships between two or more variables (for example, level of advertising and brand loyalty). Note also that the choice of research design is dependent on how much we already know about the problem and research objective. The less we know, the more likely it is that we should use exploratory research. Causal research, on the other hand, should only be used when we know a fair amount about the problem and we are looking for causal relationships among variables associated with the problem or the research objectives. We shall see how these basic research objectives are best handled by the various research designs. Table 4.1 shows the three types of research designs and the basic research objective that would prescribe a given design.[3]

■ The choice of research design is dependent on how much we already know about the problem and the research objectives. The less we know, the more likely it is that we should use exploratory research.

## Research Design: A Caution

We pause here, before discussing the three types of research design, to warn you about thinking of research design solely in a step-by-step fashion. Some may think that it is implied in this discussion that the order in which the designs are presented—that is, exploratory, descriptive, and causal—is the order in which these designs should be carried out. This is incorrect. First, in some cases, it may be perfectly legitimate to begin with any one of the three designs and to use only that one design. Second, research is an "iterative" process; by conducting one research project, we learn that we may need additional research, and so on. This may mean that we need to utilize multiple research designs. We could very well find, for example, that after conducting descriptive research, we need to go back and conduct exploratory research. Third, if multiple designs are used in any particular order (if there is an order), it makes sense to first conduct exploratory research, then descriptive research, and finally causal research. The only reason for this order pattern is that each subsequent design requires greater knowledge about the problem and research objectives on the part of the researcher. Therefore, exploratory research may give one the information needed to conduct a descriptive study, which, in turn, may provide the information necessary to design a causal experiment.

## Exploratory Research

■ Exploratory research is most commonly unstructured, informal research that is undertaken to gain background information about the general nature of the research problem.

**Exploratory research** is most commonly unstructured, informal research that is undertaken to gain background information about the general nature of the research problem. By unstructured, we mean that exploratory research does not have a formalized

**Table 4.1**
The Basic Research Objective and Research Design

| Research Objective | Appropriate Design |
| --- | --- |
| To gain background information, to define terms, to clarify problems and hypotheses, to establish research priorities | Exploratory |
| To describe and measure marketing phenomena | Descriptive |
| To determine causality, to make "if–then" statements | Causal |

set of objectives, sample plan, or questionnaire. It is usually conducted when the researcher does not know much about the problem and needs additional information or desires new or more recent information. Often exploratory research is conducted at the outset of research projects. It is considered informal because, unlike some research designed to test hypotheses or measure the reaction of one variable to a change in another variable, exploratory research can be accomplished by simply reading a magazine or even observing a situation. For example, an 18-year-old college student, sitting in his car in line at the McDonald's drive-through awaiting a cheeseburger, saw an old dilapidated truck, loaded with junk, with the sign "Mark's Hauling." This observation set in motion Brian Scudamore's ideas to launch a new type of junk service called "1-800-Got-Junk." Soon he was making so much money that he dropped out of college. The company expected revenues of $12.6 million in 2003.[4] Exploratory research is very flexible in that it allows the researcher to investigate whatever sources he or she desires and to the extent he or she feels is necessary in order to gain a good feel for the problem at hand.

> ■ Exploratory research is usually conducted when the researcher does not know much about the problem and needs additional information or desires new or more recent information.

## Uses of Exploratory Research

Exploratory research is used in a number of situations: to gain background information, to define terms, to clarify problems and hypotheses, and to establish research priorities.

> ■ Exploratory research is used in a number of situations: to gain background information, to define terms, to clarify problems and hypotheses, and to establish research priorities.

### Gain Background Information

When very little is known about the problem or when the problem has not been clearly formulated, exploratory research may be used to gain much-needed background information. Even for very experienced researchers it is rare that some exploratory research is not undertaken to gain current, relevant background information. There is far too much to be gained to ignore exploratory information.

> ■ When very little is known about the problem or when the problem has not been clearly formulated, exploratory research may be used to gain much-needed background information.

### Define Terms

Exploratory research helps to define terms and concepts. By conducting exploratory research to define a question such as "What is 'bank image'?" the researcher quickly learns that bank image is composed of several components—perceived convenience of location, loan availability, friendliness of employees, and so on. Not only would exploratory research identify the components of bank image, but it could also demonstrate how these components may be measured.

> ■ Exploratory research helps to define terms and concepts.

### Clarify Problems and Hypotheses

Exploratory research allows the researcher to define the problem more precisely and to generate hypotheses for the upcoming study. For example, exploratory research on measuring bank image reveals the issue of different groups of bank customers. Banks have three types of customers: retail customers, commercial customers, and other banks for which services are performed for fees. This information is useful in clarifying the problem of the measurement of bank image because it raises the issue of which customer group's version of bank image should be measured.

Exploratory research can also be beneficial in the formulation of **hypotheses**, which are statements taken for true for the purpose of argument or investigation. Hypotheses often describe the speculated relationships among two or more variables.

> ■ Exploratory research allows the researcher to define the problem more precisely and to generate hypotheses for the upcoming study.

Formally stating hypotheses prior to conducting a research study is very important to ensure that the proper variables are measured. Once a study has been completed, it may be too late to state which hypotheses are desirable to test.

### Establish Research Priorities

■ Exploratory research can help a firm prioritize research topics in order of importance.

Exploratory research can help a firm prioritize research topics in order of importance. A summary account of complaint letters by retail store may tell management where to devote their attention. One furniture store chain owner decided to conduct research on the feasibility of carrying office furniture after some exploratory interviews with salespeople revealed that their customers often asked for directions to stores carrying office furniture.

## Methods of Conducting Exploratory Research

A variety of methods are available to conduct exploratory research. These include secondary data analysis, experience surveys, case analysis, focus groups, and projective techniques.

### Secondary Data Analysis

■ A common method of conducting exploratory research is to examine existing information.

■ For some examples of secondary data often used in marketing research, see **www.secondarydata.com**, a Web site developed by Decision Analyst, Inc.

By **secondary data analysis**, we refer to the process of searching for and interpreting existing information relevant to the research objectives. Secondary data are data that have been collected for some other purpose. Your library and the Internet are full of secondary data, which include information found in books, journals, magazines, special reports, bulletins, newsletters, and so on. An analysis of secondary data is often the "core" of exploratory research.[5] This is because there are many benefits to examining secondary data, and the costs are typically minimal. Furthermore, the costs for search time of such data are being reduced every day as more and more computerized databases become available. Knowledge of and ability

Exploratory research in the form of discussions with employees led a furniture store owner to add business furniture.

to use these databases are already mandatory for marketing researchers. You will learn more about secondary data in Chapter 5.

## Experience Surveys

The term **experience surveys** refers to gathering information from those thought to be knowledgeable on the issues relevant to the research problem. Volvo, believing that autos have been designed by and for males, asked 100 women what they wanted in a car. They found some major differences and plan on introducing a "Volvo for women."[6] If the research problem deals with difficulties encountered when buying infant clothing, then surveys of mothers or fathers with infants may be in order. Experience surveys differ from surveys conducted as part of descriptive research in that there is usually no formal attempt to ensure that the survey results are representative of any defined group of subjects. Nevertheless, useful information can be gathered by this method of exploratory research.

The term *experience surveys* refers to gathering information from those thought to be knowledgeable on the issues relevant to the research problem.

## Case Analysis

By **case analysis**, we refer to a review of available information about former situations that have some similarities to the present research problem. Usually, there are few research problems that do not have some similarities to some situation in the past.[7] Even when the research problem deals with a radically new product, there are often some similar past experiences that may be observed. For example, when cellular telephones were invented but not yet on the market, many companies attempted to forecast the rate of adoption by looking at adoption rates of consumer electronic products such as televisions and VCRs. A wireless communications company, 21st Century Telesis, used data from a low-power, neighborhood phone system that was very successful in Japan to help it market cellular phones to young people in Japan.[8] Researchers must be cautious in using former case examples for current problems. For example, cases dealing with technology-based products just a few years ago may be irrelevant today. The Internet and the widespread use of computers have totally changed the public's use of and attitudes toward technical products and services.

Researchers should use former similar case situations cautiously when trying to make applications from them to the present research objectives.

## Focus Groups

A popular method of conducting exploratory research is through **focus groups**, which are small groups of people brought together and guided by a moderator through an unstructured, spontaneous discussion for the purpose of gaining information relevant to the research problem.[9] Although focus groups should encourage openness on the part of the participants, the moderator's task is to ensure the discussion is "focused" on some general area of interest. For example, the Piccadilly Cafeteria chain periodically conducts focus groups all around the country. The conversation may seem freewheeling, but the purpose of the focus group may be to learn what people think about some specific aspect of the cafeteria business, such as the perceived quality of cafeteria versus traditional restaurant food. This is a useful technique for gathering some information from a limited sample of respondents. The information can be used to generate ideas, to learn the respondents' "vocabulary" when relating to a certain type of product, or to gain some insights into basic needs and attitudes.[10] You can get in-depth insights into focus groups by reading Marketing Research Application 4.1.

Focus groups are small groups of people brought together and guided by a moderator through an unstructured, spontaneous discussion for the purpose of gaining information relevant to the research objectives.

## MARKETING RESEARCH APPLICATION 4.1

### Understanding Focus Groups

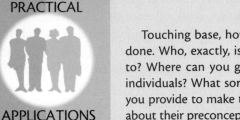

PRACTICAL

APPLICATIONS

Companies and organizations constantly update, reposition, redesign, or add totally new items to what they offer their constituents so that they might better serve the needs and interests of

those on whom they rely. Whether they are looking for consumers to buy their products, association members to re-up for another year, stockholders to add them to their portfolios, patrons to donate, or patients to bring their maladies, corporate types have long known that you either grow and flourish, or you die.

The cost of innovation is high, but the cost of errant innovation is even higher. So today, most institutions rely on some sort of face-to-face marketing research to help them touch base with their target from time to time to make sure whatever they are working on is as compelling as they would like it to be.

Touching base, however, is easier said than done. Who, exactly, is it that you want to talk to? Where can you gain open access to such individuals? What sort of environment should you provide to make them comfortable talking about their preconceptions, desires, and honest reactions to your ideas? Is it possible to have an environment with all the technology that's required today to present one's case (teleconferencing, AV-display, presentation space) that's warm enough to keep ordinary people at ease for some time?

How do you record the details of those conversations so that you can analyze what they say in pursuit of your own understanding?

Fieldwork, Inc., is a company devoted to helping corporate entities of all sorts reach and relate to their constituents in a comfortable but efficient and purposeful manner. Fieldwork has three divisions. One of those divisions is comprised of a collection of focus group facilities (16) found in major metros throughout the United States.

So what's a focus group facility and how does it work?

A focus group facility is an office comprised of interviewing suites—each of which is approximately 1,000 square feet (two large hotel rooms). Each suite has a conference room where focus groups take place and a "back room" where interested parties can observe and listen (via piped-in sound system). Video and audio recording equipment is hardwired into the suite so that a record of what transpires can be taken. That record goes to the client to be analyzed later. The personal identities of respondents (last names, addresses, phone numbers, etc.) are not made available unless permission has been granted ahead of time.

Finding the right people to talk to is frequently a complex task. Let me cite an example. A major restaurant chain is introducing a new line of barbequed entrees, but before they go to the enormous expense of contracting with their meat vendors, printing up new menus, developing advertising, and so forth, they hire a research firm to do some focus groups regarding how appealing this new line is and how well it "fits" under the current brand umbrella.

Who does the research firm want us to recruit? First of all we need people who eat out with some regularity. People who go to casual dining restaurants (the type the client has). People who aren't vegetarians. Perhaps, people who have been to one of the client's restaurants in the past six months, so they aren't totally clueless as to what the current brand umbrella really is. Furthermore, clients don't want people who are involved in any way with industries related to their own—they don't want to deal with "experts" or alert their competitors as to what they have in mind.

But there are more issues than that. They need people who are articulate in English. They need people who aren't such focus group habitués so that their point of view has become more like a professional respondent's than a "real" consumer's might be. But most importantly, they want people who represent a broad range of demographic, psychometric, or sociometric characteristics from that geographic area.

Keeping it all straight is the business of fieldwork. Getting the right people to show up at the right time in the right frame of mind to talk openly with strangers and doing so without violating their need for privacy is perhaps the biggest challenge a field facility has. Along the way, we have to maintain separation between client and respondent since clients frequently require that respondents be uninformed about who is sponsoring the research, not because they want to be clandestine about it, but because they don't want responses to be biased by knowing who is behind the mirror listening in.

In fact, much of what takes place in a focus group needs to be held in confidence. Every day we are dealing in intellectual property that is not only proprietary but, because these are new ideas just being considered, they are very susceptible to being picked up and perhaps utilized by competitive institutions. One of our primary tasks, then, is to have a high level of security throughout every aspect of our organization.

The recruiting process is an iterative one. The nature of the recruit may, itself, give insights and force changes into the nature of the recruiting process. We may find, for example that when we ask people in Chicago about barbequed food (where there's a strong Southern influence), they have a totally different take on what it means than do those in Seattle (where there's a strong Asian influence). Part of our job is to keep in daily contact with our clients to let them know how the recruiting process is going. It's not at all uncommon for a client to direct us to change one or more of our recruiting specifications midstream in response to what's happened so far.

After the recruiting is accomplished, we play host to various constituencies ourselves. Clients may represent a manufacturer, his ad agency and public relations associates, a design firm and a research house each represented by one or two people often flying in from several different cities. Then we have respondents who arrive hungry and need to be fed before they go in to chat for a few hours. It's a major logistical effort but the truth is, it's our favorite part of the process—it's where we get to meet clients, hear about their efforts—it's that point in time when we get to see our hard work begin to pay off.

A focus group facility is a social place. It's full of life, and interesting ideas float around. Respondents may arrive with a little trepidation the first time they come to a focus group but they almost always leave with a smile and a request that they be considered in the near future for another opportunity to be a focus group participant.

Molly Turner-Lammers, Fieldwork Seattle, Inc.; adapted with permission, Fieldwork Seattle, Inc.

Focus groups have been popular for a number of years. They represent 85% to 90% of the total money spent on qualitative research.[11] **Qualitative research** involves collecting, analyzing, and interpreting data by observing what people do and say.[12] Observations and statements are in a qualitative or nonstandardized form. Qualitative data can be quantified but only after a translation process has taken place. While focus groups make up a large percentage of qualitative studies, other methods include the following: **depth interviews**, defined as probing questions posed one-on-one to a subject by a trained interviewer so as to gain ideas as to what the respondent is thinking or why they behave in a certain way; **protocol analysis**, defined as placing a respondent in a decision-making setting and asking them to verbalize everything they consider when making a purchase decision; **projective techniques**, which are discussed in the following section;[13] and **ethnographic research**, borrowed from anthropology and defined as a detailed, descriptive study of a group and its behavior, characteristics, culture, etc.[14] Ethnography employs several different types of research, including immersion, participant observation, and informal and ongoing in-depth interviewing. Ethnographers pay close attention to words, metaphors, symbols, and stories people use to explain their lives and communicate with one another.[15]

Qualitative research involves collecting, analyzing, and interpreting data by observing what people do and say.

Qualitative research includes not only focus groups but depth interviews, projective techniques, protocol analysis, and ethnographic research.

■ Focus groups may be either traditional or nontraditional.

■ Focus-group facilities have a one-way mirror that allows clients in an adjoining room to watch the focus group without influencing what the focus-group members say or do.

■ Focus-group participants are interviewed by moderators, often referred to as Qualitative Research Consultants (QRs or QRCs).

■ Go to Interactive Learning at the end of this chapter and learn more about the Qualitative Research Consultants Association.

■ Focus groups generate fresh ideas, allow clients to observe the participants, are applicable to a wide variety of issues, and allow researchers to obtain information from "hard-to-reach" subpopulations.

■ Focus groups are not representative and it is sometimes difficult to interpret the results of focus groups. The moderator's report is subjective and the cost per focus-group participant is high.

■ Focus groups should be considered when the research question is one requiring something to be described.

**How Focus Groups Work.** Focus groups can be of several types. **Traditional focus groups** select about 6 to 12 people and meet in a dedicated room, with a one-way mirror for client viewing, for about two hours. In recent years, **nontraditional focus groups** have emerged, which can differ from traditional focus groups in many ways: They may be online, with clients observing on computer monitors in distant locations, or they may have up to 50 respondents, or allow client interaction with participants, or last four or five hours, or take part outside dedicated facilities such as in a park.[16] A marketing research firm offering traditional focus groups typically will have a **focus-group facility**, which is a set of rooms especially designed for focus groups. The focus group is conducted in a room that seats about 10 people (optimum size is thought to be somewhere between 6 and 12 participants) and a moderator. A wall in the room has what seems to be a large mirror but is a one-way mirror. The one-way mirror allows clients in the adjoining room to watch the focus group without influencing what the focus-group members say or do. Focus-group members may be recruited randomly but are more often recruited from the focus-group facility's database of potential respondents. Focus-group companies exert great efforts to recruit potential participants. They often use clubs or church group lists from which to recruit. While payment varies, it is not uncommon for a participant to be paid $40 to $60 for participating in a one-and-one-half- to two-hour-long focus group.[17] Focus-group participants are interviewed by **moderators**, often referred to as **Qualitative Research Consultants (QRs or QRCs)**.[18] QRCs have the responsibility of creating an atmosphere that is conducive to openness, yet they must make certain that participants do not stray too far from the central focus of the study. QRCs must also prepare a **focus-group report**, which summarizes the information provided by the focus-group participants relative to the research questions. There is a professional organization of QRCs at **www.qrca.org.**

**Advantages of Focus Groups.** The four major advantages of focus groups are: (1) they generate fresh ideas; (2) they allow clients to observe their participants; (3) they may be directed at understanding a wide variety of issues such as reactions to a new food product, brand logo, or television ad; and (4) they allow fairly easy access to special respondent groups such as lawyers or doctors (it may otherwise be very difficult to find a representative sample of these groups).

**Disadvantages of Focus Groups.** There are three major disadvantages to focus groups: (1) focus groups do not constitute representative samples; therefore, caution must be exercised in generalizing findings from them; (2) it is sometimes difficult to interpret the results of focus groups; the moderator's report of the results is based on a subjective evaluation of what was said during the focus group; and (3) the cost per participant is high though the total spent on focus-group research is generally a fraction of what may be spent on quantitative research.

**When Should Focus Groups Be Used?** When the research objective is to describe, rather than predict, focus groups may be an alternative. Consider the following situations: A company wants to know, "How do we 'speak' to our market; what language and terms do the customers use?" "What are some new ideas for an ad campaign?" "Will a new service they are developing have appeal to customers and how can we improve it?" "How can we better package our product?"[19] In all these cases,

A focus group facility at Baltimore Research. Here you can see the viewing room where clients can observe participants in the focus group room.

focus groups can describe the terms customers use, their ideas for ads, why a service appeals to them, and so on.

**When Should Focus Groups Not Be Used?** Because focus groups are based on a small number of persons who are not representative of some larger population, care must be exercised in using focus groups. If the research objective is to predict, focus groups should not be used. For example, if we show 12 people in a focus group a new-product prototype and find that 6 say they are going to buy it, can we predict that 50% of the population will buy our product? Hardly. Likewise, if our research is going to dictate a major, expensive decision for our company, we probably should not use focus groups. If the decision is that important, research that is representative of some population with some known margin of error (quantitative research) should be used.

■ Focus groups should not be used when the research question requires a prediction or when a major decision, affecting the livelihood of the company, rests upon the results of a focus group.

### Projective Techniques

Projective techniques, borrowed from the field of clinical psychology, seek to explore hidden consumer motives for buying goods and services by asking participants to project themselves into a situation and then to respond to specific questions regarding the situation. One example of such a technique is the sentence completion test. A respondent is given an incomplete sentence such as "John Smith would never dye his hair because …" By completing the sentence, ostensibly to represent the feelings of the fictitious Mr. Smith, the respondent projects himself or herself into the situation. Another example is the "cartoon test." A respondent is given a cartoon with an

■ Projective techniques seek to explore hidden consumer motives for buying goods and services by asking participants to project themselves into a situation and then to respond to specific questions regarding the situation.

empty balloon (used to capture statements made by cartoon characters) above a cartoon character and is asked to state what the cartoon character is saying by filling in the balloon. Marketers know that, by using the cartoon test, respondents are more likely to make self-revealing statements such as "I don't care if I am dying my hair, I'm not going to look old!" Or, "I don't care if I am getting old, I'm not going to stoop to dying my hair!" More likely, if asked directly, respondents will make statements such as "Some people do [dye their hair] and some people don't," "I don't care what other people do." This illustrates the value of projective techniques; by talking about "others," respondents may divulge feelings about themselves that they may not divulge in a direct question. As one marketing researcher put it: "With projective techniques, they [consumers] lay down their defenses…. The window to their psyche is opening up."[20] Projective techniques are the least used of the different types of exploratory research but nevertheless can play an important role given the right problem and research objective.

A concluding word about exploratory research is that some form of it should almost always be used at least to some extent. Why? Exploratory research, particularly secondary data analysis, is fast. You can conduct quite a bit of exploratory research online within a matter of minutes using online databases or using a search engine to surf the net. Second, compared to collecting primary data, exploratory research is cheap. Finally, sometimes exploratory research either provides information to meet the research objective or assists in gathering current information necessary to conduct either a descriptive or causal research design. Therefore, few researchers embark on a research project without doing some exploratory research.

## Descriptive Research

**Descriptive research** is undertaken to describe answers to questions of who, what, where, when, and how. When we wish to know *who* our customers are, *what* brands they buy and in what quantities, *where* they buy the brands, *when* they shop, and *how* they found out about our products, we turn to descriptive research. Descriptive research is also desirable when we wish to project a study's findings to a larger population. If a descriptive study's sample is representative, the findings may be used to predict some variable of interest such as sales.

## Classification of Descriptive Research Studies

There are two basic descriptive research studies available to the marketing researcher: cross sectional and longitudinal. **Cross-sectional studies** measure units from a sample of the population at only one point in time.

A study measuring your attitude toward adding a required internship course in your degree program, for example, would be a cross-sectional study. Your attitude toward the topic is measured at *one point in time*. Cross-sectional studies are very prevalent in marketing research, outnumbering longitudinal studies and causal studies. Because cross-sectional studies are one-time measurements, they are often described as "snapshots" of the population.

As an example, many magazines survey a sample of their subscribers and ask them questions such as their age, occupation, income, educational level, and so on. These sample data, taken at one point in time, are used to describe the readership

### Margin notes

■ Exploratory research should almost always be used, because it is fast, inexpensive, and may help in designing the proper descriptive or causal research study.

■ Descriptive research is undertaken to describe answers to questions of who, what, where, when, and how.

■ There are two types of descriptive studies: cross-sectional studies and longitudinal studies.

■ Cross-sectional studies measure units from a sample of the population at only one point in time.

■ Because cross-sectional studies are one-time measurements, they are often described as "snapshots" of the population.

of the magazine in terms of demographics. Cross-sectional studies normally employ fairly large sample sizes, so many cross-sectional studies are referred to as sample surveys.

**Sample surveys** are cross-sectional studies whose samples are drawn in such a way as to be representative of a specific population. ABC News often conducts surveys on some topic of interest to report on the evening news. The surveys' samples are drawn such that ABC may report that the results are representative of the population of the United States and that the results have, for example, a "margin of error of + or − 3%." So sample surveys may be designed in such a way that their results are representative and accurate, within some margin of error, of the true values in the population. (You will learn how to do this by studying this book.) Sample surveys require that their samples be drawn according to a prescribed plan and to a predetermined number. Later on, you will learn about these sampling plans and sample size techniques (Chapter 10).

As an example of a cross-sectional study, many companies test their proposed advertising by using "storyboards." A storyboard consists of several drawings depicting the major scenes in a proposed ad, as well as the proposed advertising copy. Companies can quickly and inexpensively test different ads' appeal, copy, and creative elements through the use of storyboards by getting consumers' reactions to them. Consumers are shown the storyboard for a proposed ad and are asked several questions, usually designed to measure their interest and understanding of the advertising message. Typically, a question is asked that measures the consumer's intentions to purchase the product after viewing the storyboard. Dirt Devil tested a proposed ad by using the AdInsights$^{SM}$ service offered by online research firm InsightExpress®. InsightExpress® allows firms to pretest promotional messages before the client firms have to spend large sums on media purchases, and they can perfect their promotional messages before they expose their messages to the competition. AdInsights$^{SM}$ may be used for all forms of promotional messages, including radio, television, and print ads. These cross-sectional studies provide client firms with useful information. In at least one situation, evaluation scores for a proposed ad were increased 219% after the ad was revised as a result of using AdInsights$^{SM}$ cross-sectional studies.

> ▨ Sample surveys are cross-sectional studies whose samples are drawn in such a way as to be representative of a specific population.

By showing a sample of online consumers proposed ads and getting their evaluations, client firms may use InsightExpress®'s AdInsights$^{SM}$ to modify promotional materials before placing them in the media. AdInsights$^{SM}$ studies are examples of cross-sectional research. Visit InsightExpress® at **www.insightexpress.com.**

By permission, InsightExpress®.

■ Longitudinal studies repeatedly measure the same sample units of a population over a period of time. Because longitudinal studies involve multiple measurements, they are often described as "movies" of the population.

■ Panels represent sample units who have agreed to answer questions at periodic intervals.

■ Several commercial marketing research firms develop and maintain consumer panels for use in longitudinal studies.

■ Visit Lightspeed Research at us.lightspeedpanel.com and Greenfield Online at www.greenfield.com.

■ Continuous panels ask panel members the same questions on each panel measurement. Discontinuous panels vary questions from one panel measurement to the next.

■ Discontinuous panels are sometimes referred to as omnibus ("including or covering many things or classes") panels.

■ The advantage of discontinuous (omnibus) panels is that they represent a group of persons who have made themselves available for research. The discontinuous panel provides clients with a source of information that may be quickly accessed for a wide variety of purposes.

**Longitudinal studies** repeatedly measure the same sample units of a population over a period of time. Because longitudinal studies involve multiple measurements, they are often described as "movies" of the population. Longitudinal studies are employed by almost 50% of businesses using marketing research.[21] To ensure the success of the longitudinal study, researchers must have access to the same members of the sample, called a panel, so as to take repeated measurements. **Panels** represent sample units who have agreed to answer questions at periodic intervals. Maintaining a representative panel of respondents is a major undertaking.

Several commercial marketing research firms develop and maintain consumer panels for use in longitudinal studies. Typically, these firms attempt to select a sample that is representative of some population. Firms such as NFOWorldwide and ACNielsen have maintained panels consisting of hundreds of thousands of households for many years. In many cases these companies will recruit panel members such that the demographic characteristics of the panel are proportionate to the demographic characteristics found in the total population according to Census Bureau statistics. Sometimes these panels will be balanced demographically not only to the United States in total but also within each of the various geographical regions. In this way, a client who wishes to get information from a panel of households in the Northwest can be assured that the panel is demographically matched to the total population in the states making up the northwestern region. Many companies maintain panels to target market segments such as "dog owners" or "kids" (ages 6 to 14; see **www.Kidzeyes.com**). Note that panels are not limited to consumer households. Panels may consist of building contractors, supermarkets, physicians, lawyers, universities, or some other entity.

Online research created the opportunity for several new companies to emerge offering panels recruited to respond to online queries. One such company is Lightspeed Research, which offers clients panels of consumer households. Greenfield Online is another firm that offers clients access to its online panel of consumers.

There are two types of panels: continuous panels and discontinuous panels. **Continuous panels** ask panel members the same questions on each panel measurement. **Discontinuous panels** vary questions from one panel measurement to the next.[22] Continuous panel examples include many of the syndicated data panels that ask panel members to record their purchases, using diaries or scanners. The essential point is that panel members are asked to record the *same* information (for example, grocery store purchases) over and over. Discontinuous panels are sometimes referred to as **omnibus panels.** (*Omnibus* means "including or covering many things or classes.") They may be used for a variety of purposes, and the information collected by a discontinuous panel varies from one panel measurement to the next. How longitudinal data are applied depends on the type of panel used to collect the data. Essentially, the discontinuous panel's primary usefulness is that it represents a large group—people, stores, or some other entity—and its members are agreeable to providing marketing research information. Discontinuous panels, like continuous panels, are also demographically matched to some larger entity, implying representativeness as well. Therefore, a marketer wanting to know how a large number of consumers, matched demographically to the total U.S. population, feel about two different product concepts may elect to utilize the services of an omnibus panel. The advantage of discontinuous (omnibus) panels is that they represent a group of persons who have made themselves available for research. In this way, then, discontinuous panels represent existing sources of information that may be quickly accessed for a wide variety of purposes.

The continuous panel is used quite differently. Usually, firms are interested in using data from continuous panels because they can gain insights into *changes in* consumers' purchases, attitudes, and so on. For example, data from continuous panels can show how members of the panel switched brands from one time period to the next. Studies examining how many consumers switched brands are known as **brand-switching studies**.

To illustrate the importance of using continuous panel data to gain insights into how consumers change brands, we compare longitudinal data taken from a continuous panel with data collected from two cross-sectional sample surveys. Figure 4.1 shows data collected from two separate cross-sectional studies, each having a household sample size of 500. (Cross-sectional data are referenced as "Survey 1" or "Survey 2.") Look at how many families used each brand in Survey 1 (red) and then see how many families used each brand in Survey 2 (blue). What would we conclude by examination of these two cross-sectional studies? (1) Pooch Plus has lost market share because only 75 families indicated that they purchased Pooch Plus in the second survey as opposed to 100 Pooch Plus families in the first survey; and (2) apparently, Pooch Plus has lost out to Milk Bone dog treat brand, which increased from 200 to 225 families. Note that Beggar's Bits remained the same. This analysis would lead most brand managers to focus on the strategies that had been used by Milk Bone (since it's "obvious" that Milk Bone took share from Pooch Plus) to increase market share for Pooch Plus.

■ Firms are interested in using data from continuous panels because they can gain insights into *changes in* consumers' purchases, attitudes, and so on.

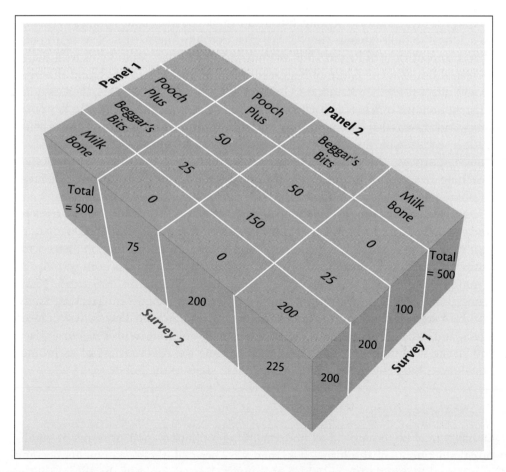

**Figure 4.1** The Advantage of Longitudinal Studies Versus Cross-Sectional Studies

Now, having reached a conclusion from the two cross-sectional surveys, let's look at the data assuming we had used longitudinal research. When we examine the longitudinal data, we reach quite a different conclusion from the one we reached by looking at the two cross-sectional studies. Looking at Panel 1 total (red) and Panel 2 total (blue), we see the same data that we saw in the two cross-sectional surveys. Panel 1 totals show us that Pooch Plus had 100 families, Beggar's Bits had 200 families, and Milk Bone had 200 families. (This is exactly the same data found in our first cross-sectional survey.) Now, we later return for a second measurement of the *same families* in Panel 2 and we find the totals are Pooch Plus, 75 families; Beggar's Bits, 200 families; and Milk Bone, 225 families. (Again, we have the same totals as shown by Survey 2 data.) But the real value of the continuous panel longitudinal data is found in the changes that occur between Panel 1 and Panel 2 measurements. With longitudinal data, we can examine how each family changed from Panel 1 to Panel 2 and, as we shall see, the ability to measure change is very important in understanding research data. To see how the families changed, look again at Panel 1 totals (red) and then look at the data *inside the figure* (green) at the Panel 2 results. In Panel 1 (red) we had 100 families using Pooch Plus. How did these families change by the time we asked for Panel 2 information? Looking at the data on the inside of the figure (green) and reading across for Pooch Plus, we see that 50 families stayed with Pooch Plus, 50 switched to Beggar's Bits, and none of the original Panel 1 Pooch Plus families switched to Milk Bone. Now look at the 200 families in Panel 1 (red) who used Beggar's Bits. In Panel 2 data (green) we see that 25 of those 200 families switched to Pooch Plus, 150 stayed with Beggar's Bits, and 25 switched to Milk Bone. Finally, all of the 200 Milk Bone families in Panel 1 stayed loyal to Milk Bone in Panel 2. So, what does this mean? It is clear that Pooch Plus is competing with Beggar's Bits and not with Milk Bone. Milk Bone's total shares increased but at the expense of Beggar's Bits, not Pooch Plus. The brand manager should direct his or her attention to Beggar's Bits, not Milk Bone. This, then, is quite different from the conclusion reached by examining cross-sectional data. The key point being made here is that because longitudinal data allow us to measure the change being made by each sample unit between time periods, we gain much richer information for analysis purposes. It is important to note, at this point, that this type of brand-switching data may be obtained only by using the continuous panel. Because different questions are asked, discontinuous panels do not allow for this type of analysis.

Another use of longitudinal data is that of market tracking. **Market-tracking studies** are those that measure some variable(s) of interest, that is, market share or unit sales over time. By having representative data on brand market shares, for example, a marketing manager can "track" how his or her brand is doing relative to a competitive brand's performance. Every three years the American Heart Association (AHA) conducts what it calls the National Acute Event Tracking Study. The AHA collects data using a panel to track changes in unaided awareness of heart attack and stroke warning signs. By tracking consumers' awareness of heart attack and stroke warning signs, the AHA can determine the effectiveness of its promotional materials designed to communicate these signs to the public.[23]

■ Market-tracking studies are those that measure some variable(s) of interest, such as market share or unit sales, over time.

## Causal Research

**Causality** may be thought of as understanding a phenomenon in terms of conditional statements of the form "If *x*, then *y*." These "if–then" statements become our way of manipulating variables of interest. For example, if the thermostat is lowered, then the air will get cooler. If I drive my automobile at lower speeds, then my gasoline mileage will increase. If I spend more on advertising, then sales will rise. As humans, we are constantly trying to understand the world in which we live. Likewise, marketing managers are always trying to determine what will cause a change in consumer satisfaction, a gain in market share, or an increase in sales. In one experiment, marketing researchers investigated how color versus noncolor and different quality levels of graphics in Yellow Page ads caused changes in consumers' attitudes toward the ad itself, the company doing the advertising, and perceptions of quality. The results showed that color and high-photographic graphics cause more favorable attitudes. But the findings differ depending on the class of product being advertised.[24] This illustrates how complex cause-and-effect relationships are in the real world. Consumers are bombarded on a daily and sometimes even hourly basis by a vast multitude of factors, all of which could cause them to act in one way or another. Thus, understanding what causes consumers to behave as they do is extremely difficult. Nevertheless, there is a high "reward" in the marketplace for even partially understanding causal relationships. Causal relationships are determined by the use of experiments, which are special types of studies. Many companies are now taking advantage of conducting experiments online.[23]

> ■ Causality may be thought of as understanding a phenomenon in terms of conditional statements of the form "if $x$, then $y$." For example, if Yellow Page ads are in color, then consumer attitudes toward the product will be higher than if the ad is in black and white.

> ■ Experiments can be conducted using online research.

## EXPERIMENTS

An **experiment** is defined as manipulating an independent variable to see how it affects a dependent variable, while also controlling the effects of additional extraneous variables. **Independent variables** are those variables which the researcher has control over *and* wishes to manipulate. Some independent variables include level of advertising expenditure, type of advertising appeal (humor, prestige), display location, method of compensating salespersons, price, and type of product. **Dependent variables**, on the other hand, are those variables that we have little or no direct control over, yet we have a strong interest in. We cannot change these variables in the same way that we can change independent variables. A marketing manager, for example, can easily change the level of advertising expenditure or the location of the display of a product in a supermarket, but he or she cannot easily change sales, market share, or level of customer satisfaction. These variables are typically dependent variables. Certainly, marketers are interested in changing these variables. But because they cannot change them directly, they attempt to change them through the manipulation of independent variables. To the extent that marketers can establish causal relationships between independent and dependent variables, they enjoy some success in influencing the dependent variables.

> ■ An experiment is defined as manipulating an independent variable to see how it affects a dependent variable, while also controlling the effects of additional extraneous variables.

> ■ Independent variables are those variables which the researcher has control over *and* wishes to manipulate. Independent variables could include level of advertising expenditure, type of advertising appeal, display location, method of compensating salespersons, price, and type of product.

> ■ Dependent variables are those variables that we have little or no direct control over, yet we have a strong interest in manipulating, such as net profits, market share, or employee or customer satisfaction.

**Extraneous variables** are those that may have some effect on a dependent variable but yet are not independent variables. To illustrate, let's say you and your friend wanted to know if brand of gasoline (independent variable) affected gas mileage in automobiles (dependent variable). Your "experiment" consists of each of you filling up your two cars, one with Brand A, the other with Brand B. At the end of the week, you learn that Brand A achieved 18.6 miles per gallon and Brand B achieved 26.8 miles per gallon. Do you have a causal relationship: Brand B gets better gas mileage than Brand A? Or could the difference in the dependent variable (gas mileage) be due to factors other than gasoline brand (independent variable)? Let's take a look at

> ■ Extraneous variables are those that may have some effect on a dependent variable but yet are not independent variables.

what these extraneous variables may be: (1) One car is an SUV and the other is a small compact. (2) One car was driven mainly on the highway and the other was driven in the city in heavy traffic. (3) One car has never had a tune-up and the other was just tuned up. We think you get the picture.

Let's look at another example. Imagine that a supermarket chain conducts an experiment to determine the effect of type of display (independent variable) on sales of apples (dependent variable). Management records sales of the apples in its regular produce bin's position and then changes (manipulates the independent variable) the position of the apples to end-aisle displays and measures sales once again. Assume sales increased. Does this mean that if we change display position of apples from the produce bins to end-aisle displays, then sales will increase? Could there be other extraneous variables that could have affected the sales of the apples? What would happen to apple sales if the weather changed from rainy to fair? If the apple industry began running ads on TV? If the season changed from summer vacation to fall? Yes, weather, industry advertising, and apples packed in school lunch boxes are viewed in this example as extraneous variables, having an effect on the dependent variable, yet themselves not defined as independent variables. As this example illustrates, it would be difficult to isolate the effects of independent variables on dependent variables without controlling for the effects of the extraneous variables. Unfortunately, it is not easy to establish causal relationships, but it can be done. In the following section, we will see how different experimental designs allow us to conduct experiments.

## Experimental Design

An **experimental design** is a procedure for devising an experimental setting such that a change in a dependent variable may be attributed solely to the change in an independent variable. In other words, experimental designs are procedures that allow experimenters to control for the effects on a dependent variable by an extraneous variable. In this way, the experimenter is assured that any change in the dependent variable was due only to the change in the independent variable.

Let us look at how experimental designs work. First, we list the symbols of experimental design:

$O$ = The measurement of a dependent variable
$X$ = The manipulation, or change, of an independent variable
$R$ = Random assignment of subjects (consumers, stores, and so on)
      to experimental and control groups
$E$ = Experimental effect, that is, the change in the dependent variable
      due to the independent variable

When a measurement of the dependent variable is taken *prior to* changing the independent variable, the measurement is sometimes called a **pretest**. When a measurement of the dependent variable is taken *after* changing the independent variable, the measurement is sometimes called a **posttest**.

There are many research designs available to experimenters. In fact, entire college courses are devoted to this one topic. But our purpose here is to illustrate the logic of experimental design, and we can do this by reviewing three designs, of which only the

■ An experimental design is a procedure for devising an experimental setting such that a change in a dependent variable may be attributed solely to the change in an independent variable.

■ You should carefully study the symbols of experimental design. Without a good grasp of the meaning of these symbols, you will have difficulty with the following sections.

Time is assumed to be represented horizontally on a continuum. Subscripts, such as $O_1$ or $O_2$, refer to different measurements made of the dependent variable. ▶

■ Measurements of the dependent variable taken prior to changing the dependent variable are called pretests and those taken after are called posttests.

last is a true experimental design. A **"true" experimental design** is one that truly isolates the effects of the independent variable on the dependent variable while controlling for effects of any extraneous variables. However, the first two designs we introduce you to are *not* true experimental designs. We introduce you to the first two designs to help you understand the real benefits of using a true experimental design. The three designs we discuss are after-only; one-group, before-after; and before-after with control group.

■ A "true" experimental design is one that truly isolates the effects of the independent variable on the dependent variable while controlling for effects of any extraneous variables.

## After-Only Design

The **after-only design** is achieved by changing the independent variable and, after some period of time, measuring the dependent variable. It is diagrammed as follows:

$$X \quad O_1$$

where $X$ represents the change in the independent variable (putting all of the apples in end-aisle displays) and the distance between $X$ and $O$ represents the passage of some time period. $O_1$ represents the measurement, a posttest, of the dependent variable (recording the sales of the apples). Now, what have you learned about causality? Not very much! Have sales gone up or down? We do not know because we neglected to measure sales prior to changing the display location. Regardless of what our sales are, there *may* have been other extraneous variables that may have had an effect on apple sales. Managers are constantly changing things "just to see what happens" without taking any necessary precautions to properly evaluate the effects of the change. Hence, the after-only design does not really measure up to our requirement for a true experimental design.

■ The after-only design is achieved by changing the independent variable and, after some period of time, measuring the dependent variable. It is not a "true" experimental design.

Designs that do not properly control for the effects of extraneous variables on our dependent variable are known as **quasi-experimental designs.** Note that in the after-only design diagram, there is no measure of $E$, the "experimental effect" on our dependent variable due solely to our independent variable. This is true in all quasi-experimental designs. Our next design, the one-group, before-after design, is also a quasi-experimental design, although it is an improvement over the after-only design.

■ Designs that do not properly control for the effects of extraneous variables on our dependent variable are known as quasi-experimental designs. There is no E, or "experimental effect," in quasi-experimental designs.

## One-Group, Before-After Design

The **one-group, before-after design** is achieved by first measuring the dependent variable, then changing the independent variable, and, finally, taking a second measurement of the dependent variable. We diagram this design as follows:

$$O_1 \quad X \quad O_2$$

The obvious difference between this design and the after-only design is that we have a measurement of the dependent variable prior to and following the change in the independent variable. Also, as the name implies, we have only one group (a group of consumers in one store) on which we are conducting our study.

As an illustration of this design, let us go back to our previous example. In this design, our supermarket manager measured the dependent variable, apple sales, prior to changing the display location. Now, what do we know about causality? We know a little more than we learned from the after-only design. We know the change in our dependent variable from time period 1 to time period 2. We at least know if sales went up, down, or stayed the same. But what if sales did go up? Can we

■ The one-group, before-after design is achieved by first measuring the dependent variable, then changing the independent variable, and, finally, taking a second measurement of the dependent variable.

■ The one-group, before-after design is also not a true experimental design; it is a quasi-experimental design.

■ Control of extraneous variables is typically achieved by the use of a second group of subjects, known as a control group.

■ By control group, we mean a group whose subjects have not been exposed to the change in the independent variable.

■ The experimental group, on the other hand, is the group that has been exposed to a change in the independent variable.

attribute the change in our dependent variable solely to the change in our independent variable? The answer is no—numerous extraneous variables, such as weather, advertising, or time of year, could have caused an increase in apple sales. With the one-group, before-after design, we still cannot measure $E$, the "experimental effect," because this design does not control for the effects of extraneous variables on the dependent variable. Hence, the one-group, before-after design is also not a true experimental design; it is a quasi-experimental design.

Control of extraneous variables is typically achieved by the use of a second group of subjects, known as a control group. By **control group**, we mean a group whose subjects have not been exposed to the change in the independent variable. The **experimental group**, on the other hand, is the group that has been exposed to a change in the independent variable. By having these two groups as part of our experimental design, we can overcome many of the problems associated with the quasi-experimental designs presented thus far. We shall use the following true experimental design to illustrate the importance of the control group.

## Before-After with Control Group

■ The before-after with control group design may be achieved by randomly dividing subjects of the experiment (in this case, supermarkets) into two groups: the control group and the experimental group. It is a "true" experimental design.

The **before-after with control group** design may be achieved by randomly dividing subjects of the experiment (in this case, supermarkets) into two groups: the control group and the experimental group. A pretest measurement of the dependent variable is then taken on both groups. Next, the independent variable is changed only in the experimental group. Finally, after some time period, posttest measurements are taken of the dependent variable in both groups. This design may be diagrammed as follows:

$$
\begin{aligned}
&\text{Experimental group } (R) \quad O_1 \ X \ O_2 \\
&\text{Control group } (R) \qquad\qquad\ O_3 \quad\ O_4 \\
&\text{where } E = (O_2 - O_1) - (O_4 - O_3).
\end{aligned}
$$

■ Note that this design assumes that the two groups, control and experimental, are equivalent in all aspects. An experimenter should take whatever steps are necessary to meet this condition of equivalency.

In this true experimental design, we have two groups. Let us assume we have 20 supermarkets in our supermarket chain. Theoretically, if we randomly divide these stores into two groups—10 in the experimental group and 10 in the control group—then the groups should be equivalent. That is, both groups should be as similar as possible, each group having an equal number of large stores and small stores, an equal number of new stores and old stores, an equal number of stores in upper-income neighborhoods and lower-income neighborhoods, and so on. Note that this design assumes that the two groups are equivalent in all aspects. An experimenter should take whatever steps are necessary to meet this condition if he or she uses this design. There are other methods for gaining equivalency besides randomization. Matching on criteria thought to be important, for example, would aid in establishing equivalent groups. When randomization or matching on relevant criteria does not achieve equivalent groups, more-complex experimental designs should be used.[26]

Looking back at our design, the $R$ indicates that we have randomly divided our supermarkets into two equal groups—one a control group, the other an experimental group. We also see that pretest measurements of our dependent variable, apple sales, were recorded at the same time for both groups of stores as noted by $O_1$

and $O_3$. Next, we see by the $X$ symbol that only in the experimental group of stores were the apples moved from the regular produce bins to end-aisle displays. Finally, posttest measurements of the dependent variable were taken at the same time in both groups of stores, as noted by $O_2$ and $O_4$.

Now, what information can we gather from this experiment? First, we know that $(O_2 - O_1)$ tells us how much change occurred in our dependent variable during the time of the experiment. But was this difference due solely to our independent variable, $X$? No, $(O_2 - O_1)$ tells us how many dollars in apple sales may be attributed to (1) the change in display location and (2) other extraneous variables, such as the weather, apple industry advertising, and so on. This does not help us very much, but what does $(O_4 - O_3)$ measure? Because it cannot account for changes in apple sales due to a change in display location (the display was not changed), then any differences in sales as measured by $(O_4 - O_3)$ must be due to the influence of other extraneous variables on apple sales. Therefore, the difference between the experimental group and the control group, $(O_2 - O_1) - (O_4 - O_3)$, results in a measure of $E$, the "experimental effect." We now know that if we change apple display locations, then apple sales will change by an amount equal to $E$. We have, through experimentation using a proper experimental design, made some progress at arriving at causality.

As we noted earlier, there are many other experimental designs, and, of course, there are almost limitless applications of experimental designs to marketing problems. An experimenter, for example, could use the before-after with-control-group design to measure the effects of different types of music (independent variable) on total purchases made by supermarket customers (dependent variable). Although we have demonstrated how valuable experimentation can be in providing us with knowledge, we should not accept all experiments as being valid. How we assess the validity of experiments is the subject of our next section.

## How Valid Are Experiments?

How can we assess the validity of an experiment? An experiment is valid if: (1) the observed change in the dependent variable is, in fact, due to the independent variable, and (2) the results of the experiment apply to the "real world" outside the experimental setting.[27] Two forms of validity are used to assess the validity of an experiment: internal and external.

**Internal validity** is concerned with the extent to which the change in the dependent variable was actually due to the independent variable. This is another way of asking if the proper experimental design was used and if it was implemented correctly. To illustrate an experiment that lacks internal validity, let us return to our apple example. In the before-after with-control-group experimental design, we made the point that the design assumes that the experimental group and the control group are, in fact, equivalent. What would happen if the researcher did not check the equivalency of the groups? Let us suppose that, by chance, the two groups of supermarkets had customers who were distinctly different regarding a number of factors such as age and income. This difference in the groups, then, would represent an extraneous variable that had been left uncontrolled. Such an experiment would lack internal validity because it could not be said that the change in the dependent variable was due solely to the change in the independent variable. Experiments lacking internal validity have little value because they produce

■ $(O_2 - O_1)$ tells us how many dollars in apple sales may be attributed to (1) the change in display location *and* (2) other extraneous variables, such as the weather, apple industry advertising, and so on.

■ Differences in sales as measured by $(O_4 - O_3)$ are only due to the influence of extraneous variables on apple sales.

■ When we calculate the difference between the experimental group and the control group, $(O_2 - O_1) - (O_4 - O_3)$, the result is $E$, the "experimental effect." $E$ is the amount of change we can expect in apple sales if we change apple display locations. We now have a causal understanding of changing the apple display.

■ An experiment is valid if: (1) the observed change in the dependent variable is, in fact, due to the independent variable, and (2) the results of the experiment apply to the "real world" outside the experimental setting.

■ Internal validity is concerned with the extent to which the change in the dependent variable was actually due to the independent variable.

■ Experiments lacking internal validity have little value.

**ETHICS**

misleading results. Sometimes organizations will conduct studies and present them as "experiments" in order to intentionally mislead others.

**External validity** refers to the extent that the relationship observed between the independent and dependent variables during the experiment is generalizable to the "real world." [28] In other words, can the results of the experiment be applied to units (consumers, stores, and so on) other than those directly involved in the experiment? There are several threats to external validity. How representative is the sample of test units? Is this sample really representative of the population? Additionally, there exist many examples of the incorrect selection of sample units for testing purposes. For example, some executives, headquartered in large cities in cold winter climates, have been known to conduct "experiments" in warmer, tropical climes during the winter. Although the experiments they conduct may be internally valid, it is doubtful that the results will be generalizable to the total population.

Another threat to external validity is the artificiality of the experimental setting itself. In order to control as many variables as possible, some experimental settings are far removed from real-world conditions.[29] If an experiment is so contrived that it produces behavior that would not likely be found in the real world, then the experiment lacks external validity.

■ If an experiment is so contrived that it produces behavior that would not likely be found in the real world, then the experiment lacks external validity.

## Types of Experiments

We can classify experiments into two broad classes: laboratory and field. **Laboratory experiments** are those in which the independent variable is manipulated and measures of the dependent variable are taken in a contrived, artificial setting for the purpose of controlling the many possible extraneous variables that may affect the dependent variable.

■ Laboratory experiments are those in which the independent variable is manipulated and measures of the dependent variable are taken in a contrived, artificial setting for the purpose of controlling the many possible extraneous variables that may affect the dependent variable.

To illustrate, let us consider a study whereby subjects are invited to a theater and shown test ads, copy A or copy B, spliced into a TV "pilot" program. Why would a marketer want to use such an artificial, laboratory setting? Such a setting is used to

Marketing researchers know how to design experiments that have both internal and external validity. Through experiments we know how an apple display affects sales.

control for variables that could affect the purchase of products other than those in the test ads. By bringing consumers into a contrived laboratory setting, the experimenter is able to control many extraneous variables. For example, you have learned why it is important to have equivalent groups (the same kind of people watching copy A as those watching copy B commercials) in an experiment. By inviting preselected consumers to the TV "pilot" showing in a theater, the experimenter can match (on selected demographics) the consumers who view copy A with those who view copy B, thus ensuring that the two groups are equal. By having the consumers walk into an adjoining "store," the experimenter easily controls other factors such as the time between exposure to the ad copy and shopping, as well as the consumers' being exposed to other advertising by competitive brands. As you have already learned, any one of these factors, left uncontrolled, could have an impact on the dependent variable. By controlling for these and other variables, the experimenter can be assured that any changes in the dependent variable were due solely to differences in the independent variable, ad copy A and copy B. Laboratory experiments, then, are desirable when the intent of the experiment is to achieve high levels of internal validity.

■ Laboratory experiments are desirable when the intent of the experiment is to achieve high levels of internal validity.

There are advantages to laboratory experiments. First, they allow the researcher to control for the effects of extraneous variables. Second, compared to field experiments, lab experiments may be conducted quickly and with less expense. Obviously, the disadvantage is the lack of a natural setting, and therefore, there is concern for the generalizability of the findings to the real world. For instance, blind taste tests of beer have found that a majority of beer drinkers favor the older beers such as Pabst, Michelob, or Coors, yet new beer brands are introduced regularly and become quite popular,[30] so the generalizability of blind taste tests is questionable.

■ The advantages of laboratory experiments are that they allow for the control of extraneous variables and they may be conducted quickly and less expensively than field experiments.

■ A disadvantage of laboratory experiments is that they are conducted in artificial settings.

**Field experiments** are those in which the independent variables are manipulated and the measurements of the dependent variable are made on test units in their natural setting. Many marketing experiments are conducted in natural settings, such as in supermarkets, malls, retail stores, and consumers' homes. Let us assume that a marketing manager conducts a *laboratory* experiment to test the differences between ad copy A, the company's existing ad copy, and a new ad copy, copy B. The results of the laboratory experiment indicate that copy B is far superior to the company's present ad copy A. But, before spending the money to use the new copy, the manager wants to know if ad copy B will really create increased sales in the real world. She elects to actually run the new ad copy in Erie, Pennsylvania, a city noted as being representative of the average characteristics of the U.S. population. By conducting this study in the field, the marketing manager will have greater confidence that the results of the study will actually hold up in other real-world settings. Note, however, that even if an experiment is conducted in a naturalistic field setting in order to enhance external validity, the experiment is invalid if it does not also have internal validity.

■ Field experiments are those in which the independent variables are manipulated and the measurements of the dependent variable are made on test units in their natural setting.

■ Even if an experiment is conducted in a naturalistic field setting in order to enhance external validity, the experiment is invalid if it does not also have internal validity.

The primary advantage of the field experiment is that of conducting the study in a naturalistic setting, thus increasing the likelihood that the study's findings will also hold true in the real world. Field experiments, however, are expensive and time consuming. Also, the experimenter must always be alert to the impact of extraneous variables, which are very difficult to control in the natural settings of field experimentation.

The example we just cited of using Erie, Pennsylvania, for a field experiment would be called a "test market." Much of the experimentation in marketing, conducted as field experiments, is known as test marketing. For this reason, test marketing is discussed in the following section.

■ The primary advantage of the field experiment is that of conducting the study in a naturalistic setting, thus increasing the likelihood that the study's findings will also hold true in the real world. Field experiments, however, are expensive and time consuming.

# TEST MARKETING

**Test marketing** is the phrase commonly used to indicate an experiment, study, or test that is conducted in a field setting. Companies may use one or several test-market cities, which are selected geographical areas in which to conduct the test. There are two broad classes of uses of test markets: (1) to test the sales potential for a new product or service, and (2) to test variations in the marketing mix for a product or service.[31]

Although test markets are very expensive and time consuming, the costs of introducing a new product on a national or regional basis routinely amount to millions of dollars. The costs of the test market are then justified if the results of the test market can improve a product's chances of success. Sometimes the test market results will be sufficient to warrant further market introductions. Sometimes the test market identifies a failure early on and saves the company huge losses. The GlobalPC, a scaled-down computer targeted for novices, was tried in test markets. The parent company, MyTurn, concluded that the test market sales results would not lead to a profit, and the product was dropped before the company experienced further losses.[32] Test markets are conducted not only to measure sales potential for a new product but also to measure consumer and dealer reactions to other marketing-mix variables. A firm may use only department stores to distribute the product in one test-market city and only specialty stores in another test-market city in order to gain some information on the best way to distribute the product. Companies can also test media usage, pricing, sales promotions, and so on through test markets. Marketing Research Application 4.2 illustrates marketers' use of test marketing.

## Types of Test Markets

Test markets have been classified into four types: standard, controlled, electronic, and simulated.[33] The **standard test market** is one in which the firm tests the product or marketing-mix variables through the company's *normal* distribution channels. A negative of this type of test market is that competitors are immediately aware of the new product or service. However, standard test markets are good indicators as to how the product will actually perform because they are conducted in real settings.

**Controlled test markets** are conducted by outside research firms that guarantee distribution of the product through prespecified types and numbers of distributors. Companies specializing in providing this service, such as RoperASW and ACNielsen, provide dollar incentives for distributors to provide them with guaranteed shelf space. Controlled test markets offer an alternative to the company that wishes to gain fast access to a distribution system set up for test-market purposes. The disadvantage is that this distribution network may or may not properly represent the firm's actual distribution system. We will look at this service again in Chapter 6 on standardized services.

**Electronic test markets** are those in which a panel of consumers has agreed to carry identification cards that each consumer presents when buying goods and services. These tests are conducted only in a small number of cities in which local retailers have agreed to participate. The advantage of the card is that as consumers buy (or do not buy) the test product, demographic information on the consumers is automatically recorded. In some cases, firms offering electronic test markets may also have the ability to link media viewing habits to panel members as well. In this way, firms using the electronic test market also know how different elements of the promotional mix

---

*Sidebar notes:*

■ *Test marketing* is the phrase commonly used to indicate an experiment, study, or test that is conducted in a field setting.

■ There are two broad classes of uses of test markets: (1) to test the sales potential for a new product or service and (2) to test variations in the marketing mix for a product or service.

■ A standard test market is one in which the firm tests the product or marketing-mix variables through the company's normal distribution channels.

■ Controlled test markets are conducted by outside research firms that guarantee distribution of the product through prespecified types and numbers of distributors.

■ Electronic test markets are those in which a panel of consumers has agreed to carry identification cards that each consumer presents when buying goods and services.

## MARKETING RESEARCH APPLICATION 4.2

PRACTICAL

APPLICATIONS

### Test Marketing Is Conducted to Determine How the Market Will React to a New Product or Service

#### ROOT BEER FLOATS FROM COKE?

Coca-Cola has introduced a new Barq's root-beer-float-flavored soft drink in Mississippi and Louisiana to test the product before a nationwide launch. Barq's Floatz is formulated to mimic a root beer float. Barq's is the top-selling root beer in the United States, and Pepsi's Mug root beer is second. The new drink is designed for those who want the flavor "treat." It is premium priced and higher in calories (150) compared to a regular, 12-ounce Coke (120 calories).[a]

#### POPCORN FURNITURE?

GLOBAL

Popcorn Furniture is the name of a company test-marketing furniture designed for children. The Thailand-based company has been testing the furniture products in schools in India. They designed stools to look like ladybugs, as well as cat and mouse chairs and ladybird tables. More products, taken from fairy tales, are being tested and are targeted at children between one and one-half and six years of age.[b]

#### MAKE MINE IRRADIATED, PLEASE!

Dairy Queen has been testing sales of irradiated ground beef patties. Irradiation reduces the risk of food poisoning. Congress has passed legislation that will allow firms to label irradiated foods as "pasteurized."[c]

#### AN SPF15 JELLYFISH BLOCKER!

GLOBAL

Zeon Healthcare has developed an anti-sting solution to fight jellyfish stings and is test-marketing the solution either by itself or with sunscreens. Called Safe Sea Marine Stinger & Jellyfish Safe Sun Block, the sunscreens come in SPF 15 and 30. These products are being test marketed in the UK.[d]

#### I'LL TELL YOU YOUR CONNECTING FLIGHT NUMBER IF YOU'LL TELL ME HOW YOU LIKED THOSE CHIPS

GLOBAL

Several airlines are creating deals with snack marketers offering to test-market and sample foods. Kraft Foods has an agreement for just such airborne tests with Southwest Airlines. Terra brand chips has deals with Jetblue, Horizon Air, American Airlines, and British Midland. Craves Candy sampled 4 million bags of Clodhoppers on Air Canada in 2003.[e]

[a] A root beer float in a bottle? (2003, June 19). *Columbus Dispatch.* Retrieved from Lexis-Nexis on December 19, 2003.
[b] Kaushik, N. (2003, July 23). Thai co introduces children's furniture. *Businessline*, p. 1.
[c] Liddle, A. (2002, May 20). DQ field tests irradiated burgers as farm bill relaxes labeling law. *Nation's Restaurant News.* vol. 36, no. 20, p. 3ff.
[d] Keep jellyfish at bay. (2003, April 1). *Community Pharmacy*, 26.
[e] Thompson, S. (2003, November 11). Snacks take flight. *Advertising Age*, vol. 73, no. 45, p. 6.

affect purchases of the new product. Firms offering this service include Information Resources, Inc., and ACNielsen. Obviously, the electronic test market offers speed, greater confidentiality, and less cost than standard or controlled test markets. However, the disadvantage is that the test market is not the real market. By virtue of having agreed to serve as members of the electronic panel, consumers in electronic test markets may be atypical. A user firm must evaluate the issue of representativeness. Also, electronic test markets are typically situated in small cities such as Eau Claire, Wisconsin,[34] which is another representativeness consideration.

**Simulated test markets (STMs)** are those in which a limited amount of data on consumer response to a new product is fed into a model containing certain assumptions regarding planned marketing programs, which generates likely product sales volume. It is claimed that IBM has suffered business failures such as the ill-fated Aptiva line of PCs because it failed to use STM research.[35] Typical STMs share the following characteristics: (1) respondents are selected to provide a sample of consumers who satisfy predetermined demographic characteristics; (2) consumers are shown commercials or print ads for the test product as well as ads for competitive products; (3) consumers are then given the opportunity to purchase, or not to purchase, the test product either in a real or simulated store environment; (4) consumers are then recontacted after they have had an opportunity to use the product in an effort to determine likelihood of repurchase, as well as other information relative to use of the product; (5) information from the preceding process is fed into a computer program that is calibrated by assumptions of the marketing mix and other elements of the environment. The program then generates output such as estimated sales volume, market share, and so on.[36]

There are many advantages to STMs. They are fast relative to standard test markets. STMs typically take only 18 to 24 weeks, compared to as many as 12 to 18 *months* for standard test markets. STMs cost only 5% to 10% of the cost of a standard test market. STMs are confidential; competitors are less likely to know about the test. Different marketing mixes may be tested, and results of STMs have shown that they can be accurate predictors of actual market response. The primary disadvantage is that STMs are not as accurate as full-scale test markets. They are very dependent on the assumptions built into the models.[37]

## Consumer Versus Industrial Test Markets

When we think of test marketing, we normally think of tests of consumer products. Test marketing, however, has been growing in the industrial market, sometimes called the B2B market. Although the techniques are somewhat different between consumer and industrial test markets, the same results are sought—the timely release of profitable products.

In consumer test markets, multiple versions of a more-or-less finished product are tested by consumers. In industrial test markets, the key technology is presented to selected industrial users, who offer feedback on desired features and product performance levels. Given this information, product prototypes are then developed and are placed with a select number of users for actual use. Users again provide feedback to iron out design problems. In this way, the new product is tried and tested under actual conditions before the final product is designed and produced for the total market. The negative side of this process is the time it takes to test the product from the beginning stages to the final, commercialized stages. During this time period, information on the new product is leaked to competitors, and the longer the product is being tested, the more investment costs increase without any revenues being generated. U.S. automakers, for example, take 48 to 60 months to design, refine, and begin production of a new car model. Japanese companies are able to do it in 30 months by having a development team made up of a combination of marketing and production people. DaimlerChrysler and 3M have experimented with this concept. In many firms, future industrial test marketing will be fully integrated with the new-product development process.[38]

## "Lead Country" Test Markets

A **lead country test market** is test marketing conducted in specific foreign countries that seem to be good predictors for an entire continent. As markets have become more global, firms are no longer interested in limiting marketing of new products and services to their domestic markets.

Colgate-Palmolive used lead country test marketing when it launched its Palmolive Optims shampoo and conditioner. The company tested the product in the Philippines, Australia, Mexico, and Hong Kong. A year later, distribution was expanded to other countries in Europe, Asia, Latin America, and Africa.[39] Colgate used two countries as test markets in 1999 to test its battery-powered Actibrush for kids. These two countries brought in $10 million in sales. Colgate moved into 50 countries in 2000 and earned $115 million in sales.[40] Korea is being used as a lead country test market for digital products and services. Seongnam is a middle-class Seoul suburb with a mix of high-rise apartment blocks, restaurants, and malls. During the next three years, municipal officials plan to transform the town of 930,000 into the world's first digital city. Multiple broadband connections will seek to do away with analog concepts—like cash and credit cards. Seongnam will start equipping citizens with digital cell phones that, in effect, pay for purchases at every store in the city. Cash-free Seongnam is one of many on-the-ground tests being launched in South Korea, a nation preoccupied with all things digital. More than half of South Korea's 15 million households have broadband service and more than 60% of Koreans carry cell phones. The country is now so wired that many companies can use entire urban populations as test markets for their latest digital products and services.[41]

> A lead country test market is test marketing conducted in specific foreign countries that seem to be good predictors for an entire continent.

## Selecting Test-Market Cities

There are three criteria that are useful for selecting test-market cities: **representativeness, degree of isolation**, and **ability to control distribution and promotion**. Because one of the major reasons for conducting a test market is to achieve external validity, the test-market city should be representative of the marketing territory in which the product will ultimately be distributed. Consequently, a great deal of effort is expended to locate the "ideal" city in terms of comparability with characteristics of the total U.S. (or other country) population. The "ideal" city is, of course, the city whose demographic characteristics most closely match the desired total market. For instance, R. J. Reynolds chose Chattanooga, Tennessee, to test-market its Eclipse "smokeless" cigarette because Chattanooga has a higher proportion of smokers than most cities, and R. J. Reynolds needed to test Eclipse with smokers.[42]

> There are three criteria that are useful for selecting test-market cities: representativeness, degree of isolation, and ability to control distribution and promotion.

When a firm test-markets a product, distribution of the product and promotion of the product are isolated to a limited geographical area, such as Tulsa, Oklahoma. If the firm advertises in the *Tulsa World* newspaper, the newspaper not only covers Tulsa but also has very little "spillover" into other sizable markets. Therefore, the company, along with its dealers, competitors, and so on, are not likely to get many calls from a nearby city wanting to know why it cannot buy the product. Distribution has been restricted to the test market, Tulsa. Some markets are not so isolated. If you were to run promotions for a product test in the *Los Angeles Times*, you would have very large spillover of newspaper readership outside the Los Angeles geographical area. Note that this would not necessarily be a problem as long as you wanted to run the test in the geographical area covered by the *Los Angeles Times* and you also had arranged for the new product to be distributed in this area.

The ability to control distribution and promotion depends on a number of factors. Are the distributors in the city being considered available and willing to cooperate? If not, is a controlled-test-market service company available for the city? Will the media in the city have the facilities to accommodate your test-market needs? At what costs?

All of these factors must be considered before selecting the test city. Fortunately, because city governments often consider it desirable to have test markets conducted in their city because it brings in additional revenues, they as well as the media typically provide a great deal of information about their city to prospective test marketers.

A good example of the application of these criteria is McDonald's test market of its all-you-can-eat breakfast bar. The test was conducted in Atlanta and Savannah, Georgia, which are representative southeastern cities where McDonald's has control over its outlets and where the promotional media are specific to those markets. The buffet was found to increase weekend family breakfast sales.[43]

## Pros and Cons of Test Marketing

The advantages of test marketing are straightforward. Testing product acceptability and marketing-mix variables in a field setting provides the best information possible to the decision maker prior to actually going into full-scale marketing of the product. Because of this, Philip Kotler has referred to test markets as the "ultimate" way to test a new product.[44] Test marketing allows for the most accurate method of forecasting future sales, and it allows firms the opportunity to pretest marketing-mix variables.

■ Test marketing allows for the most accurate method of forecasting future sales, and it allows firms the opportunity to pretest marketing-mix variables.

■ Test markets do not yield infallible results.

There are, however, several negatives to test marketing. First, test markets do not yield infallible results. There have been many instances in which test-market results have led to decisions that proved wrong in the marketplace. No doubt there have probably been many "would-be successful" products withheld from the marketplace due to poor performances in test markets. Much of this problem, however, is not due to anything inherent in test marketing; rather, it is a reflection of the complexity and changeability of consumer behavior. Accurately forecasting consumer behavior is a formidable task. Also, competitors intentionally try to sabotage test markets. Firms will often flood a test market with sales promotions if they know a competitor is test-marketing a product. When PepsiCo tested Mountain Dew Sport drink in Minneapolis in 1990, Quaker Oats Company's Gatorade counterattacked with a deluge of coupons and ads. Mountain Dew Sport was yanked from the market, although Pepsi says Gatorade had nothing to do with the decision.[45] These activities make it even more difficult to forecast the normal market's response to a product.

■ Test markets are expensive, expose the new product or service to competitors, and take time to conduct.

Another problem with test markets is their cost. Estimates are that the costs exceed several hundred thousand dollars even for limited test markets. Test markets involving several test cities and various forms of promotion can easily reach well over six figures. Finally, test markets bring about exposure of the product to the competition. Competitors get the opportunity to examine product prototypes and to see the planned marketing strategy for the new product via the test market. If a company spends too much time testing a product, it runs the risk of allowing enough time for a competitor to bring out a similar product and to gain the advantage of being first in the market. In spite of these problems, the value of the information from test marketing makes test marketing a worthwhile endeavor.

Finally, test markets may create ethical problems. Companies routinely report test-marketing results to the press, which allows them access to premarket publicity. But are negatives found in the test market always reported, or do we hear only the good news? Companies, eager to get good publicity, may select test-market cities that they feel will return favorable results. Perhaps the company already has a strong brand and market power in the market. Is this method of getting publicity ethical? The *Wall Street Journal* has addressed these issues, and the Advertising Research Foundation has published "Guidelines for Public Use of Market and Opinion Research" in an attempt to make reporting of test markets more candid.[46]

## SUMMARY

*Research design* refers to a set of advance decisions made to develop the master plan to be used in the conduct of the research project. There are three general research designs: exploratory, descriptive, and causal. Each one of these designs has its own inherent approaches. The significance of studying research design is that, by matching the research objective with the appropriate research design, a host of research decisions may be predetermined. Therefore, a research design serves as a "blueprint" for researchers. Selecting the appropriate research design depends, to a large extent, on the research objectives and how much information is already known about the problem. If very little is known, exploratory research is appropriate. Exploratory research is unstructured, informal research that is undertaken to gain background information; it is helpful for more clearly defining the research problem. Exploratory research is used in a number of situations: to gain background information, to define terms, to clarify problems and hypotheses, and to establish research priorities. Reviewing existing literature, surveying individuals knowledgeable in the area to be investigated, relying on former similar case situations, conducting focus groups, and projective techniques are methods of conducting exploratory research. Focus groups are conducted by having a small group of people guided by a moderator through a spontaneous, unstructured conversation that focuses on a research problem. Focus-group research is a type of qualitative research. Other forms of qualitative research include in-depth interviews, protocol analysis, projective techniques, and ethnographic research. Focus groups should be used when there is something that needs to be described. When something needs to be predicted, focus groups should not be used. Exploratory research should almost always be used because it is fast, inexpensive, and sometimes resolves the research objective or is helpful in carrying out descriptive or causal research.

If concepts, terms, and so on are already known and the research objective is to describe and measure phenomena, then descriptive research is appropriate. Descriptive research measures marketing phenomena and answers the questions of who, what, where, when, and how. Descriptive studies may be conducted at one point in time (cross sectional), or several measurements may be made on the same sample at different points in time (longitudinal). Longitudinal studies are often conducted using panels. Panels represent sample units who have agreed to answer questions at periodic intervals. Continuous panels are longitudinal studies in which sample units are asked the same questions repeatedly. Brand-switching tables may be prepared based on data from continuous panels. Market-tracking studies may be conducted using data from continuous panels.

The second type of panel used in longitudinal research is the discontinuous panel. Discontinuous panels, sometimes called omnibus panels, are those in which the sample units are asked different questions. The main advantage of the discontinuous panel is that research firms have a large sample of persons who are willing to answer whatever questions they are asked. The demographics of panel members are often balanced to the demographics of the larger geographical areas they are to represent, such as a region or the entire United States. Marketing research firms such as NFOWorldwide and ACNielsen have maintained panels for many years. Online survey research firms such as Lightspeed and Greenfield Online offer clients the use of online panels of respondents.

Sometimes the research objective requires the researcher to determine causal relationships between two or more variables. Causal relationships provide relationships such as "If $x$, then $y$." Causal relationships may be discovered only through special studies called experiments. Experiments allow us to determine the effects of a variable, known as an independent variable, on another variable, known as a dependent variable. Experimental designs are necessary to ensure that the effect we observe in our dependent variable is due, in fact, to our independent variable and not to other variables known as extraneous variables. The validity of experiments may be assessed by internal validity and external validity.

Laboratory experiments are particularly useful for achieving internal validity, whereas field experiments are better suited for achieving external validity. Test marketing is a form of field experimentation. Test-market cities are selected on the basis of their representativeness, isolation, and the degree to which market variables such as distribution and promotion may be controlled. Various types of test markets exist (standard, controlled, electronic, simulated, consumer, industrial, and lead country) and, although test markets garner much useful information, they are expensive and not infallible.

## KEY TERMS

Exploratory design (p. 101)
Exploratory research (p. 102 and 104)
Experimental design (p. 102)
Causal research (p. 102)
Research design (p. 103)
Hypotheses (p. 105)
Secondary data analysis (p. 106)
Experience surveys (p. 107)
Case analysis (p. 107)
Focus groups (p. 107)
Qualitative research (p. 109)
Depth interviews (p. 109)
Protocol analysis (p. 109)
Projective techniques (p. 109)
Ethnographic research (p. 109)
Traditional focus group (p. 110)
Nontraditional focus group (p. 110)
Focus-group facility (p. 110)
Moderators (p. 110)
Qualitative Research Consultants
  (QRs or QRCs) (p. 110)
Focus-group report (p. 110)
Descriptive research (p. 112)
Cross-sectional studies (p. 112)
Sample surveys (p. 113)

Longitudinal studies (p. 114)
Panels (p. 114)
Continuous panels (p. 114)
Discontinuous panels (p. 114)
Omnibus panels (p. 114)
Brand-switching studies (p. 115)
Market-tracking studies (p. 116)
Causality (p. 116)
Experiment (p. 117)
Independent variables (p. 117)
Dependent variables (p. 117)
Extraneous variables (p. 117)
Experimental design (p. 118)
Pretest (p. 118)
Posttest (p. 118)
"True" experimental design (p. 119)
After-only design (p. 119)
Quasi-experimental designs (p. 119)
One-group, before-after design (p. 119)
Control group (p. 120)
Experimental group (p. 120)
Before-after with control group (p. 120)
Internal validity (p. 121)
External validity (p. 122)
Laboratory experiments (p. 122)

Field experiments (p. 123)

Test marketing (p. 124)

Standard test market (p. 124)

Controlled test markets (p. 124)

Electronic test markets (p. 124)

Simulated test markets (STMs) (p. 125)

Lead country test market (p. 126)

Representativeness (p. 127)

Degree of isolation (p. 127)

Ability to control distribution and promotion (p. 127)

## REVIEW QUESTIONS

1 How would you match research designs with various research objectives?

2 Give some examples illustrating the uses of exploratory research.

3 What type of research design answers the questions of who, what, where, when, and how?

4 What are the differences between longitudinal studies and cross-sectional studies?

5 In what situation would a continuous panel be more suitable than a discontinuous panel? In what situation would a discontinuous panel be more suitable than a continuous panel?

6 Explain why studies of the "if–then" variety are considered to be causal studies.

7 What is the objective of good experimental design? Explain why certain designs are called quasi-experimental designs.

8 Explain the two types of validity in experimentation and also explain why different types of experiments are better suited for addressing one type of validity versus another.

9 Distinguish among the various types of test marketing.

## APPLICATION QUESTIONS

10 Think of a past job that you have held. List three areas in which you, or some other person in the organization, could have benefited from having information generated by research. What would be the most appropriate research design for each of the three areas of research you have listed?

11 You are no doubt familiar with Internet search engine companies that find online sources pertaining to words, phrases, or questions that users type in. Can you identifiy research problems likely to be addressed by a search engine company such as Google? What type of research design would you recommend for these problems?

12 Design an experiment. Select an independent variable and a dependent variable. What are some possible extraneous variables that may cause problems? Explain how you would control for the effects these variables may have on your dependent variable. Is your experiment a valid one?

13 The Maximum Company has invented an extra-strength, instant coffee brand to be called "Max-Gaff" and positioned to be stronger tasting than any competing brands. Design a taste-test experiment that compares Max-Gaff to the two leading instant coffee brands to determine which brand consumers consider to taste the strongest. Identify and diagram your experiment. Indicate how the experiment is to be conducted, and assess the internal and external validity of your experiment.

**14** Coca-Cola markets PowerAde as a sports drink that competes with Gatorade. Competition for sports drinks is fierce where they are sold in the coolers of convenience stores. Coca-Cola is thinking about using a special holder that fits in a standard convenience-store cooler but moves PowerAde to eye level and makes it more conspicuous than Gatorade. Design an experiment that determines whether the special holder increases the sales of PowerAde in convenience stores. Identify and diagram your experiment. Indicate how the experiment is to be conducted and assess the internal and external validity of your experiment.

**15** SplitScreen is a marketing research company that tests television advertisements. SplitScreen has an agreement with a cable television company in a medium-sized city in Iowa. The cable company can send up to four different television ads simultaneously to different households. SplitScreen also has agreements with the three of the largest grocery store chains, which will provide scanner data to SplitScreen. About 25% of the residents have SplitScreen scan cards that are scanned when items are bought at the grocery store and that allow SplitScreen to identify who bought which grocery products. For allowing SplitScreen access to their television hookups and their grocery-purchase information, residents receive bonus points that can be used to buy products in a special points catalog. Identify and diagram the true experimental design possible using the SplitScreen system. Assess the internal and external validity of SplitScreen's system.

# INTERACTIVE LEARNING

Go to the Qualitative Research Consultants Association Web site at **www.qrca.org**. Find their mission and read their "ethics and practices." Finally, learn how to find a list of moderators for a topic or type of business such as retail, banking, medical. Visit the Web site at **www.prenhall.com/burnsbush**. For this chapter, work through the Self-Study Quizzes, and get instant feedback on whether you need additional studying. On the Web site, you can review the chapter outlines and case information for Chapter 4.

| CASE 4.1 | ||| **Quality Research Associates** |

Sam Fulkerson of Quality Research Associates reviewed notes of meetings with his clients during the last week.

*Monday/A.M.* Discussion with Janey Dean, Director of Marketing for the Hamptons Bank. Dean is interested in knowing more about a bank image study. Informed her that we had not conducted such a study but that I would meet with her in a week and discuss how to proceed. Dean wants to hire us for advice; her own staff may actually do the image study. Next meeting set for 15th at 2:30 p.m.

*Tuesday/P.M.* Met with Cayleigh Rogers, Business Manager for Wesleyan College. College is considering a football team and the president wants some indication from alums if they favor it and if they will be willing to send in a donation to help with start-up costs. The president of the college also wants to know if present students will support the football team. Call him back for follow-up meeting.

*Wednesday/A.M.* Met with Lawrence Brown of M&M Mars. Brown is brand manager for a new candy bar and he needs advice on promotional methods in the candy bar business. Specifically, he would like to know what promotional methods have been used over the last five years by candy bar brands and how those promotions impacted sales. Advised Brown I would contact some other research suppliers and get back to him.

*Wednesday/P.M.* Tom Greer visited office. Tom also with M&M Mars. Company interested in going into cereal line and wants information fast on how consumers will react to candy-flavored cereal that company has developed. Company's own taste tests have been favorable but Greer wants reaction from a larger sample of consumers from around the country. Would like this information within a month. Important: Company already has the samples ready for mailing.

*Thursday/A.M.* Meeting with Phyllis Detrick of McBride's Markets. McBride has a chain of 150 supermarkets in eight states. Company is spending several million dollars a year on advertising. Detrick wants to know what she can do with the advertising copy and layout of the ads that will generate the most attention. She conducted some exploratory research and found that potential consumers who were reading the paper never even recalled seeing the McBride ads. Specifically, she wants to know if adding color is worth the expense. Will color ads generate greater attention? We set up joint meeting with the McBride Advertising Manager, who will bring all of their newspaper ads in for the last six months.

*Thursday/P.M.* Meeting with Carolyn Phillips, French Yarbrough, and Jeff Rogers. All three are part of a start-up company which has been working on a new toothbrush storage and sanitation device. The new product steam-sanitizes the toothbrushes overnight to make them virtually germ free. Two years ago we conducted exploratory research in the form of focus groups. We followed that up with a survey of a representative sample of households within the city. The survey showed the respondents a picture of the device and asked them if they would be willing to pay $x$ to buy it. Thus far, all had gone well and all studies indicated "go." Now, Phillips, Yarbrough, and Rogers think they are ready for introducing the product to the country. They have had several discussions with large retail chains. All of the chain buyers are interested but they want more evidence that the market will accept the devices. One chain buyer said, "I want to know if people will walk in our stores and really buy these off the shelf." Also, Phillips, Yarbrough, and Rogers have narrowed their national promotion campaigns down to two choices, but they aren't certain which one will gain them the most customers.

*Friday/A.M.* No client meetings. Work on research designs.

1 What research design do you think Sam Fulkerson should select for each of his clients?

2 For each research design you specify in question 1, describe the reason(s) you selected it.

---

## CASE 4.2 ||| Your Integrated Case

### College Life E-Zine

*In Chapter 3 we presented the third installment of the College Life E-Zine case to you. Here, we return to a portion of that installment:*

Bob stated that ORS could also provide information that would help determine potential subscribers' preferences for various types of features in the e-zine.

Don said, "Some hard data would be very helpful to us in making those decisions. We have to remember not to put ourselves in the place of our customers. We haven't been college students in several years now! I've been thinking about the different types of features we can offer and I'll bring the list of ideas to our work session tonight."

Bob said, "That sounds great. We may also want to consider doing some focus groups right away with college students. They're likely to have some great ideas about exactly what they would like to see in the e-zine. Focus groups may give you some good ideas on what to name your e-zine as well, and they'll give us some idea about students' willingness to accept the $15-per-month subscription fee."

1 Explain why it may be beneficial to conduct qualitative research, such as focus groups, prior to conducting quantitative research, such as the survey of college students at State U.

2 Explain why you believe this particular problem—determining the types of features for the e-zine—would be suitable for a focus group.

3 What limitations do you think focus-group research will have in this situation?

## CHAPTER 5

# ACCESSING SECONDARY DATA AND ONLINE INFORMATION DATABASES

## USING SECONDARY DATA TO MAKE BETTER DECISIONS

In the late 1990s, Mark Eberhard was the Southeastern Regional Sales Manager with Advanced Interactive Systems located in Seattle, WA. The company developed interactive shooting simulators, specifically to track live fire projectiles used in commercial and law enforcement indoor ranges. While marketing this technology, he visited over 250 indoor firing ranges. Upon reflection he observed that most of the shooting ranges were small, independently owned, "hobbyist" operations. He felt there might be an opportunity in the industry for a national brand chain of shooting ranges, each of which was designed based upon consumer preferences, and run using modern management tools.

- To learn how to distinguish between secondary and primary data
- To learn the uses of secondary data and how to classify different types of secondary data
- To understand both internal and external databases and their structure
- To understand the advantages and disadvantages of secondary data
- To learn how to evaluate secondary data
- To learn how to find secondary data, including search strategies needed for searching online information databases
- To know the contents of some of the major sources of secondary data provided by the government and private sources

Being a retired Marine officer, Mark was well versed on firearms, and had an intrinsic interest in marksmanship. He wondered if a chain of modern firing ranges would make a successful entrepreneurial investment. He asked himself some basic questions: Were firing ranges growing or declining in popularity? Since firing ranges are often used by hunters, he

Mark Eberhard, American
Marksman Group (AM), Inc.

wondered if hunting, of all types, was growing or declining. What about the general public's attitude toward firearms? Are American sentiments toward firearms favorable or will negative sentiment push Congress to pass legislation restricting the use of firearms? These are basic questions potential entrepreneurs should ask about the industry they are planning to enter. Is this a viable industry? Is it growing or declining? Fortunately, for most of these types of questions secondary data are available.

It didn't take Mark Eberhard long to find that the firing range industry had a trade association, the National Shooting Sports Foundation (NSSF). Trade associations often gather secondary data from various sources and make this information available to members or those who are thinking about entering the industry. NSSF, for example, gathers data from the U.S. Fish and Wildlife Service on the number of hunting licenses. These data are also available by state, which allows users to pinpoint the largest concentrations of hunters. Furthermore, the data are available for many years, which allows users to look at 20-year, 10-year, and 5-year trends. Since excise taxes are charged on the sale of firearms and ammunition, Eberhard was able to examine secondary data showing sales of weapons and ammunition over several years. The Bureau of Alcohol, Tobacco, Firearms, and Explosives (ATF) also publishes data on firearm licenses by state. The ATF also publishes an annual report which shows how many firearms (pistols, rifles, shotguns, etc.) are manufactured each year, as well as the number of firearms imported and exported.

Mark also looked at other information, such as the declining number of firearms deaths published by the National Safety Council, and the low incidence of sports injury due to hunting, paintball, trap and skeet shooting, and archery published by American Sports Data, Inc. After studying this secondary data, Mark Eberhard believed the outlook for the firing range industry was good to excellent. He continued to gather more secondary data, but eventually realized he needed data that was not available. He would have to collect primary data; data gathered for the first time for the purpose at hand. However, the secondary data he had studied would help him formulate the right questions for his primary data collection.

Mark Eberhard continues in the development of American Marksman Group, Inc., whose mission is to provide an extraordinary shooting experience for individuals of all levels of expertise. He relies on secondary data to assess factors related to the demand for firing ranges and to assess the profitability of the American Marksman Group concept. You can visit American Marksman Group at **www.americanmarksman.com**.

*Where We Are:*
1 **Establish the need for marketing research**
2 **Define the problem**
3 **Establish research objectives**
4 **Determine research design**
5 **Identify information types and sources**

Our American Marksman example illustrates the usefulness of secondary data in making better decisions. Mark Eberhard relied heavily on secondary data to determine the future potential of firing ranges in this country. When he needed to gather primary data, his knowledge of the secondary data was helpful in determining what information he needed and how to ask the right question. In this chapter, you will learn how to distinguish secondary data from primary data. We then illustrate the usefulness of secondary data and discuss how it may be classified. We will introduce you to the advantages and disadvantages of secondary data and point out key secondary data resources for marketing research. We will then introduce you to some strategies for effectively and efficiently searching for secondary data, including strategies for searching online information databases. Finally, we point out some of the most important secondary data sources for marketing researchers.[1]

## SECONDARY DATA

### Primary Versus Secondary Data

As presented in Chapter 3, data needed for marketing management decisions can be grouped into two types: primary and secondary. **Primary data** refers to information that is developed or gathered by the researcher specifically for the research project at hand.

**Secondary data** have previously been gathered by someone other than the researcher and/or for some other purpose than the research project at hand. As commercial firms, government agencies, or community service organizations record transactions and business activities, they are creating a written record of these activities in the form of secondary data. When consumers fill out warranty cards or register their boats, automobiles, or software programs, this information is stored in the form of secondary data. It is available for someone else's *secondary* use. The evolution of the Internet has done more to bring fast and easy access of secondary data to end users than anything else since Gutenberg's printing press. Since the mid-1980s virtually all documents have been electronically produced, edited, stored, and made accessible to users. For several years, firms have concentrated on bringing this information to users through specialized services. Today many of these firms offer these services via the Internet. Although some services are available only through a subscription, the Internet provides an incredible stock of free secondary data. Yet, with all the information available to Internet users today, this will likely be viewed as very primitive when Internet2 becomes widely available. Some experts say that the information highway today compares to what Internet2 will offer in the same way that a cart path compares to an eight-lane superhighway![2] We think secondary data access through the Internet, another form of online research, will continue to grow and become more and more important in the marketing researcher's toolbox.

> ■ **Primary data** refers to information that is developed or gathered by the researcher specifically for the research project at hand.

> ■ **Secondary data** have previously been gathered by someone other than the researcher and/or for some other purpose than the research project at hand.

> ■ Secondary data access through the Internet, another form of online research, will continue to grow and become more and more important in the marketing researcher's toolbox.

### Uses of Secondary Data

There are so many uses of secondary data that it is rare for a marketing research project to be conducted without including some secondary data. Some projects may be totally based upon secondary data. The applications of secondary data range from predicting very broad changes in a culture's "way of life" to very specific applications such as selecting a street address location for a new car wash. Decision Analyst, Inc., a marketing research firm, has a Web site devoted entirely to secondary data. Suggested applications include economic-trend forecasting, corporate intelligence, international data, public opinion, and historical data, among others. Marketers are very interested in knowing secondary data in terms of demographic data to help them

■ There are so many uses of secondary data that it is rare for a marketing research project to be conducted without including some secondary data. Some projects may be totally based upon secondary data.

■ Go to www.secondarydata .com at Decision Analyst, Inc., to see the many uses of secondary data for marketing research.

*Decision Analyst, Inc.*

forecast the size of the market in a newly proposed market territory. A researcher may use secondary data to determine the population and growth rate in almost any geographical area. Government agencies are interested in knowing secondary data to help them make public policy decisions. The Department of Education needs to know how many 5-year-olds will enter the public school system next year. Health care planners need to know how many senior citizens will be eligible for Medicare during the next decade. Sometimes secondary data can be used to evaluate market performance. For example, since gasoline and fuel taxes collected per gallon are available in public records, petroleum marketers can easily determine the volume of fuels consumed in a county. Articles are written on virtually every topic and this storehouse of secondary data is available to marketers who want to understand a topic more thoroughly even though they themselves may not have firsthand experience. A wealth of secondary data is available concerning the lifestyles, including purchasing habits, of demographic groups. Since these demographic groups tend to make similar purchases and have similar attitudes, they have been scrutinized by marketers. The most significant of these demographic groups for decades has been the "baby boomer" population, defined as those born between 1946 and 1964. As the "boomers" enter middle- and senior-age status, other demographic groups, such as the Gen Xers, are also studied by marketers. Our Marketing Research Application 5.1 illustrates how secondary data on demographic groups are important to marketers.

## MARKETING RESEARCH APPLICATION 5.1

PRACTICAL

APPLICATIONS

### Born Between 1977 and 1994? You're a Gen Yer!

Much secondary marketing research seeks demographic information. Derived from the Greek word *demos*, "demographics" refers to the study of the population. Normally included are population size, density, growth, income, ethnic background, housing, and retail sales, among other factors. Demographic analysis based upon age offers many insights into the marketplace and it is highly predictable. We know today how many 16-year-olds there will be in 2021! For many decades marketers have followed baby boomers, persons born from 1946 to 1964. Boomers make up a large percentage of the population, and their demands in the marketplace have followed them through the years. In the 1950s there was a huge demand for schools to educate boomers coming of school age. Textbooks, Boy and Girl Scout uniforms, and toys experienced high growth rates. Rock and Roll replaced Frank Sinatra, Perry Como, and Dean Martin when the young boomers reached their teens. The recording industry

faced a large market of boomers between 12 and 18 years of age who wanted an alternative to their parents' preferences for Big Band and crooner music. Elvis Presley met the demands of this new market better than anyone else. Indeed, one could argue that if it hadn't been for the young boomers demanding a change in music, Elvis would have had a normal life driving a truck in Memphis. As the boomers aged, they created unprecedented, but predictable, demands on colleges and universities, the job market, housing, recreation, and now, retirement- and health-related goods and services.

There is a new force in demographics. Gen Y represents a group almost as large as the boomers and is expected to be as powerful as a shaper of business decisions in the future. Though there is some disagreement among demographers as to the exact size, most agree that Gen Yers represent the 72 million Americans born between 1977 and 1994. The estimated spending income of this group is $187 billion annually. But, unlike the Boomers, Gen Yers may prove to be the most unpredictable and marketing-resistant group known to U.S. marketers. With many in their early 20s, a large percentage of Gen Yers are still living at home with their parents. They shun traditional media in preference for video games, DVDs, and Web sites.

Because Gen Yers represent such a large population and still influence their younger counterparts, marketers are keenly interested in them. Honda tried to target them with its Element, which they positioned as a "dorm room on wheels." Chrysler did the same with its PT Cruiser. Gen Yers were not impressed. Both cars sold but to a much older market. Gen Yers, however, are predictable when it comes to technology. They are heavy users of all forms of technology. Cell phone manufacturers are watching Gen Yers closely to identify hot new trends for the rest of the market. Cell phones featuring video and speaker attachments are already on the market. Jupiter Research reports that 18- to 24-year-olds spend an average of 10 hours a week online, 10 hours watching TV, and 5 hours listening to the radio. They also spend considerably more time online messaging, playing games, and downloading music than their older counterparts.

Gen Yers, having been exposed to 3,000 marketing messages a day (making some 23 million in their lives thus far), are immune to traditional advertising. One advertiser said that when you do a focus group with 21-year-olds, they tell you the advertiser's strategy. In other words, they see right through the ads. Instead of viewing ads for information, as the boomers do, they view them for entertainment. Advertisers, to get their attention, must make the ads entertaining, using word-of-mouth and stealth marketing.

Gen Yers are viewed as being a powerful force in the market today. They not only influence their younger siblings, but, surprisingly, they influence their boomer parents. MTV reports, for example, that parents are watching rocker Ozzie Osbourne and his family right along with their Gen Y kids! Marketers will rely heavily on secondary data to track Gen Yers in the years ahead.

*Source:* Portions adapted from Weiss, M. J. (2003, September 1). To be or not to be. *American Demographics*. Retrieved from LexisNexis on October 30, 2003.

# CLASSIFICATION OF SECONDARY DATA

Since so much secondary information is available, every marketing researcher must learn to properly manage these data. However, the stock of information available can be overwhelming. Marketing researchers must learn to properly handle secondary data. They must know the classifications of secondary data as well as their advantages and disadvantages, and they must know how to evaluate the information available to them.

## Internal Secondary Data

Secondary data may be broadly classified as either internal or external. **Internal secondary data** are data that have been collected within the firm. Such data include sales records, purchase requisitions, and invoices. Obviously, a good marketing researcher always determines what internal information is already available. You may recall from Chapter 1 that we referred to internal data analysis as being part of the internal reports system of a firm's marketing information system (MIS). Today a major source of internal data is databases that contain information on customers, sales, suppliers, and any other facet of business a firm may wish to track. Kotler defines **database marketing** as the process of building, maintaining, and using customer (*internal*) databases and other (*internal*) databases (products, suppliers, resellers) for the purpose of contacting, transacting, and building relationships.[3] The use of internal databases has grown dramatically for several years.

■ Internal secondary data are data that have been collected within the firm. Such data include sales records, purchase requisitions, and invoices.

### Internal Databases

Before we discuss internal and external databases, we should understand that a **database** refers to a collection of data and information describing items of interest.[4] Each unit of information in a database is called a **record**. A record could represent a customer, a

■ A database refers to a collection of data and information describing items of interest to the database owner.

■ Databases are composed of records that represent a unit of information. Subcomponents of information in records are called fields.

supplier, a competitive firm, a product, an individual inventory item, and so on. Records are composed of subcomponents of information called **fields**. As an example, a company having a database of customers would have *records* representing each customer. Typical *fields* in a customer database would include name, address, telephone number, e-mail address, products purchased, dates of purchases, locations where purchased, warranty information, and any other information the company thought was important. Although you can have a noncomputerized database, the majority of databases are computerized because they contain large amounts of information and their use is facilitated by computer capability to edit, sort, and analyze the mass of information.

**Internal databases** are databases consisting of information gathered by a company, typically during the normal course of business transactions. Marketing managers normally develop internal databases about customers, but databases may be kept on any topic of interest, such as products, members of the sales force, inventory, maintenance, and supplier firms. Companies gather information about customers when they inquire about a product or service, make a purchase, or have a product serviced. Think about the information you may have provided to marketing firms: your name, address, telephone number, fax number, e-mail address, credit card number, your banking institution and account number, and so on. Coupled with a knowledge of what products you have purchased in the past and with other information provided by government and other commercial sources, many companies know quite a bit about you. Companies use their internal databases for purposes of direct marketing and to strengthen relationships with customers; this is called **CRM, customer relationship management**.[5]

Internal databases can be quite large, and dealing with the vast quantities of data they contain can be a problem. **Data mining** is the name for software that is now available to help managers make sense out of seemingly senseless masses of information contained in databases.[6] However, even simple databases in small businesses can be invaluable. Databases can tell managers which products are selling, report inventories, and profile customers by SKU. Coupled with geodemographic information systems (GIS), databases can provide maps indicating zip codes in which the most profitable and least profitable customers reside. Internal databases, built with information collected during the normal course of business, can provide invaluable insights for managers. We shall discuss GIS more completely in the next chapter.

■ Internal databases, built with information collected during the normal course of business, can provide invaluable insights for managers.

What companies do with information collected for their internal databases can present ethical problems. Should your credit card company share the information on what types of goods and services you bought with anyone who wants to buy that information? Should your Internet service provider be able to store information on which Internet sites you visit? As more consumers have grown aware of these privacy issues, more companies have adopted privacy policies.[7]

■ What companies do with information collected in their internal databases can present ethical problems.

## External Secondary Data

### Published Sources

**External secondary data** are data obtained from outside the firm. We classify external data into three sources: (1) *published*, (2) *syndicated services data*, and (3) *databases*. **Published sources** are those sources of information that are prepared for public distribution and are normally found in libraries or through a variety of other entities such as trade associations, professional organizations, or companies. Published sources are available in a number of formats including print, CD-ROM, and online via the Internet. Many publications that were formerly available in print only are becoming available in electronic format. Magazines available electronically are called e-zines; journals are called e-journals. Published sources of secondary information come from the government (*Census of the Population*), nonprofit organizations (chambers of commerce, colleges and universities), trade and professional associations (CASRO, AMA, IMRO, MRA), and for-profits (*Sales & Marketing Management* magazine, Prentice Hall, Inc., McGraw-Hill, and research firms). Many research firms publish secondary information in the form of books, newsletters, white papers, special reports, magazines, or journals such as *Quirk's Marketing Research Review*. See Marketing Research Application 5.2.

■ **Published sources are those sources of information that are prepared for public distribution and are normally found in libraries or through a variety of other entities.**

## MARKETING RESEARCH APPLICATION 5.2

### PRACTICAL APPLICATIONS

### A Published Source of Secondary Information: *Quirk's Marketing Research Review*

Tom Quirk, after 20 years of marketing research experience, started *Quirk's Marketing Research Review* in 1986. The mission of the magazine has remained steadfast: to provide practical, valuable, and useful information to the marketing research industry. Each issue contains cases, practical examples, expert advice on research techniques, and information on the latest new product information as well as survey findings. Special issues address topics such as advertising research, B2B research, customer satisfaction, health care research, international research, Internet research and technology, among others.

In addition to publishing *Quirk's Marketing Research Review*, Quirk's also publishes nine specialty directories of research providers and a directory of all marketing research providers in the *Researcher SourceBook™*.

Tom Quirk's vision to provide information to marketing research professionals has grown to become a significant source of secondary information for researchers. Quirk's has over 16,000 subscribers in countries all over the world. You can visit Quirk's at **www.quirks.com.** By permission, *Quirk's Marketing Research Review*

■ Understanding the function
of different types of publications
can help you find the secondary
data you need.

The sheer volume of published sources makes searching this type of secondary data difficult. However, understanding the function of the different types of publications can be of great help to you in successfully searching published secondary information sources. Table 5.1 depicts the different types of publications and gives you their functions as well as an example.

**Table 5.1**

Understanding the
Functions of Different
Types of Publications
Can Make You a Better
User of Secondary Data

### 1. Reference Guides
Function: Refer to *types* of other reference sources and recommend specific titles. Guides tell you where to look to find different types of information.

Example: *Encyclopedia of Business Information Sources.* Detroit: Galegroup, 1970–2001.

### 2. Indexes and Abstracts
Function: List periodical articles by subject, author, title, keyword, etc. Abstracts also provide summaries of the articles. Indexes allow you to search for periodicals by the topic of your research.

Example: *ABI/Inform.* Ann Arbor, MI: Proquest, 1971–present.

### 3. Bibliographies
Function: List varied sources such as books, journals, etc., on a particular topic. Tell you what is available, in several sources, on a topic.

Example: *Recreation and Entertainment Industries, an Information Source Book.* Jefferson, NC: Macfarland, 2000.

### 4. Almanacs, Manuals, and Handbooks
Function: These types of sources are "deskbooks" that provide a wide variety of data in a single handy publication.

Example: *Wall Street Journal Almanac.* New York: Ballantine Books, Annual.

### 5. Dictionaries
Function: Define terms and are sometimes available for special subject areas.

Example: *Concise Dictionary of Business Management.* New York: Routledge, 1999.

### 6. Encyclopedias
Function: Provide essays, usually in alphabetical order, by topic.

Example: *Encyclopedia of Busine$$ and Finance.* New York: Macmillan, 2001.

### 7. Directories
Function: List companies, people, products, organizations, etc., usually providing brief information about each entry.

Example: *Career Guide: Dun's Employment Opportunities Directory.* Parsippany, NJ: Dun's Marketing Services Annual.

### 8. Statistical Sources
Function: Provide numeric data, often in tables, pie charts, and bar charts.

Example: *Handbook of U.S. Labor Statistics.* Lanham, MD: Bernan Press, Annual.

**9. Biographical Sources**
Function: Provide information about people. Useful for information on CEOs, etc.

Example: *D&B Reference Book of Corporate Management.* Bethlehem, PA: Dun & Bradstreet, 2001.

**10. Legal Sources**
Function: Provide information about legislation, regulations, and case law.

Example: *United States Code.* Washington, DC: Government Printing Office.

Today many libraries enter their holdings of books and other publications in electronic records whose fields are searchable electronically. These electronic libraries allow researchers to search secondary data quickly, conveniently, inexpensively, and thoroughly. Most electronic libraries have information available in two broad categories: catalogs and indexes. A **catalog** consists of a list of a library's holdings of books. (Catalogs sometimes also list the periodicals to which the library subscribes.) Therefore, catalogs are useful for finding *books* by subject, author, title, date of publication, or publisher. **Indexes** are records compiled from periodicals and contain information on the contents of periodicals recorded in fields such as author, title, keywords, date of publication, name of periodical, and so on. Sometimes an index contains the entire contents of the periodical (called full-text indexes). Such indexes are not normally constructed by a library. Rather, they are provided by companies that make them available to libraries or other organizations. We shall talk more about these when we discuss online information databases.

■ A catalog consists of a list of a library's holdings of books.

■ Indexes are records compiled from periodicals and contain information on the contents of periodicals recorded in fields such as author, title, keywords, date of publication, name of periodical, and so on.

### Syndicated Services Data

**Syndicated services data** are provided by firms that collect data in a standard format and make them available to subscribing firms. Such data are typically highly specialized and are not available in libraries for the general public.

The suppliers syndicate (sell) the information to multiple subscribers, thus making the costs more reasonable to any one subscriber. Examples include Arbitron's radio listenership data, Nielsen Media Research's Television Rating Index, and Information Resources Inc.'s InfoScan report of products sold in retail stores. In all these cases, these firms supply subscribing firms with external secondary data. We devote more attention to syndicated data services firms in Chapter 6.

■ Syndicated services data are provided by firms that collect data in a standard format and make them available to subscribing firms. Such data are typically highly specialized and are not available in libraries for the general public.

■ Go to Interactive Learning at the end of the chapter and learn more about Nielsen Media Research's Television Rating Index.

### External Databases

**External databases** are databases supplied by organizations outside the firm. They may be used as sources for secondary data. Some of these databases are available in printed format, but, in recent years, many databases have become available online. **Online information databases** are sources of secondary data searchable by search engines online. Some online databases are available free of charge and are supplied as a service by a host organization. However, many online information databases are available from commercial sources that provide subscribers password (or IP address identification) access for a fee. These databases have grown dramatically since the 1980s. During the 1990s and early 2000s, many of the companies supplying external databases of secondary data merged. We have fewer companies but each one is much larger, with the larger firms offering subscribers access to billions of records of

■ External databases are databases supplied by organizations outside the firm, and they may be used as sources for secondary data.

■ Online information databases are sources of secondary data searchable by search engines online. Examples include Factiva, LexisNexis, Proquest, and Gale Group.

information. Different databases are often packaged together by vendors that produce the software that retrieves the information. Sometimes called "aggregators" or "data-banks," these services or vendors may offer a wide variety of indexes, directories, and statistical and full-text files all searched by the same search logic. Such services include Factiva, Gale Group, Proquest, First Search, LexisNexis, and Dialog, among others. Business databases comprise a significant proportion of these data banks.

## ADVANTAGES OF SECONDARY DATA

■ The five advantages of secondary data are that secondary data can be obtained quickly and inexpensively, are usually available, enhance primary data collection, and can sometimes achieve the research objective.

### Secondary Data Can Be Obtained Quickly

There are five main advantages of using secondary data. First, secondary data can be *obtained quickly*, in contrast to collecting primary data, which may take several months from beginning to end. You can go to the Internet and quickly find a great deal of secondary data at no expense.

### Secondary Data Are Inexpensive Relative to Primary Data

Second, collecting secondary data is *inexpensive* when compared to collecting primary data. Though there are certainly costs of collecting secondary data, these costs are but a fraction of the costs of collecting primary data. Primary data collection is seldom achieved without spending at least a few thousand dollars, and, depending on the research objective, may cost hundreds of thousands or even millions of dollars. Even purchasing secondary data from commercial vendors is inexpensive relative to primary data.

### Secondary Data Are Usually Available

A third advantage of secondary data is that they are *usually available*. No matter what the problem area may be, someone somewhere has probably dealt with it, and some information is available that will help the researcher's task. Availability is one reason that many predict secondary data will grow in importance in marketing research applications. Not only is the data growing but the ability to search billions of records to find the right data is improving with computer technology.

### Secondary Data Enhance Primary Data

As our chapter-opening vignette describes, secondary data *enhance existing primary data*. Simply because researchers use secondary data does not mean that they will not collect primary data. In fact, in almost every case, the researcher's task of primary data collection is aided by first collecting secondary data. A secondary data search can familiarize the researcher with the industry, including its sales and profit trends, major competitors, and the significant issues facing the industry.[8] A secondary data search can identify concepts, data, and terminology that may be useful in conducting primary research. A bank's management, for example, hired a marketing research firm, and together, management and the research team decided to conduct a survey measuring the bank's image among its customers. A check of the secondary information available on the measurement of bank image identified the components of bank image for the study. Also, the research team, after reviewing secondary information, determined there were *three* sets of bank customers: retail customers, commercial accounts, and other correspondent banks. When the researchers mentioned this to bank management, the original objectives of the primary research were changed in order to measure the bank's image among all three customer groups.

## Secondary Data May Achieve the Research Objective

Finally, not only are secondary data faster to obtain, more convenient to use, and less expensive to gather than primary research, but they also may achieve the research objective! For example, a supermarket chain marketing manager wants to allocate TV ad dollars to the 12 TV markets in which the chain owns supermarkets. A quick review of secondary data will show him or her that data on retail sales of food is available by TV market area. Allocating the TV budget based on the percentage of food sales in a given market would be an excellent way to solve the manager's problem and satisfy the research objective.

# DISADVANTAGES OF SECONDARY DATA

Although the advantages of secondary data almost always justify a search of this information, there are caveats associated with secondary data. Five of the problems associated with secondary data include *incompatible reporting units, mismatch of the units of measurement, differing definitions used to classify the data, the timeliness of the secondary data*, and *the lack of information needed to assess the credibility of the data reported*. These problems exist because secondary data have not been collected specifically to address the researcher's problem at hand but have been collected for some other purpose. Consequently, the researcher must determine the extent of these problems before using the secondary data. This is done by evaluating the secondary data. We discuss the first four disadvantages in the following paragraphs. Evaluation of secondary data is discussed in the next section.

## Incompatible Reporting Units

Secondary data are provided in reporting units such as county, city, metro area or MSA, state, region, zip code, and so on. Marketing Research Application 5.3 introduces us to a new government reporting unit, Core-Based Statistical Areas. A researcher's use of secondary data often depends on whether the reporting unit matches the researcher's need. For example, a researcher wishing to evaluate market areas for the purpose of consideration for expansion may be pleased with data reported at the county level. A great deal of secondary data are available at the county level. But what if another marketer wishes to evaluate a two-mile area around a street address which is proposed as a site location for a retail store? County data would hardly be adequate. Another marketer wishes to know the demographic makeup of each zip code in a major city in order to determine which zip codes to target for a direct-mail campaign. Again, county data would be incompatible. While incompatible reporting units are often problems in using secondary data, more and more data are available today in multiple reporting units. Data at the

■ Secondary data are provided in reporting units such as county, MSA, state, region, zip code, and so on. A researcher's use of secondary data often depends on whether the reporting unit matches the researcher's need.

## MARKETING RESEARCH APPLICATION 5.3

PRACTICAL

APPLICATIONS

### Geographical Reporting Units Used by the U.S. Census Bureau

*What are Core-based Statistical Areas?*

Core-based Statistical Areas, or CBSAs, are geographic reporting units used by the Census Bureau. CBSAs are made up of two smaller units, Metropolitan and Micropolitan Statistical Areas (SAs). Metropolitan and micropolitan statistical areas are defined in terms of whole counties or county equivalents, including the six New England states. As of June 6, 2003, there are 362 metropolitan statistical areas and 560 micropolitan statistical areas in the United States. Metropolitan SAs are defined by the Office of Management and Budget (OMB) as having at least one urbanized area of 50,000 or more population, plus adjacent territory that has a high degree of social and economic integration with the core as measured by commuting ties. Micropolitan SAs are a new set of statistical areas that have at least one urban cluster of at least 10,000 but less than 50,000 population, plus adjacent territory that has a high degree of social and economic integration with the core MSA as measured by commuting ties.

*Why do we have Metropolitan and Micropolitan SAs?*

The metropolitan area (MA) program has provided standard statistical area definitions at the metropolitan level for 50 years. In the 1940s, it became clear that the value of data produced at that level by federal government agencies would be greatly enhanced if agencies used a single set of geographic definitions for the Nation's metropolitan areas. The OMB's predecessor, the Bureau of the Budget, led the effort to develop what were then called "standard metropolitan areas," also known as MSAs in time for their use in 1950 census reports.

The general concept of an MA is that of an area containing a large population nucleus and adjacent communities that have a high degree of integration with that nucleus. This general concept has remained essentially the same since MAs were first defined before the 1950 census. OMB establishes and maintains MAs solely for statistical purposes.[a]

*Why do MAs change?*

The MA standards are reviewed and, if warranted, revised in the years preceding each decennial census. Periodic review of the MA standards is necessary to ensure their continued usefulness and relevance. The current review of the MA standards—the Metropolitan Area Standards Review Project (MASRP)—is the sixth such review; it has been especially thorough, reflecting as a first priority users' concerns with the conceptual and operational complexity of the standards that have evolved over the decades. Other key concerns behind the particularly thorough nature of MASRP's efforts have been: (1) whether modifications to the standards over the years have permitted them to stay abreast of changes in population distribution and activity patterns, (2) whether advances in computer applications permit consideration of new approaches to defining areas, and (3) whether there is a practical way to capture a more complete range of U.S. settlement and activity patterns than the current MA standards capture.

[a]The evolution of the standards for defining MAs was discussed in detail in OMB's **Federal Register** Notice of December 21, 1998, "Alternative Approaches to Defining Metropolitan and Nonmetropolitan Areas" (63 FR 70526–70561). Table 1 of the December Notice summarized the evolution of MA standards since 1950. (The December Notice is available on the OMB Web site.)

Zip+4 level are becoming more available. Also, as we will see in the next chapter, GIS offers marketers access to data in arbitrarily defined reporting units. The latter would be very useful for the marketer wishing to know the demographics within a two-mile ring around a street address. Nevertheless, sometimes secondary data are available, but in the wrong reporting unit.

## Measurement Units Do Not Match

Sometimes secondary data are reported in measurement units that do not match the measurement unit needed by the researcher. In analyzing markets, for example, marketing researchers are typically interested in income levels. Available studies of income may measure income in several ways: total income, income after taxes, household income, and per capita income. Or consider a research project that needs to categorize businesses by size in terms of square footage. Secondary data sources, however, classify businesses in terms of size according to sales volume, number of employees, profit level, and so on. Much information in the United States is recorded in American units of measurement (feet, pounds, etc.), yet most of the rest of the world uses metric units (meter, kilograms, etc.). The United States is slowly becoming metric.[9]

> ■ Sometimes measurement units reported in secondary data do not match the unit needed by the researcher. For example, income is reported as per capita instead of per household.

## Class Definitions Are Not Usable

The class definitions of the reported data may not be usable to a researcher. Secondary data are often reported by breaking a variable into different classes and reporting the frequency of occurrence in each class. For example, the "Survey of Buying Power" reports a variable, effective buying income (EBI), in three classes. The first class reports the percentage of households having an EBI between $20,000 and $34,999, and the final class reports the percentage of households having an EBI of $50,000 and over. For most studies, these classifications are applicable. However, it is doubtful that Beneteau, Inc., a manufacturer of sailing yachts in South Carolina, could use these income classifications to help it target potential customer markets. Because Beneteau's average customer is thought to have an EBI in excess of $75,000, Beneteau could not use the data reported because of the way the EBI classes were defined. What does the researcher do? Typically, if you keep looking, you can find what you need. For example, Beneteau can obtain secondary data that would solve its problem by purchasing *Demographics USA*, published by the producers of the "Survey of Buying Power." It would find that *Demographics USA* provides information on EBI up through categories of $150,000 or more.[10]

> ■ Secondary data are often reported by breaking a variable into different classes and reporting the frequency of occurrence in each class. Sometimes the classes reported are not useful for the researcher's purpose.

## Data Are Outdated

Sometimes a marketing researcher will find information reported with the desired unit of measurement and the proper classifications, but the data are "out-of-date." Some secondary data are published only once. However, even for secondary data that are published at regular intervals, the time that passed since the last publication can be a problem when applying the data to a current problem. Ultimately, the researcher must make the decision as to whether or not to use the data.

> ■ Sometimes, the "right" secondary data is found but it is dated. Researchers must always decide if they should use outdated secondary data.

# EVALUATING SECONDARY DATA

Hopefully, you have learned that not everything you read is true. In order to properly use secondary data, you must evaluate that information before you use it as a basis for decision making. A reader must be most cautious when using an Internet source, because few quality standards are applied to most Internet sites. To determine the reliability of secondary information, marketing researchers must evaluate it. This is done by answering the following five questions:

- ■ What was the purpose of the study?
- ■ Who collected the information?
- ■ What information was collected?

- How was the information obtained?
- How consistent is the information with other information?[11]

A discussion of each question follows.

## What Was the Purpose of the Study?

Studies are conducted for a purpose. Unfortunately, studies are sometimes conducted in order to "prove" some position or advance the special interest of those conducting the study. Many years ago, chambers of commerce were known for publishing data that exaggerated the size and growth rates of their communities. They did this to "prove" that their communities were a good choice for new business locations. However, after a few years, they learned that few people trusted chamber data, and today chambers of commerce publish reliable and valid data. But the lesson is that you must be very careful to determine whether the entity publishing the data acted in a fair and unbiased manner. Consider the example of disposable diapers. The disposable diaper industry was created in the 1960s. Environmental concerns became alarming as information became available about the forecasts of huge mountains of disposable diapers that would take 50 years to decompose. Consequently, during the late 1980s, the number of customers buying old-fashioned cloth diapers doubled. Also, more than a dozen state legislatures were considering various bans, taxes, and even warning labels on disposable diapers. Then "research studies" were produced on the environmental effects of disposable versus cloth diapers. It seemed that the "new" research proved that cloth diapers, by adding detergent by-products to the water table, were more harmful to the environment than the everlasting plastic disposables! Soon after several of these studies were made available to legislators, the movement against disposables was dead. Who conducted the studies? Procter & Gamble. P&G, owning the lion's share of the market for disposable diapers, commissioned the consulting firm of Arthur D. Little, Inc., to conduct a study of disposable versus cloth diapers. The study found that disposable diapers were no more harmful to the environment than reusable cotton diapers. Another favorable study for the disposables was conducted by Franklin Associates, whose research showed disposables were not any more harmful than cloth diapers. But who sponsored this study? The American Paper Institute, an organization with major interests in disposable diapers. But wait, before you become too critical of the disposable diaper folks, let's consider some other "scientific" studies. In 1988, a study was published that showed disposable diapers as being "garbage" and contributing to massive buildups of waste that was all but impervious to deterioration. Who sponsored this study? The cloth diaper industry! Another study published in 1991 found cloth diapers to be environmentally superior to disposable diapers. Guess who sponsored this study?[12] Right! The cloth diaper industry.

## Who Collected the Information?

Even when you are convinced that there is no bias in the purpose of the study, you should question the competence of the organization that collected the information. Why? Simply because organizations differ in terms of the resources they command and their quality control. But how do you determine the competency of the organization that collected the data? First, ask others who have more experience in a given industry. Typically, credible organizations are well known in those industries for which they conduct studies. Second, examine the report itself. Competent firms will almost always provide carefully written and detailed explanations of the procedures and methods used in collecting the information contained in the report. Third, contact previous clients of the firm. Have they been satisfied with the quality of the work performed by the organization?

## What Information Was Collected?

There are many studies available on topics such as economic impact, market potential, feasibility, and the like. But what exactly was measured in these studies that constitutes impact, potential, or feasibility? There are many examples of studies that claim to provide information on a specific subject but, in fact, measure something quite different. Consider a study conducted by a transit authority on the number of riders on its bus line. On examination of the methodology used in the study, the number of riders, was not counted at all. Rather, the number of tokens was counted. Since a single rider may use several tokens on a single destination route requiring transfers to other buses, the study overestimated the number of riders. Or consider a study of "advertising effectiveness." How was effectiveness measured? Was it the sales of the product the next week after the ad was run? Was it the percentage of consumers who named the brand name the day after the ad was run? Is this distinction important? It may be or it may not be, depending on how the study's user intends to use the information. The important point here is that the user should discover exactly what information was collected.

## How Was the Information Obtained?

You should be aware of the methods used to obtain information reported in secondary sources. What was the sample? How large was the sample? What was the response rate? Was the information validated? As you will learn throughout this book, there are many alternative ways of collecting primary data and each may have an impact on the information collected. Remember that, even though you are evaluating secondary data, this information was gathered as primary data by some organization. Therefore, the alternative ways of gathering the data had an impact on the nature and quality of the data. It is not always easy to find out how the secondary data were gathered. However, as noted earlier, most reputable organizations that provide secondary data also provide information on their data collection methods. If this information is not readily available and your use of the secondary data is very important to your research project, you should make the extra effort to find out how the information was obtained.

## How Consistent Is the Information with Other Information?

In some cases, the same secondary data are reported by multiple, independent organizations, which provides an excellent way to evaluate secondary data sources. Ideally, if two or more independent organizations report the same data, you can have greater confidence in the validity and reliability of the data. Demographic data, for example, for metropolitan areas (MAs), counties, and most municipalities, are widely available from more than one source. If you are evaluating a survey that is supposedly representative of a given geographic area, you may want to compare the characteristics of the sample of the survey with the demographic data available on the population.

> ■ Research studies are often published and become part of secondary data. However, not all research studies are conducted in a totally objective manner. You must ask who conducted the study.

> ■ It may be very important to know exactly what was measured in a report before using the results.

> ■ Evaluate the method used to collect the primary data that is now available to you as secondary data. You will be much better at doing this when you finish this course.

If you know, based on U.S. census data, that there are 45% males and 55% females in a city, and a survey, which is supposed to be representative of that city, reports a sample of 46% males and 54% females, then you can be more confident in the survey data. It is indeed rare, however, that two organizations will report exactly the same results. Here you must look at the magnitude of the differences and determine what you should do. If all independent sources report very large differences of the same variable, then you may not have much confidence in any of the data. You should look carefully at what information was collected, how it was collected, and so on for each reporting source. For example, if you were to get the number of businesses in a county from Survey Sampling, Inc., and compare that number to the number of businesses reported by the governmental publication *County Business Patterns (CBP)*, you would see a marked difference. Specifically, Survey Sampling's number of businesses would be much larger than the number reported by *CBP*. Why?[13] The answer is found by asking the questions "What information was actually collected?" and "How was this information obtained?" As it turns out, neither organization actually counts the numbers of businesses in a given area. *CBP* counts the number of firms submitting payroll information on their employees. Some firms may not report this information, and other small firms with "no paid employees" (whose owners are the employees) are excluded from *CBP* data. Therefore, the *CBP* surrogate indicator used to count the number of business firms is going to have a downward bias because it does not count all firms. On the other hand, Survey Sampling counts the number of business firms by adding up the number of businesses listed in the Yellow Pages.

> ■ If two or more sources of secondary data differ, you should investigate why they differ. Did they measure the same entity? Did they use different methods to collect their data?

This brings up the question "What is a business firm?" One franchise organization may run the McDonald's in a city, yet the Yellow Pages lists nine locations. Is this one business or nine? Survey Sampling would list this as nine separate businesses. Therefore, Survey Sampling's estimates of the number of businesses has an upward bias. Which data source should be used? It would depend on the purpose of your study and how the information would be used. Either source of information may be appropriate for use as long as the user understands exactly what the information represented. The key point is that you must adequately evaluate the various data sources so that you are in a position to select the information that will give you the most valid and reliable results.

A final word about evaluating information sources is that you may be able to get some help in terms of evaluations by others. For example, books are often reviewed and those reviews are published. Also, many journals contain articles that are reviewed by editorial board members to assess their quality before publication. Also, journals typically do not accept advertising and, consequently, may be more objective in printing information that may not be favorable to other interests. However, it is far more difficult to evaluate other sources of secondary data such as magazine articles, Web sites, or special reports.

## LOCATING SECONDARY DATA SOURCES

How does one go about the actual task of locating secondary data sources? We suggest you follow the approach outlined here.[14]

*Step 1 Identify what you wish to know and what you already know about your topic.* This is the most important step in searching for information. Without having a clear understanding of what you are seeking, you will undoubtedly have difficulties. Clearly define your topic: relevant facts, names of researchers or organizations associated with the topic, key papers and other publications with which you are already familiar, and any other information you may have.

*Step 2 Develop a list of key terms and names.* These terms and names will provide access to secondary sources. Unless you already have a very specific topic of interest, keep this initial list long and quite general. Use business dictionaries and handbooks to help develop your list. Be flexible. Every time a new source is consulted, you may have to use a new selection of terms.

In printed sources as well as databases, it is important to use correct terminology to locate the most relevant resources. In many cases, the researcher must think of related terms or synonyms for a topic. For example, one database may use the term *pharmaceutical industry* to describe that industry, whereas another may use the term *drug industry*. In addition, the source may require that a broader term be used. *Pharmaceutical industry* may be listed as part of the *chemical industry*. However, there may be a need to use a narrower term. For example, if one is researching a database on the drug industry, it would be foolish to put in the term *drugs* because almost everything in that database would include that term. Perhaps a specific drug may be a wiser choice.

Many databases have lists of the terms or subject headings they assign to records of information, such as books or articles. These lists are called thesauri, dictionaries, or subject headings lists. In most library catalogs the Library of Congress (LC) Subject Headings are used. These are standard (sometimes called controlled) terms that are consistently used to describe a particular subject. For example, the term *real property* is standard in the LC Subject Headings instead of the term *real estate*. Using a standard subject heading should result in a more efficient search. Marketing Research Application 5.4 shows you how to find a standard subject heading using *ABI Inform*.

## MARKETING RESEARCH APPLICATION 5.4

PRACTICAL

APPLICATIONS

### Finding a Standard Subject Heading: A Way to Improve Your Information Searching Skills

How many times have you used an online information service database only to end up frustrated that you could not find what you really needed? Problems of two types occur. First, you get thousands of "hits," which requires that you read through huge amounts of information still searching for what you wanted to find in the first place. Second, you get information that has your key search terms contained within the article but the articles do not have anything to do with what you really want. Sound familiar? You need to learn an important skill in searching online information databases: finding the standard subject heading.

Imagine that you had several persons who were well trained in evaluating and interpreting the contents of information sources such as books, manuals, special reports, magazine articles, journal articles, and so on. Next, imagine if you had these well-trained persons to look through everything that has been published and to place all the books, articles, reports, and so on that pertained to your topic in one stack. So, you now have all publications on your topic in one category and now imagine that this information is all scanned into an electronic database that you can now search using any one or a combination of search strategies. Wow! Think this would improve your information search skills? The good news is that this has already been done for you. You just need to learn how to take advantage of what we shall call standard subject headings.

Databases have a field called the subject field. When a new piece of information arrives, be it a book, journal article, or whatever, that information is evaluated to determine its subject matter. For example, let's say that an article is entitled "Miami Blues." The title can be very misleading. In fact, if someone were doing a search about blues music, this article would appear in a results list (along with thousands of other nonrelevant information sources). But why is it misleading? Because the subject of the article is really about *real estate* in Miami. If you were interested in finding information about real estate, chances are you would not find this book using key terms in the title field of your database search engine. But, because those "people who are working for you" have looked over this article and correctly placed it in the category of real estate, we are going to find it. So, **standard subject headings** are specific words or phrases that are used to properly categorize the subject matter of records as they are entered into databases. Let's see how you would do it using *ABI Inform*, an index to business journals.

In *ABI Inform*, there is a list of standard subject headings that one can locate by using the advanced search screen and selecting "browse lists" and then "subjects." In the following example, we submit the words *real estate*. If that term is listed, then it can be used in a search by subject field.

In the next example, the searcher is using the term *real estate* as a subject term (not as a keyword in any field) to make sure the emphasis of the articles retrieved is on real estate. The searcher combines it with the word *Florida* (as a keyword in any field) to further narrow the search. Please notice that the searcher got to this screen by selecting "search methods" at the top of the screen and then "guided screen."

Finally, the search retrieves the results as indicated in the following example. Notice that item 3 entitled "Miami Blues" is a title that would not have been recognizable as an article about real estate. Also notice that the presence of the camera image before the item means that the full-text article is available online.

Although this is just one database from several hundred, a good researcher learns to look for lists of *standard subject headings* whether they are called thesaurus terms, subject headings, terms, and so on. It is also important to check all guide screens and instructions that are made available by each database. Notice that in the preceding example the instructions are listed under the tab marked "Search Guide." Happy searching!

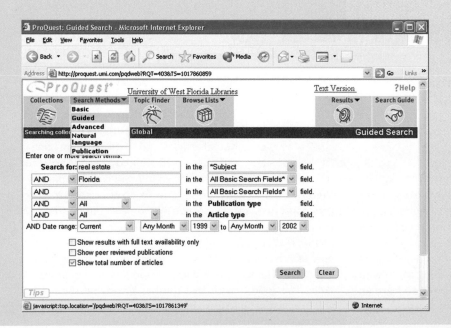

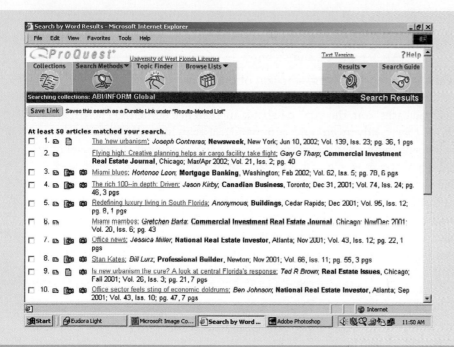

Keyword searching is usually available for searching a database, but using a keyword often retrieves too many false results. A keyword search means that the computer will retrieve a record that has that word anywhere in the record. For example, if someone is searching for the word *banks*, it could be the name of a person, a business, type of bank, a bank of dirt (hill), or any other use of that word. To avoid false results, the searcher may simply want to search one field in the record, as described later in "Field Searching." Keywords may also be used to lead one to better terms to use. If one retrieves a long list of sources, it is wise to select an item that is relevant and examine its record to identify the standard subject heading assigned to that item. Submitting that subject heading should retrieve a much more relevant list of sources (see Marketing Research Application 5.4).

*Step 3 Begin your search using several of the library sources such as those listed in Table 5.2.* If you need help in selecting the appropriate sources or databases, refer to Table 5.1 and review the functions of different types of publications.

## Search Strategies Used for Searching Online Information Databases

To better understand how to search online databases, the researcher should understand how databases are organized. A common vendor, also known as an aggregator or databank, may provide many databases. For example, the vendor Proquest provides *ABI Inform* and the *Wall Street Journal*. An actual hierarchy exists in the organization of these databases. For example:

> We pause at step 3 to discuss search strategies in more depth.

Top level = Databank (sometimes called "aggregator"), e.g., Proquest

Second level = Databases, e.g., *ABI Inform*

Third level = Records, that is, the units describing each item in the database

Fourth level = Fields, that is, parts of the record, such as author, title, NAICS number, and so on

Fifth level = Words or numbers—the text of the fields

Usually all databases from the same databank are searched similarly. There may be several methods (basic, advanced, and command) of searching databases. A basic search is usually sufficient when searching for books in a catalog or when searching small databases; however, it is often advisable to use the advanced mode when searching for journal articles or complex ideas, so that search refinements can be employed.

Most databanks employ the same search features, but other databanks may use different symbols or interfaces to retrieve results. An interface is the "look and feel" of the database that actually helps the searcher know how to submit a search. Each database has a help screen, and these are always useful. The following examples of the search techniques are those for a typical library catalog, but each databank, such as First Search, Factiva, and others, may use different searching symbols to accomplish the same results.

## Boolean Logic

**Boolean logic** allows the establishment of relationships between words and terms in most databases. Typical words used as operators in Boolean logic are AND, OR, and NOT. The following examples illustrate the use of Boolean logic:

| Operator | Requirements | Examples |
|----------|--------------|----------|
| AND | Both terms are retrieved | chemical AND industry<br>Exxon AND financial |
| OR | Either term is retrieved | drug OR pharmaceutical<br>outlook OR forecast |
| NOT | Eliminates records containing the term | Cherokee NOT jeeps<br>drugs NOT alcohol |

## Field Searching

**Field searching** refers to searching records in a database by one or more of its fields. Databases are collections of records, which consist of fields designated to describe certain parts of the record. Searching "by field" may make a search more efficient.

For example, if a title is known, a search of the title field should find the desired record. Terms entered as "subjects" may be restricted to specific subject headings (e.g., Library of Congress Subject Headings in most library catalogs), depending on the database. Most databases also allow the use of keyword searching, which searches every word in a record.

Most electronic databases employ the same search strategies for searching databases, but they often vary in the keystrokes designated to perform the search.

For example, on the Internet, the keyword *"real estate"* should be submitted with quotes surrounding the phrase so that the exact sequence of words will be searched; however, to get the same keyword phrase in some library catalogs, one would submit *real ADJ estate*.

## Proximity Operators

The preceding *"real estate"* example demonstrates one of the proximity operators that are available to enhance keyword searching. **Proximity operators** allow the searcher to indicate how close and in which order two or more words are to be positioned within the record. Examples of proximity operators are:

| Operator | Requirements | Examples |
|----------|--------------|----------|
| ADJ | Adjoining words in order | Electronic ADJ commerce |
| NEAR | Adjoining words in any order | Bill NEAR Gates |
| SAME | Both terms are located in the field of the record | Microsoft SAME legal |

## Truncation

Another feature of database searching is **truncation**, which allows the root of the word to be submitted, retrieving all words beginning with that root. The term *forecast?* would retrieve *forecasting, forecasts, forecaster*, and so on. The question mark is the truncation symbol for some databases, but other databases may use an asterisk, a plus sign, a dollar sign, or other symbols. In some cases truncation symbols may not be useful. For example, if one wanted *cat* in singular or plural, submitting *cat?* would retrieve *cat, cats, catch, catastrophe*, and so on. Using the search *cat OR cats* would be preferred.

## Nesting

It is essential that the computer translate the search statement correctly. **Nesting** is a technique that indicates the order in which a search is to be done. For example, if one wishes to search for microcomputers or personal computers in Florida, one would submit *Florida AND (microcomputer? OR personal ADJ computer?)*, indicating that *Florida* should be combined with either term. The parenthesis nests the two terms as one. Without the parentheses, *Florida* would be combined with *microcomputer*, but every instance of the words *personal computer* would be added to the results. In search engines, there are text boxes that serve much like parentheses to aid in keeping similar terms together.

## Limiting

**Limiting** allows for restricting searches to only those database records that meet specified criteria. For example, searches may be limited to a search of records containing a specific language, location, format, or date. These limitations are usually available on the advanced search screen of databases. When searching for current materials, the date limitation is most important to retrieve the correct results.

■ Now, we return to our steps in locating secondary data sources with step 4.

*Step 4  Compile the literature you have found and evaluate your findings.* Is it relevant to your needs? Perhaps you are overwhelmed by information. Perhaps you have found little that is relevant. Rework your list of keywords and authors. If you have had little success or your topic is highly specialized, consult specialized directories, encyclopedias, and so on, such as the ones listed in this chapter. Again, the librarian may be able to recommend the most appropriate source for your needs.

*Step 5  If you are unhappy with what you have found or are otherwise having trouble and the reference librarian has not been able to identify sources, use an authority.* Identify some individual or organization that might know something about the topic. Such publications as *Who's Who in Finance and Industry*, *Consultants and Consulting Organizations Directory*, *Encyclopedia of Associations*, *Industrial Research Laboratories in the United States*, and *Research Centers Directory* may help you identify people or organizations that specialize in your topic. Do not forget university faculty, government officials, and business executives. Such individuals are often delighted to be of help.

There are several keys to a successful search. First, be well informed about the search process. Reading this chapter is a good place to start. Second, you must be devoted to the search. Don't expect information to fall into your lap; be committed to finding the information. Finally, there is no substitute for a good, professional librarian. Do not be afraid to ask for advice.

*Step 6  Report results.* Locating data may be successful, but if the information is not properly transmitted to the reader, the research is worthless. It is important to outline the paper or report, correctly compose it, and accurately reference the sources that were used. See Chapter 15 for instructions on how to properly write a research report.

## KEY SOURCES OF SECONDARY DATA FOR MARKETERS

We hope you understand by now that there are thousands of sources of secondary data that may be relevant to business decisions. In Table 5.2 we provide you with some of these major sources that are useful in marketing research. However, there are a few sources that are so important that they deserve special attention. In the next few paragraphs, we give you additional information about Census 2000 and other government publications, the North American Industrial Classification System (NAICS), which is replacing the Standard Industrial Classification (SIC) system, the "Survey of Buying Power," *Demographics USA*, and *The Lifestyle Market Analyst*.

### Census 2000: Census of the Population

The United States Decennial Census, the **Census of the Population**, is considered the "granddaddy" of all market information. Even though the census is conducted only once every 10 years, census data serve as a baseline for much marketing information

**Table 5.2**

Secondary Information
Sources on Marketing

## I. Reference Guides
### Encyclopedia of Business Information Sources
Detroit: Gale Group, Annual. For the researcher, this lists marketing associations, advertising agencies, research centers, agencies, and sources relating to various business topics. It is particularly useful for identifying information about specific industries.

## II. Indexes
### ABI Inform
Ann Arbor, MI: Proquest, 1982. Available online, this database indexes and abstracts major journals relating to a broad range of business topics. Electronic access to many full-text articles is also available.

### Business File ASAP
Detroit: Gale Group, 1982. Available online and on CD-ROM. This index covers primarily business and popular journals and includes some full-text articles.

### Wilson Business Full Text
New York: H. W. Wilson, Co., 1982. Available online. This basic index is useful for indexing the major business journals further back in time than other indexes.

### Business Source Premier
Birmingham: Ebsco, 1965–. Business Source Premier provides full text back to 1965, and searchable cited references back as far as 1998. Business Source Premier offers full text coverage in all disciplines of business, including marketing, management, MIS, POM, accounting, finance, and economics. Additional full-text, nonjournal content includes market research reports, industry reports, country reports, company profiles, and SWOT analyses.

### IBISWorld Industry Market Research
http://www.ibisworld.com/. IBISWorld is America's largest collection of Industry Market Research Reports, analyzing more than 97% of the U.S. economy. There are over 700 reports, published at the five-digit NAICS code level. Each IBISWorld report is 25–30 pages long and updated up to four times a year, depending on the popularity of the industry, by a team of industry specialists and economists to ensure they include the freshest data and reflect the current state of an industry. The IBISWorld Industry Reports are a gold mine of information about industries at a very detailed level. One of the valuable features is the linkage among industries that show how each industry is related to others "upstream" and "downstream."

### Gale's Ready Reference Shelf
Gale's Ready Reference Shelf provides integrated access to 355,000 entries culled from the databases of 14 of Gale's most popular reference directories:

*Directories in Print*
*Directory of Special Libraries and Information Centers*
*Encyclopedia of American Religions*
*Encyclopedia of Associations: National Organizations of the U.S.*
*Encyclopedia of Associations: International Organizations*
*Encyclopedia of Associations: Regional, State, and Local Organizations*
*Encyclopedia of Governmental Advisory Organizations*
*Gale Directory of Databases*

**Table 5.2**
*(Continued)*

*Gale Directory of Publications and Broadcast Media*
*Newsletters in Print*
*Publishers Directory*
*Research Centers Directory*
*International Research Centers Directory*
*Government Research Centers Directory*

### III. Dictionaries and Encyclopedias
***Dictionary of Marketing Terms***
Hauppauge, NY: Barron's, 2000. Prepared by Jane Imber and Betsy Ann Toffler, this dictionary includes brief definitions of popular terms in marketing.

***Encyclopedia of Consumer Brands***
Detroit: St. James Press, 1994. For consumable products, personal products, and durable goods, this source provides detailed descriptions of the history and major developments of major brand names.

### IV. Directories
***Bradford's Directory of Marketing Research Agencies and Management Consultants in the United States and the World***
Middleberg, VA: Bradford's, Biennial. Indexed by type of service, this source gives scope of activity for each agency and lists names of officers.

***Broadcasting and Cable Yearbook***
New Providence, NJ: R. R. Bowker, Annual. A directory of U.S. and Canadian television and radio stations, advertising agencies, and other useful information.

***Directories in Print***
Detroit: Gale Research, Annual. Provides detailed information on business and industrial directories, professional and scientific rosters, online directory of databases, and other lists. This source is particularly useful for identifying directories associated with specific industries or products.
Also available online in Gale's *Ready Reference Shelf.*

***Gale Directory of Publications and Broadcast Media***
Detroit: Gale Research, Annual. A geographic listing of U.S. and Canadian newspapers, magazines, and trade publications, as well as broadcasting stations. Includes address, edition, frequency, circulation, and subscription and advertising rates.
Also available online in Gale's *Ready Reference Shelf.*

### V. Statistical Sources
***Datapedia of the United States, 2004***
Lanham, MD: Bernan Press, 2004. Based on the *Historical Statistics of the United States from Colonial Times* and other statistical sources, this volume presents hundreds of tables reflecting historical and, in some cases, forecasting data on numerous demographic variables relating to the United States.

***Demographics USA—***
Trade Dimensions International, Inc.: Annual. A compilation of data which includes statistics on population, income, retail sales, effective buying income, etc., for counties, cities, zip codes and Core-based Statistical Areas. (This source is discussed at length later in this chapter.)

*Editor and Publisher Market Guide*
New York: Editor and Publisher, Annual. Provides market data for more than 1,500 U.S. and
Canadian newspaper cities covering facts and figures about location, transaction, population,
households, banks, autos, etc.

*Market Share Reporter*
Detroit: Gale Research, Annual. Provides market share data on products and service industries
in the United States. Also available online in Gale's *Business and Company Resource Center.*

*Standard Rate and Data Service*
Des Plaines, IL: SRDS, Monthly. In the SRDS monthly publications (those for consumer
magazine and agrimedia, newspapers, spot radio, spot television) marketing statistics are
included at the beginning of each state section.

that is provided in the "in-between" years. Firms providing secondary data commercially, such as ESRI and the "Survey of Buying Power," make adjustments each year to report current information. Besides market data, census data are used to make governmental decisions in areas such as highway construction, health care services, educational needs, and, of course, redistricting.

The taking of a census of the U.S. population began in 1790. Prior to 1940, everyone had to answer all the questions that the census used. In 1940, the long form—a longer questionnaire that goes out to only a sample of respondents—was introduced as a way to collect more data, more rapidly, and without increasing respondent burden. In Census 2000, the long form went to one in six housing units. As a result, much of the census data are based on statistical sampling. A great deal of effort went into promoting Census 2000 to the citizenry of the United States due to growing concerns over privacy and declining participation rates in the census since 1970.[15] You can view census data online at **www.census.gov**.

■ The United States Decennial Census is considered the "granddaddy" of all market information. Even though the census is conducted only once every 10 years, census data serve as a baseline for much marketing information that is provided in the "in-between" years.

■ The census is composed of a short form, which every household received, and a long form, which was sent to one in six households. You can see both forms at www.census.gov.

## Other Government Publications

The U.S. government publishes a huge volume of secondary data. Most of these publications are produced in the U.S. Government Printing Office (GPO). You can visit its Web site at **www.gpoaccess.gov/index.html**. The *Statistical Abstract of the United States* is a convenient source of statistical secondary data, and it is now available to you online at **www.census.gov/statab/www**.

## North American Industry Classification System (NAICS)

The **North American Industry Classification System (NAICS)** is pronounced "nakes" and is not actually a source in and of itself. By this, we mean that NAICS is not information per se; rather, it is a coding system that can be used to access information. All marketing research students should be familiar with it because it will be used by so many secondary data sources. NAICS is replacing the **Standard Industrial Classification (SIC) system**. (We discuss both here because data based on the SIC will be around for several years.) The SIC was created in the mid-1930s when the government required all agencies gathering economic and industrial data to use the same system for classifying businesses. The SIC was a system that classified establishments by the type of activity in which they were engaged. Codes, describing a type of business activity, were used to collect, tabulate, summarize, and publish data. Each industry was assigned a code number and all firms within that particular industry reported all activities (sales, employment, etc.) by this assigned code. The SIC divides all establishments into 11 divisions. Divisions are then subdivided into a second level of classification, "major groups." Major groups are numbered consecutively 01 through 99. Division A, for example, contains major groups 01 through 09. A major group within Division A is agricultural production—crops; this is major group 01. Division B contains major groups 10 through 14: 10 is metal mining, 11 is coal mining, and so on. Each major group is further divided into two other categories, which provide greater specificity of classification.[16]

■ Visit the NAICS site, which allows you to convert SIC codes to NAICS codes, at www.census.gov/epcd/www/naics.html.

■ The SIC is being replaced by NAICS as a result of the North American Free Trade Agreement (NAFTA).

The SIC is being replaced by NAICS as a result of the North American Free Trade Agreement (NAFTA). The system will allow reports conducted by the Mexican, Canadian, and U.S. governments to share a common language for easier comparisons of international trade, industrial production, labor costs, and other statistics. NAICS will have improvements over the SIC and yet will allow for comparative analyses with past SIC-based data. In fact, Dun & Bradstreet is marketing software that provides a crossover from SIC codes to NAICS codes.[17] NAICS will classify businesses based on similar production processes; special attention is being given to classifying emerging industries such as services and high technology, and more classifications will be assigned to certain industry groups such as restaurants. Under the SIC, all restaurants—beaneries, caterers, hamburger stands, and five-star restaurants—fall under the same category: Eating and Drinking Places. NAICS will break this down into several categories, which will be more useful to researchers.[18]

■ NAICS groups the economy into 20 broad sectors as opposed to the 11 SIC divisions.

NAICS groups the economy into 20 broad sectors as opposed to the 11 SIC divisions. Many of these new sectors reflect recognizable parts of the SIC, such as the Utilities and Transportation section broken out from the SIC Transportation, Communications, and Utilities division. Because the service sector of the economy has grown so much in recent years, the SIC division for Services Industries has been broken into several new sectors, including Professional, Scientific, and Technical Services; Management, Support, Waste Management, and Remediation Services; Education Services; Health and Social Assistance; Arts, Entertainment, and Recreation; and Other Services except Public Administration. Other new NAICS sectors are composed of combinations of pieces from more than one SIC division. For example, the new information sector is composed of components from Transportation, Communications, and Utilities (broadcasting and telecommunications); Manufacturing (publishing); and Services Industries (software publishing, data processing, information services, and motion pictures and sound recording).

■ The NAICS uses a six-digit classification code instead of the old SIC four-digit code.

The NAICS uses a six-digit classification code instead of the old SIC four-digit code. The additional two digits allow for far greater specificity in identifying special types of firms. However, the six-digit code is not being used by all three NAFTA countries. The three countries agreed on a standard system using the first five digits, and the sixth digit is being used by each country in a manner allowing for special user needs in each country. Note that the NAICS code doesn't tell you anything per se. However, knowing a NAICS number that represents a type of business will allow you to find all kinds of secondary information about the firms in that business.

■ Knowing a NAICS number that represents a type of business will allow you to find all kinds of secondary information about the firms in that business.

## "Survey of Buying Power"

The "Survey of Buying Power" (SBP) has been published annually for several decades in *Sales & Marketing Management Magazine*. However, due to acquisition, it appears that the SBP will no longer be published. Instead, the information contained in the SBP will be included in *Demographics USA*. Since this information is very useful, we provide a complete discussion of this secondary information in the following paragraphs. *Demographics USA* contains data for the United States on population, income, and retail sales for food, eating and drinking places, appliances, and automotives. These data are broken up into metropolitan (MSA), county, and city levels, and media market levels. Five-year projections are also provided. Because the data for the survey are extrapolated from census data, the data are current with each year's publication. In addition to the general data, the survey also reports the **effective buying income (EBI)** and the **buying power index (BPI)**.

■ Data formerly published as the "Survey of Buying Power" in *Sales & Marketing Management* magazine is now published in *Demographics USA*.

*EBI* is defined as disposable personal income. It is equal to gross income less taxes and, therefore, reflects the effective amount of income available for expenditure on goods and services. This is important because taxes differ widely depending on geographic location. *BPI* is an indicator of the relative market potential of a geographic area. It is based on the factors that make up a market: people, ability to buy, and willingness to buy. The BPI is an index number that represents a market's percentage of the total buying power in the United States.

■ BPI is an indicator of the relative market potential of a geographic area. The BPI is an index number that represents a market's percentage of the total buying power in the United States.

### How to Calculate the Buying Power Index (BPI)

The BPI is one of the main reasons that managers and researchers find the "Survey of Buying Power" so useful. With all the demographic information available to marketers, the BPI is useful because it takes the three factors making up a market (people, ability to buy, and willingness to buy) and calculates those factors into a quantitative index that represents the buying power of a market. We provide you the formula and illustrate how to calculate the BPI as follows:

$$BPI = (\text{Population of Market Area A/Total U.S. Population}) \times 2$$
$$+ (\text{EBI of Market Area A/Total U.S. EBI}) \times 5$$
$$+ (\text{Retail Sales of Market Area A/Total U.S. Retail Sales}) \times 3$$

The market areas that can be selected are regions, states, counties, MSAs, cities, or DMAs (Designated Market Areas represent television markets). Population is used to represent the market factor *people*. EBI is used to represent the market factor *ability to buy*. However, since *willingness to buy*, the third market factor, is a mental construct representing something consumers are going to do in the future, the "Survey of Buying Power" (SBP) uses a surrogate indicator of what consumers will buy. The surrogate is past retail sales, which is used because what people bought yesterday is a good indicator of what they will buy today. The foregoing formula gives you the BPI, which, as we've said, is an index number. For example, the BPI for a large market, such as Chicago or Los Angeles, may be around 3.3333.

This means that 3.3333% of the nation's total buying power is within that market. Casper, Wyoming, may have a BPI around 0.026. This means that Casper has 0.026% of the nation's buying power.

**Advantages of the "Survey of Buying Power."** First, a major advantage of the SBP is that it provides demographic data that is updated each year. Second, it also provides five-year projections each year. Third, by calculation of the index numbers making up the BPI, the SBP quantifies markets. Like all index numbers, the BPI is useful when used to evaluate a market over a time period. This could be achieved by plotting the BPI for a market over a five-year period. In this way, a manager or researcher would have an indication as to the trend in buying power for that market area. A second useful way to use the BPI is to compare one market with other markets. The BPI represents a quantifiable measure of markets' buying power and, therefore, is an objective measure that is useful for comparing markets. Specific uses of the BPI include selection of new markets, dividing markets into sales territories having equal buying power, and allocating media expenditure based on the potential buying power in a market. A fourth advantage of the SBP is that it is inexpensive and easy to access.

**Disadvantages of the SBP.** There are two weaknesses of using data reported in the "Survey of Buying Power." As we mentioned earlier, one disadvantage of using secondary data is that the data are not classified in categories useful to the user. The example we gave was that data for EBI is reported in the SBP in only three categories, the last being $50,000 and over. However, limited categories of data formerly reported in the SBP are overcome by using *Demographics USA*. A second disadvantage of the SBP lies in the logic of the calculation of the BPI. The BPI is a general index in that it uses the entire population, all levels of EBI, and total retail sales in a market area. However, for some products, a general BPI may not be an accurate predictor of buying power. Again, this former limitation is now addressed by other indexes provided in *Demographics USA*.

## Demographics USA

As we have already noted, another useful source of secondary data is found in the publication **Demographics USA**.[19] *Demographics USA* not only provides much more detailed information but it also overcomes some of the disadvantages of the former SBP. First, as we noted earlier, the SBP has a limited number of categories by which it reports data. *Demographics USA* expands these categories. For example, it reports EBI in seven categories, with the highest category being "$150,000 and above." Instead of providing only the general BPI, *Demographics USA* offers other market indexes, such as **total business BPI**, **high-tech BPI**, **manufacturing BPI**, **BPI for economy-priced products**, **BPI for moderate-priced products**, **BPI for premium-priced products**, **BPI for business-to-business markets**, and **BPI for high-tech markets**.

Even with these additional choices of market indexes, some firms may want to calculate their own customized BPI. A **customized BPI** is an index that uses market factors selected for their relevancy to a particular product or service in terms of how they best represent the buying power for that particular product or service. As an example, let's suppose you were making a decision to locate new dealerships for

Major advantages of the SBP are that it provides demographic data that is updated each year and provides five-year projections and the BPI, which quantifies markets.

Former disadvantages of the SBP are now partially remedied by *Demographic USA*.

*Demographics USA* provides much detailed information and it also overcomes some of the disadvantages of the former SBP.

Instead of providing only the general BPI, *Demographics USA* offers other market indexes.

a new luxury automobile. Which markets represent the highest buying power for a luxury automobile? You might be predisposed to using the premium-priced-products index from *Demographics USA,* but let's say you want an even better indicator of buying power for your very expensive new luxury car. A customized BPI may consist of (1) households with incomes of $75,000 or more, (2) automobile sales, and (3) households with householder 35 to 64 years old. Of course, you would now have the problem of actually calculating your customized BPI for each market you want to consider. Another advantage of *Demographics USA* is the specificity of the geographic detail of the reporting units. In addition to providing the standard reporting units (MSAs, DMAs, etc.), *Demographics USA* also provides data by zip code and information about the business market, such as the number of establishments within nine business categories (e.g., agriculture, manufacturing, retailing, and services).

■ A customized BPI is an index that uses market factors selected for their relevancy to a particular product or service in terms of how they best represent the buying power for that particular product or service.

### The Lifestyle Market Analyst

A unique source of secondary data is **The Lifestyle Market Analyst**. This printed source of information analyzes several dozen lifestyle categories such as Avid Book Readers, Own a Cat, Take Cruise Ship Vacations, Golf, Own a Camcorder, Have Grandchildren, Shop by Catalog/Mail, Stock/Bond Investments, Improving Health, and Donate to Charitable Causes. Information is organized into sections that have different objectives. First, you can examine markets (defined as DMAs). Not only will you get some standard demographic data for the DMA, but you will also be able to determine the dominant (and least dominant) lifestyles in that market. This information helps "paint a personality portrait" of a market for users who otherwise see only a sea of numbers describing markets. Another section of the book focuses on each lifestyle. There you will find the demographic profile of the participants in that lifestyle category as well as other information. For example, to understand the lifestyle of a bicycling enthusiast, one may answer the following questions:

■ What are the demographics of bicyclists?
■ In what other activities are bikers involved?
■ Which markets have the heaviest concentration of bikers?
■ Which magazines do bikers read?

■ *The Lifestyle Market Analyst* is a printed source of information that analyzes several dozen lifestyle categories such as Avid Book Readers, Own a Cat, Take Cruise Ship Vacations, and Golf.

As another example, a *Lifestyle Market Analyst* profile of boating/sailing enthusiasts reveals that they also enjoy scuba diving, snow skiing, recreational vehicles, vacation property, and fishing, but they have little interest in devotional reading or needlework. Obviously this type of consumer is an appropriate target for outdoor equipment sales.

## SUMMARY

Data may be grouped into two categories: primary and secondary. Primary data are gathered specifically for the research project at hand. Secondary data are data that have been previously gathered for some other purpose. There are many uses of secondary data in marketing research, and sometimes secondary data are all that is needed to achieve the research objectives. Secondary data may be internal, meaning they are data already gathered *within* the firm for some other purpose. Data collected and stored from sales receipts, such as types, quantities, and prices of goods or services purchased; customer names; delivery addresses; shipping dates; salesperson making the sale; and so on, would be an example of internal secondary data. Storing internal data in electronic databases has become increasingly popular and may be used for database marketing. Databases are composed of records, which contain subcomponents of information called fields. Companies use information recorded in internal databases for purposes of direct marketing and to strengthen relationships with customers. The latter is a process known as CRM, customer relationship management. External secondary data are data obtained from sources outside the firm. These data may be classified as (1) published, (2) syndicated services data, and (3) databases. There are different types of published secondary data, such as reference guides, indexes and abstracts, bibliographies, almanacs, manuals and handbooks, and so on. Different types of secondary data have different functions, and understanding the different functions is useful in researching secondary data. Syndicated services data are provided by firms that collect data in a standard format and make them available to subscribing firms. An example would be Nielsen Media Research's Television Rating Index. Online information databases are sources of secondary data searchable by search engines online. When several databases are offered under one search engine, the service is called either an aggregator or a data bank. Examples include LexisNexis and Proquest.

Secondary data have the advantages of being quickly gathered, being readily available, being relatively inexpensive, adding helpful insights should primary data be needed, and sometimes being all that is needed to achieve the research objective. Disadvantages are that the data are often reported in incompatible reporting units (county data are reported when zip code data are needed), measurement units do not match researchers' needs (household income is reported and per capita income is needed), class definitions are incompatible with the researchers' needs (income is reported in classes up to $50K but the researchers need to know what percent of the population earns $75K or more), and secondary data may be outdated. Evaluation of secondary data is important; researchers must ask certain questions in order to ensure the integrity of the information they use: What was the true purpose of the study? Who collected the information? What information was collected? How was the information obtained? Is the information compatible with other information?

Finding secondary data involves understanding what you need to know and understanding key terms and names associated with the subject. Indexes and bibliographies may first be consulted; they list sources of secondary information by subject. Consult the sources and evaluate the information. Make use of computerized data searches from databases, if available. A good way to increase your success when searching online information databases is to learn how to find standard subject headings. Seek the services of a reference librarian to help you improve your searching skills.

Using online information databases requires understanding how these databases are organized and the fundamental search strategies used, including Boolean logic, field searching, proximity operators, truncation, nesting, and limiting. Knowing how to find standard subject headings within a database is a key to successful information searching.

Examples of important secondary data for business decisions are the *Census of the Population* from the U.S. Bureau of the Census and the *Statistical Abstract of the United States,* both of which are available online. The North American Industry Classification System (NAICS) is replacing the Standard Industrial Classification (SIC) system as the government's classification system for business. Because NAICS groups businesses into 20 sectors (instead of the 11 used by the SIC) and uses codes of up to six digits to classify businesses (instead of the four-digit code used by the SIC), NAICS offers a classification system that is much better at specifying types of industries. The former "Survey of Buying Power" (SBP) data are now being published in *Demographics USA.* The buying power index (BPI) measures the buying power of various geographical markets in the United States. *Demographics USA* is updated annually. In addition to calculating the BPI, *Demographics USA* provides several other indexes to quantify the buying power of both industrial and retail markets. Firms may also calculate customized BPIs that are specifically formulated to measure the buying power for their specific product or service. *The Lifestyle Market Analyst* is a unique publication in that it provides information on lifestyles. It contains information on several dozen lifestyle categories, such as bicycling enthusiasts, dog owners, snow-skiing enthusiasts, and so on. Demographic profiles of each lifestyle are reported along with what other lifestyle interests (and noninterests) apply.

# KEY TERMS

Primary data (p. 137)
Secondary data (p. 137)
Internal secondary data (p. 139)
Database marketing (p. 139)
Database (p. 139)
Record (p. 139)
Fields (p. 140)
Internal databases (p. 140)
CRM, customer relationship management (p. 140)
Data mining (p. 140)
External secondary data (p. 140)
Published sources (p. 140)
Catalog (p. 143)
Indexes (p. 143)
Syndicated services data (p. 143)
External databases (p. 143)
Online information databases (p. 143)
Standard subject headings (p. 152)
Boolean logic (p. 154)
Field searching (p. 154)
Proximity operators (p. 155)
Truncation (p. 155)

Nesting (p. 155)
Limiting (p. 155)
*Census of the Population* (p. 156)
*Statistical Abstract of the United States* (p. 159)
North American Industry Classification System (NAICS) (p. 159)
Standard Industrial Classification (SIC) system (p. 159)
"Survey of Buying Power" (p. 161)
Effective buying income (EBI) (p. 161)
Buying power index (BPI) (p. 161)
*Demographics USA* (p. 162)
Total business BPI (p. 162)
High-tech BPI (p. 162)
Manufacturing BPI (p. 162)
Economy-, Moderate-, and Premium-priced products BPI (p. 162)
Business-to-business BPI (p. 162)
High-tech markets BPI (p. 162)
Customized BPI (p. 162)
*The Lifestyle Market Analyst* (p. 163)

## REVIEW QUESTIONS

1. Describe how secondary data may add value to primary data.
2. What are secondary data, and how do they differ from primary data?
3. Describe some uses of secondary data.
4. How would you classify secondary data?
5. What is a database and how are databases organized?
6. What is database marketing and what is CRM?
7. What are three types of external secondary data?
8. What is the difference between a library catalog and an index?
9. What are online information databases? Name three of them.
10. What are the five advantages of secondary data? Discuss the disadvantages of secondary data.
11. How would you go about evaluating secondary data? Why is evaluation important?
12. Discuss how you would go about locating secondary data in your own library.
13. What is a standard subject heading? Explain why knowing how to find a standard subject heading would help increase your information searching skills when using online information databases.
14. What is meant by Boolean logic? Proximity operators?
15. Why would searching by field help you efficiently search online information databases?
16. Describe the purposes of the *U.S. Census of the Population*.
17. Briefly identify some sources of secondary data.

## APPLICATION QUESTIONS

18. Go to your library and find a copy of the "Survey of Buying Power." Find the BPI for your county. Explain what this number represents. Discuss why it would be a useful number in evaluating a market.
19. Go online to your favorite search engine (e.g., Ask Jeeves, Google, Yahoo, etc.) and enter "demographics." Go to some of these sites and describe the kind of information you are receiving. Why would this information be considered secondary data?
20. Access the *Statistical Abstract of the United States* online and find information relevant to any topic you are presently studying in your coursework.
21. Select an industry and go to the NAICS Web site identified in this chapter. Find the NAICS number that represents your industry. Discuss how you could use this number.
22. Suppose you were the marketing director for a luxury car manufacturer. Discuss what factors you would consider in building a customized BPI that could be used to evaluate markets for future dealerships.
23. Go to **www.easidemographics.com**. Look for their sample studies and find an example of a ring study. What disadvantage of printed secondary data does this feature overcome?
24. Explain how a marketer of boats could use *The Lifestyle Market Analyst*.

# INTERACTIVE LEARNING

Visit the Nielsen Media Research Web site at **www.nielsenmediaresearch .com** and read about their television ratings service. What do you think was the most watched television program in a recent week? You can find the answers on the Web site. You will likely be surprised!

Visit the Web site at **www.prenhall.com/burnsbush**. For this chapter, work through the Self-Study Quizzes and get instant feedback on whether you need additional studying. On the Web site, you can review the chapter outlines and case information for Chapter 5.

---

## CASE 5.1    ||| Pure-Aqua Systems

Ronny McCall and Lucy Moody were considering a new business of supplying residential homes with bottled water. They knew the public was growing wary of tap water, and they also knew that many consumers were aware that about one-third of the bottled water purchased in stores was actually bottled tap water. They had investigated a new distillation system based upon heating water and collecting the condensation. Such a system has the advantage of producing the cleanest water. Even water taken from sewage water, once heated and recondensed, is perfectly clean. Traditional distillation systems operated at high costs, but McCall and Moody had developed a new system that could distill large quantities of water at costs comparable to other water-filtering systems. The two entrepreneurs scanned secondary information for clues as to how the public opinions were changing in terms of their attitudes toward tap water. The problem with some of the information they found was that the secondary information was reported for markets outside their proposed area of operation, Pensacola, Florida.

Lucy, always searching secondary information sources, found an article in the local newspaper about a new study conducted by the local university in a joint venture with a marketing research firm. The two had worked together to create a panel of consumers that were reportedly representative of the two-county MSA that Lucy and Ronny had targeted as their market. Excited, Lucy told Ronny about the story and, together,

they went to the Web site at **www.uwf.edu/panel**. There they found results of a study conducted in November 2003 that asked a key question important to Lucy and Ronny's bottled-water venture. The question asked the respondents to rate the tap water quality in their home. The two were startled at the results. In one county almost 24% had rated the tap water as either "bad" or "poor." They knew that home-delivered water companies were successful in other markets for which they had discovered secondary data showing that as little as 10% of the population rated the tap water as "bad" or "poor."

McCall and Moody discussed what the survey results meant to them. Was this an indication that there was a need for their service in the Pensacola market area? "Wait a minute," said Ronny. "Before we go ahead and invest our nest egg in this project, how do we know these secondary data are really representative of the population?"

1 How would you evaluate the secondary data referred to in this study (without visiting the Web site)?

2 Go to the Web site (**www.uwf.edu/panel**) and search for information that would help you evaluate the secondary data reported. What can you find to either support or refute the representativeness of the data?

3 Given your answers to questions 1 and 2 above, do you think Ronny McCall and Lucy Moody should continue to investigate their proposed bottled-water venture?

## CASE 5.2 ||| Apple Supermarkets, Inc.

Apple Supermarkets operates 68 supermarkets in 12 states. The location philosophy has always been to cluster stores in larger cities to gain economies of scale through newspaper and TV advertising. All 68 stores are contained within 36 Core-based Statistical Areas. Of the total promotion budget, about 50% goes to newspaper and another 40% goes to televisions. The remaining 10% is normally allocated to local opportunities such as donations to sponsor a community activity (local Little League baseball team or a church bazaar). The newspaper budget had been allocated three months before Tony arrived but it was time to make the allocation to the managers for the TV budget.

Tony Tampary is the new VP of Marketing for Apple Supermarkets. Historically, there was no VP of Marketing. Rather, the VP of Operations allocated funds to the local supermarket managers and let them make their own marketing decisions about where and when to run company ads and spend money on local sponsorship of community events. Tony thought this procedure should continue as he had many other duties and didn't feel these decisions should be made centrally. He felt the managers were in the best position to know the local competition as well as the local media choices, not to mention the best community events to sponsor. However, Tony was concerned about how the promotion budget had been allocated to the stores in the past, because the VP of Operations hadn't put a great deal of thought into the issue. Once he had received the total promotional budget figure from the CFO, he pretty much allocated the same percentage to each store that had been allocated in the past. When Tony analyzed these allocations, he realized there were some notable discrepancies. In some cases, smaller stores were receiving larger promotion budgets than much larger stores. When he asked the Operations VP how this could have happened the reply was, "Well, I started out several years ago giving them whatever they got the previous year. But, each year I would get a call from a few managers saying they wanted more because they wanted to do some special things in the coming year. I never readjusted those budgets. Once they went up I suppose they continued getting a larger share from then on. It seemed to work OK, no one ever

complained, though I guess a few of the managers were pretty insistent on getting more year after year." Tony was afraid the budgets weren't allocated to the stores that had the most potential. Rather, the budgets were allocated based on the "squeaky wheel gets the grease" method. The managers who had learned that they would get money just by asking, kept asking. Other managers, not realizing this, kept operating with the funds they were allocated.

Tony was determined to allocate the promotional budget in a way that would more likely increase the firm's ROI. He knew there wasn't much he could do about the newspaper budgets that had already been allocated, but he wanted to improve the allocation of the TV budget. He had some experience with trying to measure advertising effectiveness and he knew it could be quite complex. For now, he had to make the allocation of the TV budget to the store managers, and he needed to do it within the week, so he really didn't have time for much research. The VP of Operations didn't have much in the way of secondary information that would be useful for marketing decisions. After work, Tony visited one of the local libraries and started looking for some useful tools that would help him make a decision. He talked with the business reference librarian, and she briefed him on the contents of the census but warned him that the data was getting to the point that it was outdated. Tony asked her for a source of current demographic data. "I need something that is applicable to this year." She told him that for many years, the *Survey of Buying Power* had been used by local business managers but the *Survey of Buying Power* was no longer in print as of 2006. Rather, the new owner, The Nielsen Company, now published another publication called *Demographics USA* which contained all the *Survey of Buying Power* information and more. She gave Tony two books. Both were *Demographics USA*, but in one, the reporting units were ZIP codes and in the other, the reporting unit was county. Tony sat down and began to examine the books.

Tony was astounded by all the information available by examining *Demographics USA* even at the ZIP code level. By reading the "Explanation of Terms" section in the beginning of the book he was able to gain an understanding of the secondary information contained in *Demographics USA*. Some of the items included:

a. Retail sales, reported in total and also by several categories, such as motor vehicle and parts dealers; furniture and home furnishing stores; electronics and appliance stores; food and beverage stores which included grocery stores, supermarkets, and other grocery (except convenience stores); gasoline stations; clothing and clothing and accessories; and so on.

b. Number of business establishments

c. Population

d. Blue collar employment

e. The Buying Power Index (BPI)

f. Effective Buying Income (EBI)

g. Households

h. Households with Cars

i. Median Age

j. Percent Change in Population (since the 2000 Census)

k. many other items

Tony was overwhelmed with the available information, but he began to focus on the geographic reporting units available to him in *Demographics USA*. He was looking at the county edition, so all information was available by county as well as by overall United States and region of the country. In addition, data was reported by CBSA (see Marketing Research Application 5.3). He also noticed that data are reported by something called DMAs. DMA stands for "Designated Market Area" and is the formal term for what is normally called a "television market." The name of the DMA is assigned according to the market of origin of the station(s) with the largest share of viewer hour; all counties whose largest viewer share is given to stations in that same market of origin are grouped together under that particular DMA. Since broadcast signals do not conform to county boundaries, the geographical areas of DMAs may cover only a portion of a given county. Essentially information for a DMA reports data for the geographical area covered by the broadcast signal for the market of origin TV stations. (See "Explanation of Terms" in any *Demographics USA* publication.)

The *Buying Power Index* (BPI) appealed to Tony. He could take the total television budget allocated to him by the CFO and allocate it first to each of the 36 CBSAs based on each CBSA's percentage of the total BPI. Once he knew how much he should allocate to each CBSA, allocations to the supermarkets within the CBSA would be easy. He could base the store allocation on past sales and make adjustments if a manager planned special promotions for the coming year. Tony would be able to gather the BPIs for each of Apple's 36 CBSAs within a few minutes. He pulled out his laptop and copied the BPI information, and made a note as to how to order his own copy to help him make allocations for other marketing decisions that would be coming up.

1. Discuss the pros and cons of Tony Tampary's decision to use the BPI to allocate the TV budget to each CBSA.

2. What changes would you suggest Tony make?

## CHAPTER 6

# STANDARDIZED INFORMATION SOURCES

---

## THE FACTS ABOUT LOYALTY PROGRAMS: THE MARITZ POLL

Maritz, one of the world leaders in research, measures public attitudes and opinions and publishes them in the Maritz Poll. Maritz studied U.S. shoppers who had made a purchase within the last 6 months in one of 11 preselected retail categories including apparel, home improvement, electronics, and so on. Firms in these categories, such as The Gap, Lowe's, and Best Buy should certainly be interested in the findings and implications of the Maritz Poll.

*Do Members of Rewards Programs Spend More?*
Maritz defined rewards programs, for the purposes of the poll, as either a store or membership program, or a private or co-labeled credit card, which award customers points, for purchases or other behaviors. They can later redeem these points for various rewards including discounts, gift certificates, merchandise, cash back, or travel. One finding is that people who are members of reward programs do spend more. Maritz notes that it may not be the reward programs that *cause*

- To learn how to distinguish standardized information from other types of information
- To know the differences between syndicated data and standardized services
- To understand the advantages and disadvantages of standardized information
- To see some of the various areas in which standardized information may be applied
- To understand some specific examples of standardized information sources in each of four areas of application
- To know the meaning of *single-source data*

customers to spend more; it could be that those who spend more intentionally join the rewards programs to gain the rewards. Even if rewards programs do not cause more buying, having customers enroll in them gives retailers a great tool because it allows them to mine the data collected from rewards programs to identify and create a dialogue with profitable customers.

*Who Are the Rewards Program Members?*

Maritz found that more women (62%) than men (54%) belong to rewards programs. They found that rewards program members are young. Seventy-one percent of those 25–34 belong to a program. Those who have kids are more likely to belong to a rewards program. Membership varies by region of the country with the highest membership (70%) in the Northeast and the lowest (37%) in the South.

For companies interested in keeping their most loyal studies, Maritz can help them make better decisions. Maritz has a division, Maritz Loyalty Marketing, that specializes in helping companies with these decisions.

*About This Study*

Maritz used a sample size of 2,178 shoppers. The study had a margin of error of $+/-2\%$. The study was published in August, 2006.

*About the Maritz Poll*

The Maritz Poll is conducted with American and European consumers on a variety of topics. The results are free to all those who visit their Web site and the results are often

published in media including the Associated Press, CNN Headline News, *Business Week, Financial Times*, Reuters, and *USA Today*, among many others. You can visit Maritz and the Maritz Poll by going to **www.maritzresearch.com**. Go to Research, then, Maritz Poll.

By permission, Maritz.

The Maritz Poll illustrates the topic of this chapter: standardized information. In this case, the Maritz Poll uses a standardized process that ensures consumer attitudes and opinions are properly measured and represented. Each poll addresses a different topic. The process of collecting the data remains the same though the data generated differ with each poll. As you will learn in this chapter, this is a form of standardized information we call standardized services. In this chapter, we are going to introduce you to the different types of standardized information: syndicated data and standardized services. We begin by defining what we mean by these types of standardized information.

# WHAT IS STANDARDIZED INFORMATION?

**Standardized information** is a type of secondary data in which the data collected and/or the process of collecting the data are standardized for all users. There are two broad classes of standardized information: syndicated data and standardized services.

**Syndicated data** are data that are collected in a standard format and made available to all subscribers. The Nielsen TV ratings, for example, consist of data on TV viewing collected using a standardized method. The resulting data are made available to anyone wishing to purchase the information. **Standardized services** refers to a standardized marketing research *process* that is used to generate information for a particular user. The Maritz Poll is a standardized process that is used to obtain current information from consumers on a variety of topics. This information is used by clients desiring to better understand their customers. We discuss both of these types of information next.

Syndicated data are a form of external, secondary data that are supplied from a common database to subscribers for a service fee. Recall from our discussion of the types of firms in the marketing research industry in Chapter 2 that we call firms providing such data syndicated data service firms. Such information is typically detailed information that is valuable to firms in a given industry and is not available in libraries. Firms supplying syndicated data follow standard research formats that enable them to collect the same standardized data over time. These firms provide subscribers with specialized, routine information needed by a given industry in the form of ready-to-use, standardized marketing data. We mentioned the Nielsen TV ratings earlier. As another example, Arbitron supplies syndicated data on the number and types of listeners to the various radio stations in each radio market. This standardized information helps advertising firms reach their target markets; it also helps radio stations define audience characteristics by providing an objective, independent measure of the size and characteristics of their audiences. With syndicated data both the process of collecting and analyzing the data and the data themselves are standardized. That is, neither is varied for the client.[1] On the other hand, standardized services rarely provide clients with standardized data. Rather, it's the *process* they are marketing. The application of that standardized process may result in different data for each client. For example, a standardized service may be measurement of customer satisfaction. Instead of a user firm trying to "reinvent the wheel" by developing its own process for measuring customer satisfaction, it may elect to use a standardized service for measuring customer satisfaction. This is also true for several other marketing research services such as test marketing, naming new brands, pricing a new product, or using mystery shoppers.

> ■ Standardized information is a type of secondary data in which the data collected and/or the process of collecting the data are standardized for all users. Two broad classes of standardized information are syndicated data and standardized services.

> ■ Syndicated data are data that are collected in a standard format and made available to all subscribers.

> ■ Standardized services refers to a standardized marketing research *process* that is used to generate information for a particular user.

> ■ With syndicated data, the data and the process used to generate the data are standardized across all users. With standardized services, the process of collecting data is standardized across all users.

# ADVANTAGES AND DISADVANTAGES OF STANDARDIZED INFORMATION

## Syndicated Data

One of the key advantages of syndicated data is *shared costs*. Many client firms may subscribe to the information; thus, the cost of the service is greatly reduced to any one subscriber firm. When costs are spread across several subscribers, other advantages

■ Advantages of syndicated data are shared costs, high quality of the data, and speed with which data are collected and made available for decision making.

result. Because syndicated data firms specialize in the collection of standard data and because their viability, in the long run, depends on the validity of the data, the *quality of the data collected is typically very high*. With several companies paying for the service, the syndicating company can go to great lengths to gather a great amount of data as well. Another advantage of syndicated data comes from the routinized systems used to collect and process the data. This means that the *data are normally disseminated very quickly* to subscribers because these syndicated data firms set up standard procedures and methods for collecting the data over and over again on a periodic basis. The more current the data, the greater their usefulness.

Although there are several advantages to syndicated data, there are some disadvantages. First, *buyers have little control over what information is collected*. Since the research is not custom research for the buyer firm, the buyer firm must be satisfied that the information received is the information needed. Are the units of measurement correct? Are the geographical reporting units appropriate? A second disadvantage is that *buyer firms often must commit to long-term contracts* when buying standardized data. Finally, there is *no strategic information advantage in purchasing syndicated data* because all competitors have access to the same information. However, in many industries, firms would suffer a serious strategic disadvantage by not purchasing the information.

■ Disadvantages of syndicated data are that there is little control over what data are collected, buyers must commit to long-term contracts, and competitors have access to the same information.

## Standardized Services

The key advantage of using a standardized service is taking advantage of the *experience of the research firm offering the service*. Often a buyer firm may have a research department with many experienced persons but no experience in a particular process that is now needed. Imagine a firm setting out to conduct a test market for the very first time. It would take the firm several months to gain the confidence needed to conduct the test market properly. Still, lessons would be learned by trial and error. Taking advantage of others' experiences with the process is a good way to minimize potential mistakes in carrying out the research process. A second advantage is the *reduced cost* of the research. Because the supplier firm conducts the service for many clients on a regular basis, the procedure is efficient and far less costly than if the buyer firm tried to conduct the service itself. A third advantage is the *speed* of the research service. The efficiency gained by conducting the service over and over translates into reduced turnaround time from start to finish of a research project. The speed at which the service is conducted by standardized services firms is usually much faster than if the buyer firm were to conduct the service on its own.

■ Advantages of standardized services are using the experience of the firm offering the service, reduced cost, and increased speed of conducting the service.

There are disadvantages of using standardized services as well. Standardized means not customized. *The ability to customize some projects is lost* when using a standardized service. Although some services offer limited customization, the ability to design a research project to fit a particular client's needs is usually sacrificed when using a standardized service. Second, *the company providing the standardized service may not know the idiosyncrasies of a particular industry*, and therefore, there is a greater burden on the client to ensure that the standardized service fits the intended situation. Client firms need to be very familiar with the service provided, including what data are collected on which population, how the data are collected, and how the data are reported, before they purchase the service.

■ Disadvantages of standardized services are the inability to customize services and the service firm's lack of knowledge about the client's industry.

# APPLICATION AREAS OF STANDARDIZED INFORMATION

Although there are many forms of standardized information that may have multiple applications, we will illustrate four major application areas in the remainder of the chapter. We will explore the use of standardized information applied to measuring consumer attitudes and opinion polls, defining market segments, conducting market tracking, and monitoring media usage and promotion effectiveness.

## Measuring Consumer Attitudes and Opinion Polls

Several firms offer measurements of consumer attitudes and opinions on various issues. The **Yankelovich Monitor**, started in 1971, measures changing social values and how these changes affect consumers. It has specialized in generational marketing and studied "matures" (seniors), baby boomers, and Generation Xers.[2] The data are syndicated, meaning they are available to anyone who wishes to purchase the data, and the information can be used for a variety of marketing management decisions. Data are collected annually through 90-minute in-home interviews and a one-hour questionnaire among 2,500 men and women aged 16 and over using a nationally representative sample.[3] The Yankelovich Monitor is available to report trends in many areas, such as energy, health foods, youth, and multicultural marketing. Of course, we already introduced you to another standardized service available at no charge to those who go to the Web site. The **Maritz Poll** has been conducted on a variety of topics including automobiles, hospitality, entertainment/leisure, pets, food/restaurants, and shopping to name a few.[4]

The **Harris poll** measures consumer attitudes and opinions on a wide variety of topics. Owned by Harris Interactive, the Harris poll started in 1963 and is one of the longest-running, most-respected surveys of consumer opinion. Harris polls are conducted on topics such as the economy, environment, politics, world affairs, legal issues, and so on. You can see some examples of recent Harris polls by going to **www.HarrisInteractive.com** and following the menu for the Harris Poll Library. The Harris poll uses a sample of 1,000 representative adults aged 18 and older. Polls are taken weekly and, because many of the same questions are asked over and over, the Harris poll can help clients identify trend lines. Since these data are standardized information, we use it as another example of syndicated data. However, client firms may have Harris Interactive conduct customized surveys.[5]

The **Gallup poll** surveys public opinion, asking questions on domestic issues, private issues, and world affairs, such as "Do you consider the income tax you have to pay this year to be fair?" (Although 85% said "yes" in 1943, only 58% said "yes" in 2002.) Business executives can track attitudes toward buying private brands or attitudes toward credit by following questions asked in the Gallup poll. The Gallup poll is available each year, and back issues covering each year begin with 1935.[6] Like Harris Interactive, the Gallup Organization can conduct customized surveys for clients. However, we treat the Gallup poll here as syndicated data since it collects attitude and opinion information and makes that information available to all who wish to purchase it. Visit its Web site, and view some poll results. This will give you an idea of the service provided by the Gallup Organization.

■ The Yankelovich Monitor measures changing social values and how these changes affect consumers. Visit Yankelovich at www.Yankelovich.com.

■ Companies can use HarrisInteractive to receive information on consumer attitudes and opinions. Go to www.HarrisInteractive.com and go the Harris Poll Library.

■ We treat the Gallup poll here as syndicated data since it collects attitude and opinion information and makes that information available to all who wish to purchase it. See examples of Gallup surveys at www.gallup.com.

## Defining Market Segments

Defining market segments requires placing customers sharing certain attributes (age, income, stage in the family life cycle, etc.) into homogenous groups or market segments. Using these categories, marketers gather information about the members of the market, compiling profiles of the attributes describing the consumers that make up each segment. Marketers can then decide which segments are presently being served or not served by the competition. They can also determine the size, growth trends, and profit potential of each segment. Using these data, a segment, or group of segments, can be targeted for marketing.

Several standardized information sources provide marketers with information about customers in the market. Some of these sources provide information on members of the industrial market, and others provide information on members of the consumer market.

### Providing Information on Members of the Industrial Market

A great deal about the industrial market can be learned through the use of the Standard Industrial Classification (SIC) system and the North American Industry Classification System (NAICS), the government's method of classifying business firms (discussed in Chapter 5). Although achieving the basic objectives of allowing you to identify, classify, and monitor standard statistics about certain member firms, the SIC falls short of allowing you to target customers in a highly specific industry. NAICS partially remedies this problem by going from the SIC's four-digit code to a six-digit code. NAICS allows users to select more specific types of firms instead of the broad categories available through SIC codes.

■ NAICS allows marketers to define industry types more specifically than the SIC system.

One standardized information service firm supplies additional information that allows the user to make even better use of the government's classification systems. **Dun's Market Identifiers (DMI)**, published by Dun & Bradsteet, provides information on over 17 million firms that it updates monthly. The real benefit of DMI is its service that provides eight-digit codes to classify businesses. By having more digits, the service can provide many more categories of firms than other classification systems. This is important if a firm is trying to target specific business firms, however narrow their classification.

■ By classifying firms using an eight-digit code, Dun & Bradstreet offers a standardized information service that allows firms to locate all firms in a narrowly defined industry group.

For example, one marketing researcher worked with a manufacturing firm, BasKet Kases, a manufacturer of wooden gift baskets, to secure a listing of all firms that wholesale gift baskets, in order to target those firms with a marketing campaign. Using the SIC Classification Manual, it was determined that SIC numbers with a 51 prefix were wholesalers of nondurable goods. By examining all of the 51 prefix descriptions, the SIC code of 5199 was found to represent wholesalers of "miscellaneous, nondurable goods," which included baskets. Without additional information, a list of firms with an SIC code of 5199 would have included wholesalers of all types of baskets, including wooden baskets for shipping fruit, freight, and so on. However, with the use of the additional codes supplied by DMI, it was found that the eight-digit code 51990603 represented "wholesalers of gift baskets," which was exactly what the researcher was seeking. By finding the firms sharing this eight-digit code, the researcher was able to identify 45 wholesale firms of gift baskets in the United States for BasKet Kases.

## Providing Information on Members of the Consumer Market

Many standardized information services are available to help marketers understand the consumer market. Information on segmenting consumers by lifestyle[7] is available through the **VALS** study, a Stanford Research Institute (SRI) survey that places consumers in segments based on their psychological and demographic characteristics. VALS stands for values and lifestyles. Some examples of these different groups of consumers include "Actualizers," who are sophisticated, successful, take-charge people with abundant resources and high self-esteem. Their possessions reflect the finer things in life. "Experiencers" are young, enthusiastic, compulsive, and rebellious. They are not committed to many beliefs and are involved in outdoor activities, sports, and social activities. They spend much of their income on fast food, clothing, videos, and movies. SRI Consulting Business Intelligence uses the VALS system to help firms identify characteristics of their customers. The VALS system is standardized in that SRI has the process for identifying consumer VALS segments. The usefulness of the concept lies in knowing in which VALS segments most of a firm's customers are categorized. For example, knowing that 80% of a firm's customers fall into one VALS segment allows firms to know much more about the values and lifestyles of their customers. You can determine your VALS segment by completing the VALS survey online at **www.sric-bi.com/VALS**. You can also learn more about the other VALS categories at this Web site.[8] VALS is now being applied in Japan.

**Geodemographics** is the term used to describe the classification of arbitrary, usually small, geographic areas in terms of the characteristics of their inhabitants. Employing computer programs called **GIS** (geodemographic information systems), geodemographers can access huge databases and construct profiles of consumers residing in geographic areas determined by the geodemographer. Instead of being confined to consumer information recorded by city, county, or state, geodemographers can produce this information for geographic areas thought to be relevant for a given marketing application (such as a proposed site for a fast-food restaurant).

Firms specializing in geodemographics combine census data with their own survey data or data that they gather from other sources. Claritas Inc. is the firm that pioneered geodemography. By accessing zip codes and census data provided in the various geographical reporting units of the census tracks, census block groups, or blocks that make up a firm's trading areas, Claritas can compile much information about the characteristics and lifestyles of the people within these trading areas. Or a firm may give Claritas a descriptive profile of its target market and Claritas can supply the firm with geographic areas that most closely match the prespecified characteristics. This service is referred to as **PRIZM** (potential ratings index for ZIP+4 markets). The PRIZM system defines every neighborhood in the United States in terms of 66 demographically and behaviorally distinct clusters. By knowing which clusters make up a firm's potential customers, Claritas can help target promotional messages to consumers making up those clusters. Marketing Research Application 6.1 gives you some background information on Claritas and describes some of its standardized services that can be used for market segmentation. Marketing Research Application 6.2 illustrates how ESRI's Community Tapestry Segmentation Service may be used to solve business problems.

■ VALS is a standardized service that offers a system for segmenting consumers by lifestyle.

■ Learn more about VALS at **www.sric-bi.com/VALS**.

■ *Geodemographics* is the term used to describe the classification of arbitrary, usually small, geographic areas in terms of the characteristics of their inhabitants.

■ Go to Interactive Learning at the end of this chapter and learn more about real-world applications of Claritas products and services.

■ Firms specializing in geodemographics combine census data with their own survey data or data that they gather from other sources. PRIZM is a standardized information service that categorizes neighborhoods in one of 66 different clusters.

## MARKETING RESEARCH APPLICATION 6.1

PRACTICAL

APPLICATIONS

### Claritas Standardized Services for Market Segmentation

Since 1971, San Diego-based Claritas has been the preeminent source of accurate, up-to-date marketing information about people, households, and businesses within any geographic area in the United States. Its target marketing services are aimed at reducing the cost of customer acquisition and growing customer value. Claritas offers industry-leading consumer segmentation systems, consulting services and software applications for site analysis, advertising sales, and customer targeting. Claritas is a division of the Nielsen Company (formerly VNU), a global information and media company with leading market positions and recognized brands in marketing information (ACNielsen), media information (Nielsen Media Research), business publications (Billboard, The Hollywood Reporter, Adweek), and trade shows. To learn more about Claritas and Nielsen products and services visit their Web sites at **www.claritas.com** and **www.nielsen.com**.

With information generated through its segmentation systems and databases, Claritas enables businesses to address key marketing issues such as:

- Who are my best customers and prospects?
- How many are there and where do they live?
- What is the most effective way to reach them?
- Which markets, locations, or industries offer the most potential?
- How should I allocate marketing resources to maximize my return on investment?

### Some Claritas Products Used for Market Segmentation:

**PRIZM NE (New Evolution)**—Defines every neighborhood in the United States at the household level in terms of 66 demographically and behaviorally distinct segments. A precision tool for lifestyle segmentation and analysis, PRIZM NE offers an easy way to identify, understand, and target consumers.

**P$YCLE NE (New Evolution)**—A market segmentation system that differentiates households in terms of financial behavior. The 58-segment system predicts which households will use which types of financial/insurance products and services.

**ConneXions NE (New Evolution)**—A classification of all U.S. households into 53 consumer segments with 10 lifestage groups to help telecommunications, Internet, cable, and satellite companies better target their rapidly expanding services.

By permission, Claritas Inc.

CLARITAS

---

We asked GIS expert Tony Burns, formerly with ESRI, to tell you about GIS and its application to retailing. In Marketing Research Application 6.3, Mr. Burns discusses GIS and describes one application of GIS—defining a trading area.

## Conducting Market Tracking

■ Tracking studies are those that monitor, or track, a variable such as sales or market share over time.

By **tracking studies** we mean studies that monitor, or track, a variable over time. For example, companies conduct market tracking to track sales of their brands as well as sales of competitors' brands over time. The "tracks" moving up and down or remaining stable serve as important monitors as to how the market is reacting to a firm's marketing mix. Many variables may be monitored in a tracking study, including market share, customer satisfaction levels, measures of promotional spending, prices, stockouts, and inventory levels.

You may ask why a company needs to know what its own sales are. Wouldn't a company know, through sales receipts, how much it has sold of a particular product? Although a company may monitor its own sales, sales measured by a firm's own sales receipts provide an incomplete picture. By monitoring only its own sales, a firm does not know what is going on in the channel of distribution. Products are not distributed instantaneously. Rather, inventories are built up and depleted at various rates among the different distributors. Just because household sales of a product increase does not mean that a producer will experience a sales increase of that product. To really know what is happening in the industry, marketers need

## MARKETING RESEARCH APPLICATION 6.2

PRACTICAL

APPLICATIONS

### Donofrio's Coffee Uses a Standardized Service to Locate Coffee Shops

Heather Donofrio had a successful chain of coffee shops targeted to young, urban professionals. Donofrio's Coffee operates in three states located in the Northeast. By carefully planning locations, Heather had never experienced a failure. Rob, Heather's husband, had started a process of franchising Donofrio's Coffee. Soon after Rob made Donofrio's Coffee available for franchising, the couple received many requests from potential franchisees. Heather knew how

important location was to the success of her business but also knew she and Rob were limited in being able to help franchisees from all over the country make the right location decision. The Donofrios needed help in choosing the most suitable locations for the new Donofrio's Coffee shops. After considering several marketing research companies, Heather decided to use the services of ESRI. David Huffman, Senior Sales Executive of ESRI's Commercial Division, explained their services to Heather. ESRI could use the **ESRI Community Tapestry** segmentation database to profile the current Donofrio's Coffee customers. Community Tapestry is a lifestyle segmentation database that classified all U.S. residential zip codes into 65 segments based on selected demographic and socioeconomic characteristics. For example, one segment is called *Laptops and Lattes*; affluent singles who rent with no home ownership and have childrearing responsibilities. Another segment is *Metro Renters*, who are young—one-third still in their 20s—well educated, and beginning their professional careers in urban areas. Other segments include *Salt of the Earth*, *Trendsetters*, and *Main Street USA*. For a broader view of markets, the 65 Community Tapestry segments can be grouped into 12 Life Mode summary groups based on similar lifestyle and lifestage patterns. For example, the seven segments in the *High Society*

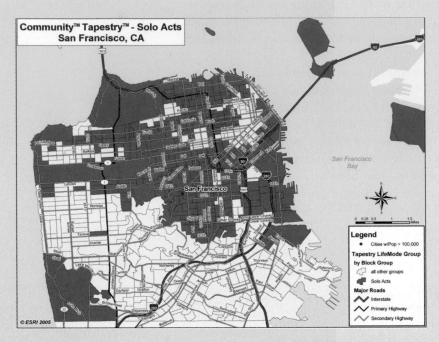

ESRI's segmentation system, Community™ Tapestry™, can identify the types of people by the neighborhoods where they live. This block group geography level map illustrates the location of metro San Franciso residents classfied in Taperstry's LifeMode *Solo Acts* summary group.
*Source*: Selected map reprinted courtesy of ESRI. Copyright © 2005 ESRI. All rights reserved.

summary group, including *Top Rung, Surburban Splendor,* and *Connoisseurs,* are the most affluent of the 65 Community Tapestry segments. The 65 segments can also be grouped into 11 Urbanization summary groups that are based on population density and affluence. Examples include *Metro Cities, Urban Outskirts,* and *Rural.* For more than 30 years ESRI has developed and refined its segmentation system methodologies.

The Donofrios were sold on ESRI's Community Tapestry segmentation when Huffman explained to them that 75% of their customers were in the *Solo Acts* Life Mode summary group, which consisted of just 5 of the 65 Tapestry segments. Further, ESRI could provide the Donofrios with a map of the United States that identified the neighborhoods in which these 5 segments dominated. By using ESRI Tapestry segmentation service, the Donofrios were ready to help franchisees locate successful Donofrio's Coffee shops.

For more information about Community Tapestry, visit: **www.esri.com/tapestry**.

■ **Tracking studies can tell a firm how well its own products are selling in retail outlets around the world and also provide sales data for competitors' products.**

to monitor the movement of goods at the retail level. Recognizing this need, market tracking is conducted at both the retail store level and at the household level. And tracking studies, as noted, also provide data on competitors' brands that otherwise would not be available to management. So, for these reasons, tracking studies are an important service provided by research firms.[9] Data are collected by scanners and by retail store audits. We provide examples of each in the following paragraphs.

### Market Tracking at the Retail Level

**Nielsen Scantrack service Scantrack®**, a service of The Nielsen Company is based on syndicated retail **scanning data** and is recognized as an industry standard in terms of providing tracking data gathered from the stores' scanners. Data are collected weekly from approximately 4,800 food, drug, and mass-merchandise stores representing about 800 different retailers and projecting to a universe of over 30,000 stores in 52 markets in the United States. Scantrack tracks thousands of products as they move through retail stores in the grocery, drug, and mass-merchandiser outlets of trade, allowing brand managers to monitor sales and market share and to evaluate marketing strategies. Scantrack reports can be provided at many different levels of information. For example, a report may be ordered for

## MARKETING RESEARCH APPLICATION 6.3

PRACTICAL

APPLICATIONS

### Why Is Geography Important in Retail Management?

GIS is a technology much like word processing or data mining. Technology has continuously played a major role in just about every business, and if it hasn't, it should. In the information age that we live in, technology's role has become increasingly important. However, for technology to be accepted into the mainstream markets, it must be beneficial, show an ROI, and be easy to use and affordable. If technology doesn't meet these requirements, it won't be adopted by businesses.

For many years, GIS wasn't a mainstream technology; in fact, just the term *geodemographic information systems* sounded too complex and difficult for any business to comprehend and resulted in GIS not being quickly integrated into organizations' day-to-day operations. GIS required staff specifically trained in GIS, and the cost justifications to do this weren't there. Businesses didn't want this complexity added to everything else they had to do to be successful. In businesses that did acquire the technology, its primary use was for sales and marketing. GIS was used more as a mapping system than as an analytical and modeling tool, and it typically wasn't integrated into other systems currently in use. Now, however, GIS is becoming part of the mainstream. Why? Because the software has become easier to use, the cost of data has come down in price, the systems are easier to use, they don't require GIS specialists, and they truly do benefit an organization. They help the bottom line, and businesses have discovered that there are certain things that only a GIS can do better than manual methods: drive-time analysis, market penetration, and trade-area delineation, to name a few. In other words, GIS is becoming mainstream because the technology criteria have been met.

The biggest advantage of GIS for retailers is that it inherently focuses the retailer's attention on where the problems are and where the solution will come from. Instead of analyzing everything in the world, GIS focuses the attention on the pieces of geography where solutions lie. Analysis such as creating the trade area and drive time cannot be done manually but adds significant value to a retailer because it defines the area of strength, market presence, and source of revenue, and gives a better understanding of customers' shopping behavior. Instead of worrying about the entire universe, a retailer can focus on the small geography and the consumers/

customers in that geography who are or who should be his or her customers. With a high degree of accuracy, the system can estimate the potential for an existing retail location as well as for a prospective location. A GIS cannot ensure victory over the competition, but it can help point retailers in the right direction and give insights about where their market or trade area is the strongest.

### CUSTOMER-BASED MARKET ANALYSIS: USING GIS TO DEFINE THE TRADING AREA

*Location, location, location* have been the three most important words in retail. Typically this has addressed the location of the store, but it has come to refer also to the location of the customer. Think about it—if you know where your customers live, you not only have more information than most retailers and a significant advantage over most of your competitors, but you also have a significant set of data that can be used to define your store trade area. You now have the ability to profile your customers, the ability to identify new store locations that have demographics similar to those of your best store, and the ability to measure your market penetration.

The customer's address is the genesis of all the power of GIS in the retail industry. It gives the location of the customer. From that location, the point can be geocoded (the address can be placed on an electronic map), and from that geocode, tremendous amounts of data become available about that point.

The proximity of customers to the retail store is important, and so is drive time to the store (i.e., the normal amount of time it takes the customers to get from their homes to the store). Retailing success is all about convenience.

A GIS is used to define the store's trade area as the area where the closest customers live. The exact cutoff is arbitrary but most retailers use a cutoff of about 50% of the total customers for the Primary Trade Area and 80% for the Secondary Trade Area. Anyone who lives outside these areas by definition lives outside the trade area. We are not excluding these outside-trade-area customers from buying in the store, but they normally are not as profitable to market to. If we marketed to all the customers who had purchased in the store in the last 12 months, and broke the results into three groups, Primary Trade Area, Secondary Trade Area, and Outside the Trade Area, the highest responders will normally be Primary, followed by Secondary, with the Outside customers responding the least.

It is important to know where your customers come from, and GIS analysis is the tool that allows us to do this.

Since there is a 50% probability of the next customer coming from the Primary Trade Area and an 80% probability that the next customer will come from the Primary/Secondary Trade Area, it is critical to learn as much as possible about those areas.

Understanding the geographies and dynamics of the retail trade area and the behavior of the consumers is critical to a retailer's success in today's extremely competitive marketplace.

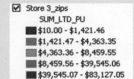

Sales aggregated to the zip code level as shown on above map

Trade area for the store shown in the example below. Trade area based on customer revenue for one year and calculated as 40%, 60%, and 80%. This shows where the revenue comes from.

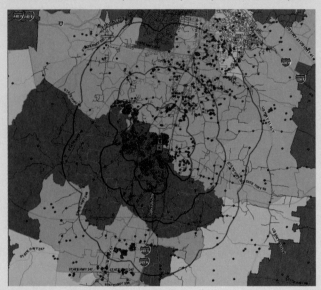

Trade areas (40%, 60%, 80%) based on customer annual spending and drive time. The underlying colors represent sales aggregated to the zip code level, with the darkest blue having the highest concentration of sales and customers. Customers are shown as red dots.

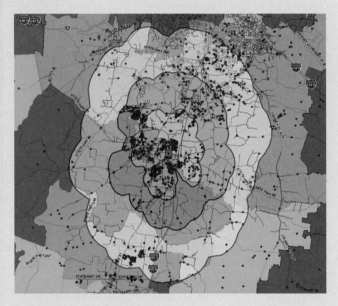

Approximately 80% of this store's revenues come from within a 20-minute-or-less drive.

Courtesy of ESRI.

■ Nielsen's Scantrack® service provides firms with tracking data based on scanner-collected data. You can learn more about Scantrack® service at **www.nielsen.com**.

just one category of products across the 52 U.S. markets.[10] Or a report can be generated for one brand in a single market. Markets can also be customized by client-specific areas of interest, commonly known as custom sales areas. Nielsen also provides services for tracking products sold in convenience stores through its **Convenience Track®** product. The Convenience Track product utilizes both scan and audit data to report for sales within this channel. Wal-Mart, dollar, club, pet, toy and home improvement stores are also tracked through the **Channel Views** product. Channel Views utilizes Nielsen's gold standard Homescan data (in-home consumer-scanned purchases) to project for channel sales for noncooperating and non-traditional channels of trade.[11]

**InfoScan.** Information Resources, Inc. (IRI), has a syndicated data service, called **InfoScan**, which gathers data by scanners in supermarkets, drugstores, and mass merchandisers. InfoScan collects data weekly in over 34,000 stores and provides subscribers access to information across many InfoScan categories. Data may be analyzed across major categories as well.[12]

The primary advantage of scanning data is that the data are available very quickly to decision makers. There is a minimum delay between the time the data are collected and the time the information is available to decision makers. The disadvantage is that a company may have products distributed through smaller stores that do not have scanners.

**Retail Store Audits.** Some tracking services do not rely solely on data collected in retail stores by scanners. **Retail store audits** also are used. In retail store audits, auditors are sent to stores and they record merchandising information needed for tracking studies. Store audits are particularly useful for smaller stores that do not have scanner equipment, such as convenience stores. Sales are estimated by calculating the following:

Beginning Inventory + Purchases Received − Ending Inventory = Sales

Auditors not only record this information for many products but also note other merchandising factors such as the level and type of in-store promotions, newspaper advertising, out-of-stock products, and shelf facings of products. Nielsen and RoperASW are two companies that provide tracking data collected by store audits. Like data collected by scanning services, data collected by audit are stored in a common database and made available to all who subscribe. The standardized information produced by these services would be examples of syndicated data.

### Market Tracking at the Household Level

Information is gathered in homes through the use of scanning devices, diaries, and audits. In-home scanner devices are provided to panel members who agree to scan the UPC codes on products they have purchased. Other services ask panel members to record purchases in diaries that are subsequently mailed back to the research firm. Finally, a few research firms collect data by actually sending auditors into homes to count and record information. Almost all of these methods rely on consumer household panels whose members are recruited for the purpose of recording and reporting their household purchases to one of the standardized data services firms. The following are examples of each method.

**IRI's Consumer Network(TM) Panel.** Information Resources, Inc., also maintains a panel of consumer households that record purchases at outlets by scanning UPC codes on the products purchased. Using IRI's handheld ScanKey scanning wand, panel members record their purchases and this information is transmitted via telephone link back to IRI. As with many panels, an advantage of this panel is that it provides not only information on products purchased but also purchase data that are linked to the demographics of the purchasers.[13]

■ IRI's InfoScan provides firms with tracking data based on scanner-collected data. Visit IRI at www.infores.com.

■ In retail store audits, auditors record merchandising information needed for tracking studies.

■ Information for tracking studies is gathered in homes using scanning devices, or through the use of diaries and even home audits.

■ IRI's Consumer Network(TM) Panel has members who scan products they purchase and send the data back to IRI to be used in tracking studies.

**Nielsen Homescan Panel.** This panel recruits members who use handheld scanners to scan all bar-coded products purchased and brought home from all outlets including warehouse clubs and convenience stores. Panel members also record the outlet at which all the merchandise was purchased and which family member made the purchase, as well as price and causal information, such as coupon usage. This panel allows Nielsen to track data on products whether they are bought in a store with or without scanners and from any store. In addition, the **Homescan Fresh Foods Panel** enables households to capture nonbarcoded perishable products. The collection of these random-weight perishables is through a codebook that contains barcodes for individual products such as bulk fruit, vegetables, cheese, and meat categories. The Homescan Panel consists of households that are demographically and geographically balanced and projectable to the total United States. In addition, local markets can be tracked. ACNielsen's Worldwide Consumer Panel Service also provides home tracking services for 21 countries around the world.

■ Learn more about Nielsen's Homescan Panel at www.nielsen.com.

**Diary**. Several companies offer tracking data collected by household diaries. Panel members are asked to complete diaries containing information such as the type of product, name brand, manufacturer or producer, model number, description, purchase price, store from which the item was purchased, and information about the person making the purchase. This information can then be used to estimate important factors such as market share, brand loyalty, brand switching, and demographic profile of purchasers. The panel members are typically balanced geographically to the United States and regions of the United States. Also, many companies have special-purpose panels. NFO, for example, has a Chronic Ailment Panel (CAP), which consists of more than 250,000 persons suffering from 60 chronic ailments. This panel offers firms involved in the health care industry valuable insights on how consumers select medical treatment. NFO also has special panels for babies, adults age 50 and over, and families that are moving.[14]

■ Some services gather tracking data by having panel members record their purchases in a household diary.

■ Some firms collect tracking data by sending auditors into panel members' homes to actually count and record data.

**Audit**. Some companies collect data from households by sending auditors into homes. NPD's Complete Kitchen Audit records ingredients, kitchen utensils, and appliances in homes. The information is provided to manufacturers of kitchen products and food producers.[15]

### Turning Market Tracking Information into Intelligence

One of the disadvantages of today's information technology is that a user of information can easily be swamped with information, producing "information overload." You can imagine the quantity of information that could flow to a manufacturer who subscribes to tracking data. The information flows in frequently and in large quantities. Various companies have created a host of products to help decision makers use vast quantities of information for intelligent decisions. Variously labeled decision support systems, data mining systems, expert systems, and the like, these systems use analytical tools to attach meaning to data, allowing managers to make decisions in response to quickly changing market conditions. Some examples include **IRI's Builder** services and

**Nielsen's CBP®**. CBP® or Category Business Planner, is a powerful, Web-based category management tool that aids managers in making faster and better decisions based on sales and in-store merchandising information of products in the consumer packaged goods industry. What is unique about CBP is that it allows a manufacturer to assess a specific retailer's performance in comparison with its competition, using the retailer's view of the marketplace (i.e., same geography and product category). This allows a manufacturer to evaluate product performance the same way a retail buyer would evaluate the manufacturer's product, allowing them to be in sync when assessing the performance of and deciding on a course of action for each product category.[16]

## Monitoring Media Usage and Promotion Effectiveness

Business firms typically conduct studies to measure their effectiveness, readership, listenership, and so on. This information is useful to firms contemplating advertising expenditures. Because there is a need for some objective measure of promotional effectiveness, several syndicated data service companies have evolved over the years to supply such information to subscribing firms. Some of these services specialize in a particular medium; a few others conduct studies on several forms of media. A discussion of both types of these organizations follows.

### Tracking Downloaded Music, Videos, and Recorded Books

Nielsen **SoundScan** tracks music downloaded online from several online music stores, such as Apple's iTunes.[17] Likewise, Nielsen **VideoScan** and **BookScan** track prerecorded videos and books. This is an example of a research firm innovating services in response to changing products and distribution systems.[18]

### Television

For many years **Nielsen Media Research** has been the major provider of TV ratings. Since 1999 Nielsen has been owned by The Nielsen Company (Formerly named VNU), which also owns the marketing research firm ACNielsen. Few TV watchers have been unaffected by Nielsen; their favorite show has been canceled or, because the rating is showed a large audience, the show has run for many years. Obviously, firms in the TV industry are constantly trying to achieve higher viewership than their competition. High viewership allows them to charge higher prices to advertise on the "more popular" programs.

Until 1987, the size and characteristics of TV audiences by program were determined by panels made up of approximately 2,000 families that recorded their TV-viewing habits in a diary or through an electronic device, the audiometer, that was attached to their TV set. Data were gathered twice a year. The data collection period became known as "sweeps" month, and this affected network and cable programming during these periods. In 1987, in an effort to gain greater objectivity, Nielsen changed the method of measuring the size and characteristics of the audiences to the **people meter**, an electronic instrument that automatically measures when a TV set is on and who is watching which channel. Family members are asked to enter their names (by codes) into the people meter each time they watch TV. Data from the people meter are transmitted directly back to Nielsen, allowing the firm to develop estimates of the size of the audience for each program by reporting the percentage of TV households viewing a given show.[19] Nielsen reports a rating and a share for each program telecast. A rating is the percentage of all the households in the United States tuned to a given program at a given time. A share is a percentage of all households watching television with a set tuned to a specific program at a specific time.

Nielsen also provides subscribers with other audience characteristic information that allows potential advertisers to select audiences that most closely match their target markets' characteristics. Ratings are reported by the number of households, by whether the women are employed outside the home, by age group for women (18+, 12–24, 18–34, 18–49, 25–54, 35–64, 55+), by age group for men (18+, 18–34, 18–49, 25–54, 35–65, 55+), and by age group of children (children ages 2 and older, ages 6 to 11, and teenagers). Nielsen also measures by ethnic origin (African American, Hispanic, or Asian).

■ Monitoring the number of persons watching TV programs is a syndicated data service provided by Nielsen.

■ The people meter records what TV program a household member is watching.

### Radio

Since 1964, radio listenership has been measured by **Arbitron**. The company's national and regional samples complete diaries reporting radio listening for one week. Diarykeepers record information in a weekly paper-and-pencil diary. They indicate the time of day; how long the station was tuned in; which station was on; where the listening was done (at home, in a car, at work, or other place); and the panel member's age, gender, and home address. Although paper-and-pencil diaries are still being used, Arbitron is transitioning to electronic measurement.

■ Arbitron provides syndicated data on radio station listening. Diarykeepers record their radio listening in pencil and paper diaries. Arbitron is transitioning to the Portable People Meter which automatically records encoded audio and video signals indicating exposure to media.

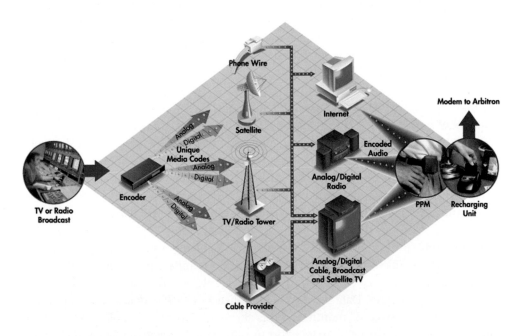

Arbitron's Portable People Meter is designed to be carried by panel members and to record encoded signals from various media sources. In this way, Arbitron can measure media exposure from multiple sources whether the panelist is in or out of their home.

By permission, Arbitron.

**The Portable People Meter™ (PPM)** system measures a panel of participants who carry a device the size of a cell phone that automatically records stations to which listeners are exposed. (We have more to say about the PPM in the upcoming section on multimedia services.) Data from the diaries are used to measure and report a number of variables indicative of radio listenership. Listenership is measured in 15-minute intervals and data are also reported by age and gender to aid in profiling audience characteristics. Subscribers to **Arbitron Radio Market Reports** can view the data online or through desktop software to select the output formats in which they wish to view the data. How can radio stations and businesses use this information to formulate marketing strategy? For instance, knowing where a person is listening may affect the type of message an advertiser wishes to use. A station with a high concentration of in-car listening may appeal to car dealers, auto parts stores, transmission repair shops, and tire stores. Understanding where the listening occurs is also helpful in determining programming elements such as traffic reports, contests, newscasts, and other information and entertainment segments. Arbitron also conducts other customized marketing research studies to suit individual clients' needs. Previously, we discussed Arbitron with regard to radio. However, Arbitron's Portable People Meter (PPM) system measures multimedia, including TV, radio, satellite radio, and online radio. The PPM system could prove to be a significant innovation in today's world, where consumers are exposed to a variety of media types in a variety of locations other than in their own living rooms. The PPM has been under development since 1992, and Arbitron has been testing the device extensively. The PPM works by embedding a code into audio signals of TV, both broadcast and cable; and radio platforms, including terrestrial, satellite, and online radio. When a survey respondent is exposed to an encoded station, the PPM captures the code identifying the medium. In the evening, respondents are asked to place their PPM in a base unit that recharges it and records the data collected so that it may be transmitted via modem to Arbitron. Arbitron panel members are encouraged to wear the PPM a minimum of 8 hours a day. The PPM may allow Arbitron to measure audiences for radio, television, cable, satellite, video games, CDs, VCR tapes, and even audio on the Internet. With recent technological advances making more media alternatives available (more channels on TV, satellite and HD radio, online streaming of audio and video, and so on), there is a growing demand for multimedia measurement services.[20]

Arbitron's Portable People Meter (PPM) could prove to be a significant innovation in today's world where consumers are exposed to a variety of media types in a variety of locations other than in their own living rooms.

## Print

**GFK's Starch Readership Service** is known as the most widely used source for measuring the extent to which magazine ads are seen and read. Starch conducts personal interviews with a minimum sample of 100 readers of a given issue of a magazine, trade publication, or newspaper. Interviews are carried out in 20 to 30 urban localities for each magazine issue analyzed. Interviews are conducted only with respondents who have read the issue prior to the interview. Therefore, Starch readership studies are not designed to determine the number of readers who read a particular issue of a magazine. Rather, Starch determines what readers saw and read in a study issue when they first looked through it. Starch studies over 25,000 ads in

400 individual print publications a year and interviews more than 40,000 people annually. Starch then uses the following readership levels in its reports:

*Noted*—the percentage of issue readers who remember having previously seen any part of the advertisement in the study issue.

*Associated*—the percentage of issue readers who not only noted the ad but also saw or read some part of it that clearly indicated the brand or advertiser.

*Read Some*—the percentage of issue readers who read any part of the ad's copy.

*Read Most*—the percentage of issue readers who read one-half or more of the written material in the advertisement.

In addition to these readership levels, Starch reports a number of other analytical measures such as an ad's rank, which shows the standing of an ad in terms of its noted and associated percentages relative to all other ads in the magazine issue. In addition to evaluating individual ads, Starch also analyzes the impact of many other variables on readership, such as ad size, number of pages, whether it is black-and-white or color, special position (cover, center spread, etc.), and product category, among several others.[21] To further help marketers make decisions about what comprises a good ad, Starch also provides another syndicated data service, called Adnorms. **Adnorms** provides readership scores by type of ads. For example, Adnorms could calculate the average readership scores for one-page, four-color computer ads appearing in *Business Week*. This allows an advertiser to compare his or her ad scores with the norm. In this way, advertising effectiveness may be assessed. Users learn the effect of ad size, color, and even copy on readership.[22]

■ GFK's Starch Readership service provides syndicated data on magazine readership. Visit GFR's Starch Ad Readership Service at www.gfkamerica.com. Go to "Products & Services." and go to GFK Starch Ad Readership studies.

### Multimedia

Some standardized information sources firms provide information on a number of media. **Simmons National Consumer Study** provides information on media usage linked to product usage. About 27,000 consumers are interviewed in the study. Media habits are related to product usage among 450 product categories, such as apparel, automotive, computers, and travel. Over 8,000 brands are studied. In addition, psychographic and demographic data are collected. The information allows users to determine the viewing/listening media habits of users of certain product categories and brands.

We discussed Arbitron with regard to radio earlier. However, Arbitron's Personal Portable Meter (PPM) is a measure of multimedia including TV, radio, and the Web. The company's development of the Personal Portable Meter (PPM) could prove to be a significant innovation in today's world, where consumers are exposed to a variety of media types in a variety of locations other than in their own living rooms. The PPM has been under development since 1992, and Arbitron has been testing the device extensively.[23] The PPM works by embedding a code into the audio portion of the signals of TV channels, radio broadcasts, and Web pages. When a survey respondent is exposed to a medium's broadcast, the PPM captures the code identifying the medium. In the evening, respondents are asked to place their PPMs in base units that recharge the unit and record the data collected so that it may be transmitted via modem to

■ Simmons National Consumer Study provides information on media usage linked to product usage. You can learn more about the services provided by Simmons by going to www.smrb.com/.

information systems, as a standardized service that defines consumer market segments. Nielsen's Scantrack® service is an example of a syndicated data source for tracking the sales of consumer product goods sold in retail stores. Other standardized services track goods by collecting data from consumer households. Arbitron radio listenership studies are an example of a syndicated data source for monitoring radio listenership.

Single-source information sources use sales data recorded by scanners at the UPC level by brand, store, date, price, and so on. Those data are then coupled with information on the buyer's demographics and media exposure. Having information on who bought what, where, when, and why in one single database may give marketers the ability to answer important cause-and-effect questions on, for example, which marketing-mix variable X caused the sale of product Y. IRI's BehaviorScan is an example of a standardized service providing single-source information. Using BehaviorScan, for example, marketers can test the effects of different TV campaigns as well as in-store promotional materials.

## KEY TERMS

Standardized information (p. 173)
Syndicated data (p. 173)
Standardized services (p. 173)
Yankelovich Monitor (p. 175)
Maritz poll (p. 175)
Harris poll (p. 175)
Gallup poll (p. 175)
Dun's Market Identifiers (DMI)
　(p. 176)
VALS (p. 177)
Geodemographics (p. 177)
GIS (p. 177)
PRIZM (p. 177)
Tracking studies (p. 178)
ESRI's Community Tapestry (p. 179)
Nielsen Scantrack service (p. 180)
Scanning data (p. 180)
Convenience Track® (p. 182)
Channel Views (p. 182)
InfoScan (p. 183)
Retail store audits (p. 183)
Homescan Fresh Foods Panel (p. 184)
IRI's Builder (p. 184)
SoundScan (p. 185)

VideoScan (p. 185)
BookScan (p. 185)
Nielsen Media Research (p. 185)
People meter (p. 185)
Arbitron (p. 186)
Portable People Meter$^{(TM)}$ (PPM)
　(p. 187)
Arbitron Radio Market Reports
　(p. 187)
GFK's Starch Readership Service
　(p. 187)
Adnorms (p. 188)
Simmons National Consumer Study
　(p. 188)
Single-source data (p. 189)
BehaviorScan (p. 189)
Project Apollo (p. 189)

# REVIEW QUESTIONS

**1** What is meant by standardized information?

**2** Distinguish between syndicated data and standardized services.

**3** What are the advantages and disadvantages of syndicated data?

**4** What are the advantages and disadvantages of standardized services?

**5** Name four broad types of applications of standardized information, and give an example of each.

**6** Explain how the standardized service Dun's Market Identifiers (DMI) could be helpful in a marketing research application.

**7** What is geodemography, and how can it be used in marketing decisions? Give an example.

**8** Explain why VALS would be considered a standardized information service.

**9** What are tracking studies? Give an example of how managers would use tracking-study data.

**10** What are the differences between Nielsen's Scantrack® service and IRI's InfoScan service?

**11** What are two panels that gather information from consumers by asking them to scan the UPC codes (bar codes) on goods they purchase and bring home?

**12** Explain how "information overload" of tracking information can be minimized through software also offered as standardized services.

**13** What standardized information service is designed to gather data on down-loaded music? Prerecorded video sales? Prerecorded book sales?

**14** What company provides syndicated data on TV ratings?

**15** What is the firm that is best known for conducting studies of radio listenership? Briefly describe the service it provides.

**16** What is single-source data?

# APPLICATION QUESTIONS

**17** Go to the Web site of three marketing research companies. Review their list of products and services offered. Which of these are standardized services? Syndicated data? Custom research offerings?

**18** Imagine you are a potential franchisee for a Donofrio's Coffee franchise (see MRA 6.2). Evaluate the Donofrios' use of the standardized service Community Tapestry to help you make your decision as to where to locate your franchise of Donofrio's Coffee.

**19** Review the kinds of information gathered by **www.gallup.com**. Go to the Web site and take a look at some of the former studies they report. How could a marketing manager use some of this information?

**20** Go to a search engine such as Google, Yahoo!, or Ask. Look up "GIS." Describe a few of the applications of GIS that some of the sites have described.

**21** Describe how a marketing manager could make use of single-source data to make (a) pricing decisions and (b) in-store promotions decisions.

22  Contact a radio or TV station or perhaps a newspaper in your town. Ask managers how they measure listenership, viewership, or readership and for what purposes they use this information. In most cases, these firms will be happy to supply you with a standard package of materials answering such questions.

23  Given what you know about syndicated services, which firm would you call on if you had the following information needs?

 a  You want to know which magazines have the heaviest readership among tennis players.

 b  You have decided to conduct a test market but you have no research department within your firm and no experience in test marketing.

 c  You need to know how a representative sample of U.S. households would answer seven questions about dental hygiene.

 d  You are thinking about a radically new advertising theme but you are very concerned about consumer reaction to the new theme. You want some idea as to how the new theme will impact sales of your frozen dinners.

# INTERACTIVE LEARNING

Go to **www.Claritas.com** and go to "Segmentation Systems." Click on "View a listing of Claritas' segmentation case studies." Select an area of interest and read a few case examples of how Claritas uses its services to solve client problems.

Visit the Web site at **www.prenhall.com/burnsbush**. For this chapter, work through the Self-Study Quizzes, and get instant feedback on whether you need additional studying. On the Web site, you can review the chapter outlines and case information for Chapter 6.

## CASE 6.1  ||| Premier Products, Inc.

Premier Products, Inc. (PPI), is a large multinational firm with several product divisions, including foods, over-the-counter drugs, and household products. The firm has over 1,000 different products and distributes through grocery stores, mass merchandisers, and convenience stores in the United States, Canada, and Western Europe. Products are marketed under different brand names but all are marked with the PPI family brand name. The company is headquartered in the United States and has six regional offices. There is a marketing research department with a staff of 26 people at company headquarters. The department is primarily responsible for quarterly reports and providing the information requests of divisional managers who are responsible for creating new products and ensuring profitable product performance. Each divisional manager, working with brand managers, develops his or her own marketing programs and makes all decisions regarding product additions and deletions, pricing, distribution, and promotion of the different brands. PPI's V.P. of Marketing Research is Stephanie Williamson.

Dale Hair, Division Manager for the Dairy Foods line of products, met with Williamson and explained she was in need of better information to help them target customers for direct-mail campaigns consisting primarily of new-product awareness messages and cents-off coupons. Hair could describe the general demographic characteristics of her primary target market thanks to previously conducted marketing research. She needed help with this for the U.S. market.

Joy Schurr, a brand manager for a line of soups, was interested in knowing what was happening in terms of consumers' attitudes toward brand name versus privately branded soups. PPI's brand, "Bowl-A-Soup," had been on the market for almost 35 years and was a well-established global brand. Schurr had been concerned about comments from many of the supermarket chain managers who were considering private brands. She wanted to know if consumer attitudes were shifting in favor of private, usually less expensive, brands versus national or global brands.

Lisa Henson, Division Manager, had a new product under development—a device for replacing lightbulbs in ceilings, which was simple to use and very effective. However, Henson was concerned that the distribution for this product would fall outside of PPI's present distribution network of supermarkets, mass merchandisers, and convenience stores. While some of the company's present mass-merchandiser customers would likely carry the product, she felt distribution would be too limited to ensure a profitable return. She was interested in knowing more about hardware stores as a possible distribution strategy for the new product. However, calling on hardware stores would be too expensive if PPI had only the one product to offer. Henson wanted to know if there were wholesalers of lightbulbs and light-related products who called upon hardware stores and other retail stores.

1 Should Stephanie Williamson assign any, or all, of these tasks to her 26-member staff?

2 Can you recommend a standardized information service that Williamson may consider for Dale Hair?

3 What would you recommend for Joy Schurr?

4 What would you recommend for Lisa Henson?

## CASE 6.2   Maggie J's Dog Treats

Maggie J's Dog Treats are sold all over the United States. Distribution is through grocery stores and a few large mass-merchandising chains such as Wal-Mart and Target Stores. Mike Hall is V.P. of marketing for the company. Hall has been concerned with the level of competition in dog treat brands in the last few months. More and more competitors are trying innovative marketing programs. Mike has commissioned an ad agency to develop a national promotional campaign. The agency has presented four different sets of TV ads, each based on a different marketing strategy. To be integrated with the TV ads is a series of in-store promotions. The four in-store promotion campaigns are each stand-alone campaigns. In other words, any one of them may be run simultaneously with any one of the four proposed TV ad campaigns.

The agency made their final presentation to Mike and the other officers of the company. Essentially they must choose between the four different TV ad/in-store promotion campaigns. Hall and the other officers are very pleased with the creative work conducted by the ad agency. All four campaigns are equally appealing. All four campaigns are consistent with the key benefits of Maggie J's treats: dogs like them and they have high nutritive value. The officers know that the selection of the right campaign is important since they are going to allocate several million dollars to the campaign. They also know it's important because they believe it is crucial for them to maintain or increase market share in light of the extreme, recent competition.

"This is a case where even a very small difference in effectiveness may play a major role in the success of our brand," says Hall. After several hours of debate it was clear that no one, even with many years in the dog treat business, could clearly determine which of the four campaigns should be selected. Finally, the Executive V.P., Jack Russell, stated, "We need to run this by Ron Spiller. He's responsible for marketing research. Maybe Ron can help us decide what to do."

The following day the officers met with Ron Spiller and reviewed the four TV ad campaigns and the four in-store promotion campaigns. Ron agreed that even a small difference in the effectiveness of the campaigns could make a significant difference in market share, profits, and ROI. Spiller also pointed out that it was possible that there could be a significant "interaction" effect between the TV campaigns and the in-store promotions. In other words, they might find that a particular TV campaign performs significantly better when it is run with a particular in-store promotion.

Maggie J's did not have their own marketing research department. However, Spiller was responsible for assisting managers in determining whether or not research was needed and in selecting the right outside supplier firm and service to use. Spiller stated that he would make some calls and gather some information from different research suppliers. A meeting was set up for the following Friday morning to consider

Spiller's proposed suggestions for conducting marketing research.

1  Do you think it is appropriate to conduct marketing research?

2  Should Ron Spiller consider a standardized information service? What are the arguments for and against using a standardized information service?

3  Should Ron Spiller consider standardized data or a standardized service?

4  Which particular standardized information service discussed in this chapter do you think Ron Spiller should recommend? Why?

# CHAPTER 7

# DECIDING ON YOUR SURVEY DATA COLLECTION METHOD

Western Wats

### WESTERN WATS USES DIFFERENT DATA COLLECTION METHODS TO SUCCESSFULLY ACHIEVE THEIR RESEARCH OBJECTIVES

Developers at a leading medical practice software company proposed an innovative use of existing technology to help manage patient communications. Management of the software company wanted to estimate the market for the proposed application, and they turned to Western Wats. The challenge was threefold: First, accurately measure future use of software most physicians had never thought about. Second, provide results in time for looming investment decisions. Third, combine one notoriously difficult survey population—physicians—with another notoriously difficult survey topic—information technology.

To tackle the first challenge, the research team relied on decades of experience, and an understanding of the practical constraints of real-world survey research. To speed up data collection and maximize response rates, Western

- To learn the four basic alternative modes for gathering survey data
- To understand the advantages and disadvantages of each of the alternative data-gathering modes
- To become knowledgeable about the details of different types of survey data collection methods such as personal interviews, telephone interviews, and computer-assisted interviews, including online surveys
- To comprehend the factors researchers consider when choosing a particular survey method
- To learn about some new, innovative methods for gathering data for special situations

Wats employed a mixed, or hybrid, mode approach of collecting data. Randomly sampled physicians were initially telephoned by research staff trained specifically to interview medical professionals. Respondents whose schedules prevented a phone interview were invited to complete the same questionnaire online at their convenience, and were immediately sent an e-mail with a secure link.

Western Wats was able to use two different modes of collecting data to achieve the research objectives. The mixed mode method allowed Western Wats to achieve an acceptable response rate and gather the data quickly, allowing the client to evaluate the final report in time to make their investment decision.

A national bank lacked consistent feedback from their high-balance business customers. Managers for that business line wanted to establish an on-going, actionable stream of customer satisfaction data, and asked Western Wats to help. While the measures were straightforward, data collection and reporting required a tailored approach.

Western Wats identified research interviewing staff who had proven experience interviewing business professionals, and then provided additional training requested by the bank. The additional training prepared the interviewers to respond to customer-respondent questions outside the survey process. The client wanted the surveyors to be able to answer questions about the bank's products and services should the respondent customers ask. Western Wats was able to collect high-quality data through personal telephone interviews which allowed for ample respondent feedback, rapport, and adaptability.

Visit Western Wats at **www.westernwats.com**.

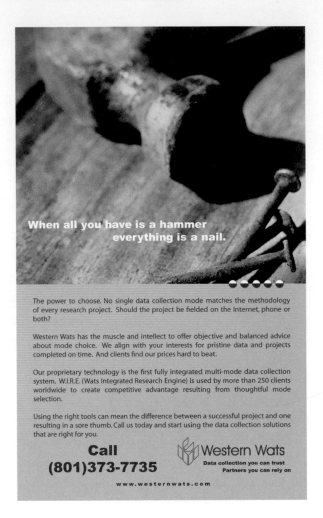

Our Western Wats example illustrates how researches select methods of data collection depending on the research objectives of a given project. As you are learning in this course, there are many different ways of conducting marketing research studies. In Chapter 4 we discussed different forms of marketing research, such as focus groups, experiments, and descriptive research. There are many ways of gathering information among these various types of studies. Respondents' behavior is observed and recorded by the researcher in observation studies. Some studies use physiological measurements, such as eye-movement-tracking devices. Other studies may use passive electronic means to gather data, such as Arbitron's PPM or the Pretesting Company's "WhisperCode," which is a device that is placed in respondents' homes and automobiles and that automatically records TV, radio, or Internet commercials to which respondents are exposed. However, in many studies, marketers must communicate with large numbers of respondents. Communication is necessary to learn what respondents are thinking—their opinions, preferences, or planned intentions. Large numbers of respondents may be required in order to collect a large enough sample of important subgroups or to ensure that the study accurately represents some larger population. A **survey** involves interviews with a large number of respondents using a predesigned questionnaire.[1] In this chapter, we focus on the various methods used to collect data for surveys.

The four basic survey modes used are: (1) person-administered surveys, (2) computer-assisted surveys, (3) self-administered surveys, and (4) mixed-mode, sometimes called "hybrid," surveys. We discuss the advantages and disadvantages of each of these methods, and we present you with the various alternative methods of collecting data within each of four basic data collection methods. For example, person-administered surveys may be conducted through mall intercepts or telephone. We discuss factors a market researcher should consider when deciding which data collection method to use. Finally, we introduce you to some innovative methods for gathering data for special situations.

# FOUR ALTERNATIVE DATA COLLECTION MODES

There are four major modes of collecting survey information from respondents: (1) Have a person ask the questions, either face-to-face or voice-to-voice, without any assistance from a computer; (2) have a computer assist or direct the questioning in a face-to-face, voice-to-voice or other survey; (3) allow respondents to fill out the questionnaire themselves, without computer assistance; (4) use some combination of two or more of the above three modes. We will refer to these four alternatives as person-administered, computer-administered, self-administered, and mixed-mode surveys, respectively. Each one has special advantages and disadvantages that we describe in general before discussing the various types of surveys found within each category. Specific advantages and disadvantages of these various types are discussed later.

## Person-Administered Surveys (Without Computer Assistance)

A **person-administered survey** is one in which an interviewer reads questions, either face-to-face or over the telephone, to the respondent and records his or her answers. It was the primary administration method for many years. However, its popularity has fallen off as communications systems have developed and computer technology has advanced. Nevertheless, person-administered surveys are still used, and we describe the advantages and disadvantages associated with these surveys next.

### Advantages of Person-Administered Surveys
Person-administered surveys have four unique advantages: They offer feedback, rapport, quality control, and adaptability.[2]

1 **Feedback.** Interviewers often must respond to direct questions from respondents during an interview. Sometimes respondents do not understand the instructions, or they may not hear the question clearly, or they might become distracted during the interview. A human interviewer may be allowed to adjust

■ There are techniques for gathering data from a relatively small group of respondents, such as observing, using mechanical devices to measure physiological response, and using passive electronic devices.

■ Sometimes marketing researchers want to communicate with respondents in order to know what they are thinking.

■ Sometimes marketing researchers need large numbers of consumers in a study in order to properly study subgroups or to have a sample size sufficient to accurately represent some larger population.

■ Surveys involve interviews with a large number of respondents using a predesigned questionnaire. This chapter focuses upon data collection methods used for surveys.

■ The four basic survey modes used are (1) person-administered surveys, (2) computer-assisted surveys, (3) self-administered surveys, and (4) mixed-mode or "hybrid." There are several alternative methods of gathering data within each of these four modes.

■ A person-administered survey is one in which an interviewer reads questions, either face-to-face or over the telephone, to the respondent and records his or her answers.

his or her questions according to verbal or nonverbal cues. When a respondent begins to fidget or look bored, the interviewer can say, "I have only a few more questions." Or if a respondent makes a comment, the interviewer may jot it down as a side note to the researcher.

2 **Rapport.** Some people distrust surveys in general, or they may have some suspicions about the survey at hand. It is often helpful to have another human being present to develop some rapport with the respondent early on in the questioning process. Another person can create trust and understanding that nonpersonal forms of data collection cannot achieve.

3 **Quality control.** An interviewer sometimes must select certain types of respondents based on gender, age, or some other distinguishing characteristic. Personal interviewers may be used to ensure respondents are selected correctly. Alternatively, some researchers feel that respondents are more likely to be truthful when they respond face-to-face.

4 **Adaptability.** Personal interviewers can adapt to respondent differences. It is not unusual, for instance, to find an elderly person or a very young person who must be initially helped step by step through the answering process in order to understand how to respond to questions. Interviewers are trained, however, to ensure that they do not alter the meaning of a question by interpreting the question to a respondent. In fact, interviewers should follow precise rules on how to adapt to different situations presented by respondents.

Marketing Research Application 7.1 illustrates how useful person-administered surveys are for selected situations.

### Disadvantages of Person-Administered Surveys

The drawbacks to using human interviewers are human error, slowness, cost, and interview evaluation.

1 **Humans make errors.** Interviewers ask questions out of sequence; they change the wording of a question, which may change the meaning of the question altogether. Humans make mistakes recording the information provided by the respondent.

2 **Slow speed.** Collecting data using human interviewers, particularly door-to-door interviewing, is slower than other modes. Although pictures, videos, and graphics can be handled by personal interviewers, they cannot accommodate them as quickly as, say, computers. Often personal interviewers simply record respondents' answers using pencil and paper, which necessitates a separate data-input step to build a computer data file. But increasing numbers of data collection companies have shifted to the use of laptop computers that immediately add the responses to a data file.

3 **High cost.** Naturally, the use of a face-to-face interviewer is more expensive than mailing the questionnaire to respondents. Ideally, personal interviewers are highly trained and skilled, and their use overcomes the expense factor. A less expensive person-administered survey is a telephone interview.

4 **Interview evaluation.** Another disadvantage of person-administered surveys is that the presence of another person may create apprehension, called "interview evaluation," among certain respondents. We discuss this concept more fully in the following section.

---

■ Personal interviewers can build rapport with respondents who are initially distrustful or suspicious.

■ Personal interviewers can adapt to differences in respondents but they must be careful not to alter the meaning of a question.

■ The disadvantages of person-administered surveys are that humans make errors, the method is slower than other methods, is the most costly, and can produce "interview evaluation" among certain respondents.

## MARKETING RESEARCH APPLICATION 7.1

PRACTICAL

APPLICATIONS

### Situations Where Personal Interviewing Is Needed to Collect Data

TAi Companies specialize in collecting data. Their facilities allow for focus groups and other marketing research studies. They have locations in New Jersey, Tampa, and Denver. OPS, Opinion Polling Service, is a division of TAi Companies that specializes in on-site (or on-location) personal interviewing when the situation dictates using personal interviewers. We asked Hal Meier, owner, to give some examples when it is best to personally interview consumers.

- XYZ chain restaurant regularly tests new menu items to discover if any can replace current offerings. Respondents fill out a survey form at the conclusion of their meal, so the survey is completed by real customers in the same setting in which the product is consumed commercially. Refusal rates are very low. It is impossible to duplicate this direct taste test in an artificial setting.
- XYZ bank asks their own customers why/whether they are using a new service (i.e., holiday layaway). Since the target population is their own customers they can easily be recruited in the bank. The incidence rate is nearly 100%: almost all intercepts qualify.
- XYZ paint company distributes through a local mass merchandiser and wants to know how their paint compares with other brands, broken down by professional painters vs. home owners. By interviewing on premises of the mass merchandiser, it is easy to identify respondents and brands they select at the paint department.

Hal Meier's basic philosophy is that, in many situations, it should be a great advantage to interview the respondent in the same setting in which they will consume or purchase the product and to have them see and hold the product instead of looking at an image on a computer screen.

Visit TAi Companies at: **www.taicompanies .com.**

By permission, TAi Companies.

**ON-SITE INTERCEPT/ INTERVIEWING BY PEOPLE WITH BOTH FEET ON THE GROUND**

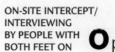
Opinion
Polling
Service

Opinion Polling Service (OPS) is the TAi division for out-of-the office on-site intercepts and interviewing. OPS is located in each TAi facility and utilizes a core group of TAi staff and specially trained "outsiders" just for this work.

OPS conducts customer surveys in banks, restaurants, stores, theme parks and many other venues. Ask for details on electronic data collections and real-time data retrieval with our "handy" PDAs.

**TAi** Companies    *We Measure Our Success In Client Satisfaction*

## Computer-Administered Surveys

As our introductory example illustrates, computer technology represents a viable option with respect to survey mode, and new developments occur almost every day. Although person-administered surveys are still the industry mainstay,

Personal interviewing is not used as much as it was in the past but still should be used if the situation calls for it. A good personal interviewer can create trust and rapport with respondents.

■ A computer-administered survey is one in which computer technology plays an essential role in the interview work. Here either the computer assists an interview or it interacts directly with the respondent.

■ In the case of Internet-based questionnaires, the computer acts as the medium by which potential respondents are approached, and it is the means by which respondents submit their completed questionnaires.

computer-administered survey methods are growing very rapidly and will rival person-administered surveys in the foreseeable future. Computer-assisted surveys are in an evolutionary state, and they are spreading to other survey types. For instance, a computer may house questions asked by a telephone interviewer, or a questionnaire may be posted on the Internet for administration. Basically, a **computer-administered survey** is one in which computer technology plays an essential role in the interview work. Here either the computer assists an interview or it interacts directly with the respondent. In the case of Internet-based questionnaires, the computer acts as the medium by which potential respondents are approached, and it is the means by which respondents submit their completed questionnaire. As with person-administered surveys, computer-administered surveys have their advantages and disadvantages.

### Advantages of Computer-Administered Surveys

There are variations of computer-administered surveys. At one extreme, the respondent answers the questions on his or her PC, often online, and the questions are tailored to his or her responses to previous questions, so there are no human interviewers. At the other end, there are computer programs in which a telephone or personal interviewer is prompted by the computer as to what questions to ask and in what sequence. Regardless of which variation is considered, at least five advantages of computer-administered surveys are evident: speed; error-free interviews; use of pictures, videos, and graphics; real-time capture of data; and reduction of anxieties caused by "interview evaluation" (respondents' concern they are not answering "correctly").

■ Computer-administered surveys are fast, error-free, capable of using pictures or graphics, able to capture data in real time, and less threatening for some respondents.

**1  Speed.** The computer-administered approach is much faster than the human interview approach. Computers can quickly jump to questions based on specific responses, they can rapidly dial random telephone numbers, and they can easily check on answers to previous questions to modify or otherwise custom-tailor the interview to each respondent's circumstances. The speed factor translates into cost savings, and there is a claim that Internet surveys are about one-half the cost of mail or phone surveys.[3]

2 **Error-free interviews.** Properly programmed, the computer-administered approach guarantees zero interviewer errors such as inadvertently skipping questions, asking inappropriate questions based on previous responses, misunderstanding how to pose questions, recording the wrong answer, and so forth. Also, the computer neither becomes fatigued nor cheats.

3 **Use of pictures, videos, and graphics.** Computer graphics can be integrated into questions as they are viewed on a computer screen. So rather than having an interviewer pull out a picture of a new type of window-unit air conditioner, for instance, computer graphics can show it from various perspectives. High-quality video windows may be programmed to appear so the respondent can see the product in use or can be shown a wide range of visual displays.

4 **Real-time capture of data.** Because respondents are interacting with the computer, the information is directly entered into a computer's data storage system and can be accessed for tabulation or other analyses at any time. Once the interviews are finished, final tabulations can be completed in a matter of minutes. This feature is so beneficial that some interview companies have telephone interviewers directly linked to computer input when they conduct their interviews.

■ The real-time capture of data by computer-administered surveys is an important advantage of this data collection method.

5 **Reduction of "interview evaluation" concern in respondents.** Interview evaluation may occur when another person is involved in the interviewing process and some respondents are apprehensive that they are answering "correctly." When involved in responding to questions in a survey, some people become anxious about the possible reaction of the interviewer to their answers. They may be concerned as to how the interviewer evaluates their responses. This may be especially present when the questions deal with personal topics such as personal hygiene, political opinions, financial matters, and even age. The presence of a human interviewer may cause them to answer differently than they would in a nonpersonal data collection mode. Some respondents, for example, try to please the interviewer by saying what they think the interviewer wants to hear. In any case, some researchers believe that respondents will provide more truthful answers to potentially sensitive topics when interacting with a machine.

■ Interview evaluation may occur because another person is conducting the interview, and his or her presence creates anxieties in respondents which may cause them to alter their normal response. Interview evaluation is more pronounced when survey topics are sensitive issues.

The advantages of using computers have created a growing demand for the use of online survey research. This has led to the growth of firms specializing in assisting companies in planning and conducting online surveys. Common Knowledge provides clients with the option to design their own surveys or utilize their programming services. They can target a sample from their online panel of millions of households and businesses, including subgroups such as consumers, B2B, healthcare, technology professionals, and teens. Common Knowledge has over 500 sample targets available and offers clients different ways to remind panelists to respond. Reminders are particularly important for low incidence targets. If necessary, Common Knowledge can use mixed-modes and call on partner panels to gain the needed responses.

## Disadvantages of Computer-Administered Surveys

The primary disadvantages of computer-assisted surveys are that they require some level of technical skill and setup costs may be significant.

1  **Technical skills required.** There is a wide range of computer-assisted methods available to marketing researchers. However, even the simplest options require some technical skills, and many of them require considerable skill to ensure the systems are operational and free of errors. Viruses, software bugs, and hardware breakdowns must be diagnosed and remedied immediately.

2  **High setup costs.** Although computer technology can result in increases in productivity, there are usually high setup costs associated with getting the systems in place and operational. Programming and debugging costs must be incurred with each survey. One software evaluator implied that two days of setup time by an experienced programmer was fairly efficient.[4] Depending on what type of computer-administered survey is under consideration, these costs, including the time factor associated with them, can render computer-administered delivery systems for surveys less attractive relative to other data collection options. At the same time, there are a number of moderate- to low-cost computer-administered options such Web-based questionnaires with user-friendly

■ The disadvantages to computer-assisted data collection are the requirement of technical skills and high setup costs.

development interfaces that are fueling the rush toward more and more online research around the world. Also, all of these disadvantages are passed on to other companies if a researcher or client uses the services of a data collection firm using some form of computer-assisted survey method.

## Self-Administered Surveys

A **self-administered survey** is one in which the respondent completes the survey on his or her own. It is different from other survey methods in that there is no agent—human or computer—administering the interview.[5] Instead, the respondent reads the questions and responds directly on the questionnaire. So, we are referring to the prototypical "pencil-and-paper" survey here. Normally, the respondent goes at his or her own pace, and in most instances he or she selects the place and time to complete the interview. He or she also may decide when the questionnaire will be returned. As with other survey methods, those that are self-administered have their advantages and disadvantages.

### Advantages of Self-Administered Surveys
Self-administered surveys have three important advantages: reduced cost, respondent control, and no interview-evaluation apprehension.

1 **Reduced cost.** By eliminating the need for an interviewer or an interviewing device such as a computer program, there can be significant savings in cost.
2 **Respondent control.** Respondents can control the pace at which they respond, so they may not feel rushed. Ideally, a respondent should be relaxed while responding, and a self-administered survey may affect this state.
3 **No interview-evaluation apprehension.** As we just noted, some respondents feel apprehensive when answering questions, or the topic may be sensitive, such as gambling,[6] smoking, or dental work.

The self-administered approach takes the administrator, whether human or computer, out of the picture, and respondents may feel more at ease. Self-administered questionnaires have been found to elicit more insightful information than face-to-face interviews.[7]

### Disadvantages of Self-Administered Surveys
The disadvantages of self-administered surveys are respondent control, lack of monitoring, and high questionnaire requirements.

1 **Respondent control.** As you can see, self-administration places control of the survey in the hands of the prospective respondent. Hence, this type of survey is subject to the possibility that respondents will not complete the survey, will answer questions erroneously, will not respond in a timely manner, or will refuse to return the survey at all.
2 **Lack of monitoring.** With self-administered surveys there is no opportunity to monitor or interact with the respondent during the course of the interview. Respondents who do not understand the meaning of a word or who are

■ Some types of computer-administered surveys incur relatively high setup costs, but others are very reasonable and easy to use.

■ A self-administered survey is one in which the respondent completes the survey on his or her own. It is different from other survey methods in that there is no agent—human or computer—administering the interview.

■ Self-administered surveys have three important advantages: reduced cost, respondent control, and no interview-evaluation apprehension.

■ The disadvantages of self-administered surveys are respondent control, lack of monitoring, and high questionnaire requirements.

■ There is potential for respondent error with self-administered surveys.

■ If respondents misunderstand or do not follow directions, they may become frustrated and quit.

confused about how to answer a question may answer improperly or get frustrated and refuse to answer at all. A monitor can offer explanations and encourage the respondent to continue.

3 **High questionnaire requirements.** Due to the absence of the interviewer or an internal computer check system, the burden of respondent understanding falls on the questionnaire itself. Not only must it have perfectly clear instructions, examples, and reminders throughout, the questionnaire must also entice the respondents to participate and encourage them to continue answering until all questions are complete. Questionnaire design is important regardless of the data collection mode. However, with self-administered surveys, clearly the questionnaire must be thoroughly checked for clarity and accuracy before data collection begins. We will learn more about designing questionnaires in Chapter 9.

■ Questionnaire design is important regardless of the data collection mode. However, with self-administered surveys, clearly the questionnaire must be thoroughly checked for clarity and accuracy before data collection begins.

## Mixed-Mode Surveys

**Mixed-mode surveys**, sometimes referred to as "hybrid" surveys, use multiple data collection methods. It has become increasingly popular to use mixed-mode surveys in recent years. Part of this popularity is due to the increasing use of online survey research. As more and more respondents have access to the Internet, the online survey, a form of computer-assisted survey, is often combined with some other method, such as telephone surveying, a form of person-administered surveying.

■ Mixed-mode surveys, sometimes referred to as "hybrid" surveys, use multiple data collection methods.

### Advantage of Mixed-Mode Surveys

1 **Multiple advantages to achieve data collection goal.** The advantage of mixed-mode surveys is that researchers are able to take the advantages of each of the various modes to achieve their data collection goals. For example, one quarterly administered panel of households uses a randomly selected sample of about 800 households. Since 50% of these households have Internet service, they may be surveyed each quarter via an online survey. This gives the panel administrators the advantage associated with online surveys: They may access all the panel households with a touch of the computer key. Also, as respondents open their e-mailed questionnaires and answer, their responses are automatically downloaded to the panel's statistical package for analysis. In order to achieve a representative sample, households without Internet service must be contacted. Households without Internet service typically have telephones. So these panel members are contacted each quarter via telephone surveys. With this mixed-mode approach, the panel administrators benefit from the advantage of the speed and low cost of online surveying as well as the advantage of reaching the total household population through using telephone surveys.[8]

■ The advantage of mixed-mode surveys is that researchers are able to use the advantages of each of the various modes to achieve their data collection goals.

### Disadvantages of Mixed-Mode Surveys

There are two primary disadvantages of using mixed-mode, or hybrid, data collection methods.

1 **Mode affects response?** One of the reasons that researchers in the past were reluctant to use mixed modes for gathering data was concern that the mode used might affect responses given by consumers. Would consumers responding to an in-home interview with a personal interviewer respond differently than a consumer responding to an impersonal, online survey? In a study conducted by Professors Green, Medlin, and Whitten, two methods of data collection were compared: online surveys versus a traditional mail survey. While the study showed no difference in the data quality, interestingly, response rates did not vary either. This is surprising since one of the major disadvantages with mail surveys is a low response rate.[9] Several other studies have been conducted to assess differences between data collection methods in mixed-mode applications.[10] But the point is that questionnaire authors must assess differences in data collected to determine if the data collection mode explains differences in responses to the research questions.

> A disadvantage of the mixed-mode survey is that the researcher must assess the effects the mode may have on response data.

2 **Additional complexity.** Using mixed modes of data collection adds to the complexities of data collection. For example, if you are conducting a survey online and by telephone, the wording of the instructions must be different to accommodate those reading instructions they themselves are to follow (for online respondents) versus someone else reading the instructions to the respondent (for telephone respondents). Further, data from the two sources will need to be integrated and care must be taken to ensure data are compatible. Responses must be coded in exactly the same way. See marketing researcher Dave Koch's specific suggestions on how to address this problem in Marketing Research Application 7.2.

> Using mixed modes of data collection adds to the complexities of data collection such as differences in instructions and integration of data from different sources.

## MARKETING RESEARCH APPLICATION 7.2

PRACTICAL

APPLICATIONS

### Managing Data Entry and Analysis Requires Special Attention When Using Mixed-Mode Data Collection

Dave Koch, Vice President of Adapt, Inc., a marketing research firm, acknowledges that today's technological advances, particularly in the area of online survey research, have provided researchers with many options for data collection. As a result, many researchers are utilizing several data collection modes, called mixed mode (or hybrid) to make certain they are reaching the right numbers and types of respondents. For example, when using an Internet survey, additional modes such as mail and telephone surveys may be used to ensure a representative sample. The end result may be data from different vendors at different times in different formats, which, as Mr. Koch warns, creates the need for paying special attention to data entry and analysis issues. Mr. Koch advises that good planning can help avoid problems and

wasted dollars due to extra use of time and company resources, and ensure project quality.

The key to success with mixed mode studies is taking time to consider back-end processing requirements when you first set up a project. Mr. Koch offers some tips:

1 Make sure you have control of the data layout at the outset. Make certain data are collected in the same format, and make sure all rating scales are consistent between data collection modes. The more specific you are on formats, the better off you will be when it comes time to analyze the data.
2 Bring the data analysis people in on your project in the initial planning stages. They can spot problems before it's too late.
3 Centralize the process of combining all the data as much as possible. Having one person responsible can help ensure data collected in different modes "fit" with each other.

**4** Since you will be using different questionnaires for each data collection mode, be sure to proofread all survey questionnaires carefully and think through the entire data analysis process before you collect data.

Koch advises us all that the key to successfully managing data from a mixed-mode study is to plan and document requirements upfront. The end results will be more efficient use of the valuable data processing resources of your company.

# DESCRIPTIONS OF DATA COLLECTION MODES

Now that you have an understanding of the pros and cons of person-, computer-, self-administered, and mixed-mode surveys, we can describe the various interviewing techniques used in each method. There are 11 different data collection methods used by marketing researchers (Table 7.1):

**1** In-home interview
**2** Mall-intercept interview
**3** In-office interview
**4** "Traditional" telephone interview
**5** Central location telephone interview
**6** Computer-assisted telephone interview (CATI)
**7** Fully computerized interview
**8** Online and other Internet-based surveys
**9** Group self-administered survey
**10** Drop-off survey
**11** Mail survey

## Person-Administered Interviews

There are at least four variations of person-administered interviews, and their differences are largely based on the location of the interview. These variations include the in-home interview, the mall-intercept interview, the in-office interview, and the telephone interview (which includes the "traditional" and central location telephone interviews).

### In-Home Interviews

Just as the name implies, an **in-home interview** is conducted in the home of the respondent. It takes longer to recruit participants for in-home interviews, and researchers must travel to and from respondents' homes. Therefore, the cost per interview is very high. Two important factors justify the high cost of in-home interviews. First, the marketing researcher must believe that personal contact is essential to the success of the interview. Second, he or she must be convinced that the in-home environment is conducive to the questioning process. In-home interviews are useful when the research objective requires respondents' physical presence to either see, read, touch, use, or interact with the research object (such as a product prototype) *and* the researcher believes that the security and comfort of respondents' homes is an important element affecting the quality of the data collected.

■ In-home interviews are useful when the research objective requires respondents' physical presence to either see, read, touch, use, or interact with the research object *and* the researcher believes that the security and comfort of respondents' homes is an important element affecting the quality of the data collected.

**Table 7.1** Ways to Gather Data

| Data Collection Method | Description |
| --- | --- |
| In-home interview | The interviewer conducts the interview in the respondent's home. Appointments may be made ahead by telephone. |
| Mall-intercept interview | Shoppers in a mall are approached and asked to take part in the survey. Questions may be asked in the mall or in the mall-intercept company's facilities located in the mall. |
| In-office interview | The interviewer makes an appointment with business executives or managers to conduct the interview at the respondent's place of work. |
| "Traditional" telephone interview | Interviewers work out of their homes to conduct telephone interviews with households or business representatives. |
| Central location telephone interview | Interviewers work in a data collection company's office using cubicles or work areas for each interviewer. Often the supervisor has the ability to "listen in" to interviews and to check that they are being conducted correctly. |
| Computer-assisted telephone interview | With a computer-assisted telephone interview, the questions are programmed for a computer screen and the interviewer then reads them off. Responses are entered directly into the computer program by the interviewer. |
| Fully computerized interview | A computer is programmed to administer the questions. Respondents interact with the computer and enter in their own answers by using a keyboard, by touching the screen, or by using some other means. |
| Online or other Internet-based survey | Respondents fill out a questionnaire that resides on the Internet, or otherwise accesses it via the Internet such as receiving an e-mail attachment or downloading the file online. |
| Group self-administered survey | Respondents take the survey in a group context. Each respondent works individually, but they meet as a group and this allows the researcher to economize. |
| Drop-off survey | Questionnaires are left with the respondent to fill out. The administrator may return at a later time to pick up the completed questionnaire, or it may be mailed in. |
| Mail survey | Questionnaires are mailed to prospective respondents who are asked to fill them out and return them by mail. |

Some research objectives require the respondents' physical presence in order to interact with the research object. A company develops a new type of countertop toaster oven that is designed to remain perfectly clean. However, in order to get the benefit of clean cooking, the oven must be configured differently for different cooking applications, and the throw-away "grease-catch foil" must be placed in just the right position to work properly. Will consumers be able to follow the instructions? This is an example of a study that would require researchers to conduct surveys in the home kitchens of the respondents. Researchers would observe respondents open the box, unwrap and assemble the device, read the directions, and cook a meal. All of this may take an hour or more. Again, respondents may not be willing to travel somewhere and spend an hour on a research project. But they would be more likely to do this in their own home.

■ In-home interviews facilitate interviewer–interviewee rapport.

## Mall-Intercept Interviews

Although the in-home interview has important advantages, it has the significant disadvantage of cost. The expense of in-home interviewer travel is high, even for local surveys. Patterned after "man-on-the-street" interviews pioneered by opinion-polling companies and other "high-traffic" surveys conducted in settings where crowds of pedestrians pass by, the **mall-intercept interview** is one in which the respondent is encountered and questioned while he or she is visiting a shopping mall. A mall-intercept company generally has its offices located within a large shopping mall, usually one that draws from a regional rather than a local market area. Typically, the interview company negotiates exclusive rights to do interviews in the mall and, thus, forces all marketing research companies that wish to do mall intercepts in that area to use that interview company's services. In any case, the travel costs are eliminated because the respondents incur the costs themselves by traveling to the mall. Mall-intercept interviewing has acquired a major role as a survey method due to its ease of implementation.[11] Shoppers are intercepted in the pedestrian traffic areas of shopping malls and either interviewed on the spot or asked to move to a permanent interviewing facility located in the mall office. Although some malls do not allow marketing research interviewing because they view it as a nuisance to shoppers, many do permit mall-intercept interviews and may rely on these data themselves to fine-tune their own marketing programs.

In addition to low cost, mall interviews have most of the advantages associated with in-home interviewing. Perhaps the most important advantage is the presence of an interviewer who can interact with the respondent.[12] However, a few disadvantages are specifically associated with mall interviewing, and it is necessary to point them out here. First, sample representativeness is an issue, for most malls draw from a relatively small area in close proximity to their location. If researchers are looking for a representative sample of some larger area, such as the county or MSA, they should be wary of using the mall intercept. Some people shop at malls more frequently than others and therefore have a greater chance of being interviewed.[13] Recent growth of nonmall retailing concepts such as catalogs and stand-alone discounters such as Wal-Mart means that more mall visitors are recreational shoppers rather than convenience-oriented shoppers, resulting in the need to scrutinize mall-intercept samples as to what consumer groups they actually represent.[14] Also, many shoppers refuse to take part in mall interviews for various reasons. Nevertheless, special selection procedures called quotas, which are described in Chapter 10, may be used to counter the problem of nonrepresentativeness.

A second shortcoming of mall-intercept interviewing is that a shopping mall does not have a comfortable home environment that is conducive to rapport and close attention to details. The respondents may feel uncomfortable because passersby stare at them; they may be pressed for time or otherwise preoccupied by various distractions outside the researcher's control. These factors may adversely affect the quality of the interview. As we indicated earlier, some interview companies attempt to counter this problem by taking respondents to special interview rooms located in the interview company's mall offices. This procedure minimizes distractions and encourages respondents to be more relaxed. Some mall-interviewing facilities have kitchens and rooms with one-way mirrors.

- Mall-intercept interviews are conducted in large shopping malls, and they are less expensive per interview than are in-home interviews.

- Mall-intercept interview companies make this method easy and popular.

- The representativeness of mall interview samples is always an issue.

- Mall-interview companies use rooms in their small headquarters areas to conduct private interviews in a relaxed setting.

- Go to Interactive Learning at the end of this chapter and discover how to locate some data collection firms in your area.

### In-Office Interviews

Although the in-home and mall-intercept interview methods are appropriate for a wide variety of consumer goods, marketing research conducted in the business-to-business or organizational market typically requires interviews with business executives, purchasing agents, engineers, or other managers. Normally, **in-office interviews** take place in person while the respondent is in his or her office, or perhaps in a company lounge area. Interviewing businesspeople face-to-face has essentially the same advantages and drawbacks as in-home consumer interviewing. For example, if Hewlett-Packard wanted information regarding user preferences for different features that might be offered in a new ultra-high-speed laser printer designed for business accounting firms, it would make sense to interview prospective users or purchasers of these printers. It would also be logical to interview these people at their places of business.

As you might imagine, in-office personal interviews incur relatively high costs. Those executives qualified to give opinions on a specific topic or individuals who would be involved in product purchase decisions must first be located. Sometimes names can be obtained from sources such as industry directories or trade association membership lists. More frequently, screening must be conducted over the telephone by calling a particular company that is believed to have executives of the type needed. However, locating those people within a large organization may be time consuming. Once a qualified person is located, the next step is to persuade that person to agree to an interview and then set up a time for the interview. This may require a sizable incentive. Finally, an interviewer must go to the particular place at the appointed time. Even with appointments, long waits are sometimes encountered and cancellations are not uncommon because businesspeople's schedules sometimes shift unexpectedly. Added to these cost factors is the fact that interviewers who specialize in businessperson interviews are more costly in general because of their specialized knowledge and abilities. They have to navigate around gatekeepers such as secretaries, learn technical jargon, and be conversant on product features when the respondent asks pointed questions or even criticizes questions as they are posed to him or her.

■ In-office interviews are conducted at executives' or managers' places of work because they are the most suitable locations.

■ In-office personal interviews incur costs due to difficulties in accessing qualified respondents.

### Telephone Interviews

As we have mentioned previously, the need for a face-to-face interview is often predicated on the necessity of the respondent's actually seeing a product, advertisement, or packaging sample. On the other hand, it may be vital that the interviewer watch the respondent to ensure correct procedures are followed or otherwise to verify something about the respondent or his or her reactions. If, however, physical contact is not necessary, telephone interviewing is an attractive option. There are a number of advantages as well as disadvantages associated with telephone interviewing.[15] The advantages of telephone interviewing are many, and they explain the popularity of phone surveys. First, the telephone is a relatively inexpensive way to collect survey data. Long-distance telephone charges are much lower than the cost of a face-to-face interview. A second advantage of the telephone interview is that it has the potential to yield a very high-quality sample. If the researcher employs random-dialing procedures and proper callback measures, the telephone approach may produce a better sample than any other survey procedure. A third and very important advantage is that telephone surveys have very quick turnaround times. Most telephone interviews are of short duration anyway, but a good interviewer may complete several interviews per

■ Advantages of telephone interviews are cost, quality, and speed.

hour. Conceivably, a study could have the data collection phase executed in a few days with telephone interviews. In fact, in the political polling industry, in which real-time information on voter opinions is essential, it is not unusual to have national telephone polls completed in a single night.

Unfortunately, the telephone survey approach has several inherent shortcomings. First, the respondent cannot be shown anything or physically interact with the research object. This shortcoming ordinarily eliminates the telephone survey as an alternative in situations requiring that the respondent view product prototypes, advertisements, packages, or anything else. A second disadvantage is that the telephone interview does not permit the interviewer to make the various judgments and evaluations that can be made by the face-to-face interviewer. For example, judgments regarding respondent income based on the home they live in and other outward signs of economic status cannot be made. Similarly, the telephone does not allow for the observation of body language and facial expressions, nor does it permit eye contact. On the other hand, some may argue that the lack of face-to-face contact is helpful. Self-disclosure studies have indicated that respondents provide more information in personal interviews, except when the topics are threatening or potentially embarrassing. Questions on alcohol consumption, contraceptive methods, racial issues, or income tax reporting will probably generate more valid responses when asked in the relative anonymity of a telephone call than when administered face-to-face.[16]

A third disadvantage of the telephone interview is that the marketing researcher is more limited in the quantity and types of information that he or she can obtain. Very long interviews are inappropriate for the telephone, as are questions with lengthy lists of response options that respondents will have difficulty remembering when they are read over the telephone. Respondents short on patience may hang up during interviews, or they may utter short and convenient responses just to speed up the interview. Obviously, the telephone is a poor choice for conducting an interview with many open-ended questions.

■ The telephone is a poor choice for conducting a survey with many open-ended questions.

A last problem with telephone interviews is the growing threat to its existence by the increased use of answering machines, caller ID, and call-blocking devices being adopted by consumers.[17] The research industry is concerned about these gatekeeping methods, and it is just beginning to study ways around them.[18] Another difficulty is that legitimate telephone interviewers must contend with the negative impression people have of telemarketers,[19] and it is too early to judge the effects of the Do Not Call legislation we discussed in Chapter 2.

■ Telephone interviewers must contend with the negative impression people have of telemarketers.

There are two types of telephone interviews: traditional and central location. As you can guess, telephone interviewing has been and continues to be greatly impacted by advances in telephone systems and communications technology. As you will see, the traditional telephone approach has largely faded away, whereas the central location approach has embraced technological advances in telephone systems.

**Traditional Telephone Interviewing.** Technology has radically changed telephone surveys; however, it is worthwhile to describe this form of telephone interviewing as a starting point. Prior to central location and computer-assisted telephone interviewing, these **traditional telephone interviews** were those that were conducted either from the homes of the telephone interviewing staff or from telephone stalls located in the data collection company's offices. Everything was done mechanically. That is, interviewers dialed the telephone number manually, they read questions off a printed questionnaire, they were responsible for following special instructions on how to administer the questions, and they checked off the respondent's answers on each questionnaire. Quality control was limited to training sessions, sometimes in the form of a dress rehearsal by administering the questionnaire to the supervisor or another interviewer, and to callback checks by the supervisor to verify that the respondent had taken part in the interview. Obviously, the traditional telephone-interview method offers great potential for errors. In addition to the possibilities of misdialing and making mistakes in administering the questions, there are potential problems of insufficient callbacks for not-at-homes, and a host of other problems. Also, because the actual hours worked while performing telephone interviews are difficult to track, most interview companies opt for a "per completion" compensation system. That is, the interviewer is compensated for each questionnaire delivered to the office that is completely filled out. As you can imagine, there have been instances of dishonest interviewers turning in falsified results.

■ Traditional telephone interviewing has great potential for errors.

A concern with traditional telephone interviewing is interviewer cheating. Although most traditional telephone interviewers are honest, only minimal control and supervision can be used with this method. Consequently, there are temptations for cheating such as turning in bogus completed questionnaires or conducting interviews with respondents who do not qualify for the survey at hand. When traditional telephone interviewing is used, checks should be more extensive and may include the following:

ETHICS

1 Have an independent party call back a sample of each interviewer's respondents to verify that they took part in the survey.
2 Have interviewers submit copies of their telephone logs to validate that the work was performed on the dates and in the time periods required.
3 If long-distance calls were made, have interviewers submit copies of their telephone bill with long-distance charges itemized to check that the calls were made properly.
4 If there is a concern about a particular interviewer's diligence, request that the interviewer be taken off the project.

A researcher should always check the accuracy and validity of interviews, regardless of the data collection method used.

**Central Location Telephone Interviewing.** This form of telephone interviewing is in many ways the research industry's standard. With **central location telephone interviewing**, a field data-collection company installs several telephone lines at one location, and the interviewers make calls from the central location. Usually, interviewers have separate enclosed work spaces and lightweight headsets that free both hands so they can record responses. Everything is done from this central location. Obviously, there are many advantages to operating from a central location. For example, resources are pooled, and interviewers can handle multiple surveys, such as calling plant managers in the afternoon and households during the evening shift.

The reasons for the prominence of the central location phone interview are savings and control. Apart from cost savings, perhaps the most important reason is quality control. To begin, recruitment and training are performed uniformly at this location. Interviewers can be oriented to the equipment, they can study the questionnaire and

■ Central location interviewing is the current telephone survey standard.

Trained interviewers conduct telephone interviews at MRSI. Visit MRSI at **www.mrsi.com**.

◼ Central location telephone interviewing affords good control of interviewers. Visit **www.mktginc.com** for an example of a limited-services marketing research firm offering central location telephone interviewing.

its instructions, and they can simulate the interview among themselves over their phone lines. Also, the actual interviewing process can be monitored. Most telephone-interviewing facilities have monitoring equipment that permits a supervisor to listen in on interviewing as it is being conducted. Interviewers who are not doing the interview properly can be spotted and the necessary corrective action can be taken. Ordinarily, each interviewer will be monitored at least once per shift, but the supervisor may focus attention on newly hired interviewers to ensure they are doing their work correctly. The fact that each interviewer never knows when the supervisor will listen in guarantees more overall diligence than would be seen otherwise. Also, completed questionnaires are checked on the spot as a further quality control; interviewers can be immediately informed of any deficiencies in filling out the questionnaire. Finally, there is control over interviewers' schedules. That is, interviewers report in and out and work regular hours, even if they are evening hours, and make calls during the time periods stipulated by the researcher as appropriate interviewing times.

## Computer-Administered Interviews

Computer technology has impacted the telephone data collection industry significantly. There are two variations of computer-administered telephone-interview systems. In one, a human interviewer is used, but in the other a computer, sometimes with a synthesized or tape-recorded voice, is used. At the same time, there are important computer-assisted interview methods that have recently emerged, which we describe in this section as well.

### Computer-Assisted Telephone Interviews (CATI)

The most advanced companies have computerized the central location telephone-interviewing process; such systems are called **computer-assisted telephone interviews (CATIs)**. Although each system is unique, and new developments occur almost daily, we can describe a typical situation. Here each interviewer is equipped with a hands-free headset and is seated in front of a computer screen that is driven by the company's computer system. Often the computer dials the prospective respondent's telephone automatically, and the computer screen provides the interviewer with the introductory comments. As the interview progresses, the interviewer moves through the questions by pressing a key or a series of keys on the keyboard. Some systems use light pens or pressure-sensitive screens. The questions and possible responses appear on the screen one at a time. The interviewer reads the question to the respondent, and then enters the response code. Then, the computer moves on to the next appropriate question. For example, an interviewer might ask if the respondent owns a dog. If the answer is "yes," there could appear a series of questions regarding what type of dog food the dog owner buys. If the answer is "no," these questions would be inappropriate. Instead, the computer program skips to the next appropriate question, which might be "Do you own a cat?" In other words, the computer eliminates the human error potential that would exist if this survey were done in the traditional paper-and-pencil telephone-interview mode. The human interviewer is just the "voice" of the computer.

> With CATI, the interviewer reads the questions off a computer screen and enters respondents' answers directly into the computer program.

The computer can even be used to customize questions. For example, in the early part of a long interview, you might ask a respondent the years, makes, and models of all cars he or she owns. Later in the interview, you might ask questions about each specific car owned. The question might come up on the interviewer's screen as follows: "You said you own a Lexus. Who in your family drives this car most often?" Other questions about this car and others owned would appear in similar fashion. Questions like this can, of course, be dealt with in a traditional or central location manual interview, but they are handled much more efficiently in the computerized version because the interviewer does not need to physically flip questionnaire pages back and forth or remember previous responses.

> With CATI, the interviewer is the "voice" of the computer.

The CATI approach also eliminates the need for editing completed questionnaires and creating computer data files by later manually entering every response with a keyboard. There is no checking for errors in completed questionnaires because there is no physical questionnaire. More to the point, in most computerized interview systems it is not permitted to enter an "impossible" answer. For example, if a question has three possible answers, with codes "A," "B," and "C," and the interviewer enters a "D" by mistake, the computer will ask for the answer to be reentered until an acceptable code is entered. If a combination or pattern of answers is impossible, the computer will not accept an answer, or it may alert the interviewer to the inconsistency and move to a series of questions that will resolve the discrepancy. Data entry for completed questionnaires is eliminated because data are entered directly into a computer file as the interviewing is completed.

> Most CATI systems are programmed to make wrong answers impossible.

This second operation brings to light another advantage of computer-assisted interviewing. Tabulations may be run at any point in the study. Such real-time reporting is impossible with pencil-and-paper questionnaires, which often entail a wait of several days following interviewing completion before detailed tabulations of the results are available. Instantaneous results available with computerized telephone interviewing provide some real advantages. Based on preliminary tabulations, certain questions may be dropped, saving time and money in subsequent interviewing. If, for example, over 90% of those interviewed answered a particular question in the same manner, there may be no need to continue asking the question.

> CATI systems permit tabulation in midsurvey.

Tabulations may also suggest the addition of questions to the survey. If an unexpected pattern of product use is uncovered in the early interviewing stages, questions can be added to further delve into this behavior. So the computer-administered telephone survey affords an element of flexibility unavailable in the traditional paper-and-pencil survey methods. Finally, managers may find the early reporting of survey results useful in preliminary planning and strategy development. Sometimes survey project deadlines run very close to managers' presentation deadlines, and advance indications of the survey's findings permit managers to organize their presentations in advance rather than all in a rush the night before. The many advantages and quick turnaround of CATI and CAPI (computer-assisted personal interviewing) make them mainstay data collection methods for many syndicated omnibus survey services.[20]

In sum, computer-administered telephone interviewing options are very attractive to marketing researchers because of the advantages of cost savings, quality control, and time savings over the paper-and-pencil method.[21]

### Fully Computerized Interviews (Not Online)

Some companies have developed **fully computerized interviews**, in which the survey is administered completely by a computer, but not online. With one such system, a computer dials a phone number and a recording is used to introduce the survey. The respondent then uses the push buttons on his or her telephone to make responses, thereby interacting directly with the computer. In the research industry, this approach is known as **completely automated telephone survey (CATS)**. CATS has been successfully employed for customer satisfaction studies, service quality monitoring, election day polls, product/warranty registration, and even in-home product tests with consumers who have been given a prototype of a new product.[22]

In another system, the respondent sits or stands in front of the computer unit and reads the instructions off the screen. Each question and its various response options appear on the screen, and the respondent answers by pressing a key or touching the screen. For example, the question may ask the respondent to rate how satisfied, on a scale of 1 to 10 (where 1 is very unsatisfied and 10 is very satisfied), he or she was the last time he or she used a travel agency to plan a family vacation. The respondent is instructed to press the key with the number appropriate to his or her degree of satisfaction. So, the respondent might press a "2" or a "7," depending on his or her experience and expectations. If, however, a "0" or some other ineligible key were pressed, the computer could be programmed to beep, indicating that the response was inappropriate, and instruct the respondent to make another entry.

All of the advantages of computer-driven interviewing are found in this approach, plus the interviewer expense or extra cost of human voice communication capability for the computer is eliminated. Because respondents' answers are saved in a file during the interview itself, tabulation can take place on a daily basis. Even if the interviews are conducted in remote locations across the United States, it is a simple matter to download the files to the central facility for daily tabulations. Some researchers believe that the research industry should move to replace pen-and-paper questionnaires with computer-based ones.[23]

### Online and Other Internet-Based Interviews

Online research may take on any of a number of faces, but the **Internet-based questionnaire**, in which the respondent answers questions online is becoming the industry standard for online surveys. Internet-based online surveys are fast, easy, and inexpensive.[24] These questionnaires accommodate all of the standard question formats, and they are very flexible, as they have the ability to present pictures, diagrams, or displays to respondents. In fact, this ability is a major reason why researchers tracking advertising effects prefer online surveys to telephone surveys, which have been a standard data collection method for advertising tracking for a great many years.[25] The researcher can check the Web site for current tabulations whenever he or she desires, and respondents can access the online survey at any time of the day or night. Online data collection has had and will continue to have a profound impact on the marketing research landscape.[26] For instance, in the case of customer satisfaction, instead of "episodic" research in which a company does a large study one time per year, it allows for "continuous market intelligence" in which the survey is posted permanently on the Web and modified as the company's strategies are implemented. Company managers can click up tabulated customer reactions on a daily basis.[27] Some researchers refer to this advantage of online surveys as "real-time research."[28]

Dr. William H. MacElroy, president of Socratic Technologies, and his associates have compared online surveys with traditional data collection methods.[29] Online surveys have important advantages of speed and low cost, plus real-time access of data; however, there are drawbacks of sample representativeness, respondent validation,

> ■ Online surveys have significant advantages over traditional surveys, and their use will increase in the future.

Just who really is answering your online survey?

With 7 years of online panel experience, we know our ithinkers

> Our panel was built one person at a time — Never through webmaster referral programs, co-registrations or mass web-site intercepts

> Respondent survey answers are validated against stored demographic information for consistency and accuracy

> Security, privacy and double opt-in best practices are strictly enforced

> Approximately 1.4 million US household members

> Survey programming and hosting also available for start-to-finish fielding solutions

[i.think_inc.]

www.ithinkinc.com    2811 McKinney Ave., Suite 218    Dallas, TX 75204    [214] 855-3777

A disadvantage of online surveys is not being able to validate who is answering the survey. ithinkinc can validate the members of their online panel.

By permission, i.thinkinc.

and difficulty in asking probing types of questions. Sample representativeness is most troublesome when global market research is involved, and firms are finding that considerable investments are required to achieve this goal.[30] Nevertheless, as Internet connectivity becomes more widespread and integrated into daily life, and as software advances to provide more flexibility and features on Web-based questionnaires, online surveys will undoubtedly become the most prevalent data collection mode. In fact, companies such as Knowledge Networks, Inc., are overcoming the sample representativeness problem by recruiting online panels whose demographic and purchasing profiles are consistent with target markets. These online panels provide accurate research data very quickly.[31]

■ Online surveys have important advantages of speed and low cost, plus real-time access of data; however, there are drawbacks of sample representativeness, respondent validation, and difficulty in asking probing types of questions.

## Self-Administered Surveys

You may be having a bit of difficulty with the "self-administered" designation, as online surveys are also taken by respondents alone, but the following survey modes are, for the most part, all paper-and-pencil situations in which the respondent fills out a static copy of the questionnaire. Probably the most popular type of self-administered survey is the mail survey; however, there are other variations—the group self-administered survey and the drop-off survey—that are discussed first.

■ With a self-administered survey, each respondent works at his or her own pace.

### Group Self-Administered Surveys

Basically, a **group self-administered survey** entails administering a questionnaire to respondents in groups, rather than individually, for convenience or to gain certain economies. One way to be more economical is to have respondents self-administer the questions. For example, 20 or 30 people might be recruited to view a TV program sprinkled with test commercials. All respondents would be seated in a viewing-room facility, and a videotape would run on a large television projection screen. Then they would be given a questionnaire to fill out regarding their recall of test ads, their reactions to the ads, and so on. As you would suspect, it is handled in a group context primarily to reduce costs and to provide the ability to interview a large number of people in a short time.

■ Group self-administered surveys economize in time and money because a group of respondents participates at the same time.

Variations for group self-administered surveys are limitless. Students can be administered surveys in their classes; church groups can be administered surveys during meetings; social clubs and organizations, company employees, movie theatre patrons, and any other group can be administered surveys during meetings, work, or leisure time. Often the researcher will compensate the group with a monetary payment as a means of recruiting the support of the group's leaders. In all of these cases, each respondent works through the questionnaire at his or her own pace. Granted, a survey administrator may be present, so there is some opportunity for interaction concerning instructions or how to respond, but the group context often discourages the respondents from asking all but the most pressing questions.

### Drop-Off Surveys

Another variation of the self-administered survey is the **drop-off survey**, in which the survey representative approaches a prospective respondent, introduces the general purpose of the survey to the prospect, and leaves it with the respondent to fill out on his or her own. Essentially, the objective is to gain the prospective respondent's

■ Drop-off surveys must be self-explanatory.

cooperation. The respondent is told the questionnaire is self-explanatory, and it will be left with him or her to fill out at leisure. Perhaps the representative will return to pick up the questionnaire at a certain time, or the respondent may be instructed to complete and return it by prepaid mail. Normally, the representative will return on the same day or the next day to pick up the completed questionnaire. In this way, a representative can cover a number of residential areas or business locations in a single day with an initial drop-off pass and a later pick-up pass. Drop-off surveys are especially appropriate for local market research undertakings in which travel is necessary but limited. They have been reported to have quick turnaround, high response rates, minimal interviewer influence on answers, and good control over how respondents are selected; plus, they are inexpensive.[32]

■ **Several variations of drop-off surveys exist.**

Variations of the drop-off method include handing out the surveys to people at their places of work and asking them to fill them out at home and then to return them the next day. Some hotel chains have questionnaires in their rooms with an invitation to fill them out and turn them in at the desk on checkout. Stores sometimes have short surveys on customer demographics, media habits, purchase intentions, or other information that customers are asked to fill out at home and return on their next shopping trips. A gift certificate drawing may even be used as an incentive to participate. As you can see, the term *drop-off* can be stretched to cover any situation in which the prospective respondent encounters the survey as though it were "dropped off" by a research representative.

## Mail Surveys

A **mail survey** is one in which the questions are mailed to prospective respondents, who are asked to fill them out and return them to the researcher by mail.[33] Part of its attractiveness stems from its self-administered aspect: There are no interviewers to recruit, train, monitor, and compensate. Similarly, mailing lists are readily available from companies that specialize in this business, and it is possible to access very specific groups of target respondents. For example, it is possible to obtain a list of physicians specializing in family practice who operate clinics in cities larger than 500,000 people. Also, one may opt to purchase computer files, printed labels, or even labeled envelopes from these companies. In fact, some list companies will even provide insertion and mailing services. There are a number of companies that sell mailing lists, and most, if not all, have online purchase options. If you want to see an example, look at Experian's Market Share Online at **www.marketshareonline.net/index.asp**. On a per-respondent basis, mail surveys are very inexpensive. In fact, they are almost always the least expensive survey method in this regard. But mail surveys incur all of the problems associated with not having an interviewer present, which we discussed earlier in this chapter.

Despite the fact that the mail survey is described as "powerful, effective, and efficient"[34] by the American Statistical Association, the mail survey is plagued by two major problems. The first is **nonresponse**, which refers to questionnaires that are not returned.[35] The second is **self-selection bias**, which means that those who do respond are probably different from those who do not fill out the questionnaire and return it; therefore, the sample gained through this method is nonrepresentative of the general population. To be sure, the mail survey is not the only survey method that suffers from nonresponse and self-selection bias. Failures to respond are found in all types of

■ **Mail surveys suffer from nonresponse and self-selection bias.**

surveys, and marketing researchers must be constantly alert to the possibilities that their final samples are somehow different from the original list of potential respondents because of some systematic tendency or latent pattern of response. Whatever the survey mode used, those who respond may be more involved with the product, they may have more education, they might be more or less dissatisfied, or they may even be more opinionated in general than the target population of concern.[36]

When informing clients of data collection alternatives, market researchers should inform them of the nonresponse problems and biases inherent in each one being considered. For example, mail surveys are notorious for low response, and those respondents who do fill out and return a mail questionnaire are likely to be different from those who do not. At the same time, there are people who refuse to answer questions over the telephone, and consumers who like to shop are more likely to be encountered in mall-intercept interviews than are those who do not like to shop. Each data collection method has its own nonresponse and bias considerations, and a conscientious researcher will help his or her client understand the dangers represented in the methods under consideration. Thus, nonresponse and the subsequent danger of self-selection bias is greatest with mail surveys, because mail surveys of households typically achieve response rates of less than 20%. Researchers have tried various tactics to increase the response rate, such as using registered mail, color, money, personalization, reminder postcards, and so on.[37] Even with these incentives, response rates are low for mail surveys.[38] Despite this situation, mail surveys are viable in countries with high literacy rates and dependable postal systems.[39] Remember, however, that consumers and business respondents are constantly changing, and the inducement that works today may not necessarily work the same way in the future. One way research companies have sought to cope with the low response rate for mail surveys is to create a mail panel in which respondents agree to respond to several questionnaires mailed to them over time, and some see this approach as a preferred option.[40] Others are shifting to Internet communication systems that are faster and cheaper. Of course, the panel members are carefully prescreened to ensure that the mail panel represents the company's target market or consumers of interest.

■ Self-selection bias means respondents who return surveys by mail may differ from the original sample.

■ When informing clients of data collection alternatives, market researchers should inform them of the nonresponse problems and biases inherent in each one being considered.

■ To cope with low response to mail surveys, some companies have turned to mail panels.

## CHOICE OF THE SURVEY METHOD

At the outset of the discussion of the various types of interviewing used in marketing research, we made the comment that the marketing researcher is faced with the problem of selecting the one survey mode that is optimal in a given situation. Each data collection method has unique advantages, disadvantages, and special features, and we have summarized them for you in Table 7.2. How do you decide which is the best survey mode for a particular research project? When answering this question, the researcher should always have as a foremost objective the quality of the data collected. Even the most sophisticated techniques of analysis cannot make up for poor data. "Garbage in, garbage out" is the time-worn phrase that reflects this concern for quality data. He or she should strive to choose a survey mode that achieves the highest quality of data allowable with the cost, time, and other special considerations involved with the research project at hand. In the following paragraphs, we will illustrate how these issues would lead to the selection of a single data collection mode.

■ In selecting a data collection mode, the researcher balances quality against cost, time, and other special considerations.

## The Survey Data Collection Time Horizon

Sometimes data must be collected within a very close deadline. There are many reasons for deadlines: A national campaign is set to kick off in four weeks and one component needs testing; an upcoming trademark infringement trial needs a survey of the awareness of the company's trademark and the trial starts in four weeks; an application deadline for a radio license with the FCC is in six weeks and a listenership study of other stations in the area must be conducted, and so on. Traditionally, if there was a very short time horizon, telephone surveys were often selected due to their speed. If the respondent had to interact with the research object, such as a product prototype, mall-intercept studies were a top choice. Today, online surveys are exceptionally fast and can accommodate all but physical handling of research objects. Magazine ads, logos, and other marketing stimuli may be evaluated in online surveys. Poor choices would be personal interviews that are door-to-door or mail surveys.

As we just noted, when time is a factor in doing research, online surveys are fast. As online surveying has matured, marketing researchers soon learned that better quality data could be achieved by collecting data from established panels consisting of respondents who had previously agreed to provide information. Panels have been widely used in the research industry to ensure high response rates. However, recruiting panel

■ A short deadline may dictate which data collection method to use.

■ By their very nature, some survey data collection methods take longer than others.

Online research. It's the most effective tool for reaching your target in today's fast-paced world. And e-Rewards Market Research can help you maximize the value of e-research better than anyone. We've become the leader in online panel quality by combining innovative technology with proven practices to deliver faster, more accurate results. We've established 15 points of quality differentiation that set us apart — and you can learn about these points at http://company.e-rewards.com/15points. You'll discover all of our unique benefits, including:

• **Respect for Research Integrity.** We're dedicated to maintaining social science standards in e-research and delivering the highest quality results.

• **Superior Client Service.** Our clients' needs come first. We hold ourselves accountable for delivering superior service by monitoring our own client satisfaction and retention rates.

• **Pay for Performance.** We guarantee our clients' satisfaction and will not accept payment for services that do not meet or exceed their expectations.

• **Powerful Panels.** Most importantly, our panels perform because we know our members — and they respond. For more details on our highly effective consumer and business panels, see the reverse.

**For more information, visit e-rewards.com/researchers or call 1-888-20-EMAIL today!**

e-Rewards has implemented 15 points of quality differentiation to their panel management in order to ensure the integrity of their panel. Read e-Rewards' 15 points of quality differentiation at: **http://researcher .e-rewards.com/15points**.

By permission, e-Rewards, Inc.

**Table 7.2**  Key Advantages and Disadvantages of Alternative Data Collection Methods

| Method | Key Advantages | Key Disadvantages | Comment |
|---|---|---|---|
| In-home interview | Conducted in privacy of the home, which facilitates interviewer–respondent rapport | Cost per interview can be high; interviewers must travel to respondents' homes | Often much information per interview is gathered |
| Mall-intercept interview | Fast and convenient data collection method | Only mall patrons are interviewed; respondents may feel uncomfortable answering questions in the mall | Mall-intercept company often has exclusive interview rights for that mall |
| In-office interview | Useful for interviewing busy executives | Relatively high cost per interview; gaining access is sometimes difficult | Useful when respondents must examine prototypes or samples of products |
| Central location telephone interview | Fast turnaround; good quality control; reasonable cost | Restricted to telephone communication | Long-distance calling is not a problem |
| CATI | Computer eliminates human interviewer error; simultaneous data input to computer file; good quality control | Setup costs can be high | Losing ground to online surveys and panels |
| Fully computerized interview | Respondent responds at his or her own pace; computer data file results | Respondent must have access to a computer or be computer literate | Many variations and an emerging data collection method with exciting prospects |
| Online questionnaire | Ease of creating and posting; fast turnaround; computer data file results | Respondent must have access to the Internet | Fastest-growing data collection method; very flexible; online analysis available |
| Group self-administered survey | Cost of interviewer eliminated; economical for assembled groups of respondents | Must find groups and secure permission to conduct the survey | Prone to errors of self-administered surveys; good for pretests or pilot tests |
| Drop-off survey | Cost of interviewer eliminated; appropriate for local market surveys | Generally not appropriate for large-scale national surveys | Many variations exist with respect to logistics and applications |
| Mail survey | Economical method; good listing companies exist | Low response rates; self-selection bias; slow | Many strategies to increase response rate exist |

members is costly and time consuming. e-Rewards® Market Research is an example of a firm that provides online panel access to clients, with over 3 million panel members. The e-Rewards panel members are recruited into the panel by invitation only and are offered valuable rewards for their time spent taking and responding to survey requests.

## The Survey Data Collection Budget

Traditionally, the least expensive method of collecting data was the mail survey. It is still a very inexpensive method of collecting data. However, it is used infrequently due to the low response rate. Online survey research is another option. There are some online survey companies that allow the client to design the questionnaire and select the target sample type and number. Surveys can be completed for a few hundred or a few thousand dollars. Insight Express is an example of such a company. However, all online surveys enjoy the advantage of being less expensive than many of the other data collection methods. Companies using online surveys must ask themselves if they can use data generated only from people with online access. And there are companies that can supply online access to representative samples made up of people who wouldn't normally have online access but have been supplied with it by the research firm. An example is Knowledge Networks. If neither of these methods, mail or online, will work, probably the next least expensive method would be the use of telephone surveying.

■ Costs vary greatly depending on the survey mode. Costs have been greatly reduced by some online survey companies.

## Incidence Rate

By **incidence rate** we are referring to the percentage of the population that possesses some characteristic necessary to be included in the survey. Rarely are research projects targeted to "everyone." In most cases, there are qualifiers for being included in a study. For example, the study may be targeted only to registered voters, or persons owning and driving their own automobile, or persons 16 years of age and older, and so on. Sometimes the incidence rate is very low. A drug company may want to interview only men above 50 with medicated cholesterol above 250. A cosmetics firm may only want to interview women who were planning facial cosmetic surgery within the next six months. In low-incidence situations such as these, certain precautions must be taken in selecting the data collection method. For example, in either of the above examples, it would be foolishly expensive to send out interviewers door-to-door looking for members who have the qualifications to participate in the study. A data collection method that can easily and inexpensively screen respondents is desirable. Online surveys, telephone surveys, and, to a lesser extent, mall surveys may be good choices.

■ The incidence rate—the percentage of the population that possesses some characteristic necessary to be included in the survey—affects the data collection mode decision.

## Cultural/Infrastructure Considerations

Data collection methods may be selected based upon different cultural considerations. This has become more of an issue as more and more marketing research companies operate around the globe. For example, in Scandinavia, residents are uncomfortable allowing strangers in their homes. Therefore, telephone and online surveying is more popular than door-to-door interviewing. On the other hand, in India fewer than 10% of the residents have a telephone, and online access is very low. Door-to-door interviewing is used often.[41] In Canada, where incentives are typically not offered to prospective respondents, there is heavy use of telephone surveys, and online research is slowly growing.[42] When a firm plans to conduct a study in a culture about which they are unfamiliar, they should consult local research firms before making the data collection method decision.

■ Culture may affect data collection mode decisions; for example, Scandinavians do not like to allow strangers in their homes.

## Type of Respondent Interaction Required

If only verbal communication is required, telephone surveys may be considered. If the respondent needs to visualize a static stimulus such as a photo of a logo or a magazine ad, mail surveys or online surveys may be considered. If the respondent needs to visualize a nonstatic stimulus such as a short video or moving graphic, online surveys may be considered. If the respondent needs to visualize a nonstatic stimulus such as a 20-minute infomercial, mailed videos (with a considerable incentive!) or mall intercepts could be considered. If the respondent is required to handle, touch, feel, or taste a product, mall intercepts may be considered. If a respondent is required to actually use a product in a realistic setting, in-home personal interviews may be considered.

# SPECIAL INNOVATIVE METHODS FOR SPECIAL SITUATIONS

Remember that we are describing the very *basic* methods of collecting data in this chapter. In practice, there are many, many alternative methods to use for gathering data. Marketing research firms are devising new, innovative methods of collecting data for special situations. For example, marketing researchers recognize there are merits in both qualitative and quantitative research, but it is rare that both are conducted. Instead, focus groups may be used to generate qualitative information, or structured surveys will be conducted to generate quantitative data. TNS NFO combined responses to online consumers' qualitative, open-ended answers with their quantitative rankings. Consumers also saw the responses of other consumers in real time, allowing them to arrive at a consensus of opinion. One of TNS NFO's clients, Hershey Chocolate, USA, was interested in learning more about product interaction among core confectionery categories as well as competing nonconfectionery categories. A study using this combined approach gathered both qualitative and quantitative data and helped Hershey gain a better understanding of consumers' preferences and willingness to substitute different categories of confectioneries. For example, the study found consumers desiring chocolate candy would not substitute gum or mints for chocolate. However, gum and mints were both considered substitutes for nonchocolate candies. Data for the study were gathered from TNS NFO's online, interactive panel, which is composed of households whose demographics are balanced with the larger population. Susan LaPointe, Director of Consumer Insights at Hershey, stated, "This methodology creatively satisfied our need for both open-end hypothesis generating and quantifiable prioritization of results. It did so in a quick and cost-effective manner." This innovative approach to collecting both qualitative and quantitative data illustrates another way in which online survey research can be utilized.

Another example of an innovation in data gathering is Affinnova's IDEA™ technology. The company has designed a system to allow consumers to create variations in product designs to suit their preferences. The company collects data from an online sample. This allows clients such as Proctor & Gamble, Kraft Foods, and Crayola to get preferences on a very large range of product design dimensions from a large sample of consumers quickly and in a cost-efficient manner. Visit the company's Web site at **www.affinova.com**.

It is important that the manager allow the marketing researcher to decide on the survey mode because he or she has a unique understanding of how question characteristics, respondent characteristics, and survey resources and objectives come into play. Choice of survey method can be made by answering the question "What data collection method will generate the most complete and generalizable information within the time horizon and without exceeding the allowable expenditure for data collection?"

■ A survey method can be chosen by answering the question "What data collection method will generate the most complete and generalizable information within the time horizon and without exceeding the allowable expenditure for data collection?"

# SUMMARY

With the exception of observation studies, in which respondents' behavior is observed and recorded by the researcher, and physiological studies, in which physiological measures such as eye movement or GSR are measured, marketing researchers must communicate with respondents in order to gather primary data. Marketing researchers refer to the process of communicating with study respondents as surveys. The four basic survey modes used are: (1) person-administered surveys, (2) computer-assisted surveys, (3) self-administered surveys, and (4) mixed-mode, sometimes called "hybrid," surveys. Person-administered survey modes are advantageous because they allow feedback, permit rapport building, facilitate certain quality controls, and capitalize on the adaptability of a human interviewer. However, they are prone to human error, slow, costly, and sometimes produce respondent apprehension known as "interview evaluation." Computer-administered interviews, on the other hand, are faster, are error-free, may have pictures or graphics capabilities, allow for real-time capture of data, and may make respondents feel more at ease because another person is not listening to their answers. Disadvantages are that technical skills are required and there may be high setup costs. Self-administered survey modes have the advantages of reduced cost, respondent control, and no interview-evaluation apprehension. The disadvantages of self-administered surveys are respondent control in that they may not complete the task or may make errors, lack of a monitor to help guide respondents, and the need to have a perfect questionnaire. Finally, mixed-mode surveys, sometimes referred to as "hybrid" surveys, use multiple data collection methods. The advantage of mixed-mode surveys is that researchers are able to take the advantages of each of the various modes to achieve their data collection goals. Disadvantages are that different modes may produce different responses to the same research question, and researchers must evaluate this. Secondly, mixed-mode methods result in greater complexities as researchers must design different questionnaires and be certain that data from different sources all come together in a common database for analysis.

We described 11 different survey data collection methods: (1) in-home interviews, which are conducted in respondents' homes; (2) mall-intercept interviews, conducted by approaching shoppers in a mall; (3) in-office interviews, conducted with executives or managers in their places of work; (4) telephone interviews, conducted by an interviewer working in his or her home; (5) telephone interviews, conducted from a central location in a telephone-interview company's facilities; (6) computer-assisted telephone interviews, in which the interviewer reads questions off a computer screen and enters responses directly into the program; (7) fully computerized interviews, in which the respondent interacts directly with a computer; (8) online and other Internet-based surveys; (9) group self-administered surveys, in which the questionnaire is handed out to a group for individual responses; (10) drop-off surveys, in which the questionnaire is left with the respondent to be completed and picked up or returned at a later time; and (11) mail surveys, in which questionnaires are mailed to prospective respondents, who are requested to fill them out and mail them back. The specific advantages and disadvantages of each data collection mode were discussed.

So, how do researchers choose the survey data collection method? Researchers must take into account several considerations when deciding on a survey data collection mode. The major concerns are: (1) the survey time horizon, (2) the survey data collection budget, (3) incidence rate, (4) cultural and infrastructure considerations, and (5) the type of respondent interaction required. Ultimately, the researcher should select the data collection mode that will result in the highest quality and quantity of information without exceeding time or budget constraints. Finally, there are many innovative methods for collecting data for special situations. NFO TNS has an online system designed to integrate qualitative with quantitative data. Affinnova's IDEA technique was presented to illustrate how the system collects data to design products based upon consumer preferences.

## KEY TERMS

Survey (p. 199)
Person-administered survey (p. 199)
Computer-administered survey (p. 202)
Interview evaluation (p. 203)
Self-administered survey (p. 205)
Mixed-mode surveys (p. 206)
In-home interview (p. 208)
Mall-intercept interview (p. 210)
In-office interviews (p. 211)
Traditional telephone interviews (p. 212)
Central location telephone interviewing (p. 213)

Computer-assisted telephone interviews (CATI) (p. 214)
Fully computerized interviews (p. 216)
Completely automated telephone survey (CATS) (p. 216)
Internet-based questionnaire (p. 216)
Group self-administered survey (p. 218)
Drop-off survey (p. 218)
Mail survey (p. 219)
Nonresponse (p. 219)
Self-selection bias (p. 219)
Incidence rate (p. 223)

## REVIEW QUESTIONS

1 What is a survey?
2 Under what conditions do marketing researchers consider using surveys?
3 What are the four basic survey modes?
4 What are the advantages of person-administered surveys over computer-administered ones?
5 What is "interview evaluation," and which survey mode is most likely to produce it?
6 Discuss the advantages and disadvantages of self-administered surveys.
7 Discuss why a researcher would or would not use a mixed-mode survey. Give an example to illustrate your points.
8 Indicate the differences among: (a) in-home interviews, (b) mall-intercept interviews, and (c) in-office interviews. What do they share in common?
9 Why are telephone surveys popular?
10 What is the difference between traditional versus central location telephone interviewing?

**11** What does CATI stand for? What does CATS stand for?

**12** What advantages do online surveys have?

**13** How does a drop-off survey differ from a mail survey?

**14** What are the major disadvantages of a mail survey?

**15** What are the major factors to be considered in the choice of the survey method?

**16** Discuss one innovative method being used to collect data for a special situation.

# APPLICATION QUESTIONS

**17** Is a telephone interview inappropriate for a survey that has as one of its objectives a complete listing of all possible advertising media a person was exposed to in the last week? Why or why not?

**18** NAPA Car Parts is a retail chain specializing in stocking and selling both domestic and foreign automobile parts. It is interested in learning about its customers, so the marketing director sends instructions to all 2,000 store managers telling them that whenever a customer makes a purchase of $150 or more, they are to write down a description of the customer who made that purchase. They are to do this just for the second week in October, writing each description on a separate sheet of paper. At the end of the week, they are to send all sheets to the marketing director. Comment on this data collection method.

**19** Discuss the feasibility of each of the types of survey modes for each of the following cases:

  **a** Faberge, Inc., wants to test a new fragrance called "Lime Brut."

  **b** Kelly Services needs to determine how many businesses expect to hire temporary secretaries to replace secretaries who go on vacation during the summer months.

  **c** The *Encyclopedia Britannica* requires information on the degree to which mothers of elementary-school-aged children see encyclopedias as worthwhile purchases for their children.

  **d** AT&T is considering a television screen phone system and wants to know people's reaction to it.

**20** With a telephone survey, when a potential respondent refuses to take part or is found to have changed his or her telephone number or moved away, it is customary to simply try another prospect until a completion is secured. It is not standard practice to report the number of refusals or noncontacts. What are the implications of this policy for the reporting of nonresponse?

**21** Compu-Ask Corporation has developed a stand-alone computerized interview system that can be adapted to almost any type of survey. It can fit on a palm-sized computer, and the respondent directly answers questions using a stylus once the interviewer has turned on the computer and started up the program. Indicate the appropriateness of this interviewing system in each of the following cases:

  **a** A survey of plant managers concerning a new type of hazardous-waste disposal system.

  **b** A survey of high school teachers to see if they are interested in a company's videotapes of educational public broadcast television programs.

  **c** A survey of consumers to determine their reactions to a nonrefrigerated variety of yogurt.

22 A researcher is pondering what survey mode to use for a client who markets a home security system for apartment dwellers. The system comprises sensors that are pressed onto all of the windows and magnetic strips that are glued to each door. Once plugged into an electric socket and activated with a switch box, the system emits a loud alarm and simulates a barking guard dog when an intruder trips one of the sensors. The client wants to know how many apartment dwellers in the United States are aware of the system, what they think of it, and how likely they are to buy it in the coming year. Which consideration factors are positive and which ones are negative for each of the following survey modes: (a) in-home interview, (b) mall-intercept survey, (c) online survey, (d) drop-off survey, and (e) CATI survey?

# INTERACTIVE LEARNING

Go to the Quirk's Web site at **www.quirks.com**. On the left margin under "Research Directories," select "Mall Facilities." Enter your metro area, or one near you, and search for the mall data collection firms near you. Then go back to the "Research Directories" and click on "Telephone Facilities." Again, enter the nearest metro area and learn what telephone data collection firms are near you.

Visit the Web site at **www.prenhall.com/burnsbush**. For this chapter, work through the Self-Study Quizzes, and get instant feedback on whether you need additional studying. On the Web site, you can review the chapter outlines and case information for Chapter 7.

| CASE 7.1 | Steward Research, Inc. |
|---|---|

Joe Steward is President of Steward Research, Inc. The firm specializes in customized research for clients in a variety of industries. The firm has a centralized location telephoning facility, and they have a division, "Steward Online," which specializes in online surveys. However, Joe often calls on the services of other research firms in order to provide his client with the most appropriate data collection method. In a meeting with four Project Directors, Joe discusses each client's special situation.

*Client 1:* A small tools manufacturer has created a new device for sharpening high-precision drill bits. High-precision drill bits are used to drill near-perfect holes in devices such as engine blocks. Such applications have demanding specifications, and drill bits may be used only a few times before being discarded. However, the new sharpening device takes the bits back to original specifications, and the bits can be resharpened and used in as many as a dozen applications. After testing the device and conducting several focus groups in order to get modifications suggestions, the client is

now ready for more information on presentation methods. The Project Director and the client have developed several different presentation formats. The client wishes to have some market evaluation of these presentations before launching a nationwide training program of the company's 125-salesperson salesforce.

*Client 2:* A regional bakery markets several brands of cookies and crackers to supermarkets throughout California, Nevada, Arizona, and New Mexico. The product category is very competitive and competitors use a great deal of newspaper and TV advertising. The bakery's V.P. of Marketing desires more analytics in making the promotional decisions for the firm. She has lamented that though she spends several million dollars a year on promotions in the four states, she has no analytic upon which to evaluate the effectiveness of the expenditures. Steward's Project Director has recommended a study that will establish some baseline measures of top-of-mind brand awareness (called TOMA, this measure of awareness is achieved by asking respondents to name the first three brands that come to mind when thinking of a product or service category, such as "cookies"), attitudes, and preferences.

*Client 3:* An inventor has developed a new device that sanitizes a toothbrush each time the brush is used and replaced in the device. The device uses steam to sanitize the brush, and lab tests have shown the mechanism to be very effective at killing virtually all germs and viruses. The inventor has approached a large manufacturer who is interested in buying the rights to the device but would like some information first. The manufacturer wants to know if people have any concerns with toothbrush sanitization and whether or not they would be willing to purchase a countertop, plug-in device to keep their toothbrush sterile. The Project Director states that the manufacturer is not interested in a sample that represents the United States. They just want to know what a few hundred people think about these issues. The inventor is anxious to supply this information very quickly before the manufacturer loses interest in the idea.

1 For each of the three clients, suggest one or more data collection methods that would be appropriate.
2 For each data collection method you select in question 1, discuss the rationale for your choice.
3 What disadvantages are inherent in the data collection methods you have recommended?

---

## CASE 7.2   |||   Your Integrated Case

### College Life E-Zine: Determining the Data Collection Method

*This is the sixth case in our integrated case series. You will find the previous College Life E-Zine cases in Chapters 1, 2, 3, 4, and 5.*

Bob Watts of ORS Research sat alone in his office late on Friday afternoon. He knew he needed to be thinking more about the research design for the college e-zine project he had been working on. Specifically, he gave some thought to the data collection method that should be used. He sketched out some considerations.

*Population targeted?* The entire student body should be considered the population. Key factor to determine is the percentage of the total students who are "very likely" to subscribe.

*Timing?* We need to go ahead and proceed with collecting this information as soon as we can. Data from the survey will allow us to estimate a number of potential subscribers, and this figure will tell us whether to proceed or not. Somewhat urgent to get this primary data collected.

*Costs?* A budget to collect data has not been confirmed . . . but we are talking about a few thousand dollars. We are constrained by the investment potential of the four investors. Not dealing with large, multinational corporation that could invest hundreds of thousands if need be.

*Cultural considerations?* Does it matter what time during the year we conduct the survey? Should not conflict with midterms or final exams. Other special considerations of college student life?

*Infrastructure considerations?* A very high percentage, nearly 100%, of the students have telephone service. On-campus students have access to high-speed Internet service. University can't tell us what percentage of the students actually are online, though they think it's fairly high. All students have an e-mail account.

*Respondent interaction?* We need to adequately describe the concept of the e-zine before we ask respondents for their intention to subscribe. We will also want their preferences for different types of e-zine features as well as information on students' buying habits, their classification, and so on. It would be nice, for "tweaking" a proposed magazine feature, to allow students to actually interact with the magazine.

*Special situations?* The university will allow us permission to use its electronic directory which has all registered students' names, telephone numbers, and e-mail addresses.

1 What data collection modes do you think should be considered?
2 What are the advantages and disadvantages of these modes?
3 Which one method do you think Bob Watts should recommend? Why?

# USING MEASUREMENT SCALES
# IN YOUR SURVEY

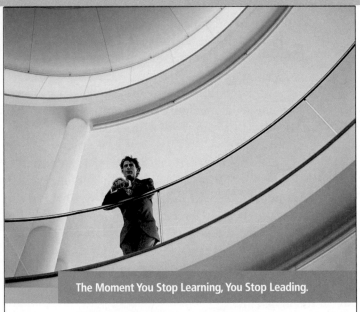

## MEASURING CUSTOMER LOYALTY

Walt Disney once said: "Do what you do so well that they will want to see it again and bring their friends." Walt Disney understood the value of retaining customers, and today's successful companies understand that it costs much less to keep a customer than to attract new customers. Firms seek to increase customer loyalty. But companies must measure customer loyalty as one of the first steps in trying to understand it and to develop strategies to increase it. As you will read in this chapter, measurement is defined as quantifying some quality or attribute of an object. In the case of customer loyalty, marketers have attempted to quantify the construct "customer loyalty" among their present customers.

There are different ways customer loyalty is measured. Almost everyone agrees that there are degrees of customer loyalty; customers don't just "have" or "not

- To examine question formats commonly used in marketing research
- To understand the basic concepts in measurement
- To learn about two types of measurement scales used by marketing researchers
- To appreciate why the type of measurement scale is important
- To become familiar with scale types commonly used in marketing research

have" customer loyalty. So, most everyone agrees the construct should not be measured using a closed-ended "yes" or "no" response, but rather, scaled response such as a 5-point or 10-point scale. However, there is disagreement as to how many scale points should be used, how many questions should be asked, and which questions should be asked in order to measure customer loyalty properly.

A common method for measuring customer loyalty is to create a loyalty index by averaging three scaled response questions. The three questions measure overall satisfaction, willingness to recommend, and likelihood to return or buy again. The three questions are normally asked using a 5-point rating scale and the average score on these three questions is used to measure customer loyalty.

A second method has been suggested by Fred Reichheld who wrote *The Ultimate Question: Driving Good Profits and True Growth*. In the book, Reichheld recommends asking only one question ("The Ultimate Question"): "How likely is it that you would recommend Company X to a friend or colleague?" and the responses are recorded on a scale ranging from 0 labeled as "Not at all likely" to 10 labeled "Extremely likely."[1] Reichheld believes this is the only question needed to measure customer loyalty.

Maritz Research specializes in customer loyalty. Their researchers believe the 5-point rating scales do not adequately discriminate among those who are loyal and those who are not. Most customers give only positive ratings; there are few negative ratings. Through researching how to best measure customer loyalty, Maritz researchers developed the

"Probability Allocation" measure which consists of the key question: "Of the next 10 times you make a purchase of <insert product class here>, how many times will you buy <insert client's brand here>?"[2]

What characteristics should we look for in "good" measurement? First, does the method used to measure the construct actually measure what it is intended to measure? If so, the measurement is said to have "validity." Secondly, will the measurement method provide a reliable result? That is, if the method identifies a customer as loyal in one measurement setting and, assuming the customer doesn't change, will the customer be identified as loyal in a second measurement? There are many other issues to look for in good measurement. Does the measure actually predict loyal and nonloyal customers?

■ **There are six basic response format options available to the researcher.**

This chapter is the first of two devoted to the questionnaire design phase of the marketing research process. Its primary goal is to develop the foundation for understanding measurement in marketing research. This is done by first describing the six question-response formats available, then defining basic concepts in measurement, and, finally, describing the various scale formats that are commonly used in marketing research.

## QUESTION-RESPONSE FORMAT OPTIONS

While it takes skill and experience to become a proficient questionnaire designer, there are some basic building blocks that you can learn quickly. One basic building block to understand is question-response formats. There are six response format options commonly found in questionnaires, and these are diagrammed in Figure 8.1.

As can be seen in Figure 8.1, there are three basic question-response formats and each one has two variations. Each of the six format options will be described in the following sections.

### Open-Ended Response Format Questions

With an **open-ended response format** question, the respondent is instructed to respond in his or her own words. That is, the response format is open-ended. This format is useful when the researcher wants the respondent to describe something in his or her own words. For example, in exploratory research situations, it is often useful to just let respondents say what is on their minds about the topic. Even in descriptive research studies, it is sometimes valuable to gather respondents' unfettered comments or answers. Sometimes the researcher wants a comment or statement from the respondent, or perhaps the researcher simply wants the respondent to indicate the name of a brand or a store. An **unaided open-ended format** does not prompt or probe the respondent beyond the initial question. When the researcher uses an **aided open-ended format**, there is a **response probe** in the form of a follow-up question instructing the interviewer to ask for additional information, saying, for

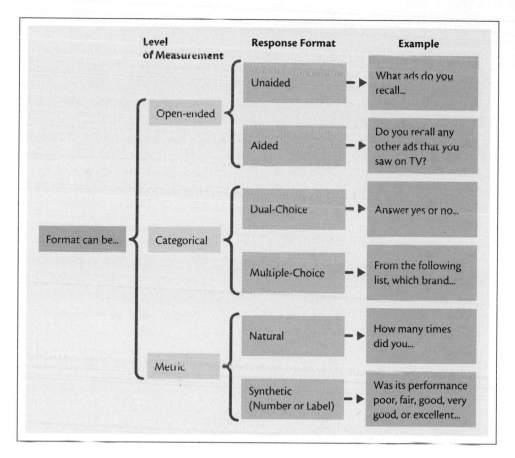

**Figure 8.1** A Diagram of the Six Question-Response Format Options

instance, "Can you think of anything else you took the last time you had a bad cold?" The intent here is to encourage the respondent to provide information beyond the initial and possibly superficial first comments.[3]

■ Question-response formats can be open-ended, categorical, or metric.

An aided open-ended response format can be used to help respondents remember what medicine they took the last time they had a bad cold.

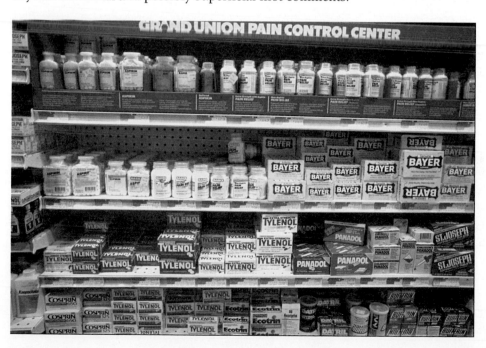

## Categorical Response Format Questions

The **categorical response format** question provides response options on the questionnaire. Categorical response formats are used when the researcher already knows the possible response to a question. By listing the response options, the researcher ensures that the respondent can answer quickly and easily.[4] A **dual-choice question** is an instance where the respondent must select one answer from only two possible alternatives, such as "yes" or "no." This is like a true–false question that you might see on a test. With a **multiple-choice category question** format, there could be several options, such as a list of several cola brands, and the respondent indicates the one that answers the question posed. So, this format is like a multiple-choice question that you might see on your next marketing research test.

Both the dual-choice and multiple-choice categorical question formats are very common on questionnaires due to the fact that they allow respondents to answer effortlessly, because the response categories are predetermined and standardized. Before we leave this section, we need to discuss the special case of the **"Check all that apply" question**. Here is an instance where what appears to be a multiple-choice category question is really a dual-choice question. Consider the following question that could appear on a questionnaire:

■ Categorical responses are either dual-choice or multiple-choice.

PRACTICAL APPLICATIONS

---

When you are purchasing a new pair of casual shoes, what features do you take into consideration? (Check all that apply.)

_____ Style

_____ Price

_____ Comfort

_____ Fit

_____ Construction

---

This question looks like a multiple-choice category question because it has several categories listed as possible responses. However, it is really a dual-choice category question because the respondent is actually answering the following five separate questions.

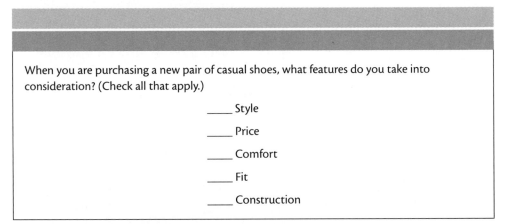

When you are purchasing a new pair of casual shoes, what features do you take into consideration? (Check "Yes" or "No" for each one.)

| | | | |
|---|---|---|---|
| a. Style | _____ Yes | _____ No |
| b. Price | _____ Yes | _____ No |
| c. Comfort | _____ Yes | _____ No |
| d. Fit | _____ Yes | _____ No |
| e. Construction | _____ Yes | _____ No |

A "check all that apply" question is in actually a series of "yes/no" dual-choice questions, but the "yes" and "no" response options are not listed on the questionnaire. The researcher knows that when a respondent checks an item, it is a "yes," and if the item is not checked, it is a "no" answer. The "check all that apply" instruction is readily understood by respondents, and this format makes the questionnaire appear less cluttered.

## Metric Response Format Questions

The **metric response question** calls for a number to be provided by the respondent or utilizes a scale developed by the researcher. "Metric" means that the answer is a number that expresses some quantity of the property being measured. With a **natural metric response format**, the respondent is asked to give a number that is the appropriate response to the property being measured, such as age, number of visits, number of dollars, etc. The **synthetic metric format** uses an artificial number to measure the property. For instance, when respondents are asked to indicate their levels of satisfaction using a scale of 1 to 10, these numbers are assigned artificially by the researcher as a convenient way for respondents to express themselves. Alternatively, synthetic metric formats may include scale descriptors such as "poor," "fair," "good," "very good," and "excellent." As you will learn shortly, these labels, or scale descriptors, are assigned artificial numbers (1, 2, 3, and so on) to represent the different gradations of the property being measured.

■ Metric responses are either natural or synthetic in nature.

## BASIC MEASUREMENT CONCEPTS

Now that you have been introduced to the six major question-response formats, we will describe the basic elements of measurement. Questionnaires are designed to collect information that is represented via **measurement**, defined as determining the description or amount of some element of interest to the researcher. For instance, a marketing manager may wish to know how a person feels about a certain product, or how much of the product he or she uses in a certain time period. This information, once compiled, can help answer specific questions such as brand usage.

■ Measurement is determining how much of a property is possessed by an object.

But what are we really measuring? We are measuring properties—sometimes called attributes or qualities—of objects. Objects include consumers, brands, stores, advertisements, or whatever construct is of interest to the researcher working with a particular manager. **Properties** are the specific features or characteristics of an object that can be used to distinguish it from another object. Of course, research objectives specify which properties are to be measured in any particular research project. When a researcher specifies the procedure to measure a property of an object, the procedure is referred to as an **operational definition**. For example, assume we are doing a survey for Canon digital cameras. In Table 8.1 you can see that we have identified six different properties—gender, age, income level, preferred brand of digital camera, evaluation of our (Canon) brand, and intention to buy our (Canon) brand. Table 8.1 illustrates the operational definition for each property, and it shows the measurement results for three different consumers who are our objects. That is, once the object's

**Table 8.1**
How Operational Definitions Lead to Measuring the Properties of Objects

| | | Measurement of 3 Different Objects | | |
|---|---|---|---|---|
| Properties | Operational Definition | Object: Mr. Able | Object: Ms. Baker | Object: Mrs. Car |
| **Gender** | Male or female? | Male | Female | Female |
| **Age** | Number of years | 35 years old | 26 years old | 40 years old |
| **Income Level** | from $0 to over $150,000, in $10,000 ranges | $30,000–$40,000 | $40,000–$50,000 | $80,000–$90,000 |
| **Preferred Brand** | Brand person bought last | Panasonic | Sony | Panasonic |
| **Evaluation of Our Brand** | Rating of "poor," "fair," "good," "very good," or "excellent" | "Good" | "Very good" | "Fair" |
| **Intention to Buy Our Brand** | How likely to purchase, using scale of "not likely" to "very likely" | "Somewhat likely" | "Very likely" | "Unlikely" |

■ An operational definition describes how a researcher will measure a property of an object.

PRACTICAL APPLICATIONS

designation on a property has been determined, we say that the object has been measured on that property.

Measurement underlies marketing research to a very great extent because researchers are keenly interested in describing marketing phenomena, and measurement is essential to this end. For instance, researchers are often given the task of finding relevant differences in the profiles of various customer types. Take, for example, a recent survey that could be used by Wrigley's Chewing Gum.[5] Wrigley's wants to measure how often people chew gum. Moreover, it is vital for target-marketing purposes to find demographic groups that are heavy gum chewers versus those who are light gum chewers. When Wrigley's discovers which consumers buy and chew gum on a regular basis (every day), it can focus its marketing efforts on

Wrigley's wants to know, "Who chews gum?"

that group in order to maximize its market share. As you can see in the table presented here, this survey measuring frequency of gum chewing shows plainly that Wrigley's prime markets are the 16–24 and 25–34 age groups.

| | Total | Age Range | | | | | |
| --- | --- | --- | --- | --- | --- | --- | --- |
| | | 16–24 | 25–34 | 35–44 | 45–54 | 55–65 | 65+ |
| Every day | 17% | **33%** | **28%** | 14% | 16% | 6% | 3% |
| Once or twice a week | 11% | **24%** | **17%** | 10% | 7% | 6% | 1% |
| Very occasionally | 25% | **28%** | **33%** | 33% | 27% | 19% | 11% |
| Never | 46% | **16%** | **22%** | 43% | 50% | 69% | 85% |
| Average | 2.0 | **2.8** | **2.5** | 1.9 | 1.9 | 1.5 | 1.2 |

When a researcher specifies an operational definition for the measurement of a property of a construct, he or she explicitly identifies the response scale's **level of measurement**, meaning that the researcher has decided whether the scale is to be open-ended, categorical, or metric. If you refer back to Figure 8.1, you will notice that we have included the headings of "Level of Measurement," "Response Format," and "Example." It is now time to describe the level of measurement in more detail.

## Open-Ended Measurement

As we indicated in our brief description of open-ended questions, researchers refrain from using these unless there are special reasons, such as conducting exploratory research. Because every respondent uses his or her own words in the responses, open-ended measures are not standardized. It is therefore the most difficult level of measurement to work with. In fact, it generally takes interpretation skills or even special computer programs to analyze open-ended responses, and for these reasons we will not dwell on open-ended measurement more than to mention it here.

## Categorical Measurement

A **categorical measure** is one where the possible responses are categories, meaning that the possible alternatives are labels that represent concrete and very different types of answers. By answering a categorical measure, a respondent is indicating to which group (or category) he or she belongs. For example, when you say "no" or "yes," you are expressing completely opposite expressions of your state of mind, so you are either in the affirmative group or the negative group. If you indicate you are a "male" or a "female," you have flatly stated what your gender group is. When you say you bought a "Domino's Pizza" the last time you ordered pizza, you belong to the Domino's Pizza buyers group, just as if you had said "Papa John's," you would belong to the Papa John's group. So, categorical measures are ones where the response options are very different from each other and the options are best envisioned as group or category labels. Also, there is practically no judgment involved for the respondent to answer a categorical measure question: The respondent simply indicates the category label that best describes him or her.

A categorical measure is used to determine what group a respondent belongs to.

## Metric Measurement

A **metric measure**, on the other hand, requires the respondent to think in terms of amounts or levels of the property being measured. We might ask how many times he or she used an ATM machine last week, how much he or she expects to pay per day for a rental car in Orlando, the person's age, or even how he or she feels about buying a wristwatch that costs $500. Metric measures have *order*, meaning that each number that can be given is larger or smaller than other numbers that can be given, and metric measures have *distance*, meaning that the numbers can be compared to see how many units separate them. For example, a metric measure for how many times he or she used an ATM machine the past week might have one respondent answering with a "2," while another respondent might respond with a "5." The number 5 is greater than the number 2 (*order*), and they are 3 units apart (*distance*).

■ A metric measure determines the amount or quantity of a property of an object.

Metric scales can be either natural or synthetic. Natural metric scales direct respondents to give a number that is appropriate or natural to the property being measured, such as the number of times, the number of dollars, the number of years, and so on. So, natural metric scales measure properties that are inherently quantitative, such as frequency (times), value (dollars), time (years), size (pounds, ounces), or the like.

A synthetic metric measure, you should recall, is one that utilizes *artificial* descriptors or numbers to indicate the amount of a property possessed by an object. For example, if we were doing research for a travel agency, we could ask respondents to use a scale of 1 to 5, where 1 means "very dissatisfied" and 5 means "very satisfied," as to how satisfied they are with the travel agency's Web site. A respondent would give a number between 1 and 5 to indicate the amount of satisfaction he or she has with the Web site. The scale is metric because it uses artificial numbers selected by the researcher that reflect relative amounts of satisfaction. The numbers 1 to 5 are artificial because they are arbitrarily selected by the researcher to represent levels of satisfaction: the researcher can select for any 1–*n* number range, such as 1–10 or even 1–100.

Researchers often use a number range such as 1–5, 1–7, 1–10, and so forth when constructing a **synthetic number metric scale**. A synthetic number has meaning only in the context of the scale from which it originates. That is, you must know the range of the scale and the property the scale is measuring in order to understand the meaning

How many times you used an ATM machine last week would be a natural metric measure of your usage.

of any number in the scale. For instance, if someone told you that he or she rates a new movie as a "5" for its action, you would not know if it was a low or a high rating until that person told you that scale's range. If it was a 1–5 scale, the 5 rating would indicate high action, but if it was a 1–10 scale, the 5 rating would denote much less action.

By the same token, we might use a **synthetic label metric scale** such as a rating scale of "poor," "fair," "good," "very good," or "excellent." Here, we are using words to indicate different gradations or levels of the respondent's opinion of the travel agency's Web site. Again, a synthetic label has meaning only in the context of the scale from which it comes. As before, this means that if someone rates the action in a new movie as "very good," you would not know whether this was the highest rating until you were told that the labels ranged from "poor" to "very good." If the labels were "poor" to "excellent," you would realize that "very good" was not the highest rating possible. The reason these labels are called metric is because they represent successive degrees, and it is customary for researchers to code them as "1," "2," "3," "4," and "5," respectively, when preparing responses for data analysis.[6] There will be more examples of synthetic label metric scales provided to you later in this chapter.

While researchers know categorical and metric scale types very well, and they can identify the types effortlessly, these labels are no doubt confusing to someone learning about them for the first time. To help you keep these four types of scales separated in your mind, we have prepared Table 8.2, which illustrates some questions that might appear in a survey. We have identified each question as dual-choice categorical, multiple-choice categorical, natural metric, or synthetic metric. Take a few minutes to examine each type of question so these four types are differentiated in your own mind.

Synthetic metric measures can be either number scales or labeled scales.

**Table 8.2**
**Examples of Questions with Categorical Scales and Metric Scales**

**A. Dual-Choice Categorical Scale Questions (Respondent selects one of two possible categories)**

1. Please indicate your gender.

_____ Male _____ Female

2. Do you recall seeing a Delta Airlines advertisement for "carefree vacations" in the past week?

_____ Yes _____ No

3. Which sports drink do you prefer after an exercise session?

_____ Gatorade _____ PowerAde

**B. Multiple-Choice Categorical Scale Questions (Respondent selects one of more than two possible categories)**

1. Check the one television brand you would probably buy next.

_____ Sony

_____ Zenith

_____ RCA

_____ Sharp

**Table 8.2**
*(Continued)*

2. What is your marital status?

_____ Married

_____ Single

_____ Divorced or Separated

_____ Other

**C. Natural Metric Scale Questions (Respondent indicates an amount or quantity in a common denomination such as years, times, dollars, etc.)**

1. Please indicate your age. _____ years

2. Approximately how many times in the last month have you purchased anything over $5 in value at a convenience store?

| 0 | 1 | 2 | 3 | 4 | 5 | More (specify:    ) |

3. How much do you think a typical purchaser of a $100,000 term life insurance policy pays per year for that policy?    $_____

**D. Synthetic Metric Scale Questions (Respondent selects a location on a graduated scale developed by the researcher)**

1. Please rate each brand in terms of its overall performance.

Brand Rating (Circle one)

|  | Poor |  |  |  |  |  | Excellent |
|---|---|---|---|---|---|---|---|
| Mont Blanc | 1 | 2 | 3 | 4 | 5 | 6 | 7 |
| Parker | 1 | 2 | 3 | 4 | 5 | 6 | 7 |
| Cross | 1 | 2 | 3 | 4 | 5 | 6 | 7 |

2. Indicate your degree of agreement with the following statements by circling the appropriate number.

| Statement | Strongly Disagree |  |  |  | Strongly Agree |
|---|---|---|---|---|---|
| a. I always look for bargains. | 1 | 2 | 3 | 4 | 5 |
| b. I enjoy being outdoors. | 1 | 2 | 3 | 4 | 5 |
| c. I love to cook. | 1 | 2 | 3 | 4 | 5 |

3. Please rate Pontiac Firebird by checking the line that best corresponds to your evaluation of each item listed.

| Slow pickup | _____ | _____ | _____ | _____ | Fast pickup |
| Good design | _____ | _____ | _____ | _____ | Bad design |
| Low price | _____ | _____ | _____ | _____ | High price |

# WHY THE LEVEL OF A SCALE IS IMPORTANT

You may ask, "Why is it important to know the level of a scale?" In other words, why should you care whether a scale is categorical or metric? The answer lies in the fact that the researcher ultimately wishes to summarize and report the findings associated with that scale. The choice of the level of measurement for a scale affects which analyses should or should not be performed. The analysis, in turn, greatly affects what may or may not be said about the property being measured. Granted, this chapter does not deal with data analysis; however, you must appreciate that when researchers wrestle with operational definitions of their scales, they are simultaneously taking into account the data analysis as well as the presentation layout they will be using in the final report. Hopefully, the following example will help to develop this appreciation.

■ The measurement level of a scale determines the proper way for the researcher to summarize findings.

To understand why the level of a scale is important, answer this question: If you asked each of 1,000 respondents about how many dollars they spend on groceries each week, how would you summarize the findings? Would you count up how many respondents gave the answer of $50, then count up how many gave $51, and so on until you had accounted for every possible dollar amount? You could do this, but it would take a great deal of effort, and even when you were done you would have a very long list of dollar amounts with how many respondents gave each amount. So, doing frequency counts for natural metric scales is an inefficient way to summarize these numbers. The appropriate way is to calculate the average and say something like "The average amount spent on groceries each week is $87.65." We were able to calculate the average because we used a metric scale where the numbers pertained to quantities of dollars.

Now, let's take the marital status question that these 1,000 respondents also answered. Recall that this is a categorical scale (Table 8.2). Would you calculate the average and say something like "The average marital status is 1.6"? No, this would be meaningless. Instead, you would say something like "Fifty percent of the respondents are married, 40% are single, and the remaining 10% are divorced or separated." That is, the appropriate summarization analysis for a categorical scale is a percentage distribution (sometimes called a frequency distribution).

To elaborate, it is appropriate for the researcher to summarize the findings of his or her study with the following guidelines. For categorical measures, the researcher should use a percentage distribution, which can be depicted as a pie chart or a bar chart. With a metric measure, the most appropriate analysis is to compute the average. As a way of introduction, Table 8.3 illustrates these guidelines.

■ Categorical scales should be summarized with percentages, while metric scales should be summarized with averages.

What would you do to summarize a question with answers that are in ranges? For example, what if you had a question that asked respondents to indicate how much they spent on their last mall shopping trip and the possible answers were "Less than $50," "Between $51 and $101," "Between $100 and $150," and so on. Read Marketing Research Application 8.1 to learn the proper way to summarize questions that have ranges such as this example. We will describe data analysis in much greater detail in later chapters.

**Table 8.3**  The Appropriate Data Analysis Is Determined by the Type of Scale

| Type of Scale | Description | Example | Appropriate Analysis |
|---|---|---|---|
| Categorical | Used to determine to which group a respondent belongs | What is your gender? | **Respondent's Gender**<br><br>Female 57%    Male 43% |
| | | Where do you recall a Domino's Pizza ad in the past month? | **Recall of Domino's Pizza Advertising**<br><br>Coupon 74.3%, Television 72.3%, Flyer 42.6%, Store Sign 39.6%, Radio 27.8%, Billboard 14.9%, Phone Book 11.9%, Magazine 8.9%, Web 4.0% |

| Type of Scale | Description | Example | Average | Std. Deviation | Minimum | Maximum |
|---|---|---|---|---|---|---|
| Metric | Used to indicate the amount or quantity | How much do you spend on pizza in a typical month? | $21.80 | $18.78 | $0 | $100 |

| Performance Aspect | Mean* |
|---|---|
| Competitive price | **3.8** |
| Hot pizza when delivered | **3.7** |
| Ease of ordering | **3.7** |
| Choice of toppings | **3.6** |
| Value for the price | **3.4** |
| Selection of pizza sizes | **3.4** |
| Amount of toppings on pizza | **3.4** |
| Promptness of delivery | **3.3** |
| Freshness of product | **3.2** |
| Condition of the crust | **3.1** |
| Variety of crusts to choose | **3.1** |
| Distinctive taste | **3.0** |

(The "How does Domino's Pizza perform on each of the following factors?" example corresponds to the Performance Aspect/Mean table above.)

*Based on a scale where 1 = "poor" and 5 = "excellent."

## MARKETING RESEARCH APPLICATION 8.1

### Using Midpoints with Ranges of Natural Metric Scales

PRACTICAL

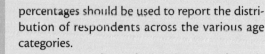

APPLICATIONS

Because respondents do not think in exact numbers, a researcher may opt to provide number ranges as response options for a natural metric scale. Alternatively, some respondents may feel slightly uncomfortable giving specifics about "sensitive topics" such as their income, age, number of alcoholic drinks consumed, amounts spent on frivolous purchases, and so on. Consider the following example.

> Please indicate your age.
> _____ Below 20 years
> _____ 20–30 years
> _____ 31–40 years
> _____ 41–50 years
> _____ 51–60 years
> _____ 61–70 years
> _____ Over 70 years

Age, of course, is a natural metric construct, as everyone is an exact number of years old. However, the researcher in this case has decided to use age ranges as the response options because age is a possibly sensitive topic. This decision has created age categories, meaning that it is a categorical scale and

percentages should be used to report the distribution of respondents across the various age categories.

However, we know that age is a natural metric variable, so how can the researcher summarize and report the average age? The answer is through the use of midpoints. The researcher would need to convert the answers into the midpoints in the following way.

| Age Ranges on Questionnaire | Calculation of Midpoint | Midpoint to Use |
|---|---|---|
| _____ Below 20 years | $0 + ((20 - 0)/2)$ | 10 |
| _____ 20–30 years | $20 + ((30 - 20)/2)$ | 25 |
| _____ 31–40 years | $31 + ((40 - 31)/2)$ | 35.5 |
| _____ 41–50 years | $41 + ((50 - 41)/2)$ | 45.5 |
| _____ 51–60 years | $51 + ((60 - 51)/2)$ | 55.5 |
| _____ 61–70 years | $61 + ((70 - 61)/2)$ | 65.5 |
| _____ Over 70 years | No calculation | 75 (75 is an arbitrary number as there is no upper limit to the "Over 70 years" range.) |

Once the appropriate midpoint is assigned to each respondent, possibly by a recoding command programmed in Excel, the average can be computed, and the researcher can report his or her best estimate of the average age of the respondents.

## COMMONLY USED SYNTHETIC METRIC SCALES

The measurement of most properties is a simple task. It is simple as long as we are measuring **objective properties**, which are physically verifiable characteristics such as age, gender, number of bottles purchased, store last visited, and so on. However, marketing researchers often desire to measure **subjective properties**, which cannot be directly observed because they are mental constructs such as a person's attitudes, opinions, or intentions. In this case, the marketing researcher must ask a respondent to translate his or her mental constructs onto an intensity continuum. To do this, the marketing researcher must develop response formats that are very clear and that are used identically by the various respondents. This process is known as **scale development**.

Scale development is principally concerned with the creation or use of synthetic metric measures.[7] There are two goals of scale development: reliability and validity. A **reliable scale** is one in which a respondent responds in the same or in a very similar manner to an identical or nearly identical question. Obviously if a question elicits wildly different answers from the same person and you know that the person is unchanged from administration to administration of the question, there is something very wrong with the question. A **valid scale**, on the other hand, is one that truly measures the construct under study. It is beyond the scope of this book to delve into reliability and validity of measures, so we will simply point out that the proper development of synthetic metric measures poses reliability and validity challenges.

■ Scale development is how researchers create reliable and valid scales.

The process of a synthetic metric scale's development can be long and difficult.[8] However, researchers are almost always under time and budget pressures, so they typically turn to scale formats with which they are familiar and ones that they no doubt have used many times before. In this section, we will describe the basic scale formats that are most common in marketing research practice and that professional marketing researchers use very frequently.

■ Market researchers use standard scales rather than inventing new ones for each research project.

## Symmetric Synthetic Scales

Many scales are designed to measure psychological properties that exist on a continuum ranging from one extreme to another in the mind of the respondent. Table 8.4 serves as a useful visual aid in illustrating the intensity continuum that underlies the measurement of these types of constructs. Notice that we are illustrating an intensity continuum that ranges from extremely negative through neutral and to extremely positive. The **neutral point** is not considered zero or an origin; instead, it is considered a midpoint along the continuum, as you can see with the numbers we have *artificially* assigned to each label for each of the three examples in Table 8.4. To relate to this visual aid, think about your own feelings about some brand. You may think it is a very good brand, so you have a strong positive rating. On the other

**Table 8.4**

The Intensity Continuum Underlying Commonly Used Symmetric Synthetic Scales

| Extremely Negative | | | Neutral | | | Extremely Positive |
|---|---|---|---|---|---|---|
| | Strongly Disagree 1 | Somewhat Disagree 2 | Neither Agree nor Disagree 3 | Somewhat Agree 4 | Strongly Agree 5 | |
| Slow Check Out | Very ____ | Somewhat ____ | No Opinion ____ | Somewhat ____ | Very ____ | Fast Check Out |
| Extremely Unfavorable 1 | Very Unfavorable 2 | Somewhat Unfavorable 3 | No Opinion 4 | Somewhat Favorable 5 | Very Favorable 6 | Extremely Favorable 7 |

hand, you may think it is a very bad brand, and you would have a strong negative rating. Finally, you might not have any opinion, in which case you would have a neutral rating. Of course, your strong feelings might not be extreme, so your rating would not be at the endpoint of the scale; it would be somewhere between the neutral position and the extreme position.

We will briefly describe three symmetric synthetic metric scales that are commonly used by marketing researchers. Remember, with symmetric scales, we are measuring attitudes, feelings, opinions, and so forth where the response can be anywhere from a strong negative to a strong positive one.

The **Likert scale** format is commonly used by marketing researchers,[9] and it is an instance where respondents are asked to indicate their degree of agreement or disagreement on a symmetric agree–disagree scale for each of a series of statements. The value of the Likert scale should be apparent because respondents are asked how much they agree or disagree with the statement. That is, the scale captures the intensity of their feelings. The following example illustrates the use of a Likert scale in a telephone interview. You should notice the directions given by the interviewer to properly administer this scale.[10]

■ Symmetric scales have counterbalancing positive and negative degrees of intensity.

■ The Likert scale format measures intensity of agreement or disagreement.

(INTERVIEWER: READ) I have a list of statements that I will read to you. As I read each one, please indicate whether you agree or disagree with it.
Are the instructions clear? (IF NOT, REPEAT)
(INTERVIEWER: READ EACH STATEMENT. WITH EACH RESPONSE, ASK) Would you say that you (dis)agree STRONGLY or just (dis)agree?

| Statement | Strongly Disagree | Disagree | Neutral | Agree | Strongly Agree |
|---|---|---|---|---|---|
| Levi's Engineered jeans are good looking. | 1 | 2 | 3 | 4 | 5 |
| Levi's Engineered jeans are reasonably priced. | 1 | 2 | 3 | 4 | 5 |
| Your next pair of jeans will be Levi's Engineered jeans. | 1 | 2 | 3 | 4 | 5 |
| Levi's Engineered jeans are easy to identify on someone. | 1 | 2 | 3 | 4 | 5 |
| Levi's Engineered jeans make you feel good. | 1 | 2 | 3 | 4 | 5 |

To use the Likert response format, borrowed from a formal scale development approach developed by Rensis Likert,[11] a researcher generates a list of statements about the construct(s) under consideration. One such statement could be "I find my bank's online bill-paying system easy to use," and another could be "The charge for my bank's online bill-paying system is reasonable." Respondents read the statements and indicate the degree of agreement or disagreement to each one. It is important that the statements not have strong evaluative words in them, such as "very," "exceptionally," or "extremely," as the statement should make a simple claim, and the respondent is the one who indicates the direction and intensity of his or her reaction to the statement.

To demonstrate how much market researchers have come to rely on the Likert scale, we will point out that consumer lifestyles are very often measured with the use

PRACTICAL
APPLICATIONS

Measuring lifestyle allows marketers to effectively target their customers.

of a lifestyle inventory composed of Likert scale questions. **Lifestyle** takes into account the values and personality traits of people as reflected in their unique activities, interests, and opinions (AIOs) toward their work, leisure time, and purchases. The underlying belief is that knowledge of consumers' lifestyles, as opposed to just demographics, offers direction for marketing decisions. Many companies use consumer lifestyles as a market-targeting tool. Lifestyle can be used to distinguish among types of purchasers, such as heavy users versus light users of a product, store patrons versus nonpatrons, or media vehicle users versus nonusers. Likert scales can assess the degree to which a person is price-conscious, fashion-conscious, an opinion giver, a sports enthusiast, child oriented, home centered, or financially optimistic. These attributes are measured by a series of AIO statements, usually in the form presented in Table 8.5.[12] Each respondent indicates his or her degree of agreement or disagreement by responding to the Likert-like categories. In some applications, the questionnaire may contain a large number of different lifestyle statements ranging from very general descriptions of the person's AIOs to very specific statements concerning particular products, brands, services, or other items of interest to the marketing researcher. Lifestyle inventories are valuable to marketers in a number of ways, not the least of which is as a market segmentation basis and tool.

■ **Lifestyle questions use the Likert scale format to measure a person's activities, interests, and opinions.**

The **semantic differential scale** is another symmetric scale that has sprung directly from the problem of translating a person's qualitative judgments into quantitative estimates. Like the modified Likert scale, this one has been borrowed from another discipline, namely semantics. The semantic differential scale contains a series of bipolar adjectives for the various properties of the object under study, and respondents indicate their impressions of each property by indicating locations along its continuum. The focus of the semantic differential is on the measurement of the meaning of an object, concept, or person. Because many marketing stimuli have meaning, mental associations, or connotations, this type of scale works very well when the marketing researcher is attempting to determine brand, store, or other images.

■ **The semantic differential is used primarily to measure brand, company, or store image.**

Table 8.5
Examples of Lifestyle
Statements on a
Questionnaire

Lifestyle is measured with the
Likert format, utilizing several
statements about
respondents' activities,
interests, and opinions.

**Please respond by circling the number that best corresponds to how much you agree or disagree with each statement.**

| Statement | Strongly Disagree | Disagree | Neither Agree nor Disagree | Agree | Strongly Agree |
|---|---|---|---|---|---|
| I shop a lot for "specials." | 1 | 2 | 3 | 4 | 5 |
| I usually have one or more outfits that are of the very latest style. | 1 | 2 | 3 | 4 | 5 |
| My children are the most important thing in my life. | 1 | 2 | 3 | 4 | 5 |
| I usually keep my house very neat and clean. | 1 | 2 | 3 | 4 | 5 |
| I would rather spend a quiet evening at home than go out to a party. | 1 | 2 | 3 | 4 | 5 |
| It is good to have a charge account. | 1 | 2 | 3 | 4 | 5 |
| I like to watch or listen to baseball or football games. | 1 | 2 | 3 | 4 | 5 |
| I think I have more self-confidence than most people. | 1 | 2 | 3 | 4 | 5 |
| I sometimes influence what my friends buy. | 1 | 2 | 3 | 4 | 5 |
| I will probably have more money to spend next year than I have now. | 1 | 2 | 3 | 4 | 5 |

The construction of a semantic differential scale begins with the determination of a concept or object to be rated. The researcher then selects bipolar pairs of words or phrases that could be used to describe the object's salient properties. Depending on the object, some examples might be "friendly–unfriendly," "hot–cold," "convenient–inconvenient," "high quality–low quality," and "dependable–undependable." The opposites are positioned at the endpoints of a continuum of intensity, and it is customary, although not mandatory, to use seven line-segment separators between each point. The respondent then indicates his or her evaluation of the performance of the object, say a brand, by checking the appropriate line. The closer the respondent checks to an endpoint on a line, the more intense is his or her evaluation of the object being measured.

**Table 8.6**
The Semantic Differential Scale Is Useful When Measuring Store, Company, or Brand Images

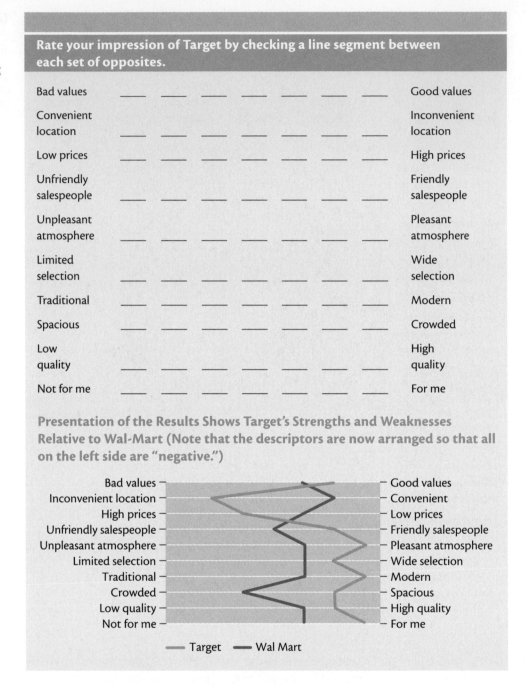

**Rate your impression of Target by checking a line segment between each set of opposites.**

| | | | | | | | | |
|---|---|---|---|---|---|---|---|---|
| Bad values | ___ | ___ | ___ | ___ | ___ | ___ | ___ | Good values |
| Convenient location | ___ | ___ | ___ | ___ | ___ | ___ | ___ | Inconvenient location |
| Low prices | ___ | ___ | ___ | ___ | ___ | ___ | ___ | High prices |
| Unfriendly salespeople | ___ | ___ | ___ | ___ | ___ | ___ | ___ | Friendly salespeople |
| Unpleasant atmosphere | ___ | ___ | ___ | ___ | ___ | ___ | ___ | Pleasant atmosphere |
| Limited selection | ___ | ___ | ___ | ___ | ___ | ___ | ___ | Wide selection |
| Traditional | ___ | ___ | ___ | ___ | ___ | ___ | ___ | Modern |
| Spacious | ___ | ___ | ___ | ___ | ___ | ___ | ___ | Crowded |
| Low quality | ___ | ___ | ___ | ___ | ___ | ___ | ___ | High quality |
| Not for me | ___ | ___ | ___ | ___ | ___ | ___ | ___ | For me |

**Presentation of the Results Shows Target's Strengths and Weaknesses Relative to Wal-Mart (Note that the descriptors are now arranged so that all on the left side are "negative.")**

Table 8.6 shows how this was done for a survey for Target, a rival of Wal-Mart. The respondents also rated Wal-Mart on the same survey. You can see that each respondent has been instructed to indicate his or her impression of various properties of each store by checking the appropriate line between the several bipolar adjective phrases. As you look at the phrases, you should note that they have been randomly flipped to avoid having all of the "good" ones on one side. This flipping procedure is used to avoid the **halo effect**, which is a general feeling about a store or brand that can bias a respondent's impressions on its specific

A semantic differential scale can be used to measure Wal-Mart's image and compare it to competitors such as Target.

properties.[13] For instance, suppose you have a very positive image of Target. If all of the positive items were on the right-hand side and all the negative ones were on the left hand side, you might be tempted to just check all of the answers on the right-hand side. But it is entirely possible that some specific aspect of the Target store might not be as good as the others. Perhaps the store is not located in a very convenient place, or the selection is not as broad as you would like. Randomly flipping positive and negative ends of the descriptors in a semantic differential scale minimizes the halo effect. There is some evidence that when respondents are ambivalent on the survey topic, it is best to use a balanced set of negatively and positively worded questions.[14]

Because it is a metric scale, one of the most appealing aspects of the semantic differential scale is the ability of the researcher to compute averages and then to plot a "profile" of the brand or company image. Each check line is assigned a number for coding. Usually, the bipolar properties are rearranged to be negative-to-positive, then numbers 1, 2, 3, and so on, beginning from the left side, are customary. Next, an average is computed for each bipolar pair. The averages are plotted as you see them, and the marketing researcher has a very nice graphical communication vehicle with which to report the findings to his or her client, as can be seen in the bottom half of Table 8.6. As you can see in our fictitious example, Target outperforms Wal-Mart in 8 of the 10 store properties, but it has a weaker image than Wal-Mart on location convenience and prices.

The **Stapel scale** is our last symmetric scale to be described. The basis of the Stapel scale format is numerical rather than verbal or visual; however, the purpose of the Stapel scale is the same as with other symmetric synthetic scales—to obtain the degree of positive or negative feeling in the mind of the respondent concerning an attribute of some object. Take a look at the following example, and you will recognize a Stapel scale easily as it has numbers that range from a minus end to a corresponding plus end, and typically include 0 as the midpoint. The respondent circles the number that best corresponds to his or her feelings on the topic.

■ When using the semantic differential scale, you should control for the "halo effect."

■ The Stapel scale uses counterbalancing positive and negative numbers for respondents to express degrees of positive or negative feelings.

**Example of a Stapel Scale**

**Rate each of the following bookstores on each factor, according to your opinion.**

| Factor | Books-a-Million | Barnes & Noble | Books, Books, & More Books |
|---|---|---|---|
| | +3 | +3 | +3 |
| | +2 | +2 | +2 |
| | +1 | +1 | +1 |
| Competitive Prices | 0 | 0 | 0 |
| | −1 | −1 | −1 |
| | −2 | −2 | −2 |
| | −3 | −3 | −3 |
| | +3 | +3 | +3 |
| | +2 | +2 | +2 |
| | +1 | +1 | +1 |
| Wide Assortment | 0 | 0 | 0 |
| | −1 | −1 | −1 |
| | −2 | −2 | −2 |
| | −3 | −3 | −3 |

A Stapel scale is a good substitute for a semantic differential scale as it is easier to construct because the researcher does not need to think of bipolar adjectives for each attribute. It is also flexible to administer as respondents do not need to "see" the scale the way they do when responding to a semantic differential scale. However, in order to use a Stapel scale properly, respondents must feel comfortable with the use of negative numbers.

Before moving on to a variation of synthetic scales, we need to address a question that may have come to your mind as you examined our various examples. All of the examples in this section have a neutral or "no opinion" option in the middle of the scale. However, you may have wondered if the "no opinion" response option is really appropriate, and our answer is "It depends."[15] We have prepared Marketing Research Application 8.2 to explain what we mean by "It depends."[16]

## Nonsymmetric Synthetic Scales

A symmetric scale is sometimes called "balanced," as it has equal amounts of positive and negative positions. But not all constructs that researchers deal with have counteropposing ends.[17] For example, suppose you were asked to indicate how important having jail bail bond protection was for you as a feature when you purchased automobile insurance. It is doubtful that you would differentiate between "extremely unimportant," "very unimportant," or "somewhat unimportant," but you could indicate

## MARKETING RESEARCH APPLICATION 8.2

### Scale Construction Tips from a Pro

PRACTICAL

APPLICATIONS

E. B. Feltser, who works as a marketing research interviewer and survey writer, explains the importance of and provides cautions for using scales in marketing research. Mr. Feltser believes that a multipoint scale is a wonderful thing; it is subtle, nicely objective, and neatly quantifiable.[a] Interviewers appreciate them because they're fast and don't entail all the typing or handwriting work associated with open-ends. It's easy to understand why they are so common in surveys.

For example, if you want to measure how satisfied customers are with a brand or a store, you can use this 5-point scale:

5 = Extremely satisfied

4 = Somewhat satisfied

3 = Neither satisfied nor dissatisfied

2 = Somewhat dissatisfied

1 = Extremely dissatisfied

That kind of symmetric construction gets a rhythm going that respondents seem to remember more easily. It is efficient as it does not repeat words ("Extremely satisfied with the brand," "Somewhat satisfied with the brand," etc.), and it is easy for the interviewer to read and say. Substituting "it" for "the brand" or leaving "with the brand" out altogether takes about half as long to read. Anything that needlessly uses up time in a survey jeopardizes its success because respondents believe that you are wasting their time.

It is important, also, to give respondents a "Don't know" option in addition to the 5-point satisfaction scale. With a "Don't know" option, a respondent who is not familiar with the brand is not forced to give an opinion. The midpoint ("Neither satisfied nor dissatisfied") is the appropriate response for someone familiar with the brand, but who is ambivalent about its performance. Now, a lot of "Neither . . . nor" responses means that the brand's performance is quite bland, not that a great many respondents have not tried it. In other words, when opting to include a "no opinion" on a scale, make sure there are respondents who legitimately have not had enough experience with the topic to have formed an opinion. Alternatively, when including a "neutral" point on a scale, it is best to assure yourself that respondents are truly ambivalent because the topic does not move them negatively or positively.

[a] Personal communication from E. B. Feltser, by permission.

how important it was to you with the response options of "not important" to "somewhat important," "very important," and "extremely important." That is, a nonsymmetric, or unbalanced, scale would be more appropriate because most people do not think in degrees of negative importance. As you can see in Figure 8.2, the symmetric scale includes the same ranges of negative as ranges of positive, and includes the neutral position on the scale. However, a nonsymmetric scale typically begins at the lowest positive position and extends to the highest positive position, plus it does not include the neutral, or "no opinion," position on the scale. We will describe three of these: the one-way labeled scale, the *n*-point scale, and the graphic rating scale.

■ A nonsymmetric scale measures positive degrees of opinions or feelings.

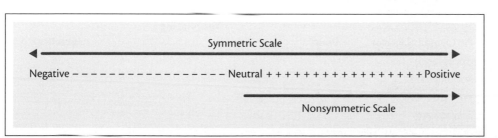

**Figure 8.2** Comparison of a Symmetric to a Nonsymmetric Synthetic Scale

The **one-way labeled scale** is one where the researcher is measuring some construct attribute with the use of labels that restrict the measure to the "positive" side. The importance scale that ran from "not important" to "extremely important" just described is a one-way labeled scale as it is primarily degrees of importance. Granted, there is a "not important" position on the scale, but this is the only instance of unimportance, and the rest of the positions on the scale are differing levels of importance. Ideally, respondents should respond to a one-way labeled scale as having equal intervals.[18]

■ A one-way labeled scale uses words to convey degrees of feeling or opinions.

**Example of a One-Way Labeled Scale**

| **How important is each of the following to you when you are deciding on a dentist?** | | | | | |
| --- | --- | --- | --- | --- | --- |
| **Factor** | **Not Important** | **Somewhat Important** | **Quite Important** | **Very Important** | **Extremely Important** |
| Lowest prices in town | ____ | ____ | ____ | ____ | ____ |
| Close to my home | ____ | ____ | ____ | ____ | ____ |
| Guaranteed painless procedures | ____ | ____ | ____ | ____ | ____ |
| Will see me right away | ____ | ____ | ____ | ____ | ____ |

The **$n$-point scale**, meaning a 5-point, 7-point, or 10-point scale format, is a popular choice for researchers measuring constructs on nonsymmetric attributes. Here is an example: Indicate how you rate the friendliness of the wait staff at Olive Garden Restaurant, where 1 means "not friendly" and 5 means "extremely friendly." It is a one-way scale that uses synthetic numbers rather than verbal labels.[19] This is the **anchored $n$-point scale**, and there are two anchors used for this type of scale. The number "1" is anchored, and the highest number, "5" in our example, is also anchored. The anchors are important as they tell the respondent the context of the scale; that is, they indicate how to translate the range of the scale into a frame of reference to which the respondent can relate. Remember, we stated earlier that synthetic numbers have meaning only in the context of the scale in which they are used.

Here is an example of an anchored 5-point scale. You should take note of how crucial it is to have good instructions that communicate the anchors and the numbers in the scale.

**Example of a 5-Point Anchored Scale**

| **Rate the performance of your book bag from 1 to 5, where 1 means "poor" and 5 means "excellent."** | | | | | |
| --- | --- | --- | --- | --- | --- |
| | | **Your Rating** | | | |
| **Performance Factor** | **Poor** | | | | **Excellent** |
| Appearance | 1 | 2 | 3 | 4 | 5 |
| Roominess | 1 | 2 | 3 | 4 | 5 |
| Waterproofing | 1 | 2 | 3 | 4 | 5 |
| Easy to carry | 1 | 2 | 3 | 4 | 5 |

Occasionally, a researcher will opt to not provide the anchors, in which case it will be an **unanchored *n*-point scale**. An example is "On a scale of 1–5, how do you rate the friendliness of Olive Garden's wait staff?" As a general rule, anchors are desirable as they stipulate concrete ends of the scale to respondents, but anchors are not mandatory.

■ An *n*-point scale uses positive numbers to convey degrees of feeling or opinions.

Here is an example of an unanchored 5-point scale[20] used by *Reader's Digest*[21] in its annual "most-trusted brands" survey conducted in various countries in Europe. As you read this example, notice the global flexibility of a simple 5-point scale. *Reader's Digest* conducts an annual consumer-trust survey each year in 18 different European countries to identify the most-trusted consumer brands in each country for at least 30 different product categories. To accomplish this end, the survey instrument asks each respondent to indicate his or her most-trusted brand in each product category. Respondents are then asked to rate each brand on an unanchored 5-point scale. The ratings are gathered for each of four aspects of trust: (1) quality, (2) value, (3) strong image, and (4) understanding customer needs.

Because of the diversity of languages in Europe and because *Reader's Digest* is published in many languages, the questionnaire is printed in 20 languages. The ability of a 5-point unanchored scale to span so many languages is, indeed, its strong point and places it high on the choice list of marketing researchers doing multinational or single-country surveys. *Reader's Digest*'s use of the simple 5-point scale of intensity demonstrates that it is applicable across Western cultures. Here is a sample of the findings of the most-trusted consumer brands in the United Kingdom in 2007. By the way, almost 28,000 people completed and returned the mail survey.

| Category | Brand |
|---|---|
| Car | Ford |
| Kitchen Appliance | Hotpoint |
| PC | Dell |
| Mobile Phone | Nokia |
| Camera | Canon |
| Holiday Company | Thomson |
| Bank/Building Society | Lloyds TSB |
| Credit Card | Visa |
| Insurance Company | Norwich Union |
| Airline | British Airways |
| Internet Company | BT |
| Petrol Retailer | Tesco |
| Vitamins | Boots |
| Pain Relief | Nurofen |
| Cold Remedy | Beechams |
| Cereal | Kellogg's |
| Hair Care | Pantene |
| Cosmetic | Boots |
| Skin Care | Nivea |
| Soap Powder | Persil |

The Trusted Brands Survey is conducted annually, and it has been expanded to cover other topics. Refer to **www.rdtrustedbrands.com** for up-to-date information on this global survey. We highly recommend that you visit this site, as it has a number of insights into European consumers, their trusted brands, Internet usage, and other valuable pieces of information about this part of the globe.

⚡ The **graphic rating scale** is the last nonsymmetric synthetic scale we will describe. Instead of labels or numbers, a graphic rating uses symbols such as smiley faces, dollar signs, thermometers, or anything else that is appropriate to the construct being measured. Typically, as can be seen in the following example, as one moves along a graphic rating scale, the symbols increase in size to connote differences in degree. Or some relevant part of the symbol—such as the smile in the smiley face or the level of the mercury in the thermometer—changes to indicate the differences in degree. Because the graphic rating scale is a picture scale, it can be used for respondents who have reading difficulties, such as children, or it might be used by a researcher to break up the monotony of labeled and numbered scales on the questionnaire.

■ A graphic rating scale uses graphic symbols to convey degrees of feeling or opinions.

PRACTICAL
APPLICATIONS

**Example of a Graphic Rating Scale**

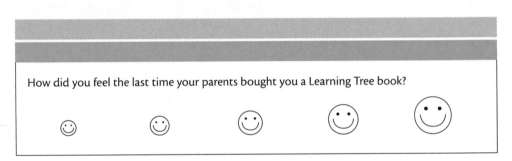

How did you feel the last time your parents bought you a Learning Tree book?

## Whether to Use a Symmetric or a Nonsymmetric Scale

You are probably confused by all the scale options we have described in this chapter and particularly as to when to use a symmetric versus a nonsymmetric scale. In reality, this decision is a judgment call on the part of the researcher, and the judgment is based on the following logic. Ideally, when a synthetic scale is used in a survey, the researcher wants respondents to use all of the scale positions, meaning that for any one question, the responses should be spread across all of the scale positions. If the researcher believes there will be very few respondents who will make use of the negative side of a symmetric scale, the researcher should opt for a nonsymmetric scale. When in doubt, a researcher can pretest both the two-sided and the one-sided versions to see whether the negative side will be used by respondents. As a general rule, it is best to pretest a symmetric scale to make sure it is being used in its entirety. Some individuals, such as Hispanics, have tendencies to use only one end of a scale,[22] and pretests should be used to find a scale that will be used appropriately.

If you choose a career in the marketing research business, you will realize that each marketing research company or marketing research department tends to rely on tried-and-true formats that they apply from study to study. There are some very good reasons for this practice of adopting a preferred question format. First, it expedites the questionnaire design process. That is, by selecting a standardized scaled-response form that has been used in several studies, there is no need to be creative and to invent a new form. This saves both time and costs. Second, by testing a scaled-response format across several studies, there is the opportunity to assess its reliability as well as its validity.

■ Include a "no opinion" option in a scale when respondents legitimately have no opinion to express.

# CHOOSING WHICH SCALE TO USE

It has been our experience that when students learn about each type of scale one-by-one, each one makes sense. However, when faced with the actual decision as to which scale to recommend in a given situation, it is difficult for neophyte marketing researchers to sort these scales out. Since you now understand the basic concepts of measurement and have become acquainted with the basic scales used by market researchers, we have provided Table 8.7 as a quick reference to our recommended scales pertaining to the constructs most often measured by market researchers. Of course, this is not a complete list of marketing constructs, but the constructs in Table 8.7 are often involved in marketing research undertakings. Also, as we indicated earlier, seasoned researchers may have preferences for other scales or variations of our recommended synthetic scales.[23]

■ Seasoned researchers develop preferences for synthetic scales that may differ from those recommended here.

**Table 8.7**
Recommended Synthetic Scales for Selected Constructs

| The following scales are recommended to neophyte researchers who are seeking ways to measure the various constructs identified. | |
|---|---|
| **Construct** | **Recommended Scale(s)** |
| **Brand Image** | **Recommend: Semantic Differential** scale using a set of bipolar adjectives |
| | Example: Refer to example on page 248. |
| | Or **Recommend: Stapel Scale** (if researcher does not wish to develop bipolar adjectives) |
| | Example: Rate Folgers Decaffeinated Coffee on ... |

|  |  |  |  |
|---|---|---|---|
| | +3 | | +3 |
| | +2 | | +2 |
| | +1 | | +1 |
| Taste | 0 | Mild on stomach | 0 |
| | −1 | | −1 |
| | −2 | | −2 |
| | −3 | | −3 |

| **Frequency of Use** | **Recommend: One-Way Labeled Scale** |
|---|---|
| | Example: How often do you buy take-out Chinese dinners? |
| | _____ Never |
| | _____ Infrequently |
| | _____ Occasionally |
| | _____ Often |
| | _____ Quite Often |
| | _____ Very Often |

**Table 8.7**
*(Continued)*

| Construct | Recommended Scale(s) |
|---|---|
| **Importance** | **Recommend: One-Way Labeled Scale** |

Example: How important is it to you that your dry-cleaning service has same-day service?

_____ Not Important

_____ Slightly Important

_____ Important

_____ Quite Important

_____ Very Important

**Intention to Purchase**   **Recommend: Symmetric Labeled Scale**

Example: The next time you buy cookies, how likely are you to buy a fat-free brand?

_____ Very Unlikely

_____ Somewhat Unlikely

_____ Neither Unlikely nor Likely

_____ Somewhat Likely

_____ Very Likely

**Lifestyle or Opinion**   **Recommend: Likert Scale** using a series of lifestyle or opinion statements

Example: Indicate how much you agree or disagree with each of the following statements.

| Statement | Strongly Disagree | Disagree | Neither Disagree nor Agree | Agree | Strongly Agree |
|---|---|---|---|---|---|
| I have a busy schedule. | | | | | |
| I work a great deal. | | | | | |

**Performance**   **Recommend: Anchored 5-Point Scale**

Example: Indicate with a number from 1 to 5, where 1 means "poor" and 5 means "excellent," as to how well you think Arby's performs on each of the following features.

| | Poor | | | | Excellent |
|---|---|---|---|---|---|
| a. Variety of items on the menu | 1 | 2 | 3 | 4 | 5 |
| b. Reasonable price | 1 | 2 | 3 | 4 | 5 |
| c. Location convenient to your home | 1 | 2 | 3 | 4 | 5 |

(With respondents who are less comfortable with number ratings, **Recommend: One-Way Labeled Scale** of "poor," "fair," "good," "very good," and "excellent.")

| Satisfaction | Recommend: Symmetric Labeled Scale |
|---|---|

Example: Based on your experience with Federal Express, how satisfied have you been with its overnight delivery service?

_____ Extremely Satisfied

_____ Somewhat Satisfied

_____ Neither Satisfied nor Unsatisfied

_____ Somewhat Unsatisfied

_____ Extremely Unsatisfied

# SUMMARY

This chapter discussed the concepts involved in measurement of the properties of objects of interest to marketing researchers. We began by reviewing the three basic question-response option formats of open-ended, categorical, and metric. We then introduced basic measurement concepts and explained that researchers want to measure properties of objects, such as consumers, and they use operational definitions to describe precisely how this measurement takes place. There are two relevant levels of measurement: categorical, where the measure is based on groups such as male versus female; and metric, where the measure is based on a quantity or amount, such as how many times a respondent used an ATM machine in the past month. Metric measures can be natural, such as the ATM example above, or synthetic, meaning that the researcher utilizes a rating scale of some sort. We explained that categorical measures are typically summarized using percents, while metric measures are summarized by using averages.

The chapter went on to describe synthetic metric scales commonly used by market researchers. We began this section by illustrating an underlying intensity-of-feeling continuum for symmetric synthetic metric scales, and we described and provided examples for three of these: the Likert scale, the semantic differential scale, and the Stapel scale. Next, we described three nonsymmetric synthetic scales where the rating scale is basically on the positive side of the intensity continuum: the one-way labeled scale, the n-point scale, and the graphic rating scale. Finally, we provided our recommended scales for a list of constructs that market researchers find themselves measuring over and over across surveys.

# KEY TERMS

Open-ended response format (p. 232)
Unaided open-ended format (p. 232)
Aided open-ended format (p. 232)
Response probe (p. 232)
Categorical response format (p. 234)
Dual-choice question (p. 234)
Multiple-choice category question (p. 234)

"Check all that apply" question (p. 234)
Metric response question (p. 235)
Natural metric response format (p. 235)
Synthetic metric format (p. 235)
Measurement (p. 235)
Properties (p. 235)
Operational definition (p. 235)

# REVIEW QUESTIONS

1 List each of the three basic question-response formats. Indicate the two variations for each one, and provide an example for each.

2 What is measurement? In your answer, differentiate an object from its properties, both objective and subjective.

3 Indicate what is an operational definition. How does a researcher use an operational definition? Provide an example of the operational definition for each of the following:
   a Store loyalty
   b Recall of a television advertisement for a particular brand
   c Use of one's debit card

4 How does reliability differ from validity? In your answer, define each term.

5 What is meant by the "level of measurement"? Identify and define the two levels of measurement described in this chapter.

6 Distinguish a synthetic number scale from a synthetic label scale. What do these two types of scales have in common, and how do they differ?

7 Answer the following question: "Why is it important for a researcher to know the level of a scale that he or she uses to measure a property of a construct of interest?"

8 Distinguish a symmetric synthetic scale from a nonsymmetric synthetic scale. Provide an example of each of these types of scales.

9 Explain what is meant by a continuum along which a subjective property of an object can be measured.

10 What are the arguments for and against the inclusion of a neutral response position in a symmetric scale?

11 Distinguish among a modified Likert scale, a semantic differential scale, and a Stapel scale.

12 What is the halo effect, and when and how does a researcher control for it?

13 What consideration should be foremost in a researcher's decision to use a symmetric synthetic rating scale versus a nonsymmetric one?

14 Distinguish among a one-way labeled scale, an $n$-point scale, and a graphic rating scale.

15 What is an "anchor" and how does an anchor give a context to an $n$-point scale?

# APPLICATION QUESTIONS

**16** Mike, the owner of Mike's Market, which is a convenience store, is concerned about low sales. He reads in a marketing textbook that the image of a store often has an impact on its ability to attract its target market. He contacts the All-Right Research Company and commissions it to conduct a study that will shape his store's image. You are charged with the responsibility of developing the store-image part of the questionnaire.

Design a semantic differential scale that will measure the relevant aspects of Mike's Market's image. In your work on this scale, you must do the following: (a) brainstorm 10 convenience store properties to be measured, (b) determine the appropriate bipolar adjectives, (c) decide on the number of scale points, and (d) indicate how the scale controls for the halo effect.

**17** Each of the following examples involves a market researcher's need to measure some construct. Devise an appropriate scale for each one. Defend the scale in terms of its level of measurement and use or nonuse of a "no opinion" or neutral response category.

**a** Mattel wants to know how preschool children react to a sing-along video game in which the child must sing along with an animated character and guess the next word in the song at various points in the video.

**b** TCBY is testing five new flavors of frozen yogurt and wants to know how its customers rate each one on sweetness, flavor strength, and richness of taste.

**c** A pharmaceutical company wants to find out how much a new federal law eliminating dispensing of free sample prescription drugs by doctors will affect their intentions to prescribe generic versus brand-name drugs for their patients.

**18** Harley-Davidson is the largest American motorcycle manufacturer, and it has been in business for several decades. Harley-Davidson has expanded into "signature" products such as shirts that prominently display the Harley-Davidson logo. Some people have a negative image of Harley-Davidson because it was the motorcycle favored by the Hell's Angels and other motorcycle gangs. There are two research questions here. First, do consumers have a negative feeling toward Harley-Davidson, and, second, are they disinclined toward the purchase of Harley-Davidson signature products such as shirts, belts, boots, jackets, sweatshirts, lighters, and key chains? Design a Likert measurement scale that can be used in a nationwide telephone study to address these two issues.

**19** Family Dollar store believes it has a niche market, and that its image in the minds of its customers is the following: *a self-service store with bargain prices and no sales hassles but with reasonably fast checkout and for household and clothing items that are functional.* Construct a Stapel scale approach that would measure Family Dollar's image to determine the extent to which customers have an opinion consistent with Family Dollar's belief.

**20** Pick any fast-food chain (such as McDonald's, KFC, etc.) and construct a scale that measures the performance of that chain's units. Use a one-way labeled scale that measures the chain on at least five performance attributes that you think are relevant. Be sure to include any instructions for the respondents.

# INTERACTIVE LEARNING

 Visit the textbook Web site at **www.prenhall.com/burnsbush**. For this chapter, use the Self-Study Quizzes and get immediate feedback on whether you need additional studying. On the Web site, you can review the chapter outlines and case information for Chapter 8.

## CASE 8.1 | Metro Toyota of Kalamazoo

The Metro Toyota dealership, located in Kalamazoo, Michigan, wanted to know how people who intended to buy a new automobile in the next 12 months viewed their purchase. The General Sales Manager called the marketing department at the University of Western Michigan and arranged for a class project to be taken on by Professor Ann Veeck's undergraduate marketing research students. Professor Veeck had a large class that semester, so she decided to divide the project into two groups and to have each group compete against the other to see which one designed and executed the better survey.

Both groups worked diligently on the survey over the semester. They met with the Metro Toyota General Sales Manager, discussed the dealership with his managers, conducted focus groups, and consulted the literature on brand, store, and company image research. Both teams conducted telephone surveys, whose findings are presented in their final reports.

The relevant findings of Professor Veeck's two marketing research teams are summarized below.

**Team One's Findings for Metro Toyota of Kalamazoo**

**Importance of Features of Dealership in Deciding to Buy There**

| Feature | Percent |
|---|---|
| Competitive prices | 86% |
| No high pressure | 75% |
| Good service facilities | 73% |
| Low-cost financing | 68% |
| Many models in stock | 43% |
| Convenient location | 35% |
| Friendly salespersons | 32% |

**Image of Metro Toyota of Kalamazoo Dealership, Percent Responding "Yes"**

| Feature | Percent |
|---|---|
| Competitive prices | 45% |
| No high pressure | 32% |
| Good service facilities | 80% |
| Low-cost financing | 78% |
| Many models in stock | 50% |
| Convenient location | 81% |
| Friendly salespersons | 20% |

**Team Two's Findings for Metro Toyota of Kalamazoo**

**Importance and Image of Metro Toyota of Kalamazoo Dealership**

| Feature | Importance[a] | Rating[b] |
|---|---|---|
| Competitive prices | 6.5 | 1.3 |
| No high pressure | 6.2 | 3.6 |
| Good service facilities | 5.0 | 4.3 |
| Low-cost financing | 4.7 | 3.9 |
| Many models in stock | 3.1 | 3.0 |
| Convenient location | 2.2 | 4.1 |
| Friendly salespersons | 2.0 | 1.2 |

[a] Based on a 7-point scale where 1 = "unimportant" and 7 = "extremely important."
[b] Based on a 5-point scale where 1 = "poor" and 5 = "excellent performance."

Professor Veeck offered to grant extra credit to each team if it gave a formal presentation of its research design, findings, and recommendations.

1 Contrast the different ways these findings can be presented in graphical form by each of Professor Veeck's research teams to the Metro Toyota management group. Which student team has the ability to present its findings more effectively? How and why?

2 What are the managerial implications apparent in each team's findings? Identify the implications and recommendations for Metro Toyota as they are evident in each team's findings.

## CASE 8.2 ||| Extreme Exposure Rock Climbing Center Faces the Krag

For the past five years, Extreme Exposure Rock Climbing Center has enjoyed a monopoly. Located in Sacramento, California, Extreme Exposure was the dream of Kyle Anderson, a former extreme sports enthusiast. Kyle's rock-climbing center has over 6,500 square feet of simulated rock walls to climb, with about 100 different routes up to a maximum of 50 vertical feet. Extreme Exposure's design permits the four major climbing types: top-roping, where the climber climbs up with a rope anchored at the top; lead-climbing, where the climber tows the rope that he or she fixes to clips in the wall while ascending; bouldering, where the climber has no rope but stays near the ground; and rappelling, where the person descends quickly by sliding down a rope. Climbers can buy day passes or monthly or yearly memberships. Shoes and harnesses can be rented cheaply, and helmets are available free of charge as all climbers must wear protective helmets. In addition to individual and group climbing classes, Extreme Exposure has several group programs, including birthday parties, a kids' summer camp, and corporate team-building classes.

Another rock-climbing center, called The Krag, will be built in Sacramento within the next six months. Kyle notes the following items about The Krag that are different from Extreme Exposure: (1) The Krag will have climbs up to a maximum of 60 vertical feet, (2) it will have a climber certification program, (3) there will be day trips to outdoor rock-climbing areas, (4) there will be group overnight and extended-stay rock-climbing trips to the Canadian Rockies, and (5) The Krag's annual membership fee will be about 20% lower than the one for Extreme Exposure.

Kyle chats with Dianne, one of his Extreme Exposure members who is in marketing, during a break in one of her climbing visits, and Dianne summarizes what she believes Kyle needs to find out about his current members. Dianne's list follows.

**Objective 1:** What is the demographic and rock-climbing profile of Extreme Exposure's members?

**Objective 2:** How satisfied are the members with Extreme Exposure's climbing facilities?

**Objective 3:** How interested are its members in (a) day trips to outdoor rock-climbing areas, (b) group overnight and/or extended-stay rock-climbing trips to the Canadian Rockies, and (c) a rock climber certification program?

**Objective 4:** What are members' opinions of the annual membership fee charged by Extreme Exposure?

**Objective 5:** Will members consider leaving Extreme Exposure to join a new rock-climbing center with climbs that are 10 feet higher than the maximum climb at Extreme Exposure?

**Objective 6:** Will members consider leaving Extreme Exposure to join a new rock-climbing center with climbs that are 10 feet higher than the maximum climb at Extreme Exposure and whose annual membership fee is 20% lower than Extreme Exposure's?

For each of Dianne's questions, identify the relevant construct and indicate how it should be measured.

# CHAPTER 9

# DESIGNING YOUR QUESTIONNAIRE

Clifford D. Scott is Associate Professor, University of Arkansas, Fort Smith. He has many years of experience in high-tech, bio-tech, and consulting. He earned a Ph.D. in Marketing from Louisiana State University and a J.D. from the University of Colorado.

## SINCE MOST CONSUMERS WANT A CAR WITH EXCELLENT FUEL ECONOMY, WOULDN'T YOU AGREE YOUR NEXT CAR WILL BE A HYBRID?

Lawyers and market researchers both ask leading questions, and both do it for the same two reasons. First, leading questions are easier. A single leading question can cut right to the point (Didn't you talk to the defendant on Tuesday at the shopping mall right after leaving home?). Getting the same information without putting words in the respondent's mouth requires a series of organized, interlocking nonleading, questions: "Did you leave home on Tuesday?" "Can you tell us where you went?" "Did you speak with anyone, and, if so, whom?" "Do you see him here today?" "Can you identify him for us?"

Second, leading questions bolster your case. A skilled questioner, whether in court or in a market study, can usually get the answers she wants. For a lawyer, that approach is fine: a lawyer is supposed to be an advocate. But a researcher is supposed to be a scientist. People risk their careers and their fortunes on the outcome of a study. If they take those risks and

- To appreciate the questionnaire design process
- To learn the four "dos" of question wording
- To understand the four "do nots" of question wording
- To learn the basics of questionnaire organization
- To comprehend precoding of questionnaires
- To understand the advantages of computer-assisted questionnaire design software

lose, they will look for someone to blame. The researcher makes an excellent target IF the study shows evidence of bias, such as leading questions. The faulty study can, and often will, come back to haunt the researcher.

This chapter will teach you how to identify and eliminate leading questions, one of the most common, and most damning, sources of bias. Looking at the question at the top of this page, clearly you would want to be "like all those other smart consumers" and buy a hybrid! Wording a question in this way would guarantee that you will get a larger percentage of respondents indicating they will buy a hybrid than if you had just asked: "If you had to select your next car today, what brand of car would you buy?" In this chapter you will learn more about the "dos and don'ts" of designing a questionnaire to avoid biased questions.

Clifford D. Scott, Ph.D., J.D.

In this chapter, you will learn the functions of a questionnaire and the process of developing questionnaires. We give you guidelines on how to word questions so that they are not biased, as was illustrated by Cliff Scott's question example you just read, and we show you how to avoid biased questions. You will also learn

■ **A questionnaire poses the survey questions to respondents.**

■ **Questionnaire design is a systematic process that requires the researcher to go through a series of considerations.**

■ **Question bias occurs when the question's wording or format influences the respondent's answer.**

how to organize a questionnaire and how to apply precodes. We introduce you to computer-assisted questionnaire design programs, and, finally, we discuss the importance of pretesting your questionnaire.[1]

## WHAT IS A QUESTIONNAIRE AND WHAT STEPS ARE TAKEN TO DEVELOP IT?

A **questionnaire** is the vehicle used to pose the questions that the researcher wants respondents to answer. As such, the questionnaire serves important functions. It translates the research objectives into specific questions that are asked of the respondents. It standardizes those questions and the response categories so that every participant responds to identical stimuli. By its wording question flow, and by its appearance, it fosters cooperation and keeps respondents motivated throughout the interview. Questionnaires serve as permanent records of the research. Finally, depending on the type of questionnaire used, it can speed up the process of data analysis.

Given that it serves all of these functions, the questionnaire is a very important element in the research process. In fact, studies have shown that questionnaire design directly affects the quality of the data collected. Even experienced interviewers cannot compensate for questionnaire defects.[2] The time and effort invested in developing a good questionnaire are well spent.[3] As you will soon learn, **questionnaire design** is a systematic process in which the researcher contemplates various question formats, considers a number of factors characterizing the survey at hand, ultimately words the various questions very carefully, and organizes the questionnaire's layout.

Figure 9.1 offers a flowchart of the various phases in a typical marketing research survey. The first two steps in the flowchart have been covered in this book. We have expanded and highlighted the questionnaire design steps, so you can see that there are some specific activities the research must execute before the questionnaire is finalized. As you can see in Figure 9.1, a questionnaire will ordinarily go through a series of drafts before it is in acceptable final form. In fact, even before the first question is constructed, the researcher mentally reviews alternative question formats to decide which ones are best suited to the survey's respondents and circumstances. As the questionnaire begins to take shape, the researcher continually evaluates each question and its response options. Changes are made, and the question's wording is reevaluated to make sure that it is asking what the researcher intends. Also, the researcher strives to minimize **question bias**, defined as the ability of a question's wording or format to influence respondents' answers.[4] We will elaborate on question development and the minimization of question bias very soon.

For now, it is important only that you realize that with a custom-designed research study, the questions on the questionnaire, along with its instructions, introduction, and general layout, are systematically evaluated for potential error and revised accordingly. Generally, this evaluation takes place at the researcher's end, and the client will not be involved until after the questionnaire has undergone considerable development and evaluation by the researcher. The client is

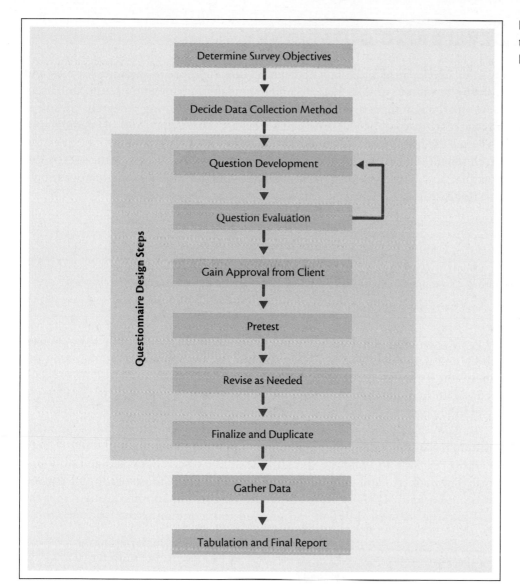

**Figure 9.1** Steps in the Questionnaire Development Process

given the opportunity to comment on the questionnaire during the client approval step, in which the client reviews the questionnaire and agrees that it covers all of the appropriate issues. This step is essential, and some research companies require the client to sign or initial a copy of the questionnaire as verification of approval. Granted, the client may not appreciate all of the technical aspects of questionnaire design, but he or she is vitally concerned with the survey's objectives and can comment on the degree to which the questions on the questionnaire appear to address these objectives. Following client approval, the questionnaire normally undergoes a pretest, which is an actual field test using a very limited sample to reveal any difficulties that might still lurk in wording, instructions, administration, and so on.[5] We describe pretesting more fully later in this chapter. Revisions are made based on the pretest results, and the questionnaire is finalized.

# DEVELOPING QUESTIONS

**Question development** is the practice of selecting appropriate response formats and wording questions so that they are understandable, unambiguous, and unbiased. Marketing researchers are very concerned with developing research questions because they measure (1) attitudes, (2) beliefs, (3) behaviors, and (4) demographics,[6] and they desire reliable and valid answers to their questions. So, question development is a tall order, but it is absolutely vital to the success of the survey. For example, how would you respond to the following question that might appear on a questionnaire?

> Have you stopped trying to beat red traffic lights when you think you have the chance?
> _____ Yes          _____ No

■ Question development is the practice of selecting appropriate response formats, and wording questions so that they are understandable, unambiguous, and unbiased.

If you say "Yes," it means you used to speed up when the traffic light showed yellow, and if you say "No," it means you are still taking chances. Either way, the conclusion is that everyone who took part in the survey drove or still drives dangerously. But we all know that not everyone drives recklessly now or drove recklessly in the past, so the question must be flawed, and it surely is.

Developing a question's precise wording is not easy. A single word can make a difference in how study participants respond to a question, and there is considerable research to illustrate this. In one study, researchers changed only one word. They asked, "Did you see *the* broken headlight?" to one group of participants, and asked, "Did you see *a* broken headlight?" to another group. Only the "the" and the "a" were different, yet the question containing the "the" produced

"Did you *see* the broken headlight?"

**Table 9.1**
Ten Words to Avoid in Question Development*

| Word | Example in a Survey Performed with Flat Screen TV Purchasers |
| --- | --- |
| All | Did you consider **all** the options before you decided to purchase your flat screen plasma TV? |
| Always | Do you **always** buy your electronics products from Gateway? |
| Any | Did you have **any** concerns about the price? |
| Anybody | Did you talk to **anybody** about flat screen televisions before you made your decision? |
| Best | What is the **best** feature on your new flat screen plasma TV? |
| Ever | Have you **ever** seen a flat screen television? |
| Every | Do you consult *Consumer Reports* **every** time you purchase a major item? |
| Most | What was the **most** important factor that convinced you it was time to make this purchase? |
| Never | Would you say that you **never** think about an extended warranty? |
| Worst | Is the high price the **worst** aspect of purchasing a flat screen plasma TV? |

*__Why avoid these words?__ These words are *extreme absolutes*, meaning that they place respondents in a situation where they must either agree fully or they must completely disagree with the extreme position in the question.

more "Don't know" and "Yes" answers than did the "a" question.[7] Our point is that as little as one word in a question can result in question bias that will distort the findings of the survey. Unfortunately, words that we use commonly in speaking to one another sometimes encourage biased answers when they appear on a questionnaire. Table 9.1 lists our "Ten Words to Avoid in Question Development."[8] Again, the point to remember is that while we use these words in everyday language, they can introduce an element of bias into a questionnaire when they are used and respondents are using a literal interpretation in their efforts to answer the questions.

As you can see by reading Table 9.1, it is important that questions do not contain subtle cues, signals, or interpretations that lead respondents to give answers that are inaccurate. Granted, not all respondents will be influenced by question wording, but if a significant minority is affected, this bias can cause the findings to be distorted or mixed, as you saw in our broken-headlight example.

■ Some words, when taken literally, introduce question bias.

What about global marketing research situations where the researcher must create questionnaires that are in diverse languages? How can a manager avoid question bias when he or she does not speak the language of the respondents? For example, a researcher working with Delta Airlines might need to design a survey that will have respondents who speak only one of the following languages: English, French, Spanish, Italian, Dutch, German, or Russian. One solution that might be put forth is to design the questionnaire in some "universal" language, such as English, that many non–native English speakers can read; however, this approach

GLOBAL

is generally unsatisfactory because there are many opportunities for miscomprehension. Instead, global marketing researchers use the following when attempting to do across-the-globe research:

- Create the questionnaire in the reseacher's native language (e.g., English),
- Translate the questionnaire into the other language (e.g., German),
- Have independent translators translate it back into the native language (e.g., from German to English) to check that the first translation was accurate,
- Revise the questionnaire based on the "back translation" (into a better German version), and
- Carefully pretest the revised questionnaire using individuals whose native tongue is the other language (e.g., natives of Germany).

## Four "Dos" of Question Wording

**The researcher uses question evaluation to scrutinize a possible question for its question bias.**

**Question evaluation** amounts to scrutinizing the wording of a question to ensure that question bias is minimized and that the question is worded such that respondents understand it and can respond to it with relative ease. As we noted earlier, question bias occurs when the phrasing of a question influences a respondent to answer unreliably or with other than perfect accuracy. Ideally, every question should be examined and tested according to a number of crucial factors known to be related to question bias. In this section, we offer four simple guidelines, or "dos," for question wording. The question should be: (1) focused, (2) simple, (3) brief, and (4) crystal clear. A discussion of these guidelines follows.

### The Question Should Be Focused on a Single Issue or Topic

**A question should be focused.**

The researcher must stay focused on the specific issue or topic. For example, take the question "What type of hotel do you usually stay in when on a trip?" The focus of this question is hazy because it does not narrow down the type of trip or when the hotel is being used. For example, is it a business or a pleasure trip? Is the hotel at a place en route or at the final destination? A more focused version is "When you are on a family vacation and stay in a hotel at your destination, what type of hotel do you typically use?" As a second example, consider how "unfocused" the following question is: "When do you typically go to work?" Does this mean when do you leave home for work or when do you actually begin work once at your workplace? A better question would be "At what time do you ordinarily leave home for work?"

### The Question Should Be Brief

**A question should be brief.**

Unnecessary and redundant words should always be eliminated. This requirement is especially important when designing questions that will be administered verbally, such as over the telephone. Brevity will help the respondent to comprehend the central question and reduce the distraction of wordiness. Here is a question that suffers from a lack of brevity: "What are the considerations that would come to your mind while you are confronted with the decision to have some type of repair done on the automatic icemaker in your refrigerator, assuming that you noticed it was not making ice cubes as well as it did when you first bought it?" A better, brief form would be "If your icemaker was not working right, how would you correct the problem?"

### The Question Should Be a Grammatically Simple Sentence If Possible

A simple sentence is preferred because it has only a single subject and predicate, whereas compound and complex sentences are busy with multiple subjects, predicates, objects, and complements. The more complex the sentence, the greater the potential for respondent error. There are more conditions to remember, and more information to consider simultaneously, so the respondent's attention may wane or he or she may concentrate on only one part of the question. To avoid these problems, the researcher should strive to use only simple sentence structure—even if two separate sentences are necessary to communicate the essence of the question. Take the question "If you were looking for an automobile that would be used by the head of your household who is primarily responsible for driving your children to and from school, music lessons, and friends' houses, how much would you and your spouse discuss the safety features of one of the cars you took for a test-drive?" A simple approach is "Would you and your spouse discuss the safety features of a new family car?" followed by (if yes), "Would you discuss safety 'very little,' 'some,' 'a good deal,' or 'to a great extent'?"

▪ A question should be as brief as possible.

### The Question Should Be Crystal Clear

All respondents should "see" the question identically. For example, the question "How many children do you have?" might be interpreted in various ways. One respondent might think of only those children living at home, whereas another might include children from a previous marriage. A better question is "How many children under the age of 18 live with you in your home?" One tactic for clarity is to develop questions that use words that are in respondents' core vocabularies. That is, the general public does not use marketing jargon such as "price point" or "brand equity," so it is best to avoid words that are vague or open to misinterpretations. To develop a crystal clear question, the researcher may be forced to slightly abuse the previous guideline of simplicity, but with a bit of effort, question clarity can be obtained with an economical number of words.[9]

▪ A question should be crystal clear.

## Four "Do Nots" of Question Wording

There are four situations in which question bias is practically assured, and it is important that you learn about these so you can avoid them or spot them when you are reviewing a questionnaire draft. Specifically, the question should not be: (1) leading, (2) loaded, (3) double-barreled, or (4) overstated.

### The Question Should Not "Lead" the Respondent to a Particular Answer

A **leading question** is worded or structured in such a way as to give the respondent a strong cue or expectation as to how to answer. Therefore, it biases responses. Consider this question: "Don't you see any problems with using your credit card for an online purchase?" The respondent is being led here because the question wording stresses one side (in this case, the negative side) of the issue. Therefore, the question "leads" respondents to the conclusion that there must be some problems, and thus they will likely agree with the question, particularly respondents who have no opinion. Rephrasing the question as "Do you see any problems with using your credit card for an online purchase?" is a much more objective request of the respondent. Here the respondent is free—that is, not led—to respond "yes" or "no." Examine the following questions for other forms of leading questions:

| | |
|---|---|
| As a Cadillac owner, you are satisfied with your car, aren't you? | This is a leading question because the wording presupposes that all Cadillac owners are satisfied. It places the respondent in a situation where disagreement is uncomfortable and singles him or her out as being different. |
| Have you heard about the satellite radio system that everyone is talking about? | This is a leading question due to its possessing the ability to condition the respondent in terms of answering in a socially desirable manner. In other words, few people would want to admit they are clueless about something "everybody is talking about." [10] |

*Do not use leading questions that have strong cues on how to answer.*

### The Question Should Not Have "Loaded" Wording or Phrasing

Leading questions are biased in that they direct the respondent to answer in a predetermined way. By contrast, loaded questions are more subtle, yet they also are biased questions. Identifying this type of bias in a question requires more judgment, because a **loaded question** has buried in its wording elements that allude to universal beliefs or rules of behavior. It may even apply emotionalism or touch on a person's inner fears. For example, a company marketing mace for personal use may use the question "Should people be allowed to protect themselves from harm by using mace as self-defense?" Obviously, most respondents will agree with the need to protect oneself from harm, and self-defense is an acceptable and well-known legal defense. Eliminating the loaded aspect of this question would result in the question "Do you think carrying a mace product is acceptable for people who are worried about being attacked?" As you can see, the phrasing of each question should be examined thoroughly to guard against the various sources of question bias error. Seasoned researchers develop a sixth sense about the pitfalls we have just described; however, because the researcher can become caught up in the research process, slips do occur. This danger explains why many researchers use "experts" to review drafts of their questionnaires. For example, it is common for the questionnaire to be designed by one employee of the research company and then given to another employee who understands questionnaire design for a thorough inspection for question bias as well as face validity, that is, if the questions "look right."

*Do not use loaded questions that have emotional overtones.*

### The Question Should Not Be "Double-Barreled"

A **double-barreled question** is really two different questions posed in one question. With two questions posed together, it is difficult for a respondent to answer either one directly. Consider a question asked of patrons at a restaurant: "Were you satisfied with the food and service?" How does the repondent answer? If they say "yes," does that mean they were satisfied with the food? The service? A combination? The question would be much improved by asking about a single item: one

"Which one of these questions should I answer?"

question for food and another question for service. Sometimes double-barreled questions are not as obvious. Look at the following question designed to ask for occupational status:

| |
|---|
| **Which term best describes you?** |
| _____ Employed full-time |
| _____ Full-time student |
| _____ Part-time student |
| _____ Unemployed |
| _____ Retired |

How does one who is retired and a full-time student answer the question? An improvement could be made by asking one question about occupational status and another about student status.[11]

■ Do not use double-barreled questions that ask two questions at the same time.

### The Question Should Not Use Words That Overstate the Condition

An **overstated question** is one that places undue emphasis on some aspect of the topic. It uses what might be considered "dramatics" to describe the topic. Avoid using words that overstate conditions. It is better to present the question in a neutral tone rather than in a strong positive or negative tone. Here is an example of an overstated question that might be found in a survey conducted for Ray-Ban sunglasses: "How much do you think you would pay for a pair of sunglasses that will protect your eyes from the sun's harmful ultraviolet rays, which are known to cause blindness?" As you can see, the overstatement concerns the effects of ultraviolet rays, and because of this overstatement, respondents will be compelled to think

Asking someone how much they would pay for a pair of sunglasses that would help prevent blindness is an overstatement.

about how much they would pay for something that can prevent their blindness and not about how much they would really pay for the sunglasses. A more toned-down and acceptable question wording would be "How much would you pay for sunglasses that will protect your eyes from the sun's rays?"

To be sure, there are other question-wording pitfalls, but if you use common sense in developing questions for your questionnaire, you will probably avoid them. For example, it is nonsensical to ask respondents questions about details they don't recall (How many and what brands of aspirin did you see the last time you bought some?); questions that invite guesses (What is the price per gallon of premium gasoline at the Exxon station on the corner?); or questions that ask them to predict their actions in circumstances they cannot fathom (How often would you go out to eat at this new, upscale restaurant that will be built 10 miles from your home?).

■ **Do not use overstated questions that use words to overemphasize the case.**

The four question errors just described are well known to researchers, and others can learn about them easily. There are unfortunate cases where it appears that questionnaire designers have deliberately used leading questions, loaded questions, or some other question wording that is biased in order to influence the survey's findings to support a particular point of view or stance. If this is done inadvertently, the questionnaire designer is woefully uninformed about the sources of question bias, but if it is done intentionally, the practice is considered to be an unethical marketing research tactic.

## QUESTIONNAIRE ORGANIZATION

Now that you have learned about question development, and specifically the guidelines and things to avoid when wording questions, we can turn to the organization of the questionnaire. Normally, the researcher creates questions by taking the research objectives in turn and developing the questions that relate to each objective. In other words, the questions are developed but not organized. **Questionnaire organization** is the sequence of statements and questions that make up a questionnaire. Questionnaire organization is an important concern because the questionnaire's appearance and the ease with which respondents complete the questions have the potential to affect the quality of the information that is gathered. Well-organized questionnaires motivate respondents to be conscientious and complete, while those that are poorly organized discourage and frustrate respondents, and may even cause them to stop answering questions in the middle of the survey. We will describe two critical aspects of questionnaire organization: the introduction and the actual flow of questions in the questionnaire body.

■ Questionnaire organization pertains to the introduction and the actual flow of questions on the questionnaire.

## The Introduction

The introduction is very important in questionnaire design. If the introduction is written to accompany a mail survey or online survey, it is normally referred to as a **cover letter**. If the introduction is to be verbally presented to a potential respondent, as in the case of a personal interview, it may be referred to as the opening comments. Of course, each survey and its target respondent group are unique, so a researcher cannot use a standardized introduction. In this section, we discuss the five functions to be provided by the introduction. Table 9.2 lists these five functions, and it provides examples of the sentences that you might find in a survey on personal money management software. As you read our descriptions of each function, refer back to the example in Table 9.2 and the brief explanation.

■ The cover letter or introduction of a questionnaire is critical to gaining cooperation to participate in the survey.

First, it is common courtesy to introduce yourself at the beginning of a survey. Note in Table 9.2 that the interviewer has identified himself or herself and the prospective respondent has been made aware that this is a bona fide survey and not a sales pitch. Additionally, the sponsor of the survey should be identified. There are two options with respect to sponsor identity. With an **undisguised survey**, the sponsoring company is identified, but with a **disguised survey**, the sponsor's name is not divulged to respondents. The choice of which approach to take depends on the survey's objectives and on whether disclosure of the sponsor's name or true intent can in some way influence respondents' answers. Another reason for disguise is to prevent alerting competitors to the survey.

■ Whether or not to use a disguised survey depends on the survey's objectives, possible undue influence caused by knowledge of the sponsor's name or intent, or desire to not alert competitors to the survey.

Second, the general purpose of the survey should be described clearly and simply. In a cover letter, the purpose may be expressed in one or two sentences. Typically, respondents are not informed of the specific purposes of the survey as it would be boring and perhaps intimidating to list all the research objectives. Consider a bank having a survey conducted by a marketing research firm. The actual purpose of the survey is to determine the bank's image relative to that of its competitors. However, the research firm need only say, "We are conducting a survey on customers' perceptions of financial institutions in this area." This satisfies the respondent's curiosity and does not divulge the name of the bank.

Third, prospective respondents must be made aware of how and why they were selected. Just a short sentence to answer the respondent's mental question of "Why me?" will suffice. Telling respondents that they were "selected at random" usually is sufficient. Of course, you should be ethical and tell them the actual method that

■ The introduction should indicate to the respondent how he or she was selected.

**Table 9.2**

The Functions of the Questionnaire Introduction

| Function | Example | Explanation |
|---|---|---|
| **Identifies the surveyor/sponsor.** | "Hello, my name is ____, and I am a telephone interviewer working with Nationwide Opinion Research Company here in Milwaukee. I am not selling anything." | The sponsor of the survey is divulged, plus the prospective respondent is made aware that this is a bona fide survey and not a sales pitch. |
| **Indicates the purpose of the survey.** | "We are conducting a survey on money management software used by individuals." | Informs prospective respondent of the topic and the reason for the call. |
| **Explains how the respondent was selected.** | "Your telephone number was generated randomly by a computer." | Notifies prospective respondent how he or she was chosen to be in the survey. |
| **Requests for/provides incentive for participation.** | "This is an anonymous survey, and I would now like to ask you a few questions about your experiences with money management computer programs. Is now a good time?" | Asks for prospective respondent's agreement to take part in the survey at this time. (Also, here, notes anonymity to gain cooperation.) |
| **Determines if respondent is suitable.** | "Do you use Quicken or Microsoft Money?" | Determines if prospective respondent qualified to take part in the survey; those who do not use either program will be screened out. |

was used. If their selection wasn't random, you should inform them as to which method was used.

Fourth, you must ask prospective respondents for their participation in the survey. With a mail survey, the cover letter might end with "Will you please take five minutes to complete the attached questionnaire and mail it back to us in the postage-paid, preaddressed envelope provided?" If you are conducting a personal interview or a telephone interview, you might say something like "I would now like to ask you a few questions about your experiences with automotive repair shops. Okay?" You should be as brief as possible yet let the respondent know that you are getting ready for him or her to participate by answering questions. This is also the appropriate time to offer an incentive to participate. **Incentives** are offers to do something for the respondent in order to increase the probability that the respondent will participate in the survey. There are various incentives that may be used by the researcher to encourage participation. As consumers have become more resistant to telemarketers and marketing researchers' pleas for information, researchers are reporting they must offer increased incentives. Offering a monetary incentive, a sample of a product, or a copy of study results are examples. Other incentives encourage respondent participation by letting them know the importance of their participation: "You are one of a select few, randomly chosen, to express your views on a new type of automobile tire." Or the topic itself can be highlighted for importance: "It is important that consumers let companies know whether or not they are satisfied."

Other forms of incentives address respondent anxieties concerning privacy. Here again, there are methods that tend to reduce these anxieties and therefore increase participation. As you can see in Table 9.2, one is is **anonymity**, in which the respondent is assured that neither the respondent's name nor any identifying designation will be associated with his or her responses. The second method is **confidentiality**, which means that the respondent's name is known by the researcher, but it is not divulged to a third party, namely, the client. Anonymous surveys are most appropriate in data collection modes where the respondent responds directly on the questionnaire. Any self-administered survey qualifies for anonymity as long as the respondent does not indicate his or her identity and provided the questionnaire does not have any covert identification-tracing mechanism. However, when an interviewer is used, appointments or callbacks are usually necessary, so there typically is an explicit designation of the respondent's name, address, telephone number, and so forth on the questionnaire. In this case, confidentiality may be required. Often questionnaires have a callback notation area for the interviewer to make notes indicating, for instance, whether the phone is busy, the respondent is not at home, or a time at which to call back when the respondent will be available. Here the respondent will ordinarily be assured of confidentiality, and it is vital that the researcher guard against the loss of that confidentiality.

A fifth function of the introduction is to qualify prospective respondents. Respondents are screened for their appropriateness to take part in the survey. **Screening questions** are used to ferret out respondents who do not meet qualifications necessary to take part in the research study.[12] Whether you screen respondents depends on the research objectives. If the survey's objective is to determine the factors used by consumers to select an automobile dealer for the purpose of purchasing a new car, you may want to screen out those who have never purchased a new car or those who have not purchased a new car within the last, say, two years. "Have you purchased a new car within the last two years?" For all those who answer "no," the survey is terminated with a polite "Thank you for your time." Some would argue that you should put the screening question early on so as not to waste the time of the researcher or the respondent. When to ask the screening question should be considered with each survey. We place screening questions as last in the introduction because we have found it awkward to begin a conversation with a prospective respondent without initially taking care of the first four items we just discussed.

The creation of the introduction should entail just as much care and effort as the development of the questions on the questionnaire. The first words heard or read by the prospective respondent will largely determine whether he or she will

■ Anonymity means the respondent is never identified with the data collected, while confidentiality means that the respondent is not to be divulged to a client or any other third party.

■ Screening questions are used to screen out respondents who do not meet the qualifications necessary to take part in the research study.

take part in the survey. It makes sense, therefore, for the researcher to labor over a cover letter or opening until it has a maximum chance of eliciting the respondent's willingness to take part in the survey. If the researcher is unsuccessful in persuading prospective respondents to take part in the survey, all of his or her work on the questionnaire itself will have been in vain.

## Question Flow

**Question flow** pertains to the sequencing of questions or blocks of questions, including any instructions, on the questionnaire. Each research objective gives rise to a question or a set of questions. As a result, questions are usually developed on an objective-by-objective basis. However, to facilitate respondents' ease in answering questions, the organization of these sets of questions should follow some understandable logic. A commonly seen sequence of questions found in questionnaires is presented in Table 9.3, and, as the table title notes, there should be a logical or commonsense order to questions on a questionnaire. To begin, as we mentioned in our discussion of the introduction's functions, the first few questions are normally screening questions that will determine whether the potential respondent qualifies to participate in the survey based on certain selection criteria that the researcher has deemed essential. Of course, not all surveys have screening questions. A survey of all charge account customers for a department store, for example, may not require screening questions. This is true because, in a sense, all potential respondents have already been qualified by virtue of having charge accounts with the store.

Once the individual is qualified by the screening questions, the next questions may serve a "warm-up" function. **Warm-up questions** are simple and easy-to-answer questions that are used to get the respondents' interest and to demonstrate the ease of responding to the research request. Ideally, warm-up questions pertain to the research objectives, but the researcher may opt for a superfluous question. For example, if the first question dealing with a research objective is difficult, a warm-up question may be used to heighten the respondent's interest so that he or she will be more inclined to deal with the harder questions that follow.

**Transitions** are statements or questions made to let the respondent know that changes in question topic or format are forthcoming. A statement such as "Now I would like to ask you a few questions about your family's TV viewing habits" is an example of a transition statement. Such statements aid in making certain that the respondent understands the line of questioning. Transitions include "skip" questions. A **skip question** is one whose answer affects which question will be answered next. For example, a transition question may be "When you bake a cake, do you usually do it from scratch or do you use a box mix?" If the person responds that he or she uses a box mix, questions asking more details about baking from scratch are not appropriate, and the questionnaire will instruct the respondent (or the interviewer, if one is being used) to skip over or to bypass those questions.

It is good practice to "bury" complicated and difficult-to-answer questions deep in the questionnaire. Scaled-response questions such as semantic differential scales, Likert-type response scales, or other questions that require some degree of mental activity such as evaluation, voicing opinions, recalling past experiences, indicating

■ Attention should be given to placing the questions in a logical sequence to ease respondent participation.

■ Warm-up questions are used near the beginning of the survey to get the respondent's interest and demonstrate the ease of responding to the research request.

■ Transitions are statements made to let the respondent know that changes in question topic or format are forthcoming.

**Table 9.3**
The Location of
Questions on a
Questionnaire
Should Be Logical

| Question Type | Question Location | Examples | Rationale |
|---|---|---|---|
| **Screens** | First questions asked | "Have you shopped at Gap in the past month?" "Is this your first visit to this store?" | Used to select the respondent types desired by the researcher to be in the survey |
| **Warm-ups** | Immediately after any screens | "How often do you go shopping?" "On what days of the week do you usually shop?" | Easy to answer; shows respondent that survey is easy to complete; generates interest |
| **Transitions (statements and questions)** | Prior to major sections of questions or changes in question format | "Now, for the next few questions, I want to ask about your family's TV viewing habits." "Next, I am going to read several statements and, after each, I want you to tell me if you agree or disagree with this statement." | Notifies respondent that the subject or format of the following questions will change |
| **Complicated and difficult-to-answer questions** | Middle of the questionnaire; close to the end | "Rate each of the following 10 stores on the friendliness of their salespeople on a scale of 1 to 7." "How likely are you to purchase each of the following items in the next three months?" | Respondent has committed himself or herself to completing the questionnaire; can see (or is told) that there are not many questions left |
| **Classification and demographic questions** | Last section | "What is the highest level of education you have attained?" | Questions that are "personal" and possibly offensive are placed at the end of the questionnaire |

intentions, or responding to "what if" questions are found here for at least two reasons. First, by the time the respondent has arrived at these questions, he or she has answered several relatively easy questions and is now caught up in a responding mode in which he or she feels some sort of commitment. Thus, even though the questions in this section require more mental effort, the person will feel more compelled to complete the questionnaire than to break it off. Second, if the questionnaire is self-administered or online, the respondent will see that only a few sections of questions remain to be answered—the end is in sight, so to speak. If the survey is being administered by an interviewer, the questionnaire will typically have prompts included for the interviewer to notify the respondent that the interview is in its last stages. Also, experienced interviewers can sense when respondents' interest levels sag, and they may voice their own prompts, if permitted, to keep the respondent on task.

◼ The more complicated and difficult-to-answer questions are placed deep in the questionnaire.

The last section of a questionnaire is traditionally reserved for classification questions. **Classification questions**, sometimes called demographic questions, are used to classify respondents into various groups for purposes of analysis. For instance, the researcher may want to classify respondents into categories based on age, gender, income level, and so on. The placement of demographic questions at the end of the questionnaire is useful because some respondents will consider certain demographic questions "personal," and they may refuse to give answers to questions about the highest level of education they attained, their income level, or marital status. In these cases, if the respondent refuses to answer, the refusal comes at the very end of the questioning process. If it occurred at the very beginning, the interview would begin with a negative vein, perhaps causing the person to think that the survey will be asking any number of personal questions, and the respondent may very well object to taking part in the survey at that point.

◼ Classification questions, sometimes called demographic questions, are used to classify respondents into various groups for purposes of analysis.

## INTEGRATED CASE

## College Life E-Zine

PRACTICAL
APPLICATIONS

Now that you have a firm grasp of questionnaire organization, you can appreciate how and why the questions and instructions appear on a well-designed questionnaire. Bob Watts, research project director for the College Life E-Zine survey, has designed such a questionnaire, and you will find it in our Marketing Research Application 9.1. Please examine this telephone survey questionnaire as it has several good examples of question wording, question flow, and necessary instructions in the questionnaire that will be used to determine the purchase behaviors and reactions of State U students to the College Life E-Zine concept. We have provided explanations for various parts of this questionnaire below the questionnaire itself.

## MARKETING RESEARCH APPLICATION 9.1

### The College Life E-Zine Survey Questionnaire

Here, you will find the complete College Life E-Zine survey questionnaire designed by Bob Watts of ORS Marketing Research. Questionnaire

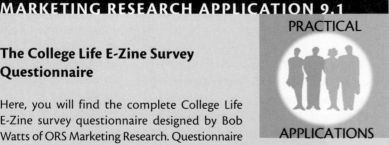

PRACTICAL
APPLICATIONS

organization and other aspects of this questionnaire are explained below.

*Hello, I am _____ with ORS, a marketing research firm. We received permission from State U to call you. We are conducting a survey about possible State U Internet services, and you were selected at random from the Student Directory. Your participation is important in that your answers will represent hundreds of your fellow students. To thank you for taking part in this survey, we will send you a coupon for a free drink and dinner entree of your choice at any one of five local restaurants. May I take a few minutes of your time to ask you some questions?*

1. Do you have Internet access?

_____ Yes _____ No **(If no, go to Question 38.)**

2. What type of Internet connection do you have where you live?

_____ High-speed cable

_____ Dial-up modem

_____ DSL

_____ Other (Specify: _____)

*We are interested in knowing about how you shop and what products and services you are planning on purchasing. Please answer the following questions with "Yes" or "No" or "Not sure."*

| Question | Yes | No | Not Sure |
|---|---|---|---|
| 3. Do you typically use coupons, "2-for-1 specials," or other promotions you see in magazines or newspapers? | _____ | _____ | _____ |
| 4. Will you purchase Regular or Diet soft drinks during the next week? | _____ | _____ | _____ |
| 5. Will you eat out at a local, non–fast-food restaurant during the week? | _____ | _____ | _____ |
| 6. Will you eat out at a local fast-food restaurant during the next week? | _____ | _____ | _____ |
| 7. Will you order a pizza to be delivered during the next week? | _____ | _____ | _____ |
| 8. Will you purchase an automobile during the next three months? | _____ | _____ | _____ |
| 9. Will you be looking for new off-campus housing for next semester? | _____ | _____ | _____ |
| 10. Will you purchase new clothes during the next month? | _____ | _____ | _____ |
| 11. Will you go out to a night entertainment establishment during the next week? | _____ | _____ | _____ |

12a. Will you make a purchase over the Internet in the next TWO MONTHS?

_____ Yes _____ No _____ Not Sure

**(If "No" or "Not Sure," skip to Question 14.)**

12b. (If "Yes" to 12a.) To the nearest $5, about how much do you think you will spend on Internet purchases in the next two months?

$_____

13. Next, I have six categories below that I will read to you. After I read them, for each one, tell me about how much you spend over the Internet on that category out of every $100 you spend on the Internet. Are my instructions clear? **(If not, repeat.)**

$_____ Books

$_____ Gifts for weddings and other special occasions

$_____ Music purchases

$_____ Financial services (insurance, loans, etc.)

$_____ Clothing

$_____ General merchandise for your home or car

$ 100 TOTAL

**(Interviewer: the total must be $100. Work with respondents to achieve this total.)**

14. Now, I want you to read the description of an "e-zine," and then ask you some questions about it.

**An e-zine is a magazine delivered to you online. We want you to think of an e-zine written especially for college students. The e-zine would include articles about your university or college as well as articles about national and world events thought to be of interest to college students. The e-zine will use state-of-the-art graphics and will have several interactive features such as interviews with campus leaders, athletes, and well-known celebrities. The e-zine would feature streaming video of local events such as previews of entertainment in some of the local night spots or even college sporting events. Some major events would be available on a "pay-per-view" basis. E-zine readers would have access to a variety of special promotions such as free coupons, admit-2-for-price-of-1 specials, and much more.**

*If the subscription price for this e-zine was $15 per month for a minimum of 6 months, how likely would you be to subscribe to it? Would you say you are "very unlikely," "somewhat unlikely," "neither likely nor unlikely," "somewhat likely," or "very likely"?*

| Very Unlikely | Somewhat Unlikely | Neither Likely nor Unlikely | Somewhat Likely | Very Likely |
|---|---|---|---|---|
| _____ | _____ | _____ | _____ | _____ |

**(Interviewer: For those responding "Unlikely" or "Neither...," go to Question 31. Otherwise, continue.)**

*We are considering a number of ideas for our e-zine and we would like some help from you in determining which features will be most preferred by our subscribers. I will read you names and brief descriptions of possible features. For each feature, please indicate your level of preference by saying "strongly do not prefer," "somewhat do not prefer," "no preference," "somewhat prefer," or "strongly prefer."*

| Feature | Strongly Do Not Prefer | Somewhat Do Not Prefer | No Preference | Somewhat Prefer | Strongly Prefer |
|---|---|---|---|---|---|
| 15. The Campus Calendar—*with prompters for important dates like Drop/Add deadlines (and you can specify other important personal dates)* | ____ | ____ | ____ | ____ | ____ |
| 16. Course & Instructor Evaluator—*Inside information about courses and instructors from students who have recently taken the course* | ____ | ____ | ____ | ____ | ____ |
| 17. Your Legislature—*Pending and passed legislative actions that affect college students* | ____ | ____ | ____ | ____ | ____ |
| 18. Popcorn Favorites—*A listing of top video rentals by category of entertainment* | ____ | ____ | ____ | ____ | ____ |
| 19. *Online "specials" from local retailing establishments where you can save dollars by using these specials* | ____ | ____ | ____ | ____ | ____ |
| 20. World & National News—*Written by college students for college students* | ____ | ____ | ____ | ____ | ____ |
| 21. My Major—*Messages from the department that is your major* | ____ | ____ | ____ | ____ | ____ |
| 22. Online Registrar—*Register, drop, add, and pay tuition online* | ____ | ____ | ____ | ____ | ____ |
| 23. My Advisor—*Messages to or from your advisor and other university officials* | ____ | ____ | ____ | ____ | ____ |
| 24. Student Government—*Streaming video of Student Government Association meetings, live and taped replays* | ____ | ____ | ____ | ____ | ____ |
| 25. Cyber-Sports—*Pay-per-view of nontelevised university sporting events at about $20 per football game and $10 for other events* | ____ | ____ | ____ | ____ | ____ |
| 26. What's Happen'n?—*Information about entertainment, cultural opportunities in the area for this week* | ____ | ____ | ____ | ____ | ____ |
| 27. Weather Today—*Local weather radar and forecast for the day and week* | ____ | ____ | ____ | ____ | ____ |
| 28. Entertainment News—*Reviews of movies, books, and theater, and celebrity news* | ____ | ____ | ____ | ____ | ____ |
| 29. Inside Sports—*The "inside scoop" from athletes and coaches throughout the conference; what big media doesn't cover* | ____ | ____ | ____ | ____ | ____ |
| 30. Cyber-Cupid—*An online university dating service* | ____ | ____ | ____ | ____ | ____ |

*In the next few questions, we want to ask you about your activities, interests, and opinions. Please tell me if you "disagree strongly," "disagree," "neither agree nor disagree," "agree," or "strongly agree" with each of the following statements that I will read.*

| Statement | Strongly Disagree | Disagree | Neither Agree nor Disagree | Agree | Strongly Agree |
|---|---|---|---|---|---|
| 31. *I am a homebody.* | ____ | ____ | ____ | ____ | ____ |
| 32. *I highly value the information I can access through the Internet.* | ____ | ____ | ____ | ____ | ____ |
| 33. *Even though I am a college student, I feel I have enough income to buy what I want.* | ____ | ____ | ____ | ____ | ____ |
| 34. *I shop a lot for "specials."* | ____ | ____ | ____ | ____ | ____ |
| 35. *I like to wear the latest styles in clothing.* | ____ | ____ | ____ | ____ | ____ |
| 36. *Keeping up with the political and economic news is not important to me.* | ____ | ____ | ____ | ____ | ____ |
| 37. *Keeping up with entertainment news is not important to me.* | ____ | ____ | ____ | ____ | ____ |

*Finally, we would like some information for classification purposes only.*

*38. What is your academic classification?*

_____ *Freshman*
_____ *Sophomore*
_____ *Junior*
_____ *Senior*
_____ *Grad Student*
_____ *Other*

*39. Do you live…*

_____ *On Campus* _____ *Off Campus*

*40. In which year were you born? 19____.*

*41. What is your GPA? ____*

*42. What is your gender?____ Male ____ Female*

*43. Do you work? _____ Yes _____ No*

**(If "yes," ask)** *How many hours per week? ____hrs.*

*44. Please tell me what is your State U college.*

_____ *Arts*
_____ *Architecture*
_____ *Business*
_____ *Computer Technology*
_____ *Education*
_____ *Engineering*
_____ *Sciences*
_____ *Music*
_____ *Nursing*
_____ *Professional Studies*

*Thank you very much for your participation in our survey.*

## EXPLANATIONS OF ASPECTS OF THE COLLEGE LIFE E-ZINE SURVEY QUESTIONNAIRE

Below, we identify various parts of the questionnaire and provide comments related to our recommendations about questionnaire organization and other specifics.

| Questionnaire Item | Explanation |
|---|---|
| 1. Do you have Internet access? | This is a *qualification/skip question* that causes the interviewer to "jump over" questions that are not relevant to respondents without Internet access, meaning that they are not qualified to be target-market members. Asking demographic questions of these respondents is a courtesy so they can be entered into the incentive drawing. |
| 2. What type of Internet connection do you have where you live? | This is an easy-to-answer *warm-up question*. |
| Questions 3–11 | All are easy-to-answer *warm-up questions* that also serve to keep the respondent motivated and interested. |
| 13. If you do purchase over the Internet, please tell us how you allocate your expenditures. | This is a *difficult-to-answer question* that is "buried" deep in the questionnaire. In fact, it may take a good deal of interviewer–respondent dialogue to effect answers that add to $100. |
| 14. Now, we want you to read the description of an "e-zine" below and then tell us how likely you would be to subscribe to an e-zine if it were available to you. | It is necessary to read this description because the e-zine does not exist. All respondents will have the identical mental picture of the e-zine being researched. |
| **(Interviewer: For those responding "Unlikely" or "Neither …", go to Question 31. Otherwise, continue.)** | First, this is a *skip instruction* for the interviewer. Only those who are "likely" to subscribe are asked the next set of questions. Second, the Instructions are *transition statements* that relate the scale to be used for the next several questions. |
| We are considering a number of ideas for our e-zine and we would like some help from you in determining which features will be most preferred by our subscribers. I will read you names and brief descriptions of possible features. For each feature, please indicate your level of preference by saying "strongly do not prefer," "somewhat do not prefer," "no preference," "somewhat prefer," or "strongly prefer." | |

| Questionnaire Item | Explanation |
|---|---|
| In the next few questions we want to ask you about your activities, interests, and opinions. Please tell me if you "disagree strongly," "disagree," "neither agree nor disagree," "agree," or "strongly agree" to each of the following statements that I will read. | This is a standard description of lifestyle questions, and the disagree–agree response scale is related with a **_transition statement_**. |
| Finally, we would like some information for classification purposes only. | This **_transition statement_** notifies the respondent that the survey is almost at an end. Also, it strongly implies that the **_demographic questions_** that follow are not to be taken personally; rather, they are for **_classification_**. |

# PRECODING THE QUESTIONNAIRE

A final task in questionnaire design is **precoding** questions, which is the placement of numbers on the question responses to facilitate data entry after the survey has been conducted. The logic of precoding is simple once you know the ground rules. The primary objective of precoding is to associate each possible response with a unique number, because numbers are easier and faster to keystroke into a computer file. Also, computer tabulation programs are more efficient when they process numbers. Table 9.4 illustrates code designations for selected questions. When words such as "yes" and "no" are used as literal response categories, precodes are normally placed alongside each response and in parentheses. For labeled scales, we recommend that the numbers match the direction of the scale. For example, notice in question 3 in Table 9.4 that the precodes are 1–4, and they match the Poor–Excellent direction of the scale. Another example would be a Strongly Disagree–Strongly Agree scale where the precodes would be 1–5. With scaled-response questions in which numbers are used as the response categories, the numbers are already on the questionnaire, so there is no need to use precodes for these questions.

■ Precodes are numbers placed with question responses to facilitate data entry and analysis.

There is one instance in which precoding becomes slightly complicated; but, again, once you learn the basic rules, the precoding is fairly easy to understand. Occasionally, a researcher uses an **"all that apply" question** that asks the respondent to select more than one item from a list of possible responses. This is the case in question 4 in Table 9.4. With "all that apply" questions, the standard approach is to have each response category option coded with a 0 or a 1. The designation "0" will be used if the category is not checked, whereas a "1" is used if it is checked by a respondent. It is as though the researcher asked each item in the list with a yes/no response (e.g., Do you usually order green peppers as topping? _____ No [0] _____ Yes [1]), but by listing them and asking "all that apply," the questionnaire is less cluttered and more efficient.

■ The precodes for an "all that apply" question are set up as though each possible response was answered with "yes" or "no."

As a final comment, we will point out that it is becoming less common for precodes to actually appear on the final questionnaire as the marketing research

**Table 9.4**
**Examples of Precodes on the Final Questionnaire**

1. Have you purchased a Godfather's pizza in the last month?

    _____ Yes (1) _____ No (2) _____ Not Sure (3)

2. The last time you bought a Godfather's pizza, did you (check only one):

    _____ Have it delivered to your house?           (1)

    _____ Have it delivered to your place of work?   (2)

    _____ Pick it up yourself?                       (3)

    _____ Eat it at the pizza parlor?                (4)

    _____ Purchase it some other way?                (5)

3. In your opinion, the taste of a Godfather's pizza is (check only one):

    _____ Poor (1)    _____ Fair (2)    _____ Good (3)    _____ Excellent (4)

4. Which of the following toppings do you typically have on your pizza? (Check all that apply.)

    _____ Green pepper    (0;1)    (*Note:* the 0;1 indicates the

    _____ Onion           (0;1)    coding system that will be used.

    _____ Mushroom        (0;1)    Typically, no precode such as this

    _____ Sausage         (0;1)    is placed on the questionnaire. Each

    _____ Pepperoni       (0;1)    response category must be defined

    _____ Hot peppers     (0;1)    as a separate question.)

    _____ Black olives    (0;1)

    _____ Anchovies       (0;1)

5. How do you rate the speediness of Godfather's in-restaurant service once you have ordered?

   (Circle the appropriate number if a 1 means very slow and a 7 means very fast.)

   | Very Slow | 1 | 2 | 3 | 4 | 5 | 6 | 7 | Very Fast |
   |-----------|---|---|---|---|---|---|---|-----------|

6. Please indicate your age: _____ Years (*Note:* No precode is used as the respondent will write in a two-digit number.)

7. Please indicate your gender.

    _____ Male (1) _____ Female (2)

industry moves toward more high-tech questionnaire design and administration. There is no need for precodes to appear on a questionnaire using computer-assisted questionnaire design programs, because the codes are embedded in the software instructions. Still, the researcher must know how to code the responses.

# COMPUTER-ASSISTED QUESTIONNAIRE DESIGN

**Computer-assisted questionnaire design** refers to software programs that allow researchers to use computer technology to develop and disseminate questionnaires and, in some cases, to retrieve and analyze data gathered by the questionnaire. Several companies have developed computer software that bridges the gap between composing questions on a word processor and generating the final, polished version complete with check boxes, radio buttons, and coded questions. Also, most of these software programs allow users to publish their questionnaires on the Internet and enable respondents to enter responses on the Internet. The data are then downloaded and made available for analysis, and practically all of these special-purpose personal computer programs generate data files that can be exported in Excel-readable format.

The following paragraphs illustrate how these computer-assisted questionnaire design programs work. First, however, let us point out that there are at least four distinct advantages of computer-assisted questionnaire design software packages: They are easier, faster, friendlier, and provide significant flexibility beyond that available with a traditional word processor.

■ Computer-assisted questionnaire design is easy, fast, friendy, and flexible.

## Questionnaire Creation

The typical computer-assisted questionnaire design program will query the user on, for example, type of question, number of response categories, whether multiple responses are permitted, if skips are to be used, and how response options will appear on the questionnaire. The survey creation feature sometimes takes the form of a menu of choices, or it might appear as a sequence of format inquiries for each section of the questionnaire. Usually, the program offers a list of question types such as closed-ended, open-ended, numeric, or scaled-response questions. The program may even have a question library feature that provides "standard" questions on constructs that researchers often measure, such as demographics, importance, satisfaction, performance, or usage. An advanced feature is an ability for the researcher to upload graphics files of various types if these are part of the research objectives. Most computer-assisted questionnaire design programs are quite flexible and allow the user to modify question formats, build blocks or matrices of questions with the identical response format, include an introduction and instructions to specific questions, and move the location of questions with great ease. Often the appearance can be modified to the designer's preferences for font, background, color, and more.

## Data Collection and Creation of Data Files

Computer-assisted questionnaire design programs create online survey questionnaires that are published on the Internet via a feature of the program. Once there, the survey is ready for respondents who are alerted to the online survey with whatever communication methods the researcher wishes to use. Normally, a data file is built as respondents take part, that is, in real time. To elaborate, each respondent accesses the online questionnaire, registers responses to the questions, and, typically, clicks on a "Submit" button at the end of the questionnaire. The submit signal prompts the program to write the respondent's answers into a data file, so the data file grows in direct proportion to and at the same rate as respondents submit their surveys. Features that block multiple submissions by the same respondent, such as requesting an e-mail address, are often available. The data file can be downloaded at the researcher's discretion, and, usually, several different formats, including Excel-readable ones, are available.

■ Computer-assisted questionnaire design programs have question types, question libraries, real-time data capture, and downloadable data sets.

## Data Analysis and Graphs

Many of the software programs for questionnaire design also have provisions for data analysis, graphic presentation, and report formats of results. Some packages offer only simplified graphing capabilities, whereas others offer different statistical analysis options. In fact, it is very useful to researchers to monitor the survey's progress with these features. The graph features vary, and some of these programs enable users to create professional-quality graphs that can be saved or embedded in word processor report files.

## PERFORMING THE PRETEST OF THE QUESTIONNAIRE

Refer back to Figure 9.1, and you will find that before finalizing the questionnaire, one last evaluation should be conducted on the entire questionnaire. Such an evaluation uses a pretest to ensure that the questions will accomplish what is expected of them. A **pretest** involves conducting a dry run of the survey on a small, representative set of respondents in order to reveal questionnaire errors before the survey is launched. It is very important that pretest participants are in fact representative, that is, selected from the target population under study. Before the questions are administered, participants are informed of the pretest, and their cooperation is requested in spotting words, phrases, instructions, question flow, or other aspects of the questionnaire that appear confusing, difficult to understand, or otherwise a problem. Normally, from 5 to 10 respondents are involved in a pretest, and the researcher looks for common problem themes across this group.[13] For example, if only one pretest respondent indicates some concern about a question, the researcher probably would not attempt modification of its wording, but if three mention the same concern, the researcher would be alerted to the need to undertake a revision. Ideally, when making revisions, researchers should place themselves in the respondent's shoes and ask the following questions: "Is the meaning of the question clear?" "Are the instructions understandable?" "Are the terms precise?" and "Are there any loaded or charged words?" However, because researchers can never completely replicate the respondent's perspective, a pretest is extremely valuable.[14]

■ A pretest is a dry run of a questionnaire to find and repair difficulties that respondents encounter while taking the survey.

## SUMMARY

This chapter described questionnaire design and some of the activities that are involved in the questionnaire design process. We noted that questionnaires serve several functions. We also advocated that the designer follow a step-by-step development process that includes question development, question evaluation, client approval, and a pretest to ensure that the questions and instructions are understandable to respondents. Certain words should be avoided in question wording, and we provided our "top 10" words that you should definitely avoid because these words are absolute extremes that force respondents to totally agree or totally disagree with the question. The objective of question development is to create questions that minimize question bias, and the four "dos" in question development stress that the ideal question is focused, simple, brief, and crystal clear. Question bias is most likely to occur when question wording is leading, loaded, double-barreled, or overstated.

The organization of questions on the questionnaire is critical, including the first statements, or introduction to the survey. The introduction should identify the sponsor of the survey, relate the survey's purpose, explain how the respondent was selected, solicit the individual's cooperation to take part, and, if appropriate, qualify him or her for taking part in the survey. We next provided general guidelines on the flow of questions on the questionnaire and pointed out the location and roles of screens, warm-ups, transitions, "difficult" questions, and classification questions. The chapter also introduced you to the notion of precoding or placing the codes to be put in the computer data file on the questionnaire itself. In addition, some companies have developed computer software that performs questionnaire design, and the chapter briefly described the features of these programs. Finally, you learned the rationale and procedure for pretesting a questionnaire.

## KEY TERMS

Questionnaire (p. 264)

Questionnaire design (p. 264)

Question bias (p. 264)

Question development (p. 266)

Question evaluation (p. 268)

Leading question (p. 269)

Loaded question (p. 270)

Double-barreled question (p. 270)

Overstated question (p. 271)

Questionnaire organization (p. 273)

Cover letter (p. 273)

Undisguised survey (p. 273)

Disguised survey (p. 273)

Incentives (p. 274)

Anonymity (p. 275)

Confidentiality (p. 275)

Screening questions (p. 275)

Question flow (p. 276)

Warm-up questions (p. 276)

Transitions (p. 276)

Skip question (p. 276)

Classification questions (p. 278)

Precoding (p. 282)

"All that apply"question (p. 282)

Computer-assisted questionnaire design (p. 284)

Pretest (p. 285)

# REVIEW QUESTIONS

1 What is a questionnaire, and what are the functions of a questionnaire?
2 What is meant by the statement that questionnaire design is a systematic process?
3 What is meant by question bias? Write two biased questions using the "bad" words in Table 9.1. Rewrite each question without using the problem word.
4 What are the four guidelines, or "dos," for question wording?
5 What are the four "do nots" for question wording? Describe each "do not."
6 What is the purpose of a questionnaire introduction, and what should it accomplish?
7 Distinguish anonymity from confidentiality.
8 Indicate the functions of: (a) screening questions, (b) warm-up questions, (c) transitions, (d) "skip" questions, and (e) classification questions.
9 What is precoding and why is it used? Relate the special precoding need with "all that apply" questions.
10 List at least three features of computer-assisted questionnaire design programs that are more advantageous to a questionnaire designer than the use of a word processor program.
11 What is the purpose of a pretest of the questionnaire and how does a researcher go about conducting a pretest?

# APPLICATION QUESTIONS

12 Listed here are five different aspects of a questionnaire to be designed for the crafts guild of Maui, Hawaii. It is to be administered by personal interviewers who will intercept tourists as they are waiting at the Maui Airport in the seating areas of their departing flight gates. Indicate a logical question flow on the questionnaire using the guidelines in Table 9.3.
   a Determine how they selected Maui as a destination.
   b Discover what places they visited in Maui and how much they liked each one.
   c Describe what crafts they purchased, where they purchased them, when they bought them, how much they paid, who made the selection, and why they bought those particular items.
   d Specify how long they stayed and where they stayed while on Maui.
   e Provide a demographic profile of each tourist interviewed.
13 The Marketing Club at your university is thinking about undertaking a money-making project. Coeds will be invited to compete and 12 will be selected to be in the "Girls of (insert your school) University" calendar. All photographs will be taken by a professional photographer and tastefully done. Some club members are concerned about the reactions of other students who might think that the calendar will degrade women. Taking each of the "do nots" of question wording, write a question that would tend to bias answers such that the responses would tend to support the view that such a calendar would be degrading. Indicate how the question is in error, and provide a version that is in better form.

14 Using the Internet, find a downloadable trial version of a computer-assisted questionnaire design program and become familiar with it. With each of the following possible features of computer-assisted questionnaire design programs, briefly relate the specifics on how the program you have chosen provides the feature.

   a Question type options
   b Question library
   c Font and appearance
   d Web uploading (sometimes called "publishing")
   e Analysis, including graphics
   f Download file format options

15 Panther Martin invents and markets various types of fishing lures. In an effort to survey the reactions of potential buyers, it hires a research company to intercept fishermen at boat launches, secure their cooperation to use a Panther Martin lure under development sometime during their fishing trip that day, meet them when they return, and verbally administer questions to them. As an incentive, each respondent will receive three lures to try that day, and five more will be given to each fisherman who answers the questions at the end of the fishing trip.

   What opening comments should be verbalized when approaching fishermen who are launching their boats? Draft a script to be used when asking these fishermen to take part in the survey.

16 Consider question 13 in the College Life E-Zine Survey Questionnaire on page 279. This question format is referred to as a "constant sum" question as the numbers provided by the respondent must sum to a constant number ($100 dollars here).

   a If the questionnaire asked, "How much did you spend last week in each category?" what misrepresentation of State U students' Internet expenditures might occur? In other words, why has Bob Watts opted to use the $100 constant-sum scale approach?
   b Note the instructions to the interviewer associated with this question. How do you envision the interviewer and respondent interacting with this question?
   c Assume that this is the second question in the questionnaire. Now, what do you envision to be the nature of the interaction and why?
   d Do you agree that difficult-to-answer questions should be located "deep" in the questionnaire? Why or why not?

# INTERACTIVE LEARNING

You can visit the textbook Web site at **www.prenhall.com/burnsbush.** Use the self-study quizzes and get instant feedback on whether or nor you need additional studying to master the material in this chapter. You can also review the chapter's major points by visiting the chapter outline and key terms.

## CASE 9.1 ||| Moe's Wraps & Subs

Moe's is a submarine sandwich shop that also offers wraps, which are sandwiches made with a tortilla rather than bread. There are seven Moe's units located in the greater metropolitan area, and Moe is thinking about setting up a franchise system to go "big-time" with nationwide coverage. A business associate recommends that Moe first conduct a baseline survey of his seven units to better understand his customers and to spot any weaknesses that he might not be aware of. Moe meets with Bob Watts of OSR Reseach, and together they agree on the following research objectives. Also, Bob has convinced Moe that a telephone survey of the greater metropolitan area is the best choice.

### Research Objectives for Moe's Wraps & Sub's Survey

1 How often do people purchase a meal at Moe's?
2 About how much do they spend there per visit (per individual)?

3 Overall, how satisfied are they with Moe's?
4 How do they rate Moe's Wraps & Subs' performance on the following various aspects?
   a Competitive price
   b Convenience of locations
   c Variety of sandwiches
   d Freshness of sandwich fillings
   e Speed of service
   f Taste of subs
   g Taste of wraps
   h Uniqueness of sandwiches
5 What recent advertising do they recall, and/or where do they recall seeing the advertising? (Moe's uses the following advertising: Yellow Pages, billboards, newspaper ads, coupons.)
6 Obtain a demographic profile of the sample.
   Design a questionnaire for the Moe's Wraps & Subs survey that will be performed by OSR Marketing Reseach under Bob Watts' direction.

## CASE 9.2 ||| Your Integrated Case

### College Life E-Zine: Questionnaire Design

*This is the seventh case in our integrated case series. You will find the previous College Life E-Zine cases in Chapters 1, 2, 3, 4, 5, and 7.*

You will find the final telephone questionnaire that Bob Watts developed for the College Life E-Zine survey in Marketing Research Application 9.1 on page 278.

Answer the following questions regarding this questionnaire:

1 Does the introduction satisfy all of its necessary functions? Why or why not?
2 Would you say that the survey was disguised or undisguised? Why do you think Bob Watts chose to indicate the sponsor in this way?
3 There are no precodes on the questionnaire. Indicate the appropriate precodes.

10

# DETERMINING SAMPLE SIZE
# AND THE SAMPLING METHOD

This Envelop Contains
**Your Secret Ballot**
(the which postage will be paid by me)
— IN —
**The Literary Digest**
NATION-WIDE POLL
**FOR**
**PRESIDENT**
VOTE AT ONCE
and Learn in Advance
of the Election Who
will be the Winner

*Literary Digest's* famous blunder was due to using a poor sampling method.

## A SURVEY THAT CHANGED SURVEY SAMPLING PRACTICE

The *Literary Digest*, an influential general interest magazine started in 1890, correctly predicted several presidential campaigns by using surveys. The world was becoming accustomed to viewing surveys as accurate predictors of future events. But the prediction the magazine made in the 1936 election was so bad that it is given credit for not only causing the collapse of the magazine (it was purchased by *Time* in 1938) but for stirring interest in refining surveying sampling techniques.

Alf Landon, the Republican candidate and Governor of Kansas was running against Democratic President Franklin D. Roosevelt. The *Literary Digest* used three lists as its sample frame for polling American voters. First, it sent a

- To become familiar with sample design terminology
- To learn how to calculate sample size
- To understand the difference between "probability" and "nonprobability" sampling methods
- To become acquainted with the specifics of four probability and four nonprobability sampling techniques

postcard to each of its two million subscribers. Secondly, it added to this sample with sample frames composed of lists of telephone owners and automobile owners.

The *Digest's* survey predicted Landon would win overwhelmingly. Roosevelt won in a landslide, taking 46 of 48 states. Only Maine and New Hampshire voted for Landon. What went wrong? The *Literary Digest* had used an unusually large sample, yet the results were terribly wrong. The answer: the sampling method was wrong. Remember, 1936 was the depths of the Great Depression. Those who could afford a magazine subscription, telephone, or automobile were much better off than the general public, and these "better off" citizens were much more likely to vote Republican. So the *Digest* was surveying, in very large numbers, voters who were mostly Republican. They didn't use a sampling method that would guarantee that Democratic voters would be just as likely to be surveyed. What this illustrates is that you must have a good sampling method. With a poor sampling method, even very large sample sizes will not produce good survey results. In contrast, other surveys using much smaller sample sizes predicted Roosevelt would win. They were ridiculed for using small samples, but their predictions were correct because they used sound sampling methods. Among those producing accurate predictions was a young man named George Gallup. The Gallup Company exists today and is still conducting accurate surveys. In this chapter you will learn how the sample method is important in producing representative results, and how the sample size is important in producing accurate survey results.[1]

nternational markets are measured in hundreds of millions of people, national markets comprise millions of individuals, and even local markets may constitute hundreds of thousands of households. To obtain information from every single person in a market is usually impossible and obviously impractical. For these reasons, marketing researchers make use of a sample. This chapter describes how researchers go about deciding sample size and taking samples. We begin with definitions of basic concepts such as population, sample, and census. To be sure, sample size determination can be complicated,[2] but we describe a simple way to calculate the desired size of a sample and illustrate how the XL Data Analyst can be used to do these calculations for you. From here, we describe sample methods and distinguish four types of probability sampling methods from four types of nonprobability sampling methods. Last, we present a step-by-step procedure for designing and taking a sample.

## BASIC CONCEPTS IN SAMPLES AND SAMPLING

■ The population is the entire group under study as defined by research objectives.

To begin, we acquaint you with some basic terminology used in sampling. The **population** is the entire group under study as specified by the research project. For example, a researcher may specify a population as "heads of households in those metropolitan areas served by Terminix who are responsible for insect pest control." A **sample** is a subset of the population that should represent that entire group. How large a sample and how to select the sample are the major topics of this chapter. A **census** is defined as an accounting of everyone in the population. Of course, a sample is used because a census is normally completely unobtainable due to time, accessibility issues, and cost.

So, researchers must use samples that represent populations, which brings us to the accuracy concerns that always occur when a sample is taken. **Sampling error** is any error in a survey that occurs because a sample is used. Sampling error is caused by two factors: (1) the method of sample selection and (2) the size of the sample. As for the latter, you will learn in this chapter that larger samples represent less sampling error than smaller samples, and that some sampling methods minimize this error, whereas others do not control it well at all regardless of the size of the sample. In order to select a sample, you will need a **sample frame**, which is some master list of all the members of the population. For instance, if a researcher had defined a population to be all shoe repair stores in the state of Montana, he or she would need a master listing of these stores as a frame from which to sample. Similarly, if the population being researched consisted of all certified public accountants (CPAs) in the United States, a sample frame for this group would be needed. In the case of shoe repair stores, a list service such as American Business Lists, of Omaha, Nebraska, which has compiled its list of shoe repair stores from Yellow Pages listings, might be used. For CPAs, the researcher could use the list of members of the American Institute of Certified Public Accountants, located in New York City, which contains a listing of all accountants who have passed the CPA exam. As we all know, lists are not perfect representations of populations, because new members are added, old ones drop off, and there may be clerical errors in the list. So, researchers understand that **sample frame error**, be it great or small, exists for sample frames in the forms of mis-, over-, or underrepresentations of the true population in a sample frame. Whenever a sample is drawn, the amount of potential sample frame error should be judged by the researcher.[3] Sometimes the only available sample frame contains much potential sample frame error, but it is used due to the lack of any other sample frame. It is a researcher's responsibility to seek out a sample frame with the least amount of error at a reasonable cost. The researcher should also apprise the client of the degree of sample frame error involved.

■ Whenever a sample is taken, the survey will reflect sampling error.

# DETERMINING SIZE OF A SAMPLE

Let's just focus on the sample error associated with size of the sample. That is, for now, let's assume that we can find a sample frame that has an acceptably low level of sample frame error, and that we can select a sample that is truly representative of the population. (We will take up sample selection methods after we discuss sample size.)

## The Accuracy of a Sample

A convenient way[4] to describe the amount of sample error due to the size of the sample, or the **accuracy of a sample**, is to treat it as a plus-or-minus percentage value.[5] That is, we can say that a sample is accurate to $\pm x\%$, such as $\pm 5\%$ or $\pm 10\%$. The interpretation of sample accuracy uses the following logic: If you use a sample size with an accuracy level of $\pm 5\%$, when you analyze your survey's findings, they will be about $\pm 5\%$ of what you would find if you performed a census. Let us give an example of this interpretation, as it is important that you understand how sample accuracy operates. We will take a sample that is representative of the population of people who bought birthday gifts in the past year, and let's say that we find that 50% of our respondents say "Yes" to the question "The last time you bought a birthday gift, did you pay more than $25?" With a sample accuracy of $\pm 5\%$, we can say that if we took a census of the population of our birthday gift givers, the percent

While directories and phone books are readily available, they may have substantial sample frame error.

**Figure 10.1** The Relationship Between Sample Size and Sample Accuracy

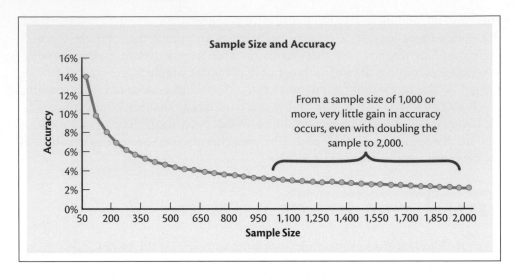

that will say "Yes" is between 45% and 55% (or 50% ± 5%). Think, for a minute, about the incredible power of a sample: We can interview a subset of the entire population, and we can extrapolate or generalize the sample's findings to the population with a ± *x*% approximation of what we would find if we took all the time, energy, and expense to interview every single member of the population.

■ The accuracy of a sample can be expressed as a ±*x*% amount.

The relationship between sample size and sample accuracy is presented graphically in Figure 10.1. In this figure, sample error (accuracy) is listed on the vertical axis and sample size is noted on the horizontal one. The graph shows the accuracy levels of samples ranging in size from 50 to 2,000. The shape of the graph shows that as the sample size increases, sample error decreases. However, you should immediately notice that the graph is not a straight line. In other words, doubling sample size does not result in halving the sample error. The relationship is a curved one. It looks a bit like a ski jump lying on its back.

There is another important property of the sample accuracy graph. As you look at the graph, note that at a sample size of around 500, the accuracy level drops below ± 5% (it is actually ± 4.4%), and it continues to decrease at a very slow rate with larger sample sizes. In other words, once a sample is greater than, say, 500, large gains in accuracy are not realized with large increases in the size of the sample. In fact, if it is already ± 4.4% in accuracy, there is not much more accuracy possible.

■ The confidence interval formula for sample size is the proper way to determine sample size.

With the lower end of the sample size axis, however, large gains in accuracy can be made with a relatively small sample size increase. For example, with a sample size of 50, the accuracy level is ± 13.9 %, whereas with a sample size of 250, it is ± 6.2%, meaning the accuracy of the 250 sample is roughly double that of the 50 sample. But as was just described, such huge gains in accuracy are not the case at the other end of the sample size scale because of the nature of the curved relationship.

## How to Calculate Sample Size

The proper way to calculate sample size is to use the **confidence interval formula for sample size** that follows.

**Sample size formula** ▶

$$n = \frac{z^2(pq)}{e^2}$$

Where    $n$ = the calculated sample size
         $z$ = standard error associated with the chosen level
               of confidence (typically, 1.96)
         $p$ = estimated percentage in the population
         $q$ = $(100\% - p)$
         $e$ = acceptable error (desired accuracy level)

The confidence interval formula for sample size is based on three elements: variability, confidence level, and desired accuracy. We will describe each in turn.

### Variability: $p$ times $q$

This formula is used if we are focusing on some categorically scaled question in the survey. For instance, when conducting a Domino's Pizza survey, our major concern might be the percentage of pizza buyers who intend to buy Domino's. There are two possible answers: "yes" or "no." If our pizza buyers population has very little **variability**, that is, if almost everyone, say, 90%, are raving Domino's Pizza fans and shout "Yes, yes, yes!" then this belief will be reflected in the sample size formula as 90% times 10%, or 900. However, if there is great variability, meaning that no two respondents agree and we have a 50%/50% split, $p$ times $q$ becomes 50% times 50%, or 2,500, which is the largest possible $p$ times $q$ number possible. (There is a different formula for when you are trying to estimate an average. However, the percentage formula is simpler and more commonly used, so we will restrict our coverage to the percentage formula.)

The use of $p = 50\%$, $q = 50\%$ is a research industry standard of sorts. As you can see, it is the most conservative $p$-$q$ combination, generating the largest sample size, so it is preferred when the researcher is uncertain or guessing about the variability. In fact, public opinion polling companies typically report the accuracy of their samples, and if you find such a report in a news article or other publication, and you reconstruct their calculation of their reported sample error, you will find that they have used 50/50. Alternatively, some researchers opt for a pilot study to determine the approximate amount of variability.[6]

■ Variability refers to how much respondents agree in their answer to a question.

PRACTICAL

APPLICATIONS

If everyone wanted the same thing on their pizza, there would be no variability.

### Level of Confidence: z

We need to decide on a **level of confidence**, and it is customary among marketing researchers to use the 95% level of confidence, in which the $z$ is 1.96. If a researcher prefers to use the 99% level of confidence, the corresponding $z$ is 2.58. We will describe how this level of confidence operates shortly.

### Desired Accuracy: e

■ Desired accuracy of a sample is expressed as *e* in the sample size calculation formula.

Lastly, the formula requires that we specify an acceptable level of sample error, meaning the ±% accuracy notion that we introduced to you. That is, the term $e$ is the amount of sample error that will be associated with the survey. It is used to indicate how close your sample percentage finding will be to the true population percentage if it were repeated many, many times.

Figure 10.2 illustrates how the level of confidence figures into sample size accuracy. There is a theoretical notion that if the survey were repeated a great many times—several thousands of times—and if you plotted the frequency distribution of each $p$ for every one of these repeated samples, the pattern would appear as a bell curve, as you see in Figure 10.2. Note that 95% of the replications would fall between the population $p$ (50% in our example in Figure 10.2) and $\pm e$.

Here is an example of a sample size calculation that you can follow to make certain that you understand how to use the sample size formula. Let us assume there is great expected variability (50%) and we want ± 3% accuracy at the 95% level of confidence.

**Sample size computed with *p* = 50%, *q* = 50%, and *e* = 3%** ▷

$$n = \frac{1.96^2 (50 \times 50)}{3^2}$$

$$= \frac{3.84(2,500)}{9}$$

$$= \frac{9,600}{9}$$

$$= 1,067$$

**Figure 10.2** How Sample Error and the 95% Level of Confidence Theoretically Operate

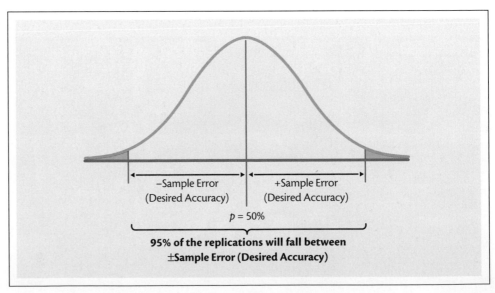

−Sample Error (Desired Accuracy)

+Sample Error (Desired Accuracy)

$p = 50\%$

**95% of the replications will fall between ±Sample Error (Desired Accuracy)**

Whenever you calculate the sample size, you are computing the number of respondents you should have participate fully in your survey. But invariably, surveys run into two difficulties that require an upward adjustment of the computed sample size. If you read Marketing Research Application 10.1, you will learn about the two problems of "incidence rate" and "nonresponse" and how to adjust the sample size to cope with these two problems. You will also find a list of other practical issues that often force researchers to make sample size adjustments.

# MARKETING RESEARCH APPLICATION 10.1

PRACTICAL

APPLICATIONS

## Adjusting Your Sample Size to Compensate for Incidence Rate, Nonresponse, and More

Suppose that Scope mouthwash wanted to find out reactions to a new formula that provides for some whitening of the teeth and a degree of tartar control as well. The researcher and Scope managers come to agree on a sample size of 500, so the researcher purchases the names of 500 individuals from a sample supply company. The survey moves along, but the data collection company that is performing the telephone interviews reports to the researcher that only 4 out of 5 people in the sample use mouthwash. In other words, the **incidence rate**, defined as the percent of individuals in the sample who qualify to take the survey, is 80%, meaning that 20%, or 100 names in the sample, are not usable. So, under this situation, the largest final sample size possible is 400.

At the same time, the data collection company manager reports to the researcher that potential respondents who qualify are refusing to take the survey. This problem is referred to as **nonresponse**, or failures by qualified respondents to take part in the survey. The data collection company estimates a refusal rate of 40%, meaning that the response rate is 60%. A response rate of 60% means that only 60% of the 400 qualified respondents will be in the final sample. The researcher is now faced with a final sample size of 240, far smaller than the desired size of 500.

To cope with the realities of incidence rate and nonresponse, researchers must make adjustments on their calculated sample sizes. A simple adjustment formula is as follows.

| **Sample size adjustment formula** | Adjusted sample size | = | Calculated sample size | × | (1/ Incidence rate %) | × | (1/ Response rate %) |
|---|---|---|---|---|---|---|---|

If you apply this formula to our Scope mouthwash example, the computations are as follows.

**Sample size adjustment example**

$$
\begin{aligned}
\text{Adjusted sample size} &= \text{Calculated sample size} \times (1/\text{Incidence rate}) \times (1/\text{Response rate}) \\
&= 500 \times (1/.8) \times (1/.6) \\
&= 500 \times 1.25 \times 1.67 \\
&= 1044
\end{aligned}
$$

So, as can be seen here, incidence rates and nonresponse can combine to have a tremendous impact on the final sample size of a survey, and astute marketing researchers will make estimates of the magnitudes of these problems and adjust the calculated sample size accordingly.

There are other factors that may force sample size adjustments. Susie Sangren, President, Clearview Data Strategy, has contributed the following list of practical constraints that researchers are likely to encounter:

- Time pressure. Often research results are needed "yesterday," meaning that the sample size may be reduced to save time.
- Cost constraint. A limited amount of money is available for the study, and limited funds translate to reduced sample size.
- Study objective. What is the purpose of the study? A decision that does not need great precision can make do with a very small sample size such as a few focus groups or a pilot study.
- Data analysis procedures. Some advanced data-analysis procedures require much-larger-than-ordinary sample sizes in order to be fully utilized.[a]

[a] Personal communication to author from Susie Sangren.

# USING THE XL DATA ANALYST TO CALCULATE SAMPLE SIZE

It is time for you to be introduced to the XL Data Analyst Excel macro software that accompanies this textbook. There is a more formal introduction in the following chapter, the first data analysis chapter in this textbook. The XL Data Analyst is primarily a set of data analysis procedures that are easy to use and interpret. But there is a computational aid included in the XL Data Analyst that pertains to sample size. For now, all you need to do is open up any Excel file that accompanies this textbook. Because the XL Data Analyst is an Excel macro, you will need to set the Excel 2003 version security at Medium or Low (*Tools—Macros—Security—* check *Medium* or *Low*). Then click on "Enable Macros" when the XL Data Analyst file loads into Excel. With Excel 2007, enable the macro content via the Security Warning feature after the file is loaded.

After the file is loaded, you will see a "Data" worksheet and a "Define Variables" worksheet, but you can ignore whatever you see on these worksheets. Instead, use the XL Data Analyst to access the "Calculate" function available in its main menu. The XL Data Analyst will calculate sample size using the confidence sample size formula we have described in this chapter. As you can see in Figure 10.3, we have "pinned" the XL Data Analyst menu item on the Excel 2007 Quick Access tool bar, and the menu sequence is Calculate—Sample Size, which opens up the selection window where you can specify the allowable error (desired sample accuracy) and the estimated percent, *p*, value. In our example, we have set the accuracy level at 4% and the estimated *p* at 60%.

Figure 10.4 reveals that the XL Data Analyst has computed the sample size for the 95% level of confidence to be 576, while for the 99% confidence level, the

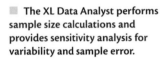

The XL Data Analyst performs sample size calculations and provides sensitivity analysis for variability and sample error.

**Figure 10.3** XL Data Analyst Setup for Sample Size Calculation

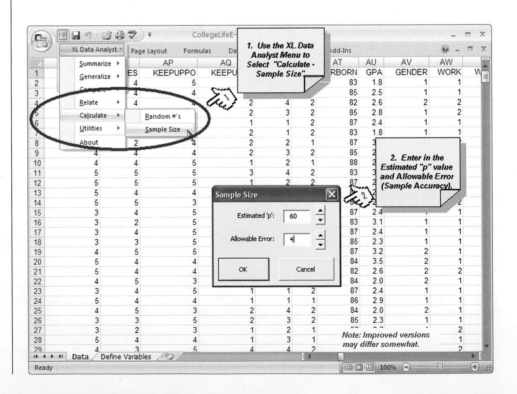

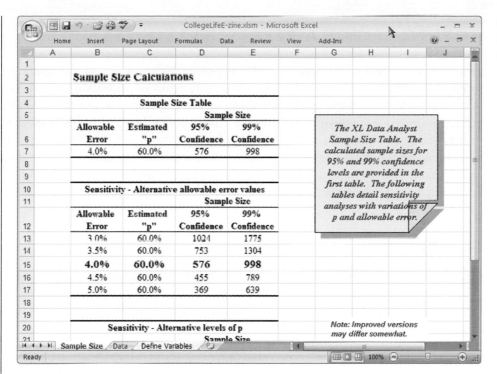

**Figure 10.4** XL Data Analyst Sample Size Calculation Output

calculated sample size is 998. There are two tables following the Sample Size Table that a researcher can use to inspect the sensitivity of the sample size to slight variations of *e* (with estimated *p* constant), ranging in our example from 3.0% to 5.0% by .5% increments, or variations in the estimated *p* (with *e* constant), ranging from 50% to 70% by 5% increments. The sensitivity analysis tables are provided so a researcher who is wrestling with a sample size decision can quickly compare the impact of small differences in his or her assumptions about variability in the population (*p*) as well as slightly loosening or tightening the sample accuracy requirements, or allowable error.

Marketing managers and other clients of marketing researchers do not have a thorough understanding of sample size. In fact, they tend to have a belief in a false "law of large sample size." That is, they often confuse the size of the sample with the representativeness of the sample. As you will soon learn in reading about sample selection procedures, the way the sample is selected, not its size, determines its representativeness. Also, as you have just learned, the accuracy benefits of excessively large samples are typically not justified by their increased costs.

It is an ethical marketing researcher's responsibility to try to educate a client on the wastefulness of excessively large samples. Occasionally, there are good reasons for having a very large sample, but whenever the sample size exceeds that of a typical national opinion poll (1,200 respondents), justification is required. Otherwise, the manager's cost will be unnecessarily inflated. Unethical researchers may recommend very large samples as a way to increase their profits, which may be set at a percentage of the total cost of the survey. They may even have ownership in the data collection company slated to gather the data at a set cost per respondent. It is important, therefore, that marketing managers know the motivations underlying the sample size recommendations of the researchers they hire.

ETHICS

■ Managers have a "large sample size" bias that ethical marketing researchers do not use for selfish advantage.

# HOW TO SELECT A REPRESENTATIVE SAMPLE

You now know that surprisingly few individuals can be chosen in a sample that represents a population with a small amount of sample error. We now turn to the selection process, for if the sample selection method is faulty or biased, our findings will be compromised. For example, if Starbucks Coffee wanted to find out how its customers feel about Starbucks coffee and other food products and it used a sample of customers drawn from those who happened to make a purchase at its Miami International Airport location on June 12, this sample would not be truly representative of all Starbucks Coffee customers. It would only represent Starbucks Coffee customers of that location in that time period.

■ Samples are typically quite small, so the selection process must not be faulty or biased.

## Probability Sampling Methods

A **random sample** is one in which every member of the population has an equal chance, or probability, of being selected into that sample. Sample methods that embody random sampling are often termed **probability sampling methods**, because the chance of selection can be expressed as a probability. We will describe four probability sampling methods: simple random sampling, systematic sampling, cluster sampling, and stratified sampling. You can use Table 10.1 as a handy reference, for it summarizes the basics of each of these sampling techniques.

**Table 10.1**

Four Different Probability Sampling Techniques

**Simple Random Sampling**
The researcher uses a table of random numbers, random digit dialing, or some other random selection procedure that guarantees each member of the population has an identical chance of being selected into the sample.

**Systematic Sampling**
Using a list of the members of the population, the researcher selects a random starting point for the first sample member. A constant "skip interval" is then used to select every other sample member. A skip interval must be used such that the entire list is covered, regardless of the starting point. This procedure accomplishes the same end as simple random sampling, and it is more efficient.

**Cluster Sampling**
The population is divided into groups called clusters, each of which must be considered to be very similar to the others. The researcher can then randomly select a few clusters and perform a census of each one. Alternatively, the researcher can randomly select more clusters and take samples from each one. This method is desirable when highly similar clusters can be easily identified.

**Stratified Sampling**
If the population is believed to have a skewed distribution for one or more of its distinguishing factors (e.g., income or product ownership), the researcher identifies subpopulations called strata. A random sample is then taken of each stratum. Weighting procedures may be applied to estimate population values such as the mean. This approach is better suited than other probability sampling methods for populations that are not distributed in a bell-shaped pattern.

Simple random sampling is like a lottery because everyone has an equal chance of being selected.

### Simple Random Sampling

With **simple random sampling**, the probability of being selected into the sample is "known" and equal for all members of the population. This sampling technique is expressed by the following formula:

Probability of selection = sample size/population size

◀ **Formula for sample selection probability**

So, with simple random sampling, if the researcher was surveying a population of 100,000 recent DVD player buyers with a sample size of 1,000 respondents, the probability of selection on any single population member into this sample would be 1,000 divided by 100,000, or 1 out of 100, calculated to be 1%. There are some variations of simple random sampling, but the table of random numbers technique best exemplifies simple random sampling.

■ Simple random sampling makes use of random numbers to select each individual into the sample.

The **random numbers technique** is an application of simple random sampling that uses the concept of a **table of random numbers**, which is a listing of numbers whose nonsystematic (or random) order is assured. Before computer-generated random numbers were widespread, researchers used physical tables that had numbers with no discernible relationship to each other. If you looked at a table of random numbers, you would not be able to see any systematic sequence of the numbers regardless of where on the table you began and whether you went up, down, left, right, or diagonally across the entries.

## USING THE XL DATA ANALYST TO GENERATE RANDOM NUMBERS

You can use the XL Data Analyst to generate your own table of random numbers. Figure 10.5 shows the menu command sequence and setup window to accomplish this end. Note that the menu sequence is "Calculate—Random #'s," and the selection window allows you to specify how many random integer numbers you want (up to 9,999),

**Figure 10.5** XL Data Analyst Setup for Random Numbers

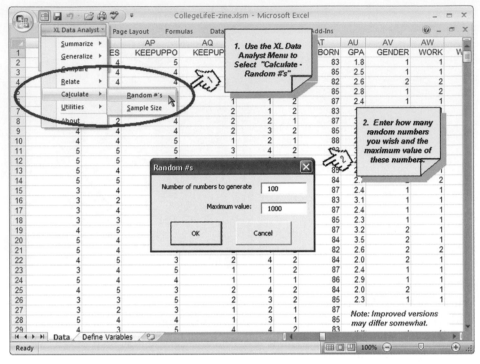

and you can also specify the largest possible value (up to 999,999,999). In our example, we have specified 100 random numbers with a maximum value of 1,000.

Figure 10.6 displays our random numbers. Notice that they are arranged in five columns. You can experiment with the random-number-table-generator function of the XL Data Analyst, and you should discover that there is no systematic pattern relating these numbers to one another.

**Figure 10.6** XL Data Analyst Output for Random Numbers

| | 100 Random Numbers | | | | |
|---|---|---|---|---|---|
| | | Random Numbers Table | | | |
| | 705 | 533 | 579 | 289 | 301 |
| | 774 | 14 | 760 | 814 | 709 |
| | 45 | 414 | 862 | 790 | 373 |
| | 961 | 871 | 56 | 949 | 364 |
| | 524 | 767 | 53 | 592 | 468 |
| | 298 | 622 | 647 | 263 | 279 |
| | 829 | 824 | 589 | 986 | 910 |
| | 226 | 695 | 980 | 243 | 533 |
| | 106 | 999 | 676 | 15 | 575 |
| | 100 | 103 | 798 | 284 | 45 |
| | 295 | 382 | 300 | 948 | 979 |
| | 401 | 278 | 160 | 162 | 646 |
| | 410 | 412 | 712 | 326 | 633 |
| | 207 | 186 | 583 | 80 | 457 |
| | 905 | 261 | 785 | 378 | 289 |
| | 919 | 631 | 627 | 428 | 97 |
| | 561 | 694 | 913 | 834 | 22 |
| | 543 | 916 | 430 | 677 | 502 |
| | 513 | 462 | 353 | 404 | 269 |
| | 55 | 243 | 979 | 60 | 390 |

The XL Data Analyst Random Numbers Table. Random numbers are provided based on the user's specification of how many and the maximum size.

Note: Improved versions may differ somewhat.

With the random numbers technique, you must have unique number values assigned to each of the members of your population. You might use social security numbers because these are unique to each person, or you may have the computer, such as in a database program, assign unique numbers to them, and do the matching work to determine what individuals are selected into the sample. Again, the use of random numbers assures the researcher that every population member who is present in the master list or file will have an equal chance of being selected into the sample.

■ With a random numbers technique, you must have unique number values assigned to all members of the population.

If a researcher is using telephone numbers and drawing a sample, this technique is referred to as **random digit dialing**. This approach is used in telephone surveys to overcome the problems of unlisted and new telephone numbers. Unlisted numbers are a growing concern not only for researchers in the United States but in all industrialized countries such as those in Europe as well.[7] In random digit dialing, telephone numbers are generated randomly with the aid of a computer. Telephone interviewers call these numbers and administer the survey to the respondent once the person has been qualified. However, random digit dialing may result in a large number of calls to nonexisting telephone numbers. A popular variation of random digit dialing that reduces this problem is the **plus-one dialing procedure**, in which numbers are selected from a telephone directory, and a digit, such as a "1," is added to each number to determine which telephone number is then dialed.

■ Random digit dialing and the "plus-one" dialing technique incorporate the simple random sampling method.

### Systematic Sampling

Before widespread use of computerized databases, researchers used hard-copy lists. In this situation, **systematic sampling** is a way to select a simple random sample from a directory or list that is much more efficient (uses less effort) than with simple random sampling, because with a physical list, the researcher must scan all the names to match up each random number. To apply the systematic sampling technique in the special case of a physical listing of the population, such as a membership directory or a telephone book, systematic sampling can be applied with less difficulty and accomplished in a shorter time period than can simple random sampling. Furthermore, in many instances, systematic sampling has the potential to create a sample that is almost identical in quality to samples created from simple random sampling.

To use systematic sampling, it is necessary to obtain a hard-copy listing of the population, but it is not necessary to have a unique identification number assigned to each member on the list. The goal of systematic sampling is to literally "skip" through the list in a systematic way, but to begin at a random starting point in the list. That is, the research calculates a "**skip interval**" using the following formula:

$$\text{Skip interval} = \text{population list size/sample size}$$

◄ **Formula for skip interval**

For example, if the skip interval is calculated to be 100, the researcher will select every 100th name in the list. This technique is much more efficient than searching for matches to random numbers. The use of this skip interval formula ensures that the entire list will be covered. The random sample requirement is implemented by the use of a **random starting point**, meaning that the researcher must use some random number technique to decide on the first name in the sample. Subsequent names are selected by using the skip interval. Because a random starting point is used, every name on the list has an equal probability of being selected into the systematic sample. If you are drawing a systematic sample from a directory of thousands of names, it would be daunting to count to, say, the 44,563rd name, so after pondering a bit, you might realize that you could draw a single random number from 1 to the number of pages in the directory to randomly select a page, then draw a random number from 1 to the number of columns on the page to select the random column, and finally, select a random number between 1 and the number of names in that column. Thus, three quickly drawn random numbers would effect the random starting point for your systematic sample.

■ Systematic sampling is more efficient than simple random sampling, and it ensures random selection of the sample.

### Cluster Sampling

Another form of probability sampling is known as **cluster sampling**, in which the population is divided into subgroups, called "clusters," each of which represents the entire population.[8] Note that the basic concept behind cluster sampling is very similar to the one described for systematic sampling, but the implementation differs. The procedure identifies identical clusters. Any one cluster, therefore, will be a satisfactory representation of the population. Cluster sampling is advantageous when there is no electronic database of the population. It is easy to administer, and cluster sampling goes a step further in striving to gain economic efficiency over simple random sampling by simplifying the sampling procedure used. We illustrate cluster sampling by describing a type of cluster sample that is sometimes referred to as "area sampling."

In **area sampling**, the researcher subdivides the population to be surveyed into geographic areas, such as census tracts, cities, neighborhoods, or any other convenient and identifiable geographic designation. The researcher has two options at this point: a one-step approach or a two-step approach. In the **one-step area sample** approach, the researcher may believe the various geographic areas to be sufficiently identical to permit him or her to concentrate his or her attention on just one area and then generalize the results to the full population. But the researcher would need to select that one area randomly and perform a census of its members. Alternatively, he or she may employ a **two-step area sample** approach to the sampling process. That is, for the first step, the researcher could select a random sample of areas, and then for the second step, he or she could decide on a probability method to sample individuals within the chosen areas. The two-step area sample approach is preferable to the one-step approach because there is always the possibility that a single cluster may be less representative than the researcher believes. But the two-step method is more costly because more areas and time are involved.[9]

■ Area sampling is a practical application of cluster sampling in which geographic areas are used to represent the clusters.

### Stratified Sampling

All of the sampling methods we have described thus far implicitly assume that the population has a normal or bell-shaped distribution for its key properties. That is, there is the assumption that every potential sample unit is a fairly good representation of the population, and any who are extreme in one way are perfectly counterbalanced by opposite extreme potential sample units. Unfortunately, in marketing research it is common to work with populations that contain unique subgroupings; you might encounter a population that is not distributed symmetrically across a normal curve. With this situation, unless you make adjustments in your sample design, you will end up with a sample that is inaccurate. One solution is **stratified sampling**, which separates the population into different subgroups and then samples all of these subgroups using a random sampling technique.

For example, let's take the case of a college that is attempting to assess how its students perceive the quality of its educational programs. A researcher has formulated the question "To what extent do you value your college degree?" The response options are along a 5-point scale, where 1 equals "not valued at all" and 5 equals "very highly valued." The population of students is defined by year: freshman, sophomore, junior, and senior. It seems reasonable to believe that the averages will differ by the respondent's year status because seniors probably value a degree more than do juniors, who value a degree more than do sophomores, and so on. At the same time, it is expected that seniors would be more in agreement (have less variability) than would underclass-persons. This belief is due to the fact that freshmen are students who are trying out college, some of whom are not serious about completing it and do not value it highly, but some of whom are intending to become doctors, lawyers, or professionals whose training will include graduate degree work as well as their present college work. The serious freshmen students would value a college degree highly, whereas the less serious ones would not, meaning that we would find much variability in the freshmen students, less variability in sophomores, still less in juniors, and the least with college seniors.

The situation might be something similar to the distributions illustrated in Figure 10.7. When you look at Figure 10.7, you will find that the average score for each class is successively higher, with freshmen at the lowest average and seniors at the highest average. Also, the bell-shaped curve for each group, or stratum, is successively narrower, meaning that there is great variability in the freshman stratum, but much less in the senior stratum of our population.

What would happen if we used a simple random sample of equal size for each of our college groups? Because sample accuracy is determined by the variability in the population—regardless of whether you assess variability by using $p$ times $q$ for categorical questions or by using the standard deviation for metric scales—in our student example, we would be least accurate with freshmen and most accurate with

▪ With stratified sampling, the population is separated into different strata and a sample is taken from each stratum.

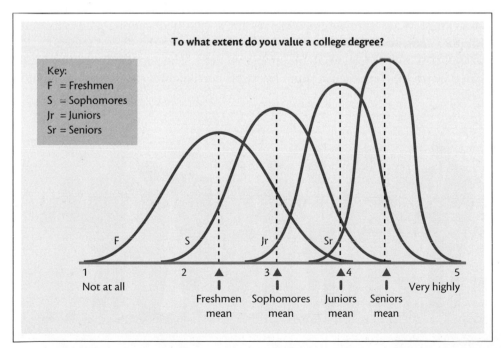

**Figure 10.7** Illustration of Four Strata in a Stratified Population of Undergraduate University Students

seniors. To state this situation differently, we would be statistically overefficient with seniors and statistically underefficient with freshmen because we would be oversampling the seniors and undersampling the freshmen. To gain overall statistical efficiency, we should draw a larger sample of freshmen and a smaller one of seniors. We might do this by allocating the sample proportionately based on the total number of the freshmen, sophomores, juniors, and seniors, each taken as a percentage of the whole college population. (Normally, there are fewer seniors than juniors than sophomores than freshmen in a college.) Thus, we would be drawing the smallest sample from the seniors group, who have the least variability in their assessments of the value of their college education, and the largest sample from the freshmen, who have the most variability in their assessments. We established in our sample size calculation section that smaller sample sizes will occur for highly similar populations (e.g, 90% times 10%), while large sample sizes will be calculated for highly dissimilar populations (e.g., 50% times 50%).

With stratified sampling, the researcher takes a **skewed population** and identifies the subgroups or **strata** contained within it based on their differences. In other words, each stratum is different from the other strata that make up the entire population. Then simple random sampling, systematic sampling, or some other type of probability sampling procedure is applied to draw a sample from each stratum. The stratum sample sizes can differ based on knowledge of the variability in each population stratum and with the aim of achieving the greatest overall sample accuracy.

How does stratified sampling result in a more accurate overall sample? There are two ways this accuracy is achieved. First, stratified sampling allows for explicit analysis of each stratum. The college degree example illustrates why a researcher would want to know about the distinguishing differences between the strata in order to assess the true picture. Each stratum represents a different response profile, and by allocating sample size based on the variability in the strata profiles, a more efficient sample design is achieved.

Second, there is a procedure that allows the estimation of the overall population average by use of a **weighted average** for a stratified sample, whose formula takes into consideration the sizes of the strata relative to the total population size and applies those proportions to the strata's averages. The population average is calculated by multiplying each stratum by its proportion and summing the weighted

■ Stratified sampling separates the population into dissimilar groups, called strata, because the researcher is working with a skewed population.

With stratified sampling, the researcher identifies subgroups or strata in the population and samples each stratum.

stratum averages. This formula results in an estimate that is consistent with the true distribution of the population when the sample sizes used in the strata are not proportionate to their shares of the population. Here is the formula that is used for two strata:

$$\text{Average}_{\text{population}} = (\text{average}_A)(\text{proportion}_A) + (\text{average}_B)(\text{proportion}_B)$$

where A signifies stratum A, and B signifies stratum B.

◀ **Formula for weighted average**

▪ Use a weighted average formula when combining strata averages taken in stratified sampling.

Here is an example. A researcher separated a population of households that rent videos on a regular basis into two strata. Stratum A was families without young children and stratum B was families with young children. When asked to use a scale of 1 = "poor" and 5 = "excellent" to rate their video rental store on its video selection, the means were computed to be 2.0 and 4.0, respectively, for the samples. The researcher knew from census information that families without young children accounted for 70% of the population, whereas families with young children accounted for the remaining 30%. The weighted mean rating for video selection was then computed as $(.7)(2.0) + (.3)(4.0) = 2.6$.

Usually, a **surrogate measure**, which is some observable or easily determined characteristic of each population member, is used to help partition or separate the population members into their various subgroupings. For example, in the instance of the college, the year classification of each student is a handy surrogate. With its internal records, the college could easily identify students in each stratum, and this determination would be the stratification method. Of course, there is the opportunity for the researcher to divide the population into as many relevant strata as necessary to capture different subpopulations. For instance, the college might want to further stratify on college of study, gender, or grade point average (GPA) ranges. Perhaps professional-school students value their degrees more than do liberal arts students, females differently from male students, and high-GPA students more than average-GPA or failing students. The key issue is that the researcher should use some basis for dividing the population into strata that results in different responses across strata. There is no need to stratify if all strata respond alike.

If the strata sample sizes are faithful to their relative sizes in the population, you have what is called a **proportionate stratified sample** design. Here you do not use the weighted formula, because each stratum's weight is automatically accounted for by its sample size. But with **disproportionate stratified sampling**, the weighted formula needs to be used, because the strata sizes do not reflect their relative proportions in the population.

## Nonprobability Sampling Methods

The four sampling methods we have described thus far embody probability sampling assumptions. In each case, the probability of any unit being selected from the population into the sample is known, and it can be calculated precisely given the sample size, population size, and strata or cluster sizes, if they are used. With a **nonprobability sampling method**, selection is not based on fairness, equity, or equal chance. One author has noted that nonprobability sampling uses human intervention, while probability sampling does not.[10] In fact, a nonprobability sampling method is inherently biased, and the researcher acknowledges that the sample is representative only to some degree that the researcher feels is sufficient under the circumstances of the survey. To be candid about it, most nonprobability sampling methods take shortcuts that save effort, time, and money, but which obliterate the equal-chance guarantee of any probability sampling method. As a result, you cannot in good conscience calculate the probability of any one person in the population being selected into a nonprobability sample.

So, why in the world would a researcher ever want to use a nonprobability sample? There are three answers to this question, and we just divulged them—effort, time, and money. Compared to random sampling techniques, nonrandom ones, meaning nonprobability sampling methods, take less effort, they are faster, and they cost less. But these savings have a cost that ethical researchers readily acknowledge, and that cost is diminished representativeness. Nonetheless, it is important that you become familiar with nonprobability sampling methods as there are instances, such as when conducting a pretest or a pilot study, when a nonrandom sampling technique is useful. Alternatively, you should be able to identify when a nonrandom sample has been utilized, so that you can make your own informed judgment as to the representativeness of the sample.

There are four nonprobability sampling methods: convenience samples, judgment samples, referral samples, and quota samples. A discussion of each method follows, and you can refer to Table 10.2, which summarizes how each of these nonprobability sampling techniques operate.

■ Nonprobability samples do not embody fairness, equity, or equal chance.

**Table 10.2**
**Four Different Nonprobability Sampling Techniques**

**Convenience Sampling**
The researcher uses a high-traffic location such as a busy pedestrian area or a shopping mall to intercept potential respondents. Sample selection error occurs in the form of the absence of members of the population who are infrequent or nonusers of that location.

**Judgment Sampling**
The researcher uses his or her judgment or that of some other knowledgeable person to identify who will be in the sample. Subjectivity enters in here, and certain members of the population will have a smaller chance of selection into the sample than will others.

**Referral Sampling**
Respondents are asked for the names or identities of others like themselves who might qualify to take part in the survey. Members of the population who are less well known, disliked, or whose opinions conflict with the respondent have a low probability of being selected into a referral sample.

**Quota Sampling**
The researcher identifies quota characteristics such as demographic or product-use factors and uses these to set up quotas for each class of respondent. The sizes of the quotas are determined by the researcher's belief about the relative size of each class of respondent in the population. Often quota sampling is used as a means of ensuring that convenience samples will have the desired proportions of different respondent classes, thereby reducing the sample selection error but not eliminating it.

## Convenience Samples

A **convenience sample** is a sample drawn at the convenience of the researcher or interviewer. Accordingly, the most convenient areas to a researcher in terms of time and effort turn out to be high-traffic areas such as shopping malls, or busy pedestrian intersections. The selection of the place and, consequently, prospective respondents is subjective rather than objective. Certain members of the population are automatically eliminated from the sampling process.[11] For instance, there are those people who may be infrequent or even nonvisitors of the particular high-traffic area being used. On the other hand, in the absence of strict selection procedures, there are members of the population who may be omitted because of their physical appearance, general demeanor, or by the fact that they are in a group rather than alone. One author states, "Convenience samples . . . can be seriously misleading."[12]

▪ A convenience sample relies on high-traffic areas where some members of the target population pass by.

Mall-intercept companies often use a convenience sampling method to recruit respondents. For example, shoppers are encountered at large shopping malls and quickly qualified with screening questions. For those satisfying the desired population characteristics, a questionnaire may be administered or a taste test performed. Alternatively, the respondent may be given a test product and asked if he or she would use it at home. A follow-up telephone call some days later solicits his or her reaction to the product's performance. In this case, the convenience extends beyond easy access of respondents into considerations of setup for taste tests, storage of products to be distributed, and control of the interviewer workforce. Additionally, large numbers of respondents can be recruited in a matter of days. The screening questions and geographic dispersion of malls may appear to reduce the subjectivity inherent in the sample design, but in fact the vast majority of the population was not there and could not be approached to take part. Yet, there are ways of controlling convenience sample selection error using a quota system, which we discuss shortly.

## Judgment Samples

A **judgment sample** is somewhat different from a convenience sample in concept because a judgment sample requires a judgment or an "educated guess" as to who should represent the population. Often the researcher or some individual helping the

With a convenience sample, the researcher selects high-traffic locations and interviews individuals who happen to be there.

▓ Judgment samples rely on someone specifying what individuals are typical or judged to be representative of the population in some way.

researcher who has considerable knowledge about the population will choose those individuals that he or she feels constitute the sample. It should be apparent that judgment samples are highly subjective and therefore prone to much error.

However, judgment samples do have special uses. For instance, in the preliminary stages of a research project, the researcher may use qualitative techniques such as depth interviews or focus groups as a means of gaining insight and understanding to the research problem. In this case, judgment sampling is a quick, inexpensive, and acceptable technique because the researcher is not seeking to generalize the findings of this sample to the population as a whole. Take, for example, a recent focus group concerning the need for a low-calorie, low-fat microwave oven cookbook. Twelve women were selected as representative of the present and prospective market. Six of these women had owned a microwave oven for 10 or more years, 3 of the women had owned the oven for less than 10 years, and 3 of the women were in the market for a microwave oven. In the judgment of the researcher, these 12 women represented the population adequately for the purposes of the focus group. It must be quickly pointed out, however, that the intent of this focus group was far different from the intent of a survey. Consequently, the use of a judgment sample was considered satisfactory for this particular phase in the research process for the cookbook. The focus group findings served as the foundation for a large-scale regional survey conducted two months later that relied on a probability sampling method.

### Referral Samples

A **referral sample** is sometimes called a "snowball sample," because it requires respondents to provide the names of additional respondents. Such lists begin when the researcher compiles a short list of potential respondents based on convenience or judgment. After each respondent is interviewed, he or she is queried about the names of other possible respondents. In this manner, additional respondents are referred by previous respondents. Or, as the other name implies, the sample grows just as a snowball grows when it is rolled downhill.

▓ Referral samples make use of respondents' volunteering names of friends and others whose names they know.

Referral samples are most appropriate when there is a limited and disappointingly short sample frame and when respondents can provide the names of others who would qualify for the survey. For example, some foreign countries have low telephone penetration or slow mail systems that make these options unsuitable, while a referral approach adds an element of trust to the approach for each new potential respondent. The nonprobability aspects of referral sampling come from the selectivity used throughout. The initial list may also be special in some way, and the primary means of adding people to the sample is by tapping the memories of those on the original list. Referral samples are often useful in industrial marketing research situations.[13]

### Quota Samples

We have saved the most commonly used nonprobability sampling method for last. The **quota sample** establishes a specific quota for various types of individuals to be interviewed. The quotas are determined through application of the research objectives and are defined by key characteristics used to identify the population. In the application of quota sampling, a fieldworker is provided with screening criteria that will classify the potential respondent into a particular quota cell. For example, if the interviewer is assigned to obtain a sample quota of 50 each for black females, black males, white females, and white males, the qualifying characteristics would be race and gender. Assuming our fieldworkers were conducting mall intercepts, each would determine through visual inspection which category the prospective respondent fits into, and would work toward filling the quota in each of the four cells. So a quota system overcomes much of the nonrepresentativeness danger inherent in convenience samples.[14]

The popularity of quota samples is attributable to the fact that they combine non-probability sampling advantages with quota controls that ensure the final sample will approximate the population with respect to its key characteristics. Quota samples are often used by consumer goods companies that have a firm grasp on the features characterizing the individuals they wish to study in a particular marketing research project. These companies often use mall-intercept data collection companies that deliver fast service at a reasonable price, and the use of quota controls guarantees that the final sample will satisfactorily represent the population that the consumer goods company has targeted for the research project. Quota samples are also used in global marketing research where communication systems are problematic. For example, most companies performing research in Latin America use quota samples.[15] When done conscientiously and with a firm understanding of the quota characteristics, quota sampling can rival probability sampling in the minds of some researchers.

■ With a quota sample, the researcher prespecifies the proportions of various types of respondents that are to be in the final sample.

■ Quota samples are the most popular nonprobability samples.

## ONLINE SAMPLING TECHNIQUES

As you know, Internet surveys are becoming popular. To be sure, sampling for Internet surveys poses special challenges,[16] but most of these issues can be addressed in the context of our probability and nonprobability sampling concepts.[17] If you understand how a particular online sampling method works, you can probably interpret the sampling procedure correctly with respect to basic sampling concepts.[18] For purposes of illustration, we will describe three types of online sampling: (1) random online intercept sampling, (2) invitation online sampling, and (3) online panel sampling.

■ Online sampling can be interpreted in the context of traditional sampling techniques.

**Random online intercept sampling** relies on a random selection of Web site visitors. There are a number of Java-based or other html-embedded routines that will select Web site visitors on a random basis such as time of day or random selection from the stream of Web site visitors. If the population is defined as Web site visitors, then this is a simple random sample of these visitors within the time frame of the survey. If the sample selection program starts randomly and incorporates a skip interval system, it is a systematic sample,[19] and if the sample program treats the population of Web site visitors like strata, it uses stratified simple random sampling as long as random selection procedures are used faithfully. However, if the population is other than Web site visitors, and the Web site is used because there are many visitors, the sample is akin to a mall-intercept sample (convenience sample).

**Invitation online sampling** is when potential respondents are alerted that they may fill out a questionnaire that is hosted at a specific Web site.[20] For example, a retail store chain may have a notice that is handed to customers with their receipts notifying them that they may go online to fill out the questionnaire. However, to avoid spam, online researchers must have an established relationship with potential respondents who expect to receive an e-mail survey. If the retail store uses a random sampling approach such as systematic sampling, a probability sample will result. Similarly, if the e-mail list is a truly representative group of the population, and the procedures embody random selection, it will constitute a probability sample. However, if in either case there is some aspect of the selection procedure that eliminates population members or otherwise overrepresents elements of the population, the sample will be a nonprobability one.

**Online panel sampling** refers to consumer or other respondent panels that are set up by marketing research companies for the explicit purpose of conducting online surveys with representative samples. There is a growing number of these companies, and online panels afford fast, convenient, and flexible access to preprofiled samples.[21] Typically, the panel company has several thousand individuals who are representative of a large geographic area, and the market researcher can specify sample parameters such as specific geographic representation, income, education, family characteristics, and so forth. The panel company then uses its database on its panel members to broadcast an e-mail notification to those panelists who qualify according to the sample parameters specified by the market researcher. Although online panel samples are not probability samples, they are used extensively by the marketing research industry.[22] In some instances, the online panel company creates the questionnaire; at other times, the researcher composes the questionnaire on the panel company's software, or some other means of questionnaire design might be used, depending on the services of the panel company. One of the greatest pluses of online panels is the high response rate, which ensures that the final sample closely represents the population targeted by the researcher. Other online sampling approaches are feasible and limited only by the creativity of the sample designers.

## SUMMARY

This chapter dealt with the sample aspects of a marketing research survey. We began by defining basic terms such as *sample*, *population*, *census*, *sampling error*, *sample frame*, and *sample frame error*. We then described the notions associated with the confidence interval method of calculating sample size. The formula for this method requires that the researcher (1) specify a sample accuracy level such as ± 3% or ± 4%; (2) estimate the variability in the population, which can be taken to be 50%/50% if the researcher is unsure; and (3) use the 95% or 99% level of confidence. You can calculate sample size with the formula or use the XL Data Analyst.

The chapter then took up sample selection methods, and it described four probability sampling methods, which are techniques that guarantee that each member of the population has an equal chance of being selected into the sample. These four techniques were: (1) simple random sampling where random numbers are employed; (2) systematic sampling that utilizes a skip interval for a sample frame list; (3) cluster sampling if the researcher can identify homogeneous groups in the population; and (4) stratified sampling, used for skewed populations. Next, four nonprobability sample methods were described, and it was pointed out for each one how its application incurs some degree of sample selection error. These techniques were (1) convenience sampling such as using a shopping mall's customer traffic as the sample frame; (2) judgment sampling, where someone arbitrarily specifies who will be in the sample; (3) referral sampling, in which case the respondents divulge the names of friends and acquaintances to the researcher; and (4) quota sampling, where the researcher attempts to minimize sample selection error by requiring that certain classes of individuals are in the sample in proportions that are believed to reflect their presence in the population.

## KEY TERMS

Population (p. 292)
Sample (p. 292)
Census (p. 292)
Sampling error (p. 292)
Sample frame (p. 292)
Sample frame error (p. 293)
Accuracy of a sample (p. 293)
Confidence interval formula for
   sample size (p. 294)
Variability (p. 295)
Level of confidence (p. 296)
Desired accuracy (p. 296)
Incidence rate (p. 297)
Nonresponse (p. 297)
Random sample (p. 300)
Probability sampling methods (p. 300)
Simple random sampling (p. 301)
Random numbers technique (p. 301)
Table of random numbers (p. 301)
Random digit dialing (p. 303)
Plus-one dialing procedure (p. 303)
Systematic sampling (p. 303)
"Skip interval" (p. 303)

Random starting point (p. 303)
Cluster sampling (p. 304)
Area sampling (p. 304)
One-step area sample (p. 304)
Two-step area sample (p. 304)
Stratified sampling (p. 304)
Skewed population (p. 306)
Strata (p. 306)
Weighted average (p. 306)
Surrogate measure (p. 307)
Proportionate stratified sample (p. 307)
Disproportionate stratified sampling
   (p. 307)
Nonprobability sampling method
   (p. 307)
Convenience sample (p. 309)
Judgment sample (p. 309)
Referral sample (p. 310)
Quota sample (p. 310)
Random online intercept sampling
   (p. 311)
Invitation online sampling (p. 311)
Online panel sampling (p. 312)

## REVIEW QUESTIONS

1 Define each of the following:
  **a** Population   **b** Sample   **c** Census   **d** Sample frame
2 Indicate the sample frame error typically found in the households listing of a telephone book.
3 Explain what is meant by the accuracy of a sample.
4 Why is $p$ taken to represent the variability of a population?
5 Why is a probability sample also a random sample?
7 How are random numbers vital to a probability sample method?
8 How is sample frame error overcome with a "plus-one" dialing procedure?
9 What single step is critical in preserving the probability characteristic of a systematic sample? Why?
10 How does cluster sampling differ from stratified sampling?
11 When is a weighted mean required for a stratified sample? Explain when and why it is not required.
12 What is convenient about a convenience sample?
13 Compare a judgment sample to a referral sample. How are they similar? How are they unlike?

**14** In order to implement a quota sample, what prior knowledge does the researcher need to have about the population?

## APPLICATION QUESTIONS

**15** Here are four populations and a potential sample frame for each one. With each pair, identify: (1) members of the population who are not in the sample frame, and (2) sample frame items that are not part of the population. Also, for each one, would you judge the amount of sample frame error to be acceptable or unacceptable?

| Population | Sample Frame |
|---|---|
| a. Buyers of Scope mouthwash | Mailing list of *Consumer Reports* subscribers |
| b. Listeners of a particular FM radio classical music station | Telephone directory in your city |
| c. Prospective buyers of a new day planner and prospective-client tracking kit | Members of Sales and Marketing Executives International (a national organization of sales managers) |
| d. Users of weatherproof decking materials (to build outdoor decks) | Individuals' names registered at a recent home and garden show |

**16** Here are some numbers that you can use to sharpen your computational skills for sample size determination. Crest toothpaste is reviewing plans for its annual survey of toothpaste purchasers. With each case that follows, calculate the sample size pertaining to the key variable under consideration. Where information is missing, provide reasonable assumptions. You can check your computations by using the sample size calculation feature of the XL Data Analyst.

| Case | Key Variable | Variability | Acceptable Error | Confidence Level |
|---|---|---|---|---|
| 1 | Market share of Crest toothpaste last year | 23% share | 4% | 95% |
| 2 | Percentage of people who brush their teeth per week | Unknown | 5% | 99% |
| 3 | How likely Crest buyers are to switch brands | 30% switched last year | 5% | 95% |
| 4 | Percentage of people who want tartar-control features in their toothpaste | 20% two years ago; 40% one year ago | 3.5% | 95% |
| 5 | Willingness of people to adopt the toothpaste | Unknown | 6% | 99% |

**17** Allbookstores.com has a used-textbook division. It buys its books in bulk from used-book buyers who set up kiosks on college campuses during final exams, and it sells the used textbooks to students who log on to the Allbookstores.com Web site via a secured credit card transaction. The used texts are then sent by United Parcel Service to the student.

The company has conducted a survey of used-book buying by college students each year for the past four years. In each survey, 1,000 randomly selected college students have been asked to indicate whether or not they bought a used textbook in the previous year. The results are as follows:

| | Years Ago | | | |
|---|---|---|---|---|
| | 1 | 2 | 3 | 4 |
| Percentage buying used text(s) | 70% | 60% | 55% | 50% |

What are the sample size implications of these data? That is, assess whether or not the survey should be continued in the coming year with a sample size of 1,000.

**18** Pet Insurers Company markets health and death benefits insurance to pet owners. It specializes in coverage for pedigreed dogs, cats, and expensive and exotic pets such as miniature Vietnamese potbellied pigs. The veterinary care costs of these pets can be high, and their deaths represent substantial financial loss to their owners. A researcher working for Pet Insurers finds that a listing company can provide a list of 15,000 names that includes all current subscribers to *Cat Lovers*, *Pedigreed Dog*, and *Exotic Pets Monthly*. If the final sample size is to be 1,000, calculate what the skip interval should be in a systematic sample for each of the following:

**a** a telephone survey using drop-down replacement of nonrespondents

**b** a mail survey with an anticipated 30% response rate (assume the incidence rate for this sample frame to be 100%)

**19** A market researcher is proposing a survey for the Big Tree Country Club, a private country club that is contemplating several changes in its layout to make the golf course more championship caliber. The researcher is considering three different sample designs as a way to draw a representative sample of the club's golfers. The three alternative designs are:

**a** Station an interviewer at the first-hole tee on one day chosen at random, with instructions to ask every 10th golfer to fill out a self-administered questionnaire.

**b** Put a stack of questionnaires on the counter where golfers check in and pay for their golf carts. There would be a sign above the questionnaires, and there would be an incentive for a "free dinner in the clubhouse" for three players who fill out the questionnaires and whose names are selected by a lottery.

**c** Using the city telephone directory, a plus-one dialing procedure would be used. With this procedure a random page in the directory would be selected, and a name on that page would be selected, both using a table of random numbers. The plus-one system would be applied to that name and every name listed after it until 1,000 golfers are identified and interviewed by telephone.

Assess the representativeness and other issues associated with this sample problem. Be sure to identify the sample method being contemplated in each case. Which sample method do you recommend using and why?

# INTERACTIVE LEARNING

You can visit the textbook Web site at **www.prenhall.com/burnsbush**. Use the self-study quizzes and get instant feedback on whether or not you need additional studying to master the material in this chapter. You can also review the chapter's major points by visiting the chapter outline and key terms.

---

**CASE 10.1** ||| **Peaceful Valley: Trouble in Suburbia**

Located on the outskirts of a large city, the suburb of Peaceful Valley comprises approximately 6,000 upscale homes. The subdivision came about 10 years ago when a developer built an earthen dam on Peaceful River and created Peaceful Lake, a meandering 20-acre body of water. The lake became the centerpiece of the development, and the first 2,000 one-half-acre lots were sold as lakefront property. Now Peaceful Valley is fully developed, with 50 streets, all approximately 1.5 miles in length, with approximately 60 houses on each street. Peaceful Valley's residents are primarily young, professional, dual-income families with one or two school-age children. A unique feature of Peaceful Valley is that there are only two entrances/exits, which have security systems that monitor vehicle traffic. As a result, Peaceful Valley is considered the safest community in the state.

But controversy has come to Peaceful Valley. The suburb's steering committee has recommended that the community build a swimming pool, tennis court, and meeting room facility on four adjoining vacant lots in the back of the subdivision. Construction cost estimates range from $1.5 million to $2 million, depending on how large the facility will be. Currently, every Peaceful Valley homeowner is billed $100 annually for maintenance, security, and upkeep of Peaceful Valley. About 75% of the residents pay this fee. To construct the proposed recreational facility, each Peaceful Valley household would be expected to pay a one-time fee of $500, and annual fees would increase to $200 based on facility maintenance cost estimates.

Objections to the recreational facility come from various quarters. For some, the one-time fee is unacceptable; for others, the notion of a recreational facility is not appealing. Some residents have their own swimming pools, belong to local tennis clubs, or otherwise have little use for a meeting room facility. Other Peaceful Valley homeowners see the recreational facility as a wonderful addition where they could have their children learn to swim, play tennis, or just hang out under supervision.

The president of the Peaceful Valley Suburb Association has decided to conduct a survey to poll the opinions and preferences of Peaceful Valley homeowners regarding the swimming pool, tennis court, and meeting room facility concept.

1   If the steering committee agrees to a survey that is accurate to ±5% and at a 95% level of confidence, what sample size should be used?

2   What sample method do you recommend? In making your recommendation, carefully consider the geographic configuration of Peaceful Valley. Provide the specifics of how each household in the sample should be selected, including what provision(s) to take if a selected household happened to be on vacation or was unwilling to take part in the survey.

3   Should the survey be a sample (of the size you calculated in question 1) or a census of Peaceful Valley homeowners? Defend your choice. Be certain to discuss any practical considerations that enter into your choice.

---

**CASE 10.2** ||| **Your Integrated Case**

**College Life E-Zine: Sample Decisions**
*This is the eighth case in our integrated case series. You will find the previous College Life E-Zine Cases in Chapters 1, 2, 3, 4, 5, 7, and 9.*

Bob Watts is on the phone with Wesley, one of our hopeful College Life E-Zine owners, discussing the sample size and selection steps of the survey. Wesley has volunteered to talk with Bob about this as he is the one who remembers most about this topic from his undergraduate studies at State U. "Okay," says Bob, "we need to make some decisions that will have some important consequences about the generalizability of our survey. As you and the others know, we have an agreement with State University officials to have access to their student data files as long as we provide them with the results of this survey, as they are very interested in partnering with the College Life E-Zine. It could off-load a lot of the State U Web site work that is planned over the next two years. They said they would work with us in any way possible to develop a sample of State U students."

Wesley says, "That's great! I knew they'd be willing to help us, since my cousin works in the State U Web site tech area, and he told me a year ago that they had so much to do that it might take five years to put it all on State U's Web site because his area is so underfunded." Wesley continues, "I actually consulted my old marketing research class notes, and I found that the typical opinion poll has a sample accuracy of from ± 3% to ± 4%. I will leave it to you to make the recommendation, however. And as for the sample selection, I'll trust it to you as well, but since we are using a telephone survey, I found in my notes that random digit dialing is a commonly used technique. But you're the expert, Bob, so whatever you come up with, we'll give it strong consideration."

Bob Watts says, "I'll take all of this under consideration and get back to you and the others next week. So long for now." Upon switching off his phone, Bob glances at his calendar and notices that the marketing research intern he hired from from State U—he has jotted her first name down—Lori—will meet with him in three days to begin her five-week rotation in his group. Somewhat devilishly, Bob thinks, "I think I'll give this Lori a test. I'll send her an e-mail with the College Life E-Zine sample decisions that are pending and see what she comes up with for our initial interview."

Here is Bob's e-mail to Lori.

To: Lori Baker, Marketing Research Intern
From: Bob Watts, Division Manager

Subject: Initial Interview
Lori:
Some time has passed since we met and I hired you as our marketing research intern this semester. You are about to begin your third and last department rotation in the company and into my department. For your initial interview with me on Friday, I am providing you with some information about a current project, and I would like you to be prepared to discuss with me your recommendations for certain sample decisions that must be made very shortly for the College Life E-Zine project (project proposal attached for your perusal—I have also included my notes with relevant communications, including the most recent one concerning sample size and method with the client group).

1 What is your recommendation as to the sample size for the survey? I suggest that you use Wesley's telephone conversation comments in deciding on your recommendation.

2 What is your reaction to a random-digit-dialing approach to select the sample of State U students? Consider that we will use a data collection company that can generate random-digit-dialing numbers easily. Does this alter your reaction to random digit dialing to any degree?

3 What if one of our budding College Life E-Zine entrepreneurs is bullish on having us just sample the technical majors at State U, such as computer science, computer and electrical engineering, information systems/decision sciences, computer graphics, and the like? What is your reaction to this sample design and why?

4 State U says it will access its electronic student files to select a sample, but it will only provide us the sample of students based on our instructions as to how to select these students. If I assign you the task of communicating to the State U technical folks how to select the sample, what steps do you propose to tell them to take to effect:
   a A simple random sample using electronic records?
   b A systematic sample using the State University Student Directory?

Have a good next few days, and I will see you at your interview at 10:00 a.m. on Friday.

Your task in analyzing this case is to take Lori's role and develop answers to each of Bob's four sampling questions for the College Life E-Zine survey.

## CHAPTER 11

# COLLECTING DATA AND SUMMARIZING WHAT YOU FOUND IN YOUR SAMPLE

## DATA ANALYSIS AT DSS RESEARCH

At DSS, when a project calls for measuring satisfaction, we often use a five-point scaled response scale with descriptors such as: "Completely Satisfied," "Very Satisfied," "Somewhat Satisfied," "Not too Satisfied," and "Not at All Satisfied." As you will learn in this chapter, we use data analysis techniques to *summarize* the results for our clients. For example, while this satisfaction scale is a metric scale and allows us to calculate means and standard deviations, we've learned that many of our clients prefer focusing on the percentages of the sample that fall in the top two categories or the top three categories. We *summarize* the data for them by reporting the percentages for each category of satisfaction. We also *summarize* by reporting the means and standard deviations to metric questions. By *summarizing* the findings we give our clients the basic descriptive statistics they need to interpret the data we have collected for them. These basic descriptive statistics are the "bread and butter" of data analysis. You will learn how to *summarize* findings in this chapter.

While summarizing data is very important, this is just the beginning of the analytics we provide DSS Research clients. Clients want to know if they can *generalize* the findings from our sample data to their entire population of customers. For example, if we determine that 43% of the sample falls in the "Completely Satisfied" and "Very Satisfied" groups, our clients

- To realize the issues involved with data collection
- To learn about the code book and how it relates to XL Data Analyst
- To see an overview of the four types of data analysis performed by market researchers
- To understand summarization data analysis, including when to use percentage, average, mode, and standard deviation
- To become acquainted with the summarize function of your XL Data Analyst
- To be introduced to our six-step data analysis and presentation approach

want to know if the 43% we are giving them is a reliable estimate of the true percentage of satisfied customers in the population. Calculating a confidence interval around the percentage allows us to answer their concerns. A confidence interval allows us to tell our clients something like: *"Our best estimate of those in the population who are either Completely or Very Satisfied is 43%. In addition, we are 95% confident that the true percentage of those who are Completely or Very Satisfied falls between 40% and 46%."* In this way we can assure the client that the results are *generalizable* to their actual customer population. You will learn how to *generalize* sample findings to the population by constructing confidence intervals in the next chapter.

Clients also need to know if there are any significant *differences* among subgroups. Are males *different* from females? Are "Heavy Usage" customers *different* from "Moderate" or "Light Usage" customers? Are customers at different client locations *different* in terms of satisfaction? To test for significant *differences* between two groups, we use t-tests. Also, when we conduct segmentation analysis for clients, we examine differences between several market segments. To analyze differences between more than two groups, we use a technique known as Analysis of Variance (ANOVA). You will learn about *differences* analysis using both t-tests and ANOVA in Chapter 13.

Clients know that satisfied customers are *related* to sales and sales are *related* to profits. Clients know that intentions of customers to buy their brand or patronize their store in the future are *related* to sales and profits. Clients also know that customers' willingness to recommend their brand or store to others is also *related* to sales and profits. Since satisfaction, intentions, and willingness to recommend are so important, clients want to know what drives these important variables. What variables are *related* to higher levels of satisfaction? What variables are *related* to increased intention to buy a client's brand? What variables are *related* to increased willingness to recommend a client's brand to others? To answer these questions we find *relationships* between variables that clients can act on, and level of satisfaction, intention, and willingness to recommend. In Chapter 14 you will learn how to use crosstabulations, correlation, and regression analysis to find these *relationships*.

At DSS Research we are capable of running the most sophisticated data analysis techniques, including multivariate analyses. How do we know which data analysis technique to use? First, we have to be knowledgeable of what data analysis tools are available and the purpose each tool serves. We also must be knowledgeable of the requirements to properly run each analysis technique. Armed with this knowledge, we examine each research objective we have carefully crafted to address the client's problem and we select the most appropriate data analysis technique to reach the research objective. By reading this and the next few chapters, and by learning the tools available to you using XL Data Analyst®, you will gain an appreciation of what professional marketing researchers do every day.

Kevin Weseman, MSMR

**Manager of Analytics**

**DSS Research**

By permission, DSS Research.

*Kevin Weseman is Manager of Analytics at DSS Research in Ft. Worth, TX. Kevin received his B.S. and MBA at the University of West Florida where he became proficient in SPSS. After a stint in the retailing industry, Kevin enrolled in the Masters of Science Marketing Research program at the University of Texas, Arlington.[1] Upon graduation Mr. Weseman received a job at DSS Research. Visit DSS Research at www.dssresearch.com*

This chapter provides background on how a researcher describes the profile of his or her sample. That is, it describes the various ways a researcher summarizes the findings in a survey sample. It will introduce you to the analyses—such as percents and averages—to use, the proper or correct time to use them, and how to communicate them to sponsors or clients who are anxiously awaiting the findings of the survey. The chapter begins our discussion of the various data analyses available to the marketing researcher. As you will soon learn, these really are devices to convert formless data into meaningful information. These techniques summarize and communicate patterns found in the data sets marketing researchers analyze. We begin the chapter by describing some issues concerning data collection that affect data coding and the code book. Next, we describe how to create a data set in Excel using our XL Data Analyst.

As an overview to data analysis, we provide a brief introduction to each of the four types of data analysis: summarizing, generalizing, seeking differences, and identifying relationships. Because this chapter deals with summarizing data, we describe the data analyses that are appropriate to summarize, or describe, categorical and metric variables. We also show you how to use the XL Data Analyst to obtain these analyses with a data set. Finally, we introduce you to our six-step approach to data analysis and presentation that will be used in all of our analysis chapters.

# ERRORS ENCOUNTERED IN THE DATA COLLECTION STAGE

Regardless of the method of data collection, the data collection stage of a marketing research project can be the source of many **nonsampling errors**, which are errors in the research process pertaining to anything except the sample size. If the researcher uses **fieldworkers**, or individuals hired to administer the survey to respondents, there are dangers of **intentional fieldworker errors** where the interviewer deliberately falsifies his or her work, such as cheating by submitting bogus completed questionnaires.[2] There are also dangers of **unintentional fieldworker errors** where the interviewer makes mistakes such as those caused by fatigue or lack of understanding of how to administer the questions. The best way to minimize fieldworker errors is to hire a reputable data collection company that has excellent training, good supervision, and built-in validation techniques,[3] to ensure that fieldworkers will be very unlikely to commit fieldworker errors.[4]

> Marketing research fieldworkers can commit intentional and/or unintentional errors while gathering data.

There are also **respondent errors**, which are errors committed by respondents when answering the questions in a survey. **Intentional respondent errors** are those committed when the respondent knowingly provides false answers or fails to give an answer. Tactics such as incentives, assuring anonymity, providing confidentiality, or follow-up validation are employed to reduce the level of intentional respondent error.[5] **Unintentional respondent errors**, on the other hand, occur when the respondent is confused, distracted, or otherwise inattentive. Here, the researcher uses tactics such as good questionnaire design, adequate pretesting of the questionnaire, "no opinion" or "unsure" response options, negatively worded items, or prompters such as "Do you have any other things that come to mind?" that minimize the amount of unintentional respondent error in a survey.

> Respondents can commit intentional and/or unintentional errors while providing answers to survey questions.

## Data Collection Errors with Online Surveys

In many ways, an online survey is similar to a self-administered questionnaire because there is no interviewer. At the same time, unless controls are in place,[6] there can be misrepresentations in online surveys. There are three data collection errors unique to online surveys: (1) multiple submissions by the same respondent, (2) bogus respondents and/or responses, and (3) misrepresentation of the population.

ONLINE

### Multiple Submissions

The typical online questionnaire is fast and easy to take. Unless there is a control in place, it is possible for a respondent to submit his or her completed questionnaire multiple times in a matter of minutes. If the person is free to submit multiple

Even with online surveys, marketing researchers must take precautions to reduce errors.

■ With online surveys researchers worry about multiple submissions, bogus responses, and misrepresentation of the target population.

responses, this error will result in an overrepresentation of that individual's views and opinions. The customary control for **multiple submissions** is to ask the respondent for his or her e-mail address, and an electronic block is activated if the e-mail address is repeated. Of course, this control does not eliminate multiple e-mail addresses from the same respondent.

### Bogus Respondents and Responses

The anonymity of the Internet can inspire individuals to log into a questionnaire site as a fictitious person or to disguise him/herself as another person. Under this disguise, the individual may feel free to give nonsense, polarized, or otherwise false responses. Coupled with the multiple submissions error, a bogus response error has the potential to create havoc with an online survey. If this concern is great, researchers turn to online panels or other options where the respondents are prequalified or preidentified in some manner to control for bogus respondents.

### Population Misrepresentation

We alluded to this problem in our sample design chapter, but it must be reiterated that all consumers are not equally Internet-connected or Web-literate. Some segments of the population—such as elderly citizens, low-income families, folks in remote areas where Internet connection is sparse and/or expensive, or technophobic people—are not good prospects for an online survey. By the same token, some individuals are more connected than others in their respective market segments. For instance, a Web-based survey of life insurance companies could result in a responding sample overrepresenting those people who are very comfortable with the Web, and underrepresenting those individuals who use the Internet infrequently.[7]

## Types of Nonresponse

**Nonresponse** is defined as a failure on the part of a prospective respondent to take part in the survey or to answer specific questions on the questionnaire. Although nonresponse was briefly described earlier in our discussion of mail surveys, we will now describe the nonresponse issue more fully and describe the various types of nonresponse that a researcher may encounter. Nonresponse has been labeled the marketing research industry's biggest problem,[8] it bedevils the polling industry,[9] and it is multinational in scope.[10] Some industry observers believe that the major problems leading to nonresponse are caused by fears of invasion of privacy, skepticism of consumers regarding the benefits of participating in research, and the use of research as a guise for telemarketing. (At this point, you may want to recall our discussion of sugging and frugging in Chapter 2.)

There are at least three different types of potential nonresponse error lurking in any survey: refusals to participate in the survey, break-offs during the interview, and refusals to answer specific questions, or item omission. Table 11.1 is a quick reference that describes each type of nonresponse.

> ■ Nonresponse occurs when a respondent refuses to take part in a survey or fails to answer a question on the survey.

> ■ There are three types of nonresponse error: refusals to participate in the survey, break-offs during the interview, and refusals to answer specific questions (item omissions).

### Refusals to Participate in the Survey

A **refusal** occurs when a potential respondent flatly rejects the offer to take part in the survey. Refusal rates for telephone surveys are estimated to be as high as 50%.[11] The reasons for refusals are many and varied. The person may be busy, he or she may have no interest in the survey, something about the interviewer's voice or approach may have turned the person off, or the refusal may simply reflect how that person always responds to surveys. Some tactics that have been found to reduce the refusal rate include making an offer to call back at a more convenient time, identifying the name of the research company (and client if possible), making the interviews as short as possible, and emphasizing that the interviewer is not selling anything.[12]

> ■ Refusals to participate in surveys are increasing worldwide.

### Break-Offs During the Interview

A **break-off** occurs when a respondent reaches a certain point, and then decides not to answer any more questions for the survey. Reasons for break-offs, as you would expect, are varied. The interview may take longer than the respondent initially believed; the topic and specific questions may prove to be distasteful or too personal; the instructions may be too confusing; a sudden interruption may occur, or

> ■ If tired, confused, or uninterested, respondents may "break off" in the middle of an interview.

| Type | Description |
|---|---|
| Refusal | A prospective respondent declines to participate in the survey. |
| Break-off | A respondent stops answering somewhere in the middle of the survey. |
| Item omission | A respondent does not answer a particular question, but continues to answer following questions. |

**Table 11.1**

Three Types of Nonresponse Encountered in a Survey

Some respondents may refuse to answer certain questions.

the respondent may choose to take an incoming call on call-waiting and stop the interview. Sometimes with self-administered surveys, a researcher will find a questionnaire that the respondent has simply stopped filling out.

It is critical that well-trained interviewers be employed to carry out the surveys. In a discussion on how to improve respondent cooperation, Howard Gershowitz, senior vice president of MKTG, said, "I think the interviewers have to be taken out of the vacuum and be included in the process. Companies that are succeeding right now realize that the interviewers are the key to their success."[13] Increasingly, research providers are focusing on improved training techniques and field audits.

### Refusals to Answer Specific Questions (Item Omission)

Even if a failure to participate or break-off situation does not occur, a researcher will sometimes find that specific questions have lower response rates than others. If a marketing researcher suspects ahead of time that a particular question, such as the respondent's annual income for last year, will have some degree of refusals, it is appropriate to include the designation "refusal" on the questionnaire. It is not wise to put these designations on self-administered questionnaires, because respondents may use this option simply as a cop-out, when they might have provided accurate answers if the designation were not there. **"Item omission"** is the phrase often used to signify that some respondents refused to answer a particular question.

Occasionally, a respondent will refuse to answer a particular question that he or she considers too personal or a private matter.

### Completed Interview

You must define a "completed" interview.

As we learned earlier, researchers will experience both break-offs and item omissions. The researcher must make a judgment call as to what is a **completed interview** meaning that even though some questions are unanswered, a sufficient number are answered to allow the questionnaire to move into the data analysis stage. The determination will vary with each marketing research project. In some cases, it may be necessary that the respondent has answered all of the questions. In others, you may adopt some decision rule to allow you to define completed versus not completed interviews. For example, in most research studies there are questions directed at the primary purpose of the study. Also, there are usually questions asked for purposes of gaining additional insights into how respondents answered the primary questions. Such secondary questions often include a list of demographic questions. Demographics, because they are more personal in nature, are typically placed at the end of the questionnaire. Because they are not the primary focus of the study, a "completed interview" may be defined as one in which all the primary questions have been answered. In this way, you will have data for your primary questions and most of the data for your secondary questions. Interviewers can then be given a specific statement as to what constitutes a completed survey such as, "If the respondent answers through question 18, you may count it as a completion." (The demographics begin with question 19.) Likewise, the researcher must adopt a decision rule for determining the extent of item omissions necessary to invalidate a survey or a particular question.

## CODING DATA AND THE DATA CODE BOOK

After questionnaires are scrutinized and completed questionnaires are identified, the researcher moves to the data entry stage of the data analysis process. **Data entry** refers to the creation of a computer file that holds the raw data taken from all of the completed questionnaires. A number of data entry options exist, ranging from manual keyboard entry of each and every piece of data to computer systems that scan entire sets of questionnaires and convert them to a data file in a matter of minutes. The most seamless data entry situations are integrated questionnaire design and analysis software programs, such as Websurveyor, that capture each respondent's answers and convert them to computer files almost immediately.

Regardless of the method, data entry requires an operation called **data coding**, defined as the identification of code values that pertain to the possible responses for each question on the questionnaire. You learned about data coding in the questionnaire design chapter where we described this same operation as "precoding." Typically, these codes are numerical because numbers are quick and easy to input, and computers work with numbers more efficiently than they do with alphanumeric codes. In large-scale projects, and especially in cases in which the data entry is performed by a subcontractor, researchers utilize a **data code book** which identifies all of the variable names and code numbers associated with each possible response to each question that makes up the data set. With a code book that describes the data file, any analyst can work on the data set, regardless of whether or not that analyst was involved in the research project during its earlier stages.

Because precoded questionnaires have the response codes identified beside the various responses, it is a simple matter to create a code book. However, we just acknowledged the fact that the researcher will no doubt encounter item omission, so what is the code to use when a missing item is encountered? The answer is that it is best to use the same code for missing data on completed questionnaires, and the easiest and most acceptable code for a missing response is to use a blank, meaning that nothing is entered for that respondent on the question that was not answered. Practically all statistical analysis programs treat a blank as "missing."

Researchers utilize a data code book when preparing and working with a computer data file.

With online surveys, such as the ones that use Qualtrics, the data file is built as respondents submit their completed online questionnaires. That is, with a Web-based survey, the codes are programmed into the html questionnaire document, but they do not appear on the questionnaire as code numbers such as those customarily placed on a paper-and-pencil questionnaire. Questions that are not answered are typically entered as a "blank" into the online survey's data base unless the researcher preprograms the software to insert a different code number. In the case of Web-based surveys, the code book is vital as it is the researcher's only map to decipher the numbers found in the data file and to match them to the answers to the questions on the questionnaire.

# INTRODUCTION TO YOUR XL DATA ANALYST

You have downloaded and used a few of the features (such as sample size determination) in the XL Data Analyst that was created to accompany this textbook. It is now time to give you a formal introduction to the XL Data Analyst. We created the XL Data Analyst so you can perform and interpret data analyses with ease. There are four reasons why we created the XL Data Analyst. First, practically everyone is acquainted with the Excel spreadsheet program that is included in Microsoft's Office Suite, so there is no need to learn a new software program. Second, commercial statistical analysis programs typically produce reams of output that is very confusing and, frankly, unnecessary for basic marketing research. We have programmed our XL Data Analyst so the findings of your analyses are plainly evident. Granted, you will need to understand some basic statistical concepts, but you will not need to memorize formulas nor deal with statistical procedures. (However, if you or your instructor wishes to look at the statistical output, you may do so.) Third, the XL Data Analyst produces tables that can be copied and pasted into word processor applications such as Microsoft Word without the need for extensive reformatting into professionally appearing tables. There are also graphs you can use or modify and copy, or you can make your own graphs in Excel. Finally, by creating a macro system for Excel, we have avoided the added cost (to you) of including a statistical program with this textbook.

■ The XL Data Analyst allows you to use Microsoft Windows features seamlessly.

## How to Get Your Data Code Book into XL Data Analyst

■ To set up the XL Data Analyst, simply enter your data and code book as directed.

Your XL Data Analyst is a Microsoft Excel program with customized features designed to perform data analyses. We will systematically introduce you to these data analyses beginning in this chapter and continuing for the next three chapters of this textbook. We have set up the XL Data Analyst with a simulated data set pertaining to your "College Life E-Zine" integrated case. In other words, the code book information for your E-Zine case data set is in your XL Data Analyst.

However, you may wish to use a different survey data set such as a course team project or a data set provided to you by your instructor, so we will describe

**Table 11.2** How to Set Up Your Data and Code Book in XL Data Analyst

| Worksheet | What | How and Where |
|---|---|---|
| **Data** | Variables | Each variable occupies a separate column. |
| | Variable Labels | A unique descriptive word in Row 1 of each variable column (e.g., Gender) |
| | Data | Numbers in the various cells of each column |
| **Define Variables** | Variable Labels | Copy *all* Variable Labels you have placed in Row 1 of the Data worksheet and *Paste Special—Paste Link* into the Define Variables worksheet beginning at cell B1. (This one-time procedure will link your variable definitions to your data set.) |
| | Variable Descriptions | You can type in or paste* a long variable description for each variable in the cell beneath its variable label (e.g., Gender of the respondent). |
| | Value Codes | Type in or paste* the related code values beneath each variable label in Row 2 with the codes separated by commas (e.g., 1, 2). |
| | Value Labels | Type in or paste* your value labels beneath each set of Value Codes in Row 3 with the value labels separated by commas and in the same order as your value codes (e.g., Male, Female). |

*In pasting from a 2nd document (e.g., a Microsoft Word document) into the Define Variables worksheet, use the Match Destination Formatting paste option to invoke the wordwrap feature.

how to set up the XL Data Analyst with the code book information for any survey. In most data analysis situations, the code book information will be input to the data file so the analysis program can access it and apply it to whatever analysis is being performed. That is, a completed data set will include variable names, variable descriptions, data value codes and data value names—each of which will be defined for you very soon. Table 11.2 lists the steps that are necessary to set up your new data set such that XL Data Analyst will produce the most useful analyses. We will describe the various steps identified in Table 11.2.

Figure 11.1 is a dual screen capture of Excel with the XL Data Analyst installed and a data set in the **Data** worksheet. We have pasted the **Define Variables** worksheet window so you can view both worksheets at the same time. As you can see in the Data worksheet, the columns include labels in the first row, meaning that each column pertains to a variable in the survey. Each row represents a respondent or a completed questionnaire. The way you set up your code book in XL Data Analyst is through the "Define Variables" worksheet. When a researcher sets up the data set for the first time in XL Data Analyst, each variable can be defined in three ways. First, there *must* be a **variable label**, or a unique, short, single-word description for that variable placed in the first row on the Data worksheet. This row is then linked (via Copy—Paste Special—Paste Link) into the Data Variables worksheet starting at cell B1.

The Define Variables worksheet accommodates the researcher's data code book as follows. There should be a **variable description**, which is a phrase or sentence that identifies the variable in more detail and refers to the question on the

**Figure 11.1** The XL Data Analyst Data Worksheet Showing Variable Names and Coded Data

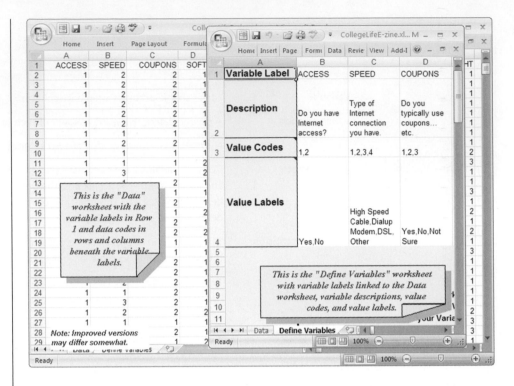

In addition to data, the XL Data Analyst requires variable labels and variable descriptions, and you can enter in value codes and value labels for categorical variables.

questionnaire. Then, depending on the nature of the variable, there can be **value codes** that are numerical values and **value labels**, which are responses that correspond to each data code number for that particular variable. You are not required to define your variables in XL Data Analyst; however, you will find that it will be much more convenient to use its menus and to read the various analyses results if you provide data labels and descriptions, and value codes and value labels where appropriate. Also, the data definition step is a one-time activity as XL Data Analyst will remember your data definitions as soon as you save your data set as an Excel file. You will see in Figure 11.1 that we have set up variable labels ACCESS, SPEED, COUPONS, and so forth with descriptions, value codes, and value labels. Note that there is a "Clean Up" utility to check your XL Data Analyst code book setup. Also, you can import a csv file if you have one.

PRACTICAL APPLICATIONS

Marketing researchers have turned to Microsoft Excel to manage data, and OzGrid Business Applications is a good example. They not only teach and tutor in Microsoft Excel, but they also use Microsoft Excel for marketing research on a daily basis. OzGrid has many clients who use their Excel add-ins to conduct marketing research. Their expert knowledge of Excel, combined with their industry experience ensures clients that OzGrid knows exactly the type of problems that are encountered in business today and how to properly analyze data to solve those problems. According to Raina Hawley of OzGrid, "Microsoft Excel is used widely in business for analyzing data for market research projects." Ms. Hawley states that "Many businesses collect data to help them make better business decisions and the use of Microsoft Excel can make the data analysis tasks simple and can automate what once took many labor-intensive hours of research."[14]

Raina Hawley oversees a staff member using Excel for a marketing research project at OzGrid.

Microsoft Excel is specifically designed for these sorts of tasks and has many useful and extremely powerful features that can aid businesses in their efforts to become successful in the marketplace. Microsoft Excel not only has many useful built-in features that can make market research easy but there are also many Microsoft Excel add-ins available on the market that have been or can be tailored to suit a company's needs. An add-in is a software product that adds extra functionality to an existing application, such as Microsoft Excel. The XL Data Analyst is an add-in that we developed to help make Microsoft Excel more useful to you for marketing research purposes. OzGrid Business Applications is far more extensive as it offers hundreds of Excel add-ins and business software designed for data analysis in all market areas through their website at **www.ozgrid.com**. OzGrid Business Applications provides training and tutoring in all aspects of Excel and Visual Basic Applications Excel, enabling their clients to become proficient users of this Microsoft Office tool.

## TYPES OF DATA ANALYSES USED IN MARKETING RESEARCH

We will show you how to use the XL Data Analyst to perform summarization analyses, but first we would like to provide you with a little background about data analyses. The complimentary processes of data coding and data entry result in a **data set**, defined as a matrix of numbers and other representations that includes all of the relevant answers of all the respondents in a survey. (You can see part of the E-Zine data set in Figure 11.1.) The researcher uses computer tools to perform various types of **data analysis**, which is defined as the process of describing a data set by computing a small number of measures that characterize the data set in ways that are meaningful to the client.[15] Data analysis accomplishes one or more of the following functions: (1) it summarizes the data, (2) it generalizes sample findings to

■ Data analysis is used to satisfy the objectives of description, generalization, differences, and relationships.

the population, (3) it compares for meaningful differences, and (4) it relates underlying patterns.[16] In other words, we are saying that there are four types of analysis objectives: description, generalization, differences, and relationships that match up with our four data analysis functions.

Now, we are going to describe the appropriate type of data analysis a researcher uses in the case of each of the four research objective types. We have developed Table 11.3 as a handy reference and also as a way to preview the various data analyses described in your textbook.

This section is an introduction to data analysis, so we will not delve into the specifics of each analysis type. But it is important to provide you with a road map of what analyses are used by researchers, and more important, when they are used. Here is a simple example that we will use throughout this section. As you know from your own experiences with unsolicited "junk" mail, credit card companies

**Table 11.3**  Research Objectives and Appropriate Types of Data Analysis

| Research Objective | Description of Analysis Appropriate to Objective | American Express College Student Survey Example |
|---|---|---|
| Description | Summarizing the sample data with:<br><br>▪ Percentages and Percentage Distribution (categorical data)<br>▪ Averages, Range, and Standard Deviation (metric data)<br>(Chapter 11) | A total of 74% of the respondents used a credit card in the past month, and the average total credit card charge was $152. |
| Generalization | Generalizing the sample findings to the population with:<br><br>▪ Hypothesis Tests<br>▪ Confidence Intervals<br>(Chapter 12) | American Express managers believed that 40% of college students own an American Express card, but this was not supported. Actually, between 18% and 28% own one. |
| Differences | Comparing averages or percents in the sample data to see if there are meaningful differences with:<br><br>▪ Percentage Difference Tests<br>▪ Averages Difference Tests<br>(Chapter 13) | A total of 25% of male college students own an American Express card, which was significantly different from 20% of female college students. However, female college students charged an average of $64, significantly more than men who charged an average of $42 on their American Express card last month. |
| Relationships | Relating variables to each other in a meaningful way with:<br><br>▪ Crosstabulations<br>▪ Correlations<br>▪ Regression Analysis<br>(Chapter 14) | College students who own American Express cards were more likely to be attending professional schools and living off campus. They earned more income than nonowners. The target market for American Express is male and female students attending private rather than public schools. |

American Express wants a summary of college students who are likely to own and use its credit card.

target college students, and they are quite successful for the most part.[17] However, one credit card company, American Express, lags far behind the other cards with respect to college student market share. So, we will take a case of a survey that American Express has commissioned to better understand the college student credit card market. (Our example here is fictitious, but we know you can relate to this example of college students' use of credit cards just as you could relate to the College Life E-Zine integrated case described in this textbook.) The survey affects a representative sample of college students from public and private universities. In Table 11.3, we have included an example of each data analysis type in the American Express survey, and we will provide more examples in the following discussions.

Now, let's connect these four objectives to their proper data analyses. But, before we do so, we need to remember an important distinction about the scales used by this researcher in the survey. In Chapter 8 we introduced you to categorical and metric scales. Recall that categorical scales have a level of measurement such that they place respondents into groups such as gender (male versus female), buyer type (buyer versus nonbuyer), marital status (single, married, separated, divorced, and so on), yes/no, and the like. A metric scale is one where the respondent indicates an amount or quantity such as how many times, how much, how long, or his or her feelings on a synthetic metric scale such as a Likert scale (disagree-agree) or a five-point anchored scale. Also in Chapter 8, we introduced you to the notion that the level of measurement dictates the *proper* data analysis. With this background revisited, we are ready to briefly describe the four types of data analysis.

■ Each data analysis type is illustrated with our American Express card example.

## Summarizing the Sample Data

With description research objectives, the researcher will summarize the data in the sample with the use of percentages or averages. In Chapter 8, we noted that if the variable under consideration is categorical, the proper summary analysis is a percentage distribution, while with a metric variable, the proper summary analysis is an average. Turning to our American Express example, two of its description

■ Summarization of data is accomplished with percents and averages.

objectives might be: (1) Do college students use credit cards and (2) if so, how much do they spend on credit card purchases per month? To summarize the data, the researcher would determine the following in the sample: (1) the percent of students who own a certain credit card and (2) the average dollars of purchases on their credit cards per month as we have computed in Table 11.3. We will describe data summarization in much greater detail later in this chapter.

## Generalizing the Findings

■ Generalization of findings is performed with hypothesis tests and/or confidence intervals.

As would be expected, the researcher will desire to generalize his or her findings so they make statements about the population that the sample represents. Generalization means that the researcher will conduct hypotheses tests and/or compute confidence intervals. Returning to our American Express survey example, the researcher could test the actual percent of students who own an American Express credit card against what the American Express executives believe is the actual percent. That is, if the American Express execs believe that 40% of college students currently own an American Express credit card, the researcher could test his or her sample percent of respondents against 40% to see if the executives' belief is supported or refuted. If this hypothesis is refuted, the researcher can compute a confidence interval as to the actual percentage of ownership of the American Express card. In Table 11.3, you will discover that the researcher found no support for the American Express executives' belief, and in fact, the researcher estimated that between 18% to 28% of college students own an American Express credit card. We will describe these two generalization data analyses in Chapter 12.

## Seeking Meaningful Differences

■ Differences analysis is done by comparing percentages or averages.

Often clients, and consequently researchers, are very interested in finding meaningful differences between groups in the sample. Such differences, when found, can offer important marketing strategy insights. With differences analysis, the researcher identifies a categorical variable (such as gender) and compares the groups represented by that variable (males versus females) by analyzing their differences on a second variable. If the second variable is categorical (use or nonuse of our brand), then the researcher will perform a percentages differences analysis; but if the second variable is metric (how many purchases in the past month), the researcher will perform an averages differences test of some sort. In our American Express survey example, the American Express executives may be interested in determining differences between male and female students, so the researcher would perform a differences test for American Express card ownership (categorical) and one for dollars spent per month (metric), comparing males to females (categorical). In Table 11.3, you will find that more male college students own American Express cards than female students, but the female students spend more per month than the male students using their American Express card. We describe differences tests in Chapter 13.

## Identifying Relationships

■ Relationship analysis involves crosstabulations, correlations, or regression analysis.

Finally, a client may wish to have a better understanding of the topics under study. The researcher can tackle relationship analysis in one of two ways. For one, he or she isolates two variables, and if the two variables are categorical, he or she will

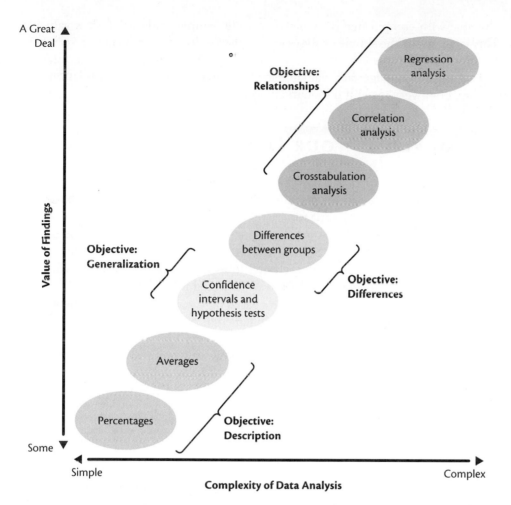

perform crosstabulation analysis, but if the two variables are metric, correlations will be used. Or the researcher may select several variables to see how they are related to a single critical variable, such as how demographics and lifestyle figure into the client's target market definition. In this case, the researcher will use regression analysis. Relationship analysis could be used to investigate student gender and American Express recognition (crosstabulation), credit card dollar expenditures and number of credit cards owned (correlation), or perhaps to determine the college student demographic and/or lifestyle factors that relate to how appealing American Express's credit card is to college students (regression). Table 11.3 notes some relationships: Specifically, college student American Express cardholders tend to be majoring in professional school curricula, they live off campus, they make more income, and attend private schools. We devote Chapter 14 to relationship analyses.

We have provided Figure 11.2 as a handy visual aid and a reference figure for you to use later as you become more familiar with the various types of data analyses. In it, we have identified two axes that underlie data analyses in general. The horizontal axis relates to the complexity of the analysis. Data analyses range from those that are very simple to those that are fairly complex. Figure 11.2 reveals that percentages are the most elementary, while regression analysis is the most complicated type of analysis you will encounter in this textbook. The vertical axis we have labeled "Value of Findings," meaning that the findings of the analysis are more valuable with complicated data analyses, while simple analyses are less valuable. This is not to say the simple analyses are not useful, for they are vital to researchers. However, as you move up the analysis balloons in Figure 11.2, the findings are typically more managerially valuable as they uncover patterns and relationships that are often very insightful to marketing managers.

# SUMMARIZING YOUR SAMPLE FINDINGS

As promised, this chapter will now delve into summarization analysis, which is the type of data analysis appropriate for description research objectives. The basic data analysis goal with all summarization is to report as few pieces of information as possible that describe the most typical response to a question. At the same time, it is vital to summarize the degree to which all of the respondents share this typical response. The typical response is referred to as the **central tendency**,[18] while the expression of how typical respondents are is referred to as **variability**.

> ■ The typical response is referred to as the central tendency.

There are two basic types of variables based on their level of measurement: categorical and metric. Because there are fundamental differences between these two, the summarization analysis is different. As a memory aid, we have prepared Table 11.4, which tells you what analysis to perform for the central tendency and the variability for categorical versus metric variables. The following sections will describe in detail the appropriate ways to summarize categorical and metric variables.

## Summarizing Categorical Variables

When the researcher is working with a variable that is at the categorical level of measurement, the appropriate central tendency to use is the mode. The **mode** is a summarization analysis measure defined as the value in a string of values that occurs most often. In other words, if you scanned a list of code numbers constituting a column for a categorical variable in a data matrix, the mode would be the number that appeared more than any other.

> ■ The number that occurs most in a set of numbers is referred to as the mode.

You should note that the mode is a relative measure of central tendency, for it does not require that a majority of responses occurred for this value. Instead, it simply specifies the value that occurs most frequently, and there is no requirement that this occurrence is 50% or more. It can take on any value as long as it is the most frequently occurring number. If a tie for the mode occurs, the distribution is considered to be "bimodal." Or it might even be "trimodal" if there is a three-way tie.

**Table 11.4**

Appropriate Summarization Analyses by Type of Scale

| Type of Scale | Central Tendency (characterizes the most typical response) | Variability (indicates how similar the responses are) |
|---|---|---|
| **Categorical Scale** (indicates a group) | Mode | Frequency or Percentage Distribution |
| **Metric Scale** (indicates an amount or quantity) | Average | Range and/or Standard Deviation |

Variability indicates how different respondents are on a common topic such as buying fresh vegetables.

In truth, summarizing the mode (or modes) is not very informative with respect to relating how typical the mode is. It is better to summarize the variability of responses to a categorical question, using a **percentage distribution**, or a summary of the percent of times each and every category appears for the entire sample. Occasionally, a **frequency distribution**, a summary of the *number* of times each and every category appears for the entire sample, is used, but a percentage distribution is much more intuitive since all of its categories will sum to 100%. Frequencies themselves are raw counts, and these frequencies are easily converted into percentages for ease of comparison. The conversion is arrived at very simply through a quick division of the frequency for each value by the total number of observations for all of the values, resulting in a percentage distribution. Glancing at a percentage distribution, a researcher or a client can easily assess the mode and the variability.

In sum, a frequency or percentage distribution affords an accounting of the responses to a categorical scale question in a data set. It quickly communicates all of the different answers in the set, and it expresses how much agreement or disagreement there is among the respondents. That is, it expresses the variability of their responses. The percentage distribution is often used here because percentages are intuitive and easy to work with. Figure 11.3 illustrates how quickly percentage distributions

■ With categorical data, one should use a frequency distribution or a percentage distribution to summarize the findings.

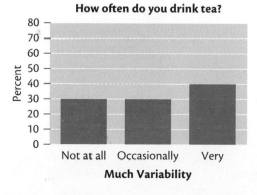

**Much Variability**

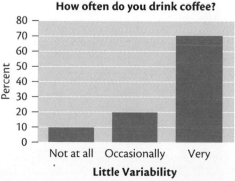

**Little Variability**

**Figure 11.3** A Bar Chart Shows Variability

communicate variability when they are converted to bar charts. For instance, if our percentage distribution happened to have a great deal of agreement in it, it would appear as a very steep, spike-shaped histogram such as the one for our "little variability" bar graph (drinking coffee); however, if the set happened to be made up of many dissimilar numbers, the bar graph would be much more spread out, with small peaks and valleys. This is the case with the "much variability" bar graph (drinking tea).

▓ Convert percentage distributions to bar charts to "see" the variability in the data.

# HOW TO SUMMARIZE CATEGORICAL VARIABLES WITH XL DATA ANALYST

To access the XL Data Analyst menu, simply click on the XL Data Analyst option on your Excel program menu and move your cursor over "Summarize." This will activate the drop-down menu under Summarize to reveal two options: "Percents" and "Averages." Since we are now dealing with categorical variables, the correct selection is "Percent." As you can see in Figure 11.4, a click on the Percent menu item will open up a selection window that you can use to select variables from your E-Zine data set. Notice that you can use the check box to have a pie graphs (Create Graph) generated along with the tables for the variables you select. When you have completed your selection by moving the variable(s) into the selected variables pane, a click on the "OK" button will cause XL Data Analyst to perform the percents summarization analysis.

▓ To summarize a variable using the XL Data Analyst, use the "Summarize" menu command.

Figure 11.5 shows the percents table generated by XL Data Analyst. As you can see, we have the variable with the description of "Respondent's classification." The result is a table with this description included in the table heading, the value labels

**Figure 11.4** Using the XL Data Analyst to Select Variables for Percents Analysis

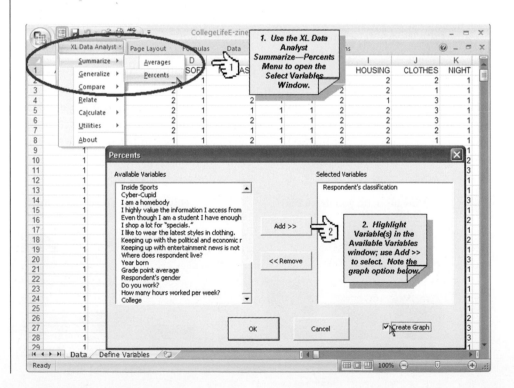

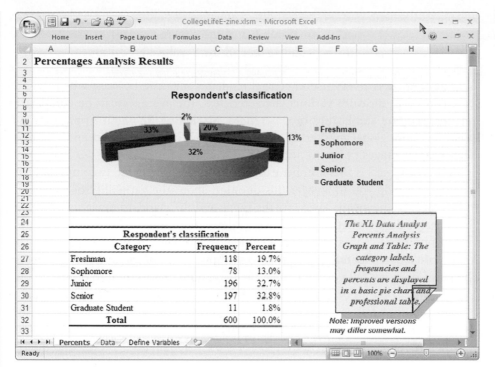

**Figure 11.5** XL Data Analyst Percents Analysis Table

such as "Freshman," "Sophomore," etc. are noted, and the frequencies and percentages are displayed. The table is formatted with a professional appearance, and you can copy and paste it into a research report or a presentation software program such as Microsoft PowerPoint. You can use Excel chart features or a chart template to create a stunning graphical presentation[19] of the findings with any XL Data Analyst percentage analysis. This work, as well, can be copied into a final report, PowerPoint, or any other compatible Windows program of your choice.

## Summarizing Metric Variables

When the researcher deals with metric variables, he or she knows that the numbers are more than mere codes. Instead, the numbers in metric variable columns in a data matrix represent real amounts reflecting quantities rather than categories. Even working with a synthetic metric variable where a labeled or number scale is used, the researcher knows that the numbers express amounts of feelings, evaluations, or opinions on the parts of the respondents. If you were given the task of identifying the central tendency number that typified all of the responses to a metric variable, you would soon realize that the best measure would be the **average**. As you can see in the formula, the average is computed by summing all of the numbers and dividing that sum by the number of respondents whose responses were included in that sum. The resulting number is the average or mean, a measure that indicates the central tendency of those values. It approximates the typical value in the set.

$$\overline{x} = \frac{\sum\limits_{i=1}^{n} x_i}{n}$$

◀ **Formula for an average**

■ With a metric variable, use the average as the measure of central tendency.

where:  $x_i$ = each individual value
 $n$ = total number of cases (sample size)
 $\Sigma$ = signifies that all the $x_i$ values are summed

The average is a very useful central tendency measure because when the same scale is used to measure various characteristics, the averages can be compared to quickly ascertain similarities or differences. Marketing Research Application 11.1 illustrates how global marketing research is quickly summarized and communicated using averages.[20]

But how typical is this number called the average? There are two summarization analyses that help you to answer this question about the variability of respondents with respect to the mean. These are the range and the standard deviation. The **range** identifies the distance between the lowest value (minimum) and the highest values in a set of numbers. That is, the range identifies the maximum and the minimum, and you can do a quick mental calculation to see how many metric units are in between. The range does not tell you how often the maximum and minimum occurred, but it does provide some information on the dispersion by indicating how far apart the extremes are found. If you find that the range is very narrow, you know that the average is typical of many respondents, but if you find the range to be very wide, it signals that the average is probably not typical of most respondents. You have to interpret "very narrow" and "very wide" in the units of the variable under study. For example, a range of 100 cents might seem to be a large number, but if you are summarizing

■ The range identifies the smallest and the largest value in a set of numbers.

## MARKETING RESEARCH APPLICATION 11.1

### Plot Averages on a Graph to Communicate Them Effectively

In global marketing, there is a debate as to whether a local country brand (national brand), a local private brand, or a global brand name is most effective. To investigate this issue, researchers in Israel asked consumers to rate shampoo on nine different product characteristics using a 1 to 7 scale where 1 meant the lowest rating and 7 corresponded to the highest rating. The respondents rated three types of brands: private, national, and global. The averages were calculated and plotted as shown on the accompanying line graph.

The graph clearly shows that local private brands are at a disadvantage to national and global brand names in all but one characteristic. However, global brands are seen as more

expensive (low rating on price). Global brands are attractive to consumers who are least price sensitive, whereas local country private brands are attractive to those consumers who are price sensitive.

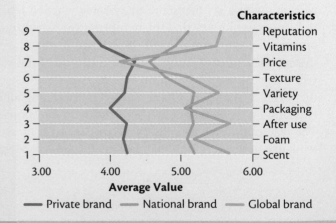

how much your respondents paid for their last Amazon.com book purchase, it would be quite small as it would represent only one dollar.

While the range is informative about the variability of responses to a metric question, it is very ambiguous as it does not tell anything about how respondents are spread across the range. For instance, are there a great many respondents whose answers are near or at the outer limits? Are there very few of them at the limits? What about the intervals between the mean and the minimum and the maximum: How are respondents situated in their answers in these intervals? The range offers no clues whatsoever as to the answers to these questions that researchers and clients sometimes ask.

To answer these important questions that one can ask about the summarization of metric data, there is another variability measure that researchers rely on, and this measure is the standard deviation. The **standard deviation** indicates the degree of variability in the metric values in such a way as to be translatable into a normal or bell-shaped curve distribution. Although marketing researchers do not always rely on the normal curve interpretation of the standard deviation, they often encounter the standard deviation on computer printouts, and they usually report it in their tables. So, it is worthwhile to digress for a moment to discuss this statistical concept.

▪ The standard deviation is a measure of variability that uses a normal or bell-shaped curve interpretation.

First, let's take a look at how a standard deviation is calculated. We have provided the formula below.

$$\text{Standard Deviation} = \sqrt{\frac{\sum\limits_{n}^{i=1}(x_i - \overline{x})^2}{n-1}}$$

◀ **Formula for a standard deviation**

where:

$x_i$ = each individual value
$\overline{x}$ = average
$n$ = total number of cases (sample size)

If you study this formula, you will realize that you first calculate the average, then you compare each respondent's value to the average by subtracting the average from it, and square that difference. It may seem strange to you to square differences, add them up, divide them by $(n-1)$, and then take the square root. However, if we did not square the differences, we would have positive and negative values, and if we summed them, there would be a cancellation effect. That is, large negative differences would cancel out large positive differences, and the numerator would end up being close to zero. But this result is contrary to what we know is the case with large differences: There is variation, which is expressed by the standard deviation. The formula remedies this problem by squaring the subtracted differences before they are summed. Squaring converts all negative numbers to positives and, of course, leaves the positives positive. Next, all of the squared differences are summed and divided by 1 less than the number of total observations in the string of values (1 is subtracted from the number of observations to achieve what is typically called an "unbiased" estimate of the standard deviation). But we now have an inflation factor to worry about because every comparison has been squared. To adjust for this, the equation specifies that the square root be taken after all other operations are performed. This final step adjusts the value back down to the original measure (e.g., units rather than squared units). By the way, if you did not take the square root at the end, the value would be referred to as the "variance." In other words, the variance is the standard deviation squared.

Now that you know how to compute a standard deviation, it is time to review the properties of a normal curve. Table 11.5 shows the properties of a bell-shaped or

**Table 11.5**

Normal Curve
Interpretation of
Standard Deviation

| Number of Standard Deviations from the Mean | Percent of Area Under Curve[a] | Percent of Area to Right (or Left)[b] |
|---|---|---|
| ±1.00 | 68% | 16.0% |
| ±1.96 | 95% | 2.5% |
| ±2.58 | 99% | 0.5% |

[a] This is the area under the curve with the number of standard deviations as the lower (left-hand) and upper (right-hand) limits and the mean equidistant from the limits.

[b] This is the area left outside of the limits described by plus or minus the number of standard deviations. Because of the normal curve's symmetric properties, the area remaining below the lower limit (left-hand tail) is exactly equal to the area remaining above the upper limit (right-hand tail).

normal distribution of values. As we have indicated in our chapter on sample size determination, the usefulness of this model is apparent when you realize that it is a symmetric distribution: Exactly 50% of the distribution lies on either side of the midpoint (the apex of the curve). With a normal curve, the midpoint is also the average. Standard deviations are standardized units of measurement that are located on the horizontal axis. They relate directly to assumptions about the normal curve. For example, the range of one standard deviation above and one standard deviation below the midpoint includes 68% of the total area underneath that curve. Because the bell-shaped distribution is a theoretical or ideal concept, this property never changes. Moreover, the proportion of area under the curve and within plus or minus any number of standard deviations from the mean is perfectly known.

For the purposes of this presentation, normally only two or three of these values are of interest to marketing researchers. Specifically, ± 2.58 standard deviations describes the range in which 99% of the area underneath the curve is found, ± 1.96 standard deviations is associated with 95% of the area underneath the curve, and ± 1.64 standard deviations corresponds to 90% of the bell-shaped curve's area. We have provided Figure 11.6 as a visual aid to the ± 1.96 standard deviations case that accounts for 95% of the area under the curve.

> ±2.58 standard deviations pertains to 99%, while ±1.96 standard deviations pertains to 95% of the area under a bell-shaped curve.

Whenever a standard deviation is reported along with an average, a specific picture should appear in your mind. Assuming that the distribution is bell shaped, the size of the standard deviation number helps you envision how similar or dissimilar the typical responses are to the average. If the standard deviation is small, the distribution is greatly compressed. On the other hand, with a large standard deviation value, the distribution is consequently stretched out at both ends.

As you might guess, marketing researchers are very comfortable with averages, percentages, standard deviations, and other statistical concepts. However, managers for whom marketing researchers work do not have the same comfort level, and it is entirely possible that a manager may misinterpret a marketing researcher's statements. For instance, if the researcher says, "The modal answer was 4," the manager might think that most or all of the respondents gave this answer. When the researcher says, "The standard deviation was 11.2," the manager may have no comprehension of what the researcher is telling him or her. Ethical research companies may use any or a combination of the following to ensure that their client managers understand the analysis terminology used by its researchers: (1) prepared handbooks or glossaries

ETHICS

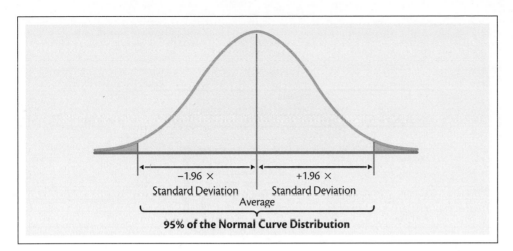

**Figure 11.6** A Normal Curve with Its 95% Properties Identified

defining marketing research terms, (2) appendices in reports that illustrate analysis concepts, (3) definitions of analysis terms embedded in reports when the manager first encounters them, or (4) footnotes or annotations with tables and figures that explain the analysis concepts used.

## HOW TO SUMMARIZE METRIC VARIABLES WITH XL DATA ANALYST

The procedure for summarizing metric variables in XL Data Analyst is identical to the one for summarizing categorical variables, except you will select "Averages" as this is the proper analysis for a metric variable. That is, click on the XL Data Analyst option on your Excel program menu and move your cursor over "Summarize." This will activate the drop-down menu under Summarize to reveal "Percents" and "Averages." Since we are now dealing with metric variables, the correct selection is "Averages." A click on the Averages menu item will open up a standard Excel selection window that you can use to select one or more metric variables. When you have completed your selection, a click on the "OK" button will cause XL Data Analyst to perform the Averages Summarization analysis. In other words, the XL Data Analyst selection procedure for Averages is identical to that for Percents, and the variables selection window looks the same as the selection window for percents that you saw in Figure 11.4, but without the Create Graph option.

To summarize a metric variable with the XL Data Analyst, use the Summarize-Averages command sequence.

Figure 11.7 shows the Averages tables generated by XL Data Analyst for the College Life E-Zine survey grade-point average variable. As you can see, this table is quite different from the Percents table, because metric data summarization involves the average, standard deviation, and range (minimum and maximum). The table in Figure 11.7 reveals that the average GPA of our 600 respondents is 2.6, while the standard deviation is .4, and the minimum and maximum are 1.5 and 4.0, respectively. If you select more than one metric variable, the variables will be included in the same table as it is most efficient to present them in this format, and the variables will be sorted in descending order

**Figure 11.7** XL Data Analyst Average Analysis Table

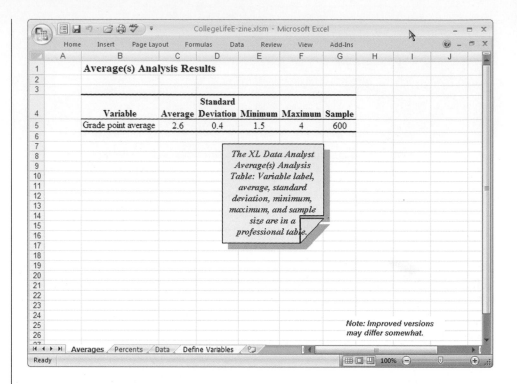

with the variable that has the highest average listed first, and the variable with the lowest average listed last. If you want to make a graph, say comparing the means of selected metric variables, you can easily create one with the Excel chart feature and use the averages in the Averages table.

## THE SIX-STEP APPROACH TO DATA ANALYSIS AND PRESENTATION

While summarization analysis is straightforward and simple to understand, the data analyses that we will describe in subsequent chapters will be a bit more complicated. In our years of performing marketing research, and, more important, teaching students like yourself how to perform and interpret data analysis, we have decided that a step-by-step process that you can apply to all data analyses is a good approach. Moreover, we have found that students are often confused with the many data analysis choices that you will soon learn. Finally, when students do select the proper data analysis, they are always challenged with the intepretation of the findings, and they have difficulties trying to present the findings in a research report.

■ Our six-step approach simplifies data analysis and interpretation of your findings.

In our six-step approach to data analysis, we are linking research objectives, data analysis, interpretation, and presentation of the findings. The approach is presented in Table 11.6. Again, summarization is straightforward, so you may think that Table 11.6 is rather elementary; however, after you have learned four or five more data analyses, you will find our step-by-step approach to be a very useful resource. You will see the six-step approach to data analysis and presentation many times again as we will use it as a guide throughout our description of data analyses in the following chapters.

What is the average GPA of our College Life E-Zine survey respondents?

**Table 11.6**  The Six-Step Approach to Data Analysis for Description Objectives

| Step | Explanation | Example from Your E-Zine Integrated Case |
| --- | --- | --- |
| **1. What is the research objective?** | Determine that you are dealing with a **Description objective.**[*] | We want a profile of our sample. |
| **2. What questionnaire question(s) is/are Involved?** | Identify the question(s), and for each one specify if it is categorical or metric. | Where do you live? (categorical)<br>How many hours do you work per week? (metric) |
| **3. What is the appropriate analysis?** | For **Description objectives**, use Percents (Categorical) or Averages (Metric). | LIVE is categorical, so we will do percents.<br>WORKHRS is metric, so we will do the average. |
| **4. How do you run it?** | Use the proper XL Data Analyst analysis: With **Description objectives**, use Summarize—Percents or Summarize—Averages. | |

**Table 11.6** *(Continued)*

| Step | Explanation | Example from Your E-Zine Integrated Case |
|------|-------------|------------------------------------------|
| **5. How do you interpret the findings?** | For **Description objectives**, report the central tendency and the variability. (XL Data Analyst Averages table or Percentages table(s)). | See tables below |

**Where does respondent live?**

| Category | Frequency | Percent |
|----------|-----------|---------|
| On Campus | 97 | 16.2% |
| Off Campus | 503 | 83.8% |
| Total | 600 | 100.0% |

| Variable | Average | Standard Deviation | Minimum | Maximum | Sample |
|----------|---------|--------------------|---------|---------|--------|
| How many hours worked per week? | 10.1 | 11.9 | 0 | 40 | 600 |

| Step | Explanation | Example from Your E-Zine Integrated Case |
|------|-------------|------------------------------------------|
| **6. How do you write/present these findings?** | With percents, paste the Percents table and/or an Excel graph for each categorical variable you want to report. With averages, modify the table with the metric variables as you see fit. | See graph and table below |

**Where does respondent live?**

16% On Campus

84% Off Campus

| Variable | Average | Standard Deviation | Sample |
|----------|---------|--------------------|--------|
| How many hours worked per week? | 10.1 | 11.9 | 600 |

\*You will learn about other analyses in subsequent chapters.

# SUMMARY

This chapter introduced you to some important issues about data collection, specifically types of errors that can occur during this step in the marketing research process. You learned about nonresponse errors, and how researchers deal with them. Next, the data entry process was described, and you read about the code book concept that researchers use to associate numbers in data sets with response categories and scales on questionnaires. As a prelude to summarization analysis, we first described the coding system and the code book that researchers maintain to translate the responses to a questionnaire into a workable data set. You became acquainted with XL Data Analyst, the Excel Analysis Macro System developed for this textbook, and you can now set up an XL Data Analyst data set with labeled variables. We next previewed the four types of statistical analysis: summarizing, generalizing, relating differences, and identifying relationships.

The bulk of the chapter took up summarization analyses, and it was pointed out that with a categorical variable, the proper analysis is to have XL Data Analyst create a percentage distribution where the mode can be quickly identified as the "typical" response. A pie or bar chart is a great visual aid for percentage distributions. In the case of a metric variable, the proper analysis is to have XL Data Analyst compute the average as the "typical" value, and the standard deviation and range are provided as clues to the variability of the responses. Finally, we introduced you to the six-step approach to data analysis and presentation that will be used throughout the analysis chapters in the textbook.

## KEY TERMS

Nonsampling errors (p. 321)
Fieldworkers (p. 321)
Intentional fieldworker errors (p. 321)
Unintentional fieldworker errors
   (p. 321)
Respondent errors (p. 321)
Intentional respondent errors (p. 321)
Unintentional respondent errors
   (p. 321)
Multiple submissions (p. 322)
Bogus respondents and responses
   (p. 322)
Population misrepresentation (p. 322)
Nonresponse (p. 323)
Refusal (p. 323)
Break-off (p. 323)
"Item omission" (p. 324)
Completed interview (p. 324)

Data entry (p. 325)
Data coding (p. 325)
Data code book (p. 325)
Variable label (p. 327)
Variable description (p. 327)
Value codes (p. 328)
Value labels (p. 328)
Data set (p. 329)
Data analysis (p. 329)
Central tendency (p. 334)
Variability (p. 334)
Mode (p. 334)
Percentage distribution (p. 335)
Frequency distribution (p. 335)
Average (p. 337)
Range (p. 338)
Standard deviation (p. 339)

## REVIEW QUESTIONS

1  What types of errors can occur during data collection?
2  Describe the various kinds of nonresponse that a researcher may encounter with a survey.
3  Indicate what data entry is and how data coding relates to data entry.
4  What is a data set and how does it appear in Excel?

5  How does one define the variables in an Excel data set so that the XL Data Analyst system will produce the most useful output?

6  Define and differentiate each of the types of data analysis.

7  What is the relationship of the four types of research objectives and the four types of data analysis?

8  What is meant by the term *central tendency*? Why is the central tendency an incomplete summarization of a variable?

9  When summarizing a categorical variable, what is the proper measure of central tendency, and why is it the proper measure?

10  When summarizing a metric variable, what is the proper measure of central tendency, and why is it the proper measure?

11  When summarizing a categorical variable, what is the proper measure of variability, and why is it the proper measure?

12  Describe how a percentage distribution is computed.

13  Describe how a standard deviation is computed.

14  When summarizing a metric variable, what is the proper measure of variability, and why is it the proper measure?

15  With reference to the formula, show how the standard deviation takes into account the typicality of every respondent.

16  What is the relationship between a standard deviation and a normal curve?

# APPLICATION QUESTIONS

17  In a survey on magazine subscriptions, respondents write in the number of magazines they subscribe to regularly. What measures of central tendency can be used? Which is the most appropriate and why?

18  A manager has commissioned research on a special marketing problem. He is scheduled to brief the board of directors on the problem's resolution in video conference tomorrow morning. The research director works late that night in the downtown San Francisco headquarters and completes the summarization data analysis, which will be sufficient for the presentation. However, less than an hour before the meeting, the manager calls him for an early-morning briefing on the survey's basic findings. The researcher looks around in his office and an idea flashes in his head. He immediately grabs a blank questionnaire. What is he about to do to facilitate the quick communication of the study's basic findings to the manager?

19  A professor asks his students how many hours they studied for the last exam. He finds that the class average is 10.5 hours and the standard deviation is 1.5 hours. The minimum is 2 hours, and the maximum is 20 hours. How would you describe the typical student's study time for this professor's last exam?

20  In a survey, Valentine's Day rose buyers are asked to indicate what color of roses they purchased for their special friends. The following table summarizes the findings.

| What color roses did you purchase last Valentine's Day? | | |
|---|---|---|
| Category | Frequency | Percent |
| Yellow Roses | 66 | 17.1% |
| White Roses | 78 | 20.3% |
| Red Roses | 159 | 41.3% |
| Mixed colors | 82 | 21.3% |
| **Total** | 385 | 100.0% |

Describe the central tendency and variability apparent in this analysis.

**21** An entrepreneur is thinking about opening an upscale restaurant. To help assess the market size, a researcher conducts a survey of individuals in the geographic target market who patronize upscale restaurants. The findings of the descriptive analysis for two questions on the survey follow.

| Variable | Average | Standard Deviation | Minimum | Maximum | Sample |
|---|---|---|---|---|---|
| Total amount spent in upscale restaurants per month | $150.11 | $32.72 | $5 | $250 | 400 |
| Average price expected to pay for an entree in an upscale restaurant | $28.87 | $5.80 | $16 | $60 | 340 |

Describe the central tendency and variability apparent in this analysis.

# INTERACTIVE LEARNING

Visit the textbook website at **www.prenhall.com/burnsbush**. For this chapter, use the self-study quizzes and get instant feedback on whether or not you need additional studying. You can also review the chapter's major points by visiting the chapter outline and key terms.

## CASE 11.1 ||| IHOP Improvement Survey

Mary Yu graduated from college in June 2003. On graduation, she took a job as a marketing research assistant with the International House of Pancakes, known as "IHOP" and headquartered in Glendale, California. When Mary began working, the marketing research department was in the middle of a huge telephone survey of IHOP patrons across North America. The objectives of the survey included: (1) determine how often and what time of day people eat at IHOP, (2) how satisfied they are with selected aspects of IHOP, (3) how satisfied they are overall with IHOP, (4) what IHOP advertising they recall, and (5) a demographic profile of the respondents.

Mary was assigned the responsibility of data analysis because she was fresh out of college. She was informed that IHOP headquarters uses a statistical analysis program called SYSStats for its data analysis. All of the 5,000 respondents' answers have been put into the computer, and all that is left is for someone to use SYSStats to perform the necessary analyses. Of course, someone has to interpret the results, too. It is Mary's responsibility to do the analysis and to interpret it. The questionnaire designers created a code sheet of the scales used in the survey. This code book is duplicated in the following table:

| Variable | Response Scale Used (data code) |
|---|---|
| Age | Actual age in years |
| Family income | Ranges in $10,000 increments male, female |
| Marital status | Single (1), married (2), other (3) |
| Family size | Number of adults; number of children under 18 living at home |
| How often they eat at IHOP | Estimated number of times per month |
| Time of day they are most likely to use IHOP | Early morning (1), midmorning (2), late morning (3), noontime (4), early afternoon (5), midafternoon (6), late afternoon (7), early evening (8), late evening (9), around midnight (10), in the wee small hours (11) |
| Satisfaction with aspects of IHOP | "Poor," "Fair," "Good," "Very Good," or "Excellent" (coded 1, 2, 3, 4, 5, respectively) |
| Overall satisfaction with IHOP | "Extremely satisfied," "Somewhat satisfied," "Neither Satisfied nor Dissatisfied," "Somewhat Dissatisfied," or "Extremely Dissatisfied" (coded 5, 4, 3, 2, 1, respectively) |
| Recall of IHOP Advertising | Yes or no for each of 8 different advertising media: television, radio, Internet, billboards, coupons, store sign, flyer, and/or phone book ad. (coded 0="No," 1="Yes") |

1 What type of descriptive data analysis should Mary instruct SYSStats to perform to determine basic patterns in the factors listed on the code sheet? For each variable, identify the type of descriptive analysis, describe its aspects, and indicate why it is appropriate.

2 Give an example of what each analysis result might "look like" and how it should be interpreted.

| CASE 11.2 | ||| | **Your Integrated Case** |
|---|---|---|

### The College Life E-Zine Survey Summarization Analysis

Bob Watts was happy to inform Sarah, Anna, Wesley, and Don that the College Life E-Zine survey data were collected and ready for analysis. Bob had other marketing research projects and meetings scheduled with present and prospective clients, so he called in his marketing intern, Lori Baker. Lori was a senior marketing major at State U., and she had taken marketing research in the previous semester. Lori had "aced" this class, which she enjoyed a great deal. Her professor had invited Bob Watts to give a talk on "a typical day in the life of a marketer researcher," and Lori had approached Bob the very next day about a marketing research internship. Like every dedicated marketing major, Lori had kept her Burns and Bush marketing research basics textbook and her XL Data Analyst software for future reference. Bob called Lori into his office and said, "Lori, it is time to do some analysis on the survey we did for the College Life E-Zine project. For now, let's just get a feel for what the data look like. I'll leave it up to your judgment as to what basic analysis to run. Let's meet tomorrow at 2:30 P.M. and see what you have found."

Your task in Case 11.2 is to take the role of Lori Baker, marketing intern. As we indicated in this chapter, the College Life E-Zine data set is included with your XL Data Analyst software that accompanies this textbook. We have used this data set in some of the examples of various types of descriptive analysis in this chapter. Now, it is time for you to use the XL Data Analyst on these and other variables in the College Life E-Zine survey data set.

1  Determine what variables are categorical, perform the appropriate descriptive analysis, and interpret it.
2  Determine what variables are metric scales, perform the appropriate descriptive analysis, and interpret it.

## CHAPTER 12

# GENERALIZING YOUR SAMPLE FINDINGS TO THE POPULATION

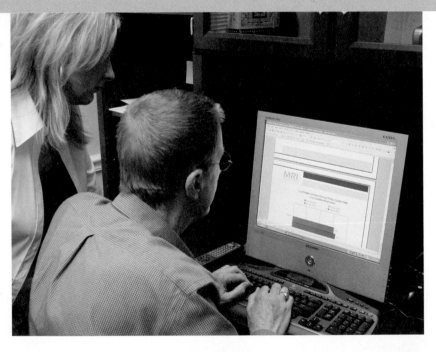

## GENERALIZING A SAMPLE STATISTIC TO THE TOTAL POPULATION AT MRI, MARKET RESEARCH INSIGHT

The photo to the left shows Verne Kennedy and Kim Alford of MRI calculating a confidence interval around a mean score on a scale measuring likelihood to subscribe to a client's service. MRI conducts research for clients in which they gather and examine sample data. When they generate statistics based upon the sample data, the clients want to know how closely the statistics represent the true population values. In other words, clients wish to know to what extent the sample statistic may be *generalized* to the total client's customer population. For example, one MRI client, an electric utility company, wanted to investigate some opportunities to offer their customers additional services. One proposed service was a plan which charged customers higher prices for electricity used during peak hours but lower prices for electricity used during off peak hours. MRI described the service to customers

- To find out what it means to generalize the findings of a survey
- To understand that a sample finding is used to estimate a population fact
- To discover how to estimate a confidence interval for a percentage or an average
- To learn how to test a hypothesis about a population percentage or an average
- To become familiar with the "Generalize" functions of the XL Data Analyst

and then asked them the likelihood they would subscribe to the service on a five-point scale ranging from "Very Likely"(5) to "Not Very Likely"(1). Since this resulted in a metric level of measurement, MRI calculated the mean response to this question as well as other proposed services. For one proposed service the mean score was 3.7.

MRI uses confidence intervals to help clients evaluate how closely the statistic represents true population values. The confidence interval provides a lower and upper interval within which we can expect the sample statistic to fall 95% of the time if we were to conduct the study over and over 100 times. Knowing that the statistic will fall within this upper and lower range 95 times out of 100 allows the client to have 95% confidence in the statistic generated from the one study. With the use of confidence intervals, MRI will now be able to make the following statement: "Our best estimate of the mean score on a 5-point scale measuring likelihood to subscribe to the service is 3.7. In addition, we can be 95% confident that the true mean in the entire customer population falls between 3.5 and 3.9." MRI's clients have confidence that the statistic, generated from just a single sample, is close to the true population value. In this chapter, you will learn how MRI calculates confidence intervals for their clients. You will learn how to calculate confidence intervals using XL Data Analyst.

By Visit MRI at
**www.mri.research.com.**

A s you learned in Chapter 11, measures of central tendency and measures of variability adequately summarize the findings of a survey. However, whenever a probability sample is drawn from a population, it is not enough to simply report the sample's descriptive statistics, for it is the population values that we want to know about. For instance, our opening vignette about MRI's use of confidence intervals reveals that, strictly speaking, it is not correct to simply report the average (or a

*Where We Are:*
1 Establish the need for marketing research
2 Define the problem
3 Establish research objectives
4 Determine research design
5 Identify information types and sources
6 Determine methods of accessing data

simple percent) found in the sample. Rather, it is better to report a range that the client understands defines the true population value or what would be found if a census were feasible.

Estimates such as these contain a certain degree of error due to the sampling process. Every sample provides some information about its population, but there is always some sample error that must be taken into account. Consequently, we begin the chapter by describing the concept of "generalization" and explaining the relationship between a sample finding and the population fact that it represents. We show you how your estimate of the population fact is more certain with larger samples and with more agreement in your respondents. From an intuitive approach, we shift to parameter estimation, where the population value is estimated with a confidence interval using specific formulas and knowledge of areas under a normal or bell-shaped curve. Specifically, we show you how to estimate a percentage confidence interval and how to estimate an average confidence interval. Our XL Data Analyst performs these estimates, and we show examples. Next, we describe the procedure and computations for a hypothesis test for a percent or an average where the sample's finding is used to determine whether a hypothesis is supported or not supported. Again the XL Data Analyst does these analyses easily, and we show examples of hypotheses tests using the XL Data Analyst.

## THE CONCEPT OF GENERALIZATION

In an earlier chapter, you learned that researchers draw samples because they do not have the time or budget necessary to conduct a census of the population under study. You also learned that a sample should be representative of its population. Finally, you should recall that a probability sample's size is determined based on the amount of error that is acceptable to the manager. It is now time to deal with this error.

> ■ Population facts are estimated using the sample's findings.

We refer to a **sample finding** whenever a percentage or average or some other analysis value is computed with a sample's data. However, because of the sample error involved, the sample finding must be considered an approximation of the **population fact**, defined as the true value when a census of the population is taken and the value is determined using all members of the population. To be sure, when a researcher follows proper sampling procedures and ensures that the sample is a good representation of the target population, the sample findings are, indeed, *best* estimates of their respective population facts. But they will always be estimates that are hindered by the sample error.

> ■ Generalization is the act of estimating a population fact from a sample finding.

**Generalization** is the act of estimating a population fact from a sample finding.[1] It is important that we define generalization because this concept will help you understand what this estimation is all about. Generalization is a form of logic in which you make an inference about an entire group based on some evidence about that group. When you generalize, you draw a conclusion from the available evidence. For example, if two of your friends each bought a new Chevrolet and they both complained about their cars' performances, you might generalize that all Chevrolets perform poorly. On the other hand, if one of your friends complained about his Chevy, whereas the other one did not, you might generalize that your friend with the problem Chevy happened to buy a lemon. Taking this a step further, your generalizations are greatly influenced by the preponderance of evidence. So, if 20 of your friends bought new Chevrolets, and they all complained about poor performance, your inference would naturally be stronger or more certain than it would be in the case of only two friends' complaining.

For our purposes, you will soon find that generalization about any population's facts is a set of procedures where the sample size and sample findings are used to make estimates of these population values. For now, let us concentrate on the sample percentage, $p$, as the sample finding we are using to estimate the population percentage, $\pi$, and see how sample size enters into statistical generalization. Suppose that Chevrolet suspected that there were some dissatisfied Chevy buyers, and it commissioned two independent marketing research surveys to determine the amount of dissatisfaction that existed in its customer group. (Of course, our Chevrolet example is entirely fictitious. We don't mean to imply that Chevrolets perform in an unsatisfactory way.)

In the first survey, 100 customers who purchased a Chevy in the last six months are called on the telephone and asked, "In general, would you say that you are satisfied or dissatisfied with the performance of your Chevrolet since you bought it?" The survey finds that 33 respondents (33%) are dissatisfied. This finding could be generalized to the total population of Chevy owners who had bought one in the last six months, and we would say that there is 33% dissatisfaction. However, we know that our sample, which, by the way, was a probability sample, must contain some sample error, and in order to reflect this, you would have to say that there is *about* 33% dissatisfaction in the population. In other words, it might actually be more or less than 33% if we did a census, because the sample finding provided us with only an estimate.

In the second survey, 1,000 respondents—that's 10 times more than in the first survey—are called on the telephone and asked the same question. This survey finds that 35% of the respondents are "dissatisfied." Again, we know that the 35% is an estimate containing sampling error, so now we would also say that the population dissatisfaction percentage is *about* 35%. This means that we have two estimates of the degree of dissatisfaction with Chevrolets. One is "about 33%" for the sample of 100, whereas the other is "about 35%" with the sample of 1,000.

How do we translate our answers (remember they include the word "about") into more accurate numerical representations? Let us say you could translate them into ballpark ranges. That is, you could translate them so we could say "33% plus or minus $x$%" for the sample of 100 and "35% plus or minus $y$%" for the sample of 1,000. How would $x$ and $y$ compare? To answer this question, think back on how your logical generalization was stronger with 20 friends than it was with 2 friends with Chevrolets. To state this in a different way, with a larger sample (more evidence), we have agreed that you would be more certain that the sample finding was accurate with respect to estimating the true population fact. In other words, with a larger sample size, you should expect the range used to estimate the true population value to be smaller. Intuitively, you should expect the range for $y$ to be smaller than the range for $x$ because you have a large sample and less sampling error. Look at Table 12.1, which illustrates how we would generalize our sample findings to the population of all Chevrolet buyers in the case of the 100 sample versus the 1,000 sample. (We will explain how to compute the ranges in Table 12.1 very shortly.)

As these examples reveal, when we make estimates of population values, such as the percentage ($\pi$) or average ($\mu$), the sample finding percent ($p$) or average ($\bar{x}$) is

Generalization is "stronger" with larger samples and less sampling error.

**Table 12.1**

A Larger Sample Size Gives You More Precision When You Generalize Sample Findings to Estimate Population Facts*

| Sample | Sample Finding | Estimated Population Fact |
|---|---|---|
| 100 randomly selected respondents | Sample finding: 33% of respondents report they are dissatisfied with their new Chevrolet. | Between 24% and 42% of all Chevrolet buyers are dissatisfied.<br><br>24%             42%<br>●————————————●<br>33% |
| 1,000 randomly selected respondents | Sample finding: 35% of respondents report they are dissatisfied with their new Chevrolet. | Between 32% and 38% of all Chevrolet buyers are dissatisfied.<br><br>32%    38%<br>●————●<br>35% |

*Fictitious example

used as the beginning point, and then a range is computed in which the population value is estimated, or generalized, to fall. The size of the sample, $n$, plays a crucial role in this computation, as you will see in all of the analysis formulas we present in this chapter.

## GENERALIZING A SAMPLE'S FINDINGS: ESTIMATING THE POPULATION VALUE

Estimation of population values is a common type of generalization used in marketing research survey analysis. This generalization process is often referred to as **"parameter estimation"** because the proper name for the population fact, or value, is the **parameter**, or the actual population value being estimated. As you might have surmised, population parameters are designated by Greek letters such as $\pi$ (percent) or $\mu$ (mean or average), while sample findings are relegated to lowercase Roman letters such as $p$ (percent) or $\bar{x}$ (average or mean). As indicated earlier, generalization is largely a reflection of the amount of sampling error believed to exist in the sample finding. When the *New York Times* conducts a survey and finds that readers spend an average of 45 minutes daily reading the *Times*, or when McDonald's determines through a nationwide sample that 60% of all breakfast buyers buy an Egg McMuffin, both companies may want to determine more accurately how close these sample findings are to the actual population parameters. We will use these two examples to explain the estimation procedures for a percentage and for an average.

■ Population facts or values are referred to as "parameters."

### How to Estimate a Population Percentage (Categorical Data)

#### Calculating a Confidence Interval
As the two examples just noted reveal, sometimes the researcher wants to estimate the population percentage (McDonald's example), and at other times, the researcher will estimate the population average (*New York Times* example). A **confidence interval** is a range (lower and upper boundary) into which the researcher believes the population

Research can estimate how many minutes people read the *New York Times* each day.

parameter falls with an associated degree of confidence (typically 95% or 99%). We will describe the way to estimate a percentage in this section. You should recall that percentages are proper when summarizing categorical variables.

▪ You estimate a population parameter using a confidence interval.

The general formula for the estimation of a population percentage is written in notation form as follows:

$$p \pm z_\alpha s_p$$

where

◁ **Formula for a population percentage estimation**

$p$ = sample percentage

$z_\alpha$ = z value for 95% or 99% level of confidence ($\alpha$ [alpha] equals either 95% or 99% level of confidence)

$s_p$ = standard error of the percentage

Typically, marketing researchers rely only on the 95% or 99% levels of confidence, which correspond to ±1.96 ($z_{.95}$), and ±2.58 ($z_{.99}$) standard errors, respectively. By far, the **most commonly used level of confidence** in marketing research is the 95% level, corresponding to 1.96 standard errors. In fact, the 95% level of confidence is usually the default level found in statistical analysis programs. So, if you wanted to be 95% confident that your range included the true population percentage, for instance, you would multiply the standard error of the percentage, $s_p$, by 1.96 and add that value to the percentage, $p$, to obtain the upper limit, and you would subtract it from the percentage to find the lower limit. Notice that you have now taken into consideration the sample statistic $p$, the variability that is in the formula for $s_p$, the sample size $n$, which is also in the formula for $s_p$, and the degree of confidence in your estimate.[2] For a 99% confidence interval, substitute 2.58 for 1.96.

▪ Most marketing researchers use the 95% level of confidence.

Table 12.2 contains the formula and lists the steps used to estimate a population percentage. This table shows that estimation of the population percentage uses the sample finding to compute a confidence interval that describes the range for the population percentage. In order to estimate a population percentage, all you need is the sample percentage, $p$, and the sample size, $n$.

**Table 12.2**

How to Estimate the
Population Value for a
Percentage

**Formula for 95%
confidence interval
estimate of a population
percentage** ▷

Here is the formula for a 95% confidence interval estimate of a population percentage. Note that we have used the formula for $s_p$ to show how the sample percent, $p$, and the sample size, $n$, are used in this estimation procedure.

$$95\% \text{ confidence interval} = p \pm 1.96\sqrt{\frac{p \times q}{n}}$$

where
$p$ = percentage
$q = \left(100\% - p\right)$
$n$ = sample size

Calculation of 95% confidence interval to estimate the population value range is as follows:

| Step | Description | Chevrolet Example ($n = 100$) |
|---|---|---|
| **Step 1** | Calculate the percentage of times respondents chose one of the categories in a categorical variable, call it $p$. (This procedure is described on page 335.) | The sample percent is found to be 33%, so $p = 33\%$ |
| **Step 2** | Subtract $p$ from 100%, call it $q$. | $100\% - 33\% = 67\%$, so $q = 67\%$ |
| **Step 3** | Multiply $p$ times $q$, divide the product by the sample size, $n$, and take the square root of that quantity. Call it the *standard error of the percentage*. | Standard error of the percentage $= \sqrt{\dfrac{pq}{n}}$  $= \sqrt{\dfrac{\left(33 \times 67\right)}{100}}$  $= 4.7\%$ |
| **Step 4** | Multiply the standard error value by 1.96. Call it the *limit*. | Limit $= 1.96 \times 4.7\%$ $= 9.2\%$ |
| **Step 5** | Take $p$; subtract the limit to obtain the *lower boundary*. Then take $p$ and add the limit to obtain the *upper boundary*. The lower boundary and the upper boundary are the *95% confidence interval* for the population percentage. | Lower boundary: $33\% - 9.2\% = 23.8\%$  Upper boundary: $33\% + 9.2\% = 42.2\%$  The *95% confidence interval* is 23.8%–42.2% |

We will do some sample calculations here to make certain that you understand how to apply the formula for the estimation of a population percentage. Let's take the McDonald's survey in which 60% of the 100 respondents were found to order an Egg McMuffin for breakfast at McDondald's. Here are the 95% and 99% confidence interval calculations.

$$p \pm z_\alpha s_p$$

$$p \pm 1.96 \times \sqrt{\frac{p \times q}{n}}$$

$$60 \pm 1.96 \times \sqrt{\frac{60 \times 40}{100}}$$

$$60 \pm 1.96 \times 4.9$$

$$60 \pm 9.6$$

$$50.4\% – 69.6\%$$

◀ **Calculation of a 95% confidence interval for a percentage**

$$p + z_\alpha s_p$$

$$p + 2.58 \times \sqrt{\frac{p \times q}{n}}$$

$$60 \pm 2.58 \times \sqrt{\frac{60 \times 40}{100}}$$

$$60 \pm 2.58 \times 4.9$$

$$60 \pm 12.6$$

$$47.4\% – 72.6\%$$

◀ **Calculation of a 99% confidence interval for a percentage**

Notice that the only thing that differs when you compare the 95% confidence interval computations to the 99% confidence interval computations in each case is $z_\alpha$. As we noted earlier, $z$ is 1.96 for 95% and 2.58 for 99% of confidence. The confidence interval is always wider for 99% than it is for 95% when the sample size is the same and variability is equal.

### Interpreting a 95% Confidence Interval

The interpretation is based on the normal curve or bell-shaped distribution that you are familiar with, and we will build on this description in this chapter. The **standard error** is a measure of the variability in a population based on the variability found in the sample. There usually is some degree of variability in the sample: Not everyone orders an Egg McMuffin, nor does everyone order coffee for breakfast. When you examine the formula for a **standard error of the percentage** (Step 3 in Table 12.2), you will notice that the size of the standard error depends on two factors: (1) the variability, denoted as $p$ times $q$, and (2) the sample size, $n$. The standard error of the percentage is large with more variability and smaller with larger samples. What you have just discovered is exactly what you agreed to when we were working with the Chevrolet example: The more you found the Chevy owners to disagree (more variability), the less certain you were about your generalization, and the more Chevy owners you heard from, the more confident you were about your generalization.

■ A confidence interval is computed with the use of the standard error measure.

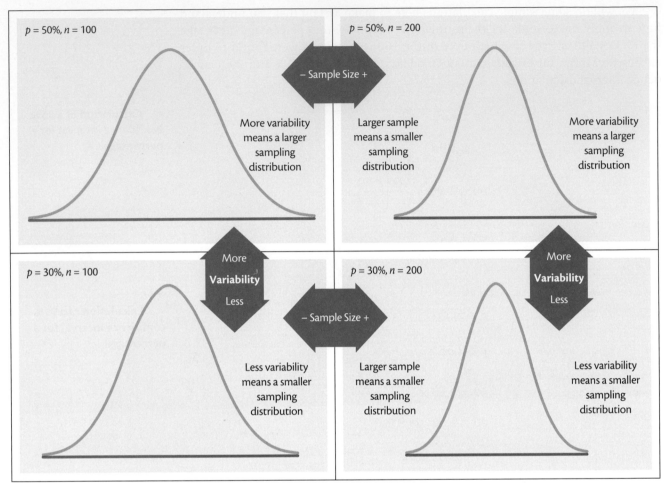

**Figure 12.1** How Variability and Sample Size Affect the Sampling Distribution

■ The sampling distribution is a theoretical concept that underlies confidence intervals.

If you theoretically took many, many samples and plotted the sample percentage, *p*, for all these samples as a frequency distribution, it would approximate a bell-shaped curve called the **sampling distribution**. The standard error is a measure of the variability in the sampling distribution based on what is theoretically believed to occur were we to take a multitude of independent samples from the same population. We are now dealing with a statistical concept, so we have created Figure 12.1 as a visual aid to help you understand how variability and sample size affect the sampling distribution.

To understand Figure 12.1, start with the upper left-hand quadrant, where the bell-shaped curve represents the case of *p* = 50% and *n* = 100. Move clockwise to the upper right-hand case of *p* = 50% and *n* = 200. Notice that the curve has become more compressed due to the increase in sample size. Now, move down to the lower right-hand case, where *p* = 30% and *n* = 200. The curve is even more compressed due to the reduced variability and large sample size. A move to the left of this quadrant is the case of *p* = 30% and *n* = 100 where the bell-shaped curve is less compressed due to the smaller sample size. Finally, moving to the upper left-hand quadrant (where we began), the curve is less compressed due to the smaller sample size (*n* = 100) and more variability (*p* = 50%).

To help you understand how confidence intervals work, Figure 12.2 compares two cases. In the first case, the standard error of the percentage is 5%, while in the second case, the standard error is 2%. Notice that the two bell-shaped normal curves reflect the

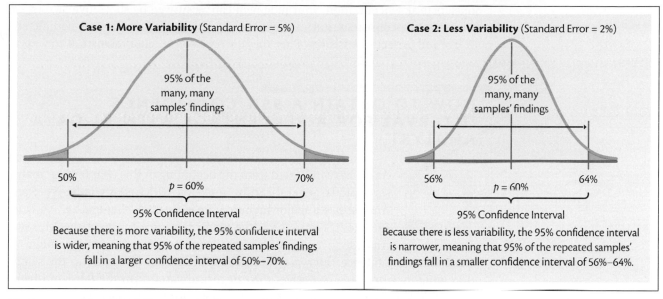

**Figure 12.2** The Variability Affects the Sampling Distribution Reflected in the 95% Confidence Interval for a Percentage

differences in variability, as the 5% curve with more variability is wider than the 2% curve that has less variability. The 95% confidence intervals are 50%–70% and 56%–64%, respectively. The larger standard error case has a larger interval, and the smaller standard error case has a smaller interval. The way to interpret a confidence interval is as follows: If you repeated your survey many, many times (thousands of times), and plotted your $p$, or percentage, found for each on a frequency distribution, it would look like a bell-shaped curve, and 95% of your percentages would fall in the confidence interval defined by the population percentage ±1.96 times the standard error of the percentage. In other words, you can be 95% confident that the population percentage falls in the range of 50% to 70% in the first case. Similarly, because the standard error is smaller (perhaps you have a larger sample in this case), you would be 95% confident that the population percentage falls in the range of 56% to 64% in the second case.

Obviously, a marketing researcher would take only one sample for a particular marketing research project, and this restriction explains why estimates must be used. Furthermore, it is the conscientious application of probability sampling techniques that allows us to make use of the sampling distribution concept. Thus, generalization procedures are direct linkages between probability sample design and data analysis. Do you remember that you had to grapple with accuracy levels when we determined sample size? Now we are on the other side of the table, so to speak, and we must use the sample size for our inference procedures. Confidence intervals must be used when estimating population values, and the size of the random sample used is always reflected in these confidence intervals.

As a final note in this section, but a note that pertains to all of the generalization analyses in this chapter, we want to remind you that the logic of statistical inference is identical to the reasoning process you go through when you weigh evidence to make a generalization or conclusion of some sort. The more evidence you have, the more precise you will be in your generalization. The only difference is that with statistical generalization we must follow rules that require the application of formulas so our estimates will be consistent with the assumptions of statistical theory. When you make

▪ Confidence intervals depend on sample size and variability found in the sample.

a nonstatistical generalization, your judgment can be swayed by subjective factors, so you may not be consistent. But in statistical estimates, the formulas are completely objective and perfectly consistent. Plus, they are based on accepted statistical concepts.

# HOW TO OBTAIN A 95% CONFIDENCE INTERVAL FOR A PERCENTAGE WITH XL DATA ANALYST

As we have indicated from the beginning of this chapter, the analysis topic is generalization, and you will find that the XL Data Analyst has a major menu command called "Generalize." As you can see in Figure 12.3, the menu sequence to direct the XL Data Analyst to compute a confidence interval for a percentage is Generalize–Confidence Interval–Percentage. This sequence opens up the selection window where you can select the categorical variable in the left-hand pane (Available Variables), and the various value labels for that variable will appear in the right-hand pane (Available Values). In our example, we will select "Do you have Internet access?" as our chosen variable in the pane on the left, and then highlight the "Yes" category in the pane on the right. Clicking "OK" will prompt the XL Data Analyst to perform the confidence interval analysis.

The XL Data Analyst confidence interval analysis for the percentage of college students with high-speed cable modem access to the Internet is provided in Figure 12.4. When you study this figure, you will find that a total of 600 respondents answered this question, and 590 of them indicated that they did have Internet

■ Use the Generalize–Confidence Interval–Percentage menu sequence of the XL Data Analyst to direct it to produce confidence intervals.

**Figure 12.3** Using the XL Data Analyst to Select a Variable Value for a Percentage Confidence Interval

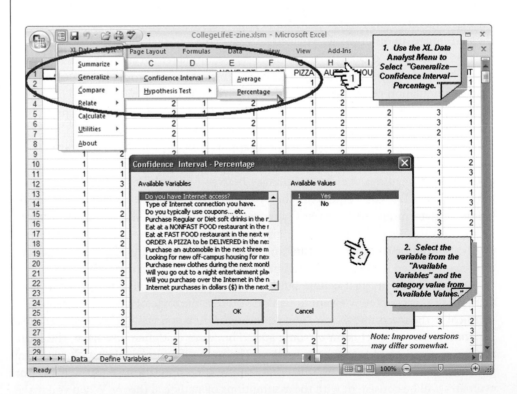

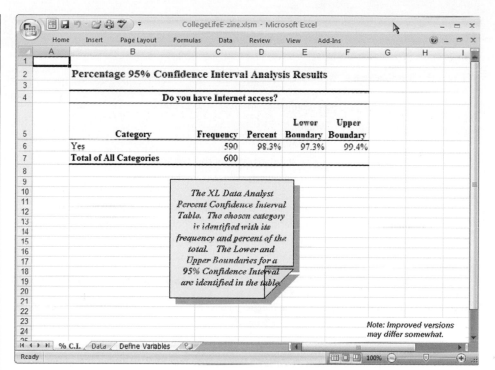

**Figure 12.4** XL Data Analyst Percentage Confidence Interval Table

access. This computes to a 98.3% value (590/600), and the table reports the lower boundary of 97.3% and the upper boundary of 99.3%, defining the 95% confidence interval for this percentage. Again, the proper interpretation of this boundary is that if we repeated our survey many, many times, 95% of the percentages found for high-speed cable connection would fall between 97.3% and 99.3%. The boundaries are so narrow for two reasons: (1) almost everyone has Internet access, so there is very little variability, and (2) the sample size is fairly large.

## How to Estimate a Population Average (Metric Data)

### Calculating a Confidence Interval for an Average

Here is the formula for the estimation of a population average in general notation.

$$\bar{x} \pm z_\alpha s_{\bar{x}}$$

◀ **Formula for a population average estimation**

where

$\bar{x}$ = sample average

$z_\alpha$ = z value for 95% or 99% level of confidence

$s_{\bar{x}}$ = standard error of the average

Table 12.3 describes how to calculate a 95% confidence interval for an average using our *New York Times* reading example, in which we found that our sample averaged 45 minutes of reading time per day.

The procedure is parallel to the one for calculating a confidence interval for a percentage, except the standard deviation is used, as it is the correct measure of variability for a metric variable. With the formula for the **standard error of the average**

■ The confidence interval for an average uses the standard deviation as the measure of variability.

**Table 12.3**
How to Estimate the
Population Value for an
Average

**Formula for 95%
confidence interval
estimate of a population
average** ▷

Here is the formula for a 95% confidence interval estimate of a population average.

$$95\% \text{ confidence interval} = \bar{x} \pm 1.96 \, s_{\bar{x}}$$

where

$\bar{x}$ = average

$s_{\bar{x}}$ = standard error of the average

$n$ = sample size

To generalize a sample average finding to estimate the population average, the process is identical to the estimation of a population percentage, except that the standard deviation is used as the measure of the variability. In the example below, we are to use the 95% level of confidence that is explained in this chapter.

| Step | Description | *New York Times* **Example ($n = 100$)** |
|------|-------------|------------------------------------------|
| **Step 1** | Calculate the average of the metric variable. (This procedure is described on page 337.) | The sample average is found to be 45 minutes. |
| **Step 2** | Calculate the standard deviation of the metric variable. (This procedure is described on page 339.) | The standard deviation is found to be 20 minutes. |
| **Step 3** | Divide the standard deviation by the square root of the sample size. Call it the *standard error of the average*. | Standard error of the average $= \dfrac{s}{\sqrt{n}}$ $= \dfrac{20}{\sqrt{n}}$ $= \dfrac{20}{\sqrt{100}}$ $= 2$ |
| **Step 4** | Multiply the standard error value by 1.96, call it the *limit*. | Limit $= 1.96 \times 2 = 3.9$ |
| **Step 5** | Take the average; subtract the limit to obtain the *lower boundary*. Then take the average and add the limit to obtain the *upper boundary*. The lower boundary and the upper boundary are the 95% *confidence interval* for the population average. | Lower boundary: $45 - 3.9 = 41.1$ minutes <br><br> Upper boundary: $45 + 3.9 = 48.9$ minutes <br><br> The *95% confidence interval* is 41.1–48.9 minutes. |

(in Table 12.3), you should note the same logic that we pointed out to you with the percentage confidence interval: The standard error of the average is large with more variability (standard deviation) and smaller with large samples ($n$).

Here is another example of the calculations of the confidence interval for an average using a sample of 100 *New York Times* readers where we have found a sample average of 45 minutes and a standard deviation of 20 minutes. The 99% confidence interval estimate is calculated as follows:

$$\bar{x} \pm z_\alpha s_{\bar{x}}$$
$$45 \pm 2.58 \times \frac{20}{\sqrt{100}}$$
$$45 \pm 2.58 \times 2$$
$$45 \pm 5.2$$
$$39.8 \text{ minutes}{-}50.2 \text{ minutes}$$

◀ **Calculation of a 99% confidence interval for an average**

Again, as with the percentage confidence intervals, the 99% confidence interval is wider because the standard error is multiplied by 2.58, while the 95% one is multiplied by the lower 1.96 value.

### Interpreting a Confidence Interval for an Average

The interpretation of a confidence interval estimate of a population average is virtually identical to the interpretation of a confidence interval estimate for a population percentage: If you repeated your survey many, many times (thousands of times), and plotted your average number of minutes of reading the *New York Times* for each sample on a frequency distribution, it would look like a bell-shaped curve, and 95% of your sample averages would fall in the confidence interval defined by the population percentage ±1.96 times the standard error of the average. In other words, you can be 95% confident that the population average falls in the range of 41.1–48.9 minutes. Of course, if the standard error is large (perhaps you have a smaller sample in this case), you would be 95% confident that the population average falls in the larger confidence interval that would result from your calculations.

▪ Interpretation of confidence intervals is identical regardless of whether you are working with a percentage or an average.

## HOW TO OBTAIN A 95% CONFIDENCE INTERVAL FOR AN AVERAGE WITH XL DATA ANALYST

If you examine Figure 12.5, you will notice that there are two options possible from "Generalize–Confidence Interval." One is for a percentage confidence interval, while the other is for an average confidence interval. The Average option opens up a Selection window that can be seen in Figure 12.5. You select your metric variable(s) by highlighting it in the left-hand pane and using the "Add>>" button to move it into the right-hand selection pane. When you click on "OK," the XL Data Analyst performs confidence interval analysis on the chosen metric variables.

In our College Life E-Zine data set example, we have selected books out of the next $100 State U students spend on the Internet, and you can see the resulting table in Figure 12.6. The average expected purchase amount is 3.6 dollars for the sample of 143 respondents who purchase items on the Internet, and the standard deviation is 2.6 dollars. (Remember, only those respondents who make purchases over the Internet answered the questions about how much they spend on books.) By default, the XL Data Analyst creates numbers with one decimal place (rounded); however, you can easily use Excel's Format–Cells operation to format the numbers in the XL Data Analyst table to be in currency, so the average is $3.62 and the boundaries are $3.19 and $4.04.

▪ The XL Data Analyst produces confidence intervals based on the 95% level of confidence.

**Figure 12.5** Using the XL Data Analyst to Select a Variable for an Average Confidence Interval

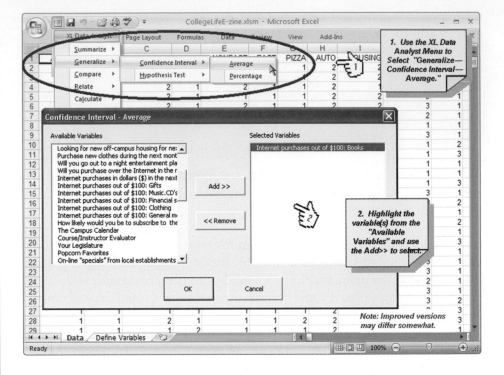

**Figure 12.6** XL Data Analyst Average Confidence Interval Table

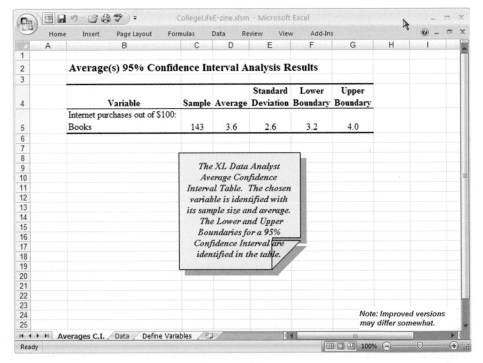

## Using the Six-Step Approach to Confidence Intervals Analysis

As a means of summarizing our discussion of confidence intervals and also to guide you when you are working with confidence intervals, we have prepared Table 12.4, which specifies how to apply our six-step analysis approach to confidence intervals.

**Table 12.4** The Six-Step Approach to Data Analysis for Generalization: Confidence Intervals

| Step | Explanation | Example (A is a categorical variable; B is a metric variable) |
|---|---|---|
| **1. What is the research objective?** | Determine that you are dealing with a **Confidence Interval Generalization objective**. | A. We want to *estimate* what percent of students at this university have high-speed modem Internet access.<br><br>B. We want to *estimate* how much students at this university who make purchases on the Internet will spend on Internet purchases in the next two months. |
| **2. What questionnaire question(s) is/are involved?** | Identify the question(s), and for each one specify whether it is categorical or metric. | A. "What type of Internet connection do you have where you live?" "High speed" is *categorical*.<br><br>B. "To the nearest $5, about how much do you think you will spend on Internet purchases in the next two months?" This is a *metric* measure. |
| **3. What is the appropriate analysis?** | To generalize a sample finding to estimate the population value, use confidence intervals. | We must use confidence intervals because we have to take into account variability and sample error. |
| **4. How do you run it?** | Use XL Data Analyst analysis: Select "Generalize–Confidence Intervals–Percentage" (categorical) or "Generalize–Confidence Interval–Average" (metric). | |

**5. How do you interpret the findings?** — The 95% confidence interval boundaries are such that if you repeated your survey many, many times and calculated the average or percent under study, 95% of the repeated findings would fall between the confidence interval boundaries.

| What type of Internet connection do you have where you live? | | | | |
|---|---|---|---|---|
| Category | Frequency | Percent | Lower Boundary | Upper Boundary |
| 1 - High-Speed Cable | 252 | 42.7% | 38.7% | 46.7% |
| **Total of All Categories** | 590 | | | |

| Variable | Sample | Average | Standard Deviation | Lower Boundary | Upper Boundary |
|---|---|---|---|---|---|
| To the nearest $5, about how much do you think you will spend on Internet purchases in the next two months? | 143 | $63.71 | $18.13 | $60.73 | $66.68 |

Notice that the values have been reformatted to currency with dollars and cents.

**Table 12.4** *(Continued)*

| Step | Explanation | Example (A is a categorical variable; B is a metric variable) |
|---|---|---|
| **6. How do you write/ present these findings?** | For a single percent or average, simply report that the 95% confidence interval is ##.# to ##.#. | A. It was determined from the sample of respondents that 42.7% of those students with Internet access have high-speed cable modem connections. The 95% confidence interval estimate for the percent of college students in the population who have Internet access with a high-speed cable modem connection is 38.7% to 46.7%.<br><br>B. For those respondents who make purchases on the Internet, the average expected amount of purchase in the next two months was found to be $63.71. The 95% confidence interval for the expected average dollar expenditure for college students in the population who make Internet purchases is $60.73 to $66.68. |

As a final comment on this topic, generalizations of survey sample findings to describe the population are useful in many ways. One important application of confidence intervals is in their use to generate market-potential estimates. We have prepared Marketing Research Application 12.1, which shows how our College Life E-Zine survey findings can be used to estimate the online-purchasing market potential of State University students.

# MARKETING RESEARCH APPLICATION 12.1

PRACTICAL

APPLICATIONS

## How to Estimate Market Potential Using a Survey's Findings

A common way to estimate total market potential is to rely on the definition of a market. A market is people with the willingness and ability to pay for a product or a service. This definition can be expressed somewhat like a formula, in the following way:

*Market potential = Population base × percent willing to buy × amount they are willing to spend*

As you should know, magazines and e-zines depend greatly on the revenues of their advertising affiliates. That is, the subscription price of *People* magazine, for instance, is a mere pittance compared to the amount of money paid by the various companies that advertise their products and services in *People*. The potential advertising affiliates for the College Life E-Zine might be persuaded to advertise on it if there is evidence that college students make purchases on the Internet. Our survey findings can be used to estimate how much State U students spend this way.

In our College Life E-Zine case, we know that the State University population base amounts to 35,000 students. We know that not all students make online purchases. In fact, we found that only 24.2% of them intend to make a purchase on the Internet in the next two months. This translates to 8,470 students. When asked how much they expect to spend on Internet purchases in that time period, we found the average to be $63.71. We can use the lower and upper boundaries of the 95% confidence interval for this average to calculate a pessimistic (lower boundary) and an optimistic (upper boundary) estimate as well as a best estimate (average) of the annual Internet-purchasing market potential of State U's student body. The calculations follow.

Using the 95% confidence intervals and the sample percentage, the total annual market potential for Internet purchases by State U students is found to be between about $3.1 million and $3.4 million per year. The best annual estimate is about $3.2 million. It is "best" because it is based on the sample average, which is the best estimate of the true population average expenditures by State U students who make Internet purchases. Of course, we realize that these are very conservative estimates for next year, as the percent of students buying on the Internet will surely increase, and the average amount they spend will most likely increase as well. We now have some convincing findings that can be used to approach potential advertising affiliates and to recruit them to use the College Life E-Zine as an advertising vehicle that will effectively target college students.

| Estimation of Internet Purchases by State University Students | | |
|---|---|---|
| **Pessimistic Estimate** | **Best Estimate** | **Optimistic Estimate** |
| 8,470 *(students who intend to make an Internet purchase in the next 2 months)* | | |
| Times $60.73 | Times $63.71 | Times $66.68 |
| = $514,383 each 2 months | = $539,624 each 2 months | = $564,780 each 2 months |
| Times 6 | | |
| = $3,086,298 per year | = $3,237,744 per year | = $3,388,680 per year |

# TESTING HYPOTHESES ABOUT PERCENTS OR AVERAGES

Sometimes someone, such as the marketing researcher or marketing manager, makes a statement about the population parameter based on prior knowledge, assumptions, or intuition. This statement, called a **hypothesis**, most commonly takes the form of an exact specification as to what the population value is. **Hypothesis testing** is a statistical procedure used to "support" (accept) or "not support" (reject) the hypothesis based on sample information.[3] With all hypothesis tests, you should keep in mind that the sample is the only source of current information about the population. Because our sample is a probability sample and therefore representative of the population, the sample results are used to determine whether or not the hypothesis about the population parameter has been supported.

> When a manager or the researcher states what he or she believes will be the sample finding *before* it is determined, this belief is called a "hypothesis."

All of this might sound frightfully technical, but it is a form of generalization that you do every day. You just do not use the words "hypothesis" or "parameter" when you do it. Here is an example to show how hypothesis testing occurs naturally. Your friend Bill does not wear his seat belt because he thinks only a few drivers actually wear them. But Bill's car breaks down, and he has to ride with his co-workers to and from work while it is being repaired. Over the course of a week, Bill rides with five different co-workers, and he notices that four out of the five buckle up. When Bill begins driving his car the next week, he begins fastening his seat belt.

PRACTICAL APPLICATIONS

> Bill's seat belt example reveals that we do intuitive hypothesis testing all of the time.

This is intuitive hypothesis testing in action; Bill's initial belief that few people wear seat belts was his hypothesis. **Intuitive hypothesis testing** (as opposed to statistical hypothesis testing) is when someone uses something he or she has observed to see if it agrees with or refutes his or her belief about that topic. Everyone uses intuitive hypothesis testing; in fact, we rely on it constantly. We just do not call it hypothesis testing, but we are constantly gathering evidence that supports or refutes our beliefs, and we reaffirm or change our beliefs based on our findings.

Bills's hyphothesis about seat belt use is about to be tested.

In other words, we generalize this new evidence into our beliefs so our beliefs will be consistent with the evidence. Read Marketing Research Application 12.2 and realize that you perform intuitive hypothesis testing a great deal.

## MARKETING RESEARCH APPLICATION 12.2

PRACTICAL

APPLICATIONS

### Intuitive Hypothesis Testing: We Do It All the Time!

People do intuitive hypothesis testing all the time to reaffirm their beliefs or to re-form them to be consistent with reality. The following diagram illustrates how people perform intuitive hypothesis testing.

Here is an everyday example. As a student taking a marketing research class, you believe that you will ace the first exam if you study hard the night before the exam. You take the exam, and you score a 70%. Ouch! It sure looks like your score does not support your belief that one cram session will be enough to earn an A grade in this course. You now realize that

your belief (your hypothesis) was wrong, and you need to study more for the next exam. Because your hypothesis was not supported, you have to come up with a new one.

You ask the student beside you, who did ace the exam, how much study time he put in. He says he studied for three solid nights before the exam. Notice that he has found evidence (his A grade) that supports his hypothesis, so he will not change his study habits belief. You, on the other hand, must change your hypothesis or suffer the consequences. Read the boxes and follow the arrows in the diagram below to see how your intuitive hypothesis testing comes out.

**Your Hypothesis**

| I believe that a single-night cram session is enough to ace the exam. This is my hypothesis. | I now believe that I need to study harder, say 3 solid nights, to ace the next exam. This is my revised hypothesis. | I will hold this belief (hypothesis) as long as I continue to ace the exams. |

**The Evidence**

| I score a 70 on the exam. Ouch! I definitely need to change my belief (hypothesis) because it is not supported by the evidence. | I score 95 on the next exam. Great! I will hold on to this hypothesis because it is supported by the evidence. |

Obviously, if you had asked Bill before his car went into the repair shop, he might have said that only a small percentage of drivers, perhaps as low as 30%, wear seat belts. His week of car rides is equivalent to a sample of five observations, and he observes that 80% of his co-workers buckle up. Because Bill's initial hypothesis is not supported by the evidence, he realizes that his hypothesis is in error, and it must be revised. If you asked Bill what percentage of drivers wear seat belts after his week of observations, he undoubtedly would have a much higher percentage in mind than his original estimate. The fact that Bill began to fasten his seat belt suggests he perceives his behavior to be out of the norm, so he has adjusted his belief and his behavior as well. In other words, his hypothesis was not supported, so Bill revised it to be consistent with what he now generalizes to be the actual case. The logic of statistical hypothesis testing is very similar to this process that Bill has just undergone.

## Testing a Hypothesis About a Percentage

Here is the formula for a percentage hypothesis test.

$$z = \frac{p - \pi_H}{s_p}$$

where
$p$    = sample percent
$\pi_H$  = hypothesized population percentage
$s_p$   = standard error of the percentage

◀ **Formula for a hypothesis test of a population percentage**

Table 12.5 provides formulas and lists the steps necessary to test a hypothesis about a percentage. Basically, hypothesis testing involves the use of four ingredients: the sample statistic ($p$ in this case), the standard error ($s_p$), the hypothesized population parameter value ($\pi_H$ in this case), and the decision to "support" or "not support" the hypothesized parameter based on a few calculations. The first two values were discussed in the section on percentage parameter estimation. The hypothesis is simply what the researcher hypothesizes the population parameter, $\pi$, to be before the research is undertaken. When these are taken into consideration by using the steps in Table 12.5, the result is a significance test for the hypothesis that determines its support (acceptance) or lack of support (rejection).

Tracking the logic of the equation for a percent hypothesis test, you can see that the sample percent ($p$) is compared to the hypothesized population percent ($\pi_H$). In this case, "compared" means "take the difference." They are compared because in a hypothesis test, one tests the **null hypothesis**, a formal statement that there is no (or null) difference between the hypothesized $\pi$ value and the $p$ value found in our sample. This difference is divided by the standard error to determine how many standard errors away from the hypothesized parameter the sample percentage falls. All the relevant information about the population as found by our sample is included in these computations. Knowledge of areas under the normal curve then comes into play to translate this distance into a determination of whether the sample finding supports (accepts) or does not support (rejects) the hypothesis.

■ A hypothesis test gives you the amount of support for your hypothesis based on your sample finding and sample size.

**Table 12.5**

How to Test a Hypothesis for a Percentage

To test a hypothesis about a percentage, you will assess how close the sample percentage is to the hypothesized population percentage. The following example uses Bill's seat belt hypothesis and tests it with a random sample of 1,000 automobile drivers.

| Step | Description | Seat Belt Example ($n = 1,000$) |
|------|-------------|-------------------------------|
| **Step 1** | Identify the percent that you (or your client) believe exists in the population. Call it $\pi_H$, or the "hypothesized percent." | Bill believes that 30% of drivers use seat belts. |
| **Step 2** | Conduct a survey and determine the sample percentage; call it $p$. (This procedure is described on page 335.) | A sample of 1,000 drivers is taken, and the sample percent for those who use seat belts is found to be 80%, so $p = 80\%$. |
| **Step 3** | Determine the *standard error of the percentage*. (This procedure is described on page 356.) | $$s_p = \sqrt{\frac{pq}{n}}$$ $$= \sqrt{\frac{(80 \times 20)}{1,000}}$$ $$= 1.26\%$$ |
| **Step 4** | Subtract $\pi_H$ from $p$ and divide this amount by the standard error of the percent. Call it $z$. | $$z = \frac{p - \pi_H}{s_p}$$ $$= \frac{(80 - 30)}{1.26}$$ $$= 39.7$$ |
| **Step 5** | Using the critical value of 1.96, determine whether the hypothesis is supported or not supported. | The computed $z$ of 39.7 is greater than the critical $z$ of 1.96, so the hypothesis is not supported. |

The example we have provided in Table 12.5 uses Bill's seat belt hypothesis that 30% of drivers buckle up their seat belts. To move our example from intuitive hypothesis testing and into statistical hypothesis testing, we have specified that Bill reads about a Harris Poll and finds that 80% of respondents in a national sample of 1,000 wear their seat belts. This is a 50% difference, but it must be translated into the number of standard errors, or $z$. In Step 4 of Table 12.5, this calculated $z$ turns out to be 39.7, but what does it mean?

As was the case with confidence intervals, the crux of hypothesis testing is the sampling-distribution concept. Our actual sample is one of the many, many theoretical samples comprising the assumed bell-shaped curve of possible sample results using the hypothesized value as the center of the bell-shaped distribution. There is a greater probability of finding a sample result close to the hypothesized mean, for example, than of finding one that is far away. But there is a critical assumption working here. We have conditionally accepted from the outset that the person who stated the hypothesis is correct. So, if our sample mean turns out to be within ±1.96 standard errors of the hypothesized mean, it supports the hypothesis maker at the 95% level of confidence because it falls within 95% of the area under the curve. As Figure 12.7 illustrates, the sampling distribution defines two areas:

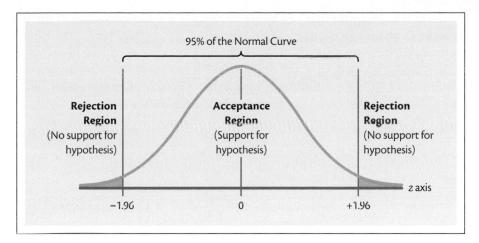

**Figure 12.7** 95% Acceptance and Rejection Regions for Hypothesis Tests

the acceptance region that resides within ±1.96 standard errors and the rejection region that is found at either end of the bell-shaped sampling distribution and outside the ±1.96 standard errors boundaries. The hypothesis test rule is simple: If the $z$ value falls in the acceptance region, there is support for the hypothesis, and if the $z$ value falls in the rejection region, there is no support for the hypothesis.

◼ The computed $z$ value is used to assess whether the hypothesis is supported or not supported.

## What Significance Level to Use and Why

Most researchers prefer to use the 95% significance level. As you have learned in this textbook and your statistics course, the critical $z$ value for the 95% level is ±1.96. Granted, you may find a researcher who prefers to use the 99% significance level; however, seasoned researchers are well aware of the ever-changing marketplace phenomena that they study, and they prefer to detect subtle changes early on. Consequently, they opt for the 95% one as it has a greater likelihood of not supporting clients' hypotheses and making them see these shifts and changes.

◼ Marketing researchers typically use the 95% level of confidence when testing hypotheses.

All you need to do is to compare the computed $z$ value to your critical value. If the computed $z$ is inside the acceptance region, you support the hypothesis, but if it falls in the rejection region, your sample fails to support the hypothesis. In Bill's seat belt case, 39.7 is greater than 1.96 or 2.58. Sorry, Bill, we do not support your hypothesis, and you should buckle up from now on.

## How Do We Know That We Have Made the Correct Decision?

But what if Bill objects to your rejection? Which is correct—the hypothesis or the researcher's sample results? The answer to this question is always the same: Sample information is invariably more accurate than a hypothesis. Of course, the sampling procedure must adhere strictly to probability sampling requirements and assure representativeness. As you can see, Bill was greatly mistaken because his hypothesis of 30% of drivers wearing seat belts was 39.7 standard errors away from the 80% finding of the national poll. If Bill wants to dispute a national sample finding reported by the Harris Poll organization, he can, but he will surely come to realize that his limited observations are much less valid than the findings of this well-respected research industry giant.

◼ Hypothesis tests assume that the sample is more representative of the population than is an unsupported hypothesis.

Here is an example that will help crystallize your understanding of the test of a hypothesis about a percentage. What percent of U.S. college students own a major credit card? Let's say that you think 3 out of 4, or 75% of college students, own a MasterCard, Visa card, or some other major credit card. A recent survey of 6,000 students on U.S. college campuses found that 65% have a major credit card.[4] The computations to test your hypotheses of 75% are as follows:

**Example of a percentage hypothesis test** ▷

$$z = \frac{p - \pi_H}{s_p}$$

$$= \frac{p - \pi_H}{\sqrt{\dfrac{pxq}{n}}}$$

$$= \frac{65 - 75}{\sqrt{\dfrac{65 \times 35}{6,000}}}$$

$$= \frac{-10}{.62}$$

$$= -16.13$$

No luck: your hypothesis is not supported because the computed $z$ value exceeds the critical value of 1.96. Yes, we realize that the result was *minus* 16.13, but the sign is irrelevant: you are comparing the absolute value of the computed $z$ to the critical value of 1.96. The true percent of U.S. college students who own a credit card is estimated to be 63.8%–66.2% at the 95% level of confidence. (We calculated the 95% confidence interval based on the sample finding.)

## Testing a Directional Hypothesis

■ A "directional" hypothesis specifies a "greater than" or "less than" value, using only one tail of the bell-shaped curve.

A **directional hypothesis** is one that indicates the direction in which you believe the population parameter falls relative to some hypothesized average or percentage. If you are testing a directional ("greater than" or "less than") hypothesis, the critical $z$ value is adjusted downward to 1.64 and 2.33 for the 95% and 99% levels of confidence, respectively. It is important that you understand that the hypothesis test formula does not change; it is only the critical value of $z$ that is changed when you are testing a directional hypothesis. This adjustment is because only one side of the bell-shaped curve is involved in what is known as a "one-tailed" test. Of course, the sample percent or average must be in the right direction away from the hypothesized value, and the computed $z$ value must meet or exceed the critical one-tailed $z$ value in order for the hypothesis to be supported.

### HOW TO TEST A HYPOTHESIS ABOUT A PERCENTAGE WITH XL DATA ANALYST

Again, we are interested in generalizing our findings to see if they support or fail to support our percentage hypothesis, so, as you can see in Figure 12.8, the menu sequence to direct the XL Data Analyst to accomplish this is Generalize–Hypothesis Test–Percentage. This

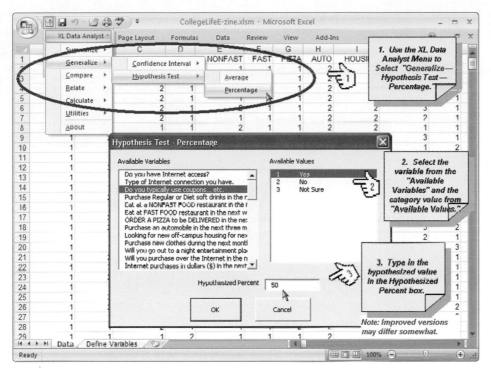

**Figure 12.8** XL Data Analyst Selection Menu for a Percentage Hypothesis Test

sequence opens up the selection window where you can select the categorical variable in the left-hand pane, and the various value labels for that variable will appear in the right-hand pane. Notice at the bottom of the selection window, there is an entry box where we will enter our "Hypothesized Percent."

In our example, we will select "Do you typically use coupons, '2-for-1 specials,' or other promotions you see in magazines or newspapers?" as our chosen variable, and then highlight the "Yes" category. We have hypothesized that 50% of our college students use these promotions. Clicking "OK" will prompt the XL Data Analyst to perform the hypothesis test.

Figure 12.9 is an annotated screenshot of an XL Data Analyst percentage hypothesis test analysis. You should immediately notice that this analysis produces a more detailed output than you have encountered thus far. First and foremost, there is a table that verifies that we have selected the "Yes" category answer for the promotions variable, and it reveals that 23.1% of our 590 respondents answered "Yes" to this question. The table also shows our hypothesized percentage of 50% so we can verify that we have entered in our hypothesized percentage correctly. Immediately following the table are the results of three hypotheses tests. The main hypothesis test finding is presented first, and the XL Data Analyst finds insufficient support for our hypothesis of 50%, so it signals that our hypothesis is "Not Supported." Next, in case we had directional hypotheses in mind, the XL Data Analyst indicates that if we hypothesized that the percent was greater than 50%, this hypothesis lacks support and it is "Not Supported," but if we had hypothesized that the population percent is less than 50%, this hypothesis is "Supported."

You should also notice that your XL Data Analyst provides the statistical values necessary to carry out the hypotheses tests. The standard error of the percentage,

■ The XL Data Analyst tests hypotheses using the 95% level of confidence.

■ The XL Data Analyst tests both directional and nondirectional hypotheses in the same analysis.

**Figure 12.9** XL Data Analyst Output Table and Results for a Percentage Hypothesis Test

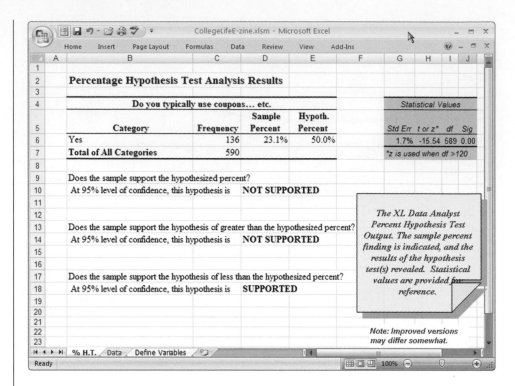

computed $z$ (or $t$) value, associated degrees of freedom for using a $t$-distribution table, and the significance level are reported in case a user wishes to use them. However, since the XL Data Analyst assesses the hypothesized percentage and indicates whether or not the hypothesis is supported by the sample at the 95% level of confidence, there is scant need to be concerned with the statistical values. These are provided for the rare case where a researcher might feel the need to inspect them.

## Is It $t$ or $z$? And Why You Do Not Need to Worry About It

PRACTICAL
APPLICATIONS

We have refrained from discussing the statistical values that appear on XL Data Analyst output, because you need to know only that it uses these values and tells you whether or not the hypothesis is supported. However, if you do inspect the statistical values, you may have noticed that there is reference to a "$t$" value and no reference to a "$z$" value. The $t$ value is agreed by statisticians to be more proper than the $z$ value,[5] but the $t$ value does not have set critical values such as 1.96. It is not important for you to understand why, but it is worthwhile to inform you that whenever XL Data Analyst performs analysis, it uses the agreed-upon best approach, and its findings are correct based on the best approach. We use the $z$ value in our explanations because it makes them simpler for you to understand as there are only a very few fixed critical values of $z$ to deal with. Also, it is customary in marketing research books to use the $z$ value formulas.

■ The XL Data Analyst correctly decides whether to use a $t$ value or a $z$ value with hypothesis tests.

## Testing a Hypothesis About an Average

Just as you learned that confidence intervals for averages follow the identical logic of confidence intervals for percentages, so is the procedure to test a hypothesis about an average identical to that for testing a hypothesis about a percent. In fact, a $z$ value is calculated using the following formula:

$$z = \frac{\bar{x} - \mu_H}{s_{\bar{x}}}$$

◀ **Formula for the test of a hypothesis about an average**

where

$\bar{x}$ = sample average

$\mu_H$ = hypothesized population average

$s_{\bar{x}}$ = standard error of the average

■ The procedure for a hypothesis test for an average is identical to one for a percentage, except the equation uses values specific to an average.

You determine whether the hypothesis is supported or not supported using this formula applied to the steps in Table 12.5.

As is our custom, we will provide a numerical example of a hypothesis test for an average. Northwestern Mutual Life Insurance Company has a college student internship program. The program allows college students to participate in an intensive training program and to become field agents in one academic term. Arrangements are made with various universities in the United States whereby students will receive college credit if they qualify for and successfully complete this program. Rex Reigen, district agent for Idaho, believed, based on his knowledge of other programs in the country, that the typical college agent will be able to earn about $2,750 in his or her first semester of participation in the program. He hypothesizes that the population parameter, that is, the average, will be $2,750. To check Rex's hypothesis, a survey was taken of current college agents, and 100 of these individuals were contacted through telephone calls. Among the questions posed was an estimate of the amount of money made in their first semester of work in the program. The sample average is determined to be $2,800, and the standard deviation is $350.

In essence, the amount of $2,750 is the hypothesized average of the sampling distribution of all possible samples of the same size that can be taken of the college agents in the country. The unknown factor, of course, is the size of the standard error in dollars. Consequently, although it is assumed that the sampling distribution will be a normal curve with the average of the entire distribution at $2,750, we need a way to determine how many dollars are within ±1 standard error of the average, or any other number of standard errors of the average for that matter. The only

How much can a college student intern make selling insurance during the summer?

■ The standard deviation and sample size are used to compute the standard error of an average.

information available that would help to determine the size of the standard error is the standard deviation obtained from the sample. This standard deviation can be used to determine a standard error with the application of the standard error formula you encountered in Step 2 of Table 12.3.

The amount of $2,800 found by the sample differs from the hypothesized amount of $2,750 by $50. Is this amount a sufficient enough difference to cast doubt on Rex's estimate? Or, in other words, is it far enough from the hypothesized average to not support the hypothesis? To answer these questions, we compute as follows (note that we have substituted the formula for the standard error of the average in the second step):

**Calculation of a test of Rex's hypothesis that Northwestern Mutual interns make an average of $2,750 in their first semester of work** ▶

$$
\begin{aligned}
z &= \frac{\bar{x} - \mu_H}{s_{\bar{x}}} \\[2mm]
&= \frac{\bar{x} - \mu_H}{\dfrac{s}{\sqrt{n}}} \\[2mm]
&= \frac{2,800 - 2,750}{\dfrac{350}{\sqrt{100}}} \\[2mm]
&= \frac{50}{35} \\[2mm]
&= 1.43
\end{aligned}
$$

**Rex's hypothesis is accepted!** ▶

The sample variability and the sample size have been used to determine the size of the standard error of the assumed sampling distribution. In this case, one standard error of the average is equal to $35. When the difference of $50 is divided by $35 to determine the number of standard errors away from the hypothesized average the sample statistic lies, the result is 1.43 standard errors. As is illustrated in Figure 12.10, 1.43 standard errors is within ±1.96 standard errors of Rex's hypothesized average. It also reveals that the hypothesis is supported because it falls in the acceptance region.

**Figure 12.10**  The Sample Findings Support the Hypothesis in This Example

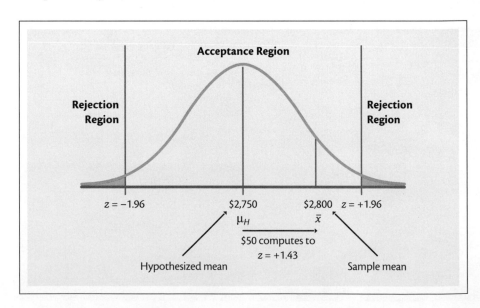

# HOW TO TEST A HYPOTHESIS ABOUT AN AVERAGE WITH XL DATA ANALYST

If the College Life E-Zine is to be successful, it must generate advertising revenues. You may not have thought about it, but all media vehicles depend on advertising revenues to be profitable, and advertisers will invest a great deal of advertising in media that effectively communicate with their target markets. Many companies see college students as a viable target market—just check out the advertising in your university newspaper or the billboards around campus to see which ones.

With our College Life E-Zine Web site, the advertising will be pop-up windows or embedded ads with hot links to the advertisers' Web sites. What types of companies should our College Life E-Zine approach to sell its online advertising space? We know (from Summarization analysis) that 24.2% of our respondents expect to make a purchase over the Internet in the next couple of months, and the survey asked these respondents to estimate how many dollars out of $100 in Internet purchases will be spent on general merchandise. Let's take the hypothesis that general merchandise will account for $20 out of each $100 of Internet purchases. If this hypothesis is supported, about 20% of the College Life E-Zine advertising recruitment effort should be aimed at general merchandise companies such as Target, Wal-Mart, Kmart, or Albertson's.

To test the hypothesis that the average will be 20 (dollars), you use the Generalize–Hypothesis Test–Average menu sequence to open up the selection window. Unlike the percentage hypothesis window, the average hypothesis test window has only one selection windowpane, as we must work with a metric variable. You will see in Figure 12.11 that we have selected the "Internet

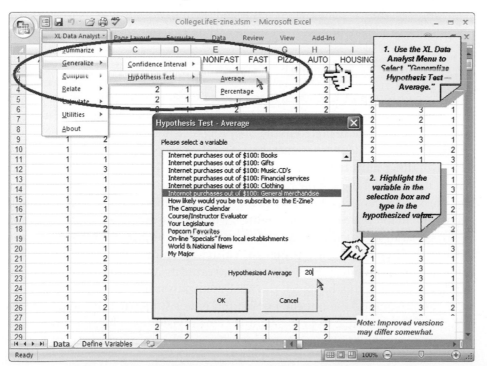

**Figure 12.11** XL Data Analyst Selection Menu for an Average Hypothesis Test

**Figure 12.12** XL Data Analyst Output Table and Results for an Average Hypothesis Test

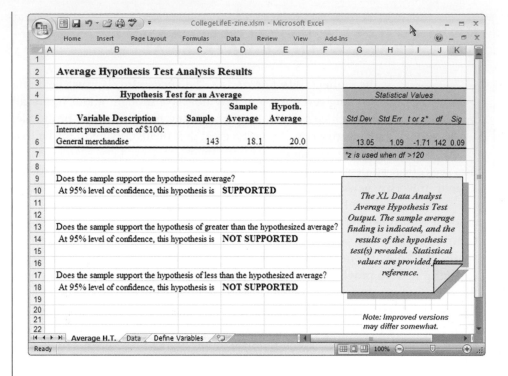

■ To have the XL Data Analyst test a hypothesis about an average, select the variable, input the hypothesized average, and click "OK."

purchases out of $100: General merchandise" variable and entered a "20" in the "Hypothesized Average" box. A click on "OK" completes our selection process.

Figure 12.12 reveals that 143 respondents answered this question (143/590 = 24.2%), and the average was found to be 18.1 (dollars). Our hypothesis of 20 dollars is supported. You should notice that if we had specified directional hypotheses, the XL Data Analyst has tested them in this analysis as well. Also, the statistical values are present in case you wish to examine them.

## Interpreting Your Hypothesis Test

How do you interpret hypothesis tests? Regardless of whether you are working with a percent hypothesis or an average hypothesis, the interpretation of a hypothesis test is again directly linked to the sampling distribution concept. If the hypothesis about the population parameter is correct or true, then a high percentage of sample findings must fall close to this hypothesized value. In fact, if the hypothesis is true, then 95% of the sample results will fall between ±1.96 standard errors of the hypothesized mean. On the other hand, if the hypothesis is incorrect, there is a strong likelihood that the sample findings will fall outside ±1.96 standard errors.

■ Interpretation of a hypothesis test is based on the sampling distribution concept.

In general, the further away the actual sample finding (percent or average) is from the hypothesized population value, the more likely the computed $z$ value will fall outside the critical range, resulting in a failure to support the hypothesis. When this happens, the XL Data Analyst tells the hypothesizer that his or her assumption about the population is not supported. It must be revised in light of the evidence from the sample. This revision is achieved through estimates of the population parameter just discussed in a previous section. These estimates can be used to provide the manager or researcher with a new mental picture of the population through confidence interval estimates of the true population value.

## Using the Six-Step Approach to Test a Hypothesis

As a means of summarizing our discussion of hypothesis tests and also to guide you when you are working with these tests, we have prepared a table that specifies how to apply our six-step analysis approach to hypothesis testing. Table 12.6 lists these six steps and provides an example of a hypothesis test for a percentage and one for a hypothesis test for an average using the College Life E-Zine survey data set.

**Table 12.6** The Six-Step Approach to Data Analysis for Generalization Objectives: Hypothesis Test

| Step | Explanation | Example (A is a categorical variable; B is a metric variable) |
|---|---|---|
| **1. What is the research objective?** | Determine that you are dealing with a **Hypothesis Test Generalization objective.*** | A. We hypothesize that 80% of college students will eat at a fast-food restaurant in the next week. <br><br> B. We hypothesize that those students who are likely (either very or somewhat likely) to subscribe to our College Life E-Zine will "Somewhat Prefer" the "Instructor & Course Evaluations" feature. |
| **2. What questionnaire question(s) is/are involved?** | Identify the question(s), and for each one specify if it is categorical or metric. | A. Will you eat at a fast-food restaurant in the next week? The answer "Yes" is *categorical*. <br><br> B. The scale is 1–5, for "Strongly Do Not Prefer," "Somewhat Do Not Prefer," "No Preference," "Somewhat Prefer," and "Strongly Prefer," respectively. This is a synthetic *metric* measure. |
| **3. What is the appropriate analysis?** | To test a hypothesis with a sample finding, use Hypothesis Test. | We must use a hypothesis test because we have to take into account variability and sample error. |
| **4. How do you run it?** | Use the proper XL Data Analyst analysis: Use "Generalize–Hypothesis Test–Percent" (categorical) or "Generalize–Hypothesis Test–Average" (metric). | |

**Table 12.6** *(Continued)*

| Step | Explanation | Example (A is a categorical variable; B is a metric variable) |
|------|-------------|----------------------------------------------------------------|
| **5. How do you interpret the findings?** | Accept or reject the hypothesis, meaning that if you repeated the survey many, many times and conducted the hypothesis test every one of these times, the hypothesis would be accepted (or rejected, depending on your sample's finding) 95% of those times. | **A. Eat at fast-food restaurant in the next week?** <br><br> See table below. <br><br> Does the sample support the hypothesized percent? <br> At 95% level of confidence, this hypothesis is **NOT SUPPORTED**. <br><br> **B. Hypothesis Test for an Average** <br><br> See table below. <br><br> At 95% level of confidence, this hypothesis is **SUPPORTED**. |
| **6. How do you write/present these findings?** | You can report that for the variable under analysis, the hypothesis of ## is accepted (or rejected depending on your sample's finding) at the 95% level of confidence. If rejected, it is proper to report the confidence interval for your sample's finding in order to estimate the true population value. | A. The hypothesis that 80% of college students will eat fast food in the coming week is not supported. The actual percentage is from 69.1% to 76.3% at the 95% level of confidence. <br><br> B. The (directional) hypothesis that those students who are likely to subscribe to our College Life E-Zine will at least "Somewhat Prefer" the "Instructor & Course Evaluations" feature is supported. |

**A. Eat at fast-food restaurant in the next week?**

| Category | Frequency | Sample Percent | Hypoth. Percent |
|----------|-----------|----------------|-----------------|
| Yes | 429 | 72.7% | 80.0% |
| **Total of All Categories** | 590 | | |

**B. Hypothesis Test for an Average**

| Variable Description | Sample | Sample Average | Hypoth. Average |
|----------------------|--------|----------------|-----------------|
| Course/Instructor Evaluator | 160 | 4.4 | 4.0 |

*You will learn about other analyses in subsequent chapters.

# SUMMARY

This chapter began by introducing you to the concept of generalization, in which you estimate a population fact with the use of a sample's finding. We moved to the notion of estimation of a population percentage or average through the use of confidence intervals. We provided the formulas for confidence intervals, examples of applications of these formulas, and instructions on how to use XL Data Analyst to compute a percentage or an average confidence interval. You learned that a confidence interval is wider with more variation but smaller with larger sample sizes. Next, we described how a researcher can test a hypothesis about a percentage or an average. That is, the researcher or manager may have a prior belief about what percent or average value exists in the population, and the sample findings can be used to assess the support or lack of support for this hypothesis. Again, we provided formulas for hypothesis tests, examples of applications of these formulas, and instructions on how to use XL Data Analyst to test hypotheses.

## KEY TERMS

Sample finding (p. 352)
Population fact (p. 352)
Generalization (p. 352)
"Parameter estimation" (p. 354)
Parameter (p. 354)
Confidence interval (p. 354)
Most commonly used level of
  confidence (p. 355)
Standard error (p. 357)

Standard error of the percentage
  (p. 357)
Sampling distribution (p. 358)
Standard error of the average (p. 361)
Hypothesis (p. 367)
Hypothesis testing (p. 367)
Intuitive hypothesis testing (p. 367)
Null hypothesis (p. 369)
Directional hypothesis (p. 372)

## REVIEW QUESTIONS

1 Distinguish between sample findings and population facts. How are they similar, and how may they differ?
2 Define "generalization," and provide an example of what you might generalize if you moved to a new city and noticed that you were driving faster than most other drivers.
3 What is a "parameter," and what is "parameter estimation"?
4 Describe how a confidence interval can be used by a researcher to estimate a population percentage.
5 What two levels of confidence are used most often, and which one is most commonly used?
6 Using the formula for a confidence interval for a percentage, indicate the role of:
   a The sample finding (percentage)
   b Variability
   c Level of confidence
7 Indicate how a researcher interprets a 95% confidence interval. Refer to the sampling distribution in your explanation.
8 In the case of a standard error of the average, indicate how it is affected by:
   a The standard deviation   b The sample size
9 What is a hypothesis and what is the purpose of a hypothesis test? With a hypothesis test, what is the "null hypothesis"?
10 How does statistical hypothesis testing differ from intuitive hypothesis testing? How are they similar?

**11** When performing a hypothesis test, what critical value of $z$ is the most commonly used one, and to what level of significance does it pertain?

**12** When the person who posited a hypothesis argues against the researcher who has performed the hypothesis test and not supported it, who should win the argument and why?

**13** Using a bell-shaped curve, show the acceptance (supported) and rejection (not supported) regions for:

**a** 95% level of confidence

**b** 99% level of confidence

**14** How does a directional hypothesis differ from a nondirectional one, and what are the two critical items to take into account when testing a directional hypothesis?

## APPLICATION QUESTIONS

**15** Here are several computation practice exercises in which you must identify which formula should be used and apply it. In each case, after you perform the necessary calculations, write your answers in the blank column.

**a** Determine confidence intervals for each of the following.

| Sample Statistic | Sample Size | Confidence Level | Your Confidence Intervals? |
|---|---|---|---|
| Mean: 150<br>  Std. Dev: 30 | 200 | 95% | |
| Percent: 67% | 300 | 99% | |
| Mean: 5.4<br>  Std. Dev: 0.5 | 250 | 99% | |
| Percent: 25.8% | 500 | 99% | |

**b** Test the following hypothesis and interpret your findings.

| Hypothesis | Sample Findings | Confidence Level | Your Test Results |
|---|---|---|---|
| Mean = 7.5 | Mean: 8.5<br>Std dev: 1.2<br>$n = 670$ | 95% | |
| Percent = 86% | $p = 95$<br>$n = 1,000$ | 99% | |
| Mean > 125 | Mean: 135<br>Std dev: 15<br>$n = 500$ | 95% | |
| Percent < 33% | $p = 31$<br>$n = 120$ | 99% | |

**16** The manager of Washington State Environmental Services Division wants a survey that will tell him how many households in the city of Seattle will voluntarily identify environmentally hazardous household materials like old cans of paint, unused pesticides, and other such materials than cannot be recycled but should be disposed of, and then transport all of their environmental hazardous items to a central disposal center located in the downtown area and open only on Sunday mornings. A random survey of 500 households determines that 20% of households would do so, and that each participating household expects to dispose of about 5 items per year with a standard deviation of 2 items. What is the value of parameter estimation in this instance?

**17** It is reported in the newspaper that a survey sponsored by *Forbes* magazine with 200 Fortune 500 company top executives has found that 75% believe that the United States trails Japan and Germany in automobile engineering. What percent of *all* Fortune 500 company top executives believe that the United States trails Japan and Germany?

**18** Alamo Rent-A-Car executives believe that Alamo accounts for about 50% of all Cadillacs that are rented. To test this belief, a researcher randomly identifies 20 major airports with on-site rental car lots. Observers are sent to each location and instructed to record the number of rental company Cadillacs observed in a four-hour period. About 500 are observed, and 30% are observed being returned to Alamo Rent-A-Car. What are the implications of this finding for the Alamo executives' belief?

# INTERACTIVE LEARNING

Visit the textbook Web site at **www.prenhall.com/burnsbush**. For this chapter, use the self-study quizzes and get quick feedback on whether or not you need additional studying. You can also review the chapter's major points by visiting the chapter outline and key terms.

▪ Load the **AutoOnline.xls** file provided for you with this textbook and use the XL Data Analyst to answer study (Case 12.1).

| CASE 12.1 | | The Auto Online Survey |

Auto Online is a Web site where prospective automobile buyers can find information about the various makes and models. Individuals can actually purchase a make and model with specific options and features online. Recently, Auto Online posted an online questionnaire on the Internet, and it mailed invitations to the last 5,000 automobile buyers who visited Auto Online. Some of these buyers bought their car from Auto Online, whereas the remaining individuals bought their autos from a dealership. However, they did visit Auto Online at least one time prior to that purchase. You may assume that the respondents to this survey are representative of the population of automobile buyers who visited the Auto Online Web site during their vehicle purchase process.

The Auto Online survey data set (and code book) is provided for you in an XL Data Analyst data file called **AutoOnline.xls**. Embedded in the questions below, we have provided copies of the relevant questions in the Auto Online survey. Your task is to use the Six-Step Approach to Data Analysis that we have described in this chapter to perform and interpret the proper analysis for each question part.

**1** In order to describe this population, estimate the population parameters for the following:

  **a** For those who have visited the Auto Online Web site, what percent found out about it from (1) an Internet banner ad, (2) Web surfing, and/or (3) a search engine?

     5 *How did you find out about Auto Online? Indicate all of the ways that you can recall.*

        \_\_\_\_ *From a friend (0,1)*

        \_\_\_\_ *Web surfing (0,1)*

        \_\_\_\_ *Theater (0,1)*

        \_\_\_\_ *Billboard (0,1)*

        \_\_\_\_ *Search engine (0,1)*

        \_\_\_\_ *Newspaper (0,1)*

        \_\_\_\_ *Internet banner ad (0,1)*

        \_\_\_\_ *Television (0,1)*

        \_\_\_\_ *Other (0,1)*

  **b** How often they make purchases online.

     2 *How often do you make purchases through the Internet?*

     *Very Often   5*

     *Often   4*

     *Occasionally   3*

     *Almost Never   2*

     *Never   1*

  **c** Number of visits they made to Auto Online.

     4 *About how many times before you bought your automobile did you visit the Auto Online Web site?*

        \_\_\_\_ *times*

  **d** The percentage who actually bought their vehicle from Auto Online.

     7 *Did you buy your new vehicle on the Auto Online Web site?*

        \_\_\_\_ *Yes (1)*   \_\_\_\_ *No (2)*

  **e** The percentage of those who felt it was a better experience than buying at a traditional dealership.

     a *If yes, was it a better experience than buying at a traditional dealership visit?*

        \_\_\_\_ *Yes (1)*   \_\_\_\_ *No (2)*

  **f** How do people feel about the Auto Online Web site?

     6 *What is your reaction to the following statements about the Auto Online Web site?*

| | Strongly Disagree | | Neutral | | Strongly Agree |
|---|---|---|---|---|---|
| *The Web site was easy to use.* | 1 | 2 | 3 | 4 | 5 |
| *I found the Web site was very helpful in my purchase.* | 1 | 2 | 3 | 4 | 5 |
| *I had a positive experience using the Web site.* | 1 | 2 | 3 | 4 | 5 |
| *I would use this Web site only for research.* | 1 | 2 | 3 | 4 | 5 |
| *The Web site influenced me to buy my vehicle.* | 1 | 2 | 3 | 4 | 5 |
| *I would feel secure to buy from this Web site.* | 1 | 2 | 3 | 4 | 5 |

**2** Auto Online principals have the following beliefs. Test these hypotheses.

**a** People will "strongly agree" to each of the first four of the eight statements concerning use of the Internet and purchase (question 3 on the questionnaire).

> 3 *Indicate your opinion on each of the following statements. For each one, please indicate if you strongly disagree, somewhat disagree, are neutral, somewhat agree, or strongly agree.*

|  | Strongly Disagree |  | Neutral |  | Strongly Agree |
|---|---|---|---|---|---|
| *I like using the Internet.* | 1 | 2 | 3 | 4 | 5 |
| *I use the Internet to research purchases I make.* | 1 | 2 | 3 | 4 | 5 |
| *I think purchasing items from the Internet is safe.* | 1 | 2 | 3 | 4 | 5 |
| *The Internet is a good tool to use when researching an automobile purchase* | 1 | 2 | 3 | 4 | 5 |
| *The Internet should not be used to purchase vehicles.* | 1 | 2 | 3 | 4 | 5 |
| *Online dealerships are just another way of getting you into the traditional dealership.* | 1 | 2 | 3 | 4 | 5 |
| *I like the process of buying a new vehicle.* | 1 | 2 | 3 | 4 | 5 |
| *I don't like to hassle with car salesmen.* | 1 | 2 | 3 | 4 | 5 |

**b** More than 90% of those buyers who say their Auto Online experience was better than buying at a traditional auto dealership will say that buying a vehicle online is "a great deal better" than buying it at a traditional dealership.

> *b If yes, indicate how much better.*
> _____ *A great deal better (1)*
> _____ *Much better (2)*
> _____ *Somewhat better (3)*
> _____ *Just a bit better (4)*

**c** Those who visit the Auto Online will…

**i** Be 35 years old,
> *13 What is your age? _____ years*

**ii** Trade in autos that are worth $10,000.

**iii** Buy cars with a sticker price of $15,000.

**iv** Actually pay $12,000 for their new automobile.
> *10 If you traded in a vehicle, approximately how much was it worth? $ _____*
> *11 What was the approximate sticker price of your new vehicle? $ _____*
> *12 What was the approximate actual price you paid for it? $ _____*

---

## CASE 12.2 ||| Your Integrated Case

### College Life E-Zine

### The College Life E-Zine Survey Generalization Analysis

*It will be useful to review the College Life E-Zine Integrated Case description in Chapter 3 as a reference to the various research objectives referred to in Case 12.2.*

This was an exciting time for our four potential Web entrepreneurs as Lori Baker, marketing intern working with Bob Watts at ORS Marketing Research, had just finished her PowerPoint presentation of the descriptive analysis results. "Wow," said Sarah, "I can see lots of things that we can do with our e-zine now that we have found all of this positive feedback about the concept. Let's get a copy of Lori's PowerPoint file and take this to the bank."

Bob, who had been sitting behind the four prospective College Life E-Zine originators during Lori's presentation, said, "Yes, the descriptive findings are impressive, and Lori's figures are certainly first-rate, but I need to remind everyone that we're dealing with a sample of State U students, so we need to take this fact into account. Do you remember our discussion about the sample size and the use of confidence intervals? We're going to need to perform generalization analyses of various sorts before you can take this survey to the bank. Specifically, we'll need to compute confidence intervals for percentages and averages, and we have some hypotheseses to test in order to feel confident about our break-even analysis."

Wesley took a quick look at Don, and then asked Bob, "Do we really need this? I mean, the descriptive findings that Lori presented are very impressive to me."

Bob answered, "I know that Lori's graphs are very professional, but part of my responsibility as a marketing researcher is to arm you with as much objective evidence as possible, and if we do the proper generalization analyses, and if they come out as we hope, your case will be airtight. No one will be able to shoot you down. My recommendation is that you take Lori's PowerPoint file and review the descriptive findings over the next week. You can discuss the many implications of these findings among yourselves. Meanwhile, Lori and I will do the necessary generalization analyses, and then you can see the findings as they pertain to the entire student body of State U. Let's meet a week from now so Lori and I can show you our findings then."

Sarah, Anna, Wesley, and Don thought about Bob's recommendation, and all quickly agreed when Anna said, "Come on, guys, we have plenty to think about, and we're a long way from launching our College Life E-Zine, so I vote that we do as Bob recommends."

After the four budding entrepreneurs left the ORS building, Bob called Lori into his office and said, "Use the XL Data Analyst to perform the following generalization analyses on the College Life E-Zine survey data set. Since you're a marketing intern, I've included some items that are not necessarily a part of our survey objectives, but which will give you some practice performing and interpreting generalization analyses.

So, I want your interpretation of each finding. Oh, and some of these are a little vague, as I want you to figure out what type of scale you're working with and what the appropriate analysis is. Let's meet early next week to see what you've found."

1  Determine 95% confidence intervals for the relevant population for each of the following:
   a  High-speed cable access
   b  Use of coupons
   c  Whether they will purchase over the Internet in the next two months
   d  How much they anticipate spending on Internet purchasing in the next two months
   e  Out of every $100 of Internet purchases, how much do State U students spend on . . .
      i.    Books
      ii.   Gifts for weddings and other special occasions
      iii.  Music/CDs
      iv.   Financial services (insurance, loans, etc.)
      v.    Clothing
      vi.   General merchandise for your home or car
   f  "Very likely" to subscribe to the College Life E-Zine
   g  Preference for the following possible e-zine features:
      i.    Popcorn Favorites
      ii.   Student Government
      iii.  What's Happen'n
   h  Living off campus
2  Test the following hypotheses:
   a  90% of State U students have some form of Internet access.
   b  50% of those with Internet access have a dial-up modem connection.
   c  70% of State U students will eat fast food in the coming week.
   d  25% will purchase new clothes next month.
   e  At least 18% of those who qualify are "very likely" to subscribe to the College Life E-Zine at a price of $15 per month.
   f  Those students who qualify will at least "somewhat prefer" the following possible E-Zine features:
      i.    On-Line Registrar
      ii.   Cyber Cupid
      iii.  Weather Today
      iv.   My Advisor

**g** "Quick Facts" on State U's Web site says that 15% of its students live on campus. Is our College Life E-Zine survey sample consistent with this fact?

**h** "Quick Facts" also states that the male/female student ratio at State U is 50/50. Is our College Life E-Zine survey sample consistent with this fact?

# CHAPTER 13

## 13

## COMPARING TO FIND DIFFERENCES IN YOUR DATA

### WHO IS AMERICA'S FAVORITE MOVIE STAR?

Popularity of celebrities is an important factor when selecting actors for starring roles in movies and when selecting the appropriate individual as spokesperson in promotional materials. The Harris Poll® reported the results of a public opinion survey that determined America's favorite movie stars. The overall winner: Denzel Washington. Tom Hanks was second, and movie legend John Wayne still occupied a high third-place position.

But what if you were a cosmetics firm or women's dress designer targeting females? You may want to ask, were there differences in popularity of movie stars depending on whether the respondent was male or female? The answer is "Yes!" The Harris Poll® reports differences based upon gender, as well as a number of other factors, including demographic groups, political ideology, and region of the country.

- To understand how market segmentation underlies differences analysis
- To learn how to assess the significance of the difference between two groups' percentages
- To learn how to assess the significance of the difference between two groups' averages
- To understand when "analysis of variance" (ANOVA) is used and how to interpret ANOVA findings
- To gain knowledge of the "Differences" analyses available with XL Data Analyst

Male: Clint Eastwood

Female: Julia Roberts

Echo Boomers (ages 18–29): Tom Hanks

Gen Xers (ages 30–41): Tom Hanks

Baby Boomers (ages 42–60): John Wayne

Matures (ages 61 and over): Julia Roberts

Conservatives: Tom Hanks and John Wayne

Liberals and Moderates: Denzel Washington

East: Clint Eastwood

West: Will Smith

South: Denzel Washington

Midwest: Brad Pitt

By examining differences among subgroups, The Harris Poll® provides users of their data with additional insights that allows greater usefulness of the research results. By understanding their target markets, marketers are in a much better position to select celebrity spokespersons by knowing these subgroup differences. In this chapter you will learn how to conduct differences analysis.

The Harris Poll® is conducted by HarrisInteractive®, a company known for high-quality surveying. You can visit The Harris Poll® results by going to www.harrisinteractive.com and clicking on "News & Events" and then "The Harris Poll."

Best actress Halle Berry and best actor Denzel Washington pose with their Academy Awards.

As you learned in Chapter 12, it is possible to make generalizations about measures of central tendency such as averages and percentages found in a probability sample survey. These generalizations, or inferences, take the form of confidence intervals or tests of hypotheses. A different type of inference concerns differences. That is, often the researcher is interested in groups, and particularly the degree to which the groups differ. For example, are college students more likely to buy a Red Bull energy drink than high school students? In this chapter, we describe the logic of differences tests, and we show you how to use XL Data Analyst to conduct various types of differences tests.

We begin this chapter by discussing why differences are important to marketing managers. Surely you have learned from our opening vignette that popular actor celebrity groups in the United States exhibit surprising differences that have profound marketing strategy implications. Next, we introduce you to differences (percentages or averages) between two independent groups, such as a comparison of high-speed cable versus DSL telephone Internet users on how satisfied they are with their Internet connection service. Next, we introduce you to ANOVA, a scary name but a simple way to compare the averages of several groups simultaneously and to quickly spot patterns of significant differences. Finally, we show you that it is possible to test whether a difference exists between the averages of two similarly scaled questions. For instance, do buyers rate a store higher in "merchandise selection" than they rate its "good values"? As in previous analysis chapters, we provide formulas and numerical examples, and also show you examples of XL Data Analyst procedures and output using the College Life E-Zine survey data set.

## WHY DIFFERENCES ARE IMPORTANT

■ Market segmentation is an important reason for analyzing differences.

One of the most vital marketing strategy concepts is market segmentation. In a nutshell, **market segmentation** holds that within a product market, there are different types of consumers who have different requirements, and these differences can be the bases of marketing strategies. For example, the Iams Company, which markets pet foods, has more than a dozen different varieties of dry dog food geared to the dog's age (puppy versus adult), weight situation (normal versus overweight), and activity (active versus inactive). Toyota Motors has 17 models, including the two-seat Spyder sports car, the four-door Avalon luxury sedan, the Highlander SUV, and the Tacoma truck. Even Boeing Airlines has seven different types of commercial jets and a separate business jet division for corporate travel. The needs and requirements of each market segment differ greatly from others, and an astute marketer will customize his or her marketing mix to each target market's unique situation.[1]

Some differences, of course, are quite obvious, but as competition becomes more intense, with aggressive market segmentation and target marketing being the watchword of most companies in an industry, there is a need to investigate differences among consumer groups for consumer marketers and among business establishments for B2B marketers. In a nutshell, market segmentation relies on the discovery of significant differences through the application of the proper data analysis. Of course, the differences must be meaningful and useful: Energetic, growing puppies need different nutritional supplements than do overweight, inactive, aging dogs with stiff joints, so Iams uses these different nutritional needs to formulate special types of dog food for these market segments.

■ **Significant differences must be meaningful and useful.**

In what might be considered an extreme example of market segmentation, Harrah's Entertainment, which operates 26 gambling casinos in 13 U.S. states, has analyzed its slot machine players—estimated to be 25 million people—and claims to have identified 90 different market segmentation types based on age, gender, game preference, casino location, and other variables.[2] This segmentation analysis has revealed that one of these segments amounts to about one-third of its customers, yet it represents 80% of revenues. Also, Harrah's claims that by custom-tailoring its marketing strategies to various market segments, it has significantly increased its market share and become more profitable.

Analyzing for significant and meaningful differences is a discovery process. That is, the marketing researcher and manager formulate the research objectives with the goal of finding useful market segmentation differences in the total market,

Harrah's uses market segmentation to target specific types of gamblers.

but there is no guarantee that significant and meaningful differences will be found. Data analysis is used to investigate for statistically significant differences, and there are rules and guidelines about how to decide when significant differences are indeed found. This chapter will inform you of the rules, and once you have learned them, you will be able to spot and interpret differences easily.[3]

Let's take the instance of a personal communication system (PCS) company like Sprint and see how a researcher might look for market segment differences. There are three ways a researcher can analyze for differences in the service Sprint customers might want: (1) compare one group to another group, such as comparing men to women customers; (2) compare three or more groups, such as people who are single, those who are married without children, those who are married with teenagers living at home, and those who are married with one or more children in college; or (3) compare how important one service feature (such as rollover minutes) is compared to another service feature (such as sharing minutes with family members). You will learn how to perform differences tests for each of these three cases in this chapter.

> ■ There are three types of differences analysis performed by market researchers.

# TESTING FOR SIGNIFICANT DIFFERENCES BETWEEN TWO GROUPS

Often a researcher will want to compare two groups that exist in the same sample. That is, the researcher may have identified two independent groups such as walk-ins versus loyal customers, men versus women, or coupon users versus those who never use coupons, and he or she may want to compare their answers to the same question. The question may use either a categorical scale or a metric scale. A categorical scale requires that the researcher compare the percentage for one group to the percentage for the other group, whereas he or she will compare averages group-to-group when a metric scale is involved. As you know by now, the formulas differ depending on whether percentages or averages are being tested. But, as you also can guess, the basic concepts involved in the formulas are identical.

## Differences Between Percentages for Two Groups

> ■ When a researcher compares two groups in a survey, it is as though a separate survey were conducted with each group.

When a marketing researcher compares two groups of respondents to determine whether or not there are statistically significant differences between them, the researcher is considering them to be two independent populations. That is, it is as though two independent surveys were administered, one for each group. The question to be answered then becomes "Are the respective parameters of these two independent populations different?" But, as always, a researcher can work only with the sample results. Therefore, the researcher falls back on statistical generalization concepts to determine whether the difference that is found between the two sample findings is a true difference between the two populations. You will shortly discover that the logic of differences tests is very similar to the logic of hypothesis testing that you learned in the previous chapter.

Gender is a demographic variable that is often used by marketers to segment their markets. Let's take the case of a video and DVD rental store that has added a line of candy, chips, pretzels, popcorn, and soft drinks. The manager pulls the sales slips from 100 randomly selected male customers and finds that 65% of them bought a snack item when they rented their movies. A different sample of 300 randomly selected female customers reveals that 40% bought a food item when they rented their movies. In other words, we have two surveys—a sample of males and a separate sample of females who rent from this video store—and we have two percentages, 65% of the men and 40% of the women, who bought munchies with their movie rentals.

Are male movie renters and females movie renters different with respect to buying snacks along with their movie rentals? It sure seems so, as there is a 25% arithmetic (65% − 40%) difference, but you cannot be completely confident of your conclusion about two populations (men and women movie renters) represented here because of sampling error. Sampling error is based on the sample sizes (100 men versus 300 women) and the variability of the percent of munchies buyers: 65% and 40%. Now, doesn't this sound very familiar to the logic we used when describing hypothesis tests?

> Differences analysis uses logic very similar to that in hypothesis tests.

To test whether a true difference exists between two group percentages, we test the null hypothesis that the difference in their population parameters is equal to zero. (We introduced you to the null hypothesis concept in Chapter 12.) The **alternative hypothesis** is that there is a true difference between the two group percentages (or averages) that we are comparing. The alternative hypothesis is, of course, the crux of market segmentation differences, so a marketing researcher is always hoping for the null hypothesis to *not* be supported. In other words, the researcher would very much like to report that significant differences were found because this is the first of the two conditions for market segmentation that we described earlier, namely, a significant difference.

> The null hypothesis holds that there is no difference between one group and the other.

To perform the test of significance of differences between two percentages, each representing a separate group (sample), the first step requires a "comparison" of the two percentages. By "comparison," we mean that you find the arithmetic difference between them. The second step requires that this difference be translated into a number of standard errors away from the hypothesized value of zero. Once the number of standard errors is known, knowledge of the area under the normal curve will yield an assessment of the support for the null hypothesis. Again, we hope this description sounds familiar to you, for it is almost exactly the same procedure used to test a hypothesis, which we described in our previous chapter. The only departure is that in the present case, we are comparing two percents from two samples ($p_1$ to $p_2$), while in a hypothesis test for a percent, we compare the hypothesized percent to the percent in the sample ($p$ to $\pi_H$).

> A differences test is a comparison of one group's percent or average to the other's by way of simple subtraction. Then this value is divided by the standard error of the difference.

Here is the formula for the test of the significance of the difference between two percentages.

$$z = \frac{p_1 - p_2}{s_{p_1-p_2}}$$

> ◀ **Formula for significance of the difference between two percentages**

where

$p_1$ = percent for sample 1
$p_2$ = percent for sample 2
$s_{p_1-p_2}$ = standard error of the difference between two percentages

Because we have two samples instead of the one that we worked with for a hypothesis test, the standard error term is calculated differently and called the **standard error of the difference between two percentages**. Here is its formula:

**Formula for the standard error of the difference between two percentages** ▷

$$s_{p_1 - p_2} = \sqrt{\frac{p_1 \times q_1}{n_1} + \frac{p_2 \times q_2}{n_2}}$$

where

$p_1$ = percent for sample 1, and $q_1 = (100 - p_1)$
$p_2$ = percent for sample 2, and $q_2 = (100 - p_2)$
$n_1, n_2$ = sample sizes for sample 1 and sample 2, respectively

Refer to Table 13.1 to follow, step-by-step, how to perform a test of the difference between two percents.

The sampling distribution under consideration now is the assumed sampling distribution of the differences between the percentages. That is, the assumption has been made that the differences have been computed for comparisons of the two sample percents for many repeated samplings. If the null hypothesis is true, this distribution of differences follows the normal curve, with an average equal to zero and a standard error equal to one. Stated somewhat differently, the procedure requires us, as before, to accept the (null) hypothesis as true until it lacks support from the statistical test. Consequently, the differences of (theoretically) hundreds of comparisons of the two sample percentages generated from many, many samplings would average zero. In other words, our sampling distribution is now the distribution of the difference between one sample and the other, taken over many, many times.

■ The standard error of the difference takes into account each group's percent and sample size.

**Table 13.1**  How to Determine If One Group's Percentage Is Different from Another Group's Percentage

Marketers are very interested in differences between groups because they offer potentially important market segmentation implications. As you might expect, the researcher assesses how close the percent for one group is to the percent for another group with a type of differences analysis. In this example, we are wondering if male movie renters differ from female ones with respect to purchases of candy, snack items, and soft drinks along with their rentals. The steps are as follows:

| Step | Description | Our Movie Rental Store Example |
|---|---|---|
| Step 1 | Determine the percent and sample size for each of your two samples. | The movie rental store manager has found that 65% of the 100 male customers buy food items, while 40% of the 300 female customers buy food items. |
| Step 2 | Compare the two percentages by taking their arithmetic difference. | The difference is 65% − 40%, or 25%. (The sign does not matter.) |
| Step 3 | Determine the *standard error of the difference between two percentages*. (This procedure is described above.) | Standard error $= \sqrt{\frac{(65 \times 35)}{100} + \frac{(40 \times 60)}{300}}$ $= 5.55\%$ |

| Step 4 | Divide the difference between the two sample percentages by the standard error of the difference between percents. Call it z. | $z = 25/5.55$ <br> $= 4.5$ |
|---|---|---|
| Step 5 | Using the critical z value, determine whether the null hypothesis is supported or not supported at your chosen level of confidence* (95% is customary, meaning a z of 1.96). | In our example, 4.5 is much larger than 1.96, so the null hypothesis is not supported. In other words, male and female movie renters are different in their purchase of food items when they rent their movies. |

\* The significance level is provided automatically by practically any analysis program that you use.

Look at Figure 13.1 and you will see that the women's and the men's populations are represented by two bell-shaped sampling distribution curves. With the women movie renters' curve, the apex is at 40%, while the men's curve apex is at 65%. This shows that if we replicated our surveys many, many times, the central value for women movie renters would be 40%, and the central value for men movie renters would be 65% who purchase a snack item with their movie rentals. In Figure 13.1 there is also the sampling distribution of the difference between two percents. Its apex is 0 to represent the null hypothesis that there is no difference between the two populations. The standard error of the difference curve has a mean of 0, and its horizontal axis is measured with standard errors such that it embodies the assumptions of a normal, or bell-shaped, curve.

If we are computing our differences test manually, we compare the computed z value with our standard z of 1.96 for a 95% level of confidence, and the computed z in Step 4 of Table 13.1 is 4.5. As you can see in Figure 13.1, 4.5 is certainly larger than 1.96. A computed z value that is larger than the critical z value amounts to no support for the null hypothesis because it falls outside the 95% area of our standard error of the difference curve. Thus, there is a statistically

■ The mean of the standard error of the differences is zero, and its distribution is a bell-shaped curve.

Do men differ from women with respect to buying snacks with their video rentals?

**Figure 13.1** Comparison of Women and Men Video Renters Sampling Distributions for Purchase of a Snack Item with His/Her Video

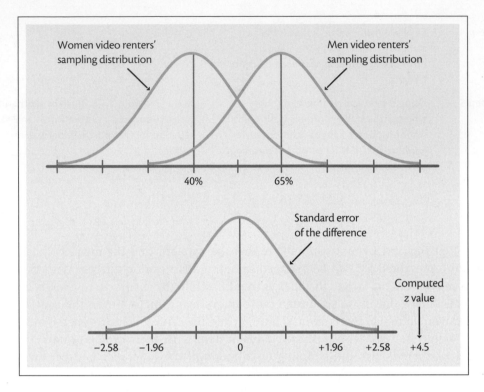

significant difference between the two percentages, and we are confident that if we repeated this comparison many, many times with a multitude of independent samples, we would conclude that there is a significant difference in at least 95% of these replications. Of course, we would never do many, many replications, but this is the statistician's basis for the assessment of significant differences between the two percents.

■ The notions in Figure 13.1 underlie all differences analyses described in this chapter.

It is important that you study and understand Figure 13.1, as the sampling distributions concept and the standard error of the difference notion underlie every differences analysis we will describe in this chapter. In fact, we will refer back to Figure 13.1 three times in this chapter for this reason rather than build new figures that demonstrate the same concepts.

Directional hypotheses are also feasible in the case of tests of statistically significant differences. The procedure is identical to directional hypotheses that are stipulated in hypothesis tests. That is, you must first look at the sign of the computed $z$ value to check that it is consistent with your hypothesized direction. Then

■ Differences analysis may be "directional" and the critical $z$ value is adjusted accordingly.

you would use a cutoff $z$ value such as 1.64 standard errors for the 95% level of confidence (2.33 standard errors for 99% level of confidence) because only one tail of the sampling distribution is being used.

There are, of course, a great many differences between men and women, but a recent study that might be of interest to our College Life E-Zine entrepreneurs compared the Internet-usage differences between men and women.[4] The differences analysis found that men are goal-directed and typically in search of information. It was determined that men want objective and accurate information that is quite detailed, and they are often seeking answers to questions that they have about products, financial issues, and their personal interest in software or hobbies. An interesting counterintuitive finding is that men do not wish to search far for answers; in fact, one might characterize them as impatient information searchers. Women Internet users, on the other hand, tend to be searching general reference topics. They also check out e-books, seek medical information, surf for cooking hints and recipes, and click on government information. Women with families look at child-rearing Web sites, and other women gravitate to social causes on the Internet.

## Differences Between Averages for Two Groups

The procedure for testing the significance of the difference between two averages from two different groups (samples) is identical to the procedure used in testing two percentages. As you can easily guess, however, the equations differ because a

## USING THE XL DATA ANALYST TO DETERMINE THE SIGNIFICANCE OF THE DIFFERENCE BETWEEN TWO GROUP PERCENTS

The XL Data Analyst can easily compare two mutually exclusive groups as to their respective percentage on a category of some variable. Let's assume that we are interested in seeing if there is a difference between male and female State University students surveyed in our College Life E-Zine case with regard to their use of coupons. That is, we want to know if the percent of women respondents who say "Yes" to intending to order a pizza delivery in the coming week is equal to the percent of men respondents who say "Yes" to this question in our survey.

Figure 13.2 shows the selection menu sequence for the XL Data Analyst to accomplish this test. Notice that you use the command sequence of Compare 2 Group Percents, and then you select the grouping variable categories of male and female for gender in this instance, and you select the target variable value of "Yes" for "Order a pizza to be delivered in the next week?" We define a **grouping variable** as the variable that is used to identify the groups that are to be compared with respect to differences. The **target variable** is the variable on which the groups will be compared. Here, gender is the grouping variable, and the "Yes" indication for the pizza-ordering question is the target variable's value.

The result of this difference analysis is found in Figure 13.3, and when you study this output, you will find that of the 320 male respondents, 82.5% indicated "yes," while of the 280 female respondents, 73.2% responded with a "yes" to the pizza question. The arithmetic difference is 9.3%, and at the bottom of the Difference Analysis Test Table, the XL Data Analyst has reported that the hypothesis of equal percents (the null hypothesis) is "Not Supported." In other words, there is a true difference with respect to ordering a delivery pizza in the next week for male versus female State U students.

■ With the XL Data Analyst, specify the grouping variable that defines the groups to compare, and then select the target variable's value that defines the nature of the comparison.

**Figure 13.2** Using the XL Data Analyst to Set Up a Two-Group Percents Analysis

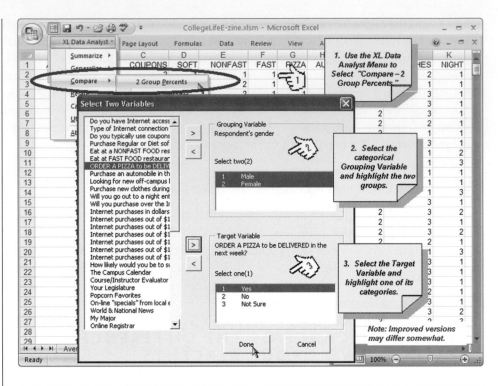

**Figure 13.3** XL Data Analyst Two-Group Percents Differences Analysis Output

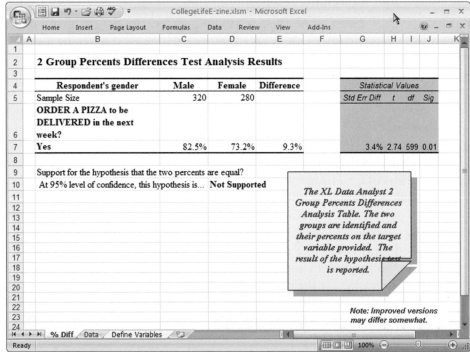

■ The procedure for comparing two group averages is identical to the one for comparing two group percents except for the substitution of appropriate formulas.

metric scale is involved. As with a percentages difference test, the average for one sample is "compared" to the average for the other sample. Recall that "compared" means "take the difference." This value is then divided by the standard error of the difference between averages. Here is the formula.

$$z = \frac{\overline{x}_1 - \overline{x}_2}{s_{\overline{x}_1 - \overline{x}_2}}$$

◀ **Formula for significance of the difference between two averages**

where
$\overline{x}_1$  = average found in sample 1
$\overline{x}_2$  = average found in sample 2
$s_{\overline{x}_1 - \overline{x}_2}$ = standard error of the difference between two averages

The standard error of the difference is easy to calculate and again relies on the variability that has been found in the samples and their sizes. The formula for the standard error of the difference between two averages is:

$$s_{\overline{x}_1 - x_2} = \sqrt{\frac{s_1^2}{n_1} + \frac{s_2^2}{n_2}}$$

◀ **Formula for the standard error of the difference between two averages**

where
$s_1$ = standard deviation in sample 1
$s_2$ = standard deviation in sample 2
$n_1$ = size of sample 1
$n_2$ = size of sample 2

To illustrate how significance of difference computations are made, we use the following example, which answers the question "Do male teens and female teens drink different amounts of sports drinks?" In a recent survey, teenagers were asked to indicate how many 20-ounce bottles of sports drinks they consume in a typical week. The descriptive statistics revealed that males consume 9 bottles on average and females consume 7.5 bottles of sports drinks on average. The respective standard deviations were found to be 2 and 1.2. Both samples were of size 100. We have prepared Table 13.2 as a step-by-step explanation of the procedures used to test the null hypothesis that males and females are equal in number of bottles of sports drink consumed in a typical week.

As we indicated earlier, Figure 13.1 illustrates how this analysis takes place. Since we are now working with averages, the two sampling distribution curves would be for the females' and males' averages, with the means of 7.5 and 9.0 under their respective apexes. The standard error of the difference curve would remain essentially as it appears in Figure 13.1, except the computed $z$ value would now be 6.43.

Patrick M. Baldasare, former President and CEO of the Response Center, a Philadelphia research and consulting firm, and Vikas Mittel, a former research analyst at the Response Center, provide some useful insights on *statistical* versus *practical* significance.[5] They say that researchers often misuse and abuse the concept of significance, for they tend to associate statistical significance with the magnitude of the result. People often think that if the difference between two numbers is significant, it must be large and therefore *must* be considered important. To remedy this misuse of the concept of significance, Baldasare and Mittel suggest that when comparing numbers, we should consider two types of significance: *statistical*

PRACTICAL

APPLICATIONS

**Table 13.2** How to Determine If One Group's Average Is Different from Another Group's Average

When metric data are being used, the researcher compares the averages. The procedure and logic are identical to that used when comparing two percents; however, the formulas differ, as averages and standard deviations are appropriate for metric data. In our example, we are investigating the possible differences between males and females with respect to the number of bottles of sports drink they drink in a typical week. The steps are described below.

| Step | Description | Our Sports Drink Example |
|------|-------------|--------------------------|
| **Step 1** | Determine the average, standard deviation, and sample size for each of your two samples. | We find that 100 males drink 9.0 bottles, while 100 females drink 7.5 bottles of sports drink per week, on the average. The standard deviations are 2.0 and 1.2, respectively. |
| **Step 2** | Compare the two averages by taking their arithmetic difference. | The difference is (9.0 − 7.5) or 1.5. (The sign does not matter.) |
| **Step 3** | Determine the *standard error of the difference between two averages*. (This procedure is described on page 399.) | $$Standard\ error = \sqrt{\frac{2^2}{100} + \frac{1.2^2}{300}}$$ $$= \sqrt{.04 + .0144}$$ $$= .233$$ |
| **Step 4** | Divide the difference between the two sample averages by the standard error of the difference between averages. Call it *z*. | $$z = \frac{1.5}{0.233}$$ $$= 6.43$$ |
| **Step 5** | Using the appropriate statistical table, determine whether the null hypothesis is accepted or rejected at your chosen level of confidence.* | In our example, the significance level would be .000, so the null hypothesis is rejected. In other words, males and females are different with respect to the number of bottles of sports drink they consume in a typical week. |

*The significance level is provided automatically by practically any analysis program that you use.

*significance* and *practical significance*. By understanding the difference between statistical and practical significance, we can avoid the pitfall that traps many in the research industry.

A *statistical* significance level of, say, 95% merely implies that, if we were to do the study over and over for 100 times, 95 times out of 100 the difference we observe now would repeat itself in the sample data. But statistical significance does not tell us anything about how important the difference is, regardless of the size of the difference we see in the observed data. *Practical* significance depends on whether or not there is a managerial application that uses the difference. That is, when the researcher reports a significant difference, it is up to the manager or the researcher working with the manager to assess the practical usefulness of the difference. When the difference is deemed to be important and useful to the marketing manager, then it has practical significance.

Researchers and executives at the American Heart Association discuss the practical meaning of data that are statistically significant.

## USING THE XL DATA ANALYST TO DETERMINE THE SIGNIFICANCE OF THE DIFFERENCE BETWEEN TWO GROUP AVERAGES

Since differences analysis is so vital to marketing research, the XL Data Analyst most definitely performs a difference analysis for the comparison of one group's average to the average of a separate group. To illustrate the operation of this analysis, we will tackle the question of whether or not differences exist in State University students' likelihoods of subscribing to the College Life E-Zine. Recall that the survey asked the question "How likely would you be to subscribe to the e-zine?" and respondents indicated their likelihood on a 5-point balanced symmetric scale where 1 = very unlikely and 5 = very likely. To illustrate the operation of the XL Data Analyst's two-group-averages comparison analysis, let's see if the average for seniors is equal to the average for freshmen. To direct the XL Data Analyst to perform this analysis, use the Compare–2 Group Averages menu sequence that will open up the selection window, as shown in Figure 13.4. Select the categorical variable into the Grouping Variable window, and highlight the two groups: Freshman and Senior. Then select the likelihood variable into the Target Variable window. (Note: You can select multiple target variables if you desire.)

Figure 13.5 contains the results of the XL Data Analyst's Two-Group Averages analysis. In the table, you can see that the Freshman and Senior averages (3.4 and 2.2, respectively) are reported along with the number of students comprising each subsample (116 and 193, respectively). The arithmetic difference of 1.2 is indicated, and the hypothesis test outcome is also indicated. In this case, the "No" signifies that the null hypothesis that there is no difference between the two averages is not supported. That is, there is a significant difference between the two averages, with freshmen students showing more interest in the College Life E-Zine than seniors at State U.

■ **To compare two group averages, specify the two groups with the grouping variable, then select the metric target variable with which the group averages will be computed.**

**Figure 13.4** Using the XL Data Analyst to Set Up a Two-Group Averages Analysis

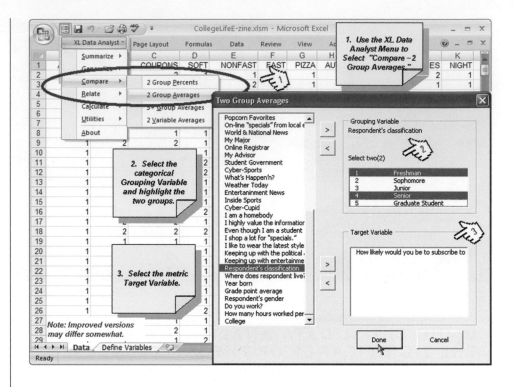

**Figure 13.5** XL Data Analyst Two-Group Averages Differences Analysis Output

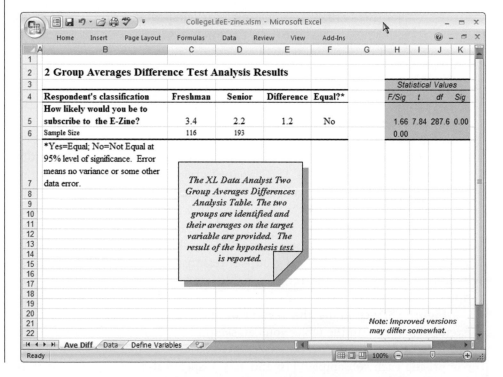

## The Six-Step Process for Analyzing Differences Between Two Groups

Thus far, we have described how to perform analysis of differences between two groups in your sample—males versus females, seniors versus freshmen, buyers versus nonbuyers, or any other two mutually exclusive groups that you can identify in your survey. You should be aware that the analysis depends on the scaling assumptions of the test variable. If the test variable is categorical, the comparison must be based on percents; whereas, when the test variable is metric, the averages are compared.

Table 13.3 walks you through our six-step analytical process for differences analysis when two groups in the sample are being compared. As you review Table 13.3, you should take note that the scaling assumptions of the target variable determine if percents are to be compared or if averages are to be compared. A categorical target variable requires a percents comparison, while a metric target variable necessitates the use of a group averages difference analysis.

**Table 13.3** The Six-Step Approach to Data Analysis for Differences Between Two Groups

| Step | Explanation | Example (A is a categorical test variable; B is a metric test variable) |
|---|---|---|
| **1. What is the research objective?** | Determine that you are dealing with a **Two-Group Differences objective**. | A. We want to determine whether students who use coupons are different from students who do not use coupons with respect to intended non–fast-food restaurant patronage in the coming weeks.<br><br>B. We want to determine if the average expected dollar Internet purchases in the next two months differ for high-speed cable modem users versus DSL users. |
| **2. What questionnaire question(s) is/are involved?** | Identify the question(s), and for each one specify whether it is categorical or metric. | A. Use/nonuse (yes versus no) of coupons is *categorical*, and intend/do not intend (yes versus no) to purchase a non–fast-food meal is *categorical*.<br><br>B. High-speed modem versus DSL are *categorical* groups, while expected dollars spent on the Internet is a *metric* measure. |
| **3. What is the appropriate analysis?** | To compare the percents or averages of two groups, use two group comparisons analysis. | We must use differences analysis because we have to take into account variability and sample error. |
| **4. How do you run it?** | Use XL Data Analyst analysis: Select "Compare–2 Group Percents" (categorical) or "Compare–2 Group Averages" (metric). | |

**Table 13.3** *(Continued)*

| Step | Explanation | Example (A is a categorical test variable; B is a metric test variable) |
|---|---|---|
| **5. How do you interpret the findings?** | The XL Data Analyst indicates percent differences are indeed, true (supported), while the average dollar amounts are not significantly different. | *(see below)* |

**Two-Group Percents Differences Test Analysis Results**

| Do you typically use coupons . . . etc. | Yes | No | Difference |
|---|---|---|---|
| Sample Size | 136 | 415 | |
| **Eat at a non–fast-food restaurant in the next week?** | | | |
| **Yes** | 70.6% | 32.3% | 38.3% |

Support for the hypothesis that the two percents are equal?

At 95% level of confidence, this hypothesis is…          **Not Supported**

**Two-Group Averages Difference Test Analysis Results**

| Variable Analyzed | High-Speed Cable | DSL | Difference | Equal?* |
|---|---|---|---|---|
| **Internet purchases in the next 2 months?** | $64.80 | $57.00 | $7.80 | Yes |
| Sample Size | 123 | 20 | | |

*Yes = Support; No = Not Support at 95% level of significance

| **6. How do you write/ present these findings?** | When significant differences are found, present them with a graph or a table (see A). When differences are not significant, state this fact (see B). | *(see below)* |
|---|---|---|

A.

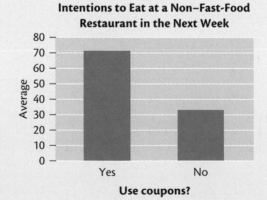

Intentions to Eat at a Non–Fast-Food Restaurant in the Next Week

B. No significant difference was found in the intended dollar amount of Internet purchases over the next two months for high-speed modem users versus DSL users.

# TESTING FOR SIGNIFICANT DIFFERENCES BETWEEN MORE THAN TWO GROUP AVERAGES

The need to understand differences between groups is fundamental not only to marketing researchers, but to other business researchers as well. Read Marketing Research Application 13.1 to see how differences analyses reveal why global businesspersons encounter difficulties when dealing with individuals who originate from different cultural regions.[6]

## MARKETING RESEARCH APPLICATION 13.1

### Analysis Reveals Ethical Philosophy Differences by Region of the Globe

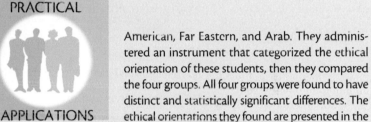

PRACTICAL APPLICATIONS

Almost every day, we read in the newspaper, see on television, or find on the Internet that the citizens of some country are angered—sometimes to the point of committing violent acts—by the policies or actions of other countries. On a more subtle level, global business partnerships often encounter opposing beliefs as to what business practices or customs are acceptable. For instance, American businesspersons are sometimes frustrated by the deliberate nature of negotiations with prospective Asian or Arab buyers, and Latin American sellers are sometimes surprised by the quick, almost impulsive, decisions of American buyers.

In an attempt to understand the underpinnings of cultural differences such as these, researchers sought to measure and compare the basic ethical orientations of university students who represented four different global regions: Anglo-American, Latin

American, Far Eastern, and Arab. They administered an instrument that categorized the ethical orientation of these students, then they compared the four groups. All four groups were found to have distinct and statistically significant differences. The ethical orientations they found are presented in the following table.

These differences reveal that American businesspersons are basically pragmatic, and they attempt to grasp the opportunity of the moment, so to speak. At the other extreme, Arab businesspersons value consistency, tradition, and formality. Asian businessmen may appear to be confused or uncertain, but it is actually ethical orientation that fosters this appearance, for they neither value the opportunity nor adhere to precedents; hence, they ponder business decisions for a considerable time. Finally, Latin American businesspersons may be opportunistic, depending on the nature of the decision at hand. Obviously, Anglo-American and Arab businesspersons have the greatest ethical orientation distance between them, so one would predict more difficulties in the business relations between companies that reside in these two global regions.

| Global Region | Ethical Orientation | Description |
|---|---|---|
| Anglo-American | Flaming utilitarian | Considers every ethical decision to be unique, so past precedents and consistency are unimportant. |
| Latin American | Moderate utilitarian | Considers some ethical decisions to be unique, so past precedents may or may not be used. |
| Far Eastern | Mugwump | Does not have a strong ethical orientation, so appears indecisive or a "fence sitter." |
| Arab | Moderate formalist | Considers past precedents to be important, so the uniqueness of each ethical decision is typically not considered. |

When a researcher wants to compare the averages of several different groups, **analysis of variance**, sometimes called **ANOVA**, should be used to accomplish such multiple comparisons. The use of the word "variance" in the name "analysis of variance" is misleading—it is not an analysis of the standard deviations of the groups. To be sure, the standard deviations are taken into consideration, and so are the sample sizes, just as you saw in all of our other statistical inference formulas. Fundamentally, ANOVA (analysis of variance) is an investigation of the differences between the group averages to ascertain whether sampling errors or true population differences explain their failure to be equal.[7] That is, the word "variance" signifies for our purposes differences between two or more groups' averages—do they vary from one another significantly? Although a term like *ANOVA* sounds frightfully technical, it is nothing more than a statistical procedure that applies when you are looking at the averages of several groups. The following sections explain to you the basic concepts involved with ANOVA and also how it can be applied to marketing research situations.

■ The test of differences among more than two groups' averages is accomplished with ANOVA.

## Why Analysis of Variance Is Preferred over Multiple Two-Group Averages Analyses

When you have two group averages to compare, you just compare the average of one group to the other's average. But when you have more than two groups, the comparisons become complicated. To illustrate, let's compare the averages of four different groups: A, B, C, and D. You will need to make the following comparisons: A:B, A:C, A:D, B:C, B:D, C:D. That is six different comparisons. It would be tedious and hard to keep track of all these if you used the two-group averages differences test we just described.

ANOVA is a very efficient, convenient analysis that does all of these tests simultaneously. That's right—you only do one test, and the results tell you where the significant differences are found. ANOVA uses some complicated formulas, and we have found from experience that market researchers do not commit them to memory. Instead, a researcher understands the basic purpose of ANOVA, and he or she is adept at interpreting ANOVA output. ANOVA's null hypothesis is that none of all the possible group-to-group averages is significantly different: that is, there is not one single significant difference that exists between any possible pair of groups. The alternative hypothesis is that at least one pair is significantly different. When the null hypothesis is not supported in an ANOVA, follow-up analysis must be applied to identify where the significant differences are found.

Again, we will not provide details on ANOVA formulas other than to say that because multiple pairs of group averages are being tested, ANOVA uses the *F* test statistic, and the significance value that appears on standard statistical output is the degree of support for the null hypothesis. As you will soon find out, the XL Data Analyst does the statistical interpretation of ANOVA and, if it finds that the null hypothesis is not supported at the 95% level of confidence, it provides a table that shows you the various group averages plus identifies which ones are significantly different.

■ ANOVA is an efficient way to compare more than two groups' averages simultaneously.

Here is an example that will help you to understand how ANOVA works and when to use it. A major department store conducts a survey, and one of the questions on the survey is "At what department did you last make a purchase for over $250?" There are four departments where significant numbers of respondents made these purchases: (1) Electronics, (2) Home and Garden, (3) Sporting Goods, and (4) Automotive. Another question on the survey is "How likely are you to purchase another item for over $250 from that department the next time?" The respondents indicate how likely they are to do this on a 7-point scale where 1 = very unlikely and 7 = very likely. To summarize the findings, the researcher calculates the average of how likely each group is to return to the department store and purchase another major item from that same department.

## How Likely Are Customers to Return?*

| Group Average** | Automotive | Electronics | Home & Garden | Sporting Goods |
|---|---|---|---|---|
| | 2.2 | 5.1 | 5.3 | 5.6 |
| **Automotive** | | Yes | Yes | Yes |
| **Electronics** | | | No | No |
| **Home & Garden** | | | | No |

*Significant differences are noted by "Yes."
**Based on a scale where 1 = very unlikely and 7 = very likely to purchase another item in this department.

The researcher who is doing the analysis decides to compare these averages statistically with ANOVA, and the findings are provided in the table you see here. When you look at this table, you will find that the Automotive Department is definitely very different from the other three departments in the store. Its average is only 2.2, while the other departments' averages range from 5.1 to 5.6. To indicate where significant differences are found, the researcher places a "Yes" notation in the cell where the group row and the group column intersect. A "No" is placed if no significant difference is found between the two group means. For instance, in our illustrative

Analysis of variance can be used to determine if shoppers have different experiences in different departments of the same store.

A researcher can see the differences (or lack of) among several groups' averages with a table based on ANOVA findings.

table, the "Yes" in the Automotive row reveals that the Automotive Department average of 2.2 is different from the Electronics Department average of 5.1. In fact, the "Yes" notations denote that the Automotive Department's average is significantly different from each of the three other departments' averages. The "No" entries denote that the averages for the other three departments are not significantly different from each other. In other words, there is a good indication that the patrons who bought an item for more than $250 from the department store's Automotive Department are not as likely to buy again as are patrons who bought from any of the three other departments.

Again Figure 13.1's notions are relevant here, except we now have four sampling distribution curves—one for each department. The Electronics, Home and Garden, and Sporting Goods sampling distribution curves would overlap a great deal, while the Automotive Department curve would stand separately on the lower end of the scale. Because ANOVA takes on all groups simultaneously, you would need to modify Figure 13.1 by adding a separate standard error of the difference curve for each of the six possible group-to-group comparisons, and you would see that the computed $z$ value was large for every Automotive Department average comparison with each of the other three departments' averages.

The search for differences among more than two groups simply translates into partitioning a large market into a number of market segments. We have provided an example of how the Canadian province of Alberta's designated travel promotion agency came to identify five visitor market segments and to ascertain meaningful differences of various types among these groups. Read Marketing Research Application 13.2 to find out what segments were determined for Travel Alberta and how it used knowledge of core similarities and market segment differences to fashion a successful promotional campaign that appealed to all five family vacation segments.[8]

GLOBAL

## MARKETING RESEARCH APPLICATION 13.2

PRACTICAL

APPLICATIONS

### Difference Analysis Reveals Five Market Segments for Alberta, Canada

The province of Alberta in western Canada is the fourth-largest Canadian province, and it is blessed with a huge variety of beautiful natural areas, including the Canadian Rockies, Banff National Park (and four other national parks), Dinosaur Valley, hundreds of lakes and streams; an overabundance of wildlife, including bighorn sheep, bison, and bears; and the attractive cities of Jasper, Edmonton, and Calgary. Alberta is an ecological wonderland in all four seasons. However, Travel Alberta, the agency charged with marketing Alberta to potential tourists, knew very little about the consumer behavior of its visitors, so it commissioned a marketing research study to better understand its market.

The survey garnered a sample size of over 3,000 respondents, and the analysts administered a number of statistical techniques. Ultimately, differences analysis revealed five separate travel-to-Alberta market segments that differed with respect to demographic factors and considerations that greatly influenced whether or not they visited Alberta. These factors also provided insight into the primary benefits each segment was seeking in its visit to Alberta. The segments and their unique profiles are summarized on the next page.

As happens with differences analyses, some differences were found, as can be seen in the demographic profiles and the key decision factors; however, no significant or meaningful differences were found in the core activities desired by the segments (experiencing Alberta's pristine mountains, forests, and many parks as well as venturing off and exploring these areas on their own). Nor were differences found for how the various segments learned about Alberta's many venues: word of mouth, meaning they listened to friends, neighbors, co-workers, and relatives about Alberta, and they had also seen newspaper stories and advertisements about Alberta.

Using its knowledge of the five market segments in its market, Travel Alberta formulated and launched its "Alberta, Made to Order" campaign that assured prospective visitors that in addition to delivering the core benefits of natural beauty and places to explore, their Alberta vacation could be customized to their particular desires and needs. The result of this campaign was that Alberta increased by 20% as a "top of the mind" travel destination over the yearlong duration of the "Alberta, Made to Order" campaign.

| | The young urban outdoor market | The indoor leisure traveler market | The children-first market | The fair weather-friends market | The older cost-conscious traveler market |
|---|---|---|---|---|---|
| **Demographics** | • Youngest segment: mid-20s | • Early 40s | • Early 40s | • Mid-40s | • Oldest segment: mid-40s |
| | • 2/3 married, but 1/4 single | • 70% married | • 2/3 married | • 2/3 married, but 1/5 single | • > 60% married |
| | • > 50% with children | • > 60% with children | • 2/3 with children | • 1/3 with children | • Fewest with children |
| **Key travel decision factors** | • School holidays | • Safety and security | • Children's sports and competitions | • Visit family and friends | • Safety and security |
| | • Cost | • Cost | • Safety and security | • Weather conditions | • Cost |
| **Activities they desire** | All segments: | | | • Mountains, forests, and parks<br>• Want to explore and do new things | |
| **Information sources about vacation areas** | All segments: | | | • Word of mouth<br>• Newspaper | |

# USING THE XL DATA ANALYST TO DETERMINE THE SIGNIFICANCE OF THE DIFFERENCE AMONG MORE THAN TWO GROUP AVERAGES

Previously, we illustrated the use of a two-group averages difference analysis by comparing the likelihood of freshmen State U respondents to subscribe to the College Life E-Zine to the likelihood of senior class respondents. As you know, there are five class categories—freshman, sophomore, junior, senior, and graduate student—and all five classes are represented in our random sample of State University students. So, this is precisely an instance where ANOVA applies. Figure 13.6 shows the menu commands and variable selection windows you use with the XL Data Analyst to set up three-plus–group averages analysis. Notice that the menu sequence is "Compare–3+ Group Averages," and the grouping variable is "respondent's classification," while the target variable is "How likely would you be to subscribe . . ."

**Figure 13.6** Using the XL Data Analyst to Set Up a Three-Plus–Group Averages Differences Analysis

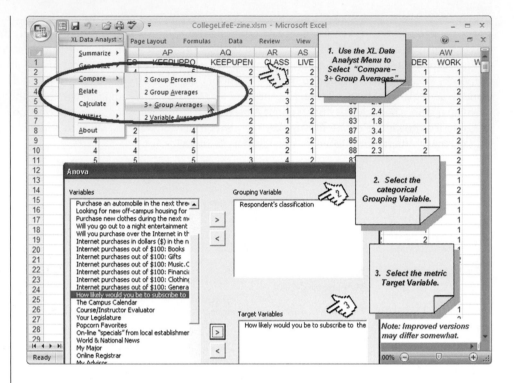

**Figure 13.7** XL Data Analyst Three-Plus–Group Averages Differences Analysis Output

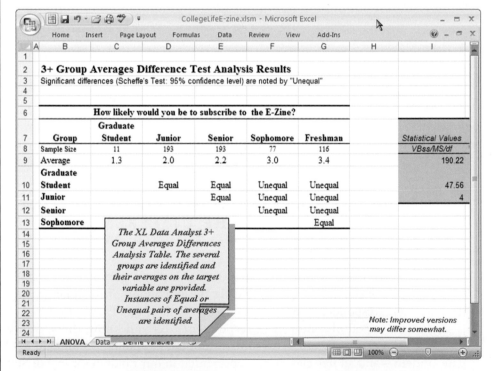

Figure 13.7 reveals that the XL Data Analyst ANOVA output is in the same table format as our introductory example on the department store purchase intentions. That is, the ANOVA output table is arranged in ascending order based on the group averages, and an "Equal" or "Unequal" is placed in the intersection cell for each possible pair of averages. An "Equal" notation means that there is a

significant difference between the two averages, while an "Unequal" designation indicates that there is no support for the null hypothesis that the two group averages are equal. Granted, the table is a bit complicated when you first examine it; however, it is much more efficient than the 10 different two-group averages differences analyses that would be necessary if ANOVA was not available.

Examine the ANOVA table output in Figure 13.7 to ensure that you can see that it is apparent that freshmen have the highest average likelihood of subscribing to the College Life E-Zine, and their average is significantly different from all other groups except sophomores. Sophomores, in turn, have an average that is significantly different from upper-class students. Finally, the averages of graduate students, seniors, and juniors are not significantly different. As with other XL Data Analyst results, the relevant statistical values are included for users with expertise and interest in examining them.

> ▪ The three-plus–group average comparison of the XL Data Analyst is an ANOVA with an output table that indicates the pair(s) of averages that are significantly different.

## The Six-Step Process for Analyzing Differences Among Three or More Groups

As we indicated early in this chapter, differences analyses are important first steps in the investigation of possible market segments. Potential market segmentation variables are any factors that uniquely identify groups in the total market and which are related to some relevant consumer behavior construct such as attitudes, perceptions, intentions, satisfaction, and so forth. With the College Life E-Zine, the vision requires an Internet connection with a high bandwidth so that graphics, pop-up ads, and other features can be experienced without lengthy loading times. We have taken the possible market segmentation variable of the type of Internet connections currently used by State University students, and used this grouping variable to compare the group averages as to how likely they are to subscribe to the College Life E-Zine. Please examine Table 13.4, which illustrates the application of our six-step analysis process to the investigation of market segmentation findings that can be relevant to our College Life E-Zine entrepreneurs.

**Table 13.4** The Six-Step Approach to Data Analysis for Differences Among Three or More Groups

| Step | Explanation | Example |
| --- | --- | --- |
| **1. What is the research objective?** | Determine that you are dealing with a **3 + Group Differences objective**. | We want to determine if there is a difference in the average likelihood of subscribing to the College Life E-Zine among different types of Internet access. |
| **2. What questionnaire question(s) is/are involved?** | Identify the question(s), and for each one specify whether it is categorical or metric. | The type of Internet access (high-speed cable, dial-up, or DSL) is *categorical*, meaning that three separate groups are identified, and the intention to subscribe is on a 1–5 metric scale. |
| **3. What is the appropriate analysis?** | To compare the averages of three or more groups, use three-plus–group comparisons analysis. | We use ANOVA because it is much more efficient than a series of two-group averages comparisons. |

**Table 13.4** *(Continued)*

| Step | Explanation | Example |
|---|---|---|
| **4. How do you run it?** | Use XL Data Analyst analysis: Select "Compare–3 + Group Averages." | |
| **5. How do you interpret the finding?** | The XL Data Analyst indicates what group averages are/are not significantly different. | |

### How Likely Would You Be to Subscribe to the E-Zine?

| Group | Dial-up | DSL | High-Speed Cable |
|---|---|---|---|
| Sample Size | 284 | 54 | 252 |
| Average | 1.8 | 2.9 | 3.1 |
| Dial-up | | Unequal | Unequal |
| DSL | | | Equal |

High-speed cable and DSL are not different, but dial-up is different from high-speed cable and from DSL connection.

| Step | Explanation | Example |
|---|---|---|
| **6. How do you write/present these findings?** | When significant differences are found, present them with a graph or a table. | |

**Intentions to Subscribe to College Life E-Zine**

*Note*: Because high-speed cable and DSL are not significantly different, a weighted average of these two group means was computed to determine the combined groups' mean of 3.1.

# TESTING FOR SIGNIFICANT DIFFERENCES BETWEEN THE AVERAGES OF TWO VARIABLES

The last differences analysis we will describe does not involve groups. Instead, it concerns comparing the average of one variable (question on the survey) to the average of another variable.[9] With this analysis, the entire sample is used, but two different variables are compared. For example, if a pharmaceuticals company was seeking to improve its cold remedy medication, a survey could be used to determine "How important is it that your cold remedy relieves your ____?" using a scale of 1 = not important and 10 = very important for each of several cold symptoms such as "congestion," "cough," or "runny nose." The question then becomes "Are any two average importance levels significantly different?" To determine the answer to this question, we must run an analysis to determine the significance of the difference between these averages. But the same respondents answered both questions, so you do not have two independent groups. Instead, you have two independent questions with one group. When you find significant differences between the averages of two variables such as ratings of importance or performance, you know that levels of the ratings are truly different in the population that the sample represents. Of course, the variables should be measured on the same scale; otherwise, you are comparing apples to oranges.

A graph of the test for the difference in the averages of two variables would appear as you have seen in Figure 13.1. You now understand that the two bell-shaped curves would be the sampling distributions of the two variables being compared, and the apex of each one would be its average in the sample. When there is a small amount of overlap for the two curves, there is a true difference in the population averages. That is, if the survey were replicated many, many times, and the averages for all these replications were graphed, they would appear similar to the bell-shaped curves in Figure 13.1, and the two averages would rarely, if ever, be equal (the null hypothesis). The formula for this statistical test is, in fact, similar to the one for the difference between two group averages. That is, the two averages are compared (take the difference), and this quantity is divided by the standard error of the difference to compute the $z$ value. You can refer to the formula for the difference between two group averages for a conceptual understanding of the computations in this analysis. The logic we described still applies, but there must be an adjustment factor (that we will not bother to discuss here) because there is only one sample involved. Directional hypothesis tests are possible as well.

■ When comparing the averages of two variables, it is important that these variables be measured with the same scale.

■ The difference analysis for the averages of two variables uses logic very similar to that used in the analysis of the difference between two group averages.

# USING THE XL DATA ANALYST TO DETERMINE THE SIGNIFICANCE OF THE DIFFERENCES BETWEEN THE AVERAGES OF TWO VARIABLES

As was indicated, the proper use of a differences test for two variables' averages requires that you select two metric variables that are measured with the same scale units. We know from our descriptive analysis that the e-zine feature of "Online 'specials' from local establishments" has the highest average preference

**Figure 13.8** Using the XL Data Analyst to Set Up a Two-Variable Averages Differences Analysis

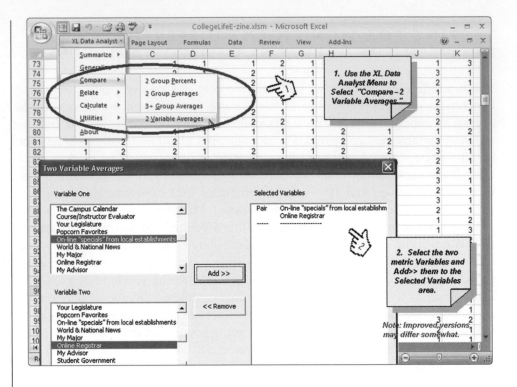

■ Use the XL Data Analyst to select the pairs of metric variables whose averages are to be compared.

rating, at 4.7, while the online registrar rating's average is 4.5. Are these two averages significantly different, or is the arithmetic difference simply a reflection of sample size error and variability in the respondents' answers? To answer this question, we can use the XL Data Analyst to perform a Two-Variables Averages comparison. The menu sequence is Compare–2 Variable Averages, which opens up the selection menu for this procedure. In Figure 13.8, you can see that two selection windows each list all of the available variables, so you must highlight a variable in the "Variable One" panel and another in the "Variable Two" panel to make a pair whose averages will be compared, and add this pair into the Selected Variables selection windowpane. You will see in Figure 13.8 that the online local specials feature and the online registrar feature are selected, and they are identified as a "pair" in the selection windowpane. (Multiple pairs may be selected in a single analysis run, if desired.)

Figure 13.9 has the resulting XL Data Analyst output for our Two-Variable Averages comparison analysis. You can see that there is a table that shows the averages of 4.7 and 4.5 for the two metric variables, and the arithmetic difference is provided. Most important, however, the XL Data Analyst has indicated in this table that the difference is a significant difference. In other words, the null hypothesis that there is no difference between these two averages is not supported. Online "specials" from local establishments are preferred more by those State University students who are likely to subscribe to the College Life E-Zine than is the online registrar feature. Of course, both features are between "somewhat prefer" and "strongly prefer" on the average, so the usefulness of this difference finding is limited as clearly both features should be included in the College Life E-Zine's features.

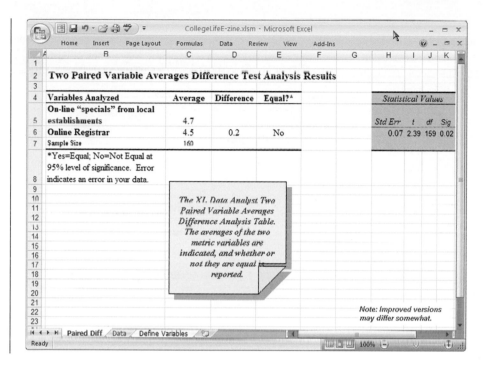

**Figure 13.9** XL Data Analyst Two-Variable Averages Differences Analysis Output

## The Six-Step Process for Analyzing Differences Between Two Variables

The assessment of significant differences between pairs of similarly measured variables is useful because it informs the researcher as to the true magnitudes of these variables. That is, when two variable averages are not significantly different, it means that the arithmetic difference between them is not a true one. If the survey were repeated many, many times, and these differences tallied, the average of the differences would be 0. However, when the null hypothesis (of no difference between the two averages) is not supported, the researcher is assured that the relative sizes of the two averages exist in the population, and the researcher can confidently report this finding to the manager.

We have prepared Table 13.5 with explanations and an example of our six-step process for the assessment of the difference between the averages of two variables.

**Table 13.5** The Six-Step Approach to Data Analysis for Differences Between Two Variables

| Step | Explanation | Example |
|---|---|---|
| **1. What is the research objective?** | Determine that you are dealing with a **Two-Variables Differences objective**. | We want to determine if there is a difference in the estimated dollars out of every $100 in Internet purchases for clothing purchases versus general merchandise purchases by State University students. |
| **2. What questionnaire question(s) is/are involved?** | Identify the question for each variable and verify that it is metric. | Respondents were requested to estimate the number of dollars out of every $100 of Internet purchases that they typically spend on clothing and on general merchandise. This is a natural metric scale in dollars. |
| **3. What is the appropriate analysis?** | To compare the averages of the two variables, use two-variable averages analysis. | We use this procedure because the two variables are measured with the same scale, and we have one group (the entire sample) that answered both questions. |

**Table 13.5** *(Continued)*

| Step | Explanation | Example |
|---|---|---|
| **4. How do you run it?** | Use XL Data Analyst analysis: Select "Compare–2 Variables Averages." | |

| **5. How do you interpret the finding?** | The XL Data Analyst indicates the two variable averages and indicates whether or not they are equal. | |

**Two Paired Variable Averages Difference Test Analysis Results**

| Variables Analyzed | Average | Difference | Equal?* |
|---|---|---|---|
| **Internet purchases out of $100: Clothing** | $25.16 | | |
| **Internet purchases out of $100: General merchandise** | $18.13 | $7.03 | No |
| Sample Size | 143 | | |

Here, the clothing purchases average of $25.16 is different from the general merchandise average of $18.13. (The averages were reformatted in Excel to appear as currency with two decimal places in this table.)

| **6. How do you write/present these findings?** | When significant differences are found, you can report them with a graph or in the text of the report. | |

**Purchases out of every $100 Internet purchases**

State University students who make purchases over the Internet typically spend about $25 out of every $100 on clothing, while they spend around $18 of every $100 on general merchandise.

# SUMMARY

The chapter began with a discussion of why differences are important to marketing managers. Basically, market segmentation implications underlie most differences analyses. It is important that differences are statistically significant, but it is also vital that they are meaningful as a basis of marketing strategy. We then described how differences between two percentages in two independent samples can be tested for statistical significance. Our presentation included formulas and a step-by-step description of how the relevant statistical values are calculated and interpreted. Then we described the analysis test procedure using averages. In addition, you were introduced to the differences analysis procedures in the XL Data Analyst that is used to determine if two groups' percentages or two groups' averages are significantly different.

When a researcher has three or more groups and wishes to compare their various averages, the correct procedure involves analysis of variance, or ANOVA. ANOVA is a technique that tests all possible pairs of averages for all the groups involved and indicates which pairs are significantly different. We did not provide ANOVA formulas, as they are quite complicated, but we showed how the XL Data Analyst is used to perform ANOVA and identify what pair(s) of group averages are significantly different. Finally, we briefly discussed the comparison of two variables' averages for significant differences. Here, the researcher is seeking to find real differences, for example, between the levels of ratings such as importance or performance that exist in the population represented by the sample being used in the analysis.

# KEY TERMS

Market segmentation (p. 390)
Alternative hypothesis (p. 393)
Standard error of the difference between two percentages (p. 394)
Grouping variable (p. 397)

Target variable (p. 397)
Standard error of the difference between two averages (p. 399)
Analysis of variance (ANOVA) (p. 406)

# REVIEW QUESTIONS

1 What are differences and why should marketing researchers be concerned with them? Why are marketing managers concerned with them?
2 What are the three ways a researcher can investigate for differences?
3 Why does the nature of the scale (categorical or metric) being used matter when performing a differences test?
4 What is the null hypothesis and what is the alternative hypothesis for a differences test?
5 When the percentages or the averages of two groups are compared, what is the nature of the comparison operation?
6 When a standard error of a difference (between percentages or averages) is computed, what two factors are taken into account, and how does each affect the size of the standard error?

7 Describe how a directional hypothesis about the difference between two percentages or two averages is tested.

8 What is ANOVA, and when is it used? Why is it "efficient"?

9 What is the null hypothesis in ANOVA?

10 How is a test of the difference between the averages of two variables different from a test of the difference between the averages of two groups with the same variable? How is it similar?

## APPLICATION QUESTIONS

11 Are the following two sample results significantly different?

| | Sample 1 | Sample 2 | Confidence Level | Your Finding? |
|---|---|---|---|---|
| a. | Mean: 10.6 | Mean: 11.7 | 95% | |
| | Std. dev: 1.5 | Std. dev: 2.5 | | |
| | $n = 150$ | $n = 300$ | | |
| b. | Percent: 45% | Percent: 54% | 99% | |
| | $n = 350$ | $n = 250$ | | |
| c. | Mean: 1,500 | Mean: 1,250 | 95% | |
| | Std. dev: 550 | Std. dev: 500 | | |
| | $n = 1,200$ | $n = 500$ | | |

12 Demonstrate your understanding of your work in question 11, above, by drawing the sampling distributions of each case—a, b, and c—in the format presented in Figure 13.1 on page 396.

13 A researcher is investigating different types of customers for a sporting goods store. In a survey, respondents have indicated how much they exercise in approximate minutes per week. These respondents have also rated the performance of the sporting goods store across 12 difference characteristics such as good value for the price, convenience of location, helpfulness of the sales clerks, and so on. The researcher used a 1–7 rating scale for these 12 characteristics, where 1 = poor performance and 7 = excellent performance. How can the researcher investigate differences in the ratings based on the amount of exercise reported by the respondents?

14 A shoe manufacturer suspects there are six market segments that it can use effectively in its target marketing: toddlers, middle-school children, high school students, young and active adults, professionals, and senior citizens. How many pairs of averages can be assessed for significant differences? Specify each separate pair.

**15** A marketing manager of a Web-based catalog sales company uses a segmentation scheme based on the incomes of target customers. The segmentation system has four segments: (1) low income, (2) moderate income, (3) high income, and (4) wealthy. The company database holds information on every customer's purchases over the past several years, and the total dollars spent is one of the prominent variables. The marketing manager finds that the average total dollar purchases for the four groups are as follows.

| Market Segment | Average Total Dollar Purchases |
|---|---|
| Low income | $101 |
| Moderate income | $120 |
| High income | $231 |
| Wealthy | $595 |

Construct a table that is based on how the XL Data Analyst presents its findings for ANOVA that illustrates that the low- and moderate-income groups are not different from each other, but the other groups are significantly different from one another.

# INTERACTIVE LEARNING

Visit the textbook Web site at **www.prenhall.com/burnsbush**. For this chapter, use the self-study quizzes and get quick feedback on whether or not you need additional studying. You can also review the chapter's major points by visiting the chapter outline and key terms.

## CASE 13.1    ‖ The *Daily Advocate* Lost Subscribers Survey

The *Daily Advocate* is a newspaper serving the Capital City area, which accounts for about 350 thousand households. The *Daily Advocate* has been the dominant daily newspaper in the area for the past 50 years. At one time, it was estimated that 9 out of 10 Capital City–area households subscribed or otherwise bought the *Daily Advocate*. In the past decade, Capital City has undergone a growth spurt due primarily to three high-technology industrial "parks" where a great many Internet, computer equipment, and biotechnology companies have located. However, the circulation of the *Daily Advocate* did not experience a corresponding spurt; in fact, the circulation peaked in 1998, and it has been slowly declining ever since. It is now estimated that only 7 out of 10 Capital City–area households subscribe to the *Daily Advocate*.

The circulation manager of the *Daily Advocate* commissions a market research study to determine what factors underlie the circulation attrition. Specifically, the survey is designed to compare current *Daily Advocate* subscribers with those who have dropped their subscriptions in the past year. A telephone survey is conducted with both sets of individuals. Following is a summary of the key findings—using a 95% level of confidence—from the study.

| Variable Analyzed | Current Subscribers | Lost Subscribers | Difference | Equal? |
|---|---|---|---|---|
| Length of residence in the city | 20.1 years | 5.4 years | 14.7 years | No |
| Length of time as a subscriber | 27.2 years | 1.3 years | 25.9 years | No |
| Watch local TV news program(s) | 87% | 85% | 2.0% | Yes |
| Watch national TV news program(s) | 72% | 79% | −7.0% | Yes |
| Obtain news from the Internet | 13% | 23% | −10.0% | No |
| Satisfaction* with … | | | | |
| Delivery of newspaper | 5.5 | 4.9 | 0.6 | Yes |
| Coverage of local news | 6.1 | 5.8 | 0.3 | Yes |
| Coverage of national news | 5.5 | 2.3 | 3.2 | No |
| Coverage of local sports | 6.3 | 5.9 | 0.4 | Yes |
| Coverage of national sports | 5.7 | 3.2 | 2.5 | No |
| Coverage of local social news | 5.8 | 5.2 | 0.6 | Yes |
| Editorial stance of the newspaper | 6.1 | 4.0 | 2.1 | No |
| Value for subscription price | 5.2 | 4.8 | 0.4 | Yes |

*Average, based on a 7-point scale where 1 = very dissatisfied and 7 = very satisfied

1 Why has the *Daily Advocate*'s circulation fallen in the face of a population boom in Capital City?

2 What marketing strategies should the *Daily Advocate* consider in order to sustain itself as the primary news vehicle in Capital City?

## CASE 13.2 ||| Your Integrated Case

### College Life E-Zine

#### The College Life E-Zine Survey: Market Segmentation Analysis

Another week has passed, and Sarah, Anna, Wesley, and Don are again treated to a PowerPoint presentation by Lori Baker, marketing intern at ORS Marketing Research. Their excitement rises to a fever pitch with the good news that even when using the lower boundary of the 95% confidence interval for the percent of students who are "very likely" to subscribe to the College Life E-Zine at $15 per month, the expected number of State University students exceeds the required break-even point of 6,000 subscriptions. In fact, the most likely estimate was about 7,800, well above the 6,000 critical value.

"I knew you would be very happy to hear Lori's generalization findings," said Bob Watts, "and I was very happy for you when Lori disclosed them to me a few days ago, for it means we are 'go' with the College Life E-Zine. Plus, you've been studying the descriptive analyses that Lori presented to you last week, and I'm sure that you have come up with the basic features that all State U prospects for the e-zine want to see, and you no doubt have some preliminary targets for the e-zine's advertising affiliates, both national and local."

Wesley replied, "Yes, we certainly do, but I want to make it so that once we have a profile of each subscriber via his or her registration, we can custom-tailor the pop-up ads and other dynamic features of our College Life E-Zine so they have the optimal effect."

"Ah," said Lori, "you must be talking about market segmentation. I recall Dr. Bush, who taught my marketing research course at State U, saying how useful various types of data analysis are in revealing meaningful market segment differences. I know the College Life E-Zine data set very well from my work sessions with it, and I can refer to my class notes or even give Dr. Bush a call if I need help. I'd like to give it a try. Of course, Bob will be overseeing my work as well. Bob, if it's okay with you, I can get right on this, and have it ready for a week from today."

Bob winks at the four e-zine entrepreneurs and says, "Are you sure you're up to it, Lori?"

Lori replies, "Absolutely!"

The very next day, Lori begins her work at ORS by outlining the differences she intends to investigate. Using Lori's questions, perform the proper data analysis on the College Life E-Zine data set using the XL Data Analyst. When you find differences, interpret them in the context of Wesley's vision for how the College Life E-Zine can be optimally effective.

Here are Lori's questions.

1 Do male State University students differ from female ones with respect to expecting to make an Internet purchase in the next two months?
2 Do on-campus State University students differ from off-campus ones with respect to expecting to make an Internet purchase in the next two months?
3 Do working State University students differ from nonworking ones with respect to expecting to make an Internet purchase in the next two months?
4 Are there differences among the various State University classes with respect to:
  a Total Internet purchases?
  b Internet purchases out of $100 (books, gifts, music, etc.)?
  c Preference for various possible e-zine features (Campus Calendar, Course/Instructor Evaluator, etc.)?
5 Are there differences among the various State University students by college with respect to:
  a Total Internet purchases?
  b Internet purchases out of $100 (books, gifts, music, etc.)?
  c Preference for various possible e-zine features (Campus Calendar, Course/Instructor Evaluator, etc.)?

## CHAPTER 14

# DETERMINING RELATIONSHIPS AMONG YOUR VARIABLES

## Maritz® RESEARCH

By permission, Maritz.

## WHICH MEASURE OF CUSTOMER LOYALTY IS MOST ASSOCIATED WITH REPEAT BUYING?

You may remember back at the beginning of Chapter 8 (Measurement) we discussed three different ways of measuring customer loyalty. The first uses three questions: (1) overall satisfaction, (2) willingness to recommend, and (3) likelihood to return or buy again. The three questions are averaged to form an index of customer loyalty. We will call this the "Three-Question" method. A second method, developed by Reichheld, asks a single question about the likelihood that a respondent would recommend Company X to a friend or colleague. We will call this the "Single-Question" method. Finally, we presented Maritz Research's

▨ To learn what is meant by a "relationship" between two variables

▨ To become familiar with a Boolean relationship, including when and why one is used

▨ To understand when and how cross-tabulations with chi-square analysis are applied

▨ To become knowledgeable about the use and interpretation of correlations

▨ To learn about the application and interpretation of regression analysis

▨ To become proficient in the use of the XL Data Analyst to execute various types of relationship analyses

"Probability Allocation" measure which asks "Of the next 10 times you make a purchase of <insert product class here>, how many times will you buy <insert client's brand here>?"

So, we have three measures of customer loyalty. Which one is best? One may answer this question by asking which of these measurement methods results in a measure that is most highly associated with customer loyalty. A "high" score should be associated with a greater number of repeat purchases, and a "low" score should be associated with fewer repeat purchases. If one measure has a greater association with actual customer loyalty, then we should have greater confidence in using the measure as a surrogate indicator of actual customer loyalty.

One method of measuring the association between two variables is called correlation. The correlation coefficient is an index number ranging from $+1.00$ to $-1.00$. A positive association means that as one variable goes up (i.e., our measure of customer loyalty score) the other variable (actual repeat purchases) goes up as well. A negative association occurs when, as one variable goes up, the other goes down. A correlation of 1.00 is perfect association. We never expect to see perfect association, but the higher the correlation coefficient, the stronger the association.

Researchers at Maritz Research wanted to determine which of the three measures were most highly associated with a measure of post-survey purchasing, so they conducted two separate studies. The first study tested nine different product and service categories with almost 1,000 respondents. The correlation coefficients for each method of measuring customer loyalty were:

Three-Question Method = .35

Single-Question Method = .26

Probability Allocation Method = .51

In a second study, conducted on mass merchandisers using a sample of almost 600 respondents, Maritz Research found the following correlation coefficients for each method of measuring customer loyalty:

Three-Question Method = .47

Single-Question Method = .36

Probability Allocation Method = .71

The good news is that all three methods are associated with the construct they purport to measure: customer loyalty. However, the strongest measure in both studies is the probability allocation method. In this chapter you will learn about correlation and the correlation coefficient.[1]

This chapter illustrates the usefulness of statistical analyses beyond generalization and differences tests. Often marketers are interested in relationships among variables. For example, Frito-Lay wants to know what kinds of people, under what circumstances, choose to buy Doritos, Fritos, and any of the other items in the Frito-Lay line. The Pontiac Division of General Motors wants to know what types of individuals would respond favorably to the various style changes proposed for the Firebird. A newspaper wants to understand the lifestyle characteristics of its prospective readers so that it is able to modify or change sections in the newspaper to better suit its audience. Furthermore, the newspaper desires information about various types of subscribers so as to communicate this information to its advertisers, helping them in copy design and advertisement placement within the various newspaper sections. For all of these cases, there are statistical procedures available, termed *relationship analyses*, that determine answers to these questions. Relationship analyses determine whether stable patterns exist between two (or more) variables; they are the central topic of this chapter.

We begin the chapter by describing what a relationship is and why relationships are useful concepts. Then we describe Boolean relationships that can exist between two categorical variables and indicate how a cross-tabulation can be used to compute a chi-square value that, in turn, can be assessed to determine whether or not a statistically significant relationship exists between the two variables. We next move to a general discussion of correlation coefficients, and we illustrate the use and interpretation of correlations. The remainder of this chapter is devoted to regression analysis, which is a powerful predictive technique and one that fosters understanding of phenomena under study. As in our previous analysis chapters, we show you how to use the XL Data Analyst to perform these analyses and how to interpret the resulting output.

# WHAT IS A RELATIONSHIP BETWEEN TWO VARIABLES?

In order to describe a relationship between two variables, we must first remind you of the scale characteristic called *description* that we introduced to you in Chapter 8. Every scale has unique descriptors, sometimes called levels, which identify the different labels of that scale. The term *levels* implies that the scale is metric, whereas the term *labels* implies that the scale is categorical. A simple categorical label is a "yes" or "no," for instance, if a respondent is a buyer (yes) or nonbuyer (no) of a particular product or service. Of course, if the researcher measured how many times a respondent bought a product, the level would be the number of times, and the scale would be metric because this scale would satisfy the assumptions of a real number scale.

A **relationship** is a consistent and systematic linkage between the levels or labels for two variables. Relationships are invaluable tools for the marketing researcher, because a relationship can be used for prediction and it fosters understanding of the phenomenon under study. For example, if Canon finds that many of its miniDV camcorder buyers have children, it will predict that those families with children who are thinking about purchasing a camcorder will be good prospects for its miniDV camcorder models. Furthermore, it seems logical that the parents are taking videos of their children, so Canon can use the promotional theme of "making memories" or "capturing special moments" because it understands that this is the primary purchasing motivation involved here.

Here is another example: If American Airlines discovers a relationship between the number of American Airlines frequent flyer miles and the amount of time that its customers spend on American's Web site, it can predict that heavy users of its Web site will also be its frequent flyers. Further, since frequent flyers take a lot of trips, they are undoubtedly checking out American's Web site for flight schedules for prospective trips or travel specials where they can use their frequent flyer miles benefits. So, if American can identify its frequent flyer Web site visitors by a registration process or cookies, it can direct pop-up advertisements or other information to them that they will be looking for.

> A relationship describes the linkage between the levels or labels for two variables.

# BOOLEAN RELATIONSHIPS AND CROSS-TABULATION ANALYSIS

## Boolean Relationships

A **Boolean relationship** is one where the presence of one variable's label is systematically related to the presence of another variable's label. You have no doubt used Boolean operators when working with search engines. For instance, if you used Google and searched for "dog AND food," it would find all the instances of Web sites that have the words "dog" and "food." That is, Google will find all of the Web sites where the pet label "dog" and the product label "food" are both present. Notice that we are working with labels here, meaning that we have specified categories, not numbers. With a Boolean relationship present, the researcher often resorts to graphical or other presentation formats to "see" the relationship.

> A graph shows a Boolean relationship quite well.

For a Boolean relationship, think about a Google search using "AND."

For example, McDonald's knows from experience that breakfast customers typically purchase coffee, whereas lunch customers typically purchase soft drinks. That is, we are using the meal variable and relating it to the choice-of-drink variable. Our labels are "morning" and "afternoon" for which meal, and "coffee" and "soft drink" for choice of drink. The relationship is in no way exclusive—there is no guarantee that a breakfast customer will always order coffee (breakfast AND coffee) or that a lunch customer will always order a soft drink (lunch AND soft drink). In general, though, this relationship exists, and Figure 14.1 presents it graphically. The Boolean relationship is simply that breakfast customers tend to purchase food items such as eggs, biscuits, and coffee, and that lunch customers tend to purchase items such as burgers, fries, and soft drinks. Notice that these Boolean relationships pairings tend to be present much of the time, but they are not 100% certainties. In other words, you might find that 80% of breakfast buyers order coffee, and that 90% of lunch buyers order a soft drink, so you could make a prediction as to what type of drink would be ordered by the next McDonald's breakfast or lunch customer that you encounter, and you would feel fairly confident that your prediction would be correct. But these relationships would not hold for every single breakfast or lunch customer, so every now and then, your prediction would not be substantiated.

■ A Boolean relationship means two variables are associated, but only in a very general sense.

## Characterizing a Boolean Relationship with a Graph

We used two pie charts in Figure 14.1 to depict the Boolean relationships in our McDonald's example. Indeed, pie charts are appropriate for categorical variables and perfectly acceptable presentation vehicles. However, it is cumbersome to create

**Figure 14.1** Example of a Boolean Relationship for the Type of Drink Ordered for Breakfast and for Lunch at McDonald's

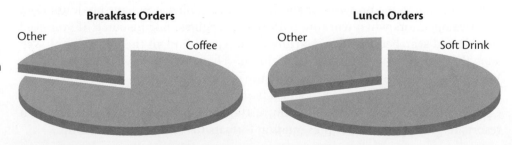

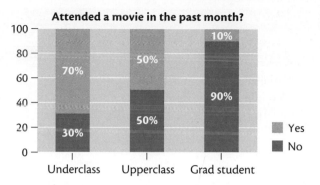

**Figure 14.2** A Boolean Relationship Illustrated with a Stacked Bar Chart

multiple pie charts in Excel and to present them as we have in Figure 14.1. An equally acceptable and more convenient graph is a stacked bar chart. With a **stacked bar chart**, two variables are shown simultaneously in the same bar graph. Each bar in the stacked bar chart stands for 100%, and it is divided proportionately by the amount of relationship that one variable shares with the other variable. In Figure 14.2 we have identified three types (labels) of college students: underclassmen, upperclassmen, and graduate students. We have also noted whether or not they have attended a movie in the past month. You can see that 70% of the underclass students have attended a movie, 50% of the upperclass students have, and only 10% of the graduate students have attended a movie in the past 30 days. In other words, one of the variables is student classification, with labels of "underclass student," "upperclass student," and "graduate student," and the other variable is attendance of a movie, with the labels of "yes" and "no." We can predict from the Boolean relationships depicted in Figure 14.2 that if we encounter a freshman or sophomore, he or she probably did attend a movie; if we encounter a junior or senior, he or she may or may not have; and if we encounter a graduate student, he or she very probably did not attend a movie. How do these relationships lead to understanding? Underclass college students are probably not knuckling down on their studies, so they have more leisure time; upperclass students are getting serious about studying as they are deep into their major courses and they are trying to increase their grade point averages to be competitive in the job market (or maybe just to graduate). Graduate students, of course, have no leisure time to speak of because they are taking difficult graduate-level courses, so they rarely go to movies.

> ▪ Pie graphs or stacked bar charts can be used to display Boolean relationships.

## Cross-Tabulation Analysis

A stacked bar chart provides a way of visualizing Boolean relationships, but you should not develop one unless you are assured that the relationship is statistically significant, meaning that the pattern of the relationship will remain essentially as it is if you replicated your survey a great many times and averaged all of the findings. The analytical technique that assesses the statistical significance of Boolean or categorical variable relationships is **cross-tabulation analysis**. With cross-tabulation, the two variables are arranged in a **cross-tabulation table**, defined as a table in which data are compared using a row-and-column format. The intersection of a row and a column is called a **cross-tabulation cell**. As you will soon see, a cross-tabulation analysis accounts for all of the relevant Boolean relationships and it is the basis for the assessment of statistical significance of the relationships.

> ▪ Use a cross-tabulation table for the data defining a possible Boolean relationship between two categorical variables.

**Table 14.1**
Cross-Tabulation Table
with Boolean
Relationships Identified

| | | Student Classification | | | |
|---|---|---|---|---|---|
| | | **Underclass Student** | **Upperclass Student** | **Graduate Student** | **Row Totals** |
| **Attended a Movie in the Past Month?** | **Yes** | 105 Underclass AND Yes | 85 Upperclass AND Yes | 5 Graduate AND Yes | 195 Underclass OR Upperclass OR Graduate AND Yes |
| | **No** | 45 Underclass AND No | 85 Upperclass AND No | 45 Graduate AND No | 175 Underclass OR Upperclass OR Graduate AND No |
| **Column Totals** | | 150 Underclass AND Yes OR No | 170 Upperclass AND Yes OR No | 50 Graduate AND Yes OR No | 370 **Grand Total:** Underclass OR Upperclass OR Graduate AND Yes OR No |

A cross-tabulation table for the stacked bar chart that we have been working with is presented in Table 14.1. Notice that we have identified the various Boolean relationships within cross-tabulation cells with rows and columns. The columns are in vertical alignment and are indicated in this table as "Underclass Student" or "Upperclass Student" or "Graduate Student," whereas the rows are indicated as "Yes" or "No" for movie attendance in the past month. In addition, we have provided a column for the Row Totals, and a row for the Column Totals. The intersection cell for the Row Totals column and the Column Totals row is called the Grand Total.

### Types of Frequencies and Percentages in a Cross-Tabulation Table

Table 14.1 is a **frequencies table** because it contains the raw counts of the various Boolean relationships found in the complete data set. From the grand total, we can see that there are 370 students in the sample, and from the row and column total cells, we can identify how many of each category of student classification (150, 170, and 50) and how many of "Yes" versus "No" movie attendees (195 and 175) are in the sample. The intersection cell for "Underclass Student" and "Yes" movie attendance reveals that there are 105 respondents found by this Boolean search, so to speak, and the other intersection cells reveal the counts of respondents found by applying their respective Boolean relationships. So, a cross-tabulation table contains the raw counts and totals pertaining to all of the relevant Boolean operations for the two categorical variables being analyzed.

Right now, you are probably wondering where all of this is going, as it is very different from the differences tests analyses, confidence intervals, and hypothesis tests you encountered in the prior chapters. In truth, Toto, we are a bit closer to Oz than we are to Kansas, but if you bear with us for a bit longer, you will master cross-tabulation analysis with ease.

◼ A frequencies table contains the raw counts of various Boolean relationships possible in a cross-tabulation.

## Chi-Square Analysis of a Cross-Tabulation Table

**Chi-square ($\chi^2$) analysis** is the examination of frequencies for two categorical variables in a cross-tabulation table to determine whether the variables have a significant relationship.[2] The chi-square analysis begins when the researcher formulates a statistical null hypothesis that the two variables under investigation are not related. Actually, it is not necessary for the researcher to state this hypothesis in a formal sense, for chi-square analysis always explicitly takes this null hypothesis into account. Stated somewhat differently, chi-square analysis always begins with the assumption that no relationship exists between the two categorical variables under analysis.

■ Chi-square analysis is used to assess the presence of a significant Boolean relationship in a cross-tabulation table.

**Observed and Expected Frequencies.** The raw counts you saw in Table 14.1 are referred to as "**observed frequencies**," as they are the counts observed by applying the Boolean operators to the data set. Long ago, someone working with cross-tabulations discovered that if you multiplied the row total times the column total and divided that product by the grand total for every cross-tabulation cell, the resulting "**expected frequencies**" would perfectly embody these cell frequencies if there was no significant relationship present. Here is the formula for the expected cell frequencies.

■ Observed frequencies are found in the sample, whereas expected frequencies are determined by chi-square analysis procedures.

$$\text{Expected cell frequency} = \frac{\text{Cell column total} \times \text{Cell row total}}{\text{Grand total}}$$

◀ **Formula for an expected cell frequency**

In other words, if you applied the above formula to compute expected frequencies, and you used these to create your stacked bar graphs, the percents of "Yes" and "No" respondents would be identical for all three student classification types: There would be no relationship to see in the graphs. So, the expected frequencies are a baseline, and if the observed frequencies are very different from the expected frequencies, there is reason to believe that a relationship does exist.

**Computed Chi-Square Value.** We will describe this analytical procedure briefly in the hope that our description adds to your understanding of cross-tabulation analysis. The observed and expected cross-tabulation frequencies are compared and the support or nonsupport of the null hypothesis is determined with the use of what is called the chi-square formula.

$$\chi^2 = \sum_{i-1}^{n} \frac{(\text{Observed}_i - \text{Expected}_i)^2}{\text{Expected}_i}$$

◀ **Chi-square formula**

where
$\text{Observed}_i$ = observed frequency in cell $i$
$\text{Expected}_i$ = expected frequency in cell $i$
$n$ = number of cells

The formula holds that each cross-tabulation cell expected frequency be subtracted from its associated observed frequency, and then that difference be squared to avoid a cancellation effect of minus and plus differences. Then the squared difference is divided by the expected frequency to adjust for differences in expected cell sizes. All of these are then summed to arrive at the computed chi-square value. We have provided a step-by-step description of this analysis[3] in Table 14.2.

**Table 14.2**  How to Determine If You Have a Significant Boolean Relationship Using Chi-Square Analysis

| Step | Description | College Students Attending Movies Example ($n = 100$) |
|------|-------------|----------------------------------------------------|
| Step 1 | Set up the cross-tabulation table and determine the raw counts for the cell known as the *observed frequencies*. | (table below) |

**Student Classification**

| | | Underclass Student | Upperclass Student | Graduate Student | Row Totals |
|---|---|---|---|---|---|
| Attended a Movie? | Yes | 105 | 85 | 5 | 195 |
| | No | 45 | 85 | 45 | 175 |
| Column Totals | | 150 | 170 | 50 | 370 |

**Step 2**  Calculate the expected frequencies using the formula:

$$\text{Expected cell frequency} = \frac{\text{Cell column total} \times \text{Cell row total}}{\text{Grand total}}$$

**Student Classification**

| | | Underclass Student | Upperclass Student | Graduate Student | Row Totals |
|---|---|---|---|---|---|
| Attended a Movie? | Yes | 79.1 | 89.6 | 26.3 | 195 |
| | No | 70.9 | 80.4 | 23.6 | 175 |
| Column Totals | | 150 | 170 | 50 | 370 |

**Step 3**  Calculate the computed chi-square value using the chi-square formula noted above.

$$\chi^2 = (105 - 79.1)^2/79.1 + (85 - 89.6)^2/89.6 + (5 - 26.3)^2/26.3 +$$
$$(45 - 70.9)^2/70.9 + (85 - 80.4)^2/80.4 + (45 - 23.6)^2/55.3$$
$$= 55.1$$

**Step 4**  Determine the critical chi-square value from a chi-square table, using the following formula: (#rows − 1) × (#columns − 1) = degrees of freedom (*df*).

$$df = (2 - 1) \times (3 - 1)$$
$$= 2$$

You would need to use your computed *df* and a chi-square distribution table to find that the critical table value is 5.99.

**Step 5**  Evaluate whether or not the null hypothesis of *no* relationship is supported.

The computed chi-square value of 55.1 is larger than the table value of 5.99, so the hypothesis is not supported. There *is* a relationship between student status and going to a movie in the past month.

By now, you should realize that whenever a statistician arrives at a computed value, he or she will most certainly be comparing it to a table value to assess its statistical significance. In Table 14.2, you will find that we did find a computed chi-square value of 55.1. We then have to consult with a chi-square value table to see if our computed chi-square value is greater than the critical table value. Much like things in Oz, the chi-square distribution is not normal, and you must calculate the *degrees of freedom* with the formula in Table 14.2 in order to know where to look in the chi-square table for the critical value. Suffice it to say that with higher degrees of freedom, the table chi-square value is larger, but there is no single value that can be memorized as in our 1.96 number for a normal distribution. A cross-tabulation can have any number of rows and columns, depending on the labels that identify the various groups in the two categorical variables being analyzed, and since the degrees of freedom are based on the number of rows and columns, there is no single critical chi-square value that we can identify for all cases.

Table 14.2 expresses that our computed value of 55.1 is, indeed, greater than the table value of 5.99, meaning that there is no support for our null hypothesis of no relationship. Yes, Dorothy, we do have a significant relationship, and we are on our way back to Kansas to draw pie charts or stacked bar graphs that portray the relationship we have discovered.

> ■ When the calculated chi-square value exceeds the critical chi-square table value, there is a significant relationship between the two variables under analysis.

### How to Interpret a Significant Cross-Tabulation Finding

As we illustrated when we introduced you to Boolean relationships, the best communication vehicle in this case is a graph, and we recommend pie charts or stacked bar graphs. Furthermore, we strongly recommend that you convert your raw counts (observed frequencies) to percentages for optimal communication.

When you determine that a significant relationship does exist (that is, there is no support for the null hypothesis of no relationship), two additional cross-tabulation tables can be calculated that are very valuable in revealing underlying relationships. The **column percentages table** divides the raw frequencies by their associated column total raw frequency. That is, the formula is as follows:

$$\text{Column cell percentage} = \frac{\text{Cell frequency}}{\text{Cell column total}}$$

> ◀ **Formula for a column cell percentage**

The **row percentages table** presents the data with the row totals as the 100% base for each. That is, a row cell percentage is computed as follows:

$$\text{Row cell percentage} = \frac{\text{Cell frequency}}{\text{Cell row total}}$$

> ◀ **Formula for a row cell percentage**

In Figure 14.3, we have calculated the column percentages and the row percentages cross-tabulation tables using our college student movie attendance cross-tabulation observed frequencies, and we have provided stacked bar charts

**Column Percents Table and Graph**

|  |  | Underclass student | Upperclass student | Graduate student |
|---|---|---|---|---|
| Attend a Movie? | No | 30% | 50% | 90% |
|  | Yes | 70% | 50% | 10% |
| Column Totals |  | 100% | 100% | 100% |

> **Figure 14.3** Illustration of Column Percents and Row Percents in a Cross-Tabulation Table
> (*Continues on next page*)

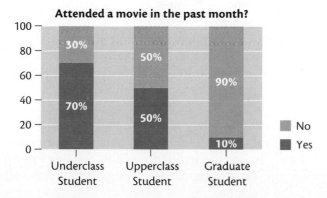

**Figure 14.3** *(Continued)*

**Row Percents Table and Graph**

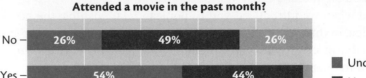

|  |  | Underclass student | Upperclass student | Graduate student | Row Totals |
|---|---|---|---|---|---|
| Attend a Movie? | No | 26% | 49% | 26% | 100% |
|  | Yes | 54% | 44% | 3% | 100% |

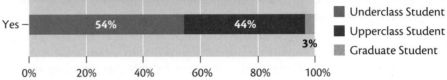

**Attended a movie in the past month?**

No — 26% 49% 26%

Yes — 54% 44% 3%

0%   20%   40%   60%   80%   100%

■ Underclass Student
■ Upperclass Student
■ Graduate Student

that portray these percentages. With the column percentages, the chart is identical to Figure 14.2, while for the row percentages, the bar chart is different. However, the relationship that we have discovered to be significant is clear regardless of which graph we inspect: Underclass students tend to go to movies, upperclass students may or may not go, and graduate students rarely take in a movie.

> ■ When a significant Boolean relationship is found, use row percentages and/or column percentages to reveal the nature of the relationship.

# HOW TO PERFORM CROSS-TABULATION ANALYSIS WITH THE XL DATA ANALYST

The XL Data Analyst performs cross-tabulation analysis and generates row and column percentage tables so that users can see the Boolean relationship patterns when they encounter a significant cross-tabulation relationship. As an exercise, consider the College Life E-Zine survey question asking respondents if they plan to purchase an automobile in the next three months. Do you think that there is a relationship to student classification? To ask this question differently, what class (freshman, sophomore, etc.) would you expect to be thinking about an automobile purchase in the next three months?

We'll use the XL Data Analyst to investigate this question. Figure 14.4 is the menu and selection window used to direct the XL Data Analyst to perform a cross-tabulation analysis. The menu sequence is Relate–Crosstabs, and this sequence opens up the selection window that you see in Figure 14.4. The "purchase an automobile . . ." question is selected into the Column windowpane, and the classification variable is clicked into the Row window pane. Actually, it does not matter which categorical variable is placed in which selection windowpane, as the XL Data Analyst will generate a row percentages table as well as a column percentages table.

> ■ Use the XL Data Analyst "Crosstabs" procedure to analyze a possible Boolean relationship between two categorical variables.

Figure 14.5 is the resulting output in the form of three tables. The first table is the Observed Frequencies table along with grand totals for rows and columns. The XL Data Analyst uses these to perform chi-square analysis, the result of which is provided immediately below the frequencies table. In this example, there is a significant relationship. The determination of a significant relationship

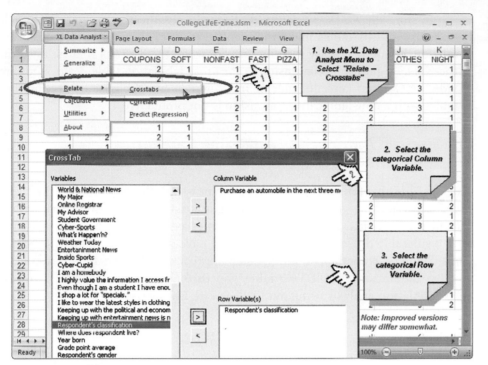

**Figure 14.4** Using the XL Data Analyst to Set Up a Cross-Tabulation Analysis

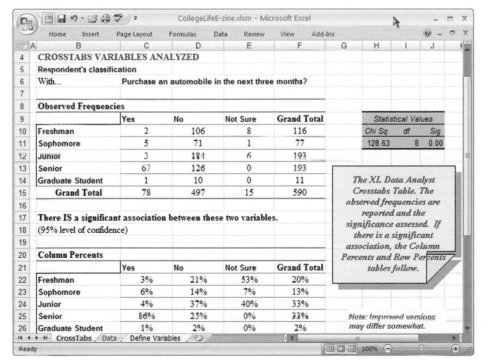

**Figure 14.5** XL Data Analyst Cross-Tabulations Analysis Output

signals that it is worthwhile to inspect the row percentages and/or the column percentages table(s) to spot the pattern of the Boolean relationship. The Column Percents table shows rather dramatically that 86% of those respondents who indicated "Yes" to the purchase question are seniors.

In sum, the XL Data Analyst has flagged a significant cross-tabulation relationship, and its tables make the identification of the nature of the Boolean relationship quite an easy task. By the way, when the XL Data Analyst finds that there is *no* significant relationship in the cross-tabulation table, it does not provide the Column Percents table or the Row Percents table, as inspecting these tables with a nonsignificant relationship is not productive.

## The Six-Step Approach to Analyzing Categorical Variables with Cross-Tabulation

Thus far, this chapter has introduced you to cross-tabulation, which is the appropriate analysis when you are investigating a possible relationship between two categorical variables. The underlying concepts associated with cross-tabulation are considerably different from those that we have described with analyses in previous chapters. Nonetheless, our six-step approach to data analysis is applicable to cross-tabulations. Table 14.3 takes you through our six steps to perform a cross-tabulation analysis using our College Life E-Zine data set.

**Table 14.3** The Six-Step Approach to Data Analysis for Cross-Tabulation Analysis

| Step | Explanation | Example |
|---|---|---|
| **1. What is the research objective?** | Determine that you are dealing with a **Relationship Objective**. | Is there a relationship between the dwelling location of State University students and their plans to purchase items on the Internet in the next two months? |
| **2. What questionnaire question(s) is/are involved?** | Identify the question for the two variables and determine their scales. | Respondents indicated their residence (on-campus or off-campus) and they indicated "Yes," "No," or "Not sure" to a question as to whether or not they think they will make an Internet purchase in the next two months. Both variables are categorical. |
| **3. What is the appropriate analysis?** | To assess the relationship between two categorical variables, use cross-tabulation analysis. | We use this procedure because the two variables are categorical, and cross-tabulation analysis is the proper one to investigate a possible Boolean relationship between them. |
| **4. How do you run it?** | Use XL Data Analyst analysis: Select "Relate–Crosstabs." | |

**5. How do you interpret the finding?**

The XL Data Analyst indicates if the relationship is significant, and if so, provides Row Percents and Column Percents tables that portray the Boolean relationship.

There is a significant association between these two variables. (95% level of confidence)

| Column Percents | Yes | No | Not Sure | Grand Total |
|---|---|---|---|---|
| On Campus | 61% | 0% | 14% | 16% |
| Off Campus | 39% | 100% | 86% | 84% |
| Grand Total | 100% | 100% | 100% | 100% |

| Row Percents | Yes | No | Not Sure | Grand Total |
|---|---|---|---|---|
| On Campus | 92% | 0% | 8% | 100% |
| Off Campus | 11% | 79% | 10% | 100% |
| Grand Total | 24% | 66% | 10% | 100% |

**6. How do you write/present these findings?**

When a significant relationship is found, you can create a graph that illustrates your finding.

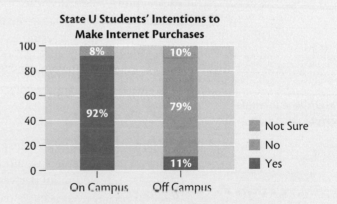

State U Students' Intentions to Make Internet Purchases

Most State University students who live on campus intend to make purchases on the Internet in the next two months, while most of those living off campus do not intend to make an Internet purchase.

# LINEAR RELATIONSHIPS AND CORRELATION ANALYSIS

We will now turn to a more precise relationship, and one that you should find easy to visualize. Perhaps the most intuitive relationship between two metric variables is a linear relationship. A **linear relationship** is a straight-line relationship. Here knowledge of the amount of one variable will automatically yield knowledge of the amount of the other variable as a consequence of applying the linear or straight-line formula that is known to exist between them. In its general form, a **straight-line formula** is as follows:

**Formula for a straight line** ▷

$$y = a + bx$$

Where:
$y =$ the variable being predicted (called the "dependent" variable)
$a =$ the intercept
$b =$ the slope
$x =$ the variable used to predict the predicted variable (called the "independent" variable)

■ The formula $y = a + bx$ describes a linear relationship between the variables $y$ and $x$.

As you can see in Figure 14.6, the **intercept** is the point on the $y$-axis that the straight line "hits" when $x = 0$, and the **slope** is the change in the line for each one-unit change in $x$. We will clarify the terms *independent* and *dependent* in a later section of this chapter.

■ A linear relationship is defined by its intercept, $a$, and its slope, $b$.

For example, South-Western Book Company hires college student representatives to work in the summer. These student representatives are put through an intensified sales training program and then are divided into teams. Each team is given a specific territory, and each individual is assigned a particular district within that territory. The student representative then goes from house to house in the district making cold calls, attempting to sell children's books. Let us assume that the amount of sales is linearly related to the number of cold calls made. In this special case, no sales calls determines zero sales, or $a = 0$, the intercept when $x = 0$. If, on average, every 10th sales call resulted in a sale and the typical sale is $62, then the average per call would be $6.20, or $b$, the slope. The linear relationship between total sales ($y$) and number of sales calls ($x$) is as follows:

**Straight-line formula example** ▷

$$y = \$0 + \$6.20x$$

Thus, if the college salesperson makes 100 cold calls in any given day, the expected total revenues would be $620 ($6.20 times 100 calls). Certainly, our student sales rep would not derive exactly $620 for every 100 calls, but the linear relationship shows what is expected to happen on average.

**Figure 14.6** The Straight-Line Relationship Illustrating the Intercept and the Slope

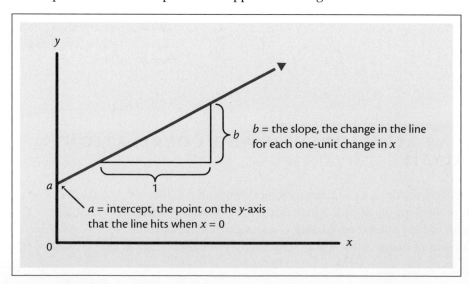

## Correlation Coefficients and Covariation

The **correlation coefficient** is an index number, constrained to fall between the range of −1.0 and +1.0, that communicates both the strength and the direction of the linear relationship between two metric variables. The amount of linear relationship between two variables is communicated by the absolute size of the correlation coefficient, whereas its sign communicates the direction of the association. A plus sign means that the relationship is such that as one variable increases, so does the other variable and vice versa. A negative sign means that as one variable increases, the other variable decreases.

Stated in a slightly different manner, a correlation coefficient indicates the degree of "covariation" between two variables. **Covariation** is defined as the amount of change in one variable systematically associated with a change in another variable. The greater the absolute size of the correlation coefficient, the greater is the covariation between the two variables, or the stronger is their relationship regardless of the sign.

■ A correlation coefficient expresses the amount of covariation between two metric variables.

We can illustrate covariation with a **scatter diagram**, which plots data pairs in an x- and y-axis graph. Here is an example: A marketing researcher is investigating the possible relationship between total company sales for Novartis, a leading pharmaceuticals sales company, in a particular territory and the number of salespeople assigned to that territory. At the researcher's fingertips are the sales figures and number of salespeople assigned for each of 20 different Novartis territories in the United States. It is possible to depict the raw data for these two variables on a scatter diagram such as the one in Figure 14.7. A scatter diagram plots the points corresponding to each matched pair of x and y variables. In this figure, the vertical axis (y) is Novartis sales for the territory and the horizontal axis (x) contains the number of salespeople in that territory.

■ A scatter diagram will portray the amount of covariation between two metric variables.

The arrangement or scatter of points appears to fall in a long ellipse. Any two variables that exhibit systematic covariation will form an ellipselike pattern on a

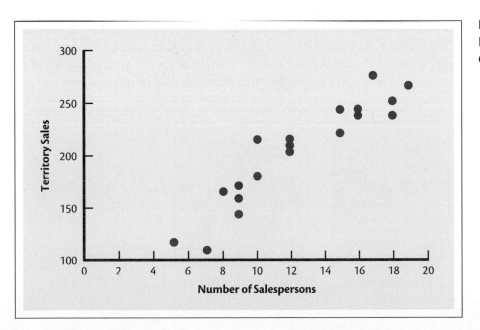

**Figure 14.7** A Scatter Diagram Showing Covariation

scatter diagram. Of course, this particular scatter diagram portrays the information gathered by the marketing researcher on sales and the number of salespeople in each territory and only that information. In actuality, the scatter diagram could have taken any shape, depending on the relationship between the points plotted for the two variables concerned.[4]

A number of different types of scatter diagram results are portrayed in Figure 14.8. Each of these scatter diagram results indicates a different degree of covariation. For instance, you can see that the scatter diagram depicted in Figure 14.8a is one in which there is no apparent association or relationship between the two variables, because the points fail to create any identifiable pattern. They are clumped into a large, formless shape. Those points in Figure 14.8b indicate a negative relationship between variable $x$ and variable $y$; higher values of $x$ tend to be associated with lower values of $y$. Those points in Figure 14.8c are fairly similar to those in Figure 14.8b, but the angle or the slope of the ellipse is different. This slope indicates a positive relationship between $x$ and $y$, because larger values of $x$ tend to be associated with larger values of $y$.

What is the connection between scatter diagrams and correlation coefficients? The answer to these questions lies in the linear relationship described earlier in this chapter. Look at Figures 14.7, 14.8b, and 14.8c and you will see that all of them form ellipses. Imagine taking an ellipse and pulling on both ends. It would stretch out and become thinner until all of its points fell on a straight line. If you happened to find some data with all of its points falling on the axis line and you computed a correlation, you would find it to be exactly 1.0 (+1.0 if the ellipse went up to the right and −1.0 if it went down to the right).

Now imagine pushing the ends of the ellipse until it became the pattern in Figure 14.8a. There would be no identifiable straight line. Similarly, there would be no systematic covariation. The correlation for a ball-shaped scatter diagram is zero because there is no discernible linear relationship. In other words, a correlation coefficient indicates the degree of covariation between two variables, and you can envision this linear relationship as a scatter diagram. The form and angle of the scatter pattern are revealed by the size and sign, respectively, of the correlation coefficient.

In our two-variables averages analysis, we cautioned you that the two variables must share the same scale: Both should be measured in dollars, number of times, the same 5-point scale, and so on. Correlation analysis has the great advantage of relating two variables that are of very different measurements. For instance, you can correlate

**The ellipital shape of a scatter diagram for two metric variables translates to the direction and size of their correlation coefficient.**

**Figure 14.8** Scatter Diagrams Illustrating Various Relationships

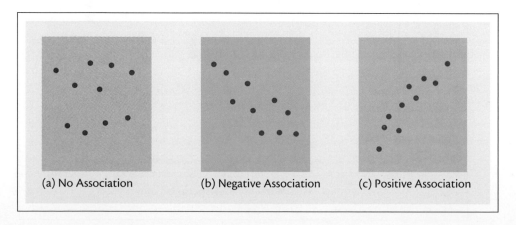

(a) No Association    (b) Negative Association    (c) Positive Association

a buyer's age with the number of times he or she purchased the item in the past year, you can correlate how many miles a commuter drives in a week to how many minutes of talk radio he or she listens to, and you can correlate how satisfied customers are with how long they have been loyal customers. You can use correlation with disparate metric scales because there is a standardization procedure in the computation of a correlation that eliminates the differences between the two measures involved.

PRACTICAL APPLICATIONS

## Statistical Significance of a Correlation

Working with correlations is a two-step process. First, you must assess the statistical significance of the correlation. If it is significant, you can take the second step, which is to interpret it. With respect to the first step, a correlation coefficient that is not statistically significant is taken to be a correlation of zero. Let us elaborate on this point. While you can always compute a correlation coefficient, you must first determine its statistical significance, and if it is *not* significant, you must consider it to be a zero correlation regardless of its computed value. To repeat, regardless of its absolute value, a correlation that is not statistically significant has no meaning at all because of the **null hypothesis for a correlation**, which states that the population correlation coefficient is equal to zero. If this null hypothesis is rejected (that is, there is a statistically significant correlation), then you can be assured that a correlation other than zero will be found in the population. But if the sample correlation is found to not be significant, the population correlation will be zero.

> With correlation analysis, the null hypothesis is that the population correlation is equal to zero.

Here is a question. If you can answer it correctly, you understand the statistical significance of a correlation. Let's say that you repeated a correlational survey many, many times and computed the average for a correlation that was not significant across all of these surveys, what would be the result? (The answer is zero, because if the correlation is not significant, the null hypothesis is true, and the population correlation is zero.)

How do you determine the statistical significance of a correlation coefficient? Tables exist that give the lowest value of the significant correlation coefficients for given sample sizes. However, most computer statistical programs will indicate the statistical significance level of the computed correlation coefficient. Your XL Data Analyst evaluates the significance and reports whether or not the correlation is significant at the 95% level of confidence.

## Rules of Thumb for Correlation Strength

After you have established that a correlation coefficient is statistically significant, we can talk about some general rules of thumb concerning the strength of the relationship. Correlation coefficients that fall between +1.00 and +.81 or between −1.00 and −.81 are generally considered to be "strong." Those correlations that fall between +.80 and +.61 or −.80 and −.61 generally indicate a "moderate" relationship. Those that fall between +.60 and +.41 or −.60 and −.41 denote a "weak" association. Any correlation that falls between the range of ±.21 and ±.40 is usually considered indicative of a "very weak" association between the variables. Finally, any correlation that is equal to or less than ±.20 is typically uninteresting to marketing researchers because it rarely identifies a meaningful association between two variables. We have provided Table 14.4 as a reference on these rules of thumb. As you use these guidelines, remember

**Table 14.4**
Rules of Thumb About Correlation Coefficient Size

| Coefficient Range | Strength of Association* |
|---|---|
| ±.81 to ±1.00 | Strong |
| ±.61 to ±.80 | Moderate |
| ±.41 to ±.60 | Weak |
| ±.21 to ±.40 | Very weak |
| ±.00 to ±.20 | None |

*Assuming the correlation coefficient is statistically significant.

■ Use Table 14.4's guidelines to judge the strength of a statistically significant correlation coefficient.

two things: First, we are assuming that the statistical significance of the correlation has been established. Second, researchers make up their own rules of thumb, so you may encounter someone whose guidelines differ slightly from those in this table.[5]

## The Pearson Product Moment Correlation Coefficient

The **Pearson product moment correlation** measures the linear relationship between two metric-scaled variables such as those depicted conceptually by our scatter diagrams. This correlation coefficient that can be computed between the two variables is a measure of the "tightness" of the scatter points to the straight line. The formula for calculating a Pearson product moment correlation is complicated, and researchers never compute it by hand, as they invariably find these on computer output. However, some instructors believe that students should understand the workings of the correlation coefficient formula, plus it is possible to describe the formula and point out how covariation is included and how the correlation coefficient's value comes to be restricted to −1.0 to +1.0. We have described this formula and pointed out these items in Marketing Research Application 14.1.

The larger the absolute size of a correlation coefficient, the stronger it is.

## MARKETING RESEARCH APPLICATION 14.1

PRACTICAL

APPLICATIONS

### How to Compute a Pearson Product Moment Correlation

Marketing researchers almost never compute statistics such as chi-square or correlation, but it is insightful to learn about this computation. The computational formula for a Pearson product moment correlation is as follows, and we will briefly describe the components of this formula to help you see how the concepts we have discussed in this chapter fit in.

**Formula for Pearson product moment correlation** ▼

$$r_{xy} = \frac{\sum_{c=1}^{n} (x_i - \bar{x})(y_i - \bar{y})}{ns_x s_y}$$

where
$x_i$ = each $x$ value
$\bar{x}$ = average of the $x$ values
$y_i$ = average $y$ value
$\bar{y}$ = average of the $y$ values
$n$ = number of paired cases
$s_x, s_y$ = standard deviations of $x$ and $y$, respectively

The numerator requires that the $x_i$ and the $y_i$ of each pair of $x$, $y$ data points be compared (via subtraction) to its average, and that these values be multiplied. The sum of all these products is referred to as the "cross-products sum," and this value represents the covariation between $x$ and $y$. Recall that we represented covariation on a scatter diagram in our introduction to correlation earlier in this section of the chapter.

The covariation is divided by the number of $xy$ pairs, $n$, to scale it down to an average per pair of $x$ and $y$ values. This average covariation is then divided by both the standard deviation of the $x$ values and the standard deviation of the $y$ values. This adjustment procedure eliminates the measurement differences in the $x$ units and the $y$ units ($x$ might be measured in years, and $y$ might be measured on a 1–10 satisfaction scale). The result constrains the correlation, $r_{xy}$, to fall within a specific range of values, and this range is between −1.0 and +1.0, as we indicated earlier as well.

## HOW TO PERFORM CORRELATION ANALYSIS WITH THE XL DATA ANALYST

A common application of correlation analysis with surveys such as the College Life E-Zine survey is its use in the investigation of relationships between lifestyle variables and consumer purchasing. In our survey, State University respondents were administered a Likert scale (5-point, stongly disagree to strongly agree) relating to their lifestyles, and one of the items was "I like to wear the latest styles in clothing." A consumer purchasing question that might be related to this lifestyle dimension is purchases of clothing via the Internet. The purchases are measured in dollars (out of every $100 spent on Internet purchases), and the Likert scale is a synthetic metric scale, so correlation analysis is appropriate.

Figure 14.9 shows the XL Data Analyst menu sequence for correlation analysis. The menu sequence is Relate–Correlate, which opens up the selection

**Figure 14.9** Using the XL Data Analyst to Set Up a Correlation Analysis

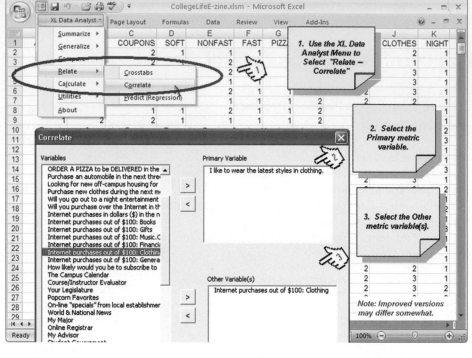

---

window. As you can see in Figure 14.9, the lifestyle question about keeping up with latest fashions is chosen as the Primary Variable, while the clothing Internet purchase variable is clicked into the Other Variable(s) window pane. (Several "other variables" can be selected in a single analysis.)

Figure 14.10 shows the resulting XL Data Analyst output for correlation. The table reveals a computed correlation of (+) .72, with a sample size of 143

**Figure 14.10** XL Data Analyst Correlation Analysis Output

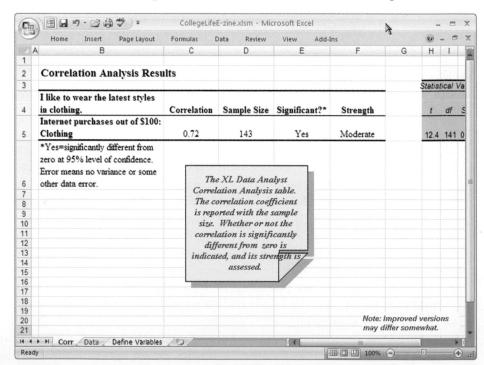

respondents, that is statistically significant from 0 (the null hypothesis) and whose strength is "moderate" based on the rules of thumb about correlation sizes presented earlier. So, yes, there is a moderate positive association between the fashion consciousness of our State University respondents who are interested in the College Life E-Zine and their purchases of clothing. These two variables covary, suggesting that if the College Life E-Zine partnered with or recruited clothing retailer advertisers whose product lines were in tune with the latest fashions, there would be good potential for success.

## The Six-Step Approach to Analyzing a Possible Linear Relationship Between Two Metric Variables

While Internet sites of all kinds are conceivable, an important aspect of the College Life E-Zine is its intended delivery of all types of information to State University students. For instance, it has the potential to provide campus calendars, instructor evaluations, registration news, online specials, sports and entertainment news, weather, and more. There is an assumption by our prospective e-zine entrepreneurs that university students are "into" obtaining information from the Web. One of the lifestyle statements in our survey was "I highly value the information I access from the Internet," and it is useful to correlate this variable with the subscription likelihood question. Table 14.5 describes the six-step analysis process used to investigate the relationship between these two variables.

**Table 14.5** The Six-Step Approach to Data Analysis for Correlation Analysis

| Step | Explanation | Example |
|---|---|---|
| 1. What is the research objective? | Determine that you are dealing with a **Relationship Objective**. | Is there a relationship between how much State University students value getting information from the Internet and how likely they are to subscribe to the College Life E-Zine? |
| 2. What questionnaire question(s) is/are involved? | Identify the question for the two variables and determine their scales. | Respondents indicated their disagreement/agreement with the Internet information value lifestyle statement using a 5-point scale, and they indicated how likely they would be to subscribe to the e-zine using a 5-point scale. Both variables are metric. |
| 3. What is the appropriate analysis? | To assess the relationship between two metric variables, use correlation analysis. | We use this procedure because the two variables are metric, and correlation analysis will assess the possible linear relationship that exists between them. |

**Table 14.5** *(Continued)*

| Step | Explanation | Example |
|------|-------------|---------|
| **4. How do you run it?** | Use XL Data Analyst analysis: Select "Relate–Correlate." | |
| **5. How do you interpret the finding?** | The XL Data Analyst indicates the significance and strength of the correlation. | *(see Correlation Analysis Results table below)* |

**Correlation Analysis Results**

| I highly value the information I access from the Internet. | Correlation | Sample Size | Significant?* | Strength |
|---|---|---|---|---|
| **How likely would you be to subscribe to the E-Zine?** | 0.77 | 590 | Yes | Moderate |

*Yes = significantly different from zero at 95% level of confidence

| Step | Explanation | Example |
|------|-------------|---------|
| **6. How do you write/present these findings?** | When a significant correlation is appreciable in its strength, you can report and interpret it in your findings. | Analysis revealed a moderately strong, significant positive correlation between State University students' value on the information they access from the Internet and their likelihood to subscribe to the College Life E-Zine. Thus, State U students who frequently use the Internet to obtain information are good prospects for the College Life E-Zine. |

# LINEAR RELATIONSHIPS AND REGRESSION ANALYSIS

**Regression analysis** is a predictive analysis technique in which two or more variables are used to predict the level of another by use of the straight-line formula, $y = a + bx$, that we described earlier. When a researcher wants to make an exact prediction based on a correlation analysis finding, he or she can turn to regression analysis. **Bivariate regression analysis** is a case in which only two variables are involved in the predictive model. When we use only two variables, one is termed *dependent* and the other is termed *independent*. The **dependent variable** is the one that is predicted, and it is customarily termed $y$ in the regression straight-line equation. The **independent variable** is the one that is used to predict the dependent variable, and it is the $x$ in the regression formula. We must quickly point out that the terms *dependent* and *independent* are arbitrary designations and are customary to regression analysis. There is no cause-and-effect relationship or true dependence between the dependent and the independent variables.

■ Regression analysis assesses the straight-line relationship between a metric dependent variable, $y$, and a metric independent variable, $x$.

## Computing the Intercept and Slope for Bivariate Regression

To compute $a$ and $b$, a statistical analysis program needs a number of observations of the various levels of the dependent variable paired with different levels of the independent variable. The formulas for calculating the slope ($b$) and the intercept ($a$) are rather complicated, but some instructors are in favor of their students understanding these formulas, so we will describe them here.

The formula for the slope, $b$, in the case of a bivariate regression is:

$$b = r_{xy} \frac{s_y}{s_x}$$

◄ **Formula for $b$, the slope, in bivariate regression**

That is, the slope is equal to the correlation of variables $x$ and $y$ times the standard deviation of $y$, the dependent variable, divided by the standard deviation of $x$, the independent variable. You should notice that the linear relationship aspect of correlation is translated directly into its regression counterpart by this formula.

When you use your data set to solve this equation for the slope, $b$, then you can calculate the intercept, $a$, with the following formula.

$$a = \bar{y} - b\bar{x}$$

◄ **Formula for $a$, the intercept, in bivariate regression**

When any statistical analysis program computes the intercept and the slope in a regression analysis, it does so on the basis of the "**least squares criterion**." The least squares criterion is a way of guaranteeing that the straight line that runs through the points on the scatter diagram is positioned so as to minimize the vertical distances away from the line of the various points. In other words, if you draw a line where the regression line is calculated and measure the vertical distances of all the points away from that line, it would be impossible to draw any other line that would result in a lower total of all of those vertical distances. So, regression analysis determines the best slope and the best intercept possible for the straight-line relationship between the independent and dependent variables for the data set that is being used in the analysis.

■ Regression analysis computes the intercept, $a$, and the slope, $b$, of a straight-line relationship between $x$ and $y$ using the "least squares criterion."

## Testing for Statistical Significance of the Intercept and the Slope

Simply computing the values for $a$ and $b$ is not sufficient for regression analysis, because the two values must be tested for statistical significance. The intercept and slope that are computed are sample estimates of population parameters of the true intercept, $\alpha$ (alpha), and the true slope, $\beta$ (beta). The tests for statistical significance are tests as to whether the computed intercept and computed slope are significantly different from zero (the null hypothesis). To determine statistical significance, regression analysis requires that a $t$ test be undertaken for each parameter estimate. The interpretation of these $t$ tests is identical to other significance tests you have seen; that is, if the computed $t$ is greater than the table $t$ value, the hypothesis is not supported, meaning that the computed intercept or slope is not zero, it is the value determined by the regression analysis.

> ■ Statistical tests determine whether or not the calculated intercept, $a$, and slope, $b$, are significantly different from zero (the null hypothesis).

## Making a Prediction with Bivariate Regression Analysis

Now, there is one more step to relate, and it is an important one. How do you make a prediction? The fact that the line is a best-approximation representation of all the points means we must account for a certain amount of error when we use the line for our predictions. The true advantage of a significant bivariate regression analysis result lies in the ability of the marketing researcher to use that information gained about the regression line through the points on the scatter diagram and to predict the value or amount of the dependent variable based on some level of the independent variable. If you examine Figure 14.11, you will see how the prediction works. The regression prediction uses a confidence interval that is based on a standard error value. To elaborate, we know that the scatter of points does not describe a perfectly straight line, because a perfect correlation of +1.0 or −1.0 almost never is found. So our regression prediction can only be an estimate.

**Figure 14.11** To Predict with Regression, Apply a Confidence Interval Around the Predicted *Y* Value(s)

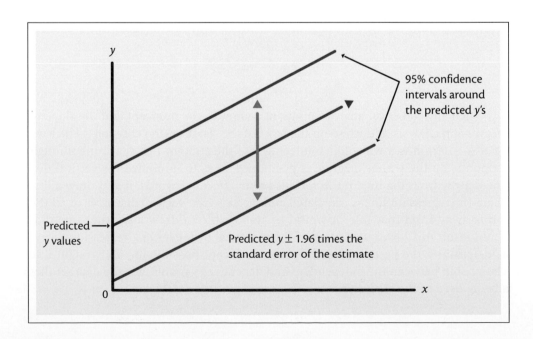

Generating a regression prediction is conceptually identical to estimating a population average. That is, it is necessary to express the amount of error by estimating a confidence interval range rather than stipulating an exact estimate for your prediction. Regression analysis provides for a **standard error of the estimate**, which is a measure of the accuracy of the predictions of the regression equation. This standard error value is analogous to the standard error of the mean you used in estimating a population average from a sample, but it is based on **residuals**, which are the differences between each predicted $y$ value for each $x$ value in the data set compared to the actual $x$ value.[6] That is, regression analysis takes the regression equation and applies it to every $x$ value and determines what you might envision as the average difference away from the associated actual $x$ value in the data set. The differences, or residuals, are translated into a standard error of estimate value, and you use the standard error of the estimate to compute confidence intervals around the predictions that you make using the regression equation. The prediction process is accomplished by applying the following equation:

■ When making a prediction with a regression equation, use a confidence interval that expresses the sample error and variability inherent in the sample used to compute the regression equation.

Predicted $y = a + bx$
Confidence interval = Predicted $y \pm (1.96 \times$ standard error of the estimate$)$

◄ **95% confidence interval for a predicted $y$ value using a regression equation**

One of the assumptions of regression analysis is that the plots on the scatter diagram will be spread uniformly and in accord with the normal curve assumptions over the regression line. The points are congregated close to the line and become more diffuse as they move away from the line. In other words, a greater percentage of the points are found on or close to the line than are found further away. The great advantage of this assumption is that it allows the marketing researcher to use his or her knowledge of the normal curve to specify the range in which the dependent variable is predicted to fall. The interpretation of these confidence intervals is identical to interpretations for previous confidence intervals: Were the same prediction made many times and an actual result determined each time, the actual results would fall within the range of the predicted value 95% of these times.

The amount a family spends on groceries is related to the number of family members.

Let us use the regression equation to make a prediction about the dollar amount of grocery purchases that would be associated with a certain family size. In this example, we have asked respondents to provide us with their approximate weekly grocery expenditures and the number of family members living in their households. A bivariate regression analysis is performed, and the regression equation is found to have an intercept of $75 and a slope of +$25. So to predict the weekly grocery expenditures for a family of four, the computations would be as follows:

**Calculation of average weekly grocery expenditures for a household of 4 individuals** ▷

$$y = a + bx$$
$$\text{Expenditures} = \$75 + (\$25 \times 4 \text{ members})$$
$$= \$75 + \$100$$
$$= \$175$$

The analysis finds a standard error of the estimate of $20, and this value is used to calculate the 95% confidence interval for the prediction.

**Calculation of 95% confidence interval for the prediction of average weekly grocery expenditures for a household of 4 individuals** ▷

$$\$175 \pm 1.96 \times \$20$$
$$\$175 \pm \$39.20$$
$$\$135.8 – \$214.2$$

The interpretation of these three numbers is as follows: For a typical family represented by the sample, the expected average weekly grocery purchases amount to $175, but because there are differences between family size and grocery purchases, the weekly expenditures would not be exactly that amount. Consequently, the 95% confidence interval reveals that the sales figure should fall between $136 and $214 (rounded values). Of course, the prediction is valid only if conditions remain the same as they were for the time period during which the original data were collected.

You may be troubled by the large range of our confidence interval, and you are right to be concerned. How precisely a regression analysis finding predicts is determined by the size of the standard error of the estimate, a measure of the variability of the predicted dependent variable. In our grocery expenditures example, the average dollars spent on groceries per week may be predicted by our bivariate regression findings; however, if we repeated the survey many, many times, and made our $175, four-member household prediction of the average dollars spent every time, 95% of these predictions would fall between $136 and $214. There is no way to make this prediction range more exact because its precision is dictated by the variability in the data. Researchers sometimes refer to the **R-square value**, which is the squared correlation coefficient between the independent and dependent variables. The $R$-square value ranges from 0 to 1, and the closer it is found to 1, the stronger is the linear relationship and the more precise will be the predictions.

▪ Researchers use the $R$-square value (the squared correlation) to judge how precise a regression analysis finding will be when used in a prediction.

There are variations of regression analysis as well as a myriad of applications. For example, researchers examined how American versus Greek university students felt when they learned of a deliberate overcharge.[7] In one situation, students learned that they had been overcharged for a new suit, by $5, $40, or $80, while in another situation students were informed that they had been overcharged for a year's membership in a health club by $25, $200, or $700. Using a form of regression called conjoint analysis, the researchers found that Greek and American college students are similar in many ways. For example, both groups felt that the suit purchase situation was more ethically offensive than the health club one. However, the Greek students saw the situations as more unethical than did the American students. Moreover, Greek students were more affected by the dollar size than were American students.

# MULTIPLE REGRESSION

Now that you have a basic understanding of bivariate regression, we will move on to an advanced regression topic. When we have completed our description of this related topic, we will instruct you on the use of the XL Data Analyst to perform regression analysis. **Multiple regression analysis** is an expansion of bivariate regression analysis such that more than one independent variable is used in the regression equation. The addition of independent variables makes the regression model more realistic because predictions normally depend on multiple factors, not just one.

The regression equation in multiple regression has the following form:

$$y = a + b_1x_1 + b_2x_2 + b_3x_3 + ... + b_mx_m$$

where

$y$ = the dependent, or predicted, variable
$x_i$ = independent variable $i$
$a$ = the intercept
$b_i$ = the slope for independent variable $i$
$m$ = the number of independent variables in the equation

◀ **Multiple regression equation**

As you can see, the addition of other independent variables has simply added $b_ix_i$'s to the equation. We still have retained the basic $y = a + bx$ straight-line formula, except now we have multiple $x$ variables, and each one is added to the equation, changing y by its individual slope. The inclusion of each independent variable in this manner preserves the straight-line assumptions of multiple regression analysis. This is sometimes known as **additivity**, because each new independent variable is added on to the regression equation. Of course, it might have a negative coefficient, but it is added on to the equation as another independent variable.

◻ **Multiple regression "adds" more independent variables to the regression equation.**

## Working with Multiple Regression

Everything about multiple regression is essentially equivalent to bivariate regression except you are dealing with more than one independent variable. The terminology is slightly different in places, and some statistics are modified to take into account the multiple aspect, but for the most part, concepts in multiple regression are analogous to those in the simple bivariate case.

Let's look at a multiple regression analysis result so you can better understand the multiple regression equation. Let's assume that we are working for Lexus, and we are trying to predict prospective customers' intentions to purchase a Lexus. We have performed a survey that included an attitude-toward-Lexus variable, a word-of-mouth variable, and an income variable. We then applied multiple regression analysis and found that these three independent variables and the intercept were statistically significant.

Here is the result.

**Lexus purchase intention multiple regression equation example** ▷

Intention to purchase a Lexus = 2
$$+ 1.0 \times \text{attitude toward Lexus (1–5 scale)}$$
$$- 0.5 \times \text{negative word of mouth (1–5 scale)}$$
$$+ 1.0 \times \text{income level (1–10 scale)}$$

This multiple regression equation says that you can predict a consumer's intention to buy a Lexus level if you know three variables: (1) attitude toward Lexus, (2) friends' negative comments about Lexus, and (3) income level using a scale with 10 income grades. Furthermore, we can see the impact of each of these variables on Lexus purchase intentions. Here is how to interpret the equation. First, the average person has a "2" intention level, or some small propensity to want to buy a Lexus. Attitude toward Lexus is measured on a 1–5 scale, and with each attitude scale point, intention to purchase a Lexus goes up 1 point. That is, an individual with a strong positive attitude of "5" will have a greater intention than one with a weak attitude of "1." With friends' objections to the Lexus (negative word of mouth) such as "A Lexus is overpriced," the intention decreases by .5 for each level on the 5-point scale. Finally, the intention increases by 1 with each increasing income level.

Here is a numerical example for a potential Lexus buyer whose attitude is 4, negative word of mouth is 3, and income is 5. (We will not use a confidence interval as we just want to illustrate how a multiple regression equation operates.)

**Calculation of Lexus purchase intention using the multiple regression equation** ▷

Intention to purchase a Lexus = 2
$$+1.0 \times 4$$
$$-.5 \times 3$$
$$+1.0 \times 5$$
$$= 9.5$$

Multiple regression is a very powerful tool, because it tells us which factors predict the dependent variable, which way (the sign) each factor influences the dependent variable, and even how much (the size of $b_i$) each factor influences it. Just as was the case in bivariate regression analysis in which we used the correlation between $y$ and $x$, it is possible to inspect the strength of the linear relationship between the independent variables and the dependent variable with multiple regression. **Multiple R**, also called the **coefficient of determination**, is a handy measure of the strength of the overall linear relationship. Just as was the case in bivariate regression analysis, the multiple regression analysis model assumes that a straight-line (plane) relationship exists among the variables. Multiple R ranges from 0 to +1.0 and represents the amount of the dependent variable "explained," or accounted for, by the combined independent variables. High multiple R values indicate that the regression plane applies well to the scatter of points, whereas low values signal that the straight-line model does not apply well.

■ Researchers use multiple R to assess how much of the dependent variable, *y*, is accounted for by the multiple regression result they have found.

Multiple $R$ is like a lead indicator of the multiple regression analysis findings. It is often one of the first pieces of information provided in a multiple regression output. Many researchers mentally convert the multiple $R$ into a percentage. For example, a multiple $R$ of .75 means that the regression findings will explain 75% of the dependent variable. The greater the explanatory power of the multiple regression finding, the better and more useful it is for the researcher. However, multiple $R$ is useful only when the multiple regression finding has only significant independent variables. There is a process called "trimming" in which researchers make iterative multiple regression analyses, systematically removing nonsignificant independent variables until only statistically significant ones remain in the analysis findings.[8]

## Using "Dummy" Independent Variables

A **dummy independent variable** is defined as one that is scaled with a categorical 0-versus-1 coding scheme. The 0-versus-1 code is traditional, but any two adjacent numbers could be used, such as 1-versus-2. The scaling assumptions that underlie multiple regression analysis require that the independent and dependent variables both be metric. However, there are instances in which a marketing researcher may want to use an independent variable that is categorical and identifies only two groups. It is not unusual, for instance, for the marketing researcher to wish to use a two-level variable, such as gender, as an independent variable, in a multiple regression problem. For instance, a researcher may want to use gender coded as 0 for male and 1 for female as an independent variable. Or you might have a buyer–nonbuyer dummy variable that you want to use as an independent variable. In these instances, it is usually permissible to go ahead and slightly violate the assumption of metric scaling for the independent variable to come up with a result that is in some degree interpretable.

It is permissible to cautiously use a few categorical variables with a multiple regression analysis.

## Three Uses of Multiple Regression

Bivariate regression is used only for prediction, whereas multiple regression can be used for (1) prediction, (2) understanding, or (3) as a screening device. You already know how to use regression analysis for prediction as we illustrated it in our bivariate regression analysis example: Use the statistically significant intercept and beta coefficient values with the levels of the independent variables you wish to use in the prediction, and then apply 95% confidence intervals using the standard error of the estimate.

However, the interpretation of multiple regression is complicated because independent variables are often measured with different units, so it is wrong to make direct comparisons between the calculated betas. For example, it is improper to directly compare the beta coefficient for family size to another for money spent per month on personal grooming, because the units of measurement are so different (people versus dollars). The most common solution to this problem is to standardize the independent variables through a quick operation that involves dividing the difference between each independent variable value and its mean by the standard deviation of that independent variable. This results in what is called the **standardized beta coefficient**. When they are standardized, direct comparisons may be made

■ Researchers study standardized beta coefficients in order to understand the relative importance of the independent variables as they impact the dependent variable.

between the resulting betas. The larger the absolute value of a standardized beta coefficient, the more relative importance it assumes in predicting the dependent variable. With standardized betas the researcher can directly compare the importance of each independent variable with others. Most statistical programs provide the standardized betas automatically.

Let's take our Lexus multiple regression example and use standardized betas for understanding. The unstandardized and standardized betas are as follows:

| Independent Variable | Attitude toward Lexus | Negative Word of Mouth | Income Level |
|---|---|---|---|
| Unstandardized beta | +1.0 | −.5 | +1.0 |
| Standardized beta | .8 | −.2 | .4 |

You should not compare the unstandardized betas, as they pertain to variables with very different scales, but you can compare the standardized betas. (Ignore the signs; just compare the absolute values.) Attitude toward Lexus is four times (.8 versus .2) more important than negative word of mouth and twice (.8 versus .4) as important as the income level, and income level is twice (.4 versus .2) as important as negative word of mouth in our understanding of what factors are related to intentions to purchase a Lexus. We now understand how vital it is for Lexus to foster strong positive attitudes, as they are apparently instrumental to positive purchase intentions. Plus, we know that Lexus does not need to worry greatly about negative comments prospective buyers might hear from friends or co-workers about Lexus, as they are less important than attitudes and income level.

A third application of multiple regression analysis is as a **screening device**, meaning that multiple regression analysis can be applied by a researcher to "narrow down" many considerations to a smaller, more manageable set. That is, the marketing researcher may be faced with a large number and variety of prospective

Multiple regression can reveal what factors are related to the purchase of a Lexus automobile.

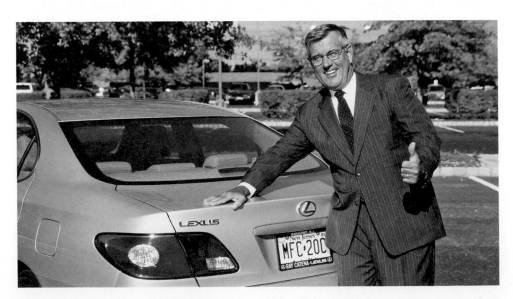

independent variables, and he or she may use multiple regression as a screening device or a way of spotting the salient (statistically significant) independent variables for the dependent variable at hand. In this instance, the intent is not to determine a prediction of the dependent variable; rather, it may be to search for clues as to what factors help the researcher understand the behavior of this particular variable. For instance, the researcher might be seeking market segmentation bases and could use regression to spot which demographic and lifestyle variables are related to the consumer behavior variable under study.

# HOW TO USE THE XL DATA ANALYST TO PERFORM REGRESSION ANALYSIS

The XL Data Analyst has been developed to allow you to perform regression analysis. If you use only one independent variable, you are working with bivariate regression, whereas when you select two or more independent variables, you have moved into the domain of multiple regression analysis. To illustrate multiple regression analysis in action, and to simultaneously familiarize you with how to direct the XL Data Analyst to perform regression analysis, we will take as our dependent variable the question "How likely would you be to subscribe to the e-zine?" that was answered by all eligible respondents in the College Life E-Zine survey. This is a metric variable because the response scale was a 5-point likelihood scale ranging from "very unlikely" to "very likely." Figure 14.12 shows the menu sequence and selection window for setting up

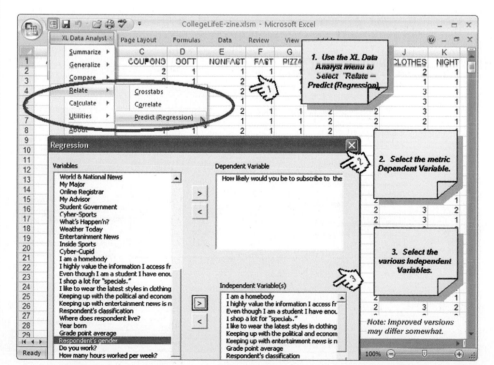

**Figure 14.12** Using the XL Data Analyst to Set Up a Multiple Regression Analysis

regression analysis with the XL Data Analyst. Notice that the menu sequence is Relate–Predict (Regression), which opens up the Regression selection window. We have selected "How likely would you be to subscribe . . ." into the Independent Variable windowpane, and we have selected some demographic factors (gender, GPA, dwelling location, and classification) and all seven of the lifestyle statements.

Figure 14.13 contains the results of this multiple regression analysis. There are two tables in Figure 14.13. First, the XL Data Analyst computes the full multiple regression analysis using all of the independent variables. It presents the beta coefficients, the standardized beta coefficients, and the result of the significance test for each independent variable's beta. Since one or more independent variables resulted in a nonsignificant beta coefficient, meaning that even though a coefficient value is reported in the first table its true population value is 0, the XL Data Analyst reruns the analysis with the nonsignificant independent variables omitted from the analysis. The final result is in the second table, where all independent variables now left in the regression analysis results have significant beta coefficients.

We can now interpret our multiple regression finding. We will first use the signs of the beta coefficients as our interpretation vehicle. For State University students, their likelihood to subscribe to the College Life E-Zine is related to three demographic factors (grade point average, class, and dwelling location) plus three lifestyle dimensions (keeping up with styles, value information from the Internet, and homebody tendency). More specifically, a State U student is more likely to lean toward subscribing if he or she has a lower GPA, is earlier in his or her university experience, and lives on campus. At the same time, students who like to keep up with styles, who value information they obtain from the Internet, and who are not homebodies are more likely to subscribe to the College Life E-Zine.

■ The XL Data Analyst removes nonsignificant independent variables in its multiple regression analysis procedure.

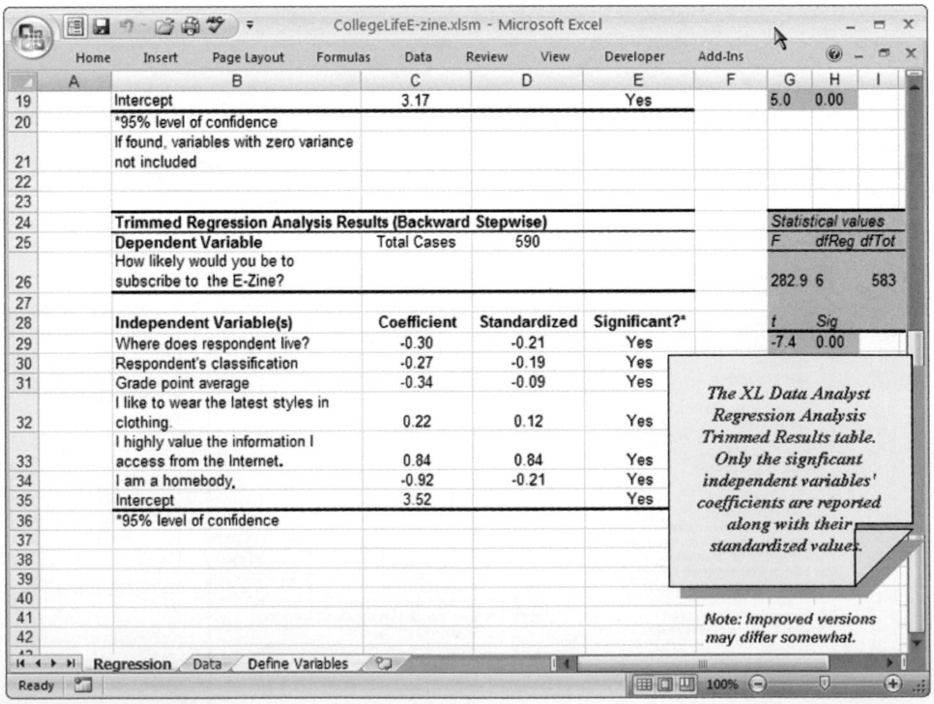

**Figure 14.13** XL Data Analyst Multiple Regression Analysis Output

Next, we can use the standard beta coefficients to better our understanding of the College Life E-Zine's appeal. A value for obtaining information from the Internet is the most important characteristic related to the appeal of the College Life E-Zine. In fact, this factor is from four to eight times more important than the other factors. Dwelling location, class status, and homebody tendency are approximately equal in importance, while fashion-consciousness and GPA are the lowest in importance. It is clear that the College Life E-Zine concept is most appealing to those State University students who trust the Internet as a ready information source, and meeting these expectations will be crucial to the success of the new e-zine.

As you learned in the introduction to this chapter, multiple regression is a powerful tool that has a number of valuable applications for marketing researchers. Here is an example of how it was applied to determine whether or not Las Vegas and Atlantic City compete for the same gambler market. A researcher compared the target market profile determined by multiple regression for Las Vegas gamblers to the one for Atlantic City gamblers.[9] Here are the interpreted findings.

PRACTICAL APPLICATIONS

| Characteristic | Las Vegas Gamblers | Atlantic City Gamblers |
|---|---|---|
| **Income** | More trips with higher income | More trips with higher income |
| **Education** | More trips with more education | More trips with more education |
| **Distance to Las Vegas** | More trips the closer he or she lives to Las Vegas | Fewer trips the closer he or she lives to Las Vegas |
| **Distance to Atlantic City** | Fewer trips the closer he or she lives to Atlantic City | More trips the closer he or she lives to Atlantic City |
| **Own home** | More trips with ownership | Not related |
| **Home in Midwest** | More trips by Midwesterners | Fewer trips by Midwesterners |
| **Home in Northeast** | Not related | More trips by Northeasterners |
| **Home in South** | Not related | Fewer trips by Southerners |
| **Retired** | More trips if retired | Not related |
| **Student** | More trips if a student | Not related |
| **Asian** | More trips if Asian | Not related |
| **Black** | Not related | More trips if Black |

The featured cells are the ones that distinguish the market segment profiles that differentiate Las Vegas from Atlantic City gamblers. Specifically, both Las Vegas and Atlantic City are drawing gamblers who live closer to their respective locations, and they both are attracting higher-income and higher-education groups. In addition, Las Vegas gamblers are more likely to be: (1) homeowners, (2) Midwesterners, (3) retired or (4) students, and (5) Asian, and not Northeasterners, Southerners, or

Blacks. Atlantic City, in contrast, is attractive to Northeasterners and Blacks, but it is definitely not attracting Midwesterners or Southerners. Compared to Las Vegas, Atlantic City is not attracting homeowners, retirees, students, or Asians. From this set of findings, the two great American gambling destinations do not compete for the same gamblers.

## The Six-Step Process for Regression Analysis

As we warned, regression analysis is the most complicated analysis taken up in this textbook, and our descriptions, while no doubt challenging to follow, provide only the most basic concepts involved with this topic. When you have gained an understanding of these basic concepts, you can use the XL Data Analyst to investigate possible insightful multiple linear relationships in your data. Table 14.6 applies our

**Table 14.6** The Six-Step Approach to Data Analysis for Regression Analysis

| Step | Explanation | Example |
|---|---|---|
| 1. What is the research objective? | Determine that you are dealing with a **Relationship Objective**. | We wish to understand the lifestyle and demographic factors that are related to State University students' purchases on the Internet. |
| 2. What questionnaire question(s) is/are involved? | Identify the question(s) for the variables and determine their scales. | Respondents indicated how much they expect to spend on Internet purchases over the next two months. This is the metric dependent variable. The independent variables consist of the lifestyle questions (metric) and some metric demographic questions (GPA, class), as well as categorical questions (gender, living location, work status). |
| 3. What is the appropriate analysis? | To assess the relationship among these variables, use regression analysis. | We use this procedure because the dependent variable is metric, and most of the independent variables are metric. The categorical questions can be treated as dummy independent variables. Multiple regression analysis will assess the linear relationship between the independent variables and the dependent variable, and it will identify the significant independent variables. |
| 4. How do you run it? | Use XL Data Analyst analysis: Select "Relate–Predict (Regression)." | |

| Independent Variable(s) | Coefficient | Standardized | Significant?* |
|---|---|---|---|
| Do you work? | −17.64 | −0.49 | Yes |
| Respondent's gender | −20.42 | −0.56 | Yes |
| Keeping up with sports and entertainment news is not important. | 2.05 | 0.14 | Yes |
| I shop a lot for "specials." | 4.68 | 0.24 | Yes |
| Even though I am a student I have enough income to buy what I want. | 5.61 | 0.23 | Yes |
| I am a homebody. | −4.24 | −0.30 | Yes |
| Intercept | 87.09 | | Yes |

*95% level of confidence

**5. How do you interpret the finding?** The XL Data Analyst indicates the significant independent variables and provides their standardized values.

**6. How do you write/present these findings?** With a significant regression finding, use the signs and sizes of the standardized beta coefficients as the basis of your interpretation.

State University students' anticipated Internet purchases levels are related to certain demographic and lifestyle factors. Interestingly, the most important variable is gender, with males purchasing more than females, while those students who do not work purchase more than working students. Heavier Internet purchasers tend not to be homebodies, they shop a good deal, and they feel they have sufficient income to buy what they want. Significant, but least important as a predictor of the anticipated level of Internet purchases, is a desire to keep up with sports and entertainment news.

six-step process to a phenomenon that is vital to the College Life E-Zine's success, namely, anticipated Internet purchases by State University students. Consult Table 14.6 to see the application of multiple regression analysis by the XL Data Analyst to gain an understanding of these purchases.

## Final Comments on Multiple Regression Analysis

There is a great deal more to multiple regression analysis, but it is beyond the scope of this textbook to delve deeper into this topic.[10] The coverage in this chapter introduces you to regression analysis, and it provides you with enough information about it to run uncomplicated regression analyses with your XL Data Analyst, identify the relevant aspects of the output, and interpret the findings. However, we have barely scratched the surface of this complex data analysis technique. There are many more assumptions, options, statistics, and considerations involved. In fact, there is so much material that whole textbooks exist on regression. Our descriptions are merely an introduction to multiple regression analysis to help you comprehend the basic notions, common uses, and interpretations involved with this predictive technique.[11]

Multiple regression is a very complicated topic that requires a great deal more study to master.

# SUMMARY

This is the last data analysis chapter in the textbook, and it deals with relationships between two or more variables and how these relationships can be useful for prediction and understanding. The first type of relationship described involved two categorical variables where the researcher deals with the co-occurrence of the labels that describe the variables. That is, a Boolean operator approach is used, and raw counts of the number of instances are computed to construct a cross-tabulation table. This table is then used in the application of chi-square analysis to evaluate whether or not a statistically significant relationship exists between the two variables being analyzed. If so, then the research turns to graphs or percentage tables to envision the nature of the relationship.

Correlation analysis can be applied to two metric variables, and the linear relationship between them can be portrayed in a scatter diagram. The correlation coefficient indicates the direction (by its sign) and the strength (by its magnitude) of the linear relationship. However, only statistically significant correlations can be interpreted, and by rules of thumb provided in the chapter, a correlation must be larger than ±.81 to be "strong."

Correlation leads to bivariate regression, in which the intercept and slope of the straight line are estimated and assessed for statistical significance. When statistically significant findings occur, the researcher can use the findings to compute a prediction, but the prediction must be cast in a confidence interval because there is invariably some error in how well the regression analysis result performs. Multiple regression analysis is appropriate when the researcher has more than one independent variable that may predict the dependent variable under study. With multiple regression, the basics of a linear relationship are retained, but there is a different slope ($b$) for each independent variable, and the signs of the slopes can be mixed. Generally, independent variables should be metric, although a few dummy-coded (e.g., 0,1) independent variables may be used in the independent variables set. A multiple regression result can be used to make predictions; moreover, with standardized beta coefficients, you can gain understanding of the phenomenon as it is permissible to compare these to each other and to interpret the relative importance of the various independent variables with respect to the behavior of the dependent variable.

# KEY TERMS

Relationship (p. 425)

Boolean relationship (p. 425)

Stacked bar chart (p. 427)

Cross-tabulation analysis (p. 427)

Cross-tabulation table (p. 427)

Cross-tabulation cell (p. 427)

Frequencies table (p. 428)

Chi-square analysis (p. 429)

"Observed frequencies" (p. 429)

"Expected frequencies" (p. 429)

Column percentages table (p. 431)

Row percentages table (p. 431)

Linear relationship (p. 435)

Straight-line formula (p. 436)

Intercept (p. 436)

Slope (p. 436)

Correlation coefficient (p. 437)
Covariation (p. 437)
Scatter diagram (p. 437)
Null hypothesis for a correlation
   (p. 439)
Pearson product moment correlation
   (p. 440)
Regression analysis (p. 444)
Bivariate regression analysis (p. 445)
Dependent variable (p. 445)
Independent variable (p. 445)

Least squares criterion (p. 445)
Standard error of the estimate (p. 447)
Residuals (p. 447)
R-square value (p. 448)
Multiple regression analysis (p. 449)
Additivity (p. 449)
Multiple R (p. 450)
Coefficient of determination (p. 450)
Dummy independent variable (p. 451)
Standardized beta coefficient (p. 451)
Screening device (p. 452)

# REVIEW QUESTIONS

1 What is a relationship between two variables, and how does a relationship help a marketing manager? Give an example using a demographic variable and a consumer behavior variable, such as satisfaction with a brand.
2 What is the basis for a Boolean relationship? What types of variables are best analyzed with a Boolean relationship and why?
3 Illustrate how a Boolean relationship is embodied in a cross-tabulation table. Provide an example using the variables of gender (categories: male and female) and vehicle type driven (SUV, sedan, sports car).
4 Describe chi-square analysis by explaining the following items:
   a Observed frequencies
   b Expected frequencies
   c Chi-square formula
5 When a researcher finds a statistically significant chi-square result for a cross-tabulation analysis, what should the researcher do next?
6 Use a scatter diagram and illustrate the covariation for the following correlations:
   a −.99
   b +.21
   c +.76
7 Explain why the statistical significance of a correlation is important. That is, what must be assumed when the correlation is found to not be statistically significant?
8 Describe the connection between a correlation and a bivariate regression analysis. In your discussion, specifically note: (1) statistical significance, (2) sign, and (3) use or application.
9 Relate how a bivariate regression analysis can be used to predict the dependent variable. In your answer, identify the independent and dependent variables, intercept, and slope. Also, give an example of how the prediction should be accomplished.
10 When a regression analysis is performed, what assures the researcher that the resulting regression equation is the best or optimal regression equation? Explain this concept.
11 How does multiple regression differ from bivariate regression? How is it similar?

**12** Define and note how each of the following is used in multiple regression:
   **a** Dummy independent variable
   **b** Standardized beta coefficients
   **c** Multiple R

**13** How should you regard your knowledge and command of multiple regression analysis that is based on its description in this chapter? Why?

## APPLICATION QUESTIONS

**14** A researcher has conducted a survey for Michelob Light beer. There are two questions in the survey being investigated in the following cross-tabulation table.

|  | Michelob Light Buyer | Michelob Light Nonbuyer | Totals |
|---|---|---|---|
| **White collar** | 152 | 8 | 160 |
| **Blue collar** | 14 | 26 | 40 |
| **Totals** | 166 | 34 | 200 |

The computed chi-square value of 81.6 is greater than the chi-square table critical value of 3.8. Interpret the researcher's findings.

**15** Following is some information about 10 respondents to a mail survey concerning candy purchasing. Construct the various different types of cross-tabulation tables that are possible. Label each table, and indicate what you find to be the general relationship apparent in the data.

| Respondent | Buy Plain M&Ms | Buy Peanut M&Ms |
|---|---|---|
| 1 | Yes | No |
| 2 | Yes | No |
| 3 | No | Yes |
| 4 | Yes | No |
| 5 | No | No |
| 6 | No | Yes |
| 7 | No | No |
| 8 | Yes | No |
| 9 | Yes | No |
| 10 | No | Yes |

**16** Morton O'Dell is the owner of Mort's Diner, which is located in downtown Atlanta, Georgia. Mort's opened up about 12 months ago, and it has experienced success, but Mort is always worried about what food items to order as inventory on a weekly basis. Mort's daughter, Mary, is an engineering student at Georgia Tech, and she offers to help her father. She asks him to provide sales data for the past 10 weeks in terms of pounds of food bought. With some difficulty, Mort comes up with the following list.

| Week | Meat | Fish | Fowl | Vegetables | Desserts |
|------|------|------|------|------------|----------|
| 1 | 100 | 50 | 150 | 195 | 50 |
| 2 | 91 | 55 | 182 | 200 | 64 |
| 3 | 82 | 60 | 194 | 209 | 70 |
| 4 | 75 | 68 | 211 | 215 | 82 |
| 5 | 66 | 53 | 235 | 225 | 73 |
| 6 | 53 | 61 | 253 | 234 | 53 |
| 7 | 64 | 57 | 237 | 230 | 68 |
| 8 | 76 | 64 | 208 | 221 | 58 |
| 9 | 94 | 68 | 193 | 229 | 62 |
| 10 | 105 | 58 | 181 | 214 | 62 |

Mary uses these sales figures to construct scatter diagrams that illustrate the basic relationships among the various types of food items purchased at Mort's Diner over the past 10 weeks. She tells her father that the diagrams provide some help in his weekly inventory ordering problem. Construct Mary's scatter diagrams with Excel to indicate what assistance they are to Mort. Perform the appropriate correlation analyses with the XL Data Analyst and interpret your findings.

**17** A pizza delivery company like Domino's Pizza wants to predict how many of its pizzas customers order per month. A multiple regression analysis finds the following statistically significant results.

| Variable | Coefficient or Value |
|----------|----------------------|
| Intercept | 2.6 |
| Pizza is a large part of my diet.* | .5 |
| I worry about calories in pizzas.* | −.2 |
| Gender (1 = female; 2 = male) | +1.1 |
| Standard error of the estimate | +.2 |

* Based on a scale where 1 = "strongly disagree," 2 = "somewhat agree," 3 = "neither agree nor disagree," 4 = "somewhat agree," and 5 = "strongly agree."

Compute the predicted number of pizzas ordered per month by each of the following three pizza customers.

**a** A man who strongly agrees that pizza is a large part of his diet but strongly disagrees that he worries about pizza calories.

**b** A woman who is neutral about pizza being a large part of her diet and who somewhat agrees that she worries about calories in pizzas.

**c** A man who somewhat disagrees that he worries about pizza calories and is neutral about pizza being a large part of his diet.

**18** Segmentation Associates, a company that specializes in using multiple regression as a means of describing market segments, conducts a survey of various types of automobile purchasers. The following table summarizes a recent study's findings. The values are the standardized beta coefficients of those segmentation variables found to be statistically significant. Where no value appears, that regression coefficient was not statistically significant.

| Segmentation Variable | Compact Automobile Buyer | Sports Car Buyer | Luxury Automobile Buyer |
| --- | --- | --- | --- |
| Demographics | | | |
| Age | −.28 | −.15 | +.59 |
| Education | −.12 | +.38 | |
| Family Size | +.39 | −.35 | |
| Income | −.15 | +.25 | +.68 |
| Lifestyle/Values | | | |
| Active | | +.59 | −.39 |
| American Pride | +.30 | | +.24 |
| Bargain Hunter | +.45 | −.33 | |
| Conservative | | −.38 | +.54 |
| Cosmopolitan | −.40 | +.68 | |
| Embraces Change | −.30 | +.65 | |
| Family Values | +.69 | | +.21 |
| Financially Secure | −.28 | +.21 | +.52 |
| Optimistic | | +.71 | +.37 |

Interpret these findings for an automobile manufacturer that has a compact automobile, a sports car, and a luxury automobile in its product line.

# INTERACTIVE LEARNING

Visit the textbook Web site at **www.prenhall.com/burnsbush**. For this chapter, use the self-study quizzes and get quick feedback on whether or not you need additional studying. You can also review the chapter's major points by visiting the chapter outline and key terms.

| CASE 14.1 | Friendly Market Versus Circle K |
| --- | --- |

Friendly Market is a convenience store located directly across the street from a Circle K convenience store. Circle K is a national chain, and its stores enjoy the benefits of national advertising campaigns, particularly the high visibility these campaigns bring. All Circle K stores have large red-and-white store signs, identical merchandise assortments, standardized floor plans, and they are open 24-7. Friendly Market, in contrast, is a one-of-a-kind "mom-and-pop" variety convenience store owned and managed by Billy Wong. Billy's parents came to the United States from Taiwan when Billy was 10 years old. After graduating from high school, Bill worked in a variety of jobs, both full- and part-time, and for most of the past 10 years, Billy has been a Circle K store employee.

In 2002, Billy made a bold move to open his own convenience store. Don's Market, a mom-and-pop convenience store across the street from the Circle K, went out of business, so Billy gathered up his life savings and borrowed as much money as he could from friends, relatives, and his bank. He bought the old Don's Market building and equipment, renamed it Friendly Market, and opened its doors for business in November 2002. Billy's core business philosophy is to greet everyone who comes in and to get to know all his customers on a first-name basis. He also watches Circle K's prices closely and seeks to have lower prices on at least 50% of the merchandise sold by both stores.

To the surprise of the manager of the Circle K across the street, Friendly Market has prospered. In 2003, Billy's younger sister, who had gone on to college

and earned an MBA degree at Indiana University, conducted a survey of Billy's target market to gain a better understanding of why Friendly Market was successful. She drafted a simple questionnaire and did the telephone interviewing herself. She used the local telephone book and called a random sample of over 150 respondents whose residences were listed within three miles of Friendly Market. She then created an XL Data Analyst data set with the following variable names and values.

| Variable Name | Value Labels |
| --- | --- |
| FRIENDLY | 0 = Do not use Friendly Market regularly; |
| | 1 = Use Friendly Market regularly |
| CIRCLEK | 0 = Do not use Circle K regularly; |
| | 1 = Use Circle K regularly |
| DWELL | 1 = Own home; 2 = Rent |
| GENDER | 1 = Male; 2 = Female |
| WORK | 1 = Work full-time; 2 = Work part-time; |
| | 3 = Retired or Do not work |
| COMMUTE | 0 = Do not pass by Friendly Market/ Circle K corner on way to work; |
| | 1 = Do pass by Friendly Market/ Circle K corner on way to work |

In addition to these demographic questions, respondents were asked if they agreed (coded 3), disagreed (coded 1), or neither agreed nor disagreed (coded 2) with each of five different lifestyle statements. The variable names and questions follow.

| Variable Name | Lifestyle Statement |
|---|---|
| BARGAIN | I often shop for bargains. |
| CASH | I always pay cash. |
| QUICK | I like quick, easy shopping. |
| KNOWME | I shop where they know my name. |
| HURRY | I am always in a hurry. |

The data set is one of the data sets accompanying this textbook. It is named "FriendlyMarket.xlsm." Use the XL Data Analyst to perform the relationship analyses necessary to answer the following questions.

1 Do customers patronize both Friendly Market and Circle K?

2 What demographic characteristics profile Friendly Market's customers? That is, what characteristics are related to patronage of Friendly Market?

3 What demographic characteristics profile Circle K's customers? That is, what characteristics are related to patronage of Circle K?

4 What is the lifestyle profile related to Friendly Market's customers?

---

## CASE 14.2     Your Integrated Case

### College Life E-Zine

### Relationships Analysis

Bob Watts and Lori Baker, marketing intern at ORS Marketing Research, are in an evaluation session. Bob has just told Lori that he is giving her the highest evaluation he has ever given to a marketing intern who has worked for him. "I am really impressed with your command of the several data analyses that you performed for our College Life E-Zine project, and your PowerPoint presentations and report tables are among the best I have ever seen. You really have a good working knowledge of those analytical techniques. As you know, we have two weeks left for your internship, but I'm submitting my evaluation to your State U marketing internship supervisor today because you've done such an excellent job."

At this, Lori responds, "Thank you so much! I've really gained a lot of experience and I'm very grateful that ORS has let me grow under your direction. I'm pretty sure that I want to be a marketing researcher, and I'll be devoting my senior year at State U to gearing up and applying to the Master of Marketing Research program at the University of Georgia."

"Oh?" says Bob. "That convinces me even more that you're the right person for the job I'm about to assign you for your last two weeks here. We need to do the final set of analyses for the College Life E-Zine project, and I'm going to let you delve into it. It involves relationship analyses using correlations and regressions, so if you handle these—especially the multiple regression analyses—as well as I believe you can, you'll have a really impressive "bullet" to add to your application. Here are the relationship objectives that I proposed to our College Life E-Zine entrepreneurs at the beginning of the project. What do you say?"

"I'll give it my very best," replies Lori.

Following are the College Life E-Zine marketing research project relationship objectives provided to Lori by Bob Watts. Use your College Life E-Zine survey data set and the XL Data Analyst to perform the appropriate relationship analyses, and interpret your findings in each instance.

1 For each of the seven lifestyle dimensions, is it related to preference for any of the 15 possible College Life E-Zine features?

**2** Find those possible College Life E-Zine features that are at least "somewhat preferred" (average of 4.0 or higher) by eligible State University students. For each one, what demographic and/or lifestyle factors are related to it and how do you interpret these relationships?

## CHAPTER 15

# PREPARING AND PRESENTING THE RESEARCH RESULTS

By permission, Burke.

A well-known researcher in the industry, Michael Lotti of Eastman Kodak, believes that "even the best research will not drive the appropriate action unless the audience understands the outcomes and implications. Researchers must create a clear, concise presentation of the results."[1] Mr. Lotti's quote underscores the significance of the final research report. The **marketing research report** is a factual message that transmits research results, vital recommendations, conclusions, and other important information to the client, who in turn bases his or her decision making on the contents of the report. This chapter deals with the essentials of writing and presenting the marketing research report.[2]

Compiling a market research report is a challenging task that plays a significant role in determining how the research results are implemented. Our example of Burke's Digital Dashboard shows how the research industry is innovating to produce online reports that meet the challenge of keeping clients current and allowing them to interact with the research project report.

- To appreciate the importance of the marketing research report
- To know what material should be included in each part of the marketing research report
- To learn the basic guidelines for writing effective marketing research reports
- To learn how to organize the written report by making effective use of headings and subheadings
- To know how to use visuals such as figures, tables, charts, and graphs
- To learn how to make pie and bar charts using XL Data Analyst and Excel
- To understand there are ethical considerations in preparing visuals
- To learn the basic principles for presenting your report orally

# THE IMPORTANCE OF THE MARKETING RESEARCH REPORT

The fact that this chapter is the final chapter in the textbook does not indicate that it is less important. On the contrary, it means that communicating the results of your research is the culmination of the entire process. Researchers must provide client value in the research report. The marketing research report is the product that represents the efforts of the marketing research team, and it may be the only part of the project that the client will see. If the report is poorly written, riddled with grammatical errors, or sloppy or inferior in any way, the quality of the research (including its analysis and information) becomes suspect and its credibility is reduced. If organization and presentation are faulty, the reader may never reach the intended conclusions. The time and effort expended in the research process are wasted if the report does not communicate effectively.

If, on the other hand, all aspects of the report are done well, the report will not only communicate properly, but it will also serve to build credibility. Marketing research users,[3] as well as marketing research suppliers,[4] agree that reporting the research results is one of the most important aspects of the marketing research process. Many managers will not be involved in any aspect of the research process but will use the report to make business decisions. Effective reporting is essential, and all of the principles of organization, formatting, good writing, and good grammar must be employed.

*Where We Are:*
1 Establish the need for marketing research
2 Define the problem
3 Establish research objectives
4 Determine research design
5 Identify information types and sources
6 Determine methods of accessing data
7 Design data collection forms
8 Determine sample plan and size
9 Collect data
10 Analyze data
11 Prepare and present the final research report

ONLINE

The marketing research report is a factual message that transmits research results, vital recommendations, conclusions, and other important information to the client, who in turn bases his or her decision making on the contents of the report.

■ The time and effort expended in the research process are wasted if the report does not communicate effectively.

# ORGANIZING THE WRITTEN REPORT

Marketing research reports are tailored to specific audiences and purposes, and you must consider both in all phases of the research process, including planning the report. Before you begin writing, then, you must answer some basic questions such as: What message do you want to communicate? What is your purpose? Who is the audience? Are there multiple audiences? What does your audience know? What does your audience need to know? What are your audience's interests, values, concerns? These and other questions must be addressed before you decide how to structure your report.

■ Reporting the research results is one of the most important aspects of the marketing research process.

When organizing the research report, it is often helpful "to get on the other side of the desk." Assume you are the reader instead of the writer. Doing so will help you see things through the eyes of your audience and increase the success of your communication. This is your opportunity to ask that basic (and very critical) question from the reader's point of view: "What's in it for me?"

■ When preparing the report, it is helpful to assume you are the reader.

Once you have answered these basic questions, you need to determine the format of your document. If the organization for which you are conducting the research has specific guidelines for preparing the document, you should follow them. However, if no specific guidelines are provided, there are certain elements that must be considered when you are preparing the report. These elements can be grouped in three sections: front matter, body, and end matter. See Table 15.1 for details.

■ Have you been given a required format to follow? If not, there are guidelines on the elements a report should contain.

**Table 15.1**

The Elements of a Marketing Research Report

A. Front Matter

    1. Title Page

    2. Letter of Authorization

    3. Letter/Memo of Transmittal

    4. Table of Contents

    5. List of Illustrations

    6. Abstract/Executive Summary

B. Body

    1. Introduction

    2. Research Objectives

    3. Method

    4. Results

    5. Limitations

    6. Conclusions, or Conclusions and Recommendations

C. End Matter

    1. Appendices

    2. Endnotes

## Front Matter

Front matter consists of all pages that precede the first page of the report.

The **front matter** consists of all pages that precede the first page of the report—the title page, letter of authorization (optional), letter/memo of transmittal, table of contents, list of illustrations, and abstract/executive summary.

## Title Page

The **title page** (Figure 15.1) contains four major items of information: (1) the title of the document, (2) the organization/person(s) for whom the report was prepared, (3) the organization/person(s) who prepared the report, and (4) the date of

**Figure 15.1** A Title Page

COLLEGE LIFE E-ZINE:
A MARKETING RESEARCH STUDY
TO DETERMINE INTENTION TO SUBSCRIBE;
PREFERENCES FOR DESIGN; ONLINE ACCESS & PURCHASES;
PRESENT & PLANNED PURCHASES; AND LIFESTYLE & DEMOGRAPHICS
OF POTENTIAL SUBSCRIBERS

Prepared for
Mr. Wesley Addington
Mr. Don Cooper
Ms. Anna Fulkerson
Ms. Sarah Stripling

Prepared by
Bob Watts
ORS Research, Inc.

April 2008

submission. If names of individuals appear on the title page, they may be in either alphabetical order or some other agreed-upon order; each individual should also be given a designation or descriptive title, if appropriate.

Though there are many jokes about titles being overly long, formal research reports should have titles that are as descriptive as possible. Note that the title of the College Life E-Zine report provides the reader with a good idea of what is contained in the report. The purpose of the title of a research report is not the same as it is for other types of publications. A newspaper article title or the title of a magazine sold on supermarket shelves has a different purpose: it should be short and catch the interest of the reader. Research report titles, on the other hand, should be informative. The title should be centered and printed in all uppercase (capital) letters. Other items of information on the title page should be centered and printed in upper- and lowercase letters. The title page is counted as page i of the front matter; however, no page number is printed on it (see Figure 15.1). On the next page, the printed page number will be ii.

■ Formal research reports should have titles that are as descriptive as possible, even if it makes the title long.

## Letter of Authorization

The **letter of authorization** is the marketing research firm's certification to do the project and is optional. It is particularly helpful in large organizations because it provides other users of the report with the name, title, and department of the individual(s) who authorized the project. It may also include a general description of the nature of the research project, completion date, terms of payment, and any special conditions of the research project requested by the client or research user. If you allude to the conditions of your authorization in the letter/memo of transmittal, the letter of authorization is not necessary in the report. However, if your reader may not know the conditions of authorization, inclusion of this document is helpful.

■ The letter of authorization is the marketing research firm's certification to do the project. Although optional, it is particularly helpful in large organizations because it provides other users with the name, title, and department of the individuals who authorized the research.

## Letter/Memo of Transmittal

Use a **letter of transmittal** to release or deliver the document to an organization for which you are not a regular employee. Use a **memo of transmittal** to deliver the document within your own organization. The letter/memo of transmittal describes the general nature of the research in a sentence or two and identifies the individual who is releasing the report. The primary purpose of the letter/memo of transmittal is to orient the reader to the report and to build a positive image of the report. It should establish rapport between the writer and receiver. It gives the receiver a person to contact if questions arise.

The writing style in the letter/memo of transmittal should be personal and slightly informal. Some general elements that may appear in the letter/memo of transmittal are a brief identification of the nature of the research, a review of the conditions of the authorization to do the research (if no letter of authorization is included), comments on findings, suggestions for further research, and an expression of interest in the project and further research. It should end with an expression of appreciation for the assignment, acknowledgment of assistance from others, and suggestions for following up. Personal observations, unsupported by the data, are appropriate.

■ Use a letter for transmittal outside your organization and a memo within your own organization.

## Table of Contents

The **table of contents** helps the reader locate information in the research report. The table of contents (Figure 15.2) should list all sections of the report that follow; each heading should read exactly as it appears in the text and should identify the number of the page on which it appears. If a section is longer than one page, list the page on which it begins. Indent subheadings under headings. All items except the title page and the table of contents are listed with page numbers in the table of contents. Front-matter pages are numbered with lowercase Roman numerals: i, ii, iii, iv, and so on. Arabic numerals (1, 2, 3) begin with the introduction section of the body of the report.

**The table of contents helps the reader locate information in the research report.**

**Figure 15.2** A Table of Contents

**Table of Contents**

| Section Title | Page |
|---|---|
| List of Illustrations | vi |
| Executive Summary | vii |
| Introduction | 1 |
| Background | 1 |
| Research Objectives | 2 |
| Limitations of the Study | 3 |
| Method | 5 |
| Definition of the Population | 5 |
| Sample Plan | 6 |
| Sample Size | 6 |
| Development of the Questionnaire | 7 |
| Data Collection Method | 8 |
| Nonsampling Error Reduction | 9 |
| Findings | 11 |
| Response Rate | 12 |
| Profile of the Sample | 14 |
| Student Connectivity | 17 |
| a. Internet Access | 18 |
| b. Type of Internet Connection | 19 |
| Student Product/Service Purchasing Habits | 21 |
| a. Use of Coupons | 22 |
| b. Soft Drinks | 23 |
| c. Non-Fast-Food Restaurants | 24 |

ii

## List of Illustrations

If the report contains tables and/or figures, include in the table of contents a **list of illustrations** along with the page numbers on which they appear. All tables and figures should be included in this list by their respective titles; this helps the reader find specific illustrations that graphically portray the information. **Tables** are words or numbers that are arranged in rows and columns; **figures** are graphs, charts, maps, pictures, and so on. Because tables and figures are numbered independently, you may have both a Figure 1 and a Table 1 in your list of illustrations. Give each a name, and list each in the order in which it appears in the report.

## Abstract/Executive Summary

Your report may have many readers. Some of them will need to know the details of your report, such as the supporting data on which you base your conclusions and recommendations. Others will not need as many details but will want to read the conclusions and recommendations. Still others with a general need to know may read only the executive summary. Therefore, the **abstract or executive summary** is a "skeleton" of your report. It serves as a summary for the busy executive or a preview for the in-depth reader. It provides an overview of the most useful information, including the conclusions and recommendations. The abstract or executive summary should be very carefully written, conveying the information as concisely as possible. It should be single-spaced and should briefly cover the general subject of the research, the scope of the research (what the research covers/does not cover), identification of the type of methodology used (e.g., a mail survey of 1,000 homeowners), conclusions, and recommendations.

## Body

The **body** is the bulk of the report. It contains an introduction to the report, an explanation of your methodology, a discussion of your results, a statement of limitations, and a list of conclusions and recommendations. Do not be alarmed by the repetition that may appear in your report. Only a few people will read it in its entirety. Most will read the executive summary, conclusions, and recommendations. Therefore, formal reports are repetitious. For example, you may specify the research objectives in the executive summary and refer to them again in the findings section as well as in the conclusions section. Also, do not be concerned that you use the same terminology to introduce the tables and/or figures. In lengthy reports, repetition actually enhances reader comprehension.

The first page of the body contains the title centered two inches from the top of the page; this page is counted as page 1, but no page number is printed on it. All other pages throughout the document are numbered consecutively.

## Introduction

The **introduction** to the marketing research report orients the reader to the contents of the report. It may contain a statement of the background situation leading to the problem, the statement of the problem, and a summary description of how the

---

**Sidebar notes:**

■ If the report contains tables and/or figures, include in the table of contents a list of illustrations along with the page numbers on which they appear.

■ Tables are words or numbers that are arranged in rows and columns; figures are graphs, charts, maps, pictures, and so on.

■ The abstract or executive summary is a "skeleton" of your report. It serves as a summary for the busy executive or a preview for the in-depth reader. It provides an overview of the most useful information, including the conclusions and recommendations.

■ The "body" of the report contains the introduction, methodology, discussion of results, limitations, and the conclusions and recommendations.

■ The first page of the body is counted as page 1, but no page number is printed on it.

research process was initiated. It should contain a statement of the general purpose of the report and also the specific objectives for the research.

**Research objectives** may be listed either as a separate section (see Table 15.1) or within the introduction section. The listing of research objectives should follow the statement of the problem, since the two concepts are closely related. The list of specific research objectives often serves as a good framework for organizing the results section of the report.

## Method

The **method** describes, in as much detail as necessary, how you conducted the research, including a description of the sample plan and sample size determination, the method of gathering data, and how the data were analyzed. Supplementary information should be placed in the appendix. If you used secondary information, you will need to document your sources (provide enough information so that your sources can be located).[5] You do not need to document facts that are common knowledge or can be easily verified. But if you are in doubt, document! **Plagiarism** refers to presenting the work of others as your own and is a serious offense. At one well-known university, 48 students were recently either expelled from the university or quit due to charges of plagiarism. The university was so diligent in prosecuting the offenders that it revoked the degrees of three of the students who had already graduated![6] Many people have lost their jobs over plagiarism. At the very least, plagiarists lose credibility.

In most cases, the method section does not need to be long. It should, however, provide the essential information your reader needs in order to understand how the data were collected and how the results were achieved. It should be detailed enough that the data collection could be replicated by others for purposes of reliability. In other words, the methodology section should be clear enough that other researchers could conduct a similar study.

## Results

The **results** section is the most important portion of your report. This section should logically present the findings of your research and be organized around your objectives for the study. The results should be presented in narrative form and accompanied by tables, charts, figures, and other appropriate visuals that support and enhance the explanation of results. Tables and figures are supportive material; they should not be overused or used as filler. Each should contain a number and title and should be referred to in the narrative.

Outline your results section before you write the report. The survey questionnaire itself can serve as a useful aid in organizing your results, because the questions are often grouped in a logical order or in purposeful sections. Another useful method for organizing your results is to individually print all tables and figures and arrange them in a logical sequence. Once you have the results outlined properly, you are ready to write the introductory sentences, definitions (if necessary), review of the findings (often referring to tables and figures), and transition sentences to lead into the next topic.

■ The introduction to the marketing research report may contain a statement of the background situation leading to the problem, the statement of the problem, and a summary description of how the research process was initiated.

■ The list of specific research objectives often serves as a good framework for organizing the results section of the report.

■ The method describes in detail how the research was conducted.

■ Plagiarism is a serious offense; it can cost you your job.

ETHICS

■ Go to Interactive Learning at the end of this chapter to learn more about what constitutes plagiarism.

■ The results section is the major portion of your report and should logically present the findings of the research.

## Limitations

Do not attempt to hide or disguise problems in your research; no research is fault-less. Always be honest and open regarding all aspects of your research. If you avoid discussing limitations, your integrity and your research are rendered suspect. Suggest what the limitations are or may be and how they impact the results. You might also suggest opportunities for further study based on the limitations. Typical **limitations** in research reports often focus on but are not limited to factors such as time, money, size of sample, and personnel. Consider the following example: "The reader should note that this study was based on a survey of students at State University. Care should be exercised in generalizing these findings to other university populations."

## Conclusions and Recommendations

Conclusions and recommendations may be listed together or in separate sections, depending on the amount of material you have to report. In any case, you should note that conclusions are not the same as recommendations. **Conclusions** are the outcomes and decisions you have reached based on your research results. **Recommendations** are suggestions for how to proceed based on the conclusions. Unlike conclusions, recommendations may require knowledge beyond the scope of the research findings themselves, that is, information on conditions within the company, the industry, and so on. Therefore, researchers should exercise caution when making recommendations. The researcher and the client should determine prior to the study whether the report is to contain recommendations. A clear understanding of the researcher's role will result in a smoother process and will help avoid conflict. Although a research user may desire the researcher to provide specific recommendations, both parties must realize that the researcher's recommendations are based solely on the knowledge gained from the research report, not familiarity with the client. Other information, if made known to the researcher, could totally change the researcher's recommendations.

If recommendations are required and if a report is intended to initiate further action, however, recommendations are the important map to the next step. Writing recommendations in a bulleted list and beginning each with an action verb help to direct the reader to the logical next step.

## End Matter

The **end matter** comprises the **appendices**, which contain additional information that the reader may refer to for further reading that is not essential to reporting the data. Appendices contain the "nice to know" information, not the "need to know." Therefore, that information should not clutter the body of the report but should instead be inserted at the end for the reader who desires or requires additional information. Tables, figures, additional reading, technical descriptions, data collection forms, and appropriate computer printouts are some elements that may appear in the appendix. (If they are critical to the reader, however, they may be included in the report itself.) Each appendix should be labeled with both a letter and a title, and each should appear in the table of contents. A reference page or endnotes (if appropriate) should precede the appendix.

---

Do not attempt to hide or disguise problems in your research; no research is faultless. Always be honest and open regarding all aspects of your research.

Conclusions are outcomes or decisions based on results. Recommendations are suggestions for how to proceed based on conclusions.

Researchers should exercise caution when making recommendations, because recommendations may require knowledge of information beyond the scope of the research project.

End matter contains additional information that the reader may refer to for further reading but that is not essential to reporting the data.

# FOLLOWING GUIDELINES AND PRINCIPLES FOR THE WRITTEN REPORT

The parts of the research report have been described. However, you should also consider their form and format and their style.

## Form and Format

Form and format concerns include headings and subheadings and visuals.

### Headings and Subheadings

In a long report, your readers need signals and signposts that help them find their way. Headings and subheadings perform this function. **Headings** indicate the topic of each section. All information under a specific heading should relate to that heading, and **subheadings** should divide that information into segments. A new heading should introduce a change of topic. Choose the kind of heading that fits your purpose— single word, phrase, sentence, question—and consistently use that form throughout the report. If you use subheadings within the divisions, the subheadings must be parallel to one another but not to the main headings. See Marketing Research Application 15.1 to learn more about how to use headings and subheadings.

> Headings and subheadings act as signals and signposts to serve as a road map for a long report.

## Visuals

**Visuals** are tables, figures, charts, diagrams, graphs, and other graphic aids. Used properly, they can dramatically and concisely present information that might otherwise be difficult to comprehend. Tables systematically present numerical data or words in columns and rows. Figures translate numbers into visual displays so that relationships and trends become comprehensible. Examples of figures are graphs, pie charts, and bar charts.

> Visuals can dramatically and concisely present information that might otherwise be difficult to comprehend.

Visuals should tell a story; they should be uncluttered and self-explanatory. Even though they are self-explanatory, the key points of all visuals should be explained in the text. Refer to visuals by number: " . . . as shown in Figure 1." Each visual should be titled and numbered. If possible, place the visual immediately below the paragraph in which its first reference appears. Or, if sufficient space is not available, continue the text and place the visual on the next page. Visuals can also be placed in an appendix. Additional information on preparing visuals is presented later in this chapter.

## Style

Consider stylistic devices when you are actually writing the sentences and paragraphs in your report. These can make the difference in whether or not your reader gets the message as you intended it. Therefore, consider the following tips for the writer:

> Stylistic devices can make the difference in whether or not your reader gets the message as you intended it.

1 A good paragraph has one main idea, and a topic sentence should state that main idea. Writing a good paragraph is a good step toward becoming a good writer. See our Marketing Research Application 15.2 to help you become a better paragraph writer.

## How Headings Can Help You Write a Professional Report

PRACTICAL

APPLICATIONS

Most students have difficulty organizing their reports. Yet, rarely will they take the time to outline their report as they were taught to do in grade school. There are few more effective methods to improving your writing skills than properly outlining before you begin writing. Below we provide you with a few key thoughts that will help you improve your writing skills through the proper use of headings.

First, before you can outline, you must do some basic planning. Go back to your research objectives. Make certain that your report addresses the research objectives that were identified at the beginning of the research project.

Second, read the information you have! Many students just start writing without reading over the information they have generated either from secondary data or even from analysis of the results in primary data collection.

Third, what information has been gathered for each of the research objectives? Organize your information into separate areas based upon how it addresses a particular research objective. For example, if one objective is to gather information on likelihood to subscribe to a new service, find that information and file it under the research objective. Was any other information gathered which addresses this objective?

Researchers at Burke, Inc., outline their client's report with headings and subheadings.

Fourth, now that you are familiar with your research objectives and the information gathered for each, start outlining the information gathered by using headings. Headings are *the* most useful way a writer can organize a paper. Headings are very useful to readers in that they serve as guideposts telling the reader where they are, where they've been, and where they are headed.

Fifth, understand your format for headings before you begin to write. We provide the following to help you with your headings. Read this and use it!

### TITLE

Titles are centered at the top of the page and are either bold-faced or underlined. Titles are normally in a larger font than the rest of the paper.

### FIRST-LEVEL HEADING

First-level headings indicate what the following section, usually consisting of several subdivisions, is about. First-level headings are centered, bold, and all caps and are usually in larger font sizes than the other material but smaller than the title.

#### Second-Level Heading

Second-level headings are centered, bold, with capitals used only on the first letter of each word. Font size may be the same as that of the rest of the report. Try to always use more than one second-level heading if you are going to use them following a first-level heading.

**Third-Level Heading**
Left-justified, third-level headings should be bold and in the same font size as the rest of the report.

**Fourth-Level Heading**. These are left-justified and on the same line as the first sentence in the paragraph. Use bold and same-sized font as the remainder of the report.

**Fifth-level headings** are in bold and are part of sentences. While this is generally the lowest level of outline you use, you can go further by indenting and numbering ideas or italicizing the first word in each item of the list.

*Source:* Portions of the above adapted from Bovée, C., and Thill, J. (2000). *Business communication today* (6th ed.). Upper Saddle River, NJ: Prentice Hall, p. 499.

## MARKETING RESEARCH APPLICATION 15.2

**PRACTICAL**

**APPLICATIONS**

### Developing Logical Paragraphs

"A **paragraph** is a group of related sentences that focus on one main idea."[a] The first sentence should include a **topic sentence**, which identifies the main idea of the paragraph. For example: "To assess whether college students would subscribe to the e-zine, respondents were asked their likelihood of subscribing to an e-zine directed at college students." Next, the **body of the paragraph** provides the main idea of the topic sentence by giving more information, analysis, or examples. For example, continuing from the topic sentence example given above: "A description of the college e-zine was read to all respondents. The description was as follows: . . . The respondents were then asked to indicate their likelihood of subscribing by selecting a choice on a 5-point response rating scale ranging from 'Very likely to subscribe' to 'Very unlikely to subscribe.' The actual scale was as follows: . . . "

Paragraphs should close with a sentence that signals the end of the topic and indicates where the reader is headed. For example: "How respondents answered the likelihood-to-subscribe

scale is discussed in the following two paragraphs." Note this last sentence contains a **transitional expression**. A transitional expression is a word, or group of words, that tells the reader where they are heading. Some examples include *following, next, second, third, at last, finally, in conclusion, to summarize, for example, to illustrate, in addition, so, therefore,* and so on.[b]

Controlling for the **length of paragraphs** should encourage good communication. As a rule, paragraphs should be short. Business communication experts believe most paragraphs should be under or around the 100-word range.[c] This is long enough for the topic sentence and three or four sentences in the body of the paragraph. The paragraph should never cover more than one main topic. For complex topics, break them into several paragraphs.

[a] Ober, S. (1998). *Contemporary business communication.* (3rd ed.). Boston: Houghton Mifflin, p. 121.
[b] Ober, S. (1998). *Contemporary business communication.* (3rd ed.). Boston: Houghton Mifflin, p. 123.
[c] Bovee, C., and Thill, J. (2000). *Business communication today.* (6th ed.). Upper Saddle River, NJ: Prentice Hall, p. 153.

2 Avoid long paragraphs (usually those with more than nine printed lines). Using long paragraphs is a strategy for burying a message, not for communicating, because most readers do not read the middle contents of long paragraphs.

3 Capitalize on white space. The lines immediately before and immediately after white space (the beginning and the end of a paragraph) are points of emphasis. So are the beginning and the end of a page. Therefore, place more important information at these strategic points.

4 Use jargon sparingly. Some of your audience may understand technical terms; others may not. When in doubt, properly define the terms for your readers. If many technical terms are required in the report, consider including a glossary of terms in an appendix to assist the less informed members of your audience.

5 Use strong verbs to carry the meaning of your sentences. Instead of "making a recommendation," "recommend." Instead of "performing an investigation," "investigate."

6 As a general rule, use the active voice. Voice indicates whether the subject of the verb is doing the action (active voice) or receiving the action (passive voice). For example, "The marketing research was conducted by Judith" uses the passive voice. "Judith conducted the marketing research" uses the active voice. Active voice is direct and forceful, and the active voice uses fewer words.

7   Eliminate extra words. Write your message clearly and concisely. Combine and reword sentences to eliminate unnecessary words. Remove opening fillers and eliminate unnecessary redundancies. For example, instead of writing "There are 22 marketing research firms in Newark," write, "Twenty-two marketing research firms are located in Newark." Instead of saying, "the end results," say, "the results."

8   Avoid unnecessary changes in tense. Tense tells if the action of the verb occurred in the past (past tense—*were*), is happening right now (present tense—*are*), or will happen in the future (future tense—*will be*). Changing tenses within a document is an error writers frequently make.

9   In sentences, keep the subject and verb close together. The farther apart they become, the more difficulty the reader has understanding the message and the greater the chance for errors in subject/verb agreement.

10  Vary the length and structure of sentences and paragraphs.

11  Use faultless grammar. If your grammar is in any way below par, you need to take responsibility for finding ways to improve. Poor grammar can result in costly errors and loss of your job. It can jeopardize your credibility and the credibility of your research. There is no acceptable excuse for poor grammar.

12  Maintain 1-inch side margins. If your report will be bound, use a $1\frac{1}{2}$-inch left margin.

13  Use the organization's preference for double or single spacing.

14  Edit carefully. Your first draft is not a finished product; neither is your second. Edit your work carefully, rearranging and rewriting until you communicate the intent of your research as efficiently and effectively as possible. Some authors suggest that as much as 50% of your production time should be devoted to improving, editing, correcting, and evaluating an already written document.[7]

15  Proofread! Proofread! Proofread! After you have finished a product, check it carefully to make sure everything is correct. Double-check names and numbers, grammar, spelling, and punctuation. Although spell-checks and grammar-checks are useful, you cannot rely on them to catch all errors. One of the best ways to proofread is to read a document aloud, preferably with a reader following along on the original. An alternative is to read the document twice—once for content and meaning and once for mechanical errors. The more important the document is, the more time and readers you need to employ for proofreading.

■ **Proofread! A good way to proofread is to have someone read the document aloud while another person follows along by reading the written document.**

## USING VISUALS: TABLES AND FIGURES

Visuals assist in the effective presentation of numerical data. The key to a successful visual is a clear and concise presentation that conveys the message of the report. The selection of the visual should match the presentation purpose for the data. Common visuals include the following.[8]

*Tables*, which identify exact values.

*Graphs and charts*, which illustrate relationships among items.

   *Pie charts*, which compare a specific part of the whole to the whole.

   *Bar charts* and *line graphs*, which compare items over time or show correlations among items.

*Flow diagrams*, which introduce a set of topics and illustrate their relationships.

*Maps*, which define locations.

*Photographs*, which present an aura of legitimacy because they are not "created" in the sense that other visuals are created. Photos depict factual content.

*Drawings*, which focus on visual details.

A discussion of some of these visuals follows.

## Tables

Tables allow the reader to compare numerical data. Effective table guidelines are as follows:

1  Do not allow computer analysis to imply a level of accuracy that is not achieved. Limit your use of decimal places (12% or 12.2% instead of 12.223%).
2  Place items you want the reader to compare in the same column, not the same row.
3  If you have many rows, darken alternate entries or double-space after every five entries to assist the reader to accurately line up items.
4  Total columns and rows when relevant.

> ■ **Tables allow the reader to compare numerical data.**

## Pie Charts

Pie charts are particularly useful for illustrating relative size or static comparisons. The **pie chart** is a circle divided into sections. Each section represents a percentage of the total area of the circle associated with one component. Today's data analysis programs easily and quickly make pie charts. We show you how to use your XL Data Analyst and Excel to make pie charts in Marketing Research Application 15.3.

> ■ **Pie charts are particularly useful for illustrating relative size or static comparisons.**

The pie chart should have a limited number of segments (four to six). If your data have many small segments, consider combining the smallest or the least important into an "other" or "miscellaneous" category. Because internal labels are difficult to read for small sections, labels for the sections should be placed outside the circle.

## MARKETING RESEARCH APPLICATION 15.3

### How to Make a Pie Chart in Excel

PRACTICAL

APPLICATIONS

So you've collected your data, conducted your analysis using your XL Data Analyst, and you now have the output that you want. If you are like other marketing researchers, you may want to enhance your written report or presentation by using some of the improved graph features on Excel 2007. This Marketing Research Application will take you step-by-step to accomplish this goal. First, do a summarization analysis using percents and request that the XL Data Analyst provide a graph. It will be a pie chart. Pie charts are useful when:

a.  Data total to 100%,
b.  When you want to visually display proportions or percentages,
c.  You don't have so many slices the chart would be hard to interpret, and
d.  You properly label your pie chart and include a legend for the slices.[1]

---

[1] For an excellent in-depth discussion on the use of pie charts, see: Fink, A. (2003). *How to report on surveys*. Thousand Oaks, CA: Sage Publications, pp. 5–9.

## Steps in Making an Enhanced Pie Chart

| Step in Excel | Illustration |
|---|---|

### Step 1: Let the XL Data Analyst make your graphs.

Use the XL Data Analyst to "Summarize" "Percents" for a categorical variable in your data set. Be sure that you have correctly set up the value codes and the value labels.

Here is the pie chart that is generated using the College Life E-Zine data set percent summarization analysis with the variable, "Type of Internet connection you have." In Excel, it is called an "Exploded Pie in 3-D."

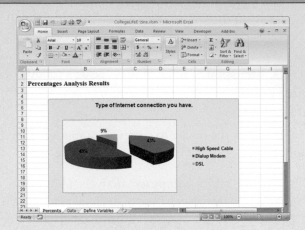

### Step 2: Change the pie chart, if you want.

If you want to change the pie chart type or use some other type if graph for this chart, click on the graph to activate it, and then use the Insert menu to open up the chart options. With the Insert menu on, click on any chart type, and select "All chart types" to see the menu of all possible charts. You can select any one of these displayed on the Insert Chart menu for your chart. Of course some chart types, such as line charts, are not appropriate for a percentage summarization table.

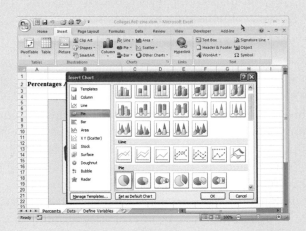

### Step 3: Make the pie slices look much better.

Assuming that the exploded pie chart is your choice, you can change the appearance of the slices. Just click on any one slice. Then left-click and chose "Format Data Series" to open up the Format Data Series options window. The 3-D format option will assist you in choosing a bevel (the edge of each pie slice) and the material (texture or smooth surface) for the slices. Here, we have chosen the circle bevel for the top and bottom of the slices, and the metal material display.

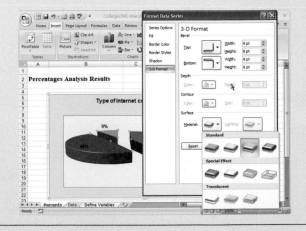

| Step in Excel | Illustration |
|---|---|

### Step 4: Format the plot area.

The plot area is the area that surrounds the pie chart slices. It is quite simple to make this part of your graph look very impressive by clicking on the plot area and then left-clicking to bring up the Excel – Format Plot Area options. Here you can use Fill Gradient fill, and then use the preset colors to select the background. Notice the wide array of preset colors available to you. You can also change the angle of the gradient. If you do not wish to use a preset plot area color, you can experiment with your own color and gradient stops.

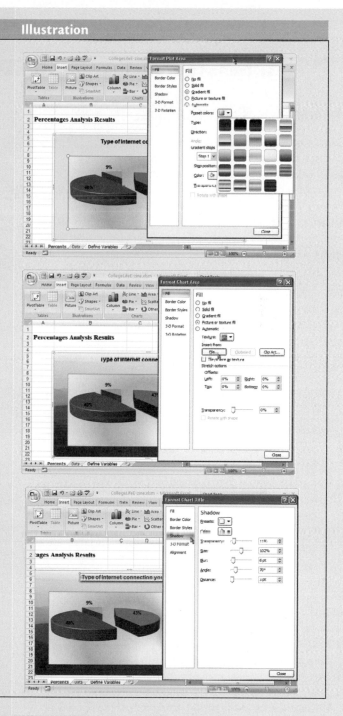

### Step 5: Consider using a picture file to personalize your graph.

Click on the outer chart area and then right-click and select Format Chart Area. The options are identical to those in Step 4, and we chose to use "Picture or texture fill." By clicking the "File" button, you can browse to find a picture file on your personal computer. The picture used in our example is just a stock one that comes with Microsoft Office, but you could use your own photos, graphics from a Web site, or any other photo file that is appropriate.

### Step 6: Enhance the chart title and legend.

If you used a picture or changed the chart area background, it is possible that the chart title and legend are now difficult to read. Both can be enhanced (separately) by selecting them via point-and-click and then using Format Chart Title or Format Legend Menus. The options are similar to those in other chart format menu windows. Of course, you can also use any of Excel's many font options to make your title and legend stand out.

   If you have a chart appearance that you want to use consistently in your report or presentation, you can save this format as a template, and use Excel's chart template feature to apply it to each of the XL Data Analyst's basic pie charts.

## Bar Charts

Several types of **bar charts** can be used and several different types are available to you in Excel. Bar charts are often used in reports because they present data in a way that is easily interpreted. They are also excellent for oral presentations. We give you specific keystroke instructions for making bar, or column, charts using your XL Data Analyst and Excel in Marketing Research Application 15.4.

## MARKETING RESEARCH APPLICATION 15.4

**PRACTICAL**

**APPLICATIONS**

### How to Make a Bar Chart in Excel

You've collected your data, conducted your analysis using your XL Data Analyst, and you now have the output that you want. You may want to enhance your written or oral report with a figure in the form of a bar chart. Bar charts are often used in marketing research reports because they are easily interpreted. Consider using them when:

a. You wish to display data on an *x*-axis and *y*-axis, and/or
b. You want to compare groups or illustrate changes over time.

When you have a limited number of bars (six or less), use a vertical bar chart (called a *Column* chart in Excel). When you have seven or more bars, consider a horizontal bar chart (called a *Bar* chart in Excel). Finally, you should properly label your bar chart.

For our example we want to compare the averages of several questions using the same metric-type scale such as the questions on the College Life E-Zine survey where respondents indicated how many dollars they would spend out of $100 Internet purchases for various types of products. So, do a Summarize—Averages analysis using all six categories in the survey. Format the averages in dollars and cents. With your cursor, select the dollar amounts and the merchandise descriptions, then use Excel's Insert menu to select the type of bar chart you want to use. This will generate a basic bar chart and open up the Cart tools function.

### Steps in Making a Bar Chart

| Step in Excel | Illustration |
|---|---|
| **Step 1: Use "Quick Layout" to select a better bar chart appearance.**<br>As you can see in the accompanying figure, the Quick Layout feature has standard templates for your bar chart, and you can select any one to automatically improve the appearance of your basic bar chart. | 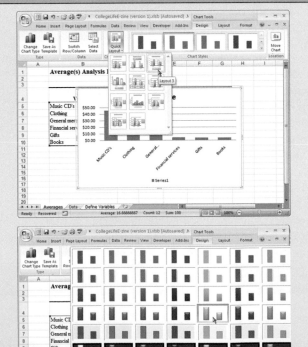 |
| **Step 2: Use chart appearance features to greatly improve the appearance of your bars.**<br>The "Design" tab opens with a great many options as to the appearance of the bars in your graph. Some options provide for a dark or grayed plot background. Note that we have selected and applied the 3-D beveled metallic green appearance for the bars. | |

| Step in Excel | Illustration |
|---|---|
| **Step 3: Use Excel's Chart features to create a professional final bar chart.**<br><br>As we described in the Marketing Research Application dealing with professional-appearing pie charts, there are many enhancements available for backgrounds, fonts, labels, and other aspects of Excel charts. These enhancements are available on practically all Excel charts, and you can use them to create a professional-quality final bar chart such as the one shown here. (Refer to our pie chart Marketing Research Application for details.)<br><br>Also, notice that there is a "Save as Template" option that will allow you to save the format of your final bar chart and apply it to other bar charts in your report or presentation. | |

# ETHICAL VISUALS

A marketing researcher should always follow the doctrine of full disclosure. An **ethical visual** is one that is totally objective in terms of how information is presented in the research report. Sometimes misrepresenting information is intentional (as when a client asks a researcher to misrepresent the data in order to promote his or her "pet project") or it may be unintentional. In the latter case, those preparing a visual are sometimes so familiar with the material being presented that they falsely assume that the graphic message is apparent to all who view it.

To ensure that you have objectively and ethically prepared your visuals, you should do the following:

> An ethical visual is one that is totally objective in terms of how information is presented in the research report.

ETHICS

1 Double- and triple-check all labels, numbers, and visual shapes. A faulty or misleading visual discredits your report and work.
2 Exercise caution if you use three-dimensional figures. They may distort the data by multiplying the value by the width and the height.
3 Make sure all parts of the scales are presented. Truncated graphs (having breaks in the scaled values on either axis) are acceptable only if the audience is familiar with the data.

# PRESENTING YOUR RESEARCH ORALLY

You may be asked to present an oral summary of the recommendations and conclusions of your research. The purpose of the **oral presentation** is to succinctly present the information and to provide an opportunity for questions and discussion.

The presentation may be accomplished through a simple conference with the client, or it may be a formal presentation to a roomful of people. In any case, says Jerry W. Thomas, CEO of Decision Analyst, research reports should "be presented orally to all key people in the same room at the same time." He believes this is important because many people don't read the research report and others may not understand all the details of the report. "An oral presentation ensures that everyone can ask questions to allow the researchers to clear up any confusion."[9] It also ensures that everyone hears the same thing.

To be adequately prepared when you present your research orally, follow these steps:

1  Identify and analyze your audience. Consider the same questions you addressed at the beginning of the research process and at the beginning of this chapter.
2  Find out the expectations your audience has for your presentation. Is the presentation formal or informal? Does your audience expect an electronic slide show?
3  Determine the key points your audience needs to hear.
4  Outline the key points, preferably on 3 × 5 cards to which you can easily refer.
5  Present your points succinctly and clearly. The written report will serve as a reference for further reading.
6  Make sure your visuals graphically and ethically portray your key points.
7  Practice your presentation. Be comfortable with what you are going to say and how you look. The more prepared you are and the better you feel about yourself, the less you will need to worry about jitters.
8  Check out the room and media equipment prior to the presentation.
9  If you are relying on an electronic device such as a computer and projector for display of PowerPoint slides, it's always a good idea to have a backup such as overheads.
10  Arrive early.
11  Be positive and confident. You are the authority; you know more about your subject than anyone else does.
12  Speak loudly enough for all in the room to hear. Enunciate clearly. Maintain eye contact and good posture. Dress appropriately.

## SUMMARY

Burke, Inc.'s online report-writing and distribution tool is called the Digital Dashboard. This is an example of online research that allows clients to see data analyzed as it is being collected. It also allows clients to interact with the data online and to analyze the data in ways that make it more meaningful for their own use.

The final stage of the marketing research process is the preparation and presentation of the marketing research report. The marketing research report is a factual message that transmits research results, vital recommendations, conclusions, and other important information to the client, who in turn bases his or her decision on the contents of the report. The report-writing and presentation stage is a very important stage of the marketing research process. This importance is attributed to the fact that, regardless of the care taken in the design and execution of the research project itself, if the report does not adequately communicate the project to the client, all is lost. In most cases, the report is the only part of the research process actually seen by the client.

Marketing research reports should be tailored to their audiences. Reports are typically organized into the categories of front matter, body, and end matter. Each of these categories has subparts, with each subpart having a different purpose. Conclusions are based on the results of the research, and recommendations are suggestions based on conclusions.

Guidelines for writing the marketing research report include proper use of headings and subheadings, which serve as signposts and signals to the reader, and proper use of visuals such as tables and figures. Style considerations include understanding the structure of paragraphs, spare use of jargon, strong verbs, active voice, consistent tense, conciseness, and varied sentence structure and length. Editing and proofreading, preferably by reading the report aloud, are important steps in writing the research report. Care should be taken to ensure that all presentations are clear and objective to the reader.

Report writers should understand the effective use of visuals such as tables and figures. Pie charts and bar charts can be effectively used to aid in communicating research results in a report. This chapter contains specific keystroke instructions on building pie charts and bar charts using XL Data Analyst and Excel. Many visual aids may be distorted so that they have a different meaning to the reader. This means that ethical considerations must be made in the preparation of the research report.

In some cases, marketing researchers are required to orally present the findings of their research project to the client. Guidelines for making an oral presentation include knowing the audience, its expectations, and the key points you wish to make; correctly preparing visuals; practicing; checking out presentation facilities and equipment prior to the presentation; having backup systems; and being positive.

# KEY TERMS

Marketing research report (p. 466)

Front matter (p. 469)

Title page (p. 469)

Letter of authorization (p. 470)

Letter of transmittal (p. 470)

Memo of transmittal (p. 470)

Table of contents (p. 471)

List of illustrations (p. 472)

Tables (p. 472)

Figures (p. 472)

Abstract/executive summary (p. 472)

Body (p. 472)

Introduction (p. 472)

Research objectives (p. 473)

Method (p. 473)

Plagiarism (p. 473)

Results (p. 473)

Limitations (p. 474)

Conclusions (p. 474)

Recommendations (p. 474)

End matter (p. 474)

Appendices (p. 474)

Headings (p. 475)

Subheadings (p. 475)

Visuals (p. 475)

Pie chart (p. 479)

Bar charts (p. 481)

Ethical visual (p. 483)

Oral presentation (p. 483)

# REVIEW QUESTIONS

1 Briefly explain three of the features of Burke, Inc.'s Digital Dashboard Online Reporting Solution.

2 Discuss the relative importance of the marketing research report to the other stages in the marketing research process.

3 What are the components of the marketing research report?

4 When should you include or omit a letter of authorization?

5 When should a letter of transmittal versus a memo of transmittal be used?

6 What is the difference between a table and a figure?

7 Why is the abstract or executive summary important?

8 What should be covered in the body of the report?

9 What are your options regarding placement of the research objectives in the report?

10 Discuss what information should be included in the methodology section of the report.

11 Discuss why it is important to properly reference others' work you have used in your report.

12 Distinguish among results, conclusions, and recommendations.

13 Why are headings and subheadings important to use?

14 Illustrate the differences between levels of headings.

15 What are guidelines to preparing tables, pie charts, and bar charts?

16 What are guidelines to preparing ethical visuals?

# APPLICATION QUESTIONS

17 Assume you have conducted a marketing research project for your university and that the project basically consists of providing them with a descriptive study of the student population. You've collected demographic information and information on students' attitudes toward various campus services and student life activities. Write a title page for the report. Would you use a memo or letter of transmittal? Write it.

18 Using your XL Data Analyst and Excel, prepare a pie chart and a bar chart using any data you have.

19 Why do you think we included a discussion of ethics in preparing visuals? If you wanted to make your pie chart or bar chart you prepared in the question above unethical, describe what you could do.

20 Now look at some of the answers you have written above. Evaluate your answers in light of the information contained in this chapter in Marketing Research Application 15.2 on developing logical paragraphs.

21 Visit your library and ask your reference librarian if he or she is aware of any marketing research reports (you can also ask for "reports written by faculty of the university") that have been placed in the library. Chances are good that you will be able to find several reports of various kinds. Examine the reports. What commonalities do they have in terms of the sections that the authors have created? Look at the sections carefully. What types of issues were addressed in the introduction section? The methodology section? How did the authors organize all of the information reported in the results section? Are recommendations different from conclusions?

# INTERACTIVE LEARNING

ETHICS

Go to **www.plagiarism.org**. Read "Plagiarism FAQs." Go to any search engine such as Google or Yahoo!. Enter "Plagiarism" in the search box. Visit some of these sites. Can you find some examples illustrating how some prominent persons have been in great difficulties because they did not cite the work of others? Visit the Web site at **www.prenhall.com/burnsbush**. For this chapter, work through the self-study quizzes, and get instant feedback on whether you need additional studying. On the Web site, you can review the chapter outlines and case information for Chapter 15.

---

## CASE 15.1  ||| Your Integrated Case

### College Life E-Zine

#### Organizing the Report

With all the data collected and the analysis nearly completed, Bob Watts started working on the final report. He knew the report itself would be the instrument that would bear the burden of properly communicating the results of the months-long research project. Bob was very concerned about writing a report that Don, Sarah, Anna, and Wesley could easily read and understand.

Bob's first thoughts in preparing the report concerned proper organization. He had several options.

■ **Organizing by Questionnaire Questions.** First, he could follow the questionnaire, making each separate question a separate division of the report. In fact, the questions themselves could serve as headings for each section. All the parties involved were thoroughly familiar with the questionnaire, and this familiarity could be an asset in organizing the report.

■ **Organizing by Research Objective.** Bob considered a second alternative for organization: grouping questions in terms of a common research objective. For example, consider the following research objective: "To gather data reflecting potential adopters' purchases of selected products and services." Data for the questions dealing with purchases or planned purchases of soft drinks, restaurants, pizza delivery, automobiles, and so on could be organized under this research objective.

■ **Organizing by Importance of Topic.** The most important topic in the survey deals with the likelihood that students will actually subscribe to the e-zine. Perhaps some of the less important questions deal with the demographic issues such as age or gender.

1 Write down the first five headings you would use in your report if you organized your paper by each one of the three methods Bob Watts is considering.
2 Which method of organization do you think Watts should use? Why?

---

## CASE 15.2  ||| Your Integrated Case

### College Life E-Zine

#### Appropriate Visuals

Bob Watts examined the questionnaire used to collect data in the College Life E-Zine project (see Chapter 9, pages 278–281). His thoughts were now concerned

with the choice of the appropriate visuals to use. Look back at the questionnaire and consider the following questions: (a) Do you have Internet access? (b) What type of Internet connection do you have where you live? (c) If you do purchase over the Internet, please tell us how you allocate your expenditures; (d) If the subscription price for this e-zine was $15 per month for a minimum of 6 months, how likely would you be to subscribe to it? (e) all the questions dealing with preferences for different types of features (i.e., *The Campus Calendar, Course/Instructor Evaluator*, etc.); (f) Year born? (g) GPA; and, finally, (h) the question asking respondents to identify their college.

1 For each of the questions identified in the case, which visual, if any, do you believe Bob Watts should select?

2 Provide a justfication for your choice of visuals.

3 Are there any questions for which you believe multiple visuals should be used?

4 Can you identify some ethical issues that could arise in terms of how an entrepreneur could use visuals to represent survey data to potential investors or bankers?

---

## CASE 15.3 ||| Your Integrated Case

### College Life E-Zine

#### PowerPoint Presentations

Back in his office at ORS, Bob Watts was putting the final touches on the College Life E-Zine project. He felt very pleased with the report and now he was beginning to think about making the oral presentation. He wanted to begin the "Survey Results" part of the presentation with the question he felt was most important to the project: the question asking potential respondents about their likelihood of subscribing to the e-zine. He felt he should start to prepare for the oral presentation by writing out his notes on the results of that question and by preparing a PowerPoint slide to present the survey data on this question.

1 Using Word, write out several of the statements that you think would be appropriate for an oral presentation to the four clients.

2 Import the statements you prepared in question 1 into PowerPoint using copy and paste. Experiment with different text colors, font sizes, and styles.

3 Using your XL Data Analyst program, run a frequency distribution on the likelihood-to-subscribe question.

4 Using XL Data Analyst, make a bar chart showing the percentage responses to each category in the question. Import the bar chart into PowerPoint.

## Chapter 1

1. Bakker, Gerben. (2003, January). Building knowledge about the consumer: The emergence of market research in the motion picture industry. Industry Overview. *Business History*, vol. 45, no. 1, 101 (29).
2. Keefe, L.M. (2004, September 15). What is the meaning of "marketing"? *Marketing News*. Chicago: American Marketing Association, 17–18.
3. Vargo, S. L., and Lusch, R. F. (2004). *Journal of Marketing*, vol. 68, no. 1, pp. 1–17.
4. Shostack, G.L. (1977). Breaking free from product marketing. *Journal of Marketing*. Shostack's original example used General Motors. vol. 41, no. 2, pg. 74.
5. Drucker, P. (1973). *Management: Tasks, responsibilities, practices.* New York: Harper & Row, pp. 64–65.
6. Kotler, P. (2003). *Marketing management* (11th ed.). Upper Saddle River, NJ: Prentice Hall, p. 19.
7. Bennett, P. D. (Ed.) (1995). *Dictionary of marketing terms* (2nd ed.). Chicago: American Marketing Association/NTC Books, p. 169.
8. Bennett, P. D. (Ed.) (1995). *Dictionary of marketing terms* (2nd ed.). Chicago: American Marketing Association/NTC Books, p. 165.
9. Clancy, K., and Krieg, P. C. (2000). *Counterintuitive marketing: Achieve great results using uncommon sense.* New York: Free Press.
10. Merritt, N. J., and Redmond, W. H. (1990). Defining marketing research: Perceptions vs. practice. *Proceedings: American Marketing Association*, 146–50.
11. Tracy, K. (1998). *Jerry Seinfeld: The entire domain.* Secaucus, NJ: Carol Publishing Group, pp. 64–65.
12. Marconi, J. (1998, June 8). What marketing aces do when marketing research tells them, "don't do it!" *Marketing News*. Also see Zangwill, W. (1993, March 8). When customer research is a lousy idea. *Wall Street Journal*, A12.
13. Heilbrunn, J. (1989, August). Legal lessons from the Delicare affair—1. United States, *Marketing and Research Today*, vol. 17, no. 3, 156–60. Also see Frederickson, P., and Totten, J. W. (1990). Marketing research projects in the academic setting: Legal liability after Beecham vs. Yankelovich, in Capello, L. M., et al., eds., *Progress in marketing thought: Proceedings of the Southern Marketing Association*, pp. 250–53.
14. See www.Mintel.com.
15. Scientific research pumps up new products: The benefits of health and wellness ingredients. (2003, March). *Stagnito's New Products Magazine*, vol. 3, no. 3, 30.
16. Lipson, S. (2001). *Giving the customer the driver's seat: The power of the research manager.* A presentation made at the American Marketing Association's 22nd Annual Marketing Research Conference, Atlanta.
17. Bruzzone, D., and Rosen, D. (2001, March). All the right moves. *Quirk's Marketing Research Review*, vol. 15, no. 3, 56–76.
18. The description of the MIS is adapted from Kotler, P. (1997). *Marketing management: Analysis, planning, implementation, and control* (9th ed.). Upper Saddle River, NJ: Prentice Hall, pp. 100ff.
19. Fine, B. (2000). Internet research: The brave new world. In C. Chakrapani (Ed.), *Marketing research: State-of-the-art perspectives* (p. 143). Chicago: American Marketing Association.
20. Grossnickle, J., and Raskin, O. (2001). *Online marketing research: Knowing your customer using the Net.* New York: McGraw Hill, p. xix.
21. Honomichl, J. (2006, June 16). Mixed bag of revenue growth in 2005. *Marketing News*, H62.
22. Fielding, M. (2007, March 1). Explore new territory: Four non-BRIC regions emerge as hot MR markets. *Marketing News*, 25ff.
23. Berkowitz, D. (2003, October 24). Harsh realities for marketing research. Retrieved from **eMarketer.com** on October 27, 2003.
24. Berkowitz, D. (2003, October 24). Harsh realities for marketing research. Retrieved from **eMarketer.com** on October 27, 2003.
25. Teinowitz, I., and Wheaton, K. (2007, March 12). Do-Not-Mail movement lurks in state legislatures. *Advertising Age.* Retrieved from **Adage.com** on March 12, 2007.
26. Honomichl, J. (2006, August 15). No great growth. *Marketing News*, H54.
27. *Marketing News*, (2003, June 9), H16.

## Chapter 2

1. Bartels, R. (1976). *The history of marketing thought* (2nd ed.). Columbus, OH: Grid, Inc., pp. 124–25.
2. Hardy, H. (1990). *The Politz papers: Science and truth in marketing research.* Chicago: American Marketing Association.
3. Bartels, R. (1976). *The history of marketing thought* (2nd ed.). Columbus, OH: Grid, Inc., p. 125.
4. Honomichl, J. (2006, August 15). No great growth. *Marketing News*, H3.
5. Honomichl, J. (2006, August 15). No great growth. *Marketing News*, H4.
6. Honomichl, J. (2006, June 15). Mixed bag of revenue growth. *Marketing News*, H3.
7. Honomichl, J. (2006, June 15). Mixed bag of revenue growth. *Marketing News*, H4
8. Malhotra, N. K. (1999). *Marketing research* (3rd ed.). Upper Saddle River, NJ: Prentice Hall, pp. 16–19.
9. Kinnear, T. C., and Root, A. R. (1994). *Survey of marketing research: Organization function, budget, and compensation.* Chicago: American Marketing Association, p. 38.
10. Kinnear, T. C., and Root, A. R. (1994). *Survey of marketing research: Organization function, budget, and compensation.* Chicago: American Marketing Association, p. 12.
11. Opinion Research Corporation. (2001, August 27). *Marketing News*, 5.
12. Honomichl, J. (2003, June 9). Honomichl top 50, Company Profiles, Synovate. *Marketing News*, H6, H8.
13. Personal communication with the authors from Creative & Response Research Service, Inc., August 12, 2003.
14. See Neal, W. D. (2002, September 16). Shortcomings plague the industry. *Marketing Research*, vol. 36, no. 19, p. 37ff.
15. These examples and the following paragraphs are based upon: Mahajan, V., and Wind, J. (1999, Fall). Rx for marketing research: A diagnosis of and prescriptions for recovery of an ailing discipline in the business world. *Marketing Research*, 7–13.
16. Clancy, K., and Krieg, P. C. (2000). *Counterintuitive marketing: Achieve great results using uncommon sense.* New York: Free Press.

17. Krum, J. R. (1978, October). B for marketing research departments. *Journal of Marketing*, vol. 42, 8–12; Krum, J. R., Rau, P. A., and Keiser, S. K. (1987–1988, December–January). The marketing research process: Role perceptions of researchers and users. *Journal of Advertising Research*, vol. 27, 9–21; Dawson, S., Bush, R. F., and Stern, B. (1994, October). An evaluation of services provided by the marketing research industry. *Service Industries Journal*, vol. 14, no. 4, 515–26; also see Austin, J. R. (1991). An exploratory examination of the development of marketing research service relationships: An assessment of exchange evaluation dimensions. In M. C. Gilly, et al. (eds.), *Enhancing knowledge development in marketing* (pp. 133–41), 1991 AMA Educators' Conference Proceedings; also see Swan, J. E., Trawick, I. F., and Carroll, M. G. (1981, August). Effect of participation in marketing research on consumer attitudes toward research and satisfaction with a service. *Journal of Marketing Research*, 356–63; also see Malholtra, N. K., Peterson, M., and Kleiser, S. B. (1999, Spring). Marketing research: A state-of-the-art review and directions for the 21st century. *Journal of the Academy of Marketing Science*, vol. 27, no. 2, 160–83.

18. Quoted in Chakrapani, C. (2001, Winter). From the editor. *Marketing Research*, vol. 13, no. 4, 2.

19. What's wrong with marketing research? (2001, Winter). *Marketing Research*, vol. 13, no. 4.

20. Dawson, S., Bush, R. F., and Stern, B. (1994, October). An evaluation of services provided by the market research industry. *Service Industries Journal*, 144, 515–26.

21. Consensus eludes certification issue. (1989, September 11). *Marketing News*, 125, 127; Stern, B., and Crawford, T. (1986, September 12). It's time to consider certification of researchers. *Marketing News*, 20–21; Stern, B. L., and Grubb, E. L. (1991). Alternative solutions to the marketing research industry's "quality control" problem. In R. L. King (ed.), *Marketing: Toward the twenty-first century* (pp. 225–29), Proceedings of the Southern Marketing Association; Jones, M. A., and McKinney, R. (1993). The need for certification in marketing research. In D. Thompson (ed.), *Marketing and education: Partners in progress* (pp. 224–29), Proceedings of the Atlantis Marketing Association. Also, for an excellent review of the pros and cons of certification, see Rittenburg, T. L., and Murdock, G. W. (1994, Spring). Highly sensitive issue still sparks controversy within the industry. *Marketing Research*, vol. 6, no. 2, 5–10. Also see Giacobbe, R. W., and Segel, M. N. (1994). Credentialing of marketing research professionals: An industry perspective. In R. Archoll and A. Mitchell (eds.), *Enhancing knowledge development in marketing* (pp. 229–301). AMA Educators' Conference Proceedings.

22. Achenbaum, A. A. (1985, June–July). Can we tolerate a double standard in marketing research? *Journal of Advertising Research*, vol. 25, RC3–7.

23. Murphy, P. E., and Laczniak, G. R. (1992, June). Emerging ethical issues facing marketing researchers. *Marketing Research*, vol. 4, no. 2, 6–11.

24. See Steinberg, M. S. (1992, June). The "professionalization" of marketing. *Marketing Research*, vol. 4, no. 2, 56. Also see McDaniel, S. W., and Solano-Mendez, R. (1993). Should marketing researchers be certified? *Journal of Advertising Research*, vol. 33, no. 4, 20–31.

25. Bernstein, S. (1990, September). A call to audit market research providers. *Marketing Research*, vol. 2, no. 3, 11–16.

26. Reidman, P. (2001, January 29). ABCi alliance begins. *Advertising Age*, vol. 72, no. 5, 38.

27. McDaniel, S., Verille, P., and Madden, C. S. (1985, February). The threats to marketing research: An empirical reappraisal.

*Journal of Marketing Research*, 74–80; Akaah, I. P., and Riordan, E. A. (1989, February). Judgments of marketing professionals about ethical issues in marketing research. *Journal of Marketing Research*, 112–120; Laczniak, G. R. and Murphy, P. E. *Marketing ethics*. Lexington, MA: Lexington Books; Ferrell, O. C., and Gresham, L. G. (1985, Summer). A contingency framework for understanding ethical decision making in marketing. *Journal of Marketing Research*, 87–96; Reidenbach, R. E., and Robin, D. P. (1990). A partial testing of the contingency framework for ethical decision making: A path analytical approach. In L. M. Capella, H. W. Nash, J. M. Starling, & R. D. Taylor (eds.), *Progress in marketing thought* (pp. 121–28), Proceedings of the Southern Marketing Association; LaFleur, E. K., and Reidenbach, R. E. (1993). A taxonomic construction of ethics decision rules: An agenda for research. In T. K. Massey, Jr. (ed.), *Marketing: Satisfying a diverse customerplace* (pp. 158–61), Proceedings of the Southern Marketing Association; Reidenbach, R. E., LaFleur, E. K., Robin, D. P., and Forest, P. J. (1993). Exploring the dimensionality of ethical judgements made by advertising professionals concerning selected child-oriented television advertising practices. In T. K. Massey, Jr. (ed.), *Marketing: Satisfying a diverse customerplace* (pp. 166–70), Proceedings of the Southern Marketing Association; and Klein, J. G., and Smith, N. C. (1994). Teaching marketing research ethics in business school classroom. In R. Achrol and A. Mitchell (eds.), *Enhancing knowledge development in marketing* (pp. 92–99), AMA Educators' Conference Proceedings.

28. Dolliver, M. (2000, July 10). Keeping honest company. *Adweek*, vol. 41, 28–29.

29. See Kelley, S., Ferrell, O. C., and Skinner, S. J. (1990). Ethical behavior among marketing researchers: An assessment. *Journal of Business Ethics*, vol. 9, no. 8, 681ff.

30. See Whetstone, J. T. (2001, September). How virtue fits within business ethics. *Journal of Business Ethics*. vol. 33, no. 2, 101–14; and Pallister, J., Nancarrow, C., and Brace, I. (1999, July). Navigating the righteous course: A quality issue. *Journal of the Market Research Society*, vol. 41, no. 3, 327–42.

31. Hunt, S. D., Chonko, L. B., and Wilcox, J. B. (1984, August). Ethical problems of marketing researcher. *Journal of Marketing Research*, vol. 21, 309–24.

32. For an excellent article on ethics, see Hunt, S. D., and Vitell, S. (1986). A general theory of marketing ethics. *Journal of Macromarketing*, 5–16.

33. Hunt, S. D., Chonko, L. B., and Wilcox, J. B. (1984, August). Ethical problems of marketing researchers. *Journal of Marketing Research*, vol. 21, 309–24.

34. For an excellent discussion of these two philosophies relative to marketing research, see Kimmel, A. J., and Smith, N. C. (2001, July). Deception in marketing research: Ethical, methodological, and disciplinary implications. *Psychology & Marketing*, vol. 18, no. 7, 672–80.

35. Ethical norms and values for marketers. *American Marketing Association*. Retrieved from **www.marketingpower.com** on March 23, 2007.

36. Bowers, D. K. (1995, Summer). Confidentiality challenges. *Marketing Research*, vol. 7, no. 3, 34–35.

37. Hunt, S. D., Chonko, L. B., & Wilcox, J. B. (1984, August). Ethical problems of marketing researcher. *Journal of Marketing Research*, vol. 21, 309–24.

38. Leaders: The lessons from Enron—Enron and auditing. (2002, February 9). *The Economist* (London), vol. 362, no. 8259, 10; and Grace, H. S., Illiano, G., Sack, R. J., and Turner, L. (2002, January). Enron and Andersen: Auditors under the microscope. *CPA Journal* (New York), vol. 72, no. 1, 8.

39. Kiecker, P. L., and Nelson, J. E. (1989). Cheating behavior by telephone interviewers: A view from the trenches. In P. Bloom, et al. (eds.), *Enhancing knowledge development in marketing* (pp. 182–88). AMA Educators' Conference Proceedings.

40. Hunt, S. D., Chonko, L. B., and Wilcox, J. B. (1984, August). Ethical problems of marketing researcher. *Journal of Marketing Research*, vol. 21, 309–24.

41. Ibid., 309–24.

42. Jarvis, S. (2002, February 4). CMOR finds survey refusal rate still rising. *Marketing News*, vol. 36, no. 3, 4. Also see Bowers, D. K. (1997). CMOR's first four years. *Marketing Research*, vol. 9, 44–45; Shea, C. Z., and LeBourveau, C. (2000, Fall). Jumping the "hurdles" of marketing research, *Marketing Research*, vol. 12, no. 3, 22–30.

43. Jarvis, S. (2002, February 4). CMOR finds survey refusal rate still rising. *Marketing News*, vol. 36, no. 3, 4.

44. 2003 Respondent cooperation and industry image study. *CMOR Topline Summary Report*. Glastonbury, CT: CMOR.

45. Kimmel, A. J., and Smith, N. C. (2001, July). Deception in marketing research: Ethical, methodological, and disciplinary implications. *Psychology & Marketing*, vol. 18, no. 7, 663–89.

46. Chavez, J. (2003, October 19). Do-not-call registry contains loopholes for some businesses. Knight Ridder/Tribune Business News. Retrieved on from BusinessFile ASAP December 7, 2003.

47. Berkowitz, D. (2003, October 24). Harsh realities for marketing research. Retrieved from **eMarketer.com** on October 27, 2003.

48. Mail abuse prevention system definition of spam. Retrieved from **www.mail-abuse.org/standard.html** on March 1, 2002.

49. New law: Is Spam on the lam? *Managing Technology*. Retrieved from **knowledge.wharton.upenn.edu** on December 6, 2003.

50. Baldinger, A., and Perterson, B. (1993, August 16). CMOR concentrates on six key areas to improve cooperation. *Marketing News*, vol. 27, no. 17, p. A15.

51. Ramasastry, A. (2003, December 5). Why the new federal "Can Spam" law probably will not work. *Find Law*. Retrieved from **CNN.com** on December 7, 2003.

52. The Senate version of the bill, S. 187, entitled "Controlling the Assault of Non-Solicited Pornography and Marketing Act of 2003, or the CAN-SPAM Act of 2003," was passed on October 22, 2003. Minor changes in the bill are expected before President Bush is asked to sign the bill into law.

53. Ramasastry, A. (2003, December 5). Why the new federal "Can Spam" law probably will not work. *Find Law*. Retrieved from **CNN.com** on December 7, 2003.

54. Gillin, D. (2001, Summer). Opt in or opt out? *Marketing Research*, 6–7.

55. The following statements are taken from the CASRO Code of Ethics, Responsibilities to Respondents; Privacy and the Avoidance of Harassment, Section 3, Internet Research. See **www.CASRO.org**.

56. See **www.bls.gov/oco/home.htm**. Retrieved on March 24, 2007.

57. Dun, T. (1999). *How research providers see it: An ARF study of practices, challenges and future opportunities*. New York: Advertising Research Foundation, p. 10.

58. See **www.bls.gov/oco/home.htm**. Retrieved on March 24, 2007.

59. *Marketing and Sales Career Directory* (4th ed.). (1993). Detroit, MI: Gale Research Inc., pp. 81–95.

## Chapter 3

1. Others have broken the marketing research process down into different numbers of steps. Regardless, there is widespread agreement that using a step-process approach is a useful tool for learning marketing research.

2. Adapted from Adler, L. (1979, September 17). Secrets of when, and when not to embark on a marketing research project. *Sales & Marketing Management Magazine*, vol. 123, 108.

3. Adapted from Adler, L. (1979, September 17). Secrets of when, and when not to embark on a marketing research project. *Sales & Marketing Management Magazine*, vol. 123, 108.

4. The operative product word: Ambitiousness. (1996, December 21). *Advertising Age*, 14; Murtaugh, P. (1998, May). Consumer research: The big lie. *Food & Beverage Marketing*, 16; and Parasuraman, A., Grewal, D., and Krishnan R. (2004). *Marketing Research*. Boston: Houghton Mifflin, pp. 41–42.

5. Koten, J., and Kilman, S. (1985, July 15). Marketing classic: How Coke's decision to offer 2 colas undid $4\frac{1}{2}$ years of planning. *Wall Street Journal*, 1.

6. Personal communication with the authors by Lawrence D. Gibson. Also see: Gibson, L. D. (1998, Spring). Defining marketing problems: Don't spin your wheels solving the wrong puzzle. *Marketing Research*, vol. 10, no. 4, 5–12.

7. Gibson, L. D. (1998, Spring). Defining marketing problems: Don't spin your wheels solving the wrong puzzle. *Marketing Research*, vol. 10, no. 4, 7.

8. Retrieved from **www.Dictionary.com** on November 13, 2003.

9. Kotler, P. (2003). *Marketing management: Analysis, planning, implementing, and control* (11th ed.). Upper Saddle River, NJ: Prentice Hall, p. 102.

10. For example, see: Gordon, G. L., Schoenbachler, D. D., Kaminski, P. F., and Brouchous, K. A. (1997). New product development: Using the salesforce to identify opportunities. *Business and Industrial Marketing*, vol. 12, no. 1, 33; and Ardjchvilj, A., Cardozo, R., and Ray, S. (2003, January). A theory of entrepreneurial opportunity identification and development. *Journal of Business Venturing*, vol. 18, no. 1, 105.

11. Personal communication with the authors by Lawrence D. Gibson. Also see: Gibson, L. D. (1998, Spring). Defining marketing problems: Don't spin your wheels solving the wrong puzzle. *Marketing Research*, vol. 10, no. 4, 5–12.

12. Gibson, L. D. (1998, Spring). Defining marketing problems: Don't spin your wheels solving the wrong puzzle. *Marketing Research*, vol. 10, no. 4, 5.

13. For example, see: Tomas, S. (1999, May). Creative problem-solving: An approach to generating ideas. *Hospital Material Management Quarterly*, vol. 20, no. 4, 33–45.

14. Kotler, P. (2003). *Marketing management: Analysis, planning, implementing, and control* (11th ed.). Upper Saddle River, NJ: Prentice Hall, p. 103.

15. Semon, T. (1999, June 7). Make sure the research will answer the right question. *Marketing News*, vol. 33, no. 12, H30.

16. Insights based on 30 years of defining the problem and research objectives in Burns, A.C. and Bush, R. F. (2006). *Marketing Research*, 5th edition. Upper Saddle River, NJ: Pearson Prentice Hall, pp. 92–93.

17. Dictionary, American Marketing Association. Retrieved from **www.marketingpower.com** on December 10, 2003.

18. Adapted from **Dictionary.com**. Retrieved on November 15, 2003. Also see Bagozzi, R. P., Phillips, L. W. (1982, September). Representing and testing organizational theories: A holistic construal. *Administrative Science Quarterly*, vol. 27, no. 3, 459.

19. For more information on proposals and reports, see Carroll, N., Mohn, M., and Land, T. H. (1989, January/February/March). A guide to quality marketing research proposals and reports. *Business*, vol. 39, no. 1, 38–40.

## Chapter 4

1. Momentum Market Intelligence performs both quantitative and qualitative research. They also offer a complete marketing intelligence system to clients. Go to their Web page at **www.mointel.com** and go to "Capabilities" to read more about the services the company offers.
2. Singleton, D. (2003, November 24). Basics of good research involve understanding six simple rules. *Marketing News*, 22–23.
3. For an excellent in-depth treatment of research design issues, see Creswell, J. (2003). *Research design: Qualitative, quantitative, and mixed methods approaches*. Thousand Oaks, CA: Sage Publications.
4. Martin, J. (2003, October 27). Cash from trash: 1–800-Got Junk? *Fortune*, vol. 148, 196.
5. Stewart, D. W. (1984). *Secondary research: Information sources and methods*. Newbury Park, CA: Sage Publications; and Davidson, J. P. (1985, April). Low cost research sources. *Journal of Small Business Management*, vol. 23, 73–77.
6. Knox, N. (2003, December 16). Volvo teams up to build what women want. *USA Today*, 1B.
7. Bonoma, T. V. Case research in marketing: Opportunities, problems, and a process. *Journal of Marketing Research*, vol. 22, 199–208.
8. Myers, J. Wireless for the 21st century. *Telephony*, vol. 231, no. 6, 24–26.
9. Greenbaum, T. I. (1988). *The practical handbook and guide in focus group research*. Lexington, MA: D.C. Heath.
10. Stoltman, J. J., and Gentry, J. W. (1992). Using focus groups to study household decision processes and choices. In R. P. Leone and V. Kumar (eds.), *AMA Educator's Conference proceedings. Vol. 3: Enhancing knowledge development in marketing* (pp. 257–63). Chicago: American Marketing Association.
11. Last, J., and Langer, J. (2003, December). Still a valuable tool. *Quirk's Marketing Research Review*, vol. 17, no. 11, 30.
12. See Bogdan, R., and Biklen, S. (1992). *Qualitative research for education: An introduction to theory and methods*. Boston: Allyn and Bacon; and Marshall, C., and Rossman, G. (1999). *Designing qualitative research*. Thousand Oaks, CA: Sage Publications.
13. For more information on qualitative techniques, see Burns, A., and Bush, R. (2002). *Marketing research: Online research applications*. Upper Saddle River, NJ: Prentice Hall, pp. 202–35.
14. Dictionary. American Marketing Association. Retrieved from **www.marketingpower.com** on December 16, 2003.
15. Taylor, C. (2003, December). What's all the fuss about? *Quirk's Marketing Research Review*, vol. 17, no. 11, 40–45.
16. Wellner, A. (2003, March). The new science of focus groups. *American Demographics*, vol. 25, no. 2, 29ff.
17. Thomas, J. (1981). Focus groups and the American dream. *White Papers, Decision Analyst, Inc.* Retrieved from **www.decisionanalyst.com** on December 16, 2003.
18. Langer, J. (2001). *The mirrored window: Focus groups from a moderator's viewpoint*. New York: Paramount Market Publishing, p. 4.
19. Langer, J. (2001). *The mirrored window: Focus groups from a moderator's viewpoint*. New York: Paramount Market Publishing, p. 11.
20. Miller, C. (1991, May 27). Respondents project, let psyches go crazy. *Marketing News*, vol. 25, no. 11, 1, 3.
21. Kinnear, T. C., and Taylor, J. R. (1991). *Marketing research: An applied approach*. New York: McGraw-Hill, p. 142.
22. Sudman, S., and Wansink, B. (2002). *Consumer panels* (2nd ed.) Chicago: American Marketing Association. This book is recognized as an authoritative source on panels.
23. Personal communication with the authors from Allison Groom, American Heart Association, March 12, 2002.
24. Lohse, G. L., and Rosen, D. L. (2002, Summer). Signaling quality and credibility in Yellow Pages advertising: The influence of color and graphics on choice. *Journal of Advertising*, vol. 30, no. 2, 73–85.
25. Wyner, G. (2000, Fall). Learn and earn through testing on the Internet: The Web provides new opportunities for experimentation. *Marketing Research*, vol. 12, no. 3, 37–38.
26. See, for example: Montgomery, D. (2001). *Design and analysis of experiments*. New York: John Wiley & Sons; and Kerlinger, F. N. (1986). *Foundations of behavioral research* (3rd ed.). New York: Holt, Rinehart, and Winston.
27. Campbell, D. T., and Stanley, J. C. (1963). *Experimental and quasi-experimental designs for research*. Chicago: Rand McNally.
28. Calder, B. J., Phillips, L. W., and Tybout, A. M. (1992, December). The concept of external validity. *Journal of Consumer Research*, vol. 9, 240–44.
29. Gray, L. R., and Diehl, P. L. (1992). *Research methods for business and management*. New York: Macmillan, pp. 387–90.
30. Doyle, J. (1994, October). In with the new, out with the old. *Beverage World*, vol. 113, no. 1576, 204–5.
31. Brennan, L. (1988, March). Test marketing. *Sales Marketing Management Magazine*, vol. 140, 50–62.
32. Miles, S. (2001, January 17). MyTurn is cutting back in unusual way. *Wall Street Journal*, Eastern edition.
33. Churchill, G. A., Jr. (2001). *Basic marketing research* (4th ed.). Fort Worth, TX: Dryden Press, pp. 144–145.
34. Spethmann, B. (1985, May 8). Test market USA. *Brandweek*, vol. 36, 40–43.
35. Clancy, K. J., and Shulman, R. S. (1995, October). Test for success. *Sales & Marketing Management Magazine*, vol. 147, no. 10, 111–115.
36. Melvin, P. (1992, September). Choosing simulated test marketing systems. *Marketing Research*, vol. 4, no. 3, 14–16.
37. Ibid. Also see Turner, J., and Brandt, J. (1978, Winter). Development and validation of a simulated market to test children for selected consumer skills. *Journal of Consumer Affairs*, 266–76.
38. Blount, S. (1992, March). It's just a matter of time. *Sales & Marketing Management*, vol. 144, no. 3, 32–43.
39. Power, C. (1992, August 10). Will it sell in Podunk? Hard to say. *Business Week*, 46–47.
40. Nelson, E. (2001, February 2). Colgate's net rose 10 percent in period, new products helped boost sales. *Wall Street Journal*, Eastern edition, B6.
41. Ihlwan, M. (2002, February 4). A nation of digital guinea pigs: Korea is a hotbed of such experiments as a cash-free city. *Business Week*, 50.
42. Greene, S. (1996, May 4). Chattanooga chosen as test market for smokeless cigarette. *Knight-Ridder/Tribune Business News*. Retrieved on March 7, 2004 from Lexis-Nexis.
43. Hayes, J. (1995, January 3). McD extends breakfast buffet test in southeast markets. *National Restaurant News*, vol. 29, no. 4, 3.
44. Kotler, P. (1991). *Marketing management: Analysis, planning, implementation, and control*. Upper Saddle River, NJ: Prentice Hall, p. 335.
45. Power, C. (1992, August 10). Will it sell in Podunk? Hard to say. *Business Week*, 46–47.
46. Murphy, P., and Laczniak, G. (1992, June). Emerging ethical issues facing marketing researchers. *Marketing Research*, 6.

## Chapter 5

1. For an example of using secondary data for a marketing research project, see Castleberry, S. B. (2001, December). Using secondary data in marketing research: A project that

melds Web and off-Web sources. *Journal of Marketing Education,* vol. 23, no. 3, 195–203.

2. Wagner, C. G. (2001, July–August). Technology: The promise of Internet2. *The Futurist,* vol. 35, no. 4, 12–13.

3. Kotler, P. (2003). *Marketing management* (11th ed.). Upper Saddle River, NJ: Prentice Hall, p. 53.

4. Senn, J. A. (1988). *Information technology in business: Principles, practice, and opportunities.* Upper Saddle River, NJ: Prentice Hall, p. 66.

5. Grisaffe, D. (2002, January 21). See about linking CRM and MR systems. *Marketing News,* vol. 36, no. 2, 13.

6. Drozdenko, R. G., and Drake, P. D. (2002). *Optimal database marketing.* Thousand Oaks, CA: Sage Publications.

7. McKim, R. (2001, September). Privacy notices: What they mean and how marketers can prepare for them. *Journal of Database Marketing,* vol. 9, no. 1, 79–84.

8. See, for example, *U.S. industrial outlook 1999.* (1999). Washington, DC: International Trade Administration, U.S. Department of Commerce.

9. Gordon, L. P. (1995). *Using secondary data in marketing research: United States and worldwide.* Westport, CT: Quorum Books, p. 24.

10. *Demographics USA* is published by Trade Dimensions International, Inc., Nielsen, Westport, CT.

11. These questions and much of the following discussion are taken from Stewart, D. W. (1984). *Secondary research: Information sources and methods.* Newbury Park, CA: Sage Publications.

12. Crossen, C. (1994). *Tainted truth: The manipulation of fact in America.* New York: Simon & Schuster, p. 140.

13. Chapman, J. (1987, February). Cast a critical eye: Small area estimates and projections sometimes can be dramatically different. *American Demographics,* vol. 9, 30.

14. These steps are updated and adapted from Stewart, D. W. (1984). *Secondary research: Information sources and methods.* Newbury Park, CA: Sage Publications, pp. 20–22, by Ms. Peggy Toifel, MSLS, MBA, University Librarian, University of West Florida, 2004.

15. America's experience with Census 2000. (2000, August). *Direct Marketing,* vol. 63, no. 4, 46–51.

16. Researchers wishing to use SIC codes should refer to the *Standard Industrial Classification Manual 1987,* rev. ed. (1987), Executive Office of the President, U.S. Office of Management and Budget, Washington, DC: U.S. Government Printing Office.

17. Winchester, J. (1998, February). Marketers prepare for switch from SIC codes. *Business Marketing,* 1, 34.

18. Boettcher, J. (1996, April–May). NAFTA prompts a new code system for industry: The death of SIC and birth of NAICS. *Database,* 42–45.

19. Information found in this section may be referenced in *Demographics USA* (2002). Chicago: Bill Communications.

## Chapter 6

1. Actually, virtually all these firms offer some customization of data analysis, and many offer varying methods of collecting data. Still, while customization is possible, these same companies provide standardized processes and data.

2. See *Rocking the ages: The Yankelovich perspective on generational marketing.* (1997). New York: Harper Business.

3. Solutions & Service/consumer trends research/monitor annually. Retrieved from **www.Yankelovich.com** on May 3, 2004.

4. You can search the Maritz Poll by going to **www.maritzresearch .com** and clicking on Maritz Poll. The polls are searchable by date, topic, or keyword.

5. Harris Poll. Retrieved from **www.HarrisInteractive.com** on May 3, 2004.

6. What does America think about? (undated publication). Wilmington, DE: Scholarly Resources, Inc.

7. Fish, D. (2000, November). Untangling psychographics and lifestyle. *Quirk's Marketing Research Review,* 138ff.

8. SRI Consulting Business Intelligence. Retrieved from **www.sric-bi.com/VALS** on May 16, 2007.

9. Stolzenberg, M. (2000, February). 10 tips on tracking research. *Quirk's Marketing Research Review,* 20–24.

10. For an example of analysis of supermarket data using Scantrack, see Heller, W. (2000, July). Surfing retail channels. *Progressive Grocer,* vol. 79, no. 7, 48–58.

11. Information supplied to the authors by Nielsen on May 17, 2007.

12. Retrieved from **www.infores.com** on May 15, 2007.

13. Combined Network consumer panel. (2007). Retrieved from **www.infores.com** on May 15, 2007.

14. Marketing minds specializing in research. (2002). Retrieved from **www.nfow.com/NFOPanel.asp** on May 16, 2002.

15. NPD group, food and beverages worldwide. (2002). Retrieved from **www.npd.com** on May 16, 2002.

16. Information supplied to the authors by Nielsen on May 17, 2007.

17. Information supplied to the authors by Nielsen on May 17, 2007.

18. Information supplied to the authors by Nielsen on May 17, 2007.

19. Repeat-viewing with people meters. *Journal of Advertising Research,* 9–13; Stoddard, L. R., Jr. (1987, October). The history of people meters. *Journal of Advertising Research,* 10–12.

20. By permission, Arbitron.

21. Information provided to the authors by RoperASW.

22. Adnorms. (2002). RoperASW, p. iv.

23. Patchen, R. H., and Kolessar, R. S. (1999, August). Out of the lab and into the field: A pilot test of the Personal Portable Meter. *Journal of Advertising Research,* vol. 39, no. 4, 55–68. Also see Moss, L. (2002, February 11). A constant companion. *Broadcasting & Cable,* vol. 132, no. 6, 17.

24. Hughes, L. Q. (2001, June 18). Buyers demand more data. *Advertising Age,* vol. 72, no. 25, 72.

25. Information supplied to the authors by Arbitron on May 17, 2007.

26. Reid, A. (2000, January 28). Is ITV's tvSPAN the holy grail adland has been waiting for? *Campaign,* 20.

27. For a review of these discussions, see Peters, B. (1990, December). The brave new world of single-source information. *Marketing Research,* vol. 2, no. 4, 16; Churchill, V. B. (1990, December). The role of ad hoc survey research in a single source world. *Marketing Research,* vol. 2, no. 4, 22–26; and Metzger, G. D. (1990, December). Single source: Yes and no (the backward view). *Marketing Research,* vol. 2, no. 4, 29.

## Chapter 7

1. Malhotra, N. (1999). *Marketing research: An applied orientation* (3rd ed.). Upper Saddle River, NJ: Prentice Hall, p. 125.

2. See Oishi, S. M. (2003). *How to conduct in-person interviews for surveys.* Thousand Oaks, CA: Sage Publications, p. 6.

3. Cleland, K. (1996, May). Online research costs about one-half that of traditional methods. *Business Marketing,* vol. 81, no. 4, B8–B9.

4. See Macer, T. (2002, December). CAVI from OpinionOne. *Quirk's Marketing Research Review*. Retrieved on March 15, 2004 from **quirks.com**.

5. Bourque, L., and Fielder, E. (2003). *How to conduct self-administered and mail surveys* (2nd ed.). Thousand Oaks, CA: Sage Publications.

6. Jang, H., Lee, B., Park, M., and Stokowski, P. A. (2000, February). Measuring underlying meanings of gambling from the perspective of enduring involvement. *Journal of Travel Research*, vol. 38, no. 3, 230–38.

7. Ericson, P. I., and Kaplan, C. P. (2000, November). Maximizing qualitative responses about smoking in structured interviews. *Qualitative Health Research*, vol. 10, no. 6, 829–40.

8. See, for example, **www.uwf.edu/panel**.

9. Green, K., Medlin, B., and Whitten, D. (2001, July/August). A comparison of Internet and mail survey methodology. *Quirk's Marketing Research Review*, 15(7), 56–59.

10. See Roy, A. (2003). Further issues and factors affecting the response rates of e-mail and mixed-mode studies. In Barone, M., et al., eds., *Enhancing knowledge development in marketing*. Proceedings: AMA Educator's Conference. Chicago: American Marketing Association, pp. 338–39; and Bachmann, D., Elfrink, J., and Vazzana, G. (1999). E-mail and snail mail face off in rematch. *Marketing Research*, vol. 11, no. 4, 11–15.

11. See Jacobs, H. (1989, Second Quarter). Entering the 1990s: The state of data collection—From a mall perspective. *Applied Marketing Research*, vol. 30, no. 2, 24–26; Lysaker, R. L. (1989, October). Data collection methods in the *U.S. Journal of the Market Research Society*, vol. 31, no. 4, 477–88; Gates, R., and Solomon, P. J. (1982, August/September). Research using the mall intercept: State of the art. *Journal of Advertising Research*, 43–50; and Bush, A. J., Bush, R. F., and Chen, H. C. (1991). Method of administration effects in mall intercept interviews. *Journal of the Market Research Society*, vol. 33, no. 4, 309–19.

12. Hornik, J., and Eilis, S. (1989, Winter). Strategies to secure compliance for a mall intercept interview. *Public Opinion Quarterly*, vol. 52, no. 4, 539–51.

13. At least one study refutes the concern about shopping frequency. See DuPont, T. D. (1987, August/September). Do frequent mall shoppers distort mall-intercept results? *Journal of Advertising Research*, vol. 27, no. 4, 45–51.

14. Bush, A. J., and Grant, E. S. (1995, Fall). The potential impact of recreational shoppers on mall intercept interviewing: An exploratory study. *Journal of Marketing Theory and Practice*, vol. 3, no. 4, 73–83.

15. Bourque, L., and Fielder, E. (2003). *How to conduct telephone interviews* (2nd ed.). Thousand Oaks, CA: Sage Publications.

16. Bush, A. J., and Hair, J. F. (1983, May). An assessment of the mall intercept as a data collection method. *Journal of Marketing Research*, vol. 22, 158–67.

17. Sheppard. J. (2000, April). Half-empty or half-full? *Quirk's Marketing Research Review*, vol. 14, no. 4, 42–45.

18. See, for example, Xu, M., Bates, B. J., and Schweitzer, J. C. (1993). The impact of messages on survey participation in answering machine households. *Public Opinion Quarterly*, vol. 57, 232–37; and Meinert, D. B., Festervand, T. A., and Lumpkin, J. R. (1992). Computerized questionnaires: Pros and cons, in King, R. L., ed., "Marketing: Perspectives for the 1990s." *Proceedings of the Southern Marketing Association*, 201–206.

19. Remington, T. D. (1993). Telemarketing and declining survey response rates. *Journal of Advertising Research*, vol. 32, no. 3, RC–6, RC–7.

20. Bos, R. (1999, November). A new era in data collection, *Quirk's Marketing Research Review*, vol. 12, no. 10, 32–40; and Fletcher, K. (1995, June 15). Jump on the omnibus. *Marketing*, 25–28.

21. Gates, R. H., and Jarboe, G. R. (Spring). Changing trends in data acquisition for marketing research. *Journal of Data Collection*, vol. 27, no. 1, 25–29; also see Synodinos, N. E., and Brennan, J. M. (1998, Summer). Computer interactive interviewing in survey research. *Psychology and Marketing*, 117–38.

22. DePaulo, P. J., and Weitzer, R. (1994, January 3). Interactive phone technology delivers survey data quickly. *Marketing News*, vol. 28, no. 1, 15.

23. Jones, P., and Palk, J. (1993). Computer-based personal interviewing: State-of-the-art and future prospects. *Journal of the Market Research Society*, vol. 35, no. 3, 221–33.

24. For a "speed" comparison, see Cobanouglu, C., Warde, B., and Moeo, P. J. (2001, Fourth Quarter). A comparison of mail, fax and Web-based survey methods. *International Journal of Market Research*, vol. 43, no. 3, 441–52.

25. Bruzzone, D., and Shellenberg, P. (2000, July/August). Track the effect of advertising better, faster, and cheaper online. *Quirk's Marketing Research Review*, vol. 14, no. 7, 22–35.

26. Sudman, S., and Blair, E. (1999, Spring). Sampling in the twenty-first century. *Academy of Marketing Science Journal*, vol. 27, no. 2, 269–77.

27. Grecco, C. (2000, July/August). Research non-stop. *Quirk's Marketing Research Review*, vol. 14, no. 7, 70–73.

28. Greenberg, D. (2000, July/August). Internet economy gives rise to real-time research. *Quirk's Marketing Research Review*, vol. 14, no. 7, 88–90.

29. MacElroy, W. H., Schchr, T., and Kaiser, S. (2001, May). *The World Wide Web and the four Ps of marketing*. German Online Research Society—DGOF e.V., GeorgElias-Mueller Institute for Psychology, University of Goettingen.

30. Taylor, H., Bremer, J., Overmeyer, C., Siegel, J. W., and Terhanian, G. (2001, Second Quarter). The record of Internet-based opinion polls in predicting the results of 72 races in the November 2000 U.S. elections. *International Journal of Market Research*, vol. 43, no. 2, 127–35.

31. Rosenblum, J. (2001, July/August). Give and take. *Quirk's Marketing Research Review*, vol. 15, no. 7, 74–77.

32. Brown, S. (1987). Drop and collect surveys: A neglected research technique? *Journal of the Market Research Society*, vol. 5, no. 1, 19–23.

33. See Bourque, L., and Fielder, E. (2003). *How to conduct self-administered and mail surveys* (2nd ed.). Thousand Oaks, CA: Sage Publications.

34. American Statistical Association (1997). ASA Series: What is a survey? More about mail surveys.

35. Nonresponse is a concern with any survey, and our understanding of refusals is minimal. See, for example, Groves, R. M., Cialdini, R. B., and Couper, M. P. (1992). Understanding the decision to participate in a survey. *Public Opinion Quarterly*, vol. 56, 475–95.

36. See, for example, McDaniel, S. W., and Verille, P. (1987, January). Do topic differences affect survey nonresponse? *Journal of the Market Research Society*, vol. 29, no. 1, 55–66; or Whitehead, J. C. (1991, Winter). Environmental interest group behavior and self-selection bias in contingent valuation mail surveys. *Growth & Change*, vol. 22, no. 1, 10–21.

37. A large number of studies have sought to determine response rates for a wide variety of inducement strategies. See, for example, Fox, R. J., Crask, M., and Kim, J. (1988, Winter). Mail questionnaires in survey research: A review of response inducement techniques. *Public Opinion Quarterly*, vol. 52,

no. 4, 467–91. Also see Yammarino, F., Skinner, S., and Childers, T. (1991). Understanding mail survey response behavior, *Public Opinion Quarterly*, vol. 55, 613–39.

38. Conant, J., Smart, D., and Walker, D. (1990). Mail survey facilitation techniques: An assessment and proposal regarding reporting practices. *Journal of the Market Research Society*, vol. 32, no. 4, 369–80.

39. Jassaume Jr., R. A., and Yamada, Y. (1990, Summer). A comparison of the viability of mail surveys in Japan and the United States. *Public Opinion Quarterly*, vol. 54, no. 2, 219–28.

40. Arnett, R. (1990, Second Quarter). Mail panel research in the 1990s. *Applied Marketing Research*, vol. 30, no. 2, 8–10.

41. Gerlotto, C. (2003, November). Learning on the go: Tips on getting international research right. *Quirk's Marketing Research Review*, vol. 17, 44.

42. Weiss, L. (2002, November). Research in Canada. *Quirk's Marketing Research Review*, vol. 16, 40.

## Chapter 8

1. Reichheld, F. (2006). *The Ultimate Question: Driving Good Profits and True Growth*. Boston, MA: Harvard Business School Press, p. 31.

2. Turner, Michelle R. (2005, January). How do you best measure and grow customer loyalty? *The Research Report*, Vol. 18. Retrieved from **www.maritzresearch.com** on March 31, 2007.

3. Sometimes open-ended questions are used to develop closed-ended questions that are used later. See, for example, Erffmeyer, R. C., and Johnson, D. A. (2001, Spring). An exploratory study of sales force automation practices: Expectations and realities. *Journal of Personal Selling and Sales Management*, vol. 21, no. 2, 167–75.

4. Fox, S. (2001, May). Market research 101. *Pharmaceutical Executive*, Supplement: *Successful Product Management: A Primer*, 34.

5. Source: A third of young people say they chew gum daily. (2001, August 23). *Marketing*.

6. Ideally, respondents should respond to the scale as having equal intervals. See, for example, Crask, M. R., and Fox, R. J. (1987). An exploration of the interval properties of three commonly used marketing research studies: A magnitude estimation approach. *Journal of the Market Research Society*, vol. 29, no. 3, 317–39.

7. Scale development requires rigorous research. See, for example, Churchill, G. A. (1979, February). A paradigm for developing better measures of marketing constructs. *Journal of Marketing Research*, vol. 16, 64–73, for method; or Ram, S., and Jung, H. S. (1990). The conceptualization and measurement of product usage. *Journal of the Academy of Marketing Science*, vol. 18, no. 1, 67–76, for an example.

8. As an example, see McMullan, R., and Gilmore, A. (2003, March). The conceptual development of customer loyalty measurement: A proposed scale. *Journal of Targeting, Measurement, and Analysis for Marketing*, vol. 11, no. 3, 230–43.

9. See, for example, Wellner, A. S. (2002, February). The female persuasion. *American Demographics*, vol. 24, no. 2, 24–29; Wasserman, T. (2002, January 7). Color me bad. *Brandweek*, vol. 43, no. 1, 2; or Wilke, M., and Applebaum, M. (2001, November 5). Peering out of the closet. *Brandweek*, vol. 42, no. 41, 26–32.

10. The order of the response scale does not seem to affect responses. See, for example, Weng, L., and Cheng, C. (2000, December). Effects of response order on Likert-type scales. *Educational and Psychological Measurement*, vol. 60, no. 6, 908–24.

11. The Likert response format, borrowed from a formal scale development approach developed by Rensis Likert, has been extensively modified and adapted by marketing researchers so much, in fact, that its definition varies from researcher to researcher. Some assume that any intensity scale using descriptors such as "strongly," "somewhat," "slightly," or the like is a Likert variation. Others use the term only for questions with agree–disagree response options.

12. Statements are taken from Wells, W. D., and Tigert, D. J. (1971). Activities, interests, and opinions. *Journal of Advertising Research*, reported in Kassarjain, H. H., and Robertson, T. S., *Perspectives in consumer behavior* (Glenview, IL: Scott Foresman, 1973), 175–76.

13. Another way to avoid the halo effect is to have subjects rate each stimulus on the same attribute and then move to the next attribute. See Wu, B. T. W., and Petroshius, S. (1987). The halo effect in store image management. *Journal of the Academy of Marketing Science*, vol. 15, no. 1, 44–51. The halo effect is real and used by companies to good advantage. See, for example, Moukheiber, Z., and Langreth, R. (2001, December 10). The halo effect. *Forbes*, vol. 168, no. 15, 66; or sites seeking advertising (the paid kind). (2002, March 11). *Advertising Age*, vol. 73, no. 10, 38.

14. Garg, R. K. (1996, July). The influence of positive and negative wording and issue involvement on responses to Likert scales in marketing research. *Journal of the Marketing Research Society*, vol. 38, no. 3, 235–46.

15. See, for example, Leigh, J. H., and Martin, C. R., Jr. (1987). "Don't know" item nonresponse in a telephone survey: Effects of question form and respondent characteristics. *Journal of Marketing Research*, vol. 29, no. 3, 317–39.

16. See also Duncan, O. D., and Stenbeck, M. (1988, Winter). No opinion or not sure? *Public Opinion Quarterly*, vol. 52, 513–25; and Durand, R. M., and Lambert, Z. V. (1988, March). Don't know responses in survey: Analyses and interpretational consequences. *Journal of Business Research*, vol. 16, 533–43.

17. Semon, T. T. (2001, October 8). Symmetry shouldn't be goal for scales. *Marketing News*, vol. 35, no. 21, 9.

18. See, for example, Crask, M. R., and Fox, R. J. (1987). An exploration of the interval properties of three commonly used marketing research studies: A magnitude estimation approach. *Journal of the Market Research Society*, vol. 29, no. 3, 317–39.

19. Some researchers claim the use of a 0–10 scale over the telephone is actually better than a 3-, 4-, or 5-point scale. See Loken, B., et al. (1987, July). The use of 0–10 scales in telephone surveys. *Journal of the Market Research Society*, vol. 29, no. 3, 353–62.

20. Personal communication with Gavin Murry, *Reader's Digest*.

21. Developed from Hiscock, J. (2002, February 14). Most trusted brands 2002. *Marketing*, 20–21.

22. Elms, P. (2000, April). Using decision criteria anchors to measure importance among Hispanics. *Quirk's Marketing Research Review*, vol. 15, no. 4, 44–51.

23. The authors are well aware of the need for multi-item scales in order to assess reliability and validity. However, practitioners rely greatly on single-item scales that have face validity. These are recommended single-item scales with face validity.

## Chapter 9

1. For examples on questionnaire development in a variety of settings go to *Google Scholar* and search "questionnaire development".

2. Susan, C. (1994). Questionnaire design affects response rate. *Marketing News*, vol. 28, H25; and Sancher, M. E. (1992).

Effects of questionnaire design on the quality of survey data. *Public Opinion Quarterly*, vol. 56, 206–17.

3. For a more comprehensive coverage of this topic, see Baker, M. J. (2003, Summer). Data collection—Questionnaire design. *Marketing Review*, vol. 3, no. 3, 343–70.

4. Babble, E. (1990). *Survey research methods* (2nd ed.). Belmont, CA: Wadsworth Publishing, pp. 131–32.

5. Hunt, S. D., Sparkman, R. D., and Wilcox, J. (1982, May). The pretest in survey research: Issues and preliminary findings. *Journal of Marketing Research*, vol. 26, no. 4, 269–73.

6. Dillman, D. A. (1978). *Mail telephone surveys: The total design method*. New York: John Wiley & Sons.

7. Loftus, E., and Zanni, G. (1975). Eyewitness testimony: The influence of the wording of a question. *Bulletin of the Psychonomic Society*, vol. 5, 86–88.

8. Adapted and modified from Payne, S. L. (1951). *The art of asking questions*. Princeton, NJ: Princeton University Press. Current source is the 1980 edition, Chapter 10.

9. For memory questions, it is advisable to have respondents recontruct specific events. See, for example, Cook, W. A. (1987, February–March). Telescoping and memory's other tricks. *Journal of Advertising Research*, vol. 27, no. 1, RC5–RC8.

10. Peterson, R. A. (2000). *Constructing effective questionnaires*. Thousand Oaks, CA: Sage Publications, Inc., p. 58.

11. Patten, M. (2001). *Questionnaire research*. Los Angeles: Pyrczak Publishing, p. 9.

12. Screens can be used to quickly identify respondents who will not answer honestly. See Waters, K. M. (1991, Spring–Summer). Designing screening questionnaires to minimize dishonest answers. *Applied Marketing Research*, vol. 31, no. 1, 51–53.

13. Normally pretests are done individually, but a focus group could be used. See Long, S. A. (1991, May 27). Pretesting questionnaires minimizes measurement error. *Marketing News*, vol. 25, no. 11, 12.

14. Response latency, or subtle hesitations in respondents, can be used as a pretest aid. See, for instance, Bassili, J. N., and Fletcher, J. F. (1991). Response-time measurement in survey research. *Public Opinion Quarterly*, vol. 55, 331–46.

## Chapter 10

1. See Bradburn, N. M., and Sudman, S. (1988). Polls and surveys: Understanding what they tell us; Cantril, A. H. (1991). The opinion connection: Polling, politics, and the press; Cantril, A. H. Public opinion polling, retrieved from **Answers.com** on April 29, 2007; Landon in a landslide: The poll that changed polling. Retrieved from **www.historymatter .gmu.edu** on April 29, 2007.

2. See, for example, Lenth, R. (2001, August). Some practical guidelines for effective sample size determination. *American Statistician*, vol. 55, no. 3, 187–93; Williams, G. (1999, April). What size sample do I need? *Australian and New Zealand Journal of Public Health*, vol. 23, no. 2, 215–17; or Cesana, B. M, Reina, G., and Marubini, E. (2001, November). Sample size for testing a proportion in clinical trials: A "two-step" procedure combining power and confidence interval expected width. *American Statistician*, vol. 55, no. 4, 288–92.

3. See, for example, Stephen, E. H., and Soldo, B. J. (1990, April). How to judge the quality of a survey. *American Demographics*, vol. 12, no. 4, 42–43.

4. We use percents throughout this chapter because they are more intuitive than averages.

5. There are myriad other considerations that can factor into sample size calculation and are beyond the scope of this book.

See, for example, Parker, R. A., and Berman, N. G. (2003, August). Sample size: More than calculations. *American Statistician*, vol. 57, no. 3, 166–71.

6. See Shiffler, R. E., and Adams, A. J. (1987, August). A correction for biasing effects of pilot sample size on sample size determination. *Journal of Marketing Research*, vol. 24, no. 3, 319–21.

7. Foreman, J., and Collins, M. (1991, July). The viability of random digit dialing in the UK. *Journal of the Market Research Society*, vol. 33, no. 3, 219–27; and Hekmat, F., and Segal, M. (1984). Random digit dialing: Some additional empirical observations, in D. M. Klein and A. E. Smith, eds., *Marketing comes of age: Proceedings of the Southern Marketing Association*, 176–80.

8. For a somewhat more technical description of cluster sampling, see Carlin, J. B., and Hocking, J. (1999, October). Design of cross-sectional surveys using cluster sampling: An overview with Australian case studies. *Australian and New Zealand Journal of Public Health*, vol. 23, no. 5, 546–51.

9. See also Sudman, S. (1985, February). Efficient screening methods for the sampling of geographically clustered special populations. *Journal of Marketing Research*, vol. 22, 20–29.

10. Bradley, N. (1999, October). Sampling for Internet surveys: An examination of respondent selection for Internet research. *Journal of the Market Research Society*, vol. 41, no. 4, 387.

11. Academic marketing researchers often use convenience samples of college students. See Peterson, R. A. (2001, December). On the use of college students in social science research: Insights from a second-order meta-analysis. *Journal of Consumer Research*, vol. 28, no. 3, 450–61.

12. Wyner, G. A. (2001, Fall). Representation, randomization, and realism. *Marketing Research*, vol. 13, no. 3, 4–5.

13. For an application of referral sampling, see Moriarity, R. T., Jr., and Spekman, R. E. (1984, May). An empirical investigation of the information sources used during the industrial buying process. *Journal of Marketing Research*, vol. 21, 137–47.

14. For a detailed description of how to select a quota sample, see Baker, M. (2002, Autumn). *Marketing Review*, vol. 3, no. 1, 103–20.

15. Paramar, A. (2003, February). Tailor techniques to each audience in Latin market. *Marketing News*, vol. 37, no. 3, 4–6.

16. The nature of sample bias for online surveys is just becoming known. See, for example, Grandcolas, U., Rettie, R., and Marusenko, K. (2003, July). Web survey bias: Sample or mode effect? *Journal of Marketing Management*, vol. 19, no. 5/6, 541–61.

17. For an historical perspective and prediction about online sampling, see Sudman, S., and Blair, E. (1999, Spring). Sampling in the twenty-first century. *Academy of Marketing Science*, vol. 27, no. 2, 269–77.

18. Internet surveys can access hard-to-reach groups. See Pro and con: Internet interviewing. (1999, Summer). *Marketing Research*, vol. 11, no. 2, 33–36.

19. See, as an example, Dahlen, M. (2001, July/August). Banner advertisements through a new lens. *Journal of Advertising Research*, vol. 41, no. 4, 23–30.

20. For a comparison of online sampling to telephone sampling, see Cooper, M. P. (2000, Winter). Web surveys: A review of issues and approaches. *Public Opinion Quarterly*, vol. 64, no. 4, 464–94.

21. Grossnickle, J., and Raskin, O. (2001, Summer). What's ahead on the Internet. *Marketing Research*, vol. 13, no. 2, 8–13.

22. Miller, T. W. (2001, Summer). Can we trust the data of online research? *Marketing Research*, vol. 13, no. 2, 26–32.

## Chapter 11

1. http://www.uta.edu/msmr.
2. These problems are international in scope. See Kreitzman, L. (1990, February 22). Market research. Virgins and groupies. *Marketing*, 35–38, for the United Kingdom.
3. There is a move in the United Kingdom for interviewer certification. See Hemsley, S. (2000, August 17). Acting the part. *Marketing Week*, vol. 23, no. 28, 37–40.
4. For a set of recommendations, see Harrison, D. E., and Krauss, S. I. (2002, October). Interviewer cheating: Implications for research on entrepreneurship in Africa. *Journal of Developmental Entrepreneurship*, vol. 3, no. 7, 319–30.
5. See also, Conrad, F., and Schober, M. (2000, Spring). Clarifying question meaning in a household survey. *Public Opinion Quarterly*, vol. 64, no. 1, 1–28.
6. Miller, T. W. (2001, September 24). Make the call: Online results are mixed bag. *Marketing News*, vol. 20, no. 35, 30–35.
7. To learn about how companies are attempting to resolve non-representativeness, see Johnson, D. W. (2002, December). Elections and public polling: Will the media get online polling right? *Psychology & Marketing*, vol. 12, no. 19, 1009.
8. Coleman, L. G. (1991, January 7). Researchers say nonresponse is single biggest problem. *Marketing News*, vol. 1, no. 25, 32–33; Landler, M. (1991, February 11). The "bloodbath" in market research. *Business Week*, 72, 74; and Jarvis, S. (2002, February 4). CMOR finds survey refusal rate still rising. *Marketing News*, vol. 3, no. 4, 36.
9. Anonymous (2003, Spring). The case for caution: This system is dangerously flawed. *Public Opinion Quarterly*, vol. 67, Issue 1, 5–17.
10. Baim, J. (1991, June). Response rates: A multinational perspective. *Marketing & Research Today*, vol. 2, no. 19, 114–119.
11. Mitchel, J. O. (2002, Fall). Telephone surveys: The next buggy whip? *LIMRA's MarketFacts Quarterly*, vol. 4, no. 21, 39.
12. Jarvis, S. (2002, February). CMOR finds survey refusal rate still rising. *Marketing News*, vol. 36, Issue 3.
13. Anonymous. (1993, August 16). The researchers' response: Four industry leaders tell how to improve cooperation. *Marketing News*, A12.
14. Personal communication, quoted by permission.
15. It is important for the researcher and client to have a partnership during data analysis. See, for example, Fitzpatrick, M. (2001, August). Statistical analysis for direct marketers—in plain English. *Direct Marketing*, vol. 64, no. 4, 54–56.
16. For an alternative presentation, see Ehrnberg, A. (2001, Winter). Data, but no information. *Marketing Research*, vol. 13, no. 4, 36–39.
17. Fitzgerald, K. (2003, June). They're baaaack: Card marketers on campus. *Credit Card Management*, vol. 3, no. 16, 18.
18. Some authors argue that central tendency measures are too sterile. See, for example, Pruden, D. R., and Vavra, T. G. (2000, Summer). Customer research, not marketing research. *Marketing Research*, vol. 12, no. 2, 14–19.
19. Gutsche, A. (2001, September 24). Visuals make the case. *Marketing News*, vol. 35, no. 20, 21–23.
20. Ghose, S., and Lowengart, O. (2001, September). Perceptual positioning of international, national and private brands in a growing international market: An empirical study. *Journal of Brand Management*, vol. 9, no. 1, 45–62.

## Chapter 12

1. In statistical jargon, one uses statistical inference (generalization) to estimate a population parameter (population fact) from the sample statistic (sampling finding).

2. Instructors may find this article useful when teaching confidence intervals: Blume, J. D., and Royall, R. M. (2003, February). Illustrating the law of large numbers (and confidence intervals). *American Statistician*, vol. 57, no. 1, 51–57.
3. We are aware of the disconnect between applied statistical testing and classical statistical testing; however, we opt for the applied approach here. Refer to Hubbard, R., Bayarri, M. J., Berk, K. N., and Carlton, M. A. (2003, August). Confusion over measures of evidence ($p$'s) versus errors ([alpha]'s) in classical statistical testing. *American Statistician*, vol. 57, no. 3, 171.
6. Dolliver, M. (2003, February 3). Studying the economics of student life today. *Adweek*, vol. 44, no. 5, 52.
5. Traditionally, statistics textbooks have advised the use of $t$ over $z$ when the sample size is 30 or less; however, since the variance is typically unknown in marketing research data, the $t$ is preferable up to 120.

## Chapter 13

1. For a contrary view, see Mazur, L. (2000, June 8). The only truism in marketing is they don't exist. *Marketing*, 20.
2. Brandt, J. R. (2003, January/February). Meet your new market. *Chief Executive*, no. 185, 8.
3. Meaningful difference is sometimes called "practical significance." See Thompson, B. (2002, Winter). "Statistical," "practical," and "clinical": How many kinds of significance do counselors need to consider? *Journal of Counseling and Development*, vol. 30, no. 1, 64–71.
4. Smith, S. M., and Whitlark, D. B. (2001, Summer). Men and women online: What makes them click? *Marketing Research*, vol. 13, no. 2, 20–25.
5. Personal communication with the author.
6. This example is based on Kumar, K., and Strandholm, K. (2002, July/August). American business education: Effect on the ethical orientation of foreign students. *Journal of Education for Business*, vol. 77, no. 6, 345–50.
7. For illumination, see Burdick, R. K. (1983, August). Statement of hypotheses in the analysis of variance. *Journal of Marketing Research*, vol. 20, 320–24.
8. This example is based on Hudson, S., and Ritchie, B. (2002, June). Understanding the domestic market using cluster analysis: A case study of the marketing efforts of Travel Alberta. *Journal of Vacation Marketing*, vol. 8, no. 3, 263–76.
9. This procedure is sometimes called a "paired samples" test. For an example of the use of paired samples $t$ tests, see Ryan, C., and Mo, X. (2001, December). Chinese visitors to New Zealand: Demographics and perceptions. *Journal of Vacation Marketing*, vol. 8, no. 1, 13–27.

## Chapter 14

1. Much of this material was adapted from: Turner, M. R. (2005, January). How do you best measure and grow customer loyalty? *The Research Report*, vol. 18. Retrieved from www.maritzresearch.com on March 31, 2007.
2. For advice on when to use chi-square analysis, see Hellebush, S. J. (2001, June 4). One chi square beats two $z$ tests. *Marketing News*, vol. 35, no. 11, 12–13.
3. Here are some articles that use cross-tabulation analysis: Burton, S., and Zinkhan, G. M. (1987, Fall). Changes in consumer choice: Further investigation of similarity and attraction effects. *Psychology in Marketing*, vol. 4, 255–66; Bush, A. J., and Leigh, J. H. (1984, April/May). Advertising on cable versus traditional television networks. *Journal of Advertising Research*, vol. 24, 33–38; and Langrehr, F. W. (1985, Summer). Consumer

images of two types of competing financial institutions. *Journal of the Academy of Marketing Science*, vol. 13, 248–64.

4. For a more advanced treatment of scatter diagrams, see Goddard, B. L. (2000, April). The power of computer graphics for comparative analysis, *Appraisal Journal*, vol. 68, no. 2, 134–41.

5. See, for example, Branch, W. (1990, February). On interpreting correlation coefficients. *American Psychologist*, vol. 45, no. 2, 296.

6. Residual analysis can take many forms. See, for example, Dempster, A. P., and Gasko-Green, M. (1981). New tools for residual analysis. *Annals of Statistics*, vol. 9, 945–59.

7. Based on Tsalikis, J., Seaton, B., and Tomaras, P. (2002, February). A new perspective on cross-cultural ethical evaluations: The use of conjoint analysis. *Journal of Business Ethics*, vol. 35, no. 4, part 2, 281–92.

8. Our description pertains to "backward" stepwise regression. We admit that this is a simplification of stepwise multiple regression.

9. Reece, W. S. (2001, February). Travelers to Las Vegas and to Atlantic City. *Journal of Travel Research*, vol. 39, no. 3, 275–84.

10. We admit that our description of regression is introductory. Two books that expand our description are Lewis-Beck, M. S. (1980). *Applied regression: An introduction*. Newbury Park, CA: Sage Publications; and Schroeder, L. D., Sjoffquist, D. L., and Stephan, P. E. (1986). *Understanding regression analysis: An introductory guide*. Newbury Park, CA: Sage Publications.

11. Regression analysis is commonly used in academic marketing research. Here are some examples: Callahan, F. X. (1982, April/May). Advertising and profits 1969–1978. *Journal of Advertising Research*, vol. 22, 17–22; Dubinsky, A. J., and Levy, M. (1989, Summer). Influence of organizational fairness on work outcomes of retail salespeople. *Journal of Retailing*, vol. 65, 221–52; Frieden, J. B., and Downs, P. E. (1986, Fall). Testing the social involvement model in an energy conservation context. *Journal of the Academy of Marketing Science*, vol. 14, 13–20; and Tellis, G. J., and Fornell, C. (1988, February). The relationship between advertising and product quality over the product life cycle: A contingency theory. *Journal of Marketing Research*, vol. 25, 64–71. For an alternative to regression analysis, see Quaintance, B. S., and Franke, G. R. (1991). Neural networks for marketing research. In King, R. L. (ed.), *Marketing: Toward the Twenty-First Century. Proceedings of the Southern Marketing Association*, 230–35.

## Chapter 15

1. Lotti, M. (2003). Practitioner viewpoint. In Burns, A., and Bush, R., *Marketing research: Online research applications*. Upper Saddle River, NJ: Prentice Hall, p. 580.

2. The authors wish to acknowledge the assistance of M. R. Howard, Ed.D., and H. H. Donofrio, Ph.D., in preparing some of the material presented in this chapter. Both are experts in business communication and report writing, and we appreciate their insights.

3. Deshpande, R., and Zaltman, G. (1982, February). Factors affecting the use of market research information: A path analysis. *Journal of Marketing Research*, vol. 19, 14–31.

4. Deshpande, R., and Zaltman, G. (1984, February). A comparison of factors affecting researcher and manager perceptions of market research use. *Journal of Marketing Research*, vol. 21, 32–38.

5. To properly cite your sources, see *MLA handbook for writers of research papers* (5th ed.). New York: Modern Language Association of America; or *Publication manual of the American Psychological Association* (5th ed.). (2001). Washington, DC: American Psychological Association.

6. Hansen, B. (2003, September 13). Combating plagiarism. *CQResearcher*. Retrieved from **http://library.eqpress.com/ eqresearcher/CQResearcher** on January 21, 2004.

7. Guffey, M. E. (2000). *Business communication: Process and product* (3rd ed.). Cincinnati: South-Western College Publishing, 103.

8. Tutee, E. R. (1983). *The visual display of quantitative information*. Cheshire, CT: Graphics Press.

9. Thomas, J. (2001, November). Executive excellence. *Marketing Research*, 11–12.

# CREDITS

## Chapter 1

Page 2: G.D.T./Getty Images Inc.—Image Bank. Page 5: Toyota Motor Sales, USA, Inc. Page 6: Courtesy NewProductWorks, A Division of the Arbor Strategy Group, **www.newproductworks.com.** Page 6: Courtesy NewProductWorks, A Division of the Arbor Strategy Group, **www.newproductworks.com.** Page 9: SEINFELD © Castle Rock Entertainment. Licensed by Warner Bros. Entertainment Inc. All Rights Reserved. Page 11. MRSI/Marketing Research Services Inc. Page12: Dutch Boy; Courtesy of Sherwin Williams. Page 22: Anthony Dunn/Ambient Images.

## Chapter 2

Page 24: Courtesy of Marketing Research Association. Page 26: Courtesty of Advertising Hall of Fame. Page 34: Courtesy of Irwin. Page 35: Courtesy of Eye Tracking, Inc. Page 40: Courtesy of Marketing Research Association. Page 41: The Burke Institute; Courtesy of The Burke Institute. Page 44 (left and right): Courtesy of Baltimore Research. Page 57: Courtesy of Marsha Medders.

## Chapter 3

Page 60: Courtesy of Bluetooth SIG. Page 67: Courtesy of Survey Sampling International. Page 68: Courtesy of Bluetooth SIG. Page 84: Courtesy of Decision Analyst.

## Chapter 4

Page 100: Courtesy of Momentum Market Intelligence. Page 101: Courtesy of Momentum Market Intelligence. Page 106: Bill Aron PhotoEdit Inc. Page 108: Courtesy of Fieldwork, Inc. Page 111: Courtesy of Baltimore Research. Page 113: Courtesy of InsightExpress. Page 122: Don and Pat Valenti/Getty Images Inc. -Stone Allstock.

## Chapter 5

Page 134: American Marksman. Page 135: American Marksman. Page 136: American Marksman

## Chapter 6

Page 170: Courtesy of Maritz Research. Page 172: Susan Werner/ Getty Images Inc. -Stone Allstock. Page 178: Courtesy of Claritas. Page 179: Courtesy of ESRI Business Information Solutions. Page 180: Courtesy of ESRI. Page 182: Courtesy of ESRI. Page 186: Courtesy of Arbitron. Page 188: Courtesy of Simmons.

## Chapter 7

Page 196: Courtesy of Western Wats. Page 198: Courtesy of Western Wats. Page 201: Courtesy of TAi Companies. Page 202: Courtesy of Stephanie Watson and Aaron Hostetler. Page 204: Courtesy of Common Knowledge Research Services. Page 214: Courtesy of MRSI. Page 217: Courtesy of i.thinkinc. Page 221: Courtesy of e-Rewards, Inc.

## Chapter 8

Page 230: Courtesy of Maritz Research. Page 233: Laima Druskis/Pearson Education/PH College. Page 236: Wm. Wrigley Jr. Company. Page 238: Steve Skjold/PhotoEdit. Page 246: Bachmann/Stock Boston. Page 249: Chris O'Meara/AP/Wide World Photos.

## Chapter 9

Page 262: Courtesy of Clifford D. Scott. Page 266: REINHARD JANKE/Peter Arnold, Inc. Page 271: JEAN LOUIS BATT/Getty Images, Inc.-Taxi. Page 272: CHIP SIMONS/Getty Images.

## Chapter 10

Page 290: Prentice Hall School Division. Page 293: David Buffington/ Getty Images, Inc. - Photodisc. Page 295: Robert Ginn/PhotoEdit. Page 301. Tony Garcia/Getty Images Inc. Stone Allstock. Page 306: Bill Robbins/Getty Images Inc. - Stone Allstock. Page 309: Jeff Greenberg/PhotoEdit.

## Chapter 11

Page 318: Courtesy of DSS. Page 320: Courtesy of DSS. Page 322: Jonathan Nourok/PhotoEdit. Page 324: Tony Freeman/PhotoEdit. Page 329 (top and margin): Courtesy of Ozgrid. Page 331: Todd Gipstein/Corbis/Bettmann. Page 335: Paul Avis/Getty Images, Inc. - Taxi. Page 343: Robert Harbison/Robert Harbison.

## Chapter 12

Courtesy of MRI Research. Page 381: Courtesy of MRI Research. Page 355: Tina Buckman/Index Stock Imagery, Inc. Page 368: Michael Newman/PhotoEdit; Courtesy of Michael Newman. Page 375: David Young-Wolff/PhotoEdit.

## Chapter 13

Page 388: Courtesy of Harris Interactive. Page 390: AP Wide World Photos. Page 391: AP Wide World Photos. Page 395: D. Young Wolff/PhotoEdit. Page 401: Courtesy of the American Heart Association. Page 407: Layne Kennedy/Corbis/Bettmann.

## Chapter 14

Page 422: Courtesy of Maritz Research. Page 426: Google. Page 440: Bill Robbins/Getty Images Inc. -Stone Allstock. Page 447: Erlanson-Messens, Britt J./Getty Images Inc. -Image Bank. Page 452: Frank LaBua/Pearson Education/PH College.

## Chapter 15

Page 466: Courtesy of Burke, Inc. Page 459: Courtesy of Burke, Inc. Page 469: Courtesy of Burke, Inc.

# NAME INDEX

Achenbaum, Alvin, 38
Adams, A. J., 295n
Alford, Kim, 350

Babble, E., 264n
Baim, J., 323n
Baldasare, Patrick M., 399–400
Bartels, Robert, 26
Bennett, P. D., 9n
Berkowitz, D., 18n, 48n
Bernstein, S., 40n
Berry, Halle, 390
Bonoma, T. V., 107n
Bourque, L., 219n
Bovée, C., 476n, 477n
Bradley, N., 307n
Brandt, John R., 391n
Brown, S., 219n
Brownell, Larry, 40
Burns, A., 109n
Burns, John, 40n
Burns, R., 109n
Bush, A. J., 210n
Bush, R. F., 38n

Calder, B. J., 122n
Chafe, Adam J., 12
Chakrapani, Chuck, 37n, 38
Chapman, J., 150n
Chavez, J., 48n
Chonko, L. B., 42n, 43n, 45n, 46n
Clancy, Kevin, 10
Cleland, K., 203n
Coleman, L. G., 323n
Collins, M., 303n
Conant, J., 220n
Crawford, I., 38n
Crossen, C., 148n

Dawson, S., 38n
DePaulo, P. J., 216n
Deshpande, R., 467n
Diehl, P. L., 122n
Disney, Walt, 230
Dolliver, M., 42n
Donnelly, Ted, 44
Drake, P. D., 140n
Drozdenko, R. G., 140n
Drucker, Peter, 6

Eberhard, Mark, 134–136
Ellis, S., 210n

Elms, P., 254n
Ericson, P. I., 205n

Feltser, E. B., 251n
Ferrell, O. C., 42n
Fielder, E., 219n
Fielding, M., 18n
Fink, A., 479n
Fish, D., 177n
Foreman, J., 303n
Fox, S., 234n

Gallup, George, 291
Gates, R. H., 216n
Gentry, J. W., 107n
Gerlotto, C., 223n
Ghose, S., 338n
Gibson, Lawrence D., 72, 74–75, 77
Gordon, L. P., 147n
Grace, H. S., 46n
Grant, F. S., 210n
Gray, L. R., 122n
Grecco, C., 217n
Greenbaum, T. I., 107n
Greenberg, D., 217n
Green, K., 207n
Greene, S., 127n
Grisaffe, D., 140n

Hanks, Tom, 388
Hansen, B., 473n
Hardy, H., 26
Hawley, Raina, 328–329
Hayes, J., 128n
Heilbrunn, J., 10n
Hiscock, J., 253n
Honomichl, Jack, 18n, 19, 26n, 27–29, 35n
Hornik, J., 210n
Hudson, S., 408n
Hughes, L. Q., 190n
Hunt, S. D., 42n, 43n, 45n, 46n

Ihlwan, M., 127n
Iliano, G., 46n

Jarboe, G. R., 216n
Jarvis, S., 47n, 323n
Jones, P., 216n

Kaplan, C. P., 205n
Kaushik, N., 125n
Kelley, S., 42n
Kennedy, Verne, 350
Kiecker, P. L., 46n

Kimmel, A. J., 47n
Kinnear, T., 29n, 30n, 114n
Knox, N., 107n
Koch, Dave, 207–208
Kolessar, R. S., 188n
Kotler, Philip, 7, 77
Krieg, Peter C., 10
Krum, J. R., 37n
Kumar, K., 105n

Laczniak, Gene, 38, 38n
Laemmie, Carl, 2–3
Landon, Alf, 290–291
Langer, J., 110n
Liddle, A., 125n
Likert, Rensis, 245n
Lipson, S., 11n
Lohse, G. L., 117n
Long, S. A., 285n
Lotti, Michael, 466
Lowengart, O., 338n
Lusch, R. F., 4–5

MacElroy, W. H., 218
Macer, T., 204n
Madden, C. S., 42n
Mahajan, Vijay, 35–37
Malhotra, Naresh, 29
Marconi, J., 10n
McDaniel, S., 42n
McKim, R., 140n
Meckley, Sean, 68
Medders, Marsha, 57–58
Medlin, B., 207n
Merritt, N. J., 10n
Merton, Robert, 26
Mill, John Stuart, 37
Miller, C., 112n
Miller, T. W., 321n
Mitchel, J. O., 323n
Mittel, Vikas, 399–400
Murphy, Patrick, 38
Murry, Gavin, 253n
Myers, J., 107n

Nelson, E., 127n
Nelson, J. E., 46n
Nielsen, A. C., 26

Ober, S., 477n

Palk, J., 216n
Parlin, Charles Coolidge, 26

**501**

## SUBJECT INDEX